W9-DEU-162

Principles of MACROECONOMICS

THIRD CANADIAN EDITION

ROBERT H. FRANK
Cornell University

BEN S. BERNANKE
Princeton University

LARS OSBERG
Dalhousie University

MELVIN L. CROSS
Dalhousie University

BRIAN K. MacLEAN
Laurentian University

McGraw-Hill
Ryerson

Toronto Montréal Boston Burr Ridge, IL Dubuque, IA Madison, WI New York San
Francisco St. Louis Bangkok Bogotá Caracas Kuala Lumpur Lisbon London Madrid
Mexico City Milan New Delhi Santiago Seoul Singapore Sydney Taipei

Principles of Macroeconomics
Third Canadian Edition

ISBN-13: 978-0-07-096532-4
ISBN-10: 0-07-096532-3

1 2 3 4 5 6 7 8 9 10 DOW 0 9

Printed and bound in the United States of America.

Vice-President and Editor-in-Chief: Joanna Cotton
Sponsoring Editor: Bruce McIntosh
Senior Marketing Manager: Joy Armitage Taylor
Developmental Editor: Daphne Scriabin
Editorial Associate: Stephanie Hess
Supervising Editor: Jessica Barnoski
Copy Editor: Julie van Tol
Production Coordinator: Sheryl MacAdam
Cover Design: Michelle Losier
Cover Image: © Digital Vision Ltd./SuperStock
Interior Design: Michelle Losier
Page Layout: Aptara, Inc.
Printer: R.R. Donnelley/Willard

Library and Archives Canada Cataloguing in Publication

Principles of macroeconomics / Robert H. Frank ... [et al.]. — 3rd Canadian ed.

Includes index.
ISBN 978-0-07-096532-4

1. Macroeconomics—Textbooks. I. Frank, Robert H.

HB172.5.P75 2009   339   C2008-906458-5

About the Authors

Robert H. Frank Professor Frank is the Henrietta Johnson Louis Professor of Management and Professor of Economics at the Johnson Graduate School of Management at Cornell University, where he has taught since 1972. His "Economic View" column appears regularly in *The New York Times*. After receiving his B.S. from Georgia Tech in 1966, he taught math and science for two years as a Peace Corps Volunteer in rural Nepal. He received his M.A. in statistics in 1971 and his Ph. D. in economics in 1972 from The University of California at Berkeley. During leaves of absence from Cornell, he has served as chief economist for the Civil Aeronautics Board (1978–1980), a Fellow at the Center for Advanced Study in the Behavioral Sciences (1992–93), and Professor of American Civilization at l'École des Hautes Études en Sciences Sociales in Paris (2000–01).

Professor Frank is the author of a best-selling intermediate economics textbook—*Microeconomics and Behavior*, Seventh Edition (Irwin/McGraw-Hill, 2008). He has published on a variety of subjects, including price and wage discrimination, public utility pricing, the measurement of unemployment spell lengths, and the distributional consequences of direct foreign investment. His research has focused on rivalry and cooperation in economic and social behavior. His books on these themes, which include *Choosing the Right Pond* (Oxford, 1995), *Passions Within Reason* (W. W. Norton, 1988), and *What Price the Moral High Ground?* (Princeton, 2004), *The Economic Naturalist* (Basic Books, 2007), and *Falling Behind* (University of California Press, 2007), have been translated into 15 languages. *The Winner-Take-All Society* (The Free Press, 1995), coauthored with Philip Cook, received a Critic's Choice Award, was named a Notable Book of the Year by *The New York Times*, and was included in *Business Week's* list of the 10 best books of 1995. *Luxury Fever* (The Free Press, 1999) was named to the *Knight-Ridder* Best Books list for 1999.

Professor Frank has been awarded an Andrew W. Mellon Professorship (1987–1990), a Kenan Enterprise Award (1993), and a Merrill Scholars Program Outstanding Educator Citation (1991). He is a co-recipient of the 2004 Leontief Prize for Advancing the Frontiers of Economic Thought. He was awarded the Johnson School's Stephen Russell Distinguished Teaching Award in 2004 and the School's Apple Distinguished Teaching Award in 2005. His introductory microeconomics course has graduated more than 7,000 enthusiastic economic naturalists over the years.

Ben S. Bernanke Professor Bernanke received his B.A. in economics from Harvard University in 1975 and his Ph.D. in economics from MIT in 1979. He taught at the Stanford Graduate School of Business from 1979 to 1985 and moved to Princeton University in 1985, where he was named the Howard Harrison and Gabrielle Snyder Beck Professor of Economics and Public Affairs, and where he served as Chairman of the Economics Department.

Professor Bernanke was sworn in on February 1, 2006, as Chairman and a member of the Board of Governors of the Federal Reserve System. Professor Bernanke also serves as Chairman of the Federal Open Market Committee, the System's principal monetary policy-making body. He was appointed as a member of the Board to a full 14-year term, which expires January 31, 2020, and to a four-year term as Chairman, which expires January 31, 2010. Before his appointment as Chairman, Professor Bernanke was Chairman of the President's Council of Economic Advisers, from June 2005 to January 2006.

Professor Bernanke's intermediate textbook, with Andrew Abel, *Macroeconomics,* Sixth Edition (Addison-Wesley, 2008) is a best seller in its field. He has authored more than 50 scholarly publications in macroeconomics, macroeconomic history, and finance. He has done significant research on the causes of the Great Depression, the role of financial markets and institutions in the business cycle, and measuring the effects of monetary policy on the economy.

Professor Bernanke has held a Guggenheim Fellowship and a Sloan Fellowship, and he is a Fellow of the Econometric Society and of the American Academy of Arts and Sciences. He served as the Director of the Monetary Economics Program of the National Bureau of Economic Research (NBER) and as a member of the NBER's Business Cycle Dating Committee. In July 2001, he was appointed Editor of the *American Economic Review*. Professor Bernanke's work with civic and professional groups includes having served two terms as a member of the Montgomery Township (N.J.) Board of Education.

Lars Osberg is currently University Research Professor, and Chair of the Department of Economics at Dalhousie University, but he began life in Ottawa, Ontario. As an undergraduate, he attended Queen's University, Kingston and the London School of Economics and Political Science. After two years working for the Tanzania Sisal Corporation as a CUSO volunteer, he went to Yale University for his Ph.D. His first book was *Economic Inequality in Canada* (1981), and the most recent is *The Economic Implications of Social Cohesion* (2003). In between, there have been eight others and two editions of an introductory textbook. He is also the author of numerous refereed articles in professional journals, book chapters, reviews, reports and miscellaneous publications. His major fields of research interest have been the extent and causes of poverty and economic inequality, with particular emphasis in recent years on social policy, social cohesion and the implications of working time, unemployment, and structural change. Among other professional responsibilities, he was president of the Canadian Economics Association in 1999–2000. Recent papers can be found at http://myweb.dal.ca/osberg/.

Melvin Cross received an Associate of Arts degree from Dawson Community College in 1968, a B.A. from the University of Montana in 1970, an M.A. from Simon Fraser University in 1972, and a Ph.D. in economics from Texas A&M University in 1976. He is an Associate Professor in the Department of Economics at Dalhousie University, which he joined in 1975. He also holds an adjunct appointment in the School of Resource and Environmental Studies and was an Associate Fellow in the Foundation Year Program of the University of King's College from 1991 to 2002. In 1994–95, he was a Visiting Adjunct Associate Professor at Queen's University and in 2002 he was a Visiting Lecturer at the University of Sydney. His teaching and research interests are in the economics of natural and environmental resources and the history of economic thought. He has taught principles of economics throughout his career. He is an author or co-author of articles in the *Canadian Journal of Fisheries and Aquatic Science, Canadian Public Policy, History of Political Economy, Marine Resource Economics,* and other journals and has been vice-president of the Atlantic Canada Economics Association since 2008.

Brian K. MacLean is Professor of Economics at Laurentian University in Sudbury, Ontario, where he has been Chair of the Department of Economics and Director of the Institute for Northern Ontario Research and Development. He speaks Japanese as a second language and has been a visiting professor at Hokkaido University in Sapporo, Japan, and at Saitama University, just outside of Tokyo, where he returns each summer to deliver a series of lectures. He has edited *Out of Control? Canada in an Unstable Financial World* (Lorimer, 1999), co-edited *The Unemployment Crisis: All for Nought?* (McGill-Queen's, 1996), and has published in the *Cambridge Journal of Economics, International Journal of Political Economy, Review of Income and Wealth, Canadian Business Economics,* and other journals. He has served on the Executive of the Canadian Economics Association, as the CEA liaison with the Canadian Women Economists Network, and as webmaster and Steering Committee member of the Progressive Economics Forum.

Dedication

For Ellen   **R. H. F.**

For Anna   **B. S. B.**

For Molly   **L. S. O.**

For Anna, Nathan, and Thomas, in memory of Carmelita   **M. L. C.**

For Kathleen and Vera, in memory of Ken   **B. K. M.**

Brief Contents

Contents

Preface

The Great Depression of the 1930s drew students to economics in search of theories to explain the world around them. If the past is any guide, the economic events of 2008—the financial crisis on Wall Street; its propagation to financial markets in Europe, Asia, and Canada; commodity price and exchange rate gyrations; and so on—will bring to our classrooms a new crop of students interested in understanding the causes and implications of these events.

Feedback from users supports our conviction that this textbook provides a different and better way to introduce beginning students to macroeconomics. This text continues to emphasize (1) an active, student-centred approach to learning; (2) economic naturalism; (3) the philosophy that evidence matters; and (4) repeated use of core principles.

ACTIVE LEARNING

Active learning by students—that is, learning based on applying new ideas until they are internalized—is an essential part of an effective learning process. By "learning" we do not just mean being able to answer a test question the next day. By the time they reach university, many students have become quite good at quick memorization. But even "A" students never fully internalize a concept unless they use it repeatedly. This textbook has been designed for instructors who strive to stimulate the intellectual curiosity of their students and thereby have an enduring impact on them. We think it useful for instructors to ask themselves, "What do I want my students to retain from this course ten or twenty years from now?" Education research shows that long-term retention depends on students seeing both the value of a concept and *actively* using it. Throughout the book we use a number of devices to foster active learning.

1. **Worked Examples.** New ideas and concepts are introduced by means of simple examples, usually numerical, which are developed step-by-step in the text. These examples display the reasoning process used to reach the economic conclusion or insight, and they provide a model for the student to apply when working exercises and problems.

EXAMPLE 4.1	Productivity and output per person in Canada, the United States, and China

In 2000, the value of Canadian economic output was approximately C$1 trillion (1000 billion). In the same year, the estimated value of U.S. output was approximately C$11.8 trillion and that of the People's Republic of China was C$1.8 trillion. The populations of Canada, the United States, and China in 2000 were about 30.8 million, 275.4 million, and 1.27 billion respectively while the numbers of employed workers in the three countries were approximately 14.9 million, 135.2 million, and 626.6 million respectively.[2]

The output per person and average labour productivity for Canada, the United States, and China in the year 2000 can be determined using the data provided above. Output per person is simply total output divided by the number of people in an economy. Average labour productivity is output divided by the number of employed workers. Doing the math, we get the following results for 2000, the year in question:

EXERCISE 12.3

The price of gold is U.S.\$930/ounce in New York and 5580 kronor/ounce in Stockholm, Sweden. If the law of one price holds for gold, what is the nominal exchange rate between the U.S. dollar and the Swedish krona?

Example 12.3 and Exercise 12.3 illustrate the application of the purchasing power parity theory. According to the **purchasing power parity (PPP) theory,** nominal exchange rates are determined as necessary for the law of one price to hold.

A particularly useful prediction of the PPP theory is that in the long run, the *currencies of countries that experience relatively high inflation will tend to depreciate against the currencies of countries that experience relatively low inflation.* To see why, we will extend the analysis in Example 12.4.

purchasing power parity (PPP) the theory that nominal exchange rates are determined as necessary for the law of one price to hold

"We're a natural, Rachel. I handle intellectual property, and you're a content-provider."

© *The New Yorker* Collection 1995 Lee Lorenz from cartoonbank.com. All Rights Reserved.

2. **Exercises.** Following many examples, and indeed throughout each chapter, we pose exercises in the running text that challenge the student to test and extend his or her understanding of the ideas being discussed. Answers to these exercises are provided at the end of the chapter, allowing immediate feedback.

3. **Anecdotes and Illustrations.** Active learning is more likely to take place when students are engaged and motivated. We begin every chapter with an anecdote that motivates the discussion, and we illustrate the ideas with memorable cartoons, photographs, and original line drawings. Most importantly, we have striven to minimize jargon and engage the student with direct, friendly writing.

4. **Recap Boxes and Summaries.** To keep students focused on the forest as well as the trees, at strategic points in each chapter we have provided "recap boxes." Recaps summarize the main ideas of the previous section. The recap boxes are also reiterated by bulleted end-of-chapter summaries, which are designed to review the most important concepts presented in the chapter.

RECAP

EXCHANGE RATES

- The *nominal exchange rate* between two currencies is the rate at which the currencies can be traded for each other. More precisely, the nominal exchange rate e for any given country is the number of units of foreign currency that can be bought for one unit of the domestic currency.

- An *appreciation* is an increase in the value of a currency relative to other currencies (a rise in e); a *depreciation* is a decline in a currency's value (a fall in e).

- An exchange rate can be either *flexible,* meaning that it varies freely according to supply and demand for the currency in the foreign exchange market, or *fixed,* meaning that its value is fixed by official government policy.

- The *real exchange rate* is the price of the average domestic good or service *relative* to the price of the average foreign good or service, when prices are expressed in terms of a common currency. A useful formula for the real exchange rate is eP/P^f, where e is the nominal exchange rate, P is the domestic price level, and P^f is the foreign price level.

- An increase in the real exchange rate implies that domestic goods are becoming more expensive relative to foreign goods, which tends to reduce exports and stimulate imports. Conversely, a decline in the real exchange rate tends to increase net exports.

---

5. **Review Questions and Problems.** Questions for review at the end of each chapter encourage the student to test his or her understanding of the main ideas of the chapter. End-of-chapter problems are carefully crafted to help students internalize and extend core concepts.

ECONOMIC NATURALISM

Economics is fascinating because of its power to explain. As an extension of the active-learning approach, we encourage students to become "economic naturalists" who employ basic economic principles to understand and explain what they see around them in the "laboratory of life."

Studying biology enables people to observe and marvel at the many details of the natural environment that would otherwise have escaped notice. For the naturalist, a walk in a quiet wood becomes an adventure. In much the same way, studying economics can enable students to see the world in which they live and work in a new light. Throughout the text, Economic Naturalist examples show students the relevance of economics to their world—how economics can help them to understand the world they live in. Keeping opportunity cost in mind, in this edition we have been more selective in our use of Economic Naturalist examples. The following are just some of the issues raised:

- Does GDP measurement by Statistics Canada ignore the underground economy?
- What is the macroeconomic impact of a sharp drop (or rise) in world oil prices?
- Why have 15 European countries adopted a common currency?
- Why did China move away from pegging the yuan to the U.S. dollar?
- What were the consequences of U.S. bank runs during the Great Depression?

Through exposure to economic naturalism, students are encouraged to pose and answer applied economic questions on their own, and they become more likely to use economics long after completing their introductory course.

ECONOMIC *Naturalist* **12.1**   Does a strong currency imply a strong economy?

Politicians and the public sometimes take pride in the fact that their national currency is "strong," meaning that its value in terms of other currencies is high or rising. Likewise, policy-makers sometimes view a depreciating ("weak") currency as a sign of economic failure. Does a strong currency necessarily imply a strong economy?

There are times, such as in 2006 in Canada, when the national currency is strong, real GDP growth is substantial, and the unemployment rate is low by historical standards. But contrary to popular opinion, there is no simple connection between the strength of a country's currency and the strength of its economy. For example, Figure 12.1 shows that the value of the Canadian dollar relative to the U.S. dollar was greater in the year 1992 than in the year 2000, though Canadian economic performance was considerably better in 2000 than in 1992, a period of deep recession and rising unemployment.

One reason a strong currency does not necessarily imply a strong economy is that an appreciating currency (an increase in e) tends to raise the real exchange rate (equal to eP/P^f), which may hurt a country's net exports. For example, if the Canadian dollar strengthens against the yen (that is, if a dollar buys more yen than before), Japanese goods will become cheaper in terms of dollars. The result may be that Canadians prefer to buy Japanese goods rather than goods produced at home. Likewise, a stronger dollar implies that each yen buys fewer dollars, so exported Canadian goods become more expensive to Japanese consumers. As Canadian goods become more expensive in terms of yen, the willingness of Japanese consumers to buy Canadian exports declines. A strong dollar may therefore imply lower sales and profits for Canadian industries that export, as well as for Canadian industries (like automobile manufacturers) that compete with foreign exporters for a share of the domestic Canadian market.

EVIDENCE MATTERS

Getting students to appreciate the power of economic models is a crucial goal of an introductory course, but students should also be made aware of the empirical evidence regarding different hypotheses. Does real GDP per capita correlate with direct measures of living standards? Do nominal interest rates tend to rise with the inflation rate? Do slowdowns in real GDP growth produce increases in the unemployment rate? Is the idea of a consumption function supported by data from Statistics Canada? Do economies with high inflation experience exchange rate depreciation? Is higher capital per worker associated with higher output per worker? Does average productivity growth necessarily translate into real wage growth? By providing evidence on questions such as these, we encourage students to view economic theories as testable hypotheses, not as unquestionable truths.

REPEATED USE OF CORE PRINCIPLES

A few core principles arise again and again in economics, especially in microeconomics, but also in macroeconomics. By repeating these core principles even in the macroeconomic chapters (4 to 17), the text enhances the likelihood that students will leave the course with a thorough appreciation of the principles. A small icon appears in the margin whenever one of the core principles is discussed, thereby reinforcing the principles many times over.

The Cost–Benefit Principle: An individual (or a firm or a society) will be better off taking an action if, and only if, the extra benefits from taking the action are greater than the extra costs.

COST–
BENEFIT

WHAT IS NEW AND IMPROVED IN THIS EDITION

NEW FEATURES

- The short-run chapters relevant to stabilization policy (Part 3) now appear before the long-run chapters on economic growth (Part 4) to make it easier for courses to follow the "short-run first" order most Canadian instructors prefer.
- Foreign exchange rate determination, so important to the Canadian economy, appears five chapters earlier in the book than in the previous edition (Chapter 12).
- Greater attention to the globally important Chinese economy in applied examples.
- New, short section on how the income-expenditure multiplier changes when imports and taxes depend on disposable income (Chapter 8).
- The already-detailed explanation of how the Bank of Canada achieves the overnight rate target is improved with the aid of an additional analytical diagram (Chapter 9).
- Expanded coverage of the consequences of extreme money supply changes (Chapter 10).
- Thorough revision of the trade chapter enhances its macro orientation and includes a new section on trade institutions (Chapter 13).
- The complementary chapters on saving and investment and on financial markets appear one after the other, their complementary nature is enhanced, and they are streamlined (Chapters 16 and 17).
- Later chapters make frequent references back to earlier chapters so that students get repeated exposure to findings such as the Fisher effect.
- Real world examples take advantage of the wider availability of international data through the World Economic Outlook Database, SourceOECD, and UNdata.

RETAINED FEATURES

- Active learning approach.
- Emphasis on prediction of real world events and explanation of real world issues.
- Careful presentation of GDP, labour force, and price level measurement issues to provide students with a strong empirical grounding.
- Compact development of the Keynesian cross model.
- Compact development of the traditional AD–AS model.
- The Bernanke/Taylor/Romer model of inflation and output determination is presented as a complement to, or substitute for, the traditional AD–AS model, depending on instructor choice.
- Thorough, lively coverage of exchange rate issues.
- Patient, systematic treatment of how the banking system creates money.

- Solid core chapter on economic growth pitched at a level appropriate for first-year students.
- Detailed application of a supply and demand model to discuss winners and losers from international trade and the impact of tariffs and quotas.
- Discussion of savings and investment and international capital flows firmly linked to real-world categories employed by Statistics Canada.
- Widespread use of Statistics Canada data with CANSIM series numbers provided.

THOROUGHLY CANADIAN MACRO

A macro textbook directed to a Canadian audience must confront head-on the interdependence of national economies. Our book places a strong *emphasis on open economy issues.* It starts with an analysis of comparative advantage as a basis for international trade (Chapter 2) and progresses to such topics as the role of Canada's flexible exchange rate in amplifying the impact of monetary policy (Chapters 9, 10, and 11), the causes and consequences of currency appreciation and depreciation (Chapter 12), international trade institutions and winners and losers from international trade (Chapter 15), the historical contribution of non-resident saving to Canadian capital formation (Chapter 16), and the connection between the current account balance and international capital flows (Chapter 17).

In addition, a Canadian macroeconomics textbook needs to introduce students to Canadian data, institutions, and policies. Beginning in Chapters 4, 5, and 6, we introduce macroeconomic data on the Canadian economy through the use of figures and tables. For example, we introduce our discussion of international trade in Chapter 15 with an empirical section on Canada's role in the global economy. In analyzing saving and investment in Chapter 16, we link the discussion to Statistics Canada data from the *National Income and Expenditure Accounts.* When we examine net capital inflows in Chapter 17, we employ data from *Canada's Balance of International Payments* and are careful to highlight the distinction between the current account balance and net exports. More generally, we have carefully documented the sources of data, and in most cases data-based figures and tables provide the relevant data series label, not just the table number, from Statistics Canada's CANSIM database. We have also included a data appendix at the end of the textbook, which uses CANSIM time series to show the major trends in the Canadian economy in recent decades. The explanatory notes for the data appendix provide an overview of the meaning and significance of the macroeconomic variables that are critical to studying the Canadian economy.

Institutions relating to monetary, fiscal, and trade policy are important to macroeconomics, and we pay particular attention to institutions of monetary policy. For example, to understand Canadian macroeconomic issues today, it is essential to understand how the Bank of Canada operates. We emphasize that the Bank's stated goal is to keep inflation in the range of 1 to 3 percent, and that the instrument the Bank uses to achieve its goal is the overnight rate target.

Relevant examples make the discussion of Canadian data, institutions, and policies come alive for students. Our Economic Naturalist examples dealing specifically with the Canadian economy answer questions such as

- Why was September 1981 an incredibly bad month for a Canadian family to take out a five-year mortgage?
- Why did the Bank of Canada cut the overnight rate target 9 times during the economic slowdown of 2000–2001?
- Why do central banks, including the Bank of Canada, try to achieve low, positive inflation rather than zero inflation?

ORGANIZATION OF TOPICS

*Principles of Macroeconomic*s is divided into four parts. Part 1 (Chapters 1, 2, and 3) introduces basic economic concepts, including the core principles. Part 2 then brings the student into the realm of macroeconomics. Chapter 4 gives an overview of the issues that macroeconomists study. Chapters 5 and 6 focus on issues of measurement: Chapter 5 looks at measures of real economic activity, such as GDP and the unemployment rate, and Chapter 6 considers measures of the price level and inflation. As preparation for our model of output and inflation rate determination, we provide students with a thorough grounding in the terminology they need in order to discuss changes in the inflation rate.

Part 3 studies the short-run behaviour of the economy, including cyclical fluctuations and stabilization policy. Chapter 7 introduces short-term fluctuations and includes descriptions of Canada's experience with recessions and expansions, the characteristic behaviour of unemployment and inflation during business cycles, and the measurement of an economy's output gap. In the short run, changes in aggregate spending can affect output. Chapter 8 looks at the relationship between planned aggregate spending and output in the very short run, when prices are fixed and firms simply meet the demand for their output. In this setting, government policies that affect planned aggregate spending, such as changes in government purchases, can help to eliminate output gaps. Maintaining the short-run focus, Chapter 9 adds monetary policy and the Bank of Canada to the story. Chapter 10 dispenses with the assumption of a fixed price level and considers output and price level determination in the context of a traditional model of aggregate demand and supply. Chapter 11 presents a model according to which an output gap substantially different from zero will eventually cause the inflation rate to change. This, in turn (via the central bank's policy reaction function), triggers a mechanism for the elimination of output gaps over time. The chapter also considers other sources of inflation, notably aggregate supply shocks and the policy dilemmas that these create. Chapter 12 extends the discussion of exchange rates and includes analysis of speculative attacks and the constraints that a fixed exchange-rate regime places on domestic monetary policy. Chapter 13 provides additional theory and evidence about money and banking and about how central banks operate. It emphasizes the severe consequences of extreme increases or decreases in the money supply.

If macroeconomic stability is achieved, then no topic in economics is more important to living standards than the sources of long-term output and productivity growth. The four chapters of Part 4 therefore deal primarily with long-term economic performance. Chapter 14 reviews the record of long-term economic growth and discusses the factors (such as rising levels of education, fixed capital formation, and improvements in technology) that have contributed to productivity growth. Chapter 15 analyzes the trade dimension of Canada's role in the global economy. It deals with trade theory, data, and institutions. Chapter 16 analyzes how saving (including non-resident saving) is related to economy-wide investment, and discusses factors affecting savings and investment decisions. Chapter 17 deals with bond and stock markets and with both the advantages and the risks associated with international capital flows.

ALTERNATIVE COURSE STRUCTURES

As our discussion of the organization of topics indicates, there is a well-developed logic to the structure and coverage of this textbook. But, naturally, each instructor will teach the material a bit differently; some will decide to cover less material, and others may prefer to teach the long-run chapters of Part 4 before the short-run chapters of Part 3. The textbook lends itself to these and other course structures. Here we will first discuss options for covering less material, regardless of the sequencing of the chapters, and then we suggest an alternative, "long-run first" path through the chapters.

Covering Less Material   What are the options for covering less material? Part 1 can be skipped, of course, if this textbook is employed in the second term of a course that covers microeconomics in the first term. We believe that instructors should cover each of the three chapters of Part 2, otherwise students may fail to develop a good grasp of what the key macroeconomic variables—GDP, the unemployment rate, and the inflation rate—really represent and of how real variables differ from nominal ones. In Part 3, Chapters 10 and 11 provide alternative macroeconomic models; Chapter 10 deals with a traditional aggregate demand–aggregate supply model of output and price level determination, whereas Chapter 11 presents a more recent model of output and inflation rate determination. Some instructors will decide to skip one of these two chapters. Chapter 13 is mainly concerned with money supply issues, and, although it deals with important matters, the chapter is not a stepping stone to later chapters—that is, it may be skipped without a loss of continuity. In Part 4, Chapter 14 on long-run economic growth is the key chapter, and most instructors will also want to cover Chapter 15 on international trade. Chapters 16 and 17 deal with topics that many students find fascinating and practical, such as stock and bond price determination, but many topics in Chapters 16 and 17 are not emphasized in other widely used textbooks, so some instructors may decide to skip one or both chapters in the interests of time.

Long-Run First Options   Some Canadian instructors like to cover the "long-run" material early in the course and, in fact, the first two editions of this textbook followed a "long-run first" approach. Instructors familiar with the second edition of this textbook who prefer a long-run first approach will be pleased to learn that this third Canadian edition retains all of the chapters from the second edition. One option for a long-run first approach would be to cover Part 1 (micro chapters), then Part 2 (measurement chapters) and Part 4 (long-run chapters), and finally Part 3 (short-run chapters). Instructors who follow this approach should be aware that some Economic Naturalist examples in the long-run chapters make reference to terms covered in the short-run chapters—for example, terms such as the Fisher effect and the purchasing power parity theory of exchange rate determination—and Chapter 15 on international trade now has a section that refers back to the short-run macro model of Chapter 8.

For instructors who would like to follow the same chapter order as they followed for the second edition of this textbook, the following list of current chapters and their former chapter numbers may be handy.

- Chapter 1 to 6 (same as in second edition)
- Chapter 7 (Chapter 11 in the second edition)
- Chapter 8 (Chapter 12 in the second edition)
- Chapter 9 (Chapter 13 in the second edition)
- Chapter 10 (Chapter 14 in the second edition)
- Chapter 11 (Chapter 15 in the second edition)
- Chapter 12 (Chapter 17 in the second edition)
- Chapter 13 (Chapter 9 in the second edition)
- Chapter 14 (Chapter 7 in the second edition)
- Chapter 15 (Chapter 16 in the second edition)
- Chapter 16 (Chapter 8 in the second edition)
- Chapter 17 (Chapter 10 in the second edition)

COMPREHENSIVE LEARNING AND TEACHING PACKAGE

FOR THE INSTRUCTOR

McGraw-Hill Ryerson has made every effort to include the support material that is most critical for you and your students.

CONNECT for Economics McGraw-Hill's **Connect** for Economics provides a complete, web-based solution that includes and expands upon the actual problem sets found at the end of each chapter. It features enhanced technology that provides a varied supply of auto-graded assignments and graphing exercises, tied to the learning objectives in the book. McGraw-Hill's Connect can be used for student practice, graded homework assignments, and formal examinations; the results are easily integrated with your course management system, including WebCT and Blackboard. Please contact your *i*Learning Sales Specialist for information on how to set up and use Connect for Economics.

LYRYX LEARNING INC
Online Learning and Assessment
lyryx.com

LYRYX for Economics   **Lyryx** Assessment for Economics is a leading-edge online assessment system, designed to support both students and instructors. The assessment takes the form of a homework assignment called a Lab. The assessments are algorithmically generated and automatically graded so that students get instant grades and feedback. New Labs are randomly generated each time, providing the student with unlimited opportunities to try a type of question. After they submit a Lab for marking, students receive extensive feedback on their work, thus promoting their learning experience.

Lyryx for the student offers algorithmically generated and automatically graded assignments. Students get instant grades and instant feedback—no need to wait until the next class to find out how well they did! Grades are instantly recorded in a grade book that the student can view.

Students are motivated to do their Labs for two reasons: first, because the results can be tied to assessment and, second, because they can try the Lab as many times as they wish prior to the due date, with only their best grade being recorded.

Instructors know from experience that if students do their economics homework, they will be successful in the course. Recent research regarding the use of Lyryx has shown that when Labs are tied to assessment, even if worth only a small percentage of the total grade of the course, students WILL do their homework—and MORE THAN ONCE!

Please contact your *i*Learning Sales Specialist for additional information on the Lyryx Assessment for Economics system. Visit **http://lyryx.com**.

CourseSmart   **CourseSmart** brings together thousands of textbooks across hundreds of courses in an eTextbook format providing unique benefits to students and faculty. By purchasing an eTextbook, students can save up to 50 percent of the cost of a print textbook; reduce their impact on the environment; and gain access to powerful Web tools for learning, including full text search, notes and highlighting, and e-mail tools for sharing notes between classmates. For faculty, CourseSmart provides instant access to review and compare textbooks and course materials in their discipline area without the time, cost, and environmental impact of mailing print examination copies. For further details contact your *i*Learning Sales Specialist or go to www.coursesmart.com.

COURSE MANAGEMENT

We offer Macroeconomics content resources for Instructors who are interested in designing their own online courses. Content cartridges are available for course management systems such as WebCT and BlackBoard. Ask your *i*Learning Sales Specialist for details.

Integrated Learning Your Integrated Learning Sales Specialist is a McGraw-Hill Ryerson representative who has the experience, product knowledge, and training, to provide the support to help you assess and integrate any of our products, technology and services into your course for optimum teaching and learning performance. The Integrated Learning Sales Specialist can show you tools that will help your students improve their grades, or help you put your entire course online—your *i*Learning Sales Specialist is there to help. Contact your local *i*Learning Sales Specialist today to learn how to maximize all of McGraw-Hill Ryerson's resources!

iLearning Services McGraw-Hill Ryerson offers a unique *i*Services package designed for Canadian faculty. Our mission is to equip providers of higher education with superior tools and resources required for excellence in teaching. For additional information, visit www.mcgrawhill.ca/highereducation/*i*services.

Teaching, Learning, and Technology Conference Series The educational environment has changed tremendously in recent years, and McGraw-Hill Ryerson continues to be committed to helping you acquire the skills you need to succeed in this new milieu. Our innovative Teaching, Technology, and Learning Conference Series brings faculty together from across Canada with 3M Teaching Excellence award winners to share teaching and learning best practices in a collaborative and stimulating environment. Pre-conference workshops on general topics, such as teaching large classes and technology integration, will also be offered. We will also work with you at your own institution to customize workshops that best suit the needs of your faculty.

The Instructor's Online Learning Centre The OLC at www.mcgrawhill.ca/olc/frankbernanke includes a password-protected Web site for Instructors.

Instructor's Resources
- **Instructor's Manual** Adapted by Teresa Cyrus of Dalhousie University, this manual is extremely useful for all teachers, but especially for those new to the job. It offers suggestions for using the Study Guides, the Test Bank, and the Economic Naturalist cases. It supplies sample syllabi with assignments, sample exams, and supplemental material. For each chapter, it provides an overview, an outline, teaching objectives, additional Economic Naturalist discussion questions, answers to textbook questions and problems, homework assignments with answers, and sample quizzes with answers.
- **Computerized Test Banks** The test banks (micro and macro) updated by Teresa Cyrus and Liza Bristow of Dalhousie University, ensure maximum flexibility in test preparation, including the reconfiguring of graphing exercises. The test banks contain more than 5000 multiple-choice questions categorized by Learning Objective, Learning Level (knowledge, comprehension, application, analysis), Type (graph, calculation, word problem), and Source (textbook, Study Guide, Web, unique).
- **PowerPoint Slides** Amy Peng of Ryerson University developed this package of dynamic slides of the important illustrations in the textbook, along with detailed, chapter-by-chapter reviews of the important ideas presented in the text.

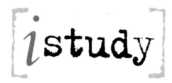

iInteract iLearn iSucceed

FOR STUDENTS

iStudy for Econ   Available 24/7: Instant feedback so you can study when you want, how you want, and where you want.

This online *iStudy* space was developed by Brennan Thompson of Ryerson University to help you master economic concepts and achieve better grades. It contains a variety of learning tools that will help you improve your problem solving skills in economics. Included are chapter overviews, interactive quizzes, and short answer questions and problems. Additionally, you will find a Cyberlecture, practice activities, and interactive graphing activities. *iStudy* offers the best, most convenient way to Interact, Learn, and Succeed.

To see a sample chapter go to the Online Learning Centre at www.mcgrawhill. ca/olc/frankbernanke. Full access to *iStudy* can be purchased at the website or by purchasing a pin code card through your campus bookstore.

Instructors: Contact your *i*Learning Sales Specialist for more information on how to make *iStudy* part of your students' success.

Student Online Learning Centre   This electronic learning aid at www. mcgrawhill.ca/olc/frankbernanke contains practise activities, separate pre- and post-tests, Economic Naturalist exercises, sample exam questions with answers, understanding questions, and chapter summaries.

ACKNOWLEDGEMENTS

The authors want to thank, first and foremost, Bruce McIntosh, our Sponsoring Editor, and Daphne Scriabin, our Developmental Editor. The entire team at McGraw-Hill Ryerson deserves credit for keeping the project moving in a timely fashion. We thank Joanna Cotton, Vice-President and Editor-in-Chief, for making this textbook a priority project. And we are grateful for the outstanding work of the McGraw-Hill Ryerson editorial and production teams.

We would like to acknowledge the role played by Mara Storey in updating data for this edition. We are extremely indebted to Teresa Cyrus, Dalhousie University, for the close reading and perceptive comments provided in her technical reviews of the manuscript. We also thank the following teachers and colleagues, whose thorough reviews and thoughtful suggestions led to innumerable substantive improvements:

Jeremiah Allen, University of Lethbridge
Natalya Brown, Nipissing University
David Gray, University of Ottawa
Don Reddick, Kwantlen University College
Robert Gateman, University of British Columbia
Rashid Khan, McMaster University
Eva Lau, University of Waterloo
Pierre-Pascal Gendron, Humber College
Laura Lamb, University of Manitoba
Eric Moon, Seneca College
James Sentance, University of Prince Edward Island
Peter Sinclair, Wilfrid Laurier University
Annie Spears, University of Prince Edward Island
Angela Trimarchi, University of Waterloo
Marianne Vigneault, Bishop's University
Mary Jane Waples, Memorial University of Newfoundland

PART 1

Introduction

Economics is a *way of thinking* about the world. Over many years economists have developed some simple principles and tools that are useful for understanding a wide range of situations, from the relatively simple economic decisions that individuals make every day to the workings of highly complex markets, such as international financial markets. A major objective of this book is to help you learn these principles and tools and also how to apply them to a variety of issues.

The three chapters of Part 1 introduce the problem of scarcity and develop six core principles that will be used throughout the book. Chapter 1 presents scarcity—the unavoidable fact that although our needs and wants are limitless, the resources available to satisfy them are limited—as the fundamental economic problem. The chapter shows that deciding whether to take an action by comparing the cost and benefit of the action is a useful approach for dealing with the inevitable trade-offs that scarcity creates. It also identifies several pitfalls that plague many decision makers. Chapter 2 goes beyond individual decision making to consider trade among both individuals and countries. An important reason for trade is that it permits people (or countries) to specialize in the production of particular goods and services, which in turn enhances productivity and raises standards of living. Finally, Chapter 3 presents an overview of the concepts of supply and demand, perhaps the most basic and familiar tools of economists.

Chapter 1 Thinking Like an Economist

How many students are in your introductory economics class? Some classes have just 20 or so. Others average 35, 100, or 200 students. At some large universities, introductory economics classes may have as many as 2000 students, while colleges and smaller universities may offer much smaller classes. What size is best?

If cost was no object, the best size for an introductory economics course, or any other course for that matter, might be only a single student. Everything could be tailored to your own background and ability, allowing you to cover the material at just the right pace. The tutorial format would also promote close communication and personal trust between you and your professor.

Why, then, have many Canadian universities reduced the number of introductory economics classes they offer while increasing the number of students per class? The simple reason is that *cost does* matter. The direct cost of providing you with your own personal introductory economics course, most notably the professor's salary and the expense of providing a classroom in which to meet, might easily top $20 000. *Someone* has to pay these costs. Since Canadian universities receive part of their revenue from governments and part from students' fees, the cost would be covered by higher tuition payments and higher tax payments.

With a larger class size, of course, the cost per student goes down. For example, in a class of 300 students, the cost of an introductory economics course might be as little as $100 per student. However, there is a trade-off. Although few students like large classes, they are significantly more affordable.

In choosing what size the introductory economics course should be, university and college administrators confront a classic economic trade-off. In making the class larger, they increase the student–faculty ratio; but, at the same time, they reduce costs per student and hence the tuition students must pay.

1.1   ECONOMICS: STUDYING CHOICE IN A WORLD OF SCARCITY

If we could always have whatever we wanted, for free, right now, we would never have to choose—all we would ever have to say is "more please," and we would get it. Unfortunately, the real world is not like that. Most things have a cost in time or money or other resources, all of which we have in only limited amounts. Scarcity means that we have to make choices. More of one good means choosing less of another. **Economics** is the study of how people make choices under conditions of scarcity and of the results of those choices for society.

That such trade-offs are widespread and important is the core problem of economics. We call this the **scarcity problem**, because the simple fact of scarcity makes trade-offs necessary. Another name for the scarcity problem might be the "no-free-lunch" idea, which comes from the observation that even a lunch that is given to you takes time to eat—time you could have spent doing other useful things.

The Scarcity Problem: Although we have boundless needs and wants, the resources available to us, including time, are limited. Scarcity means that we have to make choices—having more of one good thing usually means having less of another.

Trade-offs require choices that involve compromises between competing interests. Cost–benefit analysis is based on the disarmingly simple principle that an action will make an individual (or a firm or a society) better off if, and only if, its benefits exceed its costs. We call this statement the **cost–benefit principle**. It is one of the core principles of economics.

The Cost–Benefit Principle: An individual (or a firm or a society) will be better off taking an action if, and only if, the extra benefits from taking the action are greater than the extra costs.

The cost–benefit principle is simple, but to apply it we need to measure costs and benefits, a task that is often difficult in practice. Nevertheless, a few simplifying assumptions can help us to demonstrate how the cost–benefit principle can be applied to the question of the "best" class size. First, suppose that because a university has only two sizes of classrooms, classes of 20 and 100 students are the only possibilities. Second, assume that the only relevant costs of offering a course are the instructor's salary and the room expense, and also that the university charges tuition equal to the cost of providing a course. If room costs are $5000 and the instructor's salary is $15 000 regardless of the class size, the costs are $200 per student for a class of 100 and $1000 per student for a class of 20. The cost of reducing class sizes from 100 to 20 students is then $800 per student ($1000 − $200 = $800).

Will administrators choose the smaller class size? If they apply the cost–benefit principle, they will realize that the smaller class size makes sense only if the value to students of attending the smaller class is at least $800 per student greater than the value of attending the larger class. Would you (or your parents) be willing to pay an extra $800 for a smaller economics class? If not, and if other students feel the same way, then maintaining the larger class size makes sense. But if you and others would be willing to pay the extra tuition, then reducing the class size to 20 makes good economic sense.

Notice that the "best" class size from an economic point of view may not be the same as the "best" size from the point of view of an educational psychologist. The difference arises because the economic definition of "best" takes into account both the benefits *and* the costs of different class sizes as perceived by you (or your

Are small classes "better" than large ones?

economics the study of how people make choices under conditions of scarcity and of the results of those choices for society

COST–BENEFIT

parents). The psychologist is only interested in the learning benefits of different class sizes. In practice, of course, different people will feel differently about the value of smaller classes. People with high incomes, for example, tend to be willing to pay more for the advantage, which helps to explain why the average class size is smaller and tuition higher at those private schools whose students come predominantly from high-income families.

We have used the cost–benefit framework to consider the question of the best class size. Next, we will use it to provide a possible reason for the gradual increase in average class size that has been taking place in Canadian colleges and universities.

Between 1990–91 and 1998–99, public operating grants to Canadian universities decreased by about 25 percent. This reduction is part of a pattern of reduced expenditures that enabled the federal government to move from large deficits in the early 1990s to large surpluses by the end of the decade. To address the shortfall, Canadian colleges and universities have increased class sizes and raised fees. By 2003–04, after adjusting for inflation, fees were about twice what they had been ten years earlier. Students today borrow more to finance their education than did students in the past.[1]

Students are paying higher fees to attend larger classes. The size of classes could be reduced if a sufficient number of students paid even higher fees, or if governments increased their funding of universities. However, universities believe that students are not willing to pay even higher fees. Governments believe that taxpayers are not willing to pay more taxes to increase the funding of postsecondary education. Apparently, an insufficient number of people are willing to bear the cost of smaller classes; thus, class sizes have increased. The increase in class size follows from a governmental position concerning deficits, not from market behaviour.

Notice that the cost–benefit principle provides a plausible explanation of why class sizes have increased. You may believe that a policy that eliminated federal deficits is appropriate. But you may also believe it would have been more fair to reduce the deficit by raising taxes rather than by cutting spending—especially the spending that kept student debt down and class sizes smaller. The cost–benefit principle helps to explain cause and effect; however, it is not helpful in determining whether a policy is distributionally fair.

1.2   APPLYING THE COST–BENEFIT PRINCIPLE

In studying choice under scarcity, it is often useful to begin with the premise that people are **rational**, which means they have well-defined goals and try to fulfill them as best they can. The cost–benefit principle is a fundamental tool for the study of how rational people make choices.

Often the only real difficulty in applying the cost–benefit principle is coming up with reasonable measures of all the relevant benefits and costs. Only in rare instances will the dollar measures be conveniently available. But the cost–benefit framework can lend structure to your thinking even when no relevant market data are available. To illustrate how we proceed in such cases, the following example asks you to decide whether to perform an action whose cost and benefits are described only in vague, qualitative terms.

rational person someone with well-defined goals who tries to fulfill those goals as best he or she can

---

[1]"Students Pay More for Less," *CAUT ACPPU Bulletin*, 48(6), June 2001, p. 1, and "Students in for a Rough Ride," *CAUT ACPPU Bulletin*, 50(7), Sept. 2003, p. A9. Students' fees are an important source of revenue and their increase has enabled many universities to prevent services from being cut even further. However, notice that if fees rise by 100 percent, a university's revenue will rise by far less than 100 percent. Suppose that 25 cents of every dollar of a university's revenue comes from students' fees, which is typical. The university raises fees by 100 percent: $1.00 \times \$0.25 = \$0.25$. Thus, a 100 percent increase in students' fees increases the university's revenue by 25 percent.

Will you be better off if you walk downtown to save $10 on a $25 computer game?

EXAMPLE 1.1

Imagine you are about to buy a $25 computer game at the nearby campus store when a friend tells you that the same game is on sale at a downtown store for only $15. If the downtown store is a 30-minute walk away, and you have no other way of getting there, where will you buy the game?

The cost–benefit principle tells us that you will buy it downtown if the benefit of doing so exceeds the cost. The benefit of taking any action is the dollar value of everything you gain by taking it. Here, the benefit of buying downtown is exactly $10, since that is the amount you will save on the purchase price of the game. The cost of taking any action is the dollar value of everything you give up by taking it. Here, the cost of buying downtown is the dollar value of the time and trouble of making the trip. But how do we estimate that dollar value?

One way is to perform the following hypothetical action. Imagine that a stranger has offered to pay you to do an errand that involves the same walk downtown (perhaps to drop off a letter for her at the post office). If she offered you a payment of, say, $100, would you accept? If so, we know that your cost of walking downtown and back must be less than $100. Now imagine her offer being reduced in small increments until you finally refuse the last offer. For example, if you agree to walk downtown and back for $9 but not for $8.99, then your perceived cost of making the trip is $9. Applying that to this case, you will be better off if you buy the game downtown, because the $10 you save (your benefit) is greater than your $9 cost of making the trip.

On the other hand, suppose that your cost of making the trip is greater than $10. In that case, the cost–benefit principle tells you to buy the game from the nearby campus store.

COST–BENEFIT

ECONOMIC SURPLUS

Suppose again that in Example 1.1 your "cost" of making the trip downtown was $9. Compared to the alternative of buying the game at the campus store, buying it downtown resulted in an **economic surplus** of $1, the difference between the benefit of making the trip and its cost. In general, you will be best off if you choose those actions that generate the largest possible economic surplus. This means taking all actions that yield a positive total economic surplus, which is just another way of restating the cost–benefit principle.

economic surplus the benefit of taking any action minus its cost

Note that just because your best choice is to buy the game downtown does not imply that you *enjoy* making the trip any more than choosing a large class means that you prefer large classes to small ones. It simply means that the trip is less unpleasant than the prospect of paying $10 extra for the game. Once again, you have faced a trade-off: in this case, the choice between a cheaper game and the free time gained by avoiding the trip.

Note also that if the time it would take to walk downtown and back has a value to you of more than $10, it is perfectly rational to decide *not* to save $10 on the computer game. Economists know that money isn't everything. But in order to compare the sizes of benefits and costs we need some common unit of measurement, and economists often use dollar values for this because they are a convenient unit. This, however, does not imply that we will always choose the alternative that costs the least or saves the most money.

OPPORTUNITY COST

Suppose, for example, that the time required for the trip downtown is the only time you have left to study for a difficult test the next day. Or suppose you are watching one of your favourite movies on cable, or that you are tired and would

opportunity cost the value of the next-best alternative that must be foregone in order to undertake the activity

love a short nap. In such cases, we say that the **opportunity cost** of making the trip, the value of what you must sacrifice to walk downtown and back, is high and you are more likely to decide against making the trip.

In this example, if watching the last hour of the movie is the most valuable opportunity that conflicts with the trip downtown, the opportunity cost of making the trip is the dollar value you place on pursuing that opportunity—that is, the largest amount you would be willing to pay to avoid missing the end of the movie. Note that the opportunity cost of making the trip is not the combined value of *all* possible activities you could have pursued, but only the value of your *best* alternative, the one you would have chosen had you not made the trip.

Throughout the text we will pose exercises like the one that follows. You will find that pausing to answer them will help you to master key concepts in economics. Because doing these exercises is not very costly (indeed, many students report that they are actually fun), the cost–benefit principle indicates that it is well worth your while to do them.

COST–
BENEFIT

EXERCISE 1.1

You would again save $10 by buying the game downtown rather than at the campus store, but your cost of making the trip is now $12, not $9. How much economic surplus would you get from buying the game downtown? Where does the cost–benefit principle tell you to buy the game?

EXAMPLE 1.2

What is the opportunity cost of selling flowers on the sidewalk?

Suppose that you are a flower seller, with a stock of cut roses that will wilt by tomorrow morning. If you do not sell them tonight, their value tomorrow will be zero. You can think of two possible places to sell your flowers: on the sidewalk outside your home or downtown in upscale romantic restaurants, where you can embarrass people into buying flowers for their dates. However, to get into these restaurants, you must give the headwaiter a $30 payoff and it will cost you $10 in extra time and bus fares to travel downtown. Suppose that you expect to sell all the flowers in about an hour wherever you are, and you expect to get about $50 for your flowers if you sell downtown. You do not have anything else to do during the time you will spend selling flowers. What would be the opportunity cost of selling them on the sidewalk? What is the least revenue from sidewalk sales that would make selling on the sidewalk your best choice?

By selling on the sidewalk, you give up the surplus that you could get by selling downtown. If you had sold the flowers downtown you would have gotten a net return of $10 ($50 revenue minus $30 payoff minus $10 in extra travel costs). So the opportunity cost of selling the flowers on the sidewalk is $10. You are better off selling on the sidewalk only if you expect to make more than $10 at that location. (Notice that this and the next example do not specify how you got the flowers. Whether you grew them yourself, bought them in the marketplace, or received them as a gift, *it does not matter*. The important thing is that the flowers will wilt by tomorrow and be valueless, hence the opportunity cost of the flowers themselves is zero.)

EXAMPLE 1.3

Suppose that you think you could sell your flowers for $8 on the sidewalk. What would be the opportunity cost of selling them downtown?

If you sell your flowers downtown, you forego $8 in revenue you could get from selling flowers on the sidewalk, and you incur $30 in payoff costs and $10 in transportation expenses. Therefore, the total value of everything you give up in order to sell downtown is $48. Your surplus from sales downtown net of all opportunity costs is $2.

Notice from Examples 1.2 and 1.3 that opportunity costs can be either *explicit* or *implicit*. An explicit opportunity cost requires an outlay or payment. For example, a payment of $30 to a headwaiter for access to customers in a restaurant is an *explicit* opportunity cost. The $30 cannot be used to purchase something else. An implicit opportunity cost does not involve an actual payment. If you choose to sell flowers downtown, you forego the opportunity to earn $8 selling flowers from the sidewalk. By sacrificing an income, you are incurring an *implicit* opportunity cost. The total opportunity cost of any action is the sum of explicit and implicit opportunity costs.

THE ROLE OF ECONOMIC MODELS

Economists often use abstract models of how an idealized rational individual would choose among competing alternatives. When doing so, they consciously ignore influences that they consider relatively unimportant in order to concentrate attention on the most important influences. Physicists often construct idealized models of physical phenomena in a similar way. If, for example, the issue is how quickly a rock dropped from the top of a tower will hit the ground, a physicist could make a fairly good prediction even if she ignored the influence of air resistance. Even though the physicist knows perfectly well that air resistance has an influence, it is small enough to be ignored in this case given the force of gravity and the density of a rock. However, if a feather is dropped air resistance *will* make a difference and must be taken into consideration. Choosing the right assumptions makes the difference between a model that performs well and one that does not.

Noneconomists are sometimes harshly critical of the economist's cost–benefit model on the grounds that people in the real world rarely conduct complex mental calculations before making simple decisions. But economists know perfectly well that people do not conduct hypothetical mental actions when they make simple decisions. All the cost–benefit principle really says is that a rational decision is one that is explicitly or implicitly based on a weighing of costs and benefits. Most of us make sensible decisions most of the time, without being consciously aware that we are weighing costs and benefits, just as most people ride a bike without being consciously aware of what keeps them from falling. Through trial and error, we gradually learn what kinds of choices tend to work best in different contexts, just as bicycle riders internalize the relevant laws of physics, usually without being consciously aware of them.

Economic models of rational behaviour analyze what individuals would do in theory if they explicitly calculated the costs and benefits of their decisions. These models are useful because they enable economists to predict the behaviour of actual individuals, who are often intuitive and implicit in their decision making but are nonetheless trying to maximize their net benefit.

Hence, most economic models are examples of *positive economics*. **Positive economics** has two dimensions. First, it offers cause-and-effect explanations of economic relationships. Second, positive economics has an empirical dimension. In principle, data can be used to confirm or refute propositions, or hypotheses, that emerge from positive economics. Data also can be used to measure the magnitude of effects that emerge from cause-and-effect relationships. Thus, we can predict that if resources available to colleges and universities are reduced, class sizes will increase. We can use data to determine whether class sizes do, in fact, increase. If they do, data can be used to determine by how much they increase. Using the cost-benefit principle to explain why class sizes have increased is an example of positive economics. Ideally, positive economics is value free.

positive economics economic analysis that offers cause-and-effect explanations of economic relationships; the propositions, or hypotheses, that emerge from positive economics can, in principle, be confirmed or refuted by data; in principle, data can also be used to measure the magnitude of effects predicted by positive economics

normative economics
economic statements that reflect subjective value judgments and that are based on ethical positions

fallacy of composition the argument that because something is true for a part, it also is true for the whole

post hoc fallacy the argument that because event A precedes event B, event A causes event B

In contrast, **normative economics** asks whether something should happen. It therefore reflects subjective value judgments and is based on ethical positions. The question of whether or not larger classes and higher fees are unfair to students is a normative issue.

Two logical errors are to be avoided when modelling economic relationships. The first, the **fallacy of composition,** occurs if one argues that what is true for a part must also be true for the whole. The statement, "If one farmer harvests a larger crop he will be better off; therefore, if all farmers harvest larger crops, all farmers will better off," is an example of the fallacy of composition. If all farmers harvest larger crops, prices may decrease by an amount that would more than offset the benefit of larger harvests. What is true for an individual is not necessarily true for an entire group.

The *post hoc* fallacy is second common logical error. The name stems from the Latin phrase *post hoc, ergo propter hoc,* meaning "after this, therefore because of this." The fallacy leads one to argue that because event A precedes event B, event A causes event B. Suppose that in a fit of anger, a person wishes that a neighbour was dead. A week later, the neighbour drops dead from a heart attack. To conclude that the wish caused the death is to commit the *post hoc* fallacy. Generally, correlation does not indicate causation. For example, the United States spends more per capita on health care than Canada does, but Canadians have a longer life expectancy than Americans have. It does not follow from these facts that larger expenditures on health care reduce life expectancy. While there might be a correlation here, various social, personal, and economic factors also play a role in determining life expectancy. Cause-and-effect and correlation are two very different things.

RATIONALITY AND IMPERFECT DECISION MAKERS

When having to decide if an action will leave you better off or not, the action could be anything from eating another cookie to choosing Capilano College over Douglas College. The cost–benefit principle says that if the benefits of the action exceed its costs, then performing the action will make you better off. However, if the benefits are less than the costs, then performing the action will make you worse off. If its benefits and costs happen to be equal, then it does not matter whether you perform the action or not.

Rational people will apply the cost–benefit principle most of the time, although probably in an intuitive and approximate way rather than through explicit and precise calculation. To the extent that people are rational, their tendency to compare costs and benefits will help economists to predict their likely behaviour. For example, we can predict that students from wealthy families are more likely than others to attend private foreign universities that offer smaller classes.

RECAP

COST–BENEFIT ANALYSIS

Scarcity is a basic fact of economic life. Because of it, having more of one good often means having less of another, the scarcity problem. Economics is devoted to studying how we can make intelligent choices in a world of scarcity.

The cost–benefit principle holds that an individual (or a firm or a society) is better off taking an action if, and only if, the extra benefit from taking the action is greater than the extra cost. The benefit of taking any action minus the cost of taking the action is called the *economic surplus* from that action.

Thus, the cost–benefit principle suggests that we take only those actions that create additional economic surplus.

Applying the cost–benefit principle requires measurement. The benefit of an action is the most you would be willing to pay someone to perform it. The cost of an action is the value of the next-best alternative that you must forego to perform the action.

1.3 THREE COMMON PITFALLS

COST–
BENEFIT

The cost–benefit principle suggests that an introductory economics course emphasizes a short list of those principles with the greatest power to predict and explain behaviour. But it also suggests that among those principles, we will focus especially on those that are most difficult to master. As we explore the cost–benefit approach in greater detail, we will emphasize the errors people commonly make when trying to implement it. People tend to ignore certain costs that are relevant to a decision at hand, for example, and sometimes they are influenced by costs that are irrelevant. Three of the most commonly encountered pitfalls concern opportunity costs, sunk costs, and the difference between average and marginal costs.

1.4 PITFALL 1: IGNORING OPPORTUNITY COSTS

Sherlock Holmes, Arthur Conan Doyle's legendary detective, was successful because he saw details that most others overlooked. In *Silver Blaze*, Holmes is called on to investigate the theft of an expensive racehorse from its stable. A Scotland Yard inspector assigned to the case asks Holmes whether some particular aspect of the crime required further study. "Yes," Holmes replies, and describes "the curious incident of the dog in the nighttime." "The dog did nothing in the nighttime," responds the puzzled inspector. But, as Holmes realized, that was precisely the problem. The watchdog's failure to bark when Silver Blaze was stolen meant that the watchdog knew the thief. This clue substantially reduced the number of suspects and eventually led to the thief's apprehension.

Opportunity costs are like dogs that fail to bark in the night.

Just as we often don't notice when a dog fails to bark, many of us tend to overlook the implicit value of activities that fail to happen. As we have seen, however, intelligent decisions require taking the value of foregone opportunities into account. What *is not* stated may be as important as what *is* explicitly stated.

RECOGNIZING THE RELEVANT ALTERNATIVE

Will you be better off if you use your frequent-flyer coupon to fly to Vancouver for winter break?

EXAMPLE 1.4

With winter break only a week away, you are still undecided about whether to fly to Vancouver and then then go to Whistler with a group of classmates from the University of Alberta. The round-trip airfare from Edmonton to Vancouver is $500. All other relevant costs for the vacation while at Whistler will total exactly $1000. The maximum you are willing to pay for the vacation is $1350. You could travel to Whistler by paying $500 to fly from Edmonton to Vancouver, or by using a frequent-flyer coupon to pay for the flight. Your only alternative use for your frequent-flyer coupon is for your plane trip to Ottawa the weekend after winter break to attend your brother's wedding. (Your coupon expires shortly thereafter.)

COST–
BENEFIT

If the Edmonton–Ottawa round-trip airfare is $400, will you be better off if you use your frequent-flyer coupon to fly to Vancouver for winter break?

The *cost–benefit* criterion tells you to go to Vancouver if the benefits of the trip exceed its costs. If not for the complication of the frequent-flyer coupon, solving this problem would be a straightforward matter of comparing the maximum price you would pay for the week at Whistler (your benefit from the trip) to the sum of all relevant costs. And since your airfare and other costs would sum to $1500, or $150 more than what you are willing to pay for the trip, you would be better off not going.

But what about the possibility of using your frequent-flyer coupon to make the trip? Using it for that purpose might make the flight to Vancouver seem free, suggesting you would reap an economic surplus of $350 by making the trip. But doing so would also mean you would have to pay $400 for your airfare to Ottawa. So the opportunity cost of using your coupon to fly to Vancouver is really $400. If you use it for that purpose, the cost of the trip still exceeds its benefit and it still fails the cost–benefit test. In cases like these, you are much more likely to decide sensibly if you ask yourself, "Will I be better off if I use my frequent-flyer coupon for this trip or save it for an upcoming trip?"

The key to using the concept of opportunity cost correctly lies in recognizing precisely what taking a given action prevents us from doing. To illustrate, suppose we modify Example 1.4 slightly, as follows:

EXAMPLE 1.5

Same as Example 1.4, except that now your frequent-flyer coupon expires in a week, so your only chance to use it will be for the flight to Vancouver. Will you be better off if you use your coupon?

Since you now have no alternative use for your coupon, the opportunity cost of using it to pay for the flight to Vancouver is zero. That means your economic surplus from the trip will be $1350 − $1000 = $350 > 0$, so the cost–benefit principle tells you to use your coupon and go to Whistler.

THE TIME VALUE OF MONEY

We saw that taking an action now can mean being unable to take some other action in the future. To take the value of future opportunities properly into account, we need to weigh future costs and benefits against present costs and benefits. As the next example illustrates, having to pay someone a dollar one year from now is not the same as having to pay someone a dollar today.

EXAMPLE 1.6

Same as Example 1.4, except that instead of flying to Ottawa, your best alternative use for your frequent-flyer coupon is a flight you expect to take one year from now, for which the airfare is $363. If your savings account pays 10 percent interest per year, does the cost–benefit principle tell you to fly to Vancouver and then go to Whistler?

How does this new information alter the opportunity cost of using your coupon to fly to Vancouver? Using it now means having to pay $363 for your flight one year from now. The opportunity cost of using the coupon now might therefore seem to be exactly $363. But this way of thinking about the coupon misses an important aspect of opportunity cost.

The question you must ask is, how much am I willing to pay *today* to avoid having to pay $363 *one year from now?* To answer this question, determine how much you need to put in your savings account today, at 10 percent annual interest, to have $363 one year from now. The answer is $330, because you will earn $33 in interest (10 percent of $330) over the next year, for a total of $363. Your economic surplus from the trip to Whistler is therefore $1350 − $1000 − $330 = $20. Therefore, the cost–benefit principle tells you to take the trip to Whistler.

EXERCISE 1.2

Would your answer to Example 1.6 have been different if the annual interest rate had been 2 percent instead of 10 percent? (*Hint:* Would a deposit of $350 in your account today earn enough money to pay for your $363 air ticket one year from now?)

Example 1.6 and Exercise 1.2 drive home the point that the opportunity cost of a dollar spent today is not the same as the opportunity cost of a dollar spent one year from now. In general, the opportunity cost of resources that are expended in the future will be lower than the opportunity cost of resources that are expended in the present. The reason involves the **time value of money**—the fact that money deposited in an interest-bearing account today will grow in value over time. Indeed, the very fact that banks and other borrowers pay interest is a consequence of the opportunity cost concept.

As simple as the concept of opportunity cost is, it is one of the most important in economics. The art in applying the concept correctly lies in being able to recognize the most valuable alternative to a given activity. And though the concept is simple, its application can be subtle. For example, if we must choose between spending a dollar today or spending a dollar tomorrow, time itself will influence opportunity cost through the time value of money.

time value of money the fact that a given dollar amount today is equivalent to a larger dollar amount in the future, because the money can be invested in an interest-bearing account in the meantime

1.5 PITFALL 2: FAILURE TO IGNORE SUNK COSTS

The opportunity cost pitfall is one in which people ignore opportunity costs. In another common pitfall, the opposite is true: people are influenced by costs that really are not opportunity costs. *The only costs that are relevant to a decision about whether to take an action are the costs that we can avoid by not taking the action.* As a practical matter, however, many decision makers appear to be influenced by **sunk costs**—costs that are beyond recovery at the moment a decision is made. For example, money spent on a nontransferable, nonrefundable airline ticket is a sunk cost.

Because sunk costs must be borne *whether or not an action is taken,* they are irrelevant to the decision of whether to take the action. The sunk cost pitfall, the mistake of being influenced by sunk costs, is illustrated clearly in the following examples.

sunk cost a cost that is beyond recovery at the moment a decision is made

Will you drive through a snowstorm to get to a hockey game?

EXAMPLE 1.7

You and your friend Joe have identical tastes. At 2 P.M. you log on to Ticketmaster and buy a $30 nonrefundable ticket to a hockey game to be played that night in Ottawa, 70 km north of your home in Smiths Falls. Joe plans to attend the same game, but he plans to buy his ticket at the game. Tickets sold at the game cost only $25 because they don't carry a Ticketmaster surcharge. (Many people nonetheless pay the higher price at Ticketmaster to be sure of getting good seats.) At 4 P.M. an unexpected snowstorm begins, making the prospect of the drive to Ottawa much less attractive than before. If both you and Joe are rational, is one of you more likely to attend the game than the other?

Since you have already bought your ticket, the $30 you spent on it is a sunk cost. It is money you cannot recover, whether you go to the game or not. In deciding whether to see the game then, the cost–benefit principle tells you to compare the benefit of seeing the game (the largest dollar amount you would be willing to pay to see it) only to those *additional* costs you must incur to see the game; that is, the opportunity cost of your time, plus whatever cost you assign to the stress of driving through the snowstorm. Whether you attend the game or not, you will never see the $30 you paid for your ticket again. Therefore, it is a sunk cost, not an opportunity cost, and you will ignore the $30 if you apply the cost–benefit principle correctly.

Joe, too, must weigh the opportunity cost of his time and the hassle of the drive in deciding whether to attend the game. But he must also weigh the $25 he will have to spend for his ticket. At the moment of deciding, therefore, the remaining costs Joe must incur to see the game are $25 higher than the remaining costs for you. And since you both have identical tastes—that is, since your respective benefits of attending the game are exactly the same—Joe is less likely to make the trip. You might think the cost of seeing the game is higher for you, since your ticket cost $30, whereas Joe's will cost only $25. But at the moment of deciding whether to make the drive, the $25 is a relevant cost for Joe, whereas your $30 is a sunk cost, and hence an irrelevant one for you.

Now suppose we change the structure of Example 1.7 slightly.

EXAMPLE 1.8	Same as Example 1.7, except now a friend gives Joe a free ticket to the game at 2 P.M. Is one of you more likely to attend the game than the other?

This time neither of you faces any additional ticket expenses at the moment you must decide whether to drive through the snowstorm. Since your respective costs and benefits are the same, your decisions about whether to make the trip will be the same if you both apply the cost–benefit principle.

According to the cost–benefit criterion, the decision to attend the game does not depend on whether someone bought a ticket or was given one. A rational economic decision maker weighs the benefit of seeing the game against only the *additional* costs he must incur to see it; in this example, the opportunity cost of time, the psychological cost, and the physical risk of driving through the snowstorm. How a person came to possess a ticket has no bearing on either the relevant benefits or the relevant costs.

Of course, a calculation of costs and benefits is not the only thing that can influence a decision. A sense of *regret* can play a powerful role as well. Suppose both Joe and his friend had purchased tickets on Ticketmaster. If only they had known that a storm was coming, they would not have spent $30 for each ticket—they would have avoided a sunk cost. To avoid regret about purchasing tickets they will not use, the two friends could drive through the storm. Indeed, it seems that people who pay cash for a ticket often feel that they must use it to avoid "wasting" $30, while those who receive a ticket free of charge are more comfortable about staying home.

RECAP ↑

THE PITFALL OF NOT IGNORING SUNK COSTS

When deciding whether to perform an action, it is important to ignore sunk costs—those costs that cannot be avoided even if the action is not taken. Even though a ticket to a concert may have cost you $100, if you have already bought it and cannot sell it to anyone else, the $100 is a sunk cost. If your decision to attend the concert is based entirely on the cost–benefit principle, sunk cost will be irrelevant.

1.6   PITFALL 3: FAILURE TO UNDERSTAND THE AVERAGE–MARGINAL DISTINCTION

As we have seen, economic decisions take proper account of opportunity costs. Because sunk costs are not opportunity costs, sunk costs are irrelevant to economic decisions and are not counted when the cost–benefit principle is applied. Further, accurate application of the cost–benefit principle is not possible if marginal costs and benefits are confused with average costs and benefits.

Often we are confronted with the choice of whether or not to engage in an activity. But in many situations, the issue is not whether to pursue the activity, but in whether or not to increase it or decrease it. The cost–benefit framework emphasizes that the only relevant costs and benefits in deciding whether to change the amount of an activity are *marginal costs* and *benefits*. Economists define the **marginal cost** of an activity as the increase in total cost that results from carrying out one additional unit of the activity. Similarly, the **marginal benefit** of an activity is the increase in total benefit that results from carrying out one more unit of the activity. In many contexts, however, people seem more inclined to compare **average costs** and **average benefits**—total cost or benefit per unit of activity. The next section shows why marginal, not average, costs and benefits are relevant.

marginal cost the increase in total cost that results from carrying out one additional unit of an activity

marginal benefit the increase in total benefit that results from carrying out one more unit of an activity

average cost total cost of undertaking *n* units of an activity divided by *n*

average benefit total benefit of undertaking *n* units of an activity divided by *n*

WEIGHING MARGINAL BENEFITS AND MARGINAL COSTS GRAPHICALLY

How much memory is worthwhile for your computer to have?

EXAMPLE 1.9

Suppose you can add random-access memory (RAM) to your computer at a cost of $300 per gigabyte. Suppose also that the value to you of an additional gigabyte of memory, measured in terms of your willingness to pay for it, is as shown by curve *MB* in Figure 1.1 How many gigabytes of memory are worth purchasing?

Curve *MB* plots the value to you of an additional gigabyte of memory (measured on the vertical axis in dollars per gigabyte) as a function of your computer's existing memory (measured on the horizontal axis in gigabytes). For example, the value of additional memory is $600 per gigabyte if your computer has one gigabyte of memory but only $300 if it has 2 gigabytes. Curve *MB* is often called the marginal benefit curve, to emphasize that it shows not the *total* value of memory but the value of having *an additional unit* of memory. (*Marginal* means extra or additional.)

Curve *MC* in Figure 1.1 shows the cost, in dollars, of adding an additional gigabyte, assumed constant at $300. This curve is often called the marginal cost curve, to emphasize that it represents not the total cost of memory but the cost of adding an additional unit. The fact that curve *MC* is horizontal at $300 means

FIGURE 1.1

The Marginal Cost and Benefit of Additional RAM

Curve *MB* plots the benefit of adding an additional gigabyte of memory. Curve *MC* plots the cost of an additional gigabyte of memory. It is rational to continue adding memory as long as the marginal benefit of memory (curve *MB*) lies above the marginal cost of memory (curve *MC*). The optimal amount of RAM is 2 gigabytes, the amount for which the marginal benefit of memory is equal to its marginal cost.

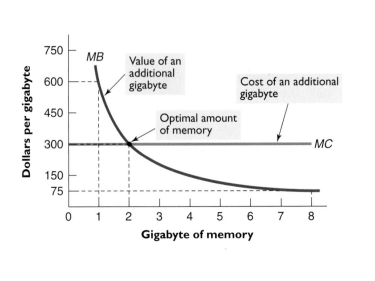

that no matter how much memory your computer has, you can always add an extra gigabyte at a cost of exactly $300. (Later on, we will consider examples in which the cost of adding additional units depends on the number of units you already have.)

Once we know the relevant marginal benefit and cost curves, finding the optimal quantity of memory is straightforward. Note in Figure 1.1 that if your computer has fewer than 2 gigabytes of memory, then the marginal benefit of adding memory (as measured by curve *MB*) is greater than its marginal cost (as measured by *MC*). So it is worthwhile to add memory if your computer currently has fewer than 2 gigabytes.

Conversely, note that if your computer has more than 2 gigabytes of memory, the marginal benefit of memory is less than its marginal cost, in which case you would have been better off buying less memory. The optimal amount of memory is thus 2 gigabytes, the amount at which the marginal benefit of memory exactly equals its marginal cost.

A common question prompted by Example 1.9 is "Why should I bother to add the second gigabyte of memory if its marginal benefit is no greater than its marginal cost?" The answer is that at any amount less than 2 gigabytes, the marginal benefit of memory exceeds its marginal cost. Suppose, for example, that your computer had only 1.9 gigabytes of memory, if that were possible. The marginal benefit of additional memory would then be greater than its marginal cost (albeit by only a tiny margin), which means that it is worthwhile to expand. The same reasoning would apply if your computer had 1.99 gigabytes, or even 1.999. So you can always do better by expanding unless you already have 2 gigabytes.[2]

---

[2]Note that in this example we treated your computer's memory bank as a perfectly divisible quantity. In practice, however, computer memory can be increased only by adding chunks of discrete size. A more realistic account of your decision of how much memory to buy for your computer would advise you to add the next chunk of memory if its benefit exceeds its cost. The optimal quantity of memory could then be an amount for which the benefit was greater than its cost. In that case, the benefit of next discrete chunk would be less than its cost.

Example 1.9 demonstrates why it is necessary to use marginal benefits and marginal costs in determining if it is worthwhile to change the amount of an activity. Next, Example 1.10 demonstrates that it may not be worthwhile to increase an activity even though its average benefit at the current level is significantly greater than its average cost. Indeed, *average cost and average benefit are irrelevant to a decision about changing the amount of an activity.*

Does the cost–benefit principle tell NASA to expand the space shuttle program from four launches per year to five?

EXAMPLE 1.10

Professor Kösten Banifoot, a prominent supporter of the NASA space shuttle program, has estimated that the gains from the program are currently $24 billion per year (an average of $6 billion per launch) and that its costs are currently $20 billion per year (an average of $5 billion per launch). True or false: If these estimates are correct, the cost–benefit principle tells NASA to expand the program. (Canadian astronauts have flown on the space shuttle, and Canada supplies components to NASA. Expansion of the space shuttle program would provide additional opportunities for Canadian science and technology.)

To decide whether an additional launch makes sense, we need to compare the cost of adding that launch with the benefit of adding it. The *average* benefit and *average* cost per launch for all shuttles launched thus far simply are not useful in deciding whether to expand the program. Of course, the average cost of the launches undertaken so far *might* be the same as the cost of adding another launch. But it also might be either higher or lower than the marginal cost of a launch. The same statement holds true regarding average and marginal benefits.

Suppose, for example, that the benefit of an additional launch is in fact the same as the average benefit per launch thus far, namely, $6 billion. Does the cost–benefit principle tell NASA to add another launch? Not if the cost of adding the fifth launch would be more than $6 billion. Suppose the relationship between the number of shuttles launched and the total cost of the program is as described in Table 1.1.

TABLE 1.1
How Cost Varies with the Number of Launches

Number of launches per year	Total costs per year ($ billions)	Marginal cost per launch ($ billions)
1	6	
		2
2	8	
		4
3	12	
		8
4	20	
		10
5	30	

At the current level of four launches per year, the average cost is $20 billion/4 = $5 billion per launch. But adding a fifth launch would raise costs from $20 billion to $30 billion, so the marginal cost of the fifth launch is $10 billion. If the benefit of an additional launch is constant at $6 billion, the cost–benefit principle does not justify increasing the number of launches. Indeed, the fourth launch itself would not be justified, since it cost $8 billion and produced only $6 billion in additional benefits. Based on the numbers shown in the table, which are completely consistent with Professor Banifoot's data on average costs and benefits, the optimal number of launches would be only three per year.

EXERCISE 1.3

Suppose the marginal benefit of each launch is $9 billion, not $6 billion. How many shuttles per year does the cost–benefit principle tell NASA to launch?

COST–
BENEFIT

RELEVANT
COSTS

The conclusion that some costs, especially marginal costs and opportunity costs, are important while others, like sunk costs and average costs, are irrelevant to economic decisions is implicit in our original explanation of the *cost–benefit principle* (an action should be taken if, and only if, the extra benefits of taking it exceed the extra costs). Yet, the pitfalls of (1) ignoring opportunity costs, (2) considering sunk costs, and (3) confusing average with marginal cost are so important that we enumerate them separately. As a result, a core principle worthy of repeated emphasis emerges:

The Principle of Relevant Costs: **In considering whether to produce or consume more of a good, what matters is the cost of one more unit (marginal cost).**

> **RECAP**
>
> **THREE IMPORTANT PITFALLS**
>
> 1. **The pitfall of ignoring opportunity costs.** When performing a cost–benefit analysis of an action, it is important to account for the full opportunity cost of the action. The opportunity cost of an action is the value of the next best alternative that is foregone by taking the action.
>
>   In calculating opportunity cost, it is important to consider the time value of money. Because money can be invested in an interest-bearing account, a dollar paid or received in the future is worth less than a dollar paid or received today.
>
> 2. **The pitfall of not ignoring sunk costs.** When deciding whether to perform an action, it is important to ignore sunk costs—costs that cannot be avoided even if the action is not taken. Even though a ticket to a game may have cost $30, if you have already bought it and cannot sell it to anyone else the $30 is a sunk cost. If your decision to attend the game is based entirely on the cost–benefit principle, you will ignore the sunk cost.
>
> 3. **The pitfall of using average instead of marginal costs and benefits.** Decision makers often have ready information about the total cost and benefit of an activity, and from these it is easy to calculate the activity's average cost and benefit. However, it is a mistake to increase an activity simply because its average benefit is greater than its average cost. Likewise, it is a mistake to decrease an activity simply because its average benefit is less than its average cost. The cost–benefit principle states that total benefit can be increased by increasing the amount of an activity if, and only if, the *marginal* benefit of the activity is greater than its *marginal* cost. Likewise, total benefit can be increased by decreasing the activity if, and only if, its *marginal* benefit is less than its *marginal* cost.

microeconomics the study of individual choice under scarcity, and its implications for the behaviour of prices and quantities in individual markets

macroeconomics the study of the performance of national economies and the policies that governments use to try to improve that performance

1.7 ECONOMICS: MICRO AND MACRO

By convention, we use the term **microeconomics** to describe the study of individual choices and of group behaviour in individual markets. **Macroeconomics**, by contrast, is the study of the performance of national economies and of the policies that governments use to try to affect that performance. Macroeconomics tries to understand the determinants of such things as the national unemployment rate, the overall price level, and the total value of national output.

In both this chapter and the next one we focus on issues that confront the individual decision maker. Further on, we will consider economic models of groups of individuals, such as all buyers or all sellers in a specific market. Later still we will turn to broader economic issues and measures.

No matter which of these levels we focus on, however, our thinking will be shaped by the fact that although economic needs and wants are effectively unlimited, the material and human resources that can be used to satisfy them are finite. Therefore, clear thinking about economic problems must always take into account the concept of trade-offs—the idea that having more of one good thing usually means having less of another. Our economy and our society are shaped to a substantial degree by the choices people make when faced with trade-offs.

1.8 THE APPROACH OF THIS TEXT

Choosing the number of students to register in each class is just one of many important decisions in planning an introductory economics course. Another decision that the *scarcity problem* applies to just as strongly concerns which of many different topics to include on the course syllabus. There is a virtually inexhaustible set of topics and issues that might be covered in an introductory course but only a limited amount of time in which to cover them. There is no free lunch; covering some topics inevitably means omitting others. Therefore, our strategy is to focus on a short list of core ideas. We promote the understanding of these ideas by returning to each of them repeatedly, in many different contexts.

Economists study the workings of the economy in part to satisfy their inherent human curiosity about how and why things happen. Economic life is all around us, every day, and coming to an understanding of it is an intellectually fascinating study, with many interesting puzzles yet to be fully solved. But greater understanding, for its own sake, is only part of the motivation of most economists. Because the economy plays such an important role in all our lives, most economists are also interested in how economic analysis can be used to improve society's well-being.

Because the basic issue underlying economic analysis is scarcity, **efficiency**—obtaining the largest possible total output from a given amount of inputs—is the first focus of economic analysis and policy. But efficiency, by itself, is never enough. The total output of society has to be divided somehow, and the well-being of each person necessarily depends on her or his particular share of it. Hence, the well-being of society as a whole depends on both the efficiency of production and the **equity** of distribution—how fairly goods are distributed among the people. The goal of economic analysis, and the objective of this text, is to increase our understanding of economic processes. Greater understanding is valuable in itself, and it can also serve a social purpose; that is, to better inform the public and private decisions aimed at improving the efficiency and equity of production and distribution.

efficiency obtaining the maximum possible output from a given amount of inputs

equity a state of impartiality and fairness

1.9 ECONOMIC NATURALISM

With the rudiments of the cost–benefit framework under your belt, you are now in a position to become an "economic naturalist," someone who uses insights from economics to help make sense of observations from everyday life. People who have studied biology are able to observe and marvel at many details of nature that would otherwise escape their notice. For example, while the novice may see only trees on a walk in the woods in early April, the biology student notices many different species of trees and understands why some are already in leaf while others are still dormant. Likewise, the novice may notice that in some animal species, males are much larger and more impressive in appearance than females, but the biology student knows that that pattern occurs only in species in which males take several mates. Natural selection favours larger males because their greater size helps them to prevail in the often bloody contests among males for access to females. By contrast, males tend to be roughly the same size as females in monogamous species, where there is much less fighting for mates.

In similar fashion, learning a few simple economic principles enables us to see the mundane details of ordinary human existence in a new light. Whereas the uninitiated often fail even to notice these details, the economic naturalist not only sees them but becomes actively engaged in the attempt to understand them by using positive economics. Let's consider an example of the type of questions that economic naturalists might pose for themselves.

ECONOMIC *Naturalist* 1.1   Why are some places littered with beer cans and wrecked cars while others are not?

Arriving in the U.K. from Nova Scotia in the summer of 2001, a visiting economic naturalist was surprised to see how much the back alleys of British towns were littered with discarded beer cans and how many abandoned cars could be seen at the side of English roads. Why did the U.K. have these problems of littering when Nova Scotia (and other Canadian provinces) did not?

The beer can litter problem has an easy explanation—in the U.K. there was no system of deposits on beverage containers, so they were often thrown away after they were emptied, and aluminium cans accumulated at the roadside and in back alleys. Although aluminium can be recycled, scrap yards did not pay enough per can to make it worthwhile for people to collect them. By contrast, in Nova Scotia (and other Canadian provinces) consumers pay a deposit on beverage containers—even if they do not bother to return their empties, the cans and bottles they discard in public places are collected and returned for the refund. Although the deposit on each container is not large, it is enough to motivate street people and kids to collect them. Although collecting discarded cans is, on an hourly basis, a poorly paid "job," it still pays more than the opportunity costs of their time. The deposit system means that discarded bottles and cans have, effectively, a market value.

It turns out that the same idea of market value explains the problem of abandoned cars in the U.K. Typically, auto wrecking yards in Canada are willing to pay a few dollars for old cars because the steel has value as scrap iron and there are often usable parts, even on an old heap. Driving (or towing) an old car to the scrap yard may be a sad event, but there are at least a few dollars to be had in recompense. However, this wasn't true in the U.K. in 2001. Because there had been a decline in the price of scrap iron, and because the British government had introduced an environmental charge for disposal of tires and car batteries, disposing of old cars cost money—if done legally. Since the low scrap iron price meant that the value of the steel and parts in a car was now less than the environmental charge for disposal, old cars became a liability rather than a small asset. Faced with this liability, some drivers in the U.K. just took off the plates and walked away from their cars (which were usually soon stripped of anything valuable and vandalized). The visiting economic naturalist observed several cars abandoned outside the front gate of an auto wrecking yard—the yard owners wanted to be paid to accept the vehicles, but the car owners did not want to actually pay to dispose of their cars. Since they could just park their cars and leave, they did.

Although littering is neither legally nor ethically defensible, it is influenced by the basic cost–benefit principle. Therefore, public policy to reduce litter has to try to ensure that the benefits to individuals of reducing litter exceeds their costs. In the U.K., government policy did not even try to influence that cost–benefit calculation to make it worthwhile to avoid beer-can littering, and the new environmental charges on automobiles backfired by increasing the private benefits of littering, thereby creating a new (and worse) environmental problem.

SUMMARY

1.1 Economics is the study of how people make choices under conditions of scarcity and of the results of those choices for society. Economic analysis of human behaviour begins with the assumption that people are rational—that they have well-defined goals and try to achieve them as best they can. In trying to achieve their goals, people normally face trade-offs. Because material and human resources are limited, having more of one good thing usually means making do with less of some other good thing.

1.2 Our focus in this chapter was on how rational people make choices between alternative courses of action. Our basic tool for analyzing these decisions is cost–benefit analysis. The cost–benefit principle says that a person will be better off by taking an action if, and only if, the benefit of that action is greater than its cost. The benefit of an action is measured as the largest dollar amount the person would be willing to pay to take the action. The cost of an action is measured as the dollar value of everything the person must give up to take the action.

1.3 Often the question is not whether to pursue an activity but rather how many units of it to pursue. In these cases, the rational actor pursues additional units as long as the marginal benefit of the activity (the benefit from pursuing an additional unit of it) exceeds its marginal cost (the cost of pursuing an additional unit of it).

1.4 Three common pitfalls can undermine economic decisions. The first involves the mistake of failing to consider opportunity costs. The opportunity cost of an activity is the value of the next-best alternative that must be foregone to engage in that activity. If people make the mistake of ignoring the value of foregone alternatives, they are much more likely to make erroneous decisions. We are less likely to make this mistake if we translate questions such as, "Should I use my one frequent-flyer coupon on the next flight I take?" into "Will I be better off if I use my one frequent-flyer coupon on the next flight, or wait and use it on another flight?"

1.5 The second pitfall involves the tendency not to ignore sunk costs. A sunk cost is a cost that is already irretrievably committed at the moment a decision must be made. In deciding whether to drive through a snowstorm to see a hockey game, the amount you have already paid for your ticket is irrelevant. In deciding whether to pursue an activity, the *only* costs and benefits that matter are the ones that will change with your pursuit of that activity. All other costs and benefits are irrelevant.

1.6 The third and final pitfall is the tendency to confuse average costs and benefits with marginal cost and benefits. A comparison of average cost with average benefit is irrelevant when making a decision to increase or decrease an activity. To apply the cost–benefit principle correctly, we must compare marginal cost with marginal benefit. A decision based on a comparison of average cost with average benefit will often be contrary to the cost–benefit principle and cause the parties affected by the decision to be worse off.

CORE

The Scarcity Problem
We have boundless needs and wants, but limited resources. Scarcity requires us to make choices among alternatives.

The Cost–Benefit Principle
An individual (or a firm or a society) will be better off by taking an action if, and only if, the extra benefits from taking the action are greater than the extra costs.

The Principle of Relevant Costs
In considering whether to produce or consume more of a good, what matters is the cost of one more unit (marginal cost).

KEY TERMS

average cost (13)	fallacy of composition (8)	opportunity cost (6)
average benefit (13)	macroeconomics (16)	positive economics (7)
economics (3)	marginal benefit (13)	*post hoc* fallacy (8)
economic surplus (5)	marginal cost (13)	rational person (4)
efficiency (17)	microeconomics (16)	sunk cost (11)
equity (17)	normative economics (8)	time value of money (11)

REVIEW QUESTIONS

1. A friend of yours on the tennis team says, "Private tennis lessons are definitely better than group lessons." Explain what you think your friend means by this statement. Then use the cost–benefit principle to explain why private lessons are not necessarily the best choice for everyone.

2. One of the two bicycle shops near campus is having a sale on new mountain bikes. Sam decides to buy his new bike from the other shop, paying $30 more in the process. Describe an example of conditions under which his decision might nonetheless be considered rational.

3. True or false: Your willingness to drive downtown to save $30 on a new appliance should depend on what fraction of the total selling price $30 is. Explain.

4. Why might someone who is trying to decide whether to see a movie be more likely to focus on the $9 ticket price than on the $20 she would fail to earn by not babysitting?

5. Many people think of their air travel as being free when they use frequent-flyer coupons. Explain why these people are likely to make wasteful travel decisions.

6. Why is a lottery ticket that pays you $10 million now worth more than a lottery ticket that pays you $1 million each year for the next 10 years?

7. Is the nonrefundable tuition payment you made to your university this semester a sunk cost? How would your answer differ if your university were to offer a full tuition refund to any student who dropped out of school during the first two months of the semester?

PROBLEMS

1. Refer to Figure 1.1 when answering questions (a) through (c).
   a. Suppose the marginal cost of a gigabyte drops from $300, as shown in Figure 1.1, to $150. What is the optimum amount of memory to install on the computer? Why?
   b. Suppose that new software makes new and more powerful applications available. What will happen to the marginal benefit curve portrayed in Figure 1.1? If the marginal cost of one gigabyte remains at $300, will the optimum amount of memory increase, decrease, or remain the same when the new software becomes available? Why?
   c. Use your answers to (a) and (b) to explain why the amount of memory installed on new computers has increased rapidly ever since personal computers were introduced.

2. The maximum price you would pay for having a freshly washed car when you go out to dinner is $6. The smallest amount for which you would be willing to wash someone else's car is $3.50. You are going out to dinner this evening, and your car is dirty. How much economic surplus would you receive from washing it?

3. To earn extra money in the summer, you grow tomatoes and sell them at the farmers' market for 30 cents per kilogram. By adding compost to your garden, you can increase your yield as shown in the following table. If compost costs 50 cents per kilogram and your goal is to make as much money as possible, how many kilograms of compost will you add?

Kilograms of compost	Kilograms of tomatoes
0	100.0
1	120.0
2	125.0
3	128.0
4	130.0
5	131.0
6	131.5

4. For each long-distance call anywhere in Canada, a new phone service will charge users 30 cents per minute for the first 2 minutes and 2 cents per minute for additional minutes in each call. Tom's current phone service charges 10 cents per minute for all calls, and his calls are never shorter than 7 minutes. If Tom's dorm switches to the new phone service, what will happen to the average length of his calls?

5. The meal plan at university A lets students eat as much as they like for a fixed fee of $500 per semester. The average student there eats 125 kg of food per semester. University B charges $500 for a book of meal tickets that entitles the student to eat 125 kg of food per semester. If the student eats more than 125 kg, he or she pays extra; if the student

eats less, he or she gets a refund. If students are rational, at which university will average food consumption be higher? At which university is more food likely to be wasted? Explain briefly.

6. Residents of your city are charged a fixed weekly fee of $6 for garbage collection. They are allowed to put out as many cans as they wish. The average household disposes of three cans of garbage per week under this plan. Now suppose that your city changes to a "tag" system. Each can of refuse to be collected must have a tag affixed to it. The tags cost $2 each and are not reusable. What effect do you think the introduction of the tag system will have on the number of bags of garbage collected in your city? Explain briefly.

7. Once a week, Smith purchases a six-pack of cola and puts it in his refrigerator for his two children. He invariably discovers that all six cans are gone on the first day. Jones also purchases a six-pack of cola once a week for his two children, but unlike Smith, he tells them that each may drink no more than three cans. Explain briefly why the cola lasts much longer at Jones's house than at Smith's.

8. Tom is a mushroom farmer. He invests all his spare cash in additional mushrooms, which grow on otherwise useless land behind his barn. The mushrooms double in weight during their first year, after which time they are harvested and sold at a constant price per kilogram. Tom's friend Dushan asks Tom for a loan of $200, which he promises to repay after 1 year. How much interest will Dushan have to pay Tom for Tom to be no worse off than if he had not made the loan? Explain briefly.

9. When John increased his computer's RAM by 64 gigabytes, the total benefit he received from using the computer went up $55. John purchased the additional memory at a cost of $4 per gigabyte, for a total cost of $48.
   a. How much economic surplus did John receive from the additional memory? Explain briefly.
   b. True or false: Because the total benefit of the additional memory was larger than its total cost, John should have added more than 4 gigabytes of memory. Explain briefly.

10. A shirt company spends $1000 per week on rent for its factory. Each shirt made at the factory requires $2 worth of cloth and $6 worth of labour and energy. If the factory produces 2000 shirts per week:
    a. What is the average cost of a shirt?
    b. What is the marginal cost of a shirt?

    If the factory produces 3000 shirts per week:
    c. What is the average cost of a shirt?
    d. What is the marginal cost of a shirt?

11. You have won a prize in a provincial lottery. In exchange for your lottery ticket, the provincial government will send you a cheque for $424 one year from now. If bank deposits pay interest at the rate of 6 percent a year, and you already have several thousand dollars in your account, what is the lowest price at which you would be willing to sell your lottery ticket today?

12. A group has chartered a bus trip to Niagara Falls. The driver's fee is $95, the bus rental $500, and the fuel charge $75. The driver's fee is nonrefundable, but the bus rental may be cancelled a week in advance at a charge of $100. At $25 a ticket, how many people must buy tickets a week before so that cancelling the trip definitely will not pay?

13. Sam bought a Trek bicycle for $800 instead of a Cannondale for $1000. Now he finds out that another bike store in town is selling the Cannondale for $800. Mikkel, Sam's friend, offers him $600 for his Trek. If Sam is a rational consumer, should he sell Mikkel his Trek and buy the Cannondale?

14. Courtney planned to travel from Ottawa to Toronto to see Shania Twain in a free Canada Day concert, and had already purchased her $50 round-trip bus ticket (nonrefundable, nontransferable) when she found out that the Tragically Hip was giving a show at the same time in Ottawa for $50. Had she known about the Tragically Hip's show before she bought her bus ticket, she would have chosen to see the Tragically Hip in her hometown. If she is a rational person and her friend Sally offers to give her one of several extra tickets she has for the Tragically Hip's show, what will she do?

15. Mandy and Tomas, who live in Calgary, have identical tastes. They both plan to attend a concert by Alanis Morisette at the Stampede Grounds. The tickets cost $20. Mandy has bought her ticket by phone using her credit card, but Tomas, who doesn't have a credit card, plans to buy his ticket at the door. On the same evening the University of Calgary announces a surprise free fireworks display on campus. If Mandy had known about the fireworks display in advance, she would not have bought the concert ticket. True or false: Assuming Mandy and Tomas are rational and that Mandy cannot resell her ticket, it follows that Mandy will go to the concert, while Tomas will go to the fireworks display. Explain briefly.

16. Do any of the following statements represent examples of the fallacy of composition? Do any of them represent examples of the *post hoc* fallacy? Explain.
   a. What is good for business is good for the country.
   b. If our city builds a new super-stadium to accommodate the Olympic Games, it will be necessary for residents to pay more taxes. However, the new stadium ensures that the next Olympic Games will be in our city. The games will generate many spinoff economic benefits: people will be hired to build various facilities and to work in them; roads and other infrastructure will be improved; and bars, restaurants, and hotels will be busier and earn greater profits. The federal and provincial governments will contribute money as well. The entire city will be better off.
   c. Students at schools that have introduced sex education programs have higher rates of sexual activity. Therefore, sex education programs cause students to engage in more sexual activity.
   d. Statistics show that as time passes, people who smoke are at greater risk of developing lung cancer than are non-smokers. Therefore, smoking increases the risk of lung cancer.
   e. If one farmer produces a bigger crop, she will be better off. Therefore, if all farmers produce bigger crops they will all be better off.
   f. A tariff on steel will protect the steel industry and increase dividends paid to owners of shares in steel corporations. The shareholders will spend their larger incomes on goods and services. As a result, the number of jobs will increase, making the entire population better off.
   g. A large part of the human population is lactose intolerant. People who are lactose intolerant suffer from health problems if they consume dairy products. This is an indicator that nature never intended humans to consume dairy products and that dairy products are unhealthy for humans. Therefore, if no one consumed any dairy products everyone would be healthier.

ANSWERS TO IN-CHAPTER EXERCISES

1.1 The benefit of buying the game downtown is again $10 but the cost is now $12, so your economic surplus from buying it downtown would be $10 − $12 = −$2. Since your economic surplus from making the trip would be negative, you are better off if you buy at the campus store.

1.2 Example 1.4 tells you that if the opportunity cost of the round-trip flight from Edmonton to Vancouver is zero, your economic surplus for the winter vacation will be $350. However, in this case your frequent-flyer coupon has an opportunity cost. Using the frequent-flyer coupon for the trip to Vancouver means having to pay $363 for your airfare one year from now. How much would you be willing to spend today to avoid paying $363 one year from now? Suppose you deposit $350 in your account today at 2 percent interest. By the end of the year, your deposit would be worth $357 (the original $350 plus $7 interest). Because that amount is not enough to pay for your $363 air ticket, the opportunity cost of using the frequent-flyer coupon now must be *more* than $350. Therefore, the cost of the trip to Vancouver is greater than its $1350 benefit, and the cost–benefit principle tells you not to go to Vancouver.

1.3 If the marginal benefit of each launch is $9 billion, the cost–benefit principle tells NASA to launch four shuttles per year. Why? The marginal benefit of the first, second, third, and fourth launch is greater than the marginal cost. The fifth launch does not pass the cost–benefit test because its marginal benefit is less than its marginal cost.

Appendix 1A Working with Equations, Graphs, and Tables

Although many of the examples and most of the end-of-chapter problems in this book are quantitative, none require mathematical skills beyond basic high-school algebra and geometry. In this brief appendix we review some of the skills you will need for dealing with these examples and problems.

The ability to translate simple verbal descriptions into the relevant equations or graphs is important. You will also need to translate tabular information into equations or graphs, and sometimes you will need to translate graphical information into a table or equation. The following examples illustrate all the tools you will need.

1A.1 USING A VERBAL DESCRIPTION TO CONSTRUCT AN EQUATION

We begin with an example that shows how to construct a long-distance telephone billing equation from a verbal description of the billing plan.

EXAMPLE 1A.1

Your long-distance telephone plan charges you $5/month plus 10 cents/minute for long-distance calls. Write an equation that describes your monthly telephone bill.

equation a mathematical expression that describes the relationship between two or more variables

variable a quantity that is free to take a range of different values

dependent variable a variable in an equation whose value is *determined by* the value taken by another variable in the equation

independent variable a variable in an equation whose value *determines* the value taken by another variable in the equation

constant (or parameter) a quantity that is fixed in value

An **equation** is a simple mathematical expression that describes the relationship between two or more **variables**—quantities that are free to assume different values in some range. The most common type of equation we'll work with contains two types of variables: **dependent variables** and **independent variables.** In this example, the dependent variable is the dollar amount of your monthly telephone bill, and the independent variable is the variable on which your bill depends, namely, the volume of long-distance calls you make during the month. Your bill also depends on the $5 monthly fee and the 10 cents/minute charge. But in this example, those amounts are *constants,* not variables. A **constant,** also called a **parameter,** is a quantity in an equation that is fixed in value, not free to vary. As the terms suggest, the dependent variable describes an outcome that depends on the value taken by the independent variable.

Once you have identified the dependent variable and the independent variable, choose simple symbols to represent them. In algebra courses, X is typically used to represent the independent variable and Y the dependent variable. Many people find it easier to remember what the variables stand for, however, if they choose symbols that are linked in some straightforward way to the quantities that the variables represent. Thus, in this example, we might use B to represent your monthly *bill* in dollars and T to represent the total *time* in minutes you spent during the month on long-distance calls.

Having identified the relevant variables and chosen symbols to represent them, you are now in a position to write the equation that links them:

$$B = 5 + 0.10T, \qquad (1A.1)$$

where B is your monthly long-distance bill in dollars and T is your monthly total long-distance calling time in minutes. The fixed monthly fee (5) and the charge per minute (0.10) are parameters in this equation. Note the importance of being clear about the units of measure. Because B represents the monthly bill in dollars, we must also express the fixed monthly fee and the per-minute charge in dollars, which is why the latter number appears in Equation 1A.1 as 0.10 rather than 10. Equation 1A.1 follows the normal convention in which the dependent variable appears by itself on the left-hand side while the independent variable or variables and constants appear on the right-hand side.

Once we have the equation for the monthly bill, we can use it to calculate how much you will owe as a function of your monthly volume of long-distance calls. For example, if you make 32 minutes of calls, you can calculate your monthly bill by simply substituting 32 minutes for T in Equation 1A.1:

$$B = 5 + 0.10(32) = 8.20. \qquad (1A.2)$$

Your monthly bill when you make 32 minutes of calls is thus equal to $8.20.

EXCERCISE 1A.1

Under the monthly billing plan described in Example 1A.1, how much would you owe for a month during which you made 45 minutes of long-distance calls?

1A.2 GRAPHING THE EQUATION OF A STRAIGHT LINE

The next example shows how to portray the billing plan described in Example 1A.1 as a graph.

Construct a graph that portrays the monthly long-distance telephone billing plan described in Example 1A.1, putting your telephone charges, in dollars per month, on the vertical axis, and your total volume of calls, in minutes per month, on the horizontal axis.

EXAMPLE 1A.2

The first step in responding to this instruction is the one we just took, namely, to translate the verbal description of the billing plan into an equation. When graphing an equation, the normal convention is to use the vertical axis to represent the dependent variable and the horizontal axis to represent the independent variable. In Figure 1A.1, we therefore put B on the vertical axis and T on the horizontal axis. One way to construct the graph shown in the figure is to begin by plotting the monthly bill values that correspond to several different total amounts of long-distance calls. For example, someone who makes 10 minutes of calls during the month would have a bill of $B = 5 + 0.10(10) = \$6$. Thus, in Figure 1A.1 the value of 10 minutes/month on the horizontal axis corresponds to a bill of \$6/month on the vertical axis (point A). Someone who makes 30 minutes of long-distance calls during the month will have a monthly bill of $B = 5 + 0.10(30) = \$8$, so the value of 30 minutes/month on the horizontal axis corresponds to \$8/month on the vertical axis (point C). Similarly, someone who makes 70 minutes of long-distance calls during the month will have a monthly bill of $B = 5 + 0.10(70) = \$12$, so the value of 70 minutes on the horizontal axis corresponds to \$12 on the vertical axis (point D). The line joining these points is the graph of the monthly billing equation, 1A.1.

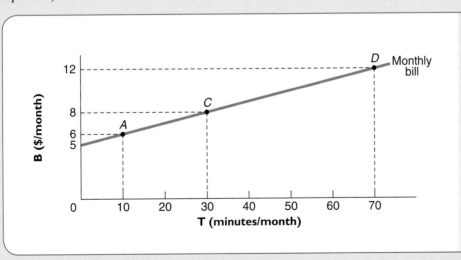

FIGURE 1A.1

The Monthly Telephone Bill in Example 1A.1
The graph of the equation $B = 5 + 0.10T$ is the straight line shown. Its vertical intercept is 5, and its slope is 0.10.

As shown in Figure 1A.1, the graph of the equation $B = 5 + 0.10T$ is a straight line. The parameter 5 is the **vertical intercept** of the line—the value of B when $T = 0$, or the point at which the line intersects the vertical axis. The

vertical intercept in a straight line, the value taken by the dependent variable when the independent variable equals zero

slope in a straight line, the ratio of the vertical distance the straight line travels between any two points *(rise)* to the corresponding horizontal distance *(run)*

parameter 0.10 is the **slope** of the line, which is the ratio of the **rise** of the line to the corresponding **run**. The ratio rise/run is simply the vertical distance between any two points on the line divided by the horizontal distance between those points. For example, if we choose points A and C in Figure 1A.1, the rise is 8 − 6 = 2 and the corresponding run is 30 − 10 = 20, so rise/run = 2/20 = 0.10. More generally, for the graph of any equation $Y = a + bX$, the parameter a is the vertical intercept and the parameter b is the slope.

1A.3 DERIVING THE EQUATION OF A STRAIGHT LINE FROM ITS GRAPH

The next example shows how to derive the equation for a straight line from a graph of the line.

EXAMPLE 1A.3

Figure 1A.2 shows the graph of the monthly billing plan for a new long-distance plan. What is the equation for this graph? How much is the fixed monthly fee under this plan? How much is the charge per minute?

FIGURE 1A.2
Another Monthly Long-Distance Plan
The vertical distance between points A and C is 12 − 8 = 4 units, and the horizontal distance between points A and C is 40 − 20 = 20, so the slope of the line is 4/20 = 1/5 = 0.20. The vertical intercept (the value of B when T = 0) is 4. So the equation for the billing plan shown is $B = 4 + 0.20T$.

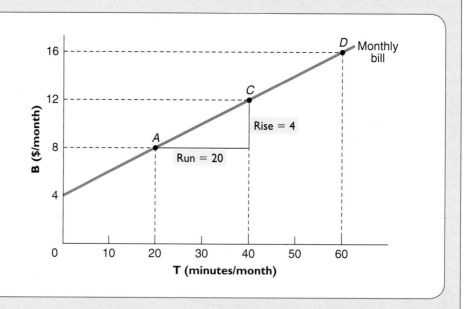

The slope of the line shown is the rise between any two points divided by the corresponding run. For points A and C, rise = 12 − 8 = 4, and run = 40 − 20 = 20, so the slope equals rise/run = 4/20 = 1/5 = 0.20. And since the horizontal intercept of the line is 4, its equation must be given by

$$B = 4 + 0.20T. \tag{1A.3}$$

Under this plan, the fixed monthly fee is the value of the bill when $T = 0$, which is $4. The charge per minute is the slope of the billing line, 0.20, or 20 cents/minute.

EXERCISE 1A.2   **Write the equation for the billing plan shown in the accompanying graph on the next page. How much is its fixed monthly fee? its charge per minute?**

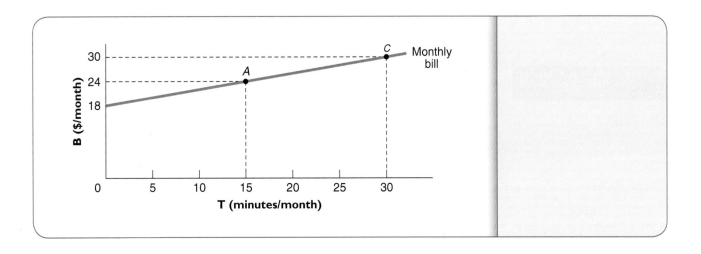

IA.4 CHANGES IN THE VERTICAL INTERCEPT AND SLOPE

Examples 1A.4 and 1A.5 and Exercises 1A.3 and 1A.4 provide practise in seeing how a line shifts with a change in its vertical intercept or slope.

Show how the billing plan whose graph is in Figure IA.2 of Example IA.3 would change if the monthly fixed fee were increased from $4 to $8.

EXAMPLE IA.4

An increase in the monthly fixed fee from $4 to $8 would increase the vertical intercept of the billing plan by $4 but would leave its slope unchanged. An increase in the fixed fee thus leads to a parallel upward shift in the billing plan by $4, as shown in Figure 1A.3. For any given number of minutes of long-distance calls, the monthly charge on the new bill will be $4 higher than on the old bill. Thus 20 minutes of calls per month cost $8 under the original plan (point A) but $12 under the new plan (point A'). And 40 minutes costs $12 under the original plan (point C), $16 under the new plan (point C'); and 60 minutes costs $16 under the original plan (point D), $20 under the new plan (point D').

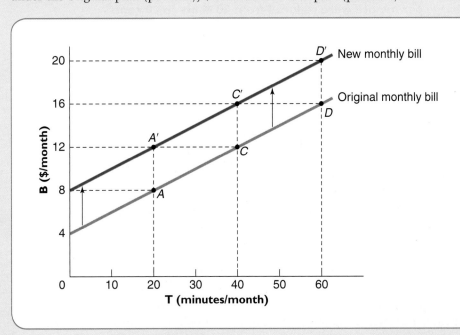

FIGURE IA.3

The Effect of an Increase in the Vertical Intercept An increase in the vertical intercept of a straight line produces an upward parallel shift in the line.

EXERCISE 1A.3

Show how the billing plan whose graph is in Figure 1A.2 would change if the monthly fixed fee were reduced from $4 to $2.

EXAMPLE 1A.5

Show how the billing plan whose graph is in Figure 1A.2 would change if the charge per minute were increased from 20 cents to 40 cents.

Because the monthly fixed fee is unchanged, the vertical intercept of the new billing plan continues to be 4. But the slope of the new plan, shown in Figure 1A.4, is 0.40, or twice the slope of the original plan. More generally, in the equation $Y = a + bX$, an increase in b makes the slope of the graph of the equation steeper.

FIGURE 1A.4

The Effect of an Increase in the Charge per Minute
Because the fixed monthly fee continues to be $4, the vertical intercept of the new plan is the same as that of the original plan. With the new charge per minute of 40 cents, the slope of the billing plan rises from 0.20 to 0.40.

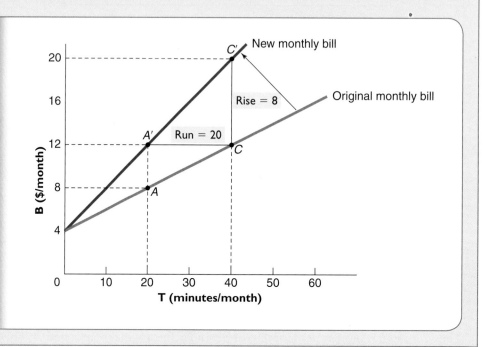

EXERCISE 1A.4

Show how the billing plan whose graph is in Figure 1A.2 would change if the charge per minute were reduced from 20 cents to 10 cents.

Exercise 1A.4 illustrates the general rule that in an equation $Y = a + bX$, a reduction in b makes the slope of the graph of the equation less steep.

1A.5   CONSTRUCTING EQUATIONS AND GRAPHS FROM TABLES

Example 1A.6 and Exercise 1A.5 show how to transform tabular information into an equation or graph.

EXAMPLE 1A.6

Table 1A.1 shows four points from a monthly long-distance telephone billing equation. If all points on this billing equation lie on a straight line, find the vertical intercept of the equation and graph it. What is the monthly fixed fee? What is the charge per minute? Calculate the total bill for a month with one hour of long-distance calls.

One approach to this problem is simply to plot any two points from the table on a graph. Since we are told that the billing equation is a straight line, that line must

TABLE 1A.1
Points on a Long-Distance Billing Plan

Long-distance bill ($/month)	Total long-distance calls (minutes/month)
10.50	10
11	20
11	30
12	40

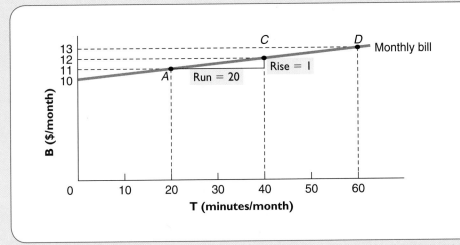

FIGURE 1A.5

Plotting the Monthly Billing Equation from a Sample of Points

Point A is taken from row 2, Table 1A.1, and point C from row 4. The monthly billing plan is the straight line that passes through these points.

be the one that passes through any two of its points. Thus, in Figure 1A.5 we use A to denote the point from Table 1A.1 for which a monthly bill of $11 corresponds to 20 minutes/month of calls (second row) and C to denote the point for which a monthly bill of $12 corresponds to 40 minutes/month of calls (fourth row). The straight line passing through these points is the graph of the billing equation.

Unless you have a steady hand, however, or use extremely large graph paper, the method of extending a line between two points on the billing plan is unlikely to be very accurate. An alternative approach is to calculate the equation for the billing plan directly. Since the equation is a straight line, we know that it takes the general form $B = f + sT$, where f is the fixed monthly fee and s is the slope. Our goal is to calculate the vertical intercept f and the slope s. From the same two points we plotted earlier, A and C, we can calculate the slope of the billing plan as $s = \text{rise/run} = 1/20 = 0.05$.

So all that remains is to calculate f, the fixed monthly fee. At point C on the billing plan, the total monthly bill is $12 for 40 minutes, so we can substitute $B = 12$, $s = 0.05$, and $T = 40$ into the general equation $B = f + sT$ to obtain

$$12 = f + 0.05(40), \tag{1A.4}$$

or

$$12 = f + 2, \tag{1A.5}$$

which solves for $f = 10$. So the monthly billing equation must be

$$B = 10 + 0.05T. \tag{1A.6}$$

For this billing equation, the fixed fee is \$10/month, the calling charge is 5 cents/minute (\$0.05/minute), and the total bill for a month with one hour of long-distance calls is $B = 10 + 0.05(60) = \$13$, just as shown in Figure 1A.5.

EXERCISE 1A.5

The following table shows four points from a monthly long-distance telephone billing plan.

Long-distance bill ($/month)	Total long-distance calls (minutes/month)
20	10
30	20
40	30
50	40

If all points on this billing plan lie on a straight line, find the vertical intercept of the corresponding equation without graphing it. What is the monthly fixed fee? What is the charge per minute? How much would the charges be for one hour of long-distance calls per month?

See www.mcgrawhill.ca/olc/frankbernanke for a brief discussion of how simultaneous equations can be used to decide which of two different long-distance billing plans is best for your purposes.

KEY TERMS

constant (24)
dependent variable (24)
equation (24)
independent variable (24)

parameter (24)
rise (26)
run (26)

slope (26)
variable (24)
vertical intercept (25)

ANSWERS TO IN-APPENDIX EXERCISES

1A.1 To calculate your monthly bill for 45 minutes of calls, substitute 45 minutes for T in Equation 1A.1 to get $B = 5.00 + 0.10(45) = \$9.50$.

1A.2 Calculating the slope using points A and C, we have rise $= 30.00 - 24.00 = 6.00$ and run $= 30.00 - 15.00 = 15.00$, so rise/run $= 6/15 = 2/5 = 0.40$. And since the horizontal intercept of the line is 18, its equation is $B = 18 + 0.40T$. Under this plan, the fixed monthly fee is \$18, and the charge per minute is the slope of the billing line, 0.40, or 40 cents/minute.

1A.3 A \$2 reduction in the monthly fixed fee would produce a downward parallel shift in the billing plan by \$2.

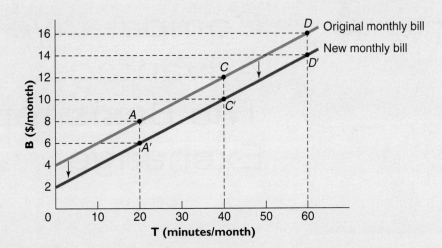

1A.4 With an unchanged monthly fixed fee, the vertical intercept of the new billing plan continues to be 4. The slope of the new plan is 0.10, half the slope of the original plan.

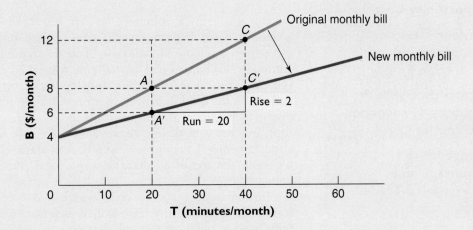

1A.5 Let the billing equation be $B = f + sT$, where f is the fixed monthly fee and s is the slope. From the first two points in the table, calculate the slope s = rise/run = 10/10 = 1. To calculate f, we can use the information in row 1 of the table to write the billing equation as $20 = f + 1(10)$ and solve for $f = 10$. So the monthly billing equation must be $B = 10 + 1.0T$. For this billing equation, the fixed fee is \$10/month, the calling charge is \$1/minute, and the total bill for a month with one hour of long-distance calls is $B = 10 + 1(60) = \$70$.

Chapter 2 Comparative Advantage: The Basis for Exchange

During a stint as a volunteer teacher in rural Nepal, a young economic naturalist employed a cook named Birkhaman, who came from a remote Himalayan village in neighbouring Bhutan. Although Birkhaman had virtually no formal education, he was spectacularly resourceful. His primary duties, to prepare food and maintain the kitchen, he performed with competence and dispatch. But he also had many other skills. He could thatch a roof, butcher a goat, and repair shoes. An able tinsmith and a good carpenter, he could sew, fix a broken alarm clock, and plaster walls. On top of all that, he was a local authority on home remedies.

Birkhaman's range of skills was broad even by Nepalese standards. But even the least skilled Nepalese villager can perform a wide range of services that most North Americans hire others to perform. The alternative to a system in which everyone is a jack of all trades is one in which people *specialize* in particular goods and services, and then satisfy their needs by trading among themselves. Economic systems based on specialization and the exchange of goods and services are generally far more productive than those with less specialization, and this is a large part of the reason why income per person in Nepal is less than 6 percent of that in Canada. Our task in this chapter is to investigate why exchange and specialization can increase economic output. In doing so we will explore why people choose to exchange goods and services in the first place, rather than having each person produce his own food, cars, clothing, shelter, and the like. We will focus first on trade between individuals and then discuss international trade.

A major focus of this chapter is what economists call *comparative advantage*. Roughly, a person has a comparative advantage at producing a particular good or service, let's say haircuts, if that person is *relatively* more efficient at producing haircuts than at producing other goods or services. We will see that we can all consume more of *every* good and service if each of us specializes in the activities at which we have a comparative advantage.

This chapter will also introduce the *production possibilities curve,* which is a graphical method of describing the combinations of goods and services that an economy can produce. The development of this tool will allow us to see much more precisely how specialization enhances the productive capacity of even the simplest economy.

Did this man perform most of his own services because he was poor, or was he poor because he performed most of his own services?

2.1 EXCHANGE AND OPPORTUNITY COST

The scarcity problem (see Chapter 1) reminds us that the opportunity cost of spending more time on any one activity is having less time available to spend on others. As the following example makes clear, this helps explain why everyone can do better by concentrating on those activities at which she performs best relative to others.

Will Eddie Greenspan be better off if he writes his own will?

EXAMPLE 2.1

Eddie Greenspan graduated from Osgoode Hall Law School in 1968 and was called to the bar in 1970. Today, he is one of Canada's top criminal defence lawyers. Greenspan has defended against charges ranging from drunk driving to murder, and his client list includes notables such as Garth Drabinsky and Conrad Black. Passionate about criminal law, Greenspan says, "I defend only innocent people because until they're convicted, everybody is presumed to be innocent," and "If they say they're innocent, they're innocent."[1] If you ever find yourself to be the underdog charged with a felony and up against a tough crown prosecutor, you will rest a little easier if Eddie Greenspan is conducting your defence.

Will a top lawyer be better off if he prepares his own will?

Although Greenspan spends virtually all of his working hours defending people accused of crimes, he also is competent to perform a much broader range of legal services. Suppose, for example, that he could prepare his own will in two hours, only half as long as it would take any other lawyer. Does that mean that Greenspan will be better off if he prepares his own will?

On the strength of his talent as a litigator, Greenspan probably earns several million dollars a year, which means that the opportunity cost of any time he spends preparing his will would be more than $1000 per hour. Lawyers who specialize in property law typically earn far less than that amount. Greenspan would have little difficulty engaging a competent property lawyer who could prepare his will for him for less than $800. So even though Greenspan's considerable skills would enable him to perform this task more quickly than another lawyer, it would not be in his interest to prepare his own will.

In the preceding example, economists would say that Greenspan has an **absolute advantage** at preparing his will but a **comparative advantage** at trial work. He has an absolute advantage at preparing his will because he can perform that task in less time than a property lawyer could. Even so, the property lawyer has a comparative advantage at preparing wills because his opportunity cost of performing that task is lower than Greenspan's.

The point of Example 2.1 is not that people whose time is valuable should never perform their own services. That example made the implicit assumption that Greenspan would have been equally happy to spend an hour preparing his will or preparing for a trial. If he was tired of trial preparation and felt it might be enjoyable to refresh his knowledge of property law, preparing his own will might

absolute advantage one person has an absolute advantage over another if he or she takes fewer hours to perform a task than the other person does

comparative advantage one person has a comparative advantage over another if his or her opportunity cost of performing a task is lower than the other person's opportunity cost

[1]Andy Halloway, "Eddie Greenspan: On Defence and the Law," *Canadian Business,* 31, January 2005, http://www.canadianbusiness.com (May 2008).

then have made perfect sense! But unless he expected to gain special satisfaction from performing that task, he would almost certainly do better to hire a property lawyer. The property lawyer would also benefit, or else she would not have offered to prepare wills for the stated price.

THE PRINCIPLE OF COMPARATIVE ADVANTAGE

One of the most important insights of economics is that when two people (or two nations) have different opportunity costs of performing various tasks, they can increase the total value of available goods and services by trading with one another. The following simple example captures the logic behind this insight.

EXAMPLE 2.2   **Will Rikke be better off if she updates her own Web page?**

Consider the case of Rikke and Beth. Rikke can update a Web page in 20 minutes or repair a bicycle in 10 minutes. Beth can update a Web page in 30 minutes or repair a bicycle in 30 minutes. Table 2.1 summarizes the data: Rikke clearly possesses an absolute advantage over Beth in both activities.

TABLE 2.1
Productivity Information for Rikke and Beth

	Time to update a Web page	Time to complete a bicycle repair
Rikke	20 minutes	10 minutes
Beth	30 minutes	30 minutes

Time used to update a Web page cannot be used to repair a bicycle, and vice versa. Thus each woman incurs an opportunity cost whenever she updates a Web page instead of repairing a bicycle. If Rikke spends 20 minutes updating a Web page, she sacrifices the opportunity to use the same 20 minutes for repairing two bicycles. The opportunity cost of each Web page that Rikke updates is therefore two bicycle repairs. If Beth were to use 30 minutes to update a Web page, she sacrifices the opportunity to use the same 30 minutes to repair a bicycle. The opportunity cost of each Web page that Beth updates is only one bicycle repair. Table 2.2 summarizes the data on the opportunity costs. The left-hand column shows that Beth's opportunity cost of updating a Web page is half the amount of Rikke's. Like the property lawyer who has a *comparative* advantage over the trial lawyer in writing wills, Beth has a *comparative* advantage over Rikke in updating Web pages.

TABLE 2.2
Opportunity Costs for Rikke and Beth

	Opportunity cost of updating a Web page	Opportunity cost of a bicycle repair
Rikke	2 bicycle repairs	0.5 Web page update
Beth	1 bicycle repair	1 Web page update

The same reasoning will provide each woman's opportunity cost of repairing bicycles. Since it takes Rikke 20 minutes to update a Web page and only 10 minutes to fix a bicycle, each bicycle repair she does prevents Rikke from updating one half of a Web page; that is, the opportunity cost of each bicycle that Rikke repairs is half a Web-page update. Similarly, the opportunity cost of each bicycle that Beth repairs is one Web-page update. For each woman, the opportunity cost of one bicycle repair is the *reciprocal* of her opportunity cost of updating a Web page. The right-hand column of Table 2.2 shows each woman's opportunity cost of one bicycle repair. Notice that Rikke has a comparative advantage over Beth in bicycle repairs.

Suppose that the community where Rikke and Beth live wants 16 Web page updates per day. If neither person specializes, and Rikke spends one half of her eight-hour workday repairing bicycles and one half updating Web pages, she can update 12 Web pages and repair 24 bicycles. Suppose Beth provides four more updates by spending two hours on Web pages, for a total 16 updates per day between them. With her remaining six hours, Beth can repair 12 bicycles. Together, Rikke and Beth repair 36 bicycles per eight-hour day. These data are summarized in Part A of Table 2.3.

TABLE 2.3
The Gains When Rikke and Beth Specialize

Part A: Without Specialization				
	Time spent updating Web pages	Number of updated Web pages	Time spent repairing bicycles	Number of bicycles repaired
Rikke	4 hours	12	4 hours	24
Beth	2 hours	4	6 hours	12
Total output		16		36

Part B: With Specialization According to Comparative Advantage				
	Time spent updating Web pages	Number of updated Web pages	Time spent repairing bicycles	Number of bicycles repaired
Rikke	0 hours	0	8 hours	48
Beth	8 hours	16	0 hours	0
Total output		16		48
Net gain with specialization		0		12

Suppose each woman had specialized according to comparative advantage. In eight hours Beth would update 16 Web pages and Rikke would repair 48 bicycles. Part B of Table 2.3 summarizes these data. With specialization, 12 more bicycles are repaired, and there is no reduction in the number of Web page updates. Specialization reduces the opportunity cost of the 16 Web page updates the community wants. Therefore, specialization creates 12 additional bicycle repairs!

Rikke is *not* better off if she updates her own Web page, even though she is a better programmer than Beth. Because she has a comparative advantage in repairing bicycles, Rikke will be better off if she specializes in repairing bicycles and hires Beth to update her Web page.

"We're a natural, Rachel. I handle intellectual
property, and you're a content-provider."

The details of Example 2.2 include the number of minutes each person needs to complete each task. However, the information necessary to compute the opportunity cost of one good in terms of another can be presented as each person's *productivity* in each task. **Productivity** is units of output per hour divided by units of input per hour. Because the information can be presented in either of these two ways, one must pay careful attention to the form in which it is presented.

productivity units of output per hour divided by units of input per hour

Exercise 2.1 below provides data on the labour productivity of Mina and Barb. Like Beth and Rikke of Example 2.2, both have skills as computer programmers and bicycle mechanics. Each woman's labour is an input to a production process. Her labour productivity is her output per hour of labour time. Thus Barb's productivity when she repairs bicycles is three repairs per hour. Barb also can update three Web pages per hour. Barb has a greater productivity in both tasks that gives her an absolute advantage over Mina in both tasks: *greater productivity* confers an *absolute* advantage. However, Barb has a *comparative* advantage in only one task because she has a lower opportunity cost than Mina does in only one task. A *lower opportunity cost* confers a *comparative* advantage. Work through Exercise 2.1 to see how to proceed when information is presented in this alternative format.

EXERCISE 2.1

Will Barb be better off if she updates her own Web page?

The following table shows the productivity rates for Barb and Mina in HTML programming and repairing bicycles. Does the fact that Barb can program faster than Mina imply that Barb will be better off if she updates her own Web page?

	Productivity in programming	Productivity in bicycle repair
Mina	2 Web page updates per hour	1 repair per hour
Barb	3 Web page updates per hour	3 repairs per hour

The principle illustrated by Examples 2.1 and 2.2 is so important that we state it formally as one of the core ideas of the course:

COMPARATIVE
ADVANTAGE

The Principle of Comparative Advantage: Total output is largest when each person (or each country) concentrates on the activities for which his or her opportunity cost is lowest.

Indeed, the gains made possible from specialization based on comparative advantage constitute the rationale for market exchange. They explain why each person does not devote 10 percent of his time to producing cars, 5 percent to growing food, 25 percent to building housing, 0.0001 percent to performing brain surgery, and so on. By concentrating on those tasks at which we are relatively most productive, together we can produce vastly more than if we all tried to be self-sufficient.

This insight brings us back to Birkhaman the cook. Though Birkhaman's versatility was marvellous, he was not nearly as good a doctor as someone who has been trained in medical school nor as good a repairman as someone who spends each day fixing things. If several people with Birkhaman's talents had joined together, each of them specializing in one or two tasks, together they would have enjoyed more and better goods and services than each could possibly have produced on his own. Although there is much to admire in the resourcefulness of people who have learned through necessity to rely on their own skills, that path is no route to economic prosperity.

SOURCES OF COMPARATIVE ADVANTAGE

At the individual level, comparative advantage often appears to be the result of inborn talent. For instance, some people seem to be naturally gifted at programming computers, while others seem to have a special knack for fixing bicycles. But nobody is born knowing how to fix bicycles. Actual ability, at a particular point in time, is always the result of innate ability plus education, training, and experience. To understand why some people, such as Eddie Greenspan, are so good at law while others are better at carpentry, we have to examine how those skills were developed. Similarly, comparative advantage at the national level may derive from differences in natural resources or from differences in society, culture, or institutions. Canada, which has one of the world's highest per capita endowments of farm and forest land, has a comparative advantage in the production of agricultural and forestry products. Likewise, topography and climate explain why Canada produces so much wheat while New Zealand has so many sheep.

Seemingly noneconomic factors can also give rise to comparative advantage. For instance, the emergence of English as the de facto world language gives English-speaking countries a comparative advantage over non-English-speaking nations in the production of books, movies, and popular music. Technological change and governmental policies can also play a role.

**www.internationalecon.com
Economics Study Centre**

ECONOMIC *Naturalist*	**2.1**	How does comparative advantage arise and why might countries not take advantage of it?

In 1890, Canadian pulp and paper was a small, insignificant industry with only very limited access to the American market. Forty years later, Canada was the world's largest papermaker and exported much of its product to the United States. Today, pulp and paper remains one of Canada's most important industries. How did Canada "create" a pulp and paper industry? How is this case relevant to today's trade disputes?

In the mid-nineteenth century, paper was produced in costly, small-scale operations. Rags, grasses, and straw provided the raw material. Beginning in 1851, a series of technological advances allowed cellulose to be isolated from wood and used as the raw material for paper. The new processes operated on a much larger scale and required large amounts of electricity. The new technology gave Canada, with its vast forests and large potential to produce hydro-electricity, a comparative advantage in the manufacture of paper. However, it was not clear that Canada would be able to benefit from its comparative advantage.

By 1900, the United States could not satisfy its growing demand for newsprint. The United States protected its pulp and paper industry from Canadian competition with high tariffs on imported pulp and paper and by imposing no duties on raw, imported pulpwood. This enabled the American pulp and paper industry to obtain inexpensive pulpwood from Canada and then to manufacture it into pulp and paper that it sold in the United States.

Under Canadian federalism, the provinces have the right to manage their natural resources. In 1902, Ontario placed an embargo on the export of pulpwood harvested from Crown lands. The embargo prevented pulpwood from being exported to the United States. No restrictions were imposed on the export of pulp and paper. The purpose was to encourage pulp and paper manufactured in Ontario to be exported to the United States. By 1915, all other provinces had taken similar measures.

The United States responded to pressure from its own pulp and paper industry by increasing its tariffs on Canadian pulp and paper. This made the Canadian product more expensive to Americans and might have defeated efforts to develop a Canadian industry by causing the Americans to buy pulp and paper elsewhere. But there was nowhere else to buy it. The higher tariffs simply caused American newspapers to pay more for Canadian newsprint. In 1913, the interests of the American newspaper industry prevailed over the interests of the American pulp and paper industry, and Congress removed the tariffs against Canadian pulp and newsprint. By 1929, Canada was producing more than twice as much newsprint as the United States and was the world's largest papermaker.

Comparative advantage obviously facilitated the creation of a Canadian pulp and paper industry, but other factors played a role, too. American demand for Canadian newsprint was growing rapidly, and the American newspaper industry's desire for access to inexpensive Canadian newsprint aligned with the interests of Canadian pulp and paper. Provincial governments undertook trade policies that capitalized on these factors. The United States removed its trade barriers to Canadian pulp and paper, and the Canadian industry flourished.[2]

For many years, Canada and the United States have engaged in a series of trade disputes over another forest product, softwood lumber. Maine and New Brunswick first disagreed about trade in softwood lumber during the 1820s, and disputes have flared periodically since then. The Softwood Lumber Agreement of 2006 ended the most recent dispute when it came into effect on October 12, 2006. Canada provides the United States with about 35 percent of its softwood lumber.

Restrictions on the importation of Canadian lumber serve the interests of the American lumber industry, but they can cost the American construction industry billions of dollars annually because they increase U.S. lumber prices.[3] The interests of Canadian lumber and American construction converge in ways that can prove useful to Canadian negotiators. However, for 20 years prior to the new agreement, the political influence of U.S. lumber producers was sufficient to cause the U.S. to take repeated trade actions against Canadian softwood lumber. The dispute provides an example of a failure to take advantage of comparative advantage due to protectionism. Some people (in this case, U.S. lumber producers) lose from greater trade, even if the potential gains from greater trade (in this case, for the U.S. construction industry) are larger than the total losses. If the losers from greater trade are not compensated for their losses, they have a self-interested reason to propose restraints on trade, and sometimes can do so successfully. The Softwood Lumber Agreement of 2006 provides that after it has been in effect for 18 months either party may terminate it with six months' notice. The dispute could flare again.[4]

> **RECAP**
>
> ### EXCHANGE AND OPPORTUNITY COST
>
> Gains from exchange are possible if trading partners have comparative advantages in producing different goods and services. An individual has a comparative advantage when his or her opportunity cost—measured in terms of other production opportunities foregone—is smaller than the corresponding opportunity costs of his or her trading partners. Maximum production is achieved if each person specializes by producing the good or service in which she has the lowest opportunity cost (the principle of comparative advantage). Comparative advantage makes specialization worthwhile even if one trading partner has an absolute advantage in every activity.

[2]Adapted from B.D. Lesser (ed.), "Canada 'Creates' a Pulp and Paper Industry," in *Four Case Studies on Aspects of the Canadian Economy,* (Halifax: Nova Scotia Department of Education, 1977), pp. 1–2. See also Kenneth Norrie and Douglas Owram, *A History of the Canadian Economy,* 2nd ed., (Toronto: Harcourt Brace & Company Canada, Ltd., 1996), pp. 256–257, 323–324.
[3]David Laband and Daowei Zhang, "America's Been Bushwhacked," *The Globe and Mail,* 16 August 2001, p. A13.
[4]See "Softwood" at www.international.gc.ca for information about the Softwood Lumber Agreement (May 2008).

2.2 COMPARATIVE ADVANTAGE AND PRODUCTION POSSIBILITIES

Comparative advantage and specialization allow an economy to produce more than if each person tries to produce a little of everything. In this section we gain further insight into the advantages of specialization by first examining an imaginary economy with only one person and then noting how economic possibilities change as new people join the economy. Along the way, we will introduce a useful graph called the *production possibilities curve*, which can be used to describe the combinations of goods and services that a particular economy can produce.

PRODUCTION POSSIBILITIES IN A ONE-PERSON ECONOMY

We begin with a hypothetical economy consisting of a single worker who can produce two goods, sugar cane and Macadamia nuts. The worker lives on a small island, and "production" consists either of cutting sugar cane that grows on the island's central valley floor or picking Macadamia nuts that grow on trees on the hillsides overlooking the valley. The more time the worker spends cutting sugar cane, the less time she has available for picking nuts. If she wants more sugar cane, then she must make do with a smaller amount of nuts. Knowing how productive she is at each activity, we can easily summarize the various combinations of sugar cane and nuts she can harvest each day if she makes full use of her available working time. This menu of possibilities is known as the **production possibilities curve.**

As the following example illustrates, constructing the production possibilities curve for a one-person economy is a straightforward matter.

production possibilities curve a graph that describes the maximum amount of one good that can be produced for every possible level of production of the other good

What is the production possibilities curve for an economy in which Susan is the only worker?

EXAMPLE 2.3

Consider a society consisting only of Susan, who allocates her production time between sugar cane and nuts. Each hour per day she devotes to cutting sugar cane yields 1.5 kg of cane, and each hour she devotes to harvesting nuts yields 3 kg of nuts. If Susan works a total of eight hours per day, describe her production possibilities curve, the graph that displays, for each level of sugar cane she cuts, the maximum amount of nuts that Susan can pick.

The vertical axis in Figure 2.1 shows Susan's daily production of sugar cane, and the horizontal axis shows her daily production of nuts. Let's begin by looking at two extreme allocations of her time. First, suppose she employs her entire workday (eight hours per day) cutting sugar cane. In that case, since she can cut 1.5 kg of sugar cane per hour, she would pick (8 hours/day)(1.5 kg/hour) = 12 kg per day of sugar cane and 0 kg of nuts. That combination of sugar cane and nuts is represented by point *A* in Figure 2.1, the vertical intercept of Susan's production possibilities curve.

Now suppose, instead, that Susan devotes all her time to picking nuts. Since she can pick 3 kg of nuts per hour, her total daily production would be (8 hours/day)(3 kg/hour) = 24 kg of nuts. That combination is represented by point *B* in Figure 2.1, the horizontal intercept of Susan's production possibilities curve. Because Susan's production of each good is exactly proportional to the amount of time she devotes to that good, the remaining points along her production possibilities curve will lie on the straight line that joins *A* and *B*.

For example, suppose that Susan devotes six hours each day to cutting sugar cane and two hours to picking nuts. She will then produce (6 hours/day)(1.5 kg/hour) = 9 kg of sugar cane and (2 hours/day)(3 kg/hour) = 6 kg of nuts per day.

FIGURE 2.1

Susan's Production Possibilities

For the production relationships given, the production possibilities curve is a straight line.

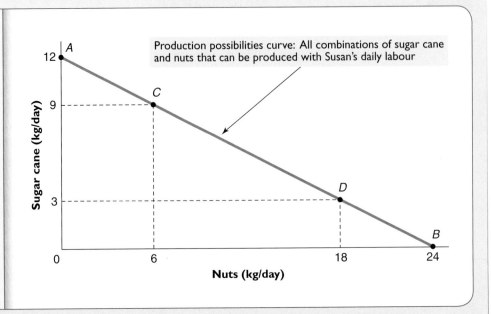

Production possibilities curve: All combinations of sugar cane and nuts that can be produced with Susan's daily labour

This is the point labelled *C* in Figure 2.1. Alternatively, if she devotes two hours to sugar cane and six hours to nuts, she will get (2 hours/day)(1.5 kg/hour) = 3 kg of sugar cane and (6 hours/day)(3 kg/hour) = 18 kg of nuts per day. This alternative combination is represented by point *D* in Figure 2.1.

Since Susan's production possibilities curve (PPC) is a straight line, its slope is constant. The absolute value of the slope of Susan's PPC is the ratio of its vertical intercept to its horizontal intercept: (12 kg of sugar cane/day)/(24 kg of nuts/day) = 1/2 kg of sugar cane/1 kg of nuts. (Be sure to keep track of the units of measure on each axis when computing this ratio.) This ratio means that Susan's opportunity cost of an additional kilogram of nuts is 1/2 kilogram of sugar cane.

Note that Susan's opportunity cost of nuts can also be expressed as the following simple formula:

$$OC_{nuts} = \frac{\text{loss in sugar cane}}{\text{gain in nuts}},$$

where loss in sugar cane means the amount of sugar cane given up and gain in nuts means the corresponding increase in nuts. Likewise, Susan's opportunity cost of sugar cane is expressed by this formula:

$$OC_{sugar\ cane} = \frac{\text{loss in nuts}}{\text{gain in sugar cane}}.$$

To say that Susan's opportunity cost of an additional kilogram of nuts is 1/2 kg of sugar cane is equivalent to saying that her opportunity cost of 1 kg of sugar cane is 2 kg of nuts.

The production possibilities curve shown in Figure 2.1 illustrates the scarcity problem—the fact that, because our resources are limited, having more of one good or service generally means having to settle for less of another (see Chapter 1). Although we generally specify the "price" of a commodity in dollar terms, economists think of the concept of price in more general terms—what a person has to give up in order to get something. If Susan wants an additional kilogram of sugar cane she can have it, but only if she is willing to give up 2 kg of nuts. If Susan is the only person in the economy, her opportunity cost of producing a good becomes, in effect, its price. Thus, the price she has to pay for an additional kilogram of sugar cane is 2 kg of nuts; or equivalently, the price she has to pay for an additional kilogram of nuts is 1/2 kg of sugar cane.

Any point that lies either on the production possibilities curve or to the left of it is said to be an **attainable point,** meaning that it can be produced with currently available resources. In Figure 2.2, for example, points *A, B, C, D,* and *E* are attainable points. Points that lie to the right of the production possibilities curve are said to be **unattainable** because they cannot be produced using currently available resources. In Figure 2.2, *F* is an unattainable point because Susan cannot produce 9 kg of sugar cane per day *and* 15 kg of nuts. Points that lie within the curve are said to be **inefficient,** because existing resources would allow for production of more of at least one good without sacrificing the production of any other good. At *E,* for example, Susan is producing only 3 kg of sugar cane per day and 6 kg of nuts, which means that she could increase her harvest of sugar cane by 6 kg per day without giving up any nuts (moving from *E* to *C*). Alternatively, Susan could pick as many as 12 additional kilograms of nuts each day without giving up any sugar cane (moving from *E* to *D*). An **efficient point** is one that lies on the production possibilities curve. At any such point, more of one good can be produced only by producing less of the other.

attainable point any combination of goods that can be produced using currently available resources

unattainable point any combination of goods that cannot be produced using currently available resources

inefficient point any combination of goods for which currently available resources enable an increase in the production of one good without a reduction in the production of the other

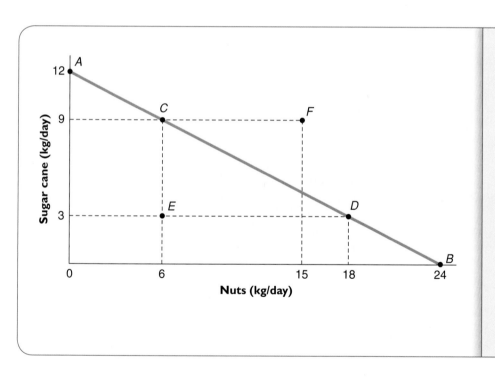

FIGURE 2.2

Attainable and Efficient Points on Susan's Production Possibilities Curve
Points that lie either on the production possibilities curve (for example, *A, C, D,* and *B*) or to its left (for example, *E*) are said to be attainable. Points that lie to the right the production possibilities curve (for example, *F*) are unattainable. Points that lie on the curve are said to be efficient, while those that lie within the curve are said to be inefficient.

Why might Susan be at point E? Perhaps she has been using a glove, which slows her down—in economic terms, she is at point E because she is using an inefficient technique. By switching to an efficient technique, she gets more of both goods.

FACTORS THAT INFLUENCE THE PRODUCTION POSSIBILITIES CURVE

To see how the slope and position of the production possibilities curve depend on an individual's productivity, let's compare Susan's PPC to that of a person who is less productive in both activities.

efficient point any combination of goods for which currently available resources do not allow an increase in the production of one good without a reduction in the production of the other

EXAMPLE 2.4   **How do changes in productivity affect the opportunity cost of nuts?**

Suppose Tom can harvest 0.75 kg of nuts for each hour he devotes to picking nuts and 0.75 kg of sugar cane for each hour he spends cutting sugar cane. If Tom is the only person in the economy, describe the economy's production possibilities curve.

We can construct Tom's PPC the same way we did Susan's. Note first that if Tom devotes an entire workday (8 hours/day) to cutting sugar cane, he harvests (8 hours/day)(0.75 kg/hour) = 6 kg of sugar cane per day and 0 kg of nuts. Therefore, the vertical intercept of Tom's PPC is *A* in Figure 2.3. If instead he devotes all his time to picking nuts, he gets (8 hours/day)(0.75 kg/hour) = 6 kg of nuts per day and no sugar cane. That means the horizontal intercept of his PPC is *B* in Figure 2.3. As before, because Tom's production of each good is proportional to the amount of time he devotes to it, the remaining points on his PPC will lie along the straight line that joins these two extreme points.

FIGURE 2.3

Tom's Production Possibilities Curve

The less productive a person is, the closer to the origin is his PPC.

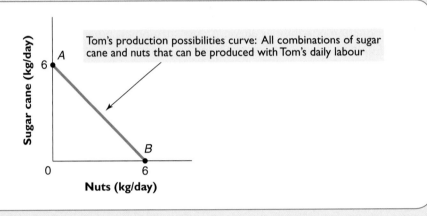

How does Tom's PPC compare with Susan's? Note that because Tom is less productive than Susan at both activities, the horizontal and vertical intercepts of Tom's PPC lie closer to the origin than do Susan's (see Figure 2.4). For Tom, the opportunity cost of an additional kilogram of nuts is 1 kg of sugar cane, which is twice Susan's opportunity cost of nuts. This difference in opportunity costs shows up as a difference in the slopes of their PPCs: the absolute value of the slope of Tom's PPC is 1, whereas Susan's is 1/2.

FIGURE 2.4

Individual Production Possibilities Curves Compared

Though Tom is less productive in both activities than Susan, Tom's opportunity cost of cutting sugar cane is only half Susan's.

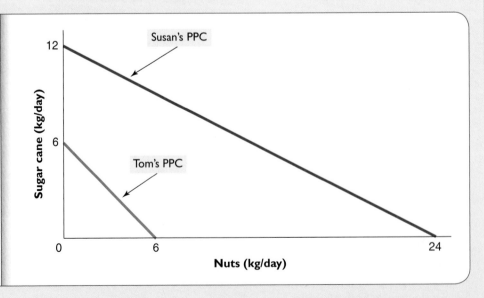

EXAMPLE 2.4

But note, too, that while Tom is absolutely less efficient than Susan at harvesting sugar cane, his opportunity cost of sugar cane is only half Susan's. Whereas Susan must give up 2 kg of nuts to pick an additional kilogram of sugar cane, Tom must give up only 1 kg. This difference in opportunity costs is another example of the concept of comparative advantage. Although Tom is *absolutely* less efficient than Susan at harvesting sugar cane, he is *relatively* more efficient. That is, Susan has an absolute advantage in both sugar cane and nuts, but Tom has a comparative advantage in sugar cane because, relative to Susan, he is even worse at picking nuts. Susan's comparative advantage is in nuts.

Notice that the principle of comparative advantage is a relative concept—one that makes sense only when the relative productivities of two or more people (or countries) are being compared. To cement this idea, work through the following exercise.

Suppose Susan can harvest 1.5 kg of sugar cane per hour or 3 kg of nuts per hour while Tom can pick 0.75 kg of sugar cane per hour and 2.25 kg of nuts per hour. What is Susan's opportunity cost of picking a kilogram of nuts? What is Tom's opportunity cost of picking a kilogram of nuts? Where does Susan's comparative advantage now lie?

EXERCISE 2.2

PRODUCTION POSSIBILITIES IN A TWO-PERSON ECONOMY

Why have we spent so much time defining comparative advantage? As the next examples illustrate, a comparative advantage arising from disparities in individual opportunity costs can create gains for everyone.

How does the one-person economy's PPC change when a second person is added?

EXAMPLE 2.5

Suppose Susan can harvest 1.5 kg of sugar cane or 3 kg of nuts per hour and Tom can harvest 0.75 kg of sugar cane or 0.75 kg of nuts per hour. If Susan and Tom are the only two people in the economy and each works eight hours per day, describe the production possibilities curve for the economy as a whole.

To construct the PPC for a two-person economy, we use an approach similar to the one we used for a one-person economy. To find the vertical intercept of the PPC, we ask how much sugar cane they would have if both Susan and Tom worked full-time harvesting sugar cane. The answer is 18 kg per day (12 kg from Susan and 6 kg from Tom), so point A in Figure 2.5 is the vertical intercept of the PPC. Similarly, if Susan and Tom both worked full-time picking nuts, they would pick 30 kg of nuts per day (24 kg from Susan and 6 from Tom). Thus point B in Figure 2.5 is the horizontal intercept of the PPC.

In contrast to the PPC for the one-person economy, however, the PPC for the two-person economy is not a straight line joining the two extreme points. To see why, suppose Susan and Tom were initially devoting all their time to harvesting sugar cane when they decided they wanted some nuts. How would they launch the production of nuts? They would want Susan to pick nuts, because her opportunity cost of picking nuts is only half Tom's. Thus, if Susan spent two hours picking nuts while Tom continued to devote all his time to sugar cane, they would lose 3 kg of sugar cane but gain 6 kg of nuts each day. Point C in Figure 2.5 represents this combination.

FIGURE 2.5

The PPC for a Two-Person Economy
Initial nut production relies on Susan, whose opportunity cost of nuts is lower than Tom's. Once Susan is fully occupied picking nuts (point *D*), additional nut production must rely on Tom.

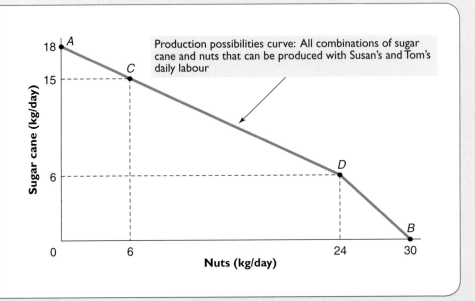

If Susan devotes all her time to picking nuts while Tom continues to spend all his time on sugar cane, they will be at *D* in Figure 2.5, which represents 6 kg of sugar cane and 24 kg of nuts per day. If they want to expand nut production any further, Tom will have to take some of his time away from sugar cane. But in doing so, they gain only one additional kilogram of nuts for each kilogram of sugar cane they lose. Notice in Figure 2.5 how the slope of the PPC changes at point *D*. To the right of point *D*, the slope of the PPC reflects Tom's opportunity cost of sugar cane rather than Susan's.

EXERCISE 2.3   **To the left of point *D* in Figure 2.5, what is the slope of the production possibilities curve, and what opportunity cost does this slope represent?**

The PPC for the two-person economy bends outward (is concave to the origin) because of individual differences in opportunity costs. As the following example shows, this distinctive shape represents expanded opportunities for both Susan and Tom.

EXAMPLE 2.6   What is the best way to achieve a given production goal?

Tom and Susan want 12 kg of sugar cane per day and 12 kg of nuts. If their productive abilities are as described in Example 2.5, what is the most effective way of dividing their labour?

Though Tom has a comparative advantage in harvesting sugar cane, even if he spends all his time harvesting sugar cane, he can cut only (8 hours/day)(0.75 kg/hour =) 6 kg per day. So Susan will have to harvest the additional 6 kg of sugar cane to achieve their production target of 12 kg. Since Susan is capable of harvesting (8 hours/day)(1.5 kg/hour) = 12 kg of sugar cane per day, she will need only four hours per day to harvest 6 kg. She can spend the remaining four hours picking nuts, which is exactly the amount of time she needs to pick their production target of 12 kg. In terms of their two-person production possibilities curve, this allocation of labour puts Susan and Tom at point *E* in Figure 2.6.

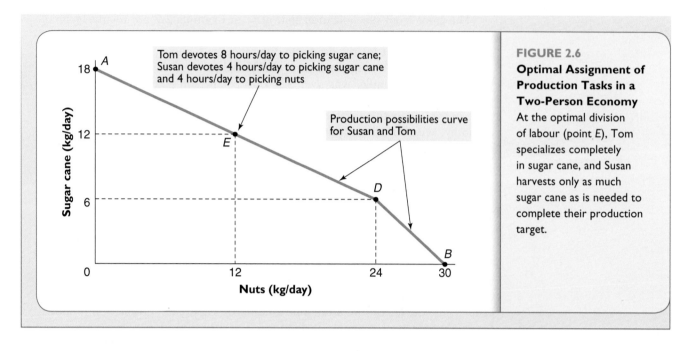

Tom devotes 8 hours/day to picking sugar cane;
Susan devotes 4 hours/day to picking sugar cane
and 4 hours/day to picking nuts

Production possibilities curve
for Susan and Tom

FIGURE 2.6

Optimal Assignment of Production Tasks in a Two-Person Economy
At the optimal division of labour (point *E*), Tom specializes completely in sugar cane, and Susan harvests only as much sugar cane as is needed to complete their production target.

Example 2.6 illustrates the general principle that when more than one opportunity is available, we are best off if we exploit the best opportunity first.

The Principle of Increasing Opportunity Cost: In expanding the production of any good, first employ those resources with the lowest opportunity cost. Only when all of the lowest cost resources are employed does it make economic sense to use resources that have higher opportunity costs.

INCREASING
OPPORTUNITY
COST

HOW MUCH DOES SPECIALIZATION MATTER?

In Example 2.6, Tom specialized completely in sugar cane, his area of comparative advantage (lowest opportunity cost). Susan did not specialize completely in picking nuts because if she had, the two would have harvested twice the nuts and half the sugar cane they wanted. Given what they wanted, Tom and Susan still did better through partial specialization than they could have if neither had specialized, as the following example demonstrates.

How much does specialization expand opportunity?

EXAMPLE 2.7

Suppose that in Example 2.6 Susan and Tom had divided their time so that each person's output consisted of half nuts and half sugar cane. How much worse off would they have been?

Tom can harvest equal quantities of both goods by spending four hours per day on the production of each, which yields (4 hours/day)(0.75 kg/hour) = 3 kg of sugar cane and (4 hours/day)(0.75 kg/hour) = 3 kg of nuts. Since Susan can harvest twice as many kilograms of nuts in an hour as she can sugar cane, to get equal quantities of both goods she must devote twice as many hours to sugar cane as to nuts. Thus, she will need to spend two-thirds of a workday (5.33 hours/day) harvesting sugar cane and one-third of a workday (2.67 hours/day) picking nuts. Her output will be (5.33 hours/day)(1.5 kg/hour) = 8 kg of sugar cane per day and (2.67 hours/day)(3 kg/hour) = 8 kg of nuts. Their combined daily production will be only 11 kg of sugar cane and 11 kg of nuts—1 kg less of each good than when they specialized.

The gains from specialization that arise in Example 2.7 are relatively small. One extra kilogram of each of two goods is worth having, but it hardly seems sufficient to account for the dramatic differences in living standards between rich and poor nations. Average income in the 20 richest countries of the world in the year 2000, for example, was over $27 000 per person compared to only $211 per person in the 20 poorest countries.[5] We will return to the role specialization plays in explaining these differences, but first we will construct a PPC for an entire economy. We also will consider factors that can cause a PPC to shift.

A PRODUCTION POSSIBILITIES CURVE FOR A MANY-PERSON ECONOMY

The process of constructing a production possibilities curve for an economy with millions of workers is really no different from the process for a one-person economy. Consider again an economy in which the only two goods are sugar cane and nuts, with sugar cane again on the vertical axis and nuts on the horizontal axis. The vertical intercept of the economy's PPC is the total amount of sugar cane that could be picked if all available workers worked full-time picking sugar cane. Thus, the maximum attainable amount of sugar cane production is shown for the hypothetical economy in Figure 2.7 as 100 000 kg per day (an amount chosen arbitrarily, for illustrative purposes). The horizontal intercept of the PPC is the amount of nuts that could be gathered if all available workers worked full-time gathering nuts, shown for this same economy as 80 000 kg per day (also an amount chosen arbitrarily). Notice that unlike the earlier examples involving one or two workers, the PPC shown in Figure 2.7 is not composed of straight line. It is a smooth curve that is bowed out from the origin.

We will say more in a moment about the reasons for this shape. But first note that a bow-shaped PPC means that the opportunity cost of producing nuts increases as the economy produces more of them. Notice, for example, that when

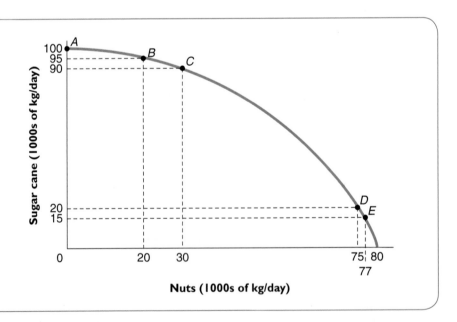

FIGURE 2.7
Production Possibilities Curve for a Large Economy
For an economy with millions of workers, the PPC bows outward from the origin.

[5]High Income Countries: Australia, Austria, Belgium, Canada, China, Hong Kong, Denmark, Finland, France, Germany, Iceland, Ireland, Japan, Luxembourg, Netherlands, Norway, Singapore, Sweden, Switzerland, United Kingdom, and United States. Low Income Countries: Burkina Faso, Burundi, Central African Rep., Chad, Ethiopia, Ghana, Guinea-Bisau, Kenya, Madagascar, Malawi, Mali, Mozambique, Myanmar, Nepal, Niger, Nigeria, Rwanda, Sierra Leone, Tanzania, and Uganda. Taken from "Average GDP per Capita In 20 High Income Countries and 20 Low Income Countries, 1970–2000," Global Policy Forum, n.d., http://www.globalpolicy.org/socecon/inequal/income/tables/gdpcompare.htm (May 2008).

the economy moves from A, where it is producing only sugar cane, to B, it gets 20 000 kg of nuts per day by giving up only 5000 kg per day of sugar cane. When nut production is increased still further, however—for example, by moving from B to C—the economy again gives up 5000 kg per day of sugar cane, yet this time gets only 10 000 additional kilograms of nuts. This pattern of increasing opportunity cost persists over the entire length of the PPC. For example, note that in moving from D to E, the economy again gives up 5000 kg per day of sugar cane but now gains only 2000 kg of nuts per day. Note, finally, that the same pattern of increasing opportunity cost applies to sugar cane. Thus, as more sugar cane is produced, the opportunity cost of producing additional sugar cane, as measured by the amount of nuts that must be sacrificed, also rises.

Why is the PPC for the multiperson economy bow shaped? The answer lies in the fact that some resources are relatively well-suited for gathering nuts while others are relatively well-suited for cutting sugar cane. If the economy is initially producing only sugar cane and wants to begin producing some nuts, which workers will it reassign? Recall Susan and Tom, the two workers discussed in Example 2.5. Tom's comparative advantage was cutting sugar cane and Susan's comparative advantage was picking nuts. If both workers were currently cutting sugar cane and you wanted to reassign one of them to gather nuts instead, whom would you send? Susan would be the clear choice, because her departure would cost the economy only half as much sugar cane as Tom's and would augment nut production by twice as much.

The principle is the same in any large multiperson economy, except that the range of differences in opportunity cost across workers is even greater than in the earlier two-worker example (Example 2.5). As we keep reassigning workers from cutting sugar cane to picking nuts, sooner or later we must withdraw even sugar specialists like Tom from cutting sugar cane. Indeed, we must eventually reassign others whose opportunity cost of producing nuts is far higher than his.

The shape of the production possibilities curve shown in Figure 2.7 illustrates the principle of increasing opportunity cost: *when increasing the production of any good, first employ those resources with the lowest opportunity cost.* This strategy will provide increased amounts of one good at the smallest possible sacrifice of other goods. In the context of our examples, using the principle of increasing opportunity cost allows each additional kilogram of nuts to be obtained with the smallest possible sacrifice of sugar cane, and vice versa.

The PPC of Figure 2.7 is a smooth curve, bowed outward from the origin, which is a contrast with the PPCs of Figures 2.5 and 2.6 which are made up of two straight lines. Each of the two straight lines has a different slope, and the slope of each line represents a set of opportunity costs associated with one worker. Consider, for example, Figure 2.5. Susan's opportunity cost of nuts is lower than Tom's and is represented by the slope of the longer line segment. Tom's opportunity cost of nuts is represented by the slope of the shorter line segment. Because Susan's opportunity cost of nuts is lower than Tom's, the slope of her section of the PPC is shallower than Tom's. Figure 2.7 is intended to represent an economy with many, perhaps millions, of workers. With many workers, individual segments of the PPC are indistinguishable. Therefore, the PPC in Figure 2.7 is a smooth curve.

RECAP

COMPARATIVE ADVANTAGE AND PRODUCTION POSSIBILITIES

For an economy that produces two goods, the *production possibilities curve* describes the maximum amount of one good that can be produced for every possible level of production of the other good. *Attainable points* are those that lie on or within the curve, and *efficient points* are those that lie along the curve. The slope of the production possibilities curve tells us the opportunity cost of producing an additional unit of the good measured along the horizontal axis. The principle of increasing opportunity cost tells us that the slope of the production possibilities curve becomes steeper as we move downward to the right. The greater the differences among individual opportunity costs, the more bow shaped the production possibilities curve will be, and the more bow shaped the production possibilities curve, the greater will be the potential gains from specialization.

2.3   FACTORS THAT SHIFT THE ECONOMY'S PRODUCTION POSSIBILITIES CURVE

As its name implies, the production possibilities curve provides a summary of the production options open to any society. At any given moment, the PPC confronts society with a trade-off. The only way people can produce and consume more nuts is to produce and consume less sugar cane. In the long run, however, it is often possible to increase production of all goods. This is what is meant when people speak of economic growth. As shown in Figure 2.8, economic growth is an outward shift in the economy's production possibilities curve. Economic growth maintained over long periods of time can greatly enhance standards of living. But this takes us back to the question we posed earlier: How do we account for the differences in living standards experienced by the world's richest and poorest nations? Economic growth can result from increases in the amount of productive resources available or from improvements in knowledge or technology that can make these resources more productive.

FIGURE 2.8

Economic Growth: An Outward Shift in the Economy's PPC
Increases in productive resources (such as labour and capital equipment) or improvements in knowledge and technology cause the PPC to shift outward. They are the main factors that drive economic growth.

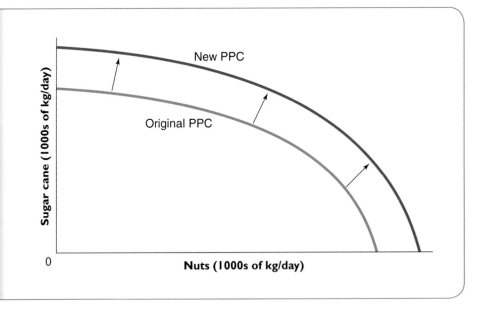

What causes the quantity of productive resources to grow in an economy? One factor is investment in new factories and equipment embodying new and more productive technology. When workers have more and better equipment to work with, their productivity increases, often dramatically. This is surely an important factor behind the differences in living standards between rich and poor countries. According to one study, for example, the value of capital investment per worker in the United States is about \$16 200, while in Nepal the corresponding figure is less than \$550.[6]

Such large differences in capital per worker do not occur all at once. They are a consequence of decades, even centuries, of differences in rates of saving and investment. Over time, even small differences in rates of investment can translate into extremely large differences in the amount of capital equipment available to each worker. Differences of this sort are often self-reinforcing: not only do higher rates of saving and investment cause income to grow, but the resulting higher income levels also make it easier to devote additional resources to savings and investment. Over time, then, even small initial productivity advantages from specialization can translate into very large income gaps.

Population growth also causes an economy's PPC curve to shift outward and thus is often listed as one of the sources of economic growth. But because population growth also generates more mouths to feed, it cannot by itself raise a country's standard of living. Indeed it may even cause a decline in the standard of living if existing population densities have already begun to put pressure on available land, water, and other scarce resources.

Perhaps the most important sources of economic growth are improvements in knowledge and technology. As economists have long recognized, such improvements often lead to higher output through increased specialization. Improvements in technology often occur spontaneously, but more frequently they are directly or indirectly the result of increases in education. They can be stimulated by opportunities in international trade.

We have shown that when individual differences in opportunity cost are present, specialization with trade will increase the quantities of the goods being produced. Our examples have been based on two individuals who produce and exchange only two goods. Real-world gains from specialization and trade often are far more spectacular than illustrated in the earlier examples. One reason is that specialization not only capitalizes on existing differences in individual skills but also deepens those skills through practise and experience. Moreover, it eliminates many of the switching and start-up costs people incur when they move back and forth among numerous tasks. These gains apply not only to people but also to the tools and equipment they use. Breaking a task down into simple steps, each of which can be performed by a different machine, greatly multiplies the productivity of individual workers.

Even in simple settings, these factors can combine to increase productivity many times over. Adam Smith, the Scottish philosopher who is remembered today as the founder of modern economics, was the first to recognize the enormousness of the gains made possible by the division and specialization of labour. Consider, for instance, his description of work in an eighteenth-century Scottish pin factory:

> One man draws out the wire, another straightens it, a third cuts it, a fourth points it, a fifth grinds it at the top for receiving the head; to make the head requires two or three distinct operations . . . I have seen a small manufactory of this kind where only ten men were employed . . . [who] could, when they exerted themselves, make among them about twelve pounds of pins in a day. There are in a pound upwards of four thousand pins of middling size. Those ten persons, therefore, could make among them upwards of forty-eight thousand pins in a day. Each person, therefore, making a tenth part of forty-eight thousand pins, might be considered as making four thousand eight hundred pins

[6]Calculated from Alan Heston, Robert Summers, and Bettina Aten, "The Penn World Table version 6.2," Center for International Comparisons of Production, Income and Prices at the University of Pennsylvania, September 2006.

in a day. But if they had all wrought separately and independently, and without any of them having been educated to this peculiar business, they certainly could not each of them have made twenty, perhaps not one pin in a day.[7]

The gains in productivity that result from specialization are indeed often prodigious. Specialization of labour enables two sorts of efficiency gains: the gain in absolute efficiency that comes from repetition (e.g., not having to switch tasks means not losing the time it takes to switch tools) and the gains from trade due to the relative efficiency of each worker specializing in the task in which they have a comparative advantage. Over time, these efficiency gains reinforce each other as experience deepens the specialized skills of each worker.

WHY HAVE SOME COUNTRIES BEEN SLOW TO SPECIALIZE?

You may be asking yourself, "If specialization is such a great thing, why don't people in poor countries like Nepal just specialize?" If so, you are in good company. Adam Smith spent many years attempting to answer precisely the same question. He summarized his explanation by writing, "The division [i.e., specialization] of labour is limited by the extent of the market."[8] In a very small market, said Smith, no one has reason to dedicate himself entirely to one occupation because a small market provides very limited opportunities to engage in trade. Smith, ever the economic naturalist, observed that work tended to be far more specialized in the large cities of England in the eighteenth century than in the rural highlands of Scotland:

> In the lone houses and very small villages which are scattered about in so desert a country as the Highlands of Scotland, every farmer must be butcher, baker and brewer for his own family. . . . A country carpenter . . . is not only a carpenter, but a joiner, a cabinet maker, and even a carver in wood, as well as a wheelwright, a ploughwright, a cart and waggon maker.[9]

In contrast, each of these same tasks was performed by a different specialist in the large English and Scottish cities of Smith's day. Scottish highlanders also would have specialized had they been able to, but the markets in which they participated were simply too small and fragmented. Smith went on to argue that economic growth would be most rapid in locations that provided easy access to ocean transportation. He also declared that the discovery of the New World and passage around the Cape of Good Hope to the east to be "the two greatest and most important events recorded in the history of mankind."[10]

What were Smith's reasons for these statements? First, ocean transportation made the whole world accessible. Second, discovery of the New World and of passage around the Cape of Good Hope made the worldwide market much larger. The small, inland villages of Scotland's Highlands were isolated from each other and from ocean transportation because overland transportation was limited to what could be provided by draft animals on very poor roads. Because the villages were isolated from all but tiny local markets, they provided extremely limited opportunities for specialization. Without specialization, the standard of living in these villages would remain where it had been for centuries.

---

[7]Adam Smith, *The Wealth of Nations*, (1776). This edition reprinted with introduction by Max Lerner and Ewin Cannan, (New York: Random House, 1969), Book I, Chapter I.
[8]Ibid. Chapter III, pp. 17–21. The quotation is from the title of this chapter.
[9]Ibid.
[10]Ibid. Book IV, Chapter VII, Part III, pp. 590–592.

Nepal is one of the most remote and isolated countries on the planet. Specialization is further limited by Nepal's rugged terrain. Exchanges of goods and services with residents of other villages can be difficult because in many cases the nearest village can be reached only after trekking hours, or even days, over treacherous Himalayan trails. Modern systems of communication and transportation have had only a limited effect in reducing this isolation. Thus the isolation of Nepal's villages is similar to the isolation of the eighteenth-century villages of Scotland's Highlands. Moreover, even though modern technology might be reducing Nepal's isolation, the process is starting in Nepal more than two centuries later than it began in the Scottish Highlands.

China and India, the world's two largest nations, provide vivid examples of how international trade and economic growth are intertwined. Since the early 1990s, both countries have experienced remarkable economic growth, and at the same time both have developed industries that send their products to markets throughout the world. A shopper who reads the labels on products sold in any retail outlet in Canada or any other country will discover that a huge variety of goods come from these two countries.

Specialization and investment are also intertwined. Without access to large markets there is little reason to invest in the specialization and productive capacity that is necessary to serve large markets. Without the capacity to serve large markets, one cannot compete in them.

HOW DOES SPECIALIZATION ENHANCE STANDARDS OF LIVING?

Specialization enhances standards of living in two ways. First, when productive activity is organized according to comparative advantage, the opportunity cost of a given amount of output is reduced, which implies that the amount of goods and services a society can obtain from its resources is increased. The greater the differences are in opportunity costs, the greater the gains are that comparative advantage and trade make available.

Second, specialization deepens existing skills through practise and experience, and it eliminates the switching and start-up costs incurred when people have to move back and forth among numerous tasks. These gains apply both to people and the tools or equipment they use. Specialization depends on investment in machinery and education, because highly skilled workers often need specialized equipment and education to carry out their tasks. Because only large markets can absorb the quantities of goods and services these workers can produce, specialization depends on access to such markets. Conversely, isolation, through its reduced access to large markets, greatly reduces specialization possibilities.

CAN WE HAVE TOO MUCH SPECIALIZATION?

As in any issue in economics, however, we should think about both costs and benefits if we want to analyze specialization. The mere fact that specialization boosts productivity does not mean that more specialization is always better than less, for specialization also entails costs. For example, most people appear to enjoy variety in the work they do, but variety tends to be one of the first casualties as workplace tasks become ever more narrowly specialized.

Indeed, Karl Marx argued forcefully that the fragmentation of workplace tasks often exacts a heavy psychological toll on workers. Thus, he wrote, "[A]ll means for the development of production . . . mutilate the laborer into a fragment of a man, degrade him to the level of an appendage of a machine, destroy every remnant of charm in his work and turn it into hated toil."[11]

[11]Karl Marx, *Das Kapital* (1856), (New York: Modern Library, 1936), pp. 708–709.

Can specialization proceed too far?

Charlie Chaplin's 1936 film, *Modern Times*, paints a vivid portrait of the psychological costs of repetitive factory work. As an assembly worker, Chaplin's only task, all day every day, is to tighten the nuts on two bolts as they pass before him on the assembly line. Finally he snaps and walks zombie-like from the factory, wrenches in hand, tightening every nut-like protuberance he encounters.

Modern Times was filmed nearly seventy years ago, and since then industrial engineers have realized that good job design involves finding the right balance between the benefits and costs of specialization. The engineers and programmers who design and produce industrial robots that now do much of the work described by Chaplin's *Modern Times* are highly specialized but they perform a variety of tasks. If you ever need brain surgery, you will be comforted if you know that, before the surgeon opens your skull, he has already exposed and successfully treated a thousand other brains. Many people make interesting and challenging careers out of highly specialized work. Besides, failure to specialize imposes its own substantial costs.

We can expect to meet life's financial obligations in the shortest time, thereby freeing up more time to do whatever else we want, if we concentrate at least a significant proportion of our efforts on those tasks that we have a comparative advantage in.

SPECIALIZATION, EXCHANGE, AND THE CIRCULAR FLOW OF INCOME AND EXPENDITURE

Specialization and exchange go together. If your professor spends most of her time teaching, she must depend on someone else to grow her food. An accountant will usually depend on someone else to make his clothes, and so on. In rich nations, because we all are highly specialized in our work, we all depend on the cooperation of many other individuals in obtaining the things we need and desire. Most of us do this by selling our labour in return for wages or salaries that we receive as money and which we can then spend to obtain the goods and services we want.

Figure 2.9 represents a very simple economy that has no government and does not engage in foreign trade. Labour is the only input used in this economy to produce goods and services. Simple though it is, Figure 2.9 is sufficient to represent the circular flow of expenditure and exchange. Households, composed of individuals, sell labour services to firms. Firms use the labour they hire to produce goods and services that they sell to households. The blue arrows in the upper half of Figure 2.9 indicate the flow of labour through the labour market to firms.

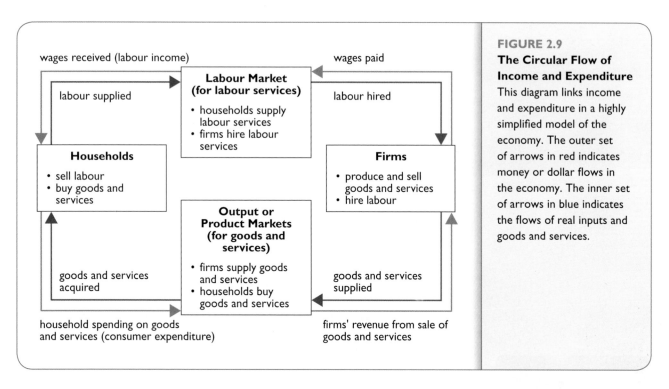

FIGURE 2.9

The Circular Flow of Income and Expenditure This diagram links income and expenditure in a highly simplified model of the economy. The outer set of arrows in red indicates money or dollar flows in the economy. The inner set of arrows in blue indicates the flows of real inputs and goods and services.

The blue arrows in the lower half indicate the flow of goods and services from firms through markets for goods and services to households. Thus, the blue inner arrows indicate a flow of real (or physical) units.

Firms pay wages and salaries to households for their labour. As indicated by the red arrows in the upper half of Figure 2.9, wages and salaries are expenditures that flow from firms through the labour market to households, where they are received as income. Red arrows in the lower half show payments flowing from households through markets for goods and services to firms. The expenditures of households are the income of firms. The red outer arrows represent monetary flows in the economy. In general, one party's expenditure is another's income.

Figure 2.9 becomes much more complicated in appearance if we make it more realistic and add boxes to represent capital markets, government, and foreign trade, and arrows to represent the flows of expenditure on, and goods received from, each. However, a simple principle remains—every transaction has both a buyer and a seller, so one person's sale is another person's purchase.

In general, every transaction can be seen from either person's point of view— either as a sale, or as a purchase. A seller will agree to a voluntary transaction only if she thinks the transaction will make her better off. The buyer also must think the transaction will make him better off. Thus, a voluntary transaction must improve the expected well-being of *both* parties. Comparative advantage and the gains from voluntary exchange underlie the ability of modern market economies to improve human well-being.

RECAP

FACTORS THAT SHIFT THE ECONOMY'S PRODUCTION POSSIBILITIES CURVE

Economic growth can be represented by an outward shift of the production possibilities curve. It can arise from an increase in the amount of productive resources available to an economy, from improvements in knowledge and technology, and from investment in capital equipment. Small differences in investment sustained by different countries over long periods of time can result in large differences in capital equipment, which contributes to large differences in material standards of living.

Specialization, investment, economic growth, and the size of markets are intertwined. While specialization enhances productivity of labour and capital equipment, it can also mean that each person becomes more dependent on fellow human beings for the goods and services that he needs or wants. Specialization also depends on access to large markets because only large markets can absorb the goods and services produced by highly specialized workers.

2.4 COMPARATIVE ADVANTAGE AND INTERNATIONAL TRADE

The same logic that leads the individuals in an economy to specialize and exchange goods with one another also leads nations to specialize and trade among themselves. As with individuals, each trading partner can benefit from exchange, even though one may be more productive than the other in absolute terms.

EXAMPLE 2.8   Can a poor nation prosper by trading?

Susan and Tom are the only two workers in Islandia, a small island nation, and their production possibilities curve is as shown in Figure 2.10. For simplicity, we will assume that each of them can produce 100 kg of nuts or 100 kg of sugar cane per hour. How does the opportunity to trade affect consumption opportunities in Islandia?

FIGURE 2.10
Production Possibilities Curve for Islandia

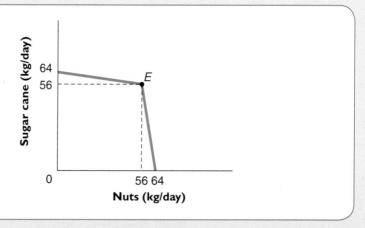

Millions of workers live in the rest of the world where the opportunity cost of a kilogram of sugar cane is 1 kg of nuts. The market price of 1 kg of sugar cane will therefore be 1 kg of nuts. (If someone tried to charge, say, 1.5 kg of nuts for a kilogram of sugar cane, consumers could simply reduce their own nut harvest by a kilogram and harvest an extra kilogram of sugar cane instead.) Because Islandia is tiny relative to the rest of the world, 1 kg of sugar cane will exchange for exactly 1 kg of nuts in a market consisting of Islandia and the rest of the world. The opportunity to trade with Islandia therefore has no perceptible impact on the rest of the world.

But it has a profound impact on Susan and Tom. Suppose they were initially at point *E* on their PPC (Figure 2.10). Without the opportunity to trade, they would have to give up 7 kg of nuts to increase sugar cane by 1 kg. But with the opportunity to trade, they can purchase 1 kg of sugar cane in exchange for only

1 kg of nuts. If Islandians started at E and sold their entire 56 kg of nuts in the world market, they could buy an additional 56 kg of sugar cane, for a total of $56 + 56 = 112$ kg of sugar cane and $56 - 56 = 0$ kg of nuts. So point A in Figure 2.11 represents their maximum possible daily consumption of sugar cane once they can engage in trade.

Similarly, if they were initially at point E on their PPC and lacked the opportunity to trade, they would have to sacrifice 7 kg of sugar cane to obtain an additional kilogram of nuts. But if they could trade, they could get an extra kilogram of nuts at a cost of just 1 kg of sugar cane. If Islandians started at E and sold their entire 56 kg of sugar cane to the rest of the world, they could buy an additional 56 kilograms of nuts, for a total of $56 + 56 = 112$ kg of nuts and $56 - 56 = 0$ kg of sugar cane. So point A in Figure 2.11 represents the maximum possible sugar cane consumption, and point B represents their maximum possible nut consumption once they can engage in trade.

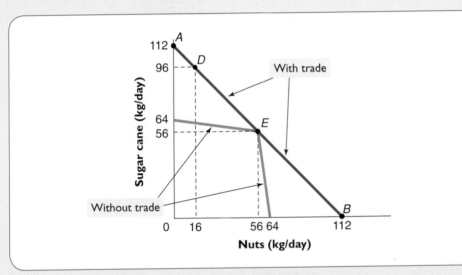

FIGURE 2.11

How Trade Expands Islandia's Menu of Possibilities
The opportunity to trade with the rest of the world greatly expands the consumption opportunities of a smaller nation.

A and B represent the two extreme points on Islandia's new menu of possibilities. By trading lesser quantities of sugar cane or nuts, it is also possible for Islandians to achieve any point along the straight line joining A and B. For example, if Islandians started at point E and sold 40 kg of nuts, they could buy an additional 40 kg of sugar cane, which would move them to point D, which has $56 + 40 = 96$ kg of sugar cane and $56 - 40 = 16$ kg of nuts. The opportunity to trade thus transforms Islandia's menu of possibilities from the PPC shown in Figure 2.10 to the one labelled AB in Figure 2.11. Trade gives Islandia the ability to consume *outside* its own production possibilities curve.

Refer to Example 2.8. What would Islandia's new menu of possibilities look like if each citizen in the rest of the world could harvest 100 kg of sugar cane per day, as before, but only 50 kg of nuts?

EXERCISE 2.4

How much does trade benefit the citizens of Islandia? The answer depends on which particular combination of sugar cane and nuts Islandians most prefer. Suppose, for example, that they most prefer the combination at point E in Figure 2.12 on the next page: 56 kg of sugar cane per day and 56 kg of nuts. The opportunity to trade would then be of no benefit to them, since that combination was available to them before trade became possible (see Figure 2.10).

But suppose that in the absence of trade, Islandians would have chosen to harvest and consume only 28 kg of sugar cane and 60 kg of nuts per day (point D

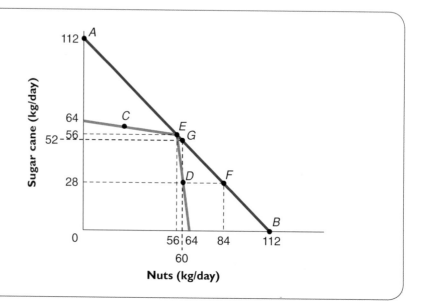

FIGURE 2.12

Gains from International Trade

If the small nation were originally at D on its PPC, the ability to trade with the rest of the world enables it to increase its consumption of nuts by 24 kg per day (moving from D to F). Alternatively, it could increase its consumption of sugar cane by 24 kg per day (moving from D to G).

in Figure 2.12). The opportunity to trade would then be very valuable indeed, for it would enable the Islandians almost to double their consumption of sugar cane without reducing their nut consumption (moving from D to G in Figure 2.12). Or they could increase their nut consumption from 60 to 84 kg per day without giving up any sugar cane (moving from D to F in Figure 2.12). The gains from trade would also be valuable if the Islandians had initially chosen to produce at a point at which the opportunity cost of a kilogram of nuts was less than 1 kg of sugar cane—say, point C in Figure 2.12. In fact, Islandia can obtain any combination on the straight line AB by producing at E and then trading with the rest of the world.

The patterns displayed in this example are at least roughly indicative of actual patterns of international trade. The volume of trade has grown substantially over time and, with some important exceptions, no single nation produces more than a small fraction of the total supply of any good or service. Thus the price at which one good exchanges for another on the world market is not much influenced by how much of a good a nation itself produces. The greater the difference between domestic opportunity costs and world opportunity costs, the more a nation benefits from the opportunity to trade with other nations.

CAN EXCLUSION FROM TRADE HURT A SMALL, POOR NATION?

The importance of trade and comparative advantage to a smaller trading partner may influence the foreign policy of the larger nation. For example, in 1959, the revolution led by Fidel Castro overthrew the government of Cuban dictator Fulgencio Batista. In 1960, while moving into the Soviet orbit, Castro expropriated all American business interests in Cuba. The United States responded early in 1961 by breaking diplomatic relations and ceasing all its trade with Cuba. Since then, the United States has not traded with Cuba, thereby maintaining economic pressure on Castro's communist government. (Sugar is Cuba's most important export.) Loss of trade with Cuba is of little consequence to the United States.

EXERCISE 2.5   **Suppose that Figure 2.11 represents Islandia's circumstances of trade with a superpower. After Islandia and the superpower have been trading for many years, a dispute between them causes trade to cease. Will this cause hardship for Islandia? How?**

IF INTERNATIONAL TRADE IS BENEFICIAL, WHY ARE FREE-TRADE AGREEMENTS SO CONTROVERSIAL?

The North American Free Trade Agreement (NAFTA) is a treaty that greatly reduces trade barriers between Canada, the United States, and Mexico. NAFTA is a contentious political issue, and discussions among world leaders about global trading arrangements are just as contentious. If international specialization and trade are so beneficial, why would anyone oppose them?

It is possible to accept the logic of comparative advantage and oppose freer trade on other grounds. Although international trade can increase the total value of goods and services produced, it does not guarantee that everyone will participate in those benefits. Some opponents of NAFTA feared that it would help Mexico exploit its comparative advantage in the production of goods made with unskilled labour. Others thought Mexican farmers could grow produce more cheaply than farmers to the north, thus putting pressure on American and Canadian farmers. Some also feared that Mexico would not honour Canadian and U.S. labour standards and environmental policies. Consumers would benefit, but unskilled workers in Canada and the United States would confront the possibility of lower wages or unemployment, and global pollution might be aggravated. Also, both Canada and Mexico would be trading with a superpower. This raised concerns that the U.S. would use trade as an instrument of foreign policy, thereby reducing the sovereignty of its smaller partners. The issue of sovereignty may be closely linked to the distribution of trade benefits. If foreigners own a large part of the small country's industry, much of the benefit of trade might flow to foreigners, not to the domestic population.

Opponents of trade agreements also fear that the agreements will lock existing patterns of comparative advantage into place, making it difficult to develop new, more desirable patterns. Recall the case of Canadian pulp and paper. The American pulp and paper industry would have preferred that Canada use its comparative advantage to supply pulpwood as raw material to the American industry. This would have been an obstacle to the development of a Canadian pulp and paper industry. Canadian provincial governments opted instead to use barriers to trade to support the development of a Canadian industry.

International trade provides access to worldwide markets and greatly increases the degree to which each of us relies on human beings living almost anywhere to provide goods and services. As an example, you might consider how many countries were involved in providing the food you will eat and the clothing you will wear in the next 24 hours. At the same time, international trade raises questions of how its benefits will be distributed among the citizens of the world, how those benefits will be used, how international trade will affect a nation's domestic policies, and so on. Chapter 15 examines international trade in much more detail.

RECAP

COMPARATIVE ADVANTAGE AND INTERNATIONAL TRADE

Nations, like individuals, can benefit from exchange, even though one trading partner may be more productive than the other in absolute terms. The greater the difference between domestic opportunity costs and world opportunity costs, the more a nation can potentially benefit from exchange with other nations. But expansions of exchange do not guarantee that each individual citizen will do better. Unskilled workers in high-wage countries may be hurt in the short run by the reduction of barriers to trade with low-wage nations. International trade may also raise issues about the distribution of benefits between trading partners, national sovereignty, and the extent to which an existing pattern of comparative advantage might change over time.

SUMMARY

2.1 One person has an *absolute* advantage over another in the production of a good if she can produce more of that good than the other person. One person has a *comparative* advantage over another in the production of a good if she is relatively more efficient than the other person at producing that good, meaning that her opportunity cost of producing it is lower than her counterpart's. Specialization based on comparative advantage is the basis for economic exchange. When each person specializes in the task at which she is relatively most efficient, the economic pie is maximized, making possible the largest slice for everyone.

2.1 At the individual level, comparative advantage may spring from differences in talent or ability or from differences in education, training, and experience. At the national level, sources of comparative advantage include these innate and learned differences, as well as differences in language, culture, institutions, climate, natural resources, and a host of other factors.

2.2 The production possibilities curve is a simple device for summarizing the possible combinations of output that a society can produce if it employs its resources efficiently. In a simple economy that produces only sugar cane and nuts, the PPC shows the maximum quantity of sugar cane production (vertical axis) possible at each level of nut production (horizontal axis). The slope of the PPC at any point represents the opportunity cost of nuts at that point, expressed in kilograms of sugar cane.

2.2 All production possibilities curves slope downward because of the scarcity problem, which implies that the only way to obtain more of one good is to accept less of another. In a nut/sugar cane economy whose workers have different opportunity costs of picking nuts, the slope of the PPC becomes steeper with increasing production of nuts and movement down the curve. This change in slope illustrates the principle of increasing opportunity cost, which states that in expanding the production of any good, a society minimizes its opportunity cost by first employing those resources that are relatively efficient at producing that good. Only when all of the lowest cost resources are employed does it make economic sense to use resources that have higher opportunity costs.

2.2 The same logic that prompts individuals to specialize in their production and to exchange goods with one another also leads nations to specialize and trade with one another. On both levels, each trading partner can benefit from an exchange, even though one may have an absolute advantage for each good. For both individuals and nations, the benefits of exchange tend to be larger the larger the differences are between the trading partners' opportunity costs.

2.3 Though international trade can raise the total value of goods and services produced, it also raises questions: How will the benefits of those goods and services be distributed among trading partners? Will national sovereignty be compromised? Will trade agreements entrench patterns of comparative advantage or will they encourage change in comparative advantage over time?

CORE

The Principle of Comparative Advantage
Total output is largest when each person (or each country) concentrates on the activities for which his or her opportunity cost is lowest.

The Principle of Increasing Opportunity Cost
In expanding the production of any good, first employ those resources with the lowest opportunity cost. Only when all of the lowest cost resources have been employed does it make economic sense to use resources that have higher opportunity costs.

KEY TERMS

absolute advantage (33)
attainable point (41)
comparative advantage (33)

efficient point (41)
inefficient point (41)
production possibilities curve (39)

productivity (36)
unattainable point (41)

REVIEW QUESTIONS

1. Explain what "having a comparative advantage" at producing a particular good or service means. What does "having an absolute advantage" at producing a good or service mean?

2. How will a reduction in the number of hours worked each day affect an economy's production possibilities curve?

3. How will technological innovations that boost labour productivity affect an economy's production possibilities curve?

4. Why does saying that people are poor because they do not specialize make more sense than saying that people perform their own services because they are poor?

5. What factors helped Canada to establish a pulp and paper industry?

6. What factors help Canada to be an exporter of grain?

7. What factors make it more difficult for Quebec to produce and sell movies, books, and popular music, compared to English-speaking Canada?

PROBLEMS

1. Consider a society whose only worker is Helen, who allocates her production time between cutting hair and baking bread. Each hour per day she devotes to cutting hair yields 4 haircuts, and each hour she devotes to baking bread yields 8 loaves of bread. If Helen works a total of 8 hours per day, graph her production possibilities curve.

2. Refer to Problem 1. Which of the points listed below is efficient? Which is attainable?
   a. 28 haircuts/day, 16 loaves/day
   b. 16 haircuts/day, 32 loaves/day
   c. 18 haircuts/day, 24 loaves/day

3. Determine whether the following statements are true or false, and briefly explain why.
   a. Toby can produce 5 L of apple cider or 70 g of feta cheese per hour. Kyle can produce 3 L of apple cider or 42 g of feta cheese per hour. Therefore, Toby and Kyle cannot benefit from specialization and trade.
   b. A doctor who can vacuum her office faster and more thoroughly than commercial cleaners is better off if she cleans her office herself.
   c. In an economy in which millions of workers each have different opportunity costs of producing two goods, the principle of comparative advantage implies that the slope of the production possibilities curve decreases in absolute value as more of the good on the horizontal axis is produced.

4. Nancy and Bill are auto mechanics. Nancy takes 4 hours to replace a clutch and 2 hours to replace a set of brakes. Bill takes 6 hours to replace a clutch and 2 hours to replace a set of brakes. If Bill and Nancy open a motor repair shop
   a. if Nancy works only on clutches, and Bill works only on brakes, both will be better off.
   b. Bill has a comparative advantage at replacing brakes.
   c. Nancy has an absolute advantage at replacing clutches.
   d. Nancy has a comparative advantage at replacing clutches.
   e. all but one of the above statements are correct.

5. Bob and Stella are a married couple. Bob takes 10 minutes to change a lightbulb and 2 minutes to fix a broken fuse. Stella takes 3 minutes to change a lightbulb and 30 seconds to fix a broken fuse. Which of the following statements is true?
   a. Stella has a comparative advantage at fixing fuses, because she can do it faster than Bob.
   b. Stella has a comparative advantage at changing lightbulbs and fixing fuses, because she can do both of them faster than Bob.
   c. Stella has an absolute advantage at changing lightbulbs and fixing fuses, because she can do both of them faster than Bob.
   d. Bob has a comparative advantage at fixing fuses, because Stella has a comparative advantage at changing lightbulbs.
   e. Stella has a comparative advantage at changing lightbulbs.

6. Kamal and Filipe are stranded together on a desert island. The raw materials on the island are suitable only for making beer and pizza, but their quantities are unlimited. What is scarce is labour. Filipe and Kamal each spend 10 hours a day making beer or pizza. The following table specifies how much beer and pizza Filipe and Kamal can produce per hour.

	Beer	Pizza
Filipe	1 bottle per hour	0.2 pizzas per hour
Kamal	1.5 bottles per hour	0.5 pizzas per hour

    a. Draw the daily production possibilities curves (PPCs) for Filipe and Kamal.

    b. Who has an absolute advantage in making pizza? in brewing beer?

    c. Who has a comparative advantage in making pizza? in brewing beer?

Now suppose their preferences are as follows: Filipe wants 2 beers and as much pizza as he can eat each day; Kamal wants 2 pizzas and as much beer as he can drink each day.

    d. If each man is self-reliant, how much beer and pizza will Filipe and Kamal eat and drink?

    e. Suppose the two men decide to trade with each other. Draw their joint PPC, and give an example of a trade that will make each of them better off.

7. Rework Problem 6 with the following changes:

    a. Each individual's productivity is shown in the table that follows, which specifies the number of hours each man needs to produce a single unit of beer and pizza.

    b. Filipe wants 6 beers and as much pizza as he can eat each day, while Kamal wants 2 pizzas and as much beer as he can drink each day.

	Production time for 1 beer	**Production time for 1 pizza**
Filipe	5/4 hours	5/3 hours
Kamal	5 hours	5/2 hours

8. Suppose Filipe and Kamal's production possibilities curves from Problem 7 are combined. What would be the maximum number of pizzas available to Filipe and Kamal if they could buy or sell in a world market in which 1 beer could be exchanged for 1 pizza? What would be the maximum number of beers available to them?

9. Inlandia and Outlandia both can produce oranges and oil. Inlandia can produce up to 10 million tonnes of oranges per week or 5 million barrels of oil, or any combination of oil and oranges along a straight-line production possibilities curve linking those two points. Outlandia can produce up to 50 million tonnes of oranges per week or 1 million barrels of oil, or any combination along a straight-line production possibilities curve linking those points.

    a. Does the principle of increasing opportunity cost apply in either of these two economies? Why or why not?

    b. Suppose Inlandia and Outlandia sign a trade agreement in which each country will specialize in the production of either oil or oranges. According to the principle of comparative advantage, which country will specialize in which commodity?

    c. If Inlandia and Outlandia are the only two economies in the world that are open to international trade, what are the maximum and minimum prices that can prevail on the world market for a tonne of oranges, in terms of barrels of oil?

10. Jay, Kay, and Dee are marooned alone on the Greek island of Skorpios. They must find a way to provide themselves with food and drinking water. The following table shows how many hours each person takes to produce one unit of food or one unit of water.

	Production time for 1 unit of food	**Production time for 1 unit of drinking water**
Jay	1 hour	2 hours
Kay	2 hours	1 hour
Dee	4 hours	6 hours

    a. If each person can work for 12 hours a day and each person provides only for himself or herself, draw their individual PPCs.

    b. Suppose Jay, Kay, and Dee decide to produce food and water cooperatively, so they can gain from trade. Draw their combined production possibilities curve.

    c. If the trio wants, in aggregate, to consume 15 units of food and 12 units of water, who will specialize in food production? Who will specialize in water production? Will anyone divide his or her time between food and water production?

    d. If the trio wants, in aggregate, to consume 6 units of water and as much food as possible, who will specialize in food and who will specialize in water? Will anyone divide his or her time between food and water production? How much food will be produced?

    e. Suppose production is as in part (c). Dee suggests dividing the output equally among the three of them. Assuming that the amounts of food that Jay and Kay get under this arrangement are exactly what each would have chosen if he or she had lived and worked alone, is each of them strictly better off when they share? Explain.

ANSWERS TO IN-CHAPTER EXERCISES

2.1

	Productivity in programming	**Productivity in bicycle repair**
Mina	2 Web page updates per hour	1 repair per hour
Barb	3 Web page updates per hour	3 repairs per hour

The entries in the table tell us that Barb has an absolute advantage over Mina in both activities. While Barb can update 3 Web pages per hour, Mina can update only 2. Barb's absolute advantage over Mina is even greater in the task of fixing bicycles—3 repairs per hour versus Mina's 1.

But, as in Example 2.2, the fact that Barb is a better programmer than Mina does not imply that Barb will be better off if she updates her own Web page. Barb's opportunity cost of updating a Web page is 1 bicycle repair, whereas Mina must give up only half a bicycle repair to update a Web page. Mina has a comparative advantage over Barb at programming, and Barb has a comparative advantage over Mina at bicycle repair.

2.2 Susan's opportunity cost of picking a kilogram of nuts is 1/2 kg of sugar cane. But Tom's opportunity cost of picking a kilogram of nuts is now only 1/3 kg of sugar cane. So Tom has a comparative advantage at picking nuts, and Susan has a comparative advantage at cutting sugar cane.

2.3 The slope to the left of point D (in absolute value) is 1/2 kg of sugar cane per kilogram of nuts, which is Susan's opportunity cost of picking nuts.

2.4 In the rest of the world, the opportunity cost of a kilogram of nuts is now 2 kg of sugar cane, not 1 kg. This means that Islandians can now buy or sell a kilogram of nuts for 2 kg of sugar cane and can buy or sell a kilogram of sugar cane for 1/2 kg of nuts. So if Islandians start at point E and sell all 56 kg of nuts they produce, they can buy an additional 112 kg of sugar cane, for a total of 168 kg of sugar cane. This would put them at point A in the diagram below. Alternatively, if they start at E and sell all 56 kg of sugar cane they produce, they can buy an additional 28 kg of nuts, for a total of 84 kg of nuts, which would put them at B. The straight line AB is their new menu of opportunities.

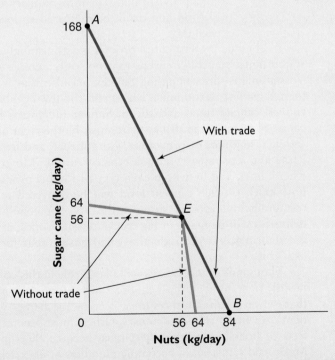

2.5 Loss of the opportunity to trade reduces Islandia's menu of consumption possibilities from AB to its own production possibilities curve. If, when it was trading, Islandia selected a combination of nuts and sugar cane significantly different from the combination represented by point E in the graph above, loss of the opportunity to trade would cause Islandia significant hardship. (If, when it was trading, Islandia selected a point on AB quite close to E, loss of trade would cause Islandia only minor inconvenience.)

Chapter 3 · Supply and Demand: An Introduction

The stock of foodstuffs on hand at any moment in Toronto's grocery stores, restaurants, and private kitchens is sufficient to feed the city's 2.5 million residents for a week at most. Since most of these residents have nutritionally adequate and highly varied diets, and since almost no food is produced within the city, provisioning Toronto requires that millions of kilograms of food and drink be delivered to locations throughout the city each day.

The entire process is astonishingly complex. For example, the system must somehow ensure that not only *enough* food is delivered to satisfy Torontonians' discriminating palates but also that it is the *right kinds* of food: there must not be too much bacon and too few eggs, or too much caviar and not enough canned tuna, and so on. Similar judgments must be made *within* each category of food and drink: there must be the right amount of Swiss cheese and the right amounts of provolone, Gorgonzola, and feta, and a different variety of herbs and seasonings for each type of cuisine. Moreover, someone must decide where, how, and by whom each type of food is produced. Someone must decide how much of each type of food will be delivered to each of the thousands of restaurants and grocery stores in the city. Someone must determine whether the deliveries will be made in big trucks or small ones, arrange that the trucks be in the right place at the right time, and ensure that fuel and qualified drivers are available.

Thousands of individuals will play a role in this collective effort. Some people, just the right number, must choose to drive food delivery trucks, rather than trucks that deliver lumber. Others must become mechanics who fix these trucks, rather than carpenters who build houses. Others must become farmers, rather than architects or bricklayers. Still others must become chefs in upscale restaurants, or at McDonald's, instead of becoming plumbers or electricians.

A great number of complex tasks must be accomplished in order to provide Torontonians with food every day. Nevertheless, the citizens of that city are able to access what they need fairly easily and consistently. Yes, a grocery store will occasionally run out of flank steak, or a waiter must sometimes tell a diner that someone else has just ordered the last serving of roast duck, but such episodes remain in memory only because they are rare.

In this chapter, we will explore the remarkable process by which markets allocate food, housing, and other goods and services. To be sure, markets are by no means perfect, and our stress on their virtues is to some extent an attempt to counteract what most economists view as an underappreciation by the general public of their remarkable strengths. We will discuss why, under fairly general circumstances, markets function smoothly. We will also discuss the circumstances under which markets, left to themselves, cannot be expected to function well.

This chapter provides a survey of how markets function. Because a major objective of economics is to understand how markets work, subsequent chapters discuss the economic role of markets in considerably more detail. Macroeconomics focuses on national economies as entire units while most of microeconomics is directly concerned with analyses of individual markets. But individual markets—labour markets, financial markets, and foreign exchange markets—also play a central role in macroeconomics. How all markets work is, therefore, a central issue for economics, even if we take as given the regulations and policies of government (e.g., food safety standards or minimum wage laws) within which markets function.

Every society, regardless of how it is organized, must answer certain basic economic questions: What goods and services will be produced? In what quantities? How? For example, how much of our limited time and other resources will we devote to building housing, how much to the production of food, and how much to providing other goods and services? What techniques will we use to produce each good? Who will do each specific task?

As well as deciding what to produce, every society must decide how to distribute the product of its efforts among its members: Who will get more and who will get less? For example, what income will the person who stocks shelves in a grocery store earn? How much will the CEO of the grocery chain receive? Will society make provision for those who cannot work; for example, a taxi driver paralyzed in a car accident? Each person's income helps determine his or her access to the goods and services a society produces. What *distribution* of income is fair? In Canada, as elsewhere, markets play a crucial role. Therefore, we need to understand how (and why) markets can often successfully answer these questions, and also how (and why) they may sometimes fail.

WHAT, HOW, AND FOR WHOM? CENTRAL PLANNING VERSUS THE MARKET

In the thousands of different societies for which records are available, basic economic issues have been decided in essentially one of two ways. One approach is to make most economic decisions centrally. An individual or small number of individuals decides on behalf of a larger group. For example, in many agrarian societies throughout history, families or other small groups consumed only those goods and services that they produced for themselves, and a single clan or family leader made most important production and distribution decisions. On an immensely larger scale, the economic organization of the former Soviet Union (and other communist countries) was also largely centralized. In so-called centrally planned communist nations, a central bureaucratic committee established production targets for the country's farms and factories, developed a master plan for how to achieve those targets (including detailed instructions concerning who was to produce what), and set up guidelines for the distribution and use of the goods and services produced.

Neither form of centralized economic organization is much in evidence today. When implemented on a small scale, as in a self-sufficient family enterprise, centralized decision making is certainly feasible. For the reasons discussed in Chapter 2, however, the jack-of-all-trades approach was doomed once it became clear how dramatically people could improve their living standards by specialization

—that is, by having each individual focus his efforts on a relatively narrow range of tasks. And with the fall of the Soviet Union and its satellite nations in the late 1980s, there are now only three communist economies left in the world: Cuba, North Korea, and China. The first two of these are experiencing severe economic stress, and China has largely abandoned any attempt to control production and distribution decisions from the centre.

In the twenty-first century we are therefore left, for the most part, with the second major form of economic system, one in which production and distribution decisions are left to individuals interacting in markets. In the so-called capitalist, or market, economies, people decide for themselves which careers to pursue and which products to produce or buy. In fact, there are few, if any, *pure* market economies today. Modern industrial countries are more properly described as *mixed economies,* meaning that goods and services are allocated by a combination of free markets, regulation, and other forms of collective control. Still, it makes sense to refer to such systems as market economies in which people are for the most part free to start businesses, to shut them down, or to sell them. Within broad limits, the distribution of goods and services is determined by individual preferences backed by individual purchasing power, which in most cases comes from the income people earn in the labour market.

www.statcan.ca/start.html
Statistics Canada

3.1 MARKETS AND PRICES

market the context in which potential buyers and sellers of a good or service can negotiate exchanges

Beginning with some basic concepts and definitions, we will explore how the interactions between buyers and sellers in markets determine the prices and quantities of the various goods and services traded in those markets. By definition, the **market** for any good is the context in which potential buyers and sellers of that good can negotiate exchanges. For any good, we specify the time and the place at which it is bought and sold. So, for example, the market for hamburgers on a given day in a given place is just the set of people (or other economic actors, like firms) potentially able to buy or sell hamburgers at that time and location.

In the market for hamburgers, sellers comprise the individuals and companies that either sell or might sell hamburgers, under the right circumstances. Similarly, buyers in this market include all individuals who buy, or might buy, hamburgers. In most parts of Canada a cooked hamburger can still be had for less than $5. How is the market price of hamburgers determined? Looking beyond hamburgers to the vast array of other goods that are bought and sold every day, we may ask why some goods are cheap and others expensive.

Adam Smith and other early economists (including Karl Marx) thought that the market price of a good was determined by its cost of production. But although costs surely do affect prices, they cannot explain why one of Pablo Picasso's paintings sells for so much more than one of A.J. Casson's. Stanley Jevons and other nineteenth-century economists tried to explain price by focusing on the value people derived from consuming different goods and services. It certainly seems plausible that people will pay a lot for a good they value highly. Yet willingness to pay cannot be the whole story either. A person deprived of water in the desert, for example, will be dead in a matter of hours, but water from a municipal system sells for a fraction of a penny per litre. By contrast, human beings can get along perfectly well without gold, and yet gold sells for hundreds of dollars per ounce.

Cost of production, or value to the consumer; which is more significant? The answer is that both matter. Writing in the late nineteenth century, the British economist Alfred Marshall was among the first to show clearly how costs and value interact to determine both the prevailing market price for a good and the amount of it that is bought and sold. His famous analogy was that demand and supply are like the two blades of a scissors, since each by itself can explain little, but together they can cut through to the essence of many issues.[1] Our task in the pages ahead will be to explore Marshall's insights and gain some practise in applying them. As a first step, we introduce the two main components of Marshall's path-breaking analysis: the supply curve and the demand curve.

THE SUPPLY CURVE

In the market for hamburgers, the **supply curve** of hamburgers is a simple schedule, or graph, that tells us, for each possible price of hamburgers, the total quantity of hamburgers of uniform quality that all hamburger sellers together would be willing to supply per period of time at that price, provided that all other things are held constant. Notice that the definition of the supply curve refers to the *quantities* of hamburgers that sellers are *willing* to *supply* at specific prices. Although they are related, the *supply curve* and the *quantity supplied* are two different concepts. **Quantity supplied** is the total amount of a good of uniform quality that all sellers together are willing to produce and sell *at a single, specific price* during a particular period of time.

What does the supply curve of hamburgers look like? The answer is based on the logical assumption that people will be willing to produce and sell hamburgers as long as the price they receive for them is sufficient to cover their opportunity costs of supplying them. Thus, if what people could earn by selling hamburgers is not sufficient to compensate them for what they could have earned if they had spent their time and invested their money in some other way, they will not sell hamburgers. Otherwise, they will. Figure 3.1 provides an illustration. It portrays a single supply curve showing the relationship between *price* and *quantity supplied*. Many points lie on this single curve. Each point on a supply curve identifies a specific quantity supplied and a corresponding, specific price. Figure 3.1 indicates that if the price is $2, the quantity of hamburgers supplied will be 8000. If the price is higher, the quantity is greater; for example, at a price of $3 each, 12 000 will be supplied.

Economists know perfectly well that some hamburgers are bigger than others (and consequently sell for a higher price), but we want to focus on the role played by prices in the market. Hence we simplify by making the assumption that we can draw a supply curve for a particular type of hamburger; for example, one made with six ounces of well-done, grade A beef and garnished with relish. The definitions of supply and quantity supplied generalize by stating the good is of uniform

supply curve a curve or schedule showing the total quantity of a good of uniform quality that sellers want to sell at each price during a particular period of time provided that all other things are held constant

quantity supplied the total amount of a good of uniform quality that all sellers are willing produce and sell at a single, specific price during a particular period of time

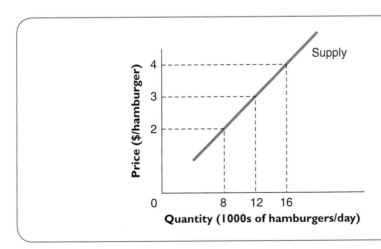

FIGURE 3.1
The Daily Supply Curve of Hamburgers in Downtown Toronto
At higher prices, sellers generally offer more units for sale. The supply curve is upward sloping.

---

[1] "We might as reasonably dispute whether it is the upper or the under blade of a pair of scissors that cuts a piece of paper, as whether value is governed by utility or cost of production." Alfred Marshall, *Principles of Economics* (1920), 8th ed., (London: Macmillan & Co Ltd, 1964), p. 290.

quality. It has specific, given characteristics. We therefore think of other, similar goods (larger or smaller hamburgers, hotdogs, etc.) as being sold in other, different markets, recognizing that because these goods cater to similar wants, the markets for them are linked.

The definition of quantity supplied also refers to a particular period of time. A quantity supplied of 8000 hamburgers per day is quite different from a quantity of 8000 hamburgers per month. Because, to be meaningful, our definition must specify the period of time during which a quantity is supplied, the label on the horizontal axis of Figure 3.1 indicates quantity supplied *per day*.

In general, people differ with respect to their opportunity costs of producing and selling hamburgers. For those with limited education and work experience, the opportunity cost of selling hamburgers is relatively low because they typically do not have a lot of high-paying alternatives. For others, the opportunity cost of selling burgers is of moderate value, and for still other people, like rock stars and professional athletes, it is prohibitively high. Because of these differences in people's opportunity costs of selling hamburgers, the daily supply curve of hamburgers will be *upward sloping* as shown in Figure 3.1, which exhibits a hypothetical supply curve for the hamburger market in downtown Toronto on a given day. (Although economists usually refer to demand and supply "curves," to keep things simple we often draw them as straight lines in our examples.)

Why is the supply curve for hamburgers upward sloping? When the price of hamburgers is low, say, $2 per hamburger, only those people whose opportunity cost of selling hamburgers is less than or equal to that amount will offer hamburgers for sale. For the supply curve shown in Figure 3.1, the quantity supplied at a price of $2 will be 8000 hamburgers per day. In that example, 8000 hamburgers is the total quantity of hamburgers offered for sale by people whose opportunity cost of selling hamburgers is $2 per hamburger or less. If the price of a hamburger were to rise above $2, however, additional sellers would find it worthwhile to offer hamburgers for sale. For example, at a price of $3, Figure 3.1 shows that the quantity of hamburgers supplied is 12 000 per day, while at a price of $4 the quantity supplied is 16 000. The higher the price, the more people find it worthwhile to supply hamburgers.

INCREASING
OPPORTUNITY
COST

The upward slope of the supply curve may be seen as a consequence of the principle of increasing opportunity cost, discussed in Chapter 2. This principle tells us that as we expand the production of hamburgers, we turn first to those suppliers whose opportunity costs of producing hamburgers are lowest and only then to others with higher opportunity costs.

Finally, a supply curve (or schedule) holds constant all things other than price and quantity supplied. The Latin words *ceteris paribus* (other things constant) are often used to indicate this assumption, one which allows us to focus on the impact of price on quantity supplied. Many things could affect actual supply in the real world; a power failure, for example, could shut down the city and temporarily eliminate the market for hamburgers. We will ignore such possibilities and impose the assumption of *ceteris paribus* in order to show how supply and demand determine the price and quantity traded. Later, we will relax the assumption of *ceteris paribus* to see the effects of factors other than price.

BOX 3.1   SUPPLY AS AN EQUATION

There are many possible ways to express something. An economic model can be explained with words, with graphs, or by using mathematical equations. If we choose to use the language of mathematics, the supply curve pictured in Figure 3.1 could also be written algebraically as

$$Q_S = a + bP_S.$$

Algebraically, we use Q_S to mean quantity supplied in *thousands* of units and P_S to mean supply price. In general, the parameter a is the horizontal intercept, and the parameter b is the reciprocal of the slope of the supply curve. The plus sign indicates a direct, positive relationship between quantity supplied and price. In the specific example of the supply schedule portrayed graphically in Figure 3.1, $a = 0$ and $b = 4$, so the supply curve also can be written algebraically as

$$Q_S = 4P_S.$$

If we measure quantity supplied in thousands of hamburgers per day and price in dollars, we can state the relationship between price and quantity supplied in any of three ways. Both the graphical representation of Figure 3.1 and the algebraic statement $Q_S = 4P_S$ are equivalent to the verbal statement, "If price increases by one dollar, quantity supplied will increase by 4000 hamburgers." The mathematical statement says the same thing as either the figure or the words do, just more compactly.[2]

THE DEMAND CURVE

The supply curve, by itself, does not tell us how many hamburgers will be sold in downtown Toronto on a given day, or at what price those hamburgers will sell. To find the prevailing price and quantity, we also need the demand curve for hamburgers in this market. The **demand curve** for hamburgers is a graph that tells us the total quantity of hamburgers that buyers want to buy at each price.[3]

Figure 3.2 graphs the daily demand for a hypothetical market for hamburgers in downtown Toronto. It shows a relationship between *price* and *quantity demanded*. Typically, a demand curve is downward sloping. The demand curve in Figure 3.2 shows that when price is high, buyers as a group are willing to purchase fewer hamburgers. Like the supply curve, the demand curve is composed of many points. Each point on the demand curve identifies a specific quantity demanded at the corresponding price. Thus, a single demand curve plots many different quantities demanded and many prices. When the price is $4, quantity demanded is 8000 hamburgers per day; when the price is $3, the quantity demanded is 12 000 hamburgers per day, and so on.

We define the demand curve in the same terms as we do the supply curve. The demand curve pertains to a good of uniform quality. Quantity demanded is specified as an amount per period of time, so the label on the horizontal axis of Figure 3.2 indicates that quantity is measured in thousands of hamburgers *per day*. Finally, the assumption of *ceteris paribus* pertains to demand just as it

demand curve a curve or schedule showing the total quantity of a good of uniform quality that buyers want to buy at each price during a particular period of time provided that all other things are held constant

[2]The reader may be perplexed by the economist's practice of placing price, the independent variable, on the vertical axis. The practice stems from Alfred Marshall, who treated quantity as the independent variable because he wanted to investigate the effect of changes in quantity on price. Such was Marshall's influence that ever since he published *Principles of Economics* in 1890, economists have placed price on the vertical axis. The work of another great economist, Leon Walras, is characteristic of practice before 1890. Walras treated price as the independent variable, and placed it on the horizontal axis. Walras may have been vexed by Marshall's influence; in his correspondence, he refers to Marshall as the "great white elephant of political economy." Marshall, *Principles of Economics*, pp. 78–85. Robert B. Ekelund, Jr. and Robert F. Hebert, *A History of Economic Theory and Method*, 5th ed. (Long Grove, Illinois: Waveland Press, Inc., 2007), pp. 383, 387–390.

[3]To be truly precise, we have to specify "hamburgers of uniform quality during a particular period of time provided that all other things are held constant." But the key idea is fairly simple: How many would people want to buy, at each price?

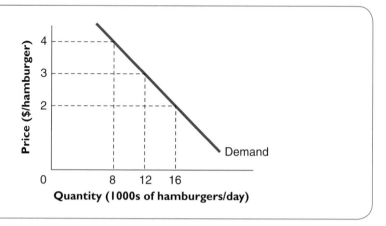

FIGURE 3.2

The Daily Demand Curve for Hamburgers in Downtown Toronto
The demand curve for any good is a generally downward-sloping function of its price. At lower prices, buyers generally want to purchase more units.

quantity demanded the total amount of a good of uniform quality purchased at a single, specific price by all buyers during a particular period of time

does to supply. A single demand curve shows the relationship between quantity demanded and price, provided that all things other than price and quantity are held constant. Therefore, we define **quantity demanded** as the total amount purchased by all buyers at a single, specific price. We will return to the question of what happens to demand when things other than price and quantity change, but first we develop the concept of market equilibrium.

BOX 3.2   DEMAND AS AN EQUATION

Demand, like supply, can be analyzed with words, with graphs, or by using equations. A linear demand curve can be represented algebraically by an equation of the form

$$Q_D = c - dP_D.$$

Quantity demanded is represented by Q_D, while P_D represents demand price. In general, the parameter c represents the horizontal intercept; i.e., the quantity of hamburgers that would be consumed if hamburgers were free. The parameter d has a minus sign because quantity demanded decreases when price increases; i.e., quantity is negatively related to price. In the specific case of the demand curve that is graphed in Figure 3.2, the demand curve can be written as the equation

$$Q_D = 24 - 4P_D.$$

In this case, Q_D represents quantity demanded in thousands of units, $c = 24$, and $d = -4$. Again, one could express it verbally: If price increases by one dollar, quantity demanded will decrease by 4000 hamburgers. Some people find it easiest to understand the relationship between quantity demanded and price when it is expressed verbally, while others prefer algebra or graphs. All are just different ways of saying the same thing.

---

equilibrium a state that occurs when all of the forces that act on all the variables in a system are in balance, exactly offsetting each other so that none of the variables in the system has any tendency to change

MARKET EQUILIBRIUM

The concept of equilibrium is employed in both the physical and social sciences and is of central importance in economic analysis. We use the term *equilibrium* to denote a state of rest. In general, a system in **equilibrium** has no tendency to change. In physics, for example, a ball hanging from a spring is said to be in equilibrium when the spring has stretched so that the upward force it exerts on the ball is exactly counterbalanced by the downward force of gravity. In economics, a market is said to be in equilibrium when no participant in the market has any desire to alter his or her behaviour so that there is no tendency for any change in either price or quantity.

If we want to determine the final position of a ball hanging from a spring, (recognizing that it may bounce for a while, but will eventually settle down) we need to find the point at which the forces of gravity and spring tension are balanced and the system is in equilibrium. Similarly, if we want to find the price at which a good will sell (the **equilibrium price**) and the quantity of it that will be sold when the market has settled down (the **equilibrium quantity**), we need to find the equilibrium in the market for that good. The basic tools for finding the equilibrium for some good in a market are the supply and demand curves for that good. The price and quantity at which the supply and demand curves for the good intersect is the equilibrium. For the hypothetical supply and demand curves for hamburgers in downtown Toronto, the equilibrium price will therefore be $3 per hamburger, and the equilibrium quantity of hamburgers sold will be 12 000 per day, as shown in Figure 3.3 which combines Figures 3.1 and 3.2.

equilibrium price and equilibrium quantity the price and quantity of a good at the intersection of the supply and demand curves for the good

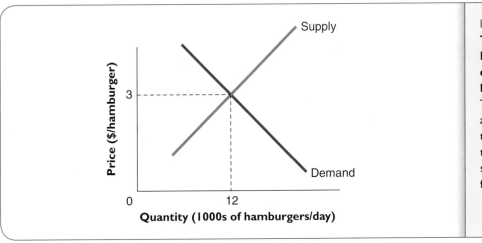

FIGURE 3.3
The Equilibrium Price and Quantity of Hamburgers in Downtown Toronto
The equilibrium quantity and price of a product are the values that correspond to the intersection of the supply and demand curves for that product.

In Figure 3.3, note that at the equilibrium price of $3 per hamburger, both sellers and buyers are "satisfied" in the following sense: buyers are buying exactly the quantity of hamburgers they want to buy at that price (12 000 per day) and sellers are selling exactly the quantity of hamburgers they want to sell (also 12 000 per day) at that price. In this **market equilibrium**, both buyers and sellers are satisfied in that, neither group faces any incentives to change their behaviour.

Note the limited sense of the term *satisfied* in the definition of market equilibrium. It does not mean that sellers would be displeased to receive a price higher than the equilibrium price. Rather, it means only that they are able to sell all they wish to sell at that price. Similarly, to say that buyers are satisfied at the equilibrium price does not mean that they would not like to have a higher income or that they would not be happy to pay less than the equilibrium price. Rather, it means only that, given their incomes, they are able to buy exactly as many units of the good as they want to at the equilibrium price.

Note also that if the price of hamburgers in our downtown Toronto market was anything other than $3, either buyers or sellers would not be satisfied. Suppose, for example, that the price of hamburgers was $4, as shown in Figure 3.4. At that price, buyers want to buy only 8000 hamburgers per day, but sellers want to sell 16 000. Since no one can force someone to buy a hamburger against his or her wishes, this means that buyers will buy only the 8000 hamburgers they want

market equilibrium occurs when all buyers and sellers are satisfied with their respective quantities at the market price

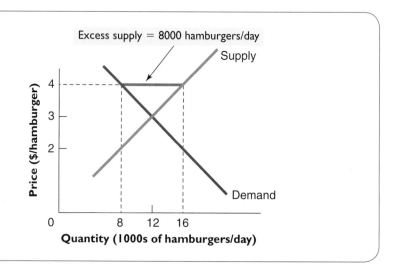

FIGURE 3.4

Excess Supply
When price exceeds the equilibrium price, there is excess supply, or surplus, that is equal to the difference between quantity supplied and quantity demanded.

excess supply, or surplus the difference between the quantity supplied and the quantity demanded when the price of a good exceeds the equilibrium price; some sellers are dissatisfied when there is excess supply

excess demand, or shortage the difference between the quantity supplied and the quantity demanded when the price of a good lies below the equilibrium price; some buyers are dissatisfied when there is excess demand

to buy. So when the price exceeds the equilibrium price, sellers will be dissatisfied. At a price of $4 in this example, the quantity supplied exceeds the quantity demanded by 8000 hamburgers. Therefore, sellers are left with an **excess supply**, or **surplus**.

Conversely, suppose that the price of hamburgers in the downtown Toronto market was less than the equilibrium price, say $2 per hamburger. As shown in Figure 3.5, buyers want to buy 16 000 hamburgers per day at that price, whereas sellers want to sell only 8000. Since sellers cannot be forced to sell hamburgers against their wishes, this time the buyers will be dissatisfied. At a price of $2 in this example, the quantity demanded exceeds the quantity supplied by 8000 hamburgers. Therefore, buyers experience an **excess demand**, or **shortage**.

Markets for goods and services often tend toward their respective equilibrium prices and quantities provided that many buyers and sellers are competing in the market. The mechanisms by which this happens are implicit in our definitions of excess supply and excess demand. Suppose, for example, that the price of hamburgers in our hypothetical market was $4, leading to excess supply as shown in Figure 3.4. Sellers are dissatisfied because they provide more hamburgers than buyers want to buy, so they have an incentive to take whatever steps they can to increase their sales. A simple strategy is for them to cut their price slightly. Thus, if one seller reduced his price from $4 to, say, $3.95 per hamburger, he could attract many of the buyers who had been paying $4 for hamburgers supplied by other sellers. Those sellers, to recover their lost business, would then have an incentive

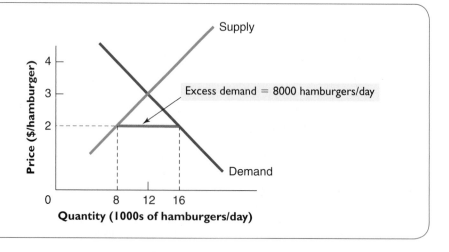

FIGURE 3.5

Excess Demand
When price lies below the equilibrium price, there is excess demand, or shortage, the difference between quantity demanded and quantity supplied.

to match the price cut. But notice that if all sellers lowered their prices to $3.95, there would still be considerable excess supply in the hamburger market. So sellers would face continuing incentives to cut their prices. This pressure to cut prices will not go away until the price falls all the way to $3. At $3, excess supply is zero.

Conversely, suppose that price starts out less than the equilibrium price, say, $2 per hamburger. This time it is the buyers who are dissatisfied. A person who cannot get all the hamburgers she wants at a price of $2 has an incentive to offer a higher price, hoping to obtain hamburgers that would otherwise have been sold to other buyers. And sellers, for their part, will be only too happy to post higher prices as long as queues of dissatisfied buyers remain.

The upshot is that price has a tendency to move to its equilibrium level under conditions of either excess supply or excess demand. And when price reaches its equilibrium level, both buyers and sellers are satisfied simultaneously since they are able to buy or sell precisely the amounts they choose, given their incomes.

We emphasize that the mere fact that buyers and sellers are satisfied in this sense does not mean that markets automatically result in the best of all possible worlds. For example, a poor person may buy one hamburger each day at a price of $3, but still be hungry; in this case, he is satisfied only in the sense that he cannot buy a second hamburger without sacrificing other urgent purchases.

It is also important to emphasize that the equilibrating process depends on competition among many buyers and sellers, all of whom are small relative to the size of the market. If all sellers are small, no seller has the ability to increase the price of hamburgers above the equilibrium price by restricting the quantity supplied. For example, if all sellers are small, no seller can raise the price of hamburgers to $4 by restricting the quantity to 8000 hamburgers per day. Why? Because at $4, other sellers will be perfectly willing to compete for buyers by increasing the quantity of hamburgers, while offering a somewhat lower price.

Similarly, if all buyers are small, no buyer can reduce price below the equilibrium price, say to $2, by announcing that they will pay no more than $2 for a hamburger. Why? Because at $2 only 8000 hamburgers/day will be supplied, and other buyers will compete for hamburgers by offering a somewhat higher price.

RECAP

MARKETS AND PRICES

The *market* for a good or service is the context in which potential buyers and sellers of the good or service can negotiate exchanges. For any given price, the *supply curve* shows the total quantity that suppliers of the good would be willing to sell, and the *demand curve* shows the total quantity that demanders would be willing to buy. Suppliers are willing to sell more at higher prices (supply curves slope upward) and demanders are willing to buy less at higher prices (demand curves slope downward).

Market equilibrium, the situation in which all buyers and sellers are satisfied with their respective quantities at the market price, occurs at the intersection of the supply and demand curves. The corresponding price and quantity are called the *equilibrium price* and the *equilibrium quantity.*

Prices and quantities tend to be driven toward their equilibrium values by the competitive actions of buyers and sellers. If the price is initially too high, resulting in excess supply, dissatisfied sellers will compete for buyers by cutting their prices to sell more. If the price is initially too low, resulting in excess demand, competition among buyers drives the price upward. This process continues until equilibrium is reached. The equilibrating process depends on competition among large numbers of small buyers and sellers.

BOX 3.3   MARKET EQUILIBRIUM: SUPPLY EQUALS DEMAND

When a market is in equilibrium, no buyer or seller wants to change their behaviour, so none of the variables in the system tend to change. Figure 3.3 presents a graphical representation of equilibrium in a simple system of supply and demand—the intersection of the supply and demand curves. The intersection of supply and demand curves is the only place where quantity supplied (Q_S) equals quantity demanded (Q_D). It therefore identifies the equilibrium quantity, which we will call Q^*. Because the supply price (P_S) equals demand price (P_D) at this intersection point, the intersection also identifies the equilibrium price, which we will call P^*.

We can represent equilibrium algebraically by using the equations for supply and demand that appear in the previous boxes. In market equilibrium we have that $P_S = P_D = P^*$ and $Q_S = Q_D = Q^*$. Therefore, by setting $Q_S = Q_D$ we can solve for P^*:

$$a + bP^* = c - dP^*.$$

The equation for supply (from Box 3.1) is on the left hand side of the equal sign, and the equation for demand (from Box 3.2) is on the right.
Solving for P^* we have that

$$P^* = \frac{(c-a)}{(b+d)} .$$

We can substitute P^* into either the equation for demand or for supply to determine Q^*. Using the demand equation, we have

$$Q^* = c - d \times \left(\frac{c-a}{b+d} \right)$$

Therefore, the equilibrium condition states that supply is equal to demand. The equilibrium quantity is Q^*. By definition, $Q_S = Q_D = Q^*$, where quantity supplied and quantity demanded are represented by Q_S and Q_D, respectively, as they were in the earlier two boxes.

If we insert the values for the parameters as stated in the two earlier boxes, we can rewrite the equilibrium condition:

$$0 + 4P^* = 24 - 4P^*.$$

Since this is one equation with one unknown, we can solve for P^* and find that $P^* = \$3$. The equilibrium value for price can be substituted into either the equation for supply or the equation for demand to determine that the equilibrium quantity is 12. Remember that Q^* is measured in thousands of units. Therefore, the equilibrium quantity actually is 12 000 hamburgers. The values for equilibrium price and quantity are consistent with what is shown in Figure 3.3.

As demonstrated here, an equilibrium of supply and demand involves the simultaneous solution of two equations. See www.mcgrawhill.ca/olc/frankbernanke for additional discussion of how two simultaneous equations are solved.

3.2   MARKETS, EQUILIBRIUM, AND EFFICIENCY

When a market is out of equilibrium, it is always possible to identify mutually beneficial but unrealized exchanges. When people have failed to take advantage of all mutually beneficial exchanges, we often say that there is "cash on the table"—the economist's metaphor for unexploited opportunities. When the price in a market is below the equilibrium price, there is cash on the table because it will always be possible for a supplier to produce an additional unit at a cost that is lower than the price buyers are willing to pay. This leads to an important result, which we will state as a core principle.

The Equilibrium Principle: A market in equilibrium leaves no unexploited opportunities for individuals.

EQUILIBRIUM

COST–
BENEFIT

The **efficient quantity** of any good is the quantity that maximizes the total economic surplus that results from producing and consuming the good. The *cost–benefit principle* tells us to keep expanding production of the good as long as the benefit of producing one more unit exceeds the cost of that additional unit. This means that the efficient quantity is that level of production for which the cost and the benefit of one more unit of the good are the same.

When the quantity of a good is less than the efficient quantity, increasing its production will increase total economic surplus. By the same token, when the quantity of a good exceeds the efficient quantity, reducing its production will increase total economic surplus. **Economic efficiency** occurs when all goods and services in the economy are produced and consumed at levels that produce the maximum economic surplus for society. The importance of efficiency leads us to express this as another core principle.

efficient quantity the quantity that results in the maximum possible economic surplus from producing and consuming the good

economic efficiency condition that occurs when all goods and services are produced and consumed at their respective socially optimal levels

The Efficiency Principle: Economic efficiency occurs when total economic surplus is maximized. Efficiency is an important social goal because, when the economic pie grows larger, everyone can potentially have a larger slice.

The efficiency principle pertains if supply and demand curves reflect all significant costs and benefits associated with production and consumption of the good.

EFFICIENCY

 RECAP

MARKETS, EQUILIBRIUM, AND EFFICIENCY

When the supply and demand curves for a good reflect all significant costs and benefits associated with the production and consumption of that good, the market equilibrium will result in the largest possible economic surplus. Economic efficiency occurs when total economic surplus is maximized. Economic efficiency is important because a larger economic pie means everyone can have a potentially larger slice.

3.3 EXPLAINING CHANGES IN PRICES AND QUANTITIES

If we know how the factors that govern supply and demand curves are changing, we can make informed predictions about how prices and the corresponding quantities will change. But when describing changing circumstances in the marketplace, we must take care to recognize some important terminological distinctions. For example, we must distinguish between the meanings of the seemingly similar expressions *change in the quantity demanded* and *change in demand*. When we speak of a **change in the quantity demanded**, we mean the change in quantity that people want to buy that occurs in response to a change in price. For instance,

change in quantity demanded a movement along the demand curve that occurs in response to a change in price

Figure 3.6(a) depicts an increase in the quantity demanded that occurs in response to a reduction in the price of tuna. When the price falls from $5 to $4 per can, the quantity demanded rises from 2000 to 4000 cans per day. By contrast, when we speak of a **change in demand**, we mean a *shift in the entire demand curve*. For example, Figure 3.6(b) depicts an increase in demand, meaning that at every price the quantity demanded is higher than before. In summary, a change in the quantity demanded refers to a movement *along* the demand curve, and a change in demand means a *shift* of the entire curve.

change in demand a shift of the entire demand curve

FIGURE 3.6

An Increase in the Quantity Demanded versus an Increase in Demand

Panel (a): An increase in quantity demanded is represented by a downward movement along the demand curve as price falls. Panel (b): An increase in demand is represented by an outward shift of the demand curve.

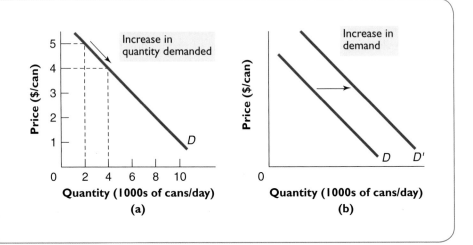

A similar terminological distinction applies on the supply side of the market. A **change in supply** means a shift in the entire supply curve, whereas a **change in the quantity supplied** refers to a movement along the supply curve. Why might the demand curve shift? Why might the supply curve shift? Shifts in either the supply curve or demand curve happen because of changes in some of the factors we have, up until now, held constant. We can use the framework of supply and demand to analyze the implications of changes in these factors.

change in supply a shift of the entire supply curve

change in quantity supplied a movement along the supply curve that occurs in response to a change in price

Alfred Marshall's supply and demand model is one of the most useful tools of the economic naturalist. Once we understand the forces that govern the placements of supply and demand curves, we are suddenly in a position to make sense of a host of interesting observations in the world around us.

SHIFTS IN THE SUPPLY CURVE

To get a better feel for how the supply and demand model enables us to predict and explain price and quantity movements, it is helpful to begin with a few simple examples. Because the supply curve is based on costs of production, anything that changes production costs will shift the supply curve and hence will result in a new equilibrium quantity and price.

EXAMPLE 3.1

What will happen to the equilibrium price and quantity of new houses if the wage rate of carpenters falls?

Suppose the initial supply and demand curves for new houses are as shown by the curves S and D in Figure 3.7, resulting in an equilibrium price of $160 000 per house and an equilibrium quantity of 40 houses per month. A decline in the wage rate of carpenters reduces the cost of making new houses, and this means

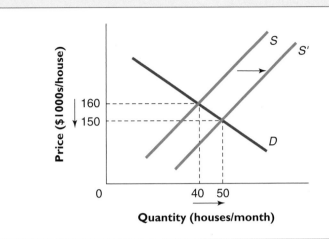

FIGURE 3.7
The Effect on the Market for New Houses of a Decline in Carpenters' Wage Rates
When input prices fall, supply shifts right, causing equilibrium price to fall and equilibrium quantity to rise.

that, for any given price of houses, more builders can profitably serve the market than before. Diagrammatically, this means a rightward shift in the supply curve of houses, from S to S'. (A rightward shift in the supply curve can also be described as a downward shift.)

Because carpenters make up only a tiny fraction of all potential home buyers, we may assume that lower wages have no significant effect on demand for houses. Thus, a reduction in carpenters' wages produces a significant rightward shift in the supply curve of houses, but no perceptible shift in the demand curve. We see from Figure 3.7 that the new equilibrium price, $150 000 per house, is lower than the original price, and the new equilibrium quantity, 50 houses per month, is higher than the original quantity.

Example 3.1 involved changes in the cost of an input in the production of a good, carpenters' labour in the production of houses. We have modified the assumption of *ceteris paribus*, all other things equal, to now mean all other things equal but one (i.e., carpenters' wage rate). As the following case illustrates, supply curves also shift when technology changes.

ECONOMIC *Naturalist* **3.1**   Why has the consumption of French fries increased substantially during the last 25 years?

Commercial techniques for peeling, cutting, cooking, and storing French fries are much more sophisticated now than they were 25 years ago. Today, raw potatoes are processed into French fries in a few large plants, frozen, and shipped to restaurants and consumers. Once in restaurants and homes, French fries are easily cooked. In the United States, consumption of potatoes has increased by about 30 percent since 1977, most of it because Americans are eating more French fries and potato chips.[4]

In Figure 3.8, the curves labelled S and D depict the supply and demand curves for French fries during the late 1970s. The curve S' represents the supply curve today. The increase in supply is the result of technological improvements in the production of French fries. As the graph shows, the equilibrium quantity of French fries has increased, and the price has decreased.

[4]David M. Cutler, Edward L. Glaeser, and Jesse M. Shapiro, "Why have Americans Become More Obese?" *Journal of Economic Perspectives, 17* (2003), p. 94.

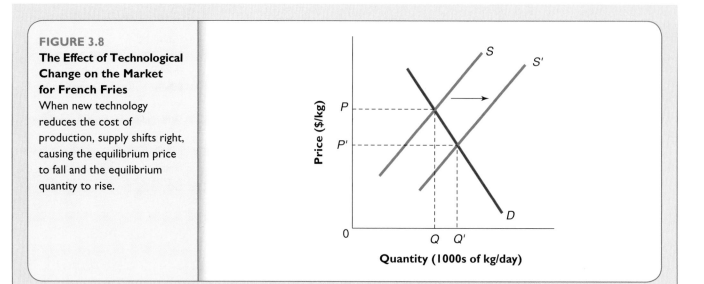

FIGURE 3.8

The Effect of Technological Change on the Market for French Fries
When new technology reduces the cost of production, supply shifts right, causing the equilibrium price to fall and the equilibrium quantity to rise.

inputs goods or services used in the process of producing a different good or service

technology the stock of knowledge, useful in producing goods and services, that is available to a society

Changes in *input* prices and technology are two of the most important factors that give rise to shifts in supply curves. **Inputs** are those items used in a production process to produce a good or service. Inputs are also sometimes referred to as factors of production or factor inputs. In Example 3.1, labour is an input used in the production of houses. The supply curve for houses in Figure 3.7 shifted to the right, or increased, because wages paid to carpenters fell, thus reducing the cost of an input in building houses. Consider another example: because petroleum is an input used in plastics production, a decrease in the price of petroleum shifts the supply curve of plastic garbage cans to the right. Garbage cans are now cheaper to produce, so there will be an increase in quantity supplied at each particular price. Generally, a reduction in the price of an input into the production of a good will increase the supply of that good. An increase in the price of an input will have the opposite effect.

Technology is the stock of knowledge, useful in producing goods and services, that is available to a society. An improvement in technology means that an increase in the stock of available knowledge has made it possible to produce more of at least one good or service from a given set of inputs. In the case of Economic Naturalist 3.1, the stock of knowledge concerning the production of French fries increased, causing an increase in the supply of French fries.

In the real world, many other factors can cause supply to shift. When we think about a change in something other than price and quantity, we are modifying the assumption of *ceteris paribus*. If we do this one thing at a time, we can analyze the impact of each change. For example, weather conditions have a major impact on the yield of crops and the supply of foodstuffs (and on the supply of other goods and services, too). If we introduce changes in the weather as a factor, we are allowing more than just price and quantity to change.

Expectations of future changes can also affect supply curves. Suppose that a drought causes an expectation that harvests at the end of the current growing season will be small. Suppliers are likely to withhold supplies from existing stocks on the *expectation* that whatever is withheld now can be sold at a higher price later. The supply curve for the current period will shift to the left, which is a reduction of supply. Supply in the current period is reduced, even though the existing stock of wheat is not affected by the drought. The drought affects only what is *expected* to be harvested later, but what is expected to happen later affects what is supplied now.

An increase in a subsidy can also shift a supply curve to the right, as can an increase in the number of firms serving a market. A reduction in a subsidy or the number of firms in a market would shift a supply curve to the left.

SHIFTS IN DEMAND

The preceding examples involved changes that gave rise to shifts in supply curves. Next, we'll look at what happens when demand curves shift. In the following example, the shift in demand results from events outside the particular market itself.

What will happen to the equilibrium price and quantity of tennis balls if court rental fees decline?

EXAMPLE 3.2

Let the initial supply and demand curves for tennis balls be as shown by the curves *S* and *D* in Figure 3.9, where the resulting equilibrium price and quantity are $1 per ball and 40 million balls per month, respectively. Tennis courts and tennis balls are what economists call **complements**, goods that are more valuable when used in combination than when used alone. Tennis balls, for example, would be of less value if there were no tennis courts on which to play. (Tennis balls would still have *some* value even without courts; e.g, to the parents who pitch them to their children for batting practice.) As tennis courts become cheaper to use, people will respond by playing more tennis, and this will increase their demand for tennis balls. A decline in court rental fees will thus shift the demand curve for tennis balls rightward to *D'*. (A rightward shift of a demand curve can also be described as an upward shift.)

complements two goods are complements in consumption if an increase in the price of one causes a leftward shift in the demand curve for the other

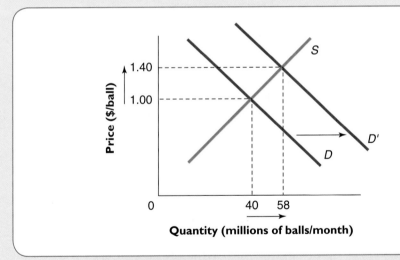

FIGURE 3.9
The Effect on the Market for Tennis Balls of a Decline in Court Rental Fees
When the price of a good's complement falls, demand for the good shifts right, causing equilibrium price and quantity to rise.

Note in Figure 3.9 that for the demand shift shown, the new equilibrium price of tennis balls, $1.40, is higher than the original price and the new equilibrium quantity, 58 million balls per month, is higher than the original quantity.

What will happen to the equilibrium price and quantity of overnight letter delivery service as more people gain access to the Internet?

EXAMPLE 3.3

Suppose that the initial supply and demand curves for overnight letter deliveries are as shown by the curves *S* and *D* in Figure 3.10 and that the resulting equilibrium price and quantity are denoted *P* and *Q*. Email messages and overnight

substitutes two goods are substitutes in consumption if an increase in the price of one causes a rightward shift in the demand curve for the other

letters are examples of what economists call **substitutes**, meaning that, in many applications at least, the two serve similar functions for people. (Many non-economists would call them substitutes, too. Economists don't *always* choose obscure terms for important concepts!) When two goods or services are substitutes, a decrease in the effective price of one will cause a leftward shift in the demand curve for the other. (A leftward shift in a demand curve can also be described as a downward shift.) An increase in Internet access is, in effect, a decline in the price of a substitute for overnight delivery for affected users. Diagrammatically, this means a leftward shift in the demand curve for overnight delivery service to D' in Figure 3.10.

FIGURE 3.10

The Effect on the Market for Overnight Letter Delivery of a Decline in the Price of Internet Access
When the price of a substitute for a good falls, demand for the good shifts left, causing equilibrium price and quantity to fall.

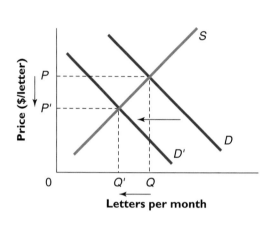

As the figure shows, both the new equilibrium price P' and the new equilibrium quantity Q' are lower than the initial values P and Q. More widespread Internet access probably will not put Purolator and UPS out of business, but it will definitely cost them many customers.

To summarize, economists define goods as substitutes if an increase in the price of one causes a rightward shift in the demand curve for the other. By contrast, goods are complements if an increase in the price of one causes a leftward shift in the demand curve for the other. The concepts of substitutes and complements enable you to answer questions like the one posed in the following exercise.

EXERCISE 3.1

How will a decline in airfares affect intercity (or long distance) bus fares and the price of hotel rooms in resort communities?

Demand curves are shifted not just by changes in the prices of substitutes and complements but also by other factors that change the amounts that people are willing to pay for a given good or service. One of the most important such factors is income.

ECONOMIC *Naturalist*   3.2   When the price of oil rises, why do prices for houses in Calgary rise?

Calgary's economy is heavily dependent on the oil industry. If the price of oil rises, oil companies respond by exploring for more oil and by developing existing oil fields more intensively. As oil companies increase their activity, more people will be drawn to Calgary, some to work in the oil industry, others to supply more goods and services to the oil industry as it expands, and still others to supply goods and services to Calgary's rising population. (For example, if more families move to Calgary, more teachers will be required.) In addition, wages and salaries will tend to be bid up to attract more workers, there will be more opportunities to work overtime, and so on. Thus, individuals will tend to have higher incomes because of the oil boom. Because of a larger population and because at least some individuals will have higher incomes (and now may be able to afford to move out of apartments into houses), the demand curve for houses will shift to the right, as shown by the demand curve labelled D' in Figure 3.11. As a result, the equilibrium price and quantity of houses, P' and Q', will be higher than before.

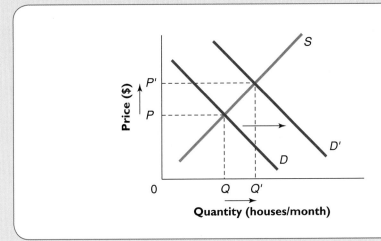

FIGURE 3.11

The Effect of an Increase in the Price of Oil on the Price of Houses in Calgary
An increase in income shifts demand for a normal good to the right, causing equilibrium price and quantity to rise.

Two factors caused the demand curve for houses in Calgary to shift to the right when the price of oil rose: the population of the city increased, and the income of individuals increased. Either factor by itself would have caused the demand curve to shift to the right; together, they reinforce each other. When incomes increase, the demand curves for most goods will shift to the right. In recognition of that fact, economists have chosen to call such goods **normal goods.**

Not all goods are normal goods, however. In fact, the demand curves for some goods actually shift leftward when income goes up, and such goods are called **inferior goods.** When would having more money tend to make you want to buy less of something? In general, this will happen in the case of goods for which there are attractive substitutes that sell for only slightly higher prices. Apartments in an unsafe, inconveniently located neighbourhood are an example. Most residents would choose to move out of such neighbourhoods as soon as they could afford to, which means that an increase in income would cause the demand for such apartments to shift leftward. Ground beef with high fat content is another example of an inferior good. For health reasons, most people prefer grades of meat with low fat content, and when they do buy high-fat meats it is usually a sign of budgetary pressure. When people in this situation receive higher incomes, they usually switch quickly to leaner grades of meat.

normal good a good whose demand curve shifts rightward when the incomes of buyers increase

inferior good a good whose demand curve shifts leftward when the incomes of buyers increase

EXERCISE 3.2   **Normal and inferior goods were defined in terms of how their demand curves are affected by an increase in income. How will a *decrease* in income affect the demand for a normal good? an inferior good?**

Preferences, or tastes, are another important factor that determines whether a given good will meet the cost–benefit test. Steven Spielberg's films *Jurassic Park* and *The Lost World* appeared to kindle a powerful, if previously latent, preference among children for toy dinosaurs. In the wake of these films, the demand for such toys shifted sharply to the right. And the same children who couldn't find enough dinosaur toys suddenly seemed to lose interest in toy designs involving horses and other present-day animals, whose respective demand curves shifted sharply to the left.

Expectations can also influence demand. For example, if many parents suddenly expect a special toy to be scarce during the holiday season, demand for the toy will increase before the holiday season.

FOUR SIMPLE RULES

For supply and demand curves that have the conventional slopes (upward sloping for supply curves, downward sloping for demand curves), the preceding examples illustrate the four basic rules that govern how shifts in supply and demand affect equilibrium prices and quantities. These rules are summarized in Figure 3.12.

FIGURE 3.12
Four Rules Governing the Effects of Supply and Demand Shifts

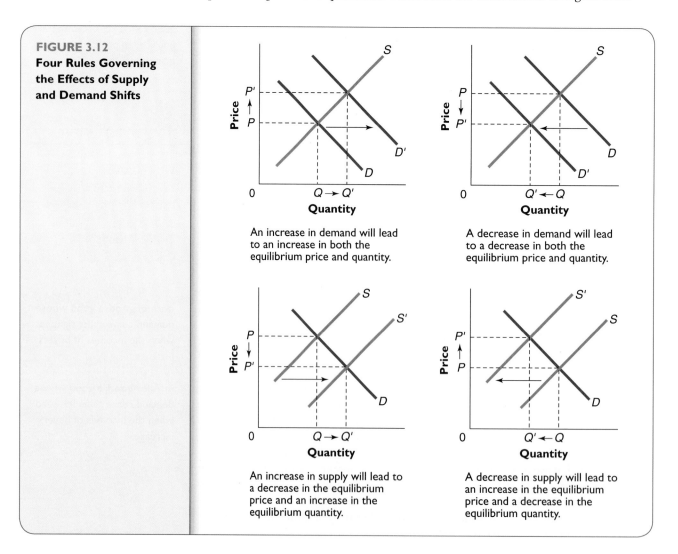

An increase in demand will lead to an increase in both the equilibrium price and quantity.

A decrease in demand will lead to a decrease in both the equilibrium price and quantity.

An increase in supply will lead to a decrease in the equilibrium price and an increase in the equilibrium quantity.

A decrease in supply will lead to an increase in the equilibrium price and a decrease in the equilibrium quantity.

The qualitative rules summarized in Figure 3.12 hold for supply or demand shifts of any magnitude, provided the curves have their conventional slopes. But although it is easy enough for textbook authors to invent examples where only one thing is happening in a market, in the real world we often observe simultaneous changes in demand and supply. As the next example demonstrates, when both supply and demand curves shift at the same time, the direction in which equilibrium price or quantity changes will depend on the relative magnitudes of the shifts.

How do shifts in *both* demand and supply affect equilibrium quantities and prices?

EXAMPLE 3.4

What will happen to the equilibrium price and quantity in the corn tortilla chip market if both the following events occur: (1) researchers discover that the oils in which tortilla chips are fried are harmful to human health, and (2) the price of corn-harvesting equipment falls?

The discovery regarding the health effects of the oils will shift the demand for tortilla chips to the left, because many people who once bought chips in the belief that they were healthful will now switch to other foods. The decline in the price of harvesting equipment will shift the supply of chips to the right, because additional farmers will now find it profitable to enter the corn market. In Figure 3.13(a) and (b), the original supply and demand curves are denoted by S and D, while the new curves are denoted by S' and D'. Note that in both parts, the shifts lead to a decline in the equilibrium price of chips.

But note also that the effect of the shifts on equilibrium quantity cannot be determined without knowing their relative magnitudes. Taken separately, the demand shift causes a decline in equilibrium quantity, whereas the supply shift causes an increase in equilibrium quantity. The net effect of the two shifts thus depends on which of the individual effects is larger. In Figure 3.13(a), the demand shift dominates, so equilibrium quantity declines. In Figure 3.13(b), the supply shift dominates, so equilibrium quantity goes up.

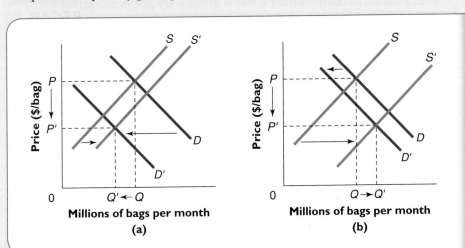

FIGURE 3.13

The Effects of Simultaneous Shifts in Supply and Demand
When demand shifts left and supply shifts right, equilibrium price falls, but equilibrium quantity may either rise [panel (b)] or fall [panel (a)].

The following exercise asks you to consider a simple variation on the problem posed in Example 3.4.

What will happen to the equilibrium price and quantity in the corn tortilla chip market if both the following events occur: (1) researchers discover that a vitamin found in corn helps protect against cancer and heart disease; and (2) a swarm of locusts destroys part of the corn crop?

EXERCISE 3.3

SUMMARY

3.1 Eighteenth-century economists tried to explain differences in the prices of goods by focusing on differences in their cost of production. But this approach cannot explain why a conveniently located house sells for more than one that is less conveniently located. Early nineteenth-century economists tried to explain price differences by focusing on differences in what buyers were willing to pay. But this approach cannot explain why the price of a lifesaving appendectomy is less than that of a surgical facelift.

3.1 Alfred Marshall's model of supply and demand explains why neither cost of production nor value to the purchaser (as measured by willingness to pay) by itself is sufficient to explain why some goods are cheap and others are expensive. To explain variations in price, we must examine the interaction of cost and willingness to pay. As we saw in this chapter, goods differ in price because of differences in their respective supply and demand curves.

3.1 The supply curve is an upward-sloping line indicating the quantity sellers will offer at any given price. The demand curve is a downward-sloping line that tells what quantity buyers will demand at any given price. Market equilibrium occurs when the quantity buyers demand at the market price is exactly the same as the quantity that sellers offer. The equilibrium price–quantity pair is the one at which the demand and supply curves intersect. In equilibrium, market price measures both the value of the last unit sold to buyers and the cost of the resources required to produce it.

3.1 When the price of a good lies above its equilibrium value, there is an excess supply, or surplus, of that good. Excess supply motivates sellers to cut their prices, and price continues to fall until the equilibrium

price is reached. When price lies below its equilibrium value, there is excess demand, or shortage. With excess demand, dissatisfied buyers are motivated to offer higher prices, and the upward pressure on prices persists until equilibrium is reached. The equilibrating process depends on competition among many small buyers and sellers. A remarkable feature of the market system is that, relying only on the tendency of people to respond in self-interested ways to market price signals, it somehow manages to coordinate the actions of literally billions of buyers and sellers worldwide.

3.3 The basic supply and demand model is a primary tool of the economic naturalist. Changes in the equilibrium price of a good, and in the amount of it traded in the marketplace, can be predicted on the basis of shifts in its supply or demand curves. The following four rules hold for any good with a downward-sloping demand curve and an upward-sloping supply curve:

1. An increase in demand will lead to an increase in equilibrium price and quantity.
2. A reduction in demand will lead to a reduction in equilibrium price and quantity.
3. An increase in supply will lead to a reduction in equilibrium price and an increase in equilibrium quantity.
4. A decrease in supply will lead to an increase in equilibrium price and a reduction in equilibrium quantity.

3.3 Incomes, tastes, population, and the prices of substitutes and complements are among the factors that shift demand schedules. Supply schedules, in turn, are primarily governed by such factors as technology, input prices, and, for agricultural products, the weather. Changes in expectations can also shift supply and demand schedules.

CORE

The Equilibrium Principle
A market in equilibrium leaves no unexploited opportunities for individuals.

The Efficiency Principle
Economic efficiency occurs when total economic surplus is maximized. Efficiency is an important social goal, because when the economic pie grows larger, everyone can have a larger slice.

KEY TERMS

change in demand (74)
change in quantity demanded (73)
change in quantity supplied (74)
change in supply (74)
complements (77)
demand curve (67)
economic efficiency (73)
efficient quantity (73)
equilibrium (68)

equilibrium price (69)
equilibrium quantity (69)
excess demand (70)
excess supply (70)
inferior good (79)
inputs (76)
market (64)
market equilibrium (69)
normal good (79)

quantity supplied (65)
quantity demanded (68)
shortage (70)
substitutes (78)
supply curve (65)
surplus (70)
technology (76)

REVIEW QUESTIONS

1. Why isn't knowing how much it costs to produce a good sufficient to predict its market price?

2. Distinguish between the meaning of the expressions "change in demand" and "change in the quantity demanded."

3. Last year a government official proposed that gasoline price controls be imposed to protect the poor from rising gasoline prices. What evidence could you consult to discover whether this proposal was enacted?

4. Explain why, in unregulated markets, the equilibrium principle suggests that excess demand and excess supply tend to be fleeting.

PROBLEMS

1. State whether the following pairs of goods are complements or substitutes. (If you think a pair is ambiguous in this respect, explain why.)
   a. Tennis courts and squash courts
   b. Squash racquets and squash balls
   c. Ice cream and chocolate
   d. Cloth diapers and disposable diapers

2. How would each of the following affect the Canadian market supply curve for wheat?
   a. A new and improved crop rotation technique is discovered.
   b. The price of fertilizer falls.
   c. The government offers new tax breaks to farmers.
   d. The Prairies suffer a drought.

3. Indicate how you think each of the following would affect demand in the indicated market:
   a. An increase in family income on the demand for winter vacations in the Caribbean
   b. A study linking beef consumption to heart disease on the demand for hamburgers
   c. A relaxation of immigration laws on the demand for elementary-school places
   d. An increase in the price of audiocassettes on the demand for CDs
   e. An increase in the price of CDs on the demand for CDs

4. A student at the University of Regina claims to have spotted a UFO outside Regina. How will his claim affect the supply of binoculars in Regina stores?

5. What will happen to the equilibrium price and quantity of oranges if the wages paid to farm workers rise?

6. How will an increase in the birthrate affect the equilibrium price of land?

7. What will happen to the equilibrium price and quantity of fish if it is discovered that fish oils help prevent heart disease?

8. What will happen to the equilibrium price and quantity of beef if the price of chicken feed increases?

9. Use supply and demand analysis to explain why hotel room rental rates near your campus during parents' weekend and graduation weekend might differ from the rates charged during the rest of the year.

10. How will a new law mandating an increase in required levels of automobile insurance affect the equilibrium price and quantity in the market for new automobiles?

11. Suppose the current issue of *The Globe and Mail* reports an outbreak of mad cow disease in Manitoba, as well as the discovery of a new breed of chicken that gains more weight from the same amount of food than existing breeds. How will these developments affect the equilibrium price and quantity of chicken sold in Canada?

12. What will happen to the equilibrium quantity and price of potatoes if population increases and a new, higher yielding variety of potato plant is developed?

13. What will happen to the equilibrium price and quantity of apples if apples are discovered to help prevent colds and a fungus kills 10 percent of existing apple trees?

14. What will happen to the equilibrium quantity and price of corn if the price of butter increases and the price of fertilizer decreases?

15. Tofu was available 25 years ago only from small businesses operating in Chinese quarters of large cities. Today tofu has become popular as a high-protein health food and is widely available in supermarkets throughout Canada. At the same time, production has evolved to become factory-based, using modern food-processing technologies. Draw a diagram with demand and supply curves depicting the market for tofu 25 years ago and the market for tofu today. Given the information above, what does the demand–supply model predict about changes in the quantity of tofu sold in Canada between then and now? What does it predict about changes in the price of tofu?

ANSWERS TO IN-CHAPTER EXERCISES

3.1 Travel by air and travel by bus are substitutes, so a decline in airfares will shift the demand for bus travel to the left, resulting in lower bus fares and fewer bus trips taken. Travel by air and the use of resort hotels are complements, so a decline in airfares will shift the demand for resort hotel rooms to the right, resulting in higher hotel rates and an increase in the number of rooms rented.

3.2 A decrease in income will shift the demand curve for a normal good to the left and will shift the demand curve for an inferior good to the right.

3.3 The vitamin discovery shifts the demand for chips to the right, and the crop losses shift the supply of chips to the left. Both shifts result in an increase in the equilibrium price of chips. But depending on the relative magnitude of the shifts, the equilibrium quantity of chips may either rise [panel (a) of the figure] or fall [panel (b) of the figure].

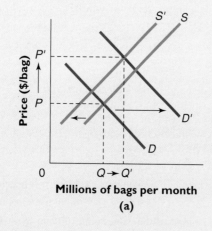

Millions of bags per month
(a)

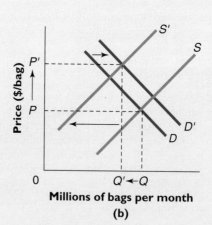

Millions of bags per month
(b)

PART 2

Macroeconomics: Issues and Data

This section introduces you to macroeconomics the study of the performance of *national* economies. Macroeconomics looks at issues such as why some economies grow more rapidly than others and why economies can experience severe slumps.

Unlike microeconomics, which focuses on the behaviour of individual households, firms, and markets, macroeconomics takes a bird's-eye view of the economy. It looks at the forest, so to speak, and not just the trees because sometimes the whole is more than the sum of the parts. So while microeconomists might study the determinants of consumer phone call spending, macroeconomists analyze the factors that determine aggregate, or total, consumer spending. Experience has shown that the macroeconimic perspective is essential for the analysis of issues such as unemployment, inflation, and economic growth.

Chapter 4 begins our discussion of macroeconomics by introducing you to some of the key macroeconomic issues and questions. These include the search for the factors that cause economies to grow, productivity to improve, and living standards to rise over long periods of time. Macroeconomists also study shorter-term fluctuations in the economy (called recessions and expansions), unemployment, inflation,

and the economic incerdependence among nations, among other topics. Macroeconomic policies—government actions to alter the overall performance of the economy—are of particular concern to macroeconomists, as the quality of macroeconomic policymaking is a major determinat of a nation's economic health.

To study phenomena like economic growth scientifically, economists must have accurate measurements. Chapters 5 and 6 continue the introduction to macroeconomics by discussing how some key macroeconomic concepts are measured and interpreted. Chapter 5 discusses two important measurs of the level of economic activity: the gross domestic product and the unemployment rate. Besides describing how these variables are constructed in practice, that chapter will also discuss how these measures are related to the living standard of the average person. Chapter 6 concerns the measurement of the price level and inflation, and it includes a discussion of the impacts that different types of price-level changes have on the economy. When you have completed Part 2 you will be familiar not only with the major questions that macroeconomists ask but also with some of the most important tools that they use in search of answers.

Chapter 4

Macroeconomics: The Bird's-Eye View of the Economy

In 1929, the Great Depression began in the United States and quickly turned into a global economic slump. With its high level of dependence on exports, Canada was hit hard by the global downturn. Between 1929 and 1933, Canada's real output declined by almost 30 percent, consumer prices fell by 23 percent, and the unemployment rate soared from 3 percent to 19.3 percent. Large numbers of Canadians became dependent on government relief for survival.

Economic conditions were even worse in some other countries. In Germany, for example, nearly a third of the labour force could not find work, and many families lost their savings as major banks collapsed. Indeed, the desperate economic situation was a factor behind Adolf Hitler's rise to power in 1933.

How could such an economic catastrophe have happened? One often-heard hypothesis is that the Great Depression in the United States was caused by wild speculation on Wall Street, which provoked the stock market crash. The hypothesis has been lent some support by Japan's experience of a decade of stagnation in the 1990s following a stock market crash. But though U.S. stock market prices were unrealistically high in 1929, there is little evidence to suggest that the fall in stock prices was a decisive cause of the Depression on its own. A similar crash in 1987 (when stock market prices fell a record 23 percent in one day—an event comparable in severity to the crash of October 1929) did not slow the U.S. economy significantly. Also, the Depression was a worldwide event, affecting even countries that did not have developed stock markets.

Another explanation for the Depression has been that capitalist economies like the United States and Canada are naturally unstable, prone to long periods of economic depression. This explanation, however, fails to account for why the Great Depression was so much worse than earlier economic slumps. It also fails to explain why the "mixed" capitalist economies that emerged from the Second World War have avoided a depression comparable to that experienced by the capitalist economies of the 1930s.

What was the decisive factor behind the Great Depression, then? Today, most economists who have studied the period attribute much of the blame to *poor economic policy-making* in the major capitalist countries. Of course, policy-makers did not set out to transform an economic downturn into a decade-long economic catastrophe. Rather, they fell prey to misconceptions of the time about how the economy worked. In other words, the Great Depression, far from being inevitable, *could have been avoided*—if only the state of economic knowledge had been better. From today's perspective, the Great Depression was to economic policy-making what the voyage of the *Titanic* was to ocean navigation.

One of the few benefits of the Great Depression was that it forced economists and policy-makers of the 1930s to recognize that there were major gaps in their understanding of how the economy works. This recognition led to the development of a new subfield within economics, called macroeconomics. As mentioned in Chapter 1, *macroeconomics* is the study of the performance of national economies and the policies governments use to try to improve that performance.

This chapter will introduce the subject matter and some of the tools of macroeconomics. Although understanding episodes like the Great Depression remains an important concern of macroeconomists, the field has expanded to include the analysis of many other aspects of national economies. Among the issues macroeconomists study are the sources of long-run economic growth and development, the causes of high unemployment, and the factors that determine the rate of inflation. Appropriately enough in a world in which economic "globalization" preoccupies business people and policy-makers, macroeconomists also study how national economies interact. Since the performance of the national economy has an important bearing on the availability of jobs, the wages workers earn, the prices they pay, and the rates of return they receive on their savings, it's clear that macroeconomics addresses bread-and-butter issues that affect virtually everyone.

In light of the world's experience during the Great Depression, macroeconomists are particularly concerned with understanding how *macroeconomic policies* work and how they should be applied. **Macroeconomic policies** are government actions designed to affect the performance of the economy as a whole (as opposed to policies intended to affect the performance of the market for a particular good or service, such as lumber or haircuts). The hope of many macroeconomists is that by improving knowledge about how government policies affect the economy, they can help current or alternative policy-makers do a better job—and avoid serious mistakes, such as those that were made during the Great Depression. On an individual level, educating people about macroeconomic policies and their effects will make for a better-informed citizenry, capable of making well-reasoned decisions in the voting booth.

macroeconomic policies government actions designed to affect the performance of the economy as a whole

4.1 THE MAJOR MACROECONOMIC ISSUES

We have defined macroeconomics as the study of the performance of the national economy as well as the policies used to improve that performance. Let's now take a closer look at some of the major economic issues that macroeconomists study.

ECONOMIC GROWTH AND LIVING STANDARDS

Although the wealthy industrialized countries (such as Canada, the United States, Japan, and the countries of Western Europe) are certainly not free from poverty, hunger, and homelessness, the typical person in those countries enjoys a standard of living better than at any previous time or place in history. By *standard of living*, we mean the degree to which people have access to goods and services that make their lives easier, healthier, safer, and more enjoyable. People with a high living standard enjoy more and better consumer goods: audio equipment, camcorders, cellular phones, and the like. But they also benefit from a longer life expectancy and better general health (the result of high-quality medical care, good nutrition, and good sanitation), from higher literacy rates (the result of greater access to education), from more time and opportunity for cultural enrichment and recreation, from more interesting and fulfilling career options, and from better working conditions. Of course, the scarcity problem will always exist—even for the citizens of a rich country, having more of one good thing means having less of another. But higher incomes make these choices much less painful than they would be otherwise. Choosing between a larger apartment and a nicer car is much easier than choosing between feeding your children adequately and sending them to school, the kind of hard choice people in the poorest nations face.

Canadians sometimes take their standard of living for granted. But we should realize that the way we live today is radically different from the way people have lived throughout most of history. The current standard of living in Canada is the result of sustained economic growth through several generations, a process of steady increase in the quantity and quality of the goods and services the economy can produce. The basic equation is simple: the more we can produce, the more we can consume, whether it be private goods, social spending, or leisure.

www.statcan.ca
Statistics Canada

To get a sense of the extent of economic growth over time, examine Figure 4.1, which shows how the output of the Canadian economy has increased since 1926. (We discuss the measure of output used here, real gross domestic product, in Chapter 5.) Although output fluctuates at times, the overall trend has been unmistakably upward. Indeed, in 2007 the output of the Canadian economy was more than 19 times what it was in 1926 and more than eight times its level in 1950. What caused this remarkable economic growth? Can it continue? Should it? These are some of the questions macroeconomists try to answer.

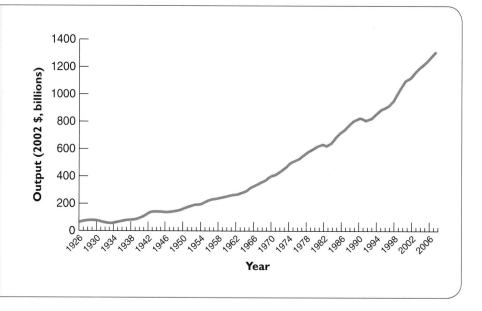

FIGURE 4.1

Output of the Canadian Economy, 1926–2007

The output of the Canadian economy has increased by more than 19 times since 1926 and by more than 8 times since 1950.

SOURCE: Statistics Canada, CANSIM series v41707175 (real GDP) and adapted from series F55 from F.H. Leacy, ed., *Historical Statistics of Canada* (hereafter *HSC*).

One reason for the growth in Canadian output over the past century has been the rapid growth of the Canadian population, and hence the number of workers available. Because of population growth, increases in *total* output cannot be equated with improvements in the general standard of living. Although increased output means that more goods and services are available, increased population implies that more people are sharing those goods and services. Because the population changes over time, output *per person* is a better indicator of the average living standard than total output.

Figure 4.2 shows output per person in Canada since 1926 (the blue line). Note that the long-term increase in output per person is smaller than the increase in total output shown in Figure 4.1 because of population growth. Nevertheless,

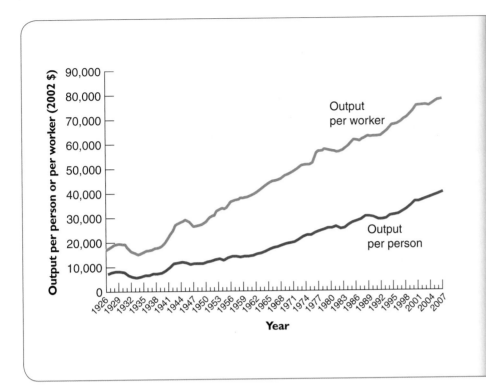

FIGURE 4.2

Output per Person and per Worker in the Canadian Economy, 1926–2007

The red line shows output per worker in the Canadian economy since 1926, and the blue line shows output per person. Relative to 1926, output per person is about 6 times greater, and output per worker is 4.2 times greater.

SOURCE: Adapted from Statistics Canada, CANSIM II series V2461119 (employment), v466668 (population), and V41707175 (real GDP); and from *HSC* series D129, A1, and F55.

the gains made over this long period are still impressive: in 2007, the value of personal goods and services consumed by a typical Canadian resident was nearly six times the value available to a typical Canadian resident back in 1926. To put this increase into perspective, Canadians no longer rely upon horse and buggy for everyday travel—according to recent estimates, more than 83 percent of Canadian households owned or leased one or more vehicles (automobiles, trucks or vans). Television ownership is taken for granted, with about 65 percent of households subscribing to cable and 23 percent to satellite. About three in four Canadian households have a computer at home, and 68 percent of all households access the Internet from home.

Nor has the rise in output been reflected entirely in increased availability of consumer goods. In health, for example, great strides have been made. The mortality rate for infants has plummeted from about 100 per 1000 live births in the 1920s to about 5 per 1000 live births. Average life expectancy has risen from 59 to 80 years (78 years for males and 83 years for females). In education, as late as 1951 over half of the Canadian population aged 15 and over had less than a Grade 9 education, while only a few percent (mostly men) had university degrees. By 1996, adults with university degrees had become more numerous than adults with less than Grade 9, and the share of degrees earned by women had surpassed 50 percent. By 2006, almost half of the population aged 25 to 64 had obtained a college or university degree.

www.statcan.ca
CANSIM

PRODUCTIVITY

While growth in output per person is closely linked to changes in what the typical person can *consume*, macroeconomists are also interested in changes in what the average worker can *produce*. Figure 4.2 shows how output per employed worker (that is, total output divided by the number of people working) has changed since 1926 (red line). The figure shows that in 2007, a Canadian worker could produce about 4.2 times the quantity of goods and services produced by a worker back in 1926, despite the fact that the workweek is now much shorter.

average labour productivity
output per employed worker

Economists define **average labour productivity** as output per employed worker.[1] As Figure 4.2 shows, average labour productivity and output per person are closely related. This relationship makes sense—as we noted earlier, the more we can produce, the more we can consume. Because of this close link to the average living standard, average labour productivity and the factors that cause it to increase over time are of major concern to macroeconomists.

It should be noted that although the typical household is more likely to experience better wages and living conditions when average labour productivity is rising, the process is not automatic. In some countries there have been whole decades during which the value of goods and services that typical households could buy actually stagnated despite rising average labour productivity. During such periods, there is a shift in the income distribution from low- and middle-income households to high-income households. (For further information, see Figure 6.1.)

Although the long-term improvement in output per worker is impressive, the *rate* of improvement has slowed somewhat since the 1970s. Between 1950 and 1973 in Canada, output per employed worker increased by 2.4 percent per year. But from 1973 to 2007, the average rate of increase in output per worker was only 1 percent per year, despite a noticeable upsurge during the 1997–2000 period. Slowing productivity growth leads to less rapid improvement in living standards, since the supply of goods and services cannot grow as quickly as it does during periods of rapid growth in productivity. Identifying the causes of productivity slowdowns and speedups is thus an important challenge for macroeconomists.

The current standard of living in Canada is not only much higher than in the past but also much higher than in many other nations today. Why do many of the world's countries, including both the developing nations of Asia, Africa, and Latin America and some countries of Eastern Europe, not enjoy living standards comparable to those of Western countries? How can these countries catch up? Once again, these are questions of keen interest to macroeconomists.

| EXAMPLE 4.1 | **Productivity and output per person in Canada, the United States, and China** |

In 2000, the value of Canadian economic output was approximately C$1 trillion (1000 billion). In the same year, the estimated value of U.S. output was approximately C$11.8 trillion and that of the People's Republic of China was C$1.8 trillion. The populations of Canada, the United States, and China in 2000 were about 30.8 million, 275.4 million, and 1.27 billion respectively while the numbers of employed workers in the three countries were approximately 14.9 million, 135.2 million, and 626.6 million respectively.[2]

The output per person and average labour productivity for Canada, the United States, and China in the year 2000 can be determined using the data provided above. Output per person is simply total output divided by the number of people in an economy. Average labour productivity is output divided by the number of employed workers. Doing the math, we get the following results for 2000, the year in question:

[1]For some purposes, such as productivity comparisons between the United States and Europe, it is useful to recognize that average labour productivity can also be measured as output divided by the number of hours worked. A country with relatively long average hours of work, such as the United States, comes out higher in international average labour productivity rankings if countries are ranked by average output per employed worker than if they are ranked by average output per hour worked.
[2]The statistics in the example are from each country's official agencies, and the output statistics are converted to a common basis using average annual exchange rates for each country. Economists often adjust the output of the Chinese economy upward by a very large amount to reflect what Chinese output would be if valued at prices prevailing in the rest of the world. They sometimes adjust Chinese employment numbers upward by a moderate amount to reflect alleged undercounting of the employed in China.

	Canada	United States	China
Output per person (C$)	$32 468	$42 847	$1429
Average labour productivity (C$)	$67 114	$87 278	$2871

Note that the larger population and hence greater number of employed workers of the United States provides a partial explanation of why U.S. output was larger than Canadian output in 2000. But U.S. output was also higher because average labour productivity was higher in that country. On the other hand, China's output was greater than Canada's solely because of China's greater population and employment figures; China's average labour productivity was much lower. But in recent years China's output has been growing much more rapidly than those of high-income countries, and China's population growth has been relatively slow in the same period. This means that the average labour productivity gap between China and high-income countries has shrunk considerably since 2000.

Even if we examine more recent data, the average labour productivity gap between China and, for example, Canada is substantial and is associated with significant differences in more direct measures of living standards. For example, according to the latest *Human Development Report* published by the United Nations, average life expectancy at birth is several years longer in Canada than in China, about 10 percent of the adult Chinese population is classified as illiterate compared to less than 1 percent in Canada, and about 12 percent of the Chinese population is classified as undernourished compared to less than 1 percent in Canada.[3] (For additional evidence of how average labour productivity differences among countries are associated with differences in direct measures of living standards, see Table 5.5.)

RECESSIONS AND EXPANSIONS

Economies do not always grow steadily; sometimes they go through periods of unusual strength or weakness. A look back at Figure 4.1 shows that although output generally grows over time, it does not always grow smoothly. (Figure 7.2, which shows growth of output per capita directly, provides a sharper picture of the often rough process of output growth.) Particularly striking is the decline in output during the Great Depression of the 1930s, followed by the sharp increase in output during the Second World War (1939–1945). But the figure shows many more moderate fluctuations in output as well.

Pronounced slowdowns in economic growth are called *recessions*; extraordinarily severe economic slowdowns, like the one that began in 1929, are called *depressions*. In Canada, major recessions occurred in 1981–1982 and 1990–1992 (find those recessions in Figure 4.1). During recessions, economic opportunities decline: jobs are harder to find, people with jobs are less likely to get wage increases, profits are lower, and more companies go out of business. Recessions are particularly hard on economically disadvantaged people, who are most likely to be thrown out of work and have the hardest time finding new jobs.

[3]See Human Development Indicators, *Human Development Report 2007/2008*, http://hdr.undp.org/en/ (May 2008).

Sometimes the economy grows quickly. These periods of economic growth are called *expansions*, and particularly strong expansions are called *booms*. During an expansion, jobs are easier to find, more people get raises and promotions, and most businesses thrive.

The alternating cycle of recessions and expansions raises some questions that are central to macroeconomics. What causes these short-term fluctuations in the rate of economic growth? What can government policy-makers do about them?

UNEMPLOYMENT

The *unemployment rate*, the fraction of the labour force who are looking for a job but can't find work, is a key indicator of the state of the labour market. When the unemployment rate is high, work is hard to find, and people who do have jobs typically find it harder to get promotions or wage increases.

Figure 4.3 shows the unemployment rate in Canada since 1921. Unemployment rises during recessions; note the dramatic spike in unemployment during the Great Depression and the increases in unemployment during the 1981–1982 and 1990–1992 recessions. But even in the so-called good times, such as the 1960s and the last few years of the 1990s, some people are unemployed. Why does unemployment rise so sharply during periods of recession? And why are there always unemployed people, even when the economy is booming?

FIGURE 4.3

The Canadian Unemployment Rate, 1921–2007

The unemployment rate measures the unemployed as a percentage of the labour force. This graph of the Canadian unemployment rate shows three major spikes since 1921: during the Great Depression of the 1930s and during the severe recessions of the early 1980s and the early 1990s.
SOURCE: Statistics Canada, CANSIM series v2062815, and adapted from *HSC* series D132 (persons without jobs and seeking work) and *HSC* series D127 (total labour force).

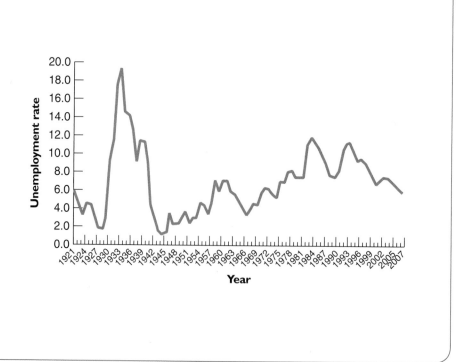

EXAMPLE 4.2   Increases in unemployment during recessions and an economic slowdown

Find the increase in Canada's monthly unemployment rate from the onset of a recession or economic slowdown to the peak unemployment rate in the three-year period thereafter. Specifically, find the increases in the unemployment rate associated with the recessions beginning in the third quarter of 1981, the second quarter of 1990, and in the slowdown beginning in mid-2000.

Unemployment-rate data are published in Statistics Canada's *Labour Force Survey*, which yields the following information:

Unemployment rate at the beginning of recession or slowdown (%)	Peak unemployment rate (%)	Increase in unemployment rate
8.3 (October 1981)	12.9 (December 1982)	+4.6
7.8 (July 1990)	11.8 (June 1993)	+4.0
6.7 (June 2000)	8.0 (January 2002)	+1.3

The unemployment rate reached a higher peak in the 1980s recession and underwent a larger percentage-point increase than in the recession of the 1990s. But the recession of the 1990s was more drawn out, and it took longer for the unemployment rate to peak. The rise in the unemployment rate during the economic slowdown of 2000–2001 was much less pronounced than in the two earlier recessions.

Though the recessions of the 1980s and 1990s have been the most severe for Canada since the Second World War, they pale in comparison to the Great Depression. Then Canada's unemployment rate increased from an annual rate of 3 percent in 1929 to an annual rate of 19.3 percent in 1933. Clearly, that 16.3-percentage-point increase in the unemployment rate belongs to a class by itself.

One question of great interest to macroeconomists is why unemployment rates differ markedly from country to country. For example, the unemployment rate in Canada prior to 1981 tended to be no higher on average than the U.S. rate. But during the 1980s, the Canadian rate averaged two percentage points higher than the U.S. rate, and in the 1990s, the gap widened to 3.8 points.

Find the most recent monthly unemployment rates for Canada and the United States. A useful source is the Web site (http://www.oecd.org/) of the Organization for Economic Cooperation and Development (OECD), an organization of high-income countries. The OECD produces standardized unemployment rates for making comparisons among its member countries. Is the Canada–U.S. unemployment rate gap narrower today than it was during the 1990s?

EXERCISE 4.1

**www.oecd.org
OECD**

INFLATION

Another important economic statistic is the rate of *inflation,* which is the rate at which prices in general increase over time. As we discuss in Chapter 6, when the inflation rate changes sharply it can alter the distribution of income between borrowers and savers. Very high inflation imposes costs on the economy, as does negative inflation (known as deflation).

In recent years inflation has been relatively low in Canada, but that has not always been the case (see Figure 4.4 for data on Canadian inflation since 1915). During the 1970s, inflation was a major public concern. Why was inflation high in the 1970s, and why is it relatively low today? What difference does it make to the average person?

FIGURE 4.4

The Canadian Inflation Rate, 1915–2007

Canada experienced double-digit inflation near the end of WWI (1917–1918 and 1920), for two years following WWII (1948 and 1951), and in the mid-1970s and early 1980s. Inflation rates have been low during the past decade but not as low as during 1930–1933, Great Depression years characterized by deflation. SOURCE: Adapted from Statistics Canada, CANSIM series v41690973.

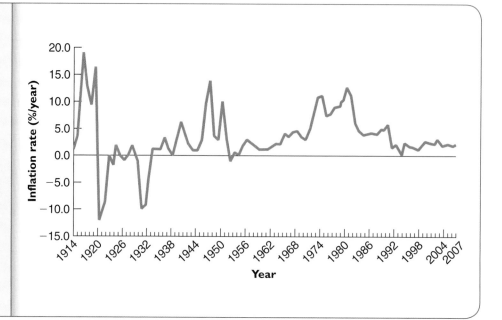

Inflation and unemployment are often linked together in policy discussions. One reason for this linkage is the oft-heard argument that unemployment can be reduced only at the cost of higher inflation and that inflation can be reduced only at the cost of higher unemployment. Another impact of inflation is that interest rates tend to be higher in periods of high inflation. The link between inflation and interest rates is discussed in Chapter 6.

ECONOMIC INTERDEPENDENCE AMONG NATIONS

National economies do not exist in isolation but are increasingly interdependent. Canada, always a trading nation, became sharply more dependent on trade during the 1990s. By 2007, Canadian exports amounted to about 35 percent of Canadian output and imports to 33 percent.

Sometimes international flows of goods and services become a matter of political concern. The Canada–U.S. Free Trade Agreement (FTA) implemented in January 1989 and the North American Free Trade Agreement (NAFTA), entered into by Canada, the United States, and Mexico in January 1994, have been the subject of intense policy debate in Canada. What are the implications—for economic growth, jobs, and income distribution—of trade agreements in which countries agree to reduce taxes or quotas on the international flow of goods and services?

A related issue is the phenomenon of *trade imbalances*, which occur when the quantity of goods and services that a country sells abroad (its *exports*) differs significantly from the quantity of goods and services its citizens buy from abroad (its *imports*). Figure 4.5 shows Canadian exports and imports since 1961, measured as a percentage of the economy's total output. Except for a brief time following the implementation of the Canada–U.S. Free Trade Agreement, Canadian exports have typically outstripped imports, creating a situation called a *trade surplus*. Given the timing of events, the *trade deficits* of the early 1990s might seem to stem from the FTA, but many economists point more to the role of the then-strong Canadian dollar, which hampered exports and encouraged imports.

While Canada tends to run trade surpluses, imports to the United States have exceeded exports since the 1970s, with the U.S. trade deficit in 2000 reaching a record high of 3.7 percent of GDP. Macroeconomists debated whether U.S. trade deficits of this magnitude were sustainable and whether the deficits pointed to

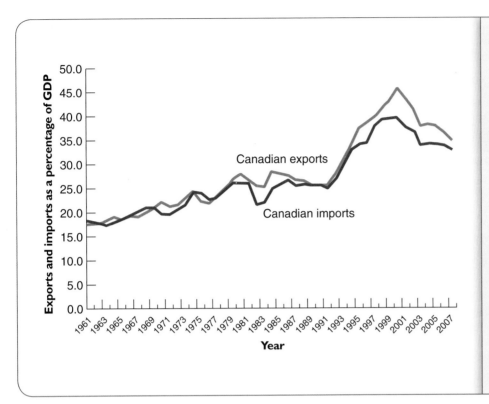

FIGURE 4.5

Exports and Imports as Shares of Canadian Output, 1961–2007

The red line shows Canadian exports as a percentage of Canadian output. The blue line shows imports relative to output. In recent decades, Canada has exported more than it has imported, though imports outstripped exports during the period 1991–1992 (when the Canadian dollar was strong and the Canada–U.S. Free Trade Agreement was being implemented). SOURCE: Adapted from Statistics Canada, CANSIM II series v646957 (imports), v646954 (exports), and v646937 (GDP).

an eventual weakening of the U.S. dollar. Starting in 2003, the U.S. dollar has weakened against most major currencies, including the Canadian dollar.

The value of one currency relative to another, known as the foreign exchange rate, is another aspect of the economic interdependence among nations. Figure 4.6 illustrates the large swings in the value of the Canada–U.S. foreign exchange rate in recent decades. Exchange rate issues are discussed in detail in Chapter 12.

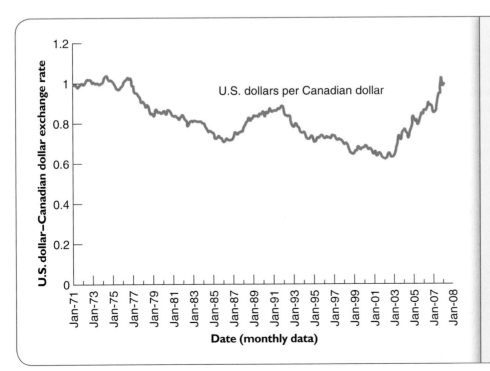

FIGURE 4.6

Canada's Exchange Rate, 1971 to early 2008

The figure expresses the value of the Canadian dollar relative to the U.S. dollar from 1971 to January 2008. The declining value of the Canadian dollar from the early 1990s until 2002 was a source of controversy in Canada. More recently, the sharply appreciating value of the Canadian dollar has become a source of controversy. SOURCE: Pacific Exchange Rate Service, http://fx.sauder.ubc.ca/.

RECAP

THE MAJOR MACROECONOMIC ISSUES

- *Economic growth and living standards* Over the past century, the industrialized nations have experienced remarkable economic growth and improvements in living standards. Macroeconomists study the reasons for this extraordinary growth and try to understand why growth rates vary markedly among nations.
- *Productivity* Average labour productivity, or output per employed worker, is a crucial determinant of living standards. Macroeconomists ask, "What causes slowdowns and speedups in the rate of productivity growth?"
- *Recessions and expansions* Economies experience periods of markedly slower or negative growth (recessions) and more rapid growth (expansions). Macroeconomists examine the sources of these fluctuations and the government policies that attempt to moderate them.
- *Unemployment* The unemployment rate is the fraction of the labour force who are looking for a job but can't find work. Unemployment rises during recessions but there are always unemployed people, even during good times. Macroeconomists study the causes of unemployment, including the reasons why it sometimes differs markedly across countries.
- *Inflation* The inflation rate is the rate at which prices in general are increasing over time. Questions macroeconomists ask about inflation include, Why does inflation vary over time and across countries? Must a reduction in inflation be accompanied by an increase in unemployment, or vice versa?
- *Economic interdependence among nations* Modern economies are highly interdependent. Related issues studied by macroeconomists include the desirability of new trade agreements, the causes and effects of trade imbalances, and exchange-rate determination.

4.2   MACROECONOMIC POLICY

We have seen that macroeconomists are interested in why different countries' economies perform differently and why a particular economy may perform well in some periods and poorly in others. Although many factors contribute to economic performance, government policy is surely among the most important. Understanding the effects of various policies and helping government officials develop better policies are important objectives of macroeconomists.

TYPES OF MACROECONOMIC POLICY

We have defined macroeconomic policies as government policies that affect the performance of the economy as a whole, as opposed to the market for a particular good or service. There are three major types of macroeconomic policy: *monetary policy, fiscal policy,* and *structural policy.*

monetary policy central bank management of interest rates to achieve macroeconomic objectives

The term **monetary policy** refers to central bank management of interest rates in order to achieve macroeconomic objectives. For reasons that we will discuss in later chapters, most economists agree that changes in interest rates affect other important economic variables, including the international value of the dollar, national output, employment, and inflation. In virtually all countries, monetary policy is controlled by a government institution called the *central bank.* In

Canada, the central bank is called the Bank of Canada. It corresponds to the Federal Reserve System in the United States.

Fiscal policy refers to decisions that determine the government's budget, including the amount and composition of government expenditures and government revenues. The balance between government spending and revenue (mainly from taxes) is a particularly important aspect of fiscal policy known as the **government budget balance.** If revenues are less than expenditures, the government budget balance is negative and is described as a **government budget deficit.** If revenues exceed expenditures, the balance is positive and described as a **government budget surplus.** Figure 4.7 shows Canada's federal government budget deficits and surpluses for the 1984–2007 period. As with monetary policy, economists generally agree that fiscal policy can have important effects on the overall performance of the economy. For example, many economists believe that contractionary fiscal policy in the 1930s contributed to the severity of the Great Depression in Canada.

Finally, the term **structural policy** includes government policies aimed at changing the underlying structure or institutions of the nation's economy. Structural policies come in many forms, from minor tinkering to ambitious overhauls of the entire economic system. The move away from central planning and toward a more market-oriented approach in many formerly communist countries, such as Poland, the Czech Republic, and Hungary, is a large-scale example of structural

fiscal policy decisions that determine the government's budget, including the amount and composition of government expenditures and government revenues

government budget balance the difference between government revenues and expenditures; it equals zero when revenues equal expenditure, is positive when revenues exceed expenditures, and is negative when revenues fall short of expenditures

government budget deficit when government revenues fall short of expenditures; that is, the government budget balance is negative

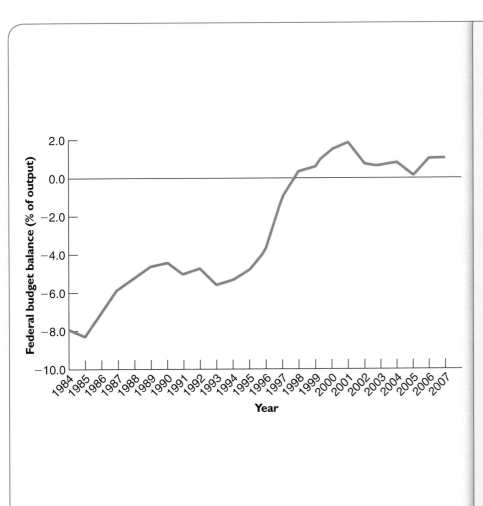

FIGURE 4.7

The Federal Government Budget Balance as a Percentage of Output, Canada, 1984–2007
The federal deficit percentage declined from the mid-1980s until the early 1990s recession, which caused it to rise again. Recovery and major federal expenditure cuts in the mid-1990s reduced deficits and produced surpluses by the end of the decade. Federal income tax cuts in 2000 reduced the surpluses but counteracted the economic slowdown of 2000–2001. SOURCE: Fiscal Reference Tables, http://www.fin.gc.ca/frt/2007/frt07_e.pdf. Department of Finance, Canada, September 2007. Reproduced with permission of the Minister of Public Works and Government Services Canada. NOTE: The year shown is the fiscal year ending in that year; e.g., 2007 stands for fiscal year 2006–2007.

government budget surplus
when government revenues
exceed expenditures; that is,
the government budget balance
is positive

structural policy government
policies aimed at changing
the underlying structure, or
institutions, of the nation's
economy

policy. Many developing countries have tried structural reforms at the urging of the International Monetary Fund. Supporters of structural policy claim that, by changing the basic characteristics of the economy or by remaking its institutions, the reforms can stimulate economic growth and improve living standards.

RECAP

MACROECONOMIC POLICY

Macroeconomic policies affect the performance of the economy as a whole. The three types of macroeconomic policy are monetary policy, fiscal policy, and structural policy. *Monetary policy,* which in Canada is under the control of the Bank of Canada, refers to interest rate changes made by the central bank. *Fiscal policy* involves decisions about the government budget, including its expenditures and tax collections. *Structural policy* refers to government actions to change the underlying structure or institutions of the economy. Structural policy can range from minor tinkering to a major overhaul of the economic system, as with the formerly communist countries that are attempting to convert to market-oriented systems.

4.3   AGGREGATION

In Chapter 1, we discussed the difference between macroeconomics, the study of national economies and microeconomics, which studies both individual economic entities (such as households and firms) and the markets for specific goods and services. The main difference between the fields is one of perspective: macroeconomists take a "bird's-eye view" of the economy, ignoring the fine details to understand how the system works as a whole. Microeconomists work instead at "ground level," studying the economic behaviour of individual households, firms, and markets. Both perspectives are essential to understanding what makes an economy work.

EXERCISE 4.2

Which of the following questions would be studied primarily by macroeconomists? By microeconomists? Explain.
   a. **Does increased government spending lower the unemployment rate?**
   b. **Does Microsoft's dominance of the software industry harm consumers?**
   c. **Should the Bank of Canada and the Department of Finance raise the midpoint of the inflation-control target range from 2 percent to something higher?**
   d. **Why did Canada's average rate of personal saving fall during the 1990s?**
   e. **Does the increase in the number of consumer products being sold over the Internet threaten the profits of conventional retailers like Zellers?**

aggregation the adding up of
individual economic variables to
obtain economy-wide totals

Although macroeconomics and microeconomics take different perspectives on the economy, the basic tools of analysis are much the same. In the chapters to come, you will see that macroeconomists apply the same core principles (see Chapters 1 to 3) as microeconomists. But macroeconomists must pay particular attention to issues of **aggregation**, the adding up of individual economic variables to obtain economy-wide totals.

For example, explaining trends in movie theatre ticket sales relative to spending on DVD and video rentals is a topic for microeconomics, not macroeconomics.

Instead, macroeconomists add up consumer spending on all goods and services during a given period to obtain *aggregate,* or total, consumer spending. And they explore connections between aggregate consumer spending and variables such as aggregate income and unemployment. Sometimes aggregation just involves suppressing the mind-boggling details to see broad trends, as in Example 4.3.

Aggregation: A national crime index	EXAMPLE 4.3

To illustrate aggregation as a process of suppressing details in order to see the bigger picture, consider an issue that is only partly economic—crime. Suppose policy-makers want to find out whether the problem of crime in Canada is getting worse. How could they do so?

Police forces and RCMP detachments keep records of crimes reported to them, so a researcher could determine, say, how many break-and-enters occurred last year in any one of dozens of jurisdictions. But data on the number of crimes of each type in each jurisdiction would produce stacks of computer output. Is there a way to add up all the crime data to get some sense of the national trend?

Aggregation is used to obtain a measure of annual criminal code offences expressed in terms of crimes per 100 000 population. For example, Statistics Canada reported that in 2006, some 8269 criminal code offences (violent crimes, property crimes, and other crimes) occurred for every 100 000 Canadians.[4] This rate represented a substantial drop from the crime rate in 1993, which was 10 594 crimes per 100 000 people. So aggregation (the adding up of many different crimes into a national total) indicates that crime decreased in Canada between 1993 and 2006.

Although aggregation of crime statistics reveals the big picture, it may obscure important details. Criminal code offences is a category lumping together relatively minor crimes such as theft with very serious crimes such as murder. Most people would agree that murder does far more damage than theft, so adding them might give a false picture of crime trends. In this case, though, the percentage decline in the overall crime rate was close to the percentage decline in the murder rate.

Sometimes, sensible aggregation involves more than just suppressing details in order to see the bigger picture—it requires recognizing that the whole can be more than the sum of the parts. In other words, sensible aggregation may require avoiding the mistake known as the *fallacy of composition.*

The fallacy of composition occurs when, for example, the assumption is made that if one fan at a sporting event can get a better view by standing up, then all fans at the event will get a better view if they all stand up at once. In economics, the **fallacy of composition** occurs when it is falsely assumed that what is true at the level of a particular individual, household, firm, or industry is necessarily true at a higher aggregate level.

fallacy of composition the mistake of falsely assuming that what is true at the level of a particular individual, household, firm, or industry is necessarily true at a higher aggregate level

A classic example of the fallacy of composition relates to microeconomics. Suppose that one potato farmer decides to put in longer hours. By working longer hours, the farmer produces a larger crop of potatoes, and thereby earns a larger income. It might seem safe to generalize that if all potato farmers worked longer hours and produced larger crops of potatoes, they would all earn larger incomes. But if a single farmer supplies more potatoes to the market, the market price for potatoes will typically be unaffected, whereas if all farmers supply more potatoes, then the price of potatoes would tend to fall (because of a rightward shift of the supply schedule, as explained in Chapter 3). The total revenues of the farmers could fall. If revenues fell, the generalization about all potato farmers in the market (the potato-farming industry) based on the experience of the one farmer would be an example of the fallacy of composition.

[4]See Statistics Canada, CANSIM II series V12397045.

An awareness of the fallacy of composition is particularly important in macroeconomics, where aggregation across the whole economy is involved. To illustrate, suppose that one Canadian becomes rich because the government of Canada issues a cheque for $1 million to compensate him for wrongful imprisonment on a murder charge. Would it be logical to generalize that everyone in Canada could become rich if the government issued cheques for $1 million to every man, woman, and child?

Macroeconomists would identify such a generalization as an example of the fallacy of composition. The total value of the cheques would exceed the current dollar value of Canada's economic output 30 times over. The government would have to pay for the cheques by printing up and issuing a tremendous amount of additional Canadian currency. The price level for the Canadian economy would soar and the value of the currency would plummet—one Canadian dollar would at most buy what a few pennies would buy today. It is true that there would be some redistribution of income. Students with loans, for example, would be able to pay them off more easily. But the average Canadian would not become richer.

RECAP

AGGREGATION

Macroeconomics, the study of national economies, differs from microeconomics, the study of individual economic entities (such as households and firms) and the markets for specific goods and services. Macroeconomists take a bird's-eye view of the economy. To study the economy as a whole, macroeconomists make frequent use of *aggregation,* the adding up of individual economic variables to obtain economy-wide totals. A cost of aggregation is that the fine details of the economic situation are obscured. Sensible aggregation sometimes requires recognizing that the whole can be more than the sum of its parts.

4.4   STUDYING MACROECONOMICS: A PREVIEW

This chapter introduced many of the key issues of macroeconomics. In the chapters to come we will look at each of these issues in more detail. The next two chapters (Chapters 5 and 6) cover the *measurement* of economic performance, including key variables like the level of economic activity, the extent of unemployment, and the rate of inflation. Obtaining quantitative measurements of the economy, against which theories can be tested, is the crucial first step in answering basic macroeconomic questions like those raised in this chapter.

In Part 3 we will study short-term economic fluctuations. Chapter 7 provides background on what happens during recessions and expansions, as well as some historical perspective. Chapter 8 discusses one important source of short-term economic fluctuations; that is, variations in aggregate spending. The chapter also shows how, by influencing aggregate spending, fiscal policy may be able to moderate economic fluctuations. The second major policy tool for stabilizing the economy, monetary policy, is the subject of Chapter 9. Chapter 10 develops a model of the simultaneous determination of the price level and of the level of output. Chapter 11 brings inflation into the analysis and discusses the circumstances under which macroeconomic policy-makers may face a short-term trade-off between inflation and unemployment.

Chapter 12 fleshes out our analysis of exchange rates between national currencies. We will discuss in detail how exchange rates are determined and how they affect the workings of the economy and macroeconomic policy. The role

played in the economy by money and banks is covered in Chapter 13. This chapter supplements the preceding chapters on monetary policy and exchange rates and provides a bridge to the long-run chapters which follow.

In Part 4 we look at economic behaviour over relatively long periods of time. Long-run economic performance is extremely important, accounting for much of the substantial differences in living standards among the inhabitants of different countries. Chapter 14 examines economic growth and productivity improvement, the fundamental determinants of the average standard of living in the long run. International trade, which has played an important role in Canada's development, is the focus of Chapter 15. In Chapter 16 we study saving and its link to the creation of new capital goods, such as factories and machines. Chapter 17 covers the role of the financial system, explains the pricing of bonds and stocks, and discusses international capital flows.

SUMMARY

4.1 Macroeconomics is the study of the performance of national economies and of the policies governments use to try to improve that performance. Some of the broad issues macroeconomists study are:

Sources of economic growth and improved living standards

Trends in *average labour productivity,* or output per employed worker

Short-term fluctuations in the pace of economic growth (recessions and expansions)

Causes and cures of unemployment and inflation

Economic interdependence among nations

4.2 To help explain differences in economic performance among countries, or in economic performance in the same country at different times, macroeconomists study the implementation and effects of macroeconomic policies.

Macroeconomic policies are government actions designed to affect the performance of the economy as a whole. Macroeconomic policies include *monetary policy* (central bank management of interest rates), *fiscal policy* (relating to decisions about the government's budget), and *structural policy* (aimed at affecting the basic structure and institutions of the economy).

4.3 Macroeconomics is distinct from microeconomics, which focuses on the behaviour of individual economic entities and specific markets. Macroeconomists make heavy use of *aggregation,* which is the adding up of individual economic variables into economy-wide totals. Aggregation allows macroeconomists to study the "big picture" of the economy, while ignoring fine details about individual households, firms, and markets. Sensible aggregation sometimes requires recognition that the whole can be more than the sum of the parts.

KEY TERMS

aggregation (100)
average labour productivity (92)
fallacy of composition (101)
fiscal policy (99)

government budget balance (99)
government budget deficit (99)
government budget surplus (100)

macroeconomic policies (89)
monetary policy (98)
structural policy (100)

REVIEW QUESTIONS

1. How did the experience of the Great Depression motivate the development of the field of macroeconomics?

2. How has Canadian economic performance differed from U.S. economic performance in recent decades?

3. Why is average labour productivity a particularly important economic variable?

4. True or false, and explain: Economic growth within a particular country generally proceeds at a constant rate.

5. True or false, and explain: Differences of opinion about economic policy recommendations can always be resolved by objective analysis of the issues.

6. If one computer chip maker increases output, it will realize increased revenue. If all computer chip makers increase output, prices will tend to fall, and this could result in reduced revenue. What is the term used for the mistake of assuming that what is true for one acting alone is also true for all acting together?

7. What type of macroeconomic policy (monetary, fiscal, structural) might include each of the following actions:

   a. A broad government initiative to reduce the country's reliance on resources and promote high-technology industries.

   b. A reduction in sales taxes like the GST.

   c. Provision of additional cash to the banking system.

   d. An attempt to reduce the government budget deficit by reducing spending.

   e. A decision by a developing country to defy the International Monetary Fund by imposing controls on international capital flows.

PROBLEMS

1. Over the next 50 years, the Japanese population is expected to decline, while the fraction of the population that is retired is expected to increase sharply. What are the implications of these population changes for total output and average living standards in Japan, assuming that average labour productivity stagnates?

2. Is it possible for average living standards to rise during a period in which average labour productivity is falling? Discuss, using a numerical example for illustration.

3. The Bureau of Economic Analysis, or BEA, is a U.S. government agency that collects a wide variety of statistics about the U.S. economy. From the BEA's home page (http://www.bea.gov) find data for the most recent year available on U.S. exports and imports of goods and services. Is the United States running a trade surplus or deficit? Calculate the ratio of the surplus or deficit to U.S. exports.

4. Which of the following would be studied by a macroeconomist? By a microeconomist?
   a. The global operations of Nortel Networks.
   b. The effect of anti-competitive business practices on energy prices.
   c. The impact of rising energy prices on inflation and growth in the Canadian economy.
   d. Inflation in developing countries.
   e. The effects of tax cuts on consumer spending.

ANSWERS TO IN-CHAPTER EXERCISES

4.1 The answer depends on current statistics.

4.2 a. Macroeconomists. Government spending and the unemployment rate are aggregate concepts pertaining to the national economy.
   b. Microeconomists. Microsoft, though large, is an individual firm.
   c. Macroeconomists. Relevant evidence would relate to the links between inflation and other macroeconomic variables.
   d. Macroeconomists. Average saving is an aggregate concept.
   e. Microeconomists. The focus is on a relatively narrow set of markets and products rather than on the economy as a whole.

Chapter 5 — Measuring Economic Activity: GDP and Unemployment

"Total economic activity was unchanged in this month, after edging up 0.1 percent last month."

"The unemployment rate held at 7.0 percent for the fourth consecutive month."

News headlines like these fill the airwaves—some TV and radio stations carry nothing else. In fact, all kinds of people are interested in economic data. The average person hopes to learn something that will be useful in a business decision, a financial investment, or a career move. The professional economist depends on economic data in much the same way that a doctor depends on a patient's vital signs—pulse, blood pressure, and temperature—to make an accurate diagnosis. To understand economic developments and to be able to give useful advice to policy-makers, business people, or union leaders, an economist simply must have up-to-date, accurate data.

Measurement of the economy dates back to the mid-seventeenth century. Not until the twentieth century, though, did economic measurement come into its own, and not until the Second World War were the foundations of modern economic measurement in place.

The Second World War was an important catalyst for the development of economic statistics since its very outcome depended on mobilization of economic resources. In the United Kingdom, for example, Richard Stone contributed to wartime planning by pioneering a comprehensive system for measuring the economy's output. He did so by making use of macroeconomic concepts developed in the 1930s by John Maynard Keynes, possibly the most influential economist of the twentieth century. In Canada, the foundations for modern-day economic statistics were established by a 1945 White Paper on Employment and Income.[1]

In this chapter and the next, we will focus on the measurement of three basic macroeconomic variables that arise in almost any discussion of the economy: the *gross domestic product* (or GDP), the *unemployment rate*, and the *inflation*

---

[1] *Employment and Income With Special Reference to the Initial Period of Reconstruction*, (Ottawa: King's Printer, April 1945).

**www.statcan.ca/english/
Gross Domestic Product
by Industry**

rate. This chapter deals primarily with the first two of these statistics. Chapter 6 deals with the inflation rate.

GDP can be expressed in three different but equivalent ways: by production (or value-added), expenditure, and income approaches. This chapter begins with the production approach to GDP measurement, the approach followed in the Statistics Canada publication *Gross Domestic Product by Industry.* The key source of GDP measurements for Canada, however, is a Statistics Canada publication called the *National Income and Expenditure Accounts.* The words "expenditure" and "income" in the title refer to the two major ways Statistics Canada obtains the same number for GDP: by adding up different categories of expenditure in the economy, or by adding up the incomes earned in producing the economy's output. The incomes earned in producing GDP, in turn, are associated with employment as defined in the *Labour Force Survey,* the source for unemployment-rate statistics.

By the end of this chapter, you will understand how official measures of output and unemployment are constructed and will have gained some insight into their strengths and limitations. Understanding the strengths and limitations of economic data is necessary background for the economic analysis in the chapters to come.

5.1 GROSS DOMESTIC PRODUCT: MEASURING THE NATION'S OUTPUT

Chapter 4 discussed the link between an economy's output and its living standard. We noted that high levels of output per worker are associated with a high standard of living. A "worker" means someone engaged in paid employment as measured by the *Labour Force Survey.*[2] But what, exactly, does "output" mean? To study economic growth and productivity scientifically, we need to be more precise about how economists define and measure an economy's output.

The most commonly used measure of an economy's output is called the *gross domestic product,* or *GDP.* GDP is intended to measure how much an economy produces in a given period, such as a quarter (three months) or a year. More precisely, **gross domestic product (GDP)** is the market value of the final goods and services produced in a country during a given period. To understand this definition, let's take it apart and examine each of its parts separately. The first key phrase in the definition is "market value."

gross domestic product (GDP)
the market value of the final goods and services produced in a country during a given period

MARKET VALUE

A modern economy produces many different goods and services, from dental floss (a good) to acupuncture (a service). To be able to talk about total output, as opposed to the output of specific items like dental floss, economists need to *aggregate* the quantities of many different goods and services into a single number. We have a ready means of adding them up if they are exchanged for money and hence also have *market prices.*

A simple example will illustrate the process. In the imaginary economy of Orchardia, total production is 4 million apples and 6 million pears.[3] One could add the number of apples to the number of pears and conclude that the total output is 10 million pieces of fruit. But would Orchardia's output then just equal the output of

[2]Someone engaged in paid employment can be an employee, an employer, or a self-employed worker without employees. A tiny fraction of the employment involved in the production of Canadian GDP, less than half a percentage point, consists of unpaid family labour on farms and in small businesses. For ease of expression, we will generally ignore this unpaid employment.

[3]To keep things simple, we are assuming that apples and pears in this imaginary economy are each of a single type. In reality, adding together, say, Spartan apples with Macintosh apples or Bartlett pears with Anjou pears, requires a similar procedure to adding apples to pears.

an economy producing 10 million blueberries? And what if Orchardia also produced 3 million pairs of shoes? What is a sensible way of adding apples and pears to shoes?

Suppose, however, we know that apples have a market price of $0.25 each, pears of $0.50 each, and shoes of $20 a pair. Then we can say that the market value of this economy's production, or its GDP, is equal to:

$$\left(4 \text{ million apples} \times \frac{\$0.25}{\text{apple}}\right) + \left(6 \text{ million pears} \times \frac{\$0.50}{\text{pear}}\right)$$

$$+ \left(3 \text{ million pears of shoes} \times \frac{\$20}{\text{pair}}\right) = \$64 \text{ million.}$$

Notice that when we calculate total output this way, the more expensive items (the shoes) receive a higher weighting than the cheaper items (the apples and pears). But this weighting is not a subjective judgment about the relative values of apples, pears, and shoes; the weights are market prices that large numbers of people have been willing to pay in millions of transactions.

Orchardia's GDP   EXAMPLE 5.1

Suppose Orchardia were to produce 3 million apples, 3 million pears, and 4 million pairs of shoes at the same market prices as in the preceding text. What is its GDP now?

Now the Orchardian GDP is equal to:

$$\left(3 \text{ million apples} \times \frac{\$0.25}{\text{apple}}\right) + \left(3 \text{ million pears} \times \frac{\$0.50}{\text{pear}}\right)$$

$$+ \left(4 \text{ million pairs of shoes} \times \frac{\$20}{\text{pair}}\right) = \$82.25 \text{ million.}$$

Notice that Orchardian GDP is higher in Example 5.1 than in the previous text, even though two of the three goods (apples and pears) are being produced in smaller quantities than before. The reason is that the good whose production has increased (shoes) is much more valuable than the goods whose production has decreased (apples and pears).

Now suppose Orchardia produces the original quantities of the three goods at the original prices ($0.25/apple, $0.50/pear, and $20/pair of shoes). In addition, suppose Orchardia produces 5 million peaches at $0.30 each. What is the GDP of Orchardia now?

EXERCISE 5.1

Market prices provide a convenient way to add together, or aggregate, the many different goods and services produced in a modern market economy. Market prices even provide the basis for valuing public-sector services, such as healthcare and education provided to the public without charge.

There are no market prices for public services provided without charge, but the paid labour and other inputs used to produce them are purchased in markets; thus non-marketed public services are valued in GDP according to the market value of the inputs used to produce them. This practice is followed by statistical agencies around the world. And if it were not followed, there would be a large category of employment as measured by the *Labour Force Survey* without a corresponding measure of output in GDP.

But the use of market prices of goods and services (or the use of market prices of inputs) does not provide a solution to all aggregation problems. For example, in a predominantly agricultural society where relatively few goods and services are traded in markets and much of agricultural production goes towards the farm households' own subsistence, an economic aggregate based only on market transactions would seriously understate the level of economic activity.[4]

Even in modern market economies, it is important to recognize that the expansion of marketed and public-sector output may come about in part through the incorporation of activities that had previously taken place outside of paid employment. For example, the growth of paid housekeeping and childcare services may represent in part a conversion of unpaid household activities into marketed output or into publicly provided services.

The opposite process can also take place. That is, reductions in marketed and public-sector output may be associated with the expansion of non-market household activity. For example, the extension of the average age of completing education results in young people spending less time in paid employment and more time studying. Or a trend to early retirement from paid employment might reduce GDP but result in an increase in, say, recreational gardening. (Time spent in unpaid housekeeping, childcare, studying, and recreational gardening is not measured by the *Labour Force Survey* or by GDP. But statistics on non-market uses of time by the working-age population have been collected intermittently by Statistics Canada through the *General Social Survey*.)

While GDP for Canada is calculated from market values the way we have done for the imaginary economy of Orchardia, not all goods and services with market value go into the GDP total. As we will see next, the GDP total includes only those goods and services that are the end products of the production process, called *final goods and services*. Otherwise, there would be a problem of counting some goods and services two or more times.

FINAL GOODS AND SERVICES

Many goods are used in the production process. Before a baker can produce a loaf of bread, grain must be grown and harvested, then the grain must be ground into flour and, together with other ingredients, baked into bread. Of the three major goods that are produced during this process—the grain, the flour, and the bread—only the bread is used by consumers. Because producing the bread is the ultimate purpose of the process, the bread is called a *final good*. In general, a **final good or service** is the end product of a process, the product or service that consumers actually use. The goods or services produced on the way toward making the final product—here, the grain and the flour—are called **intermediate goods or services.**

final goods or services consumed by the ultimate user; because they are the end products of the production process, they are counted as part of GDP

intermediate goods or services used up in the production of final goods and services and therefore not counted as part of GDP

Since we are interested in measuring only those items that are of direct economic value, *only final goods and services are included in GDP*. Intermediate goods and services are *not* included. To illustrate, suppose that the grain from the previous example has a market value of $0.50 (the price the milling company paid for the grain). The grain is then ground into flour, which has a market value of $1.20 (the price the baker paid for the flour). Finally, the flour is made into a loaf of fine French bread, worth $2 at the local store. In calculating the contribution of these activities to GDP, would we want to add together the values of the grain, the flour, and the bread? No, because the grain and flour are intermediate goods, valuable only because they can be used to make bread. So, in this example the total contribution to GDP is $2, the value of the loaf of bread, the final product.

Example 5.2 illustrates the same distinction but this time with a focus on services.

---

[4]One way to deal with this problem is to impute a value to agricultural output produced by farm households for their own consumption. The statistical agencies of many countries include such an imputation in their calculation of GDP.

The hair stylist and her assistant

EXAMPLE 5.2

Your hair stylist charges $20 for a haircut. In turn, she pays her assistant $4 per haircut in return for sharpening the scissors, sweeping the floor, and other chores. For each haircut given, what is the total contribution of the hair stylist and her assistant, taken together, to GDP?

The answer to this problem is $20, the price of the haircut. The haircut is counted in GDP because it is the final service, the one that actually has value to the final user. The services provided by the assistant have value only because they contribute to the production of the haircut, and thus they are not counted as a final service in GDP.

A process that is equivalent to adding together the value of all final goods and services is adding up the *value added* by all firms in the production process. The **value added** by any firm equals the market value of its product or service minus the cost of inputs purchased from other firms. Table 5.1 provides the relevant data from the simple example of the $2-per-loaf French bread. The value added by the grain supplier was $0.50 because the grain was sold to the flour miller for $0.50 and was assumed to require no intermediate goods for its production. The value added by the flour miller was $0.70, the difference between the value of the flour sold to the bakery and the cost of the grain used to produce the flour. Finally, the value added by the bakery was $0.80, the difference between the price for which the bread was sold as a final good and the cost to the bakery of purchasing the flour (assumed to be the sole intermediate good utilized by the bakery). Notice that the sum of value added by the three firms is $2, which equals the market value of the bread.

value added for any firm, the market value of its product or service minus the cost of inputs purchased from other firms

TABLE 5.1
Value Added in Bread Production

Firm	Revenue	− Cost of intermediate goods	= Value added
Grain supplier	$0.50	$0.00	$0.50
Flour miller	$1.20	$0.50	$0.70
Bakery	$2.00	$1.20	$0.80
Total			$2.00

A special type of good that is difficult to classify as intermediate or final is a *capital good*. A **capital good** is a long-lived good, which is itself produced and used only to produce other goods and services. Factories and machines are examples of capital goods. Capital goods do not fit the definition of final goods, since their purpose is to produce other goods. On the other hand, they are not used up during the production process, except over a very long period, so they are not exactly intermediate goods either. For purposes of measuring GDP, statistical agencies have agreed to classify newly produced capital goods as final goods. Otherwise, a country that invested in its future by building modern factories and buying new machines would be counted as having a lower GDP than a country that devoted all its resources to producing consumer goods.

capital good long-lived good, which is itself produced and used to produce other goods and services

We have now established that GDP is equal to the market value of final goods and services. Let's look at the last part of the definition, "produced within a country during a given period."

PRODUCED WITHIN A COUNTRY DURING A GIVEN PERIOD

The word *domestic* in the term *gross domestic product* tells us that GDP is a measure of economic activity within a given country. Thus, only production that takes place within the country's borders is counted. For example, the GDP of Canada includes the market value of all cars produced within Canadian borders, even though the cars are made in foreign-owned plants. Looked at another way, cars produced in Canada by a U.S.-based company like General Motors are *not* counted in U.S. GDP.

We have seen that GDP is intended to measure the amount of production that occurs during a given period, normally the calendar year. For this reason, only goods and services that are actually produced during a particular year are included in the GDP for that year. Example 5.3 and Exercise 5.2 illustrate.

EXAMPLE 5.3	The sale of a house and GDP

A 20-year-old house is sold to a young family for $100 000. The family pays the real estate agent a 6 percent commission. What is the contribution of this transaction to GDP?

Because the house was not produced during the current year, its value is *not* counted in this year's GDP. (The value of the house was included in the GDP 20 years earlier, the year the house was built.) In general, purchases and sales of existing assets, such as old houses or used cars, do not contribute to the current year's GDP. However, the $6000 fee paid to the real estate agent represents the market value of the agent's services in helping the family find the house and make the purchase. Since those services were provided during the current year, the agent's fee *is* counted in current-year GDP.

EXERCISE 5.2   **Lotta Doe sells 100 shares of stock in Benson Buggywhip for $50 per share. She pays her broker a 2 percent commission for executing the sale. How does Lotta's transaction affect the current-year GDP?**

RECAP ⬆

MEASURING GDP

Gross domestic product (GDP) equals

the market value
GDP is basically an aggregate of the market values of the many goods and services produced in the economy. The services provided by government employees are typically not provided at market prices, so they are included in GDP at the government's cost of producing them. Goods and services produced by unpaid household labour for use within the household—everything from meal preparation to mowing the lawn—are not included in GDP.

of final goods and services
Final goods and services (which include capital goods, such as factories and machines) are counted in GDP. Intermediate goods and services, which are used up in the production of final goods and services, are not counted. In practice, the value of final goods and services is determined by the value-added method. The value added by any firm equals the firm's revenue from selling its product minus the cost of inputs purchased from other firms. Summing the value added by all firms in the production process yields the value of the final good or service.

produced in a country during a given period
Only goods and services produced within a nation's borders are included in GDP, and only those produced during the current year (or the portion of the value produced during the current year) are counted as part of the current-year GDP.

5.2 THE EXPENDITURE METHOD FOR MEASURING GDP

GDP is a measure of the quantity of goods and services *produced* by an economy. But any good or service that is produced will also be *purchased* and used by some economic agent—a consumer buying Christmas gifts or a firm investing in new machinery, for example. For many purposes, knowing not only how much is produced, but who uses it and how, is important.

Economic statisticians divide the users of the final goods and services that make up the GDP for any given year into four categories: *households, firms, governments,* and the *foreign sector* (that is, foreign purchasers of domestic products). They assume that all the final goods and services that are produced in a country in a given year will be purchased and used by members of one or more of these four groups. Furthermore, the amounts that purchasers spend on various goods and services should be equal to the market values of those goods and services. As a result, GDP can also be measured by adding up the total amount spent by each of the four groups on final goods and services and subtracting spending on imported goods and services.

Corresponding to the four groups of final users are four components of expenditure: consumption, private-sector investment, government purchases, and net exports. That is, households consume, firms engage in private-sector investment, governments make government purchases, and the foreign sector buys the nation's exports. Table 5.2 gives the dollar values for each of these components for the Canadian economy in 2007. As the table shows, GDP for Canada in 2007 was over $1.5 trillion, which is roughly $46 400 per person. Detailed definitions of the components of expenditure and their principal subcomponents follow. As you read through them, refer to Table 5.2 to get a sense of the relative importance of each type of spending.

Consumption, or personal expenditure, is spending by households on goods and services, such as food, clothing, and entertainment. Consumption is divided into four subcomponents:

consumption spending by households on goods and services, such as food, clothing, and entertainment

- *Durable goods*, or consumer durables, are long-lived goods such as cars and furniture purchased for household use. Note that new houses are not treated as consumer durables but as part of private-sector investment.

- *Semi-durable goods* are consumer goods that would typically be used on multiple occasions and be expected to last for a year or more. Examples are clothing and footwear.

- *Non-durable goods* are consumer goods that would typically be used only once or be expected to last less than a year. Examples are food, gasoline, and heating fuel purchased by households.

- *Services*, a large component of consumer spending, include everything from haircuts and taxi rides to legal and financial services.

Not all personal spending is counted as consumption in GDP. For example, if you give change to a homeless person, the act is considered a private transfer, reducing your income and increasing the income of the homeless person, not as a payment for goods or services received. Similarly, allowances paid by parents to children are considered transfers, not payments for services rendered.

TABLE 5.2

Expenditure Components of Canadian GDP, 2007 (billions of dollars)

Component and Principal Subcomponent Names	Principal Subcomponent Values	Component Values	Macroeconomic Symbols	Percentage of GDP
Consumption		854.0	C	**55.8%**
Durable goods	111.9			
Semi-durable goods	70.4			
Non-durable goods	205.7			
Services	466.0			
Private-Sector Investment		297.6	I	**19.4%**
Non-residential structures and equipment	189.0			
Residential structures	108.6			
Business investment in inventories	7.2			
Government Purchases		341.8	G	**22.3%**
Net government current expenditure on goods and services	298.1			
Government gross fixed capital formation	43.7			
Net exports		31.3	NX	**2.0%**
Exports	534.7			
Imports	−503.4			
Statistical discrepancy	−0.3	−0.3		**−0.02%**
Total:				
Gross Domestic Product	1531.4	1531.4	Y	**100%**

SOURCE: Adapted from the Statistics Canada CANSIM database, http://cansim2.statcan.ca. Table 380-0002 and from the Statistics Canada Web site, http://www40.statcan.ca/101/cst01/econ04.htm.

NOTE: The statistical discrepancy is used to reconcile GDP from the expenditure approach with GDP from the income approach. If one approach leads to a higher estimate than the other, then half of the difference between the two is added to the lower value and half is subtracted from the higher value. The table omits government inventory investment, which is so small its GDP share rounds to zero. Components do not add to totals exactly as a result of rounding and this minor omission.

private-sector investment
spending by firms on final goods and services, primarily capital goods and housing

Private-sector investment, sometimes called business investment or simply investment, is spending by firms on final goods and services, primarily capital goods and housing. Private-sector investment is divided into three subcomponents:

- Investment in *non-residential structures and equipment*, or non-residential gross fixed capital formation, is the purchase by firms of new capital goods such as machinery, factories, office buildings, shopping malls, and transportation equipment. (Remember that for the purposes of calculating GDP long-lived capital goods are treated as final goods rather than as intermediate goods.) Firms buy capital goods to increase their capacity to produce. A new car will be treated as a consumer durable falling under consumption if purchased for family use but as an investment in equipment if purchased by a taxi company as an addition to its fleet.

- Investment in *residential structures*, or housing investment, refers to purchases of new dwellings, regardless of whether the dwelling is a new house purchased by a family for personal use or a new apartment building purchased by a landlord to earn rental income. In many respects, purchases

of new houses by families are like their purchases of consumer durables and could be classified as consumption. But national accounting experts have decided otherwise, as a matter of convention. For GDP accounting purposes, residential investment is treated as an investment by the business sector.

- *Business investment in inventories,* or inventory investment, refers to changes in company inventories. The goods a firm produces but does not sell during the current period are treated, for accounting purposes, as if the firm had bought those goods from itself. This is a smart accounting twist for making sure that production equals expenditure—that all the goods produced are also sold. Inventory investment will take a negative value if the value of inventories on hand falls over the course of a year. Inventories of a firm tend to build up (positive inventory investment) if there is an unanticipated decline in sales and tend to run down (negative inventory investment) when there is an unanticipated increase in sales.

People often refer to purchases of financial assets, such as stocks or bonds, as investments. For an individual buying a stock or bond with the hope of financial gain, the stock or bond may seem like an investment promising to yield a financial return. But for the economy as a whole, the stock or bond is a piece of paper or a computer entry representing an asset for the buyer and a liability for the seller. Its purchase is not equivalent to the formation of *new* physical capital or inventories that we have labelled private-sector investment. The everyday use of the term investment for purchases of financial assets, then, is very different from the definition of investment employed in GDP. Whereas economists usually use the term "real" to distinguish inflation-adjusted values from "nominal" ones, as explained below, they also use the term "real investment" to describe this formation of new physical capital or inventories and to contrast it with "financial investment."

government purchases
purchases by federal, provincial, and municipal governments of final goods and services; government purchases do not include *government transfer payments*, nor do they include interest paid on the public debt

Government purchases are purchases by federal, provincial, and municipal governments of final goods (such as computers) and services (such as teaching in public schools). Government purchases in GDP are a subset of all spending recorded in government budgets. Government purchases do *not* include *government transfer payments*, which are payments made by the government in return for which no current goods or services are received. Examples of transfer payments (which, again, are *not* included in government purchases but are included in government budgets) are old age security benefits, employment insurance benefits, and social assistance payments. Interest paid on the public debt is another type of transfer. It is also excluded from government purchases in GDP but is recorded, of course, in government budgets.

Government purchases are divided into two major subcomponents:

- *Net government current expenditure on goods and services* consists of purchases of office supplies and the services of government employees. Department of National Defence spending on warships, military aircraft, weapons, and the like also falls into this category.

- *Government gross fixed capital formation,* or government investment in fixed capital, corresponds to government purchases of new structures and equipment, including waterworks, sewage systems, roads, harbours, and airports. It includes the portion of Department of National Defence spending on durable assets that could be used for civilian purposes, such as docks, roads, hospitals, and transport aircraft.

For some purposes, it is useful to combine private-sector investment and government investment into a single total. For example, in discussing economy-wide saving and capital formation in Chapter 16, we will examine how Statistics Canada combines private-sector investment and government investment into a category of economy-wide investment called *gross investment*. But, as shown above, private-sector investment and government investment are treated as different types of expenditures in calculating GDP by the expenditure approach.

net exports exports minus imports

Net exports equal exports minus imports, where

- *exports* are domestically produced final goods and services that are sold abroad (or to visiting tourists), and

- *imports* are purchases by domestic buyers of goods and services that were produced abroad. Imports are subtracted from exports to find the net amount of spending on domestically produced goods and services.

A country's net exports reflect the net demand by the rest of the world for its goods and services. Net exports can be negative, since imports can exceed exports in any given year. The annual net exports of the United States, for example, have been consistently negative for over two decades. As Table 5.2 showed, Canada's net exports were positive in 2007. (Figure 4.5 showed that Canada's net exports have traditionally been positive.)

The relationship between GDP and expenditures on goods and services can be summarized by an equation. Let

$$
\begin{aligned}
Y &= \text{gross domestic product, or output,} \\
C &= \text{consumption expenditure,} \\
I &= \text{private-sector investment,} \\
G &= \text{government purchases,} \\
NX &= \text{net exports.}
\end{aligned}
$$

Using these symbols, we can write that GDP equals the sum of the four types of expenditure algebraically:

$$Y = C + I + G + NX.$$

> **RECAP** ↑
>
> ## EXPENDITURE COMPONENTS OF GDP
>
> GDP can be expressed as the sum of expenditures on domestically produced final goods and services. The four types of expenditure that are counted in the GDP, and the economic groups that make up each type of expenditure, are as follows:
>
> | Who makes the expenditure? | Type of expenditure | Examples |
> |---|---|---|
> | Households | Consumption | Food, clothes, haircuts, new cars |
> | Firms | Private-sector invesment | New factories and equipment, new houses, increases in inventory stocks |
> | Governments | Government purchases | New school buildings, roads, docks, salaries of civil servants |
> | Foreign sector | Net exports, or exports minus imports | Exported manufactured goods, resource exports, financial services provided by domestic residents to foreigners |

Measuring GDP by production and by expenditure   EXAMPLE 5.4

Suppose that an economy produces 1 000 000 automobiles valued at $15 000 each. Of these, 700 000 are sold to consumers, 200 000 are sold to businesses, 50 000 are sold to the government, and 25 000 are sold abroad. No automobiles are imported. The automobiles left unsold at the end of the year are held in inventory by the auto producers. Find GDP in terms of (a) the market value of production and (b) the components of expenditure. You should get the same answer both ways.

The market value of the production of final goods and services in this economy is 1 000 000 autos times $15 000 per auto, or $15 billion.

To measure GDP in terms of expenditure, we must add spending on consumption, private-sector investment, government purchases, and net exports. Consumption is 700 000 autos multiplied by $15 000, or $10.5 billion. Government purchases are 50 000 autos multiplied by $15 000, or $0.75 billion. Net exports are equal to exports (25 000 autos at $15 000, or $0.375 billion) minus imports (zero), so net exports are $0.375 billion.

But what about private-sector investment? Here we must be careful. The 200 000 autos that are sold to businesses, worth $3 billion, count as investment. But notice, too, that the auto companies produced 1 000 000 automobiles but sold only 975 000 (700 000 + 200 000 + 50 000 + 25 000). Hence 25 000 autos were unsold at the end of the year and were added to the automobile producers' inventories. This addition to producer inventories (25 000 autos at $15 000, or $0.375 billion) counts as inventory investment, which is part of total private-sector investment. Thus total private-sector investment spending equals the $3 billion worth of autos sold to businesses plus the $0.375 billion in inventory investment, or $3.375 billion.

To recap, in this economy consumption is $10.5 billion, private-sector investment (including inventory investment) is $3.375 billion, government purchases equal $0.75 billion, and net exports are $0.375 billion. Summing these four components of expenditure yields $15 billion—the same value for GDP that we got by calculating the market value of production.

EXERCISE 5.3

Extending Example 5.4, suppose that 25 000 of the automobiles purchased by households are imported rather than domestically produced. Domestic production remains at 1 000 000 autos valued at $15 000 each. Once again, find GDP in terms of (a) the market value of production and (b) the components of expenditure.

5.3 GDP AND THE INCOMES OF CAPITAL AND LABOUR

We have seen that the GDP can be thought of equally well as a measure of total value added or as a measure of total expenditure. Either method of calculating GDP gives the same final answer. A third way to think of GDP is in terms of the incomes it can be broken down into. Broadly speaking, GDP can be divided into labour income and capital income.

As Table 5.3 demonstrates, however, Statistics Canada divides income into more than just two broad categories. Pay particular attention to the following five components, the first corresponding closely to labour income and the other four corresponding roughly to capital income (though the third component also includes labour income):

- *Wages, salaries, and supplementary labour income* is the largest single income component of income-based GDP. Supplementary labour income is another word for the monetary value of fringe benefits.

TABLE 5.3
Income Components of Canadian GDP, 2007 (billions of dollars)

Component Names	Values	Percentage of GDP
Wages, salaries, and supplementary labour income	782.3	51.1%
Corporate and like profits before taxes	210.4	13.7%
Net farm and small business income	90.4	5.9%
Interest and miscellaneous investment income	68.7	4.5%
Taxes less subsidies on factors of production	66.9	4.4%
Subtotal:		
Net Domestic Product at basic prices	1237.1	80.8%
Plus:		
Capital consumption allowances	193.8	12.7%
Taxes less subsidies on products	100.1	6.5%
Statistical discrepancy	0.3	0.02%
Total:		
Gross Domestic Product at market prices	1531.3	100%

SOURCE: Adapted from the Statistics Canada CANSIM database, http://cansim2.statcan.ca. Table 380-0001 and from the Statistics Canada Web site, http://www40.statcan.ca/101/cst.01/econ03.htm.

NOTE: The statistical discrepancy is equal in magnitude and opposite in sign to the one shown in Table 5.2. The table omits a very small inventory valuation adjustment from the components but not from the total for Net Domestic Product at basic prices. Statistics Canada, *Gross Domestic Product by Industry*, July 2001, Catalogue no. 15-001-XIE, Appendix IIa, pp. 106–107, explains the difference between basic prices and the formerly employed concept of "factor cost."

- *Corporate and like profits before taxes* is a term we have used to group together the net earnings of private-sector corporations and government business enterprises after deducting an allowance (see *capital consumption allowances* below) for the consumption of fixed capital. This category includes corporate income paid out as dividends.

- *Net farm and small business income* is a term we have used to group together the net income of farmers and net income of unincorporated businesses. This category also includes most rental income.

- *Interest and miscellaneous investment income* is basically interest and other investment income (excluding dividends), less net investment income received from abroad, less interest on the public debt.

- *Capital consumption allowances* are, as the name implies, allowances for using up fixed capital in the production process. Capital consumption is also called depreciation. Roughly speaking, **capital consumption allowances** correspond to that part of income required to replace the fixed capital used up in production. Capital consumption allowances are the major source of difference between gross and net domestic product.[5]

capital consumption allowances accounting allowances for the using up of fixed capital in the production process

Figure 5.1 may help you visualize the three equivalent ways of thinking about GDP: the market value of production, the total value of expenditure, and the sum of labour income and capital income. Figure 5.1 also roughly captures the relative importance of the components of expenditure and of income.

Income and expenditure are equal in magnitude. Recall that there is a circular flow relationship between them. Figure 2.9 presented the circular flow of income and expenditure in a highly simplified model of the economy featuring labour as the only input and consumer goods and services as the only output. The revenue that firms received from selling consumer goods and services depended on the expenditure of households, which in turn depended on the wages that households

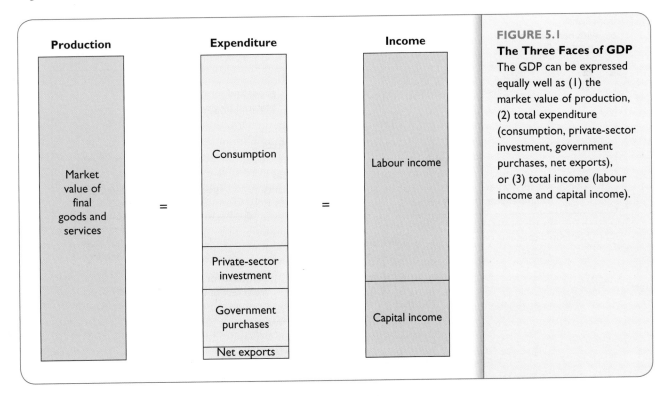

FIGURE 5.1
The Three Faces of GDP
The GDP can be expressed equally well as (1) the market value of production, (2) total expenditure (consumption, private-sector investment, government purchases, net exports), or (3) total income (labour income and capital income).

[5]We will see in Chapter 16 that in special Statistics Canada accounts dealing with economy-wide saving and investment, capital consumption allowances are mainly attributed to corporations, but also to government, households, and unincorporated businesses.

received from firms. Figure 5.2 provides a circular flow diagram with more detail than was given in Figure 2.9. It is still a simplified model in that it does not take into account, for example, financial markets and the sources of income (interest and dividends) associated with bonds, stocks, and other financial instruments. (Financial markets are discussed in Part 4.) But in addition to households and firms, Figure 5.2 accounts for the government sector and the rest of the world

FIGURE 5.2

The Circular Flow of Income and Expenditure Revisited

This diagram links income and expenditure in a model of the economy that includes firm, household, government, and rest of the world (foreign) sectors. The red arrows indicate money or dollar flows in the economy. The blue arrows indicate the flow of real inputs and goods and services.

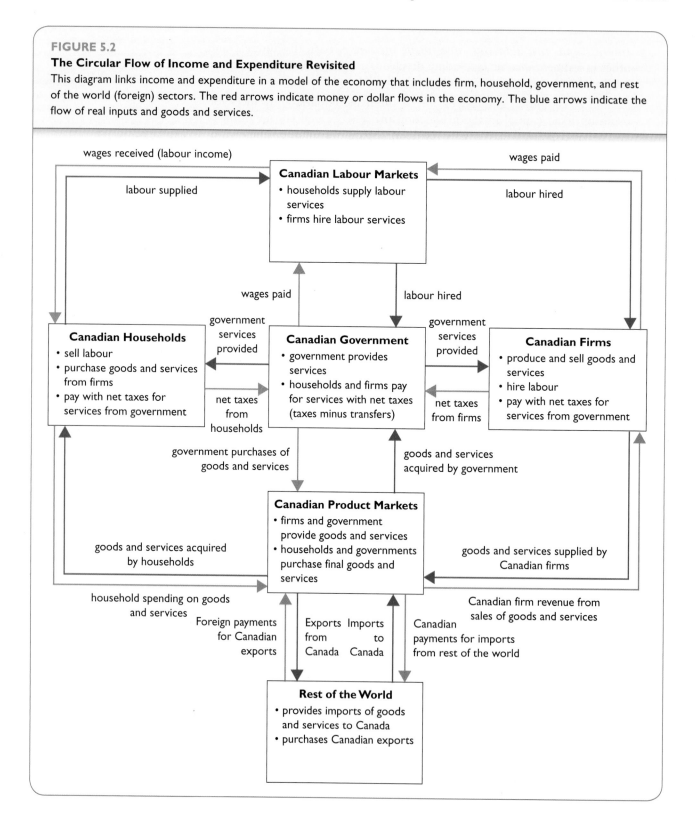

(or foreign sector) and thereby deals with additional flows of income and expenditure. Although the income and expenditure approaches to GDP measurement provide a more realistic representation of the economy than Figures 2.9 and 5.2, they too are based upon the circular flow of income and expenditure.

ECONOMIC *Naturalist*	5.1	Does GDP measurement ignore the underground economy?

It is commonly assumed that economic activities conducted "underground" in order to evade tax officials or law enforcement officers are not captured in GDP. It is true that GDP does not capture all underground activity. But a careful Statistics Canada study concluded that measured underground activity could make up as much as 1.5 percent of official Canadian GDP.[6] This is not surprising if you understand the basics of GDP measurement, such as that GDP can be measured by three different approaches, and that even the income approach is not only based upon tax returns.

For example, the method of estimating residential rents is to multiply the stock of rented dwellings by the average monthly rent paid by tenants, based upon answers to questions about rent asked in the monthly *Labour Force Survey*. Even if a high percentage of landlords cheated on their tax returns, the value of rents recorded in GDP would be quite accurate.

GDP will also pick up some underground transactions because of the way intermediate goods and services are treated in the national accounts. Suppose that a contractor pays an electrician under the table to wire a house. The electrician will not declare the income, and the value added by the electrician will be underestimated. But the house will still be sold for its market value, so the value added by the contractor will be overestimated. Provided Statistics Canada has good statistics on housing sales, the estimate of total value added will be correct.

In other cases, the underground activity may require significant amounts of an input that is measured in GDP. Suppose that someone grows marijuana at home using electric lamps for artificial light and then sells the marijuana in underground transactions. GDP will not pick up the marijuana sales directly. The extra electricity usage will be misclassified as personal consumption rather than as an intermediate input for producing marijuana. But the electricity consumption will add to the GDP total and serve as a rough proxy for the marijuana production.

5.4 NOMINAL GDP VERSUS REAL GDP

As a measure of the total production of an economy over a given period, such as a particular year, GDP is useful in comparisons of economic activity in different places. For example, GDP data for the year 2008, broken down by province, could be used to compare aggregate production in Ontario and Quebec or in British Columbia and Alberta during that year. However, economists are interested in comparing levels of economic activity not only in different *locations* but *over time* as well.

Using GDP to compare economic activity at two different points in time may give misleading answers, however, as the following example shows. Suppose for the sake of illustration that the economy produces only pizzas and calzones. The prices and quantities of the two goods in the years 2002 and 2008 are shown in Table 5.4. If we calculate GDP in each year as the market value of production, we find that GDP for 2002 is

$$\left(10 \text{ pizzas} \times \frac{\$10}{\text{pizza}}\right) + \left(15 \text{ calzones} \times \frac{\$5}{\text{calzone}}\right) = \$175.$$

The GDP for 2008 is

$$\left(20 \text{ pizzas} \times \frac{\$12}{\text{pizza}}\right) + \left(30 \text{ calzones} \times \frac{\$6}{\text{calzone}}\right) = \$420.$$

Comparing the GDP for the year 2008 to the GDP for the year 2002, we might conclude that it is 2.4 times greater ($420/$175).

[6]Statistics Canada, *The Size of the Underground Economy in Canada*, Catalogue 13-603E, No. 2.

TABLE 5.4
Prices and Quantities in 2002 and 2008

	Quantity of pizzas	Price of pizzas	Quantity of calzones	Price of calzones
2002	10	$10	15	$5
2008	20	$12	30	$6

But look more closely at the data given in Table 5.4. Can you see what is wrong with this conclusion? The quantities of both pizzas and calzones produced in the year 2008 are exactly twice the quantities produced in the year 2002. If economic activity, as measured by actual production of both goods, exactly doubled over the 6 years, why do the calculated values of GDP show a greater increase?

The answer, as you also can see from the table, is that prices as well as quantities rose between 2002 and 2008. Because of the increase in prices, the *market value* of production grew more over those 6 years than the *physical volume* of production. So in this case, GDP is a misleading gauge of economic growth during the 2002–08 period, since the physical quantities of the goods and services produced in any given year, not the dollar values, are what determine people's economic well-being. Indeed, if the prices of pizzas and calzones had risen 2.4 times between 2002 and 2008, GDP would have risen 2.4 times as well, with no increase in physical production! In that case, the claim that the economy's (physical) output had more than doubled during the 6-year period would obviously be wrong.

As this example shows, if we want to use GDP to compare economic activity at different points in time, we need some method of excluding the effects of price changes. In other words, we need to adjust for inflation. To do so, economists use a common set of prices to value quantities produced in different years. The standard approach is to pick a particular year, called the *base year*, and use the prices from that year to calculate the market value of output. When GDP is calculated using the prices from a base year, rather than the current year's prices, it is called **real GDP**, to emphasize its concern with real physical production. Real GDP is also called constant-dollar GDP. It is GDP adjusted for inflation. To distinguish real GDP, in which quantities produced are valued at base-year prices, from GDP valued at current-year prices, economists refer to the latter measure as **nominal GDP**.

real GDP a measure of GDP in which the quantities produced are valued at the prices in a base year rather than at current prices

nominal GDP a measure of GDP in which the quantities produced are valued at current-year prices; nominal GDP measures the *current dollar value* of production

---

EXAMPLE 5.5   Calculating the change in real GDP over the 2002–2008 period

Using data from Table 5.4 and assuming that 2002 is the base year, find real GDP for the years 2008 and 2002. By how much did real output grow between 2002 and 2008?

To find real GDP for the year 2008, we must value the quantities produced that year using the prices in the base year, 2002. Using the data in Table 5.4,

Year 2008 real GDP = (year 2008 quantity of pizzas × year 2002 price of pizzas) + year 2008 quantity of calzones × year 2002 price of calzones)

= (20 × $10) + (30 × $5)

= $350.

The real GDP of this economy in the year 2008 is $350. What is the real GDP for 2002?

By definition, the real GDP for 2002 equals 2002 quantities valued at base-year prices. The base year in this example happens to be 2002, so real GDP for 2002 equals 2002 quantities valued at 2002 prices, which is the same as nominal GDP for 2002. In general, in the base year, real GDP and nominal GDP are the same. We already found nominal GDP for 2002, $175, so that is also the real GDP for 2002.

We can now determine how much real production has actually grown over the 6-year period. Since real GDP was $175 in 2002 and $350 in 2008, the physical volume of production doubled between 2002 and 2008. This conclusion makes good sense, since Table 5.4 shows that the production of both pizzas and calzones exactly doubled over the period. By using real GDP, we have eliminated the effects of price changes and obtained a reasonable measure of the actual change in physical production over the 6-year span.

Of course, the production of all goods will not necessarily grow in equal proportion, as in Example 5.5. Exercise 5.4 asks you to find real GDP when pizza and calzone production grow at different rates.

EXERCISE 5.4

Suppose production and prices of pizzas and calzones in 2002 and 2008 are as follows:

	Quantity of pizzas	Price of pizzas	Quantity of calzones	Price of calzones
2002	10	$10	15	$5
2008	30	$12	30	$6

These data are the same as those in Table 5.4, except that pizza production has tripled rather than doubled between 2008 and 2002. Find real GDP in 2008 and 2002, and calculate the growth in real output over the 6-year period. (Continue to assume that 2002 is the base year.)

If you complete Exercise 5.4, you will find that the growth in real GDP between 2002 and 2008 reflects a sort of average of the growth in physical production of pizzas and calzones. Real GDP therefore remains a useful measure of overall production, even when the production of different goods and services grows at different rates.

The method of calculating real GDP just described was followed for many years by Statistics Canada. However, as of May 2001, Statistics Canada switched to more complicated method for determining real GDP called the *chain Fisher real GDP method*.[7] The new method, which updates prices each quarter, makes the official real GDP data less sensitive to the particular base year chosen. But the results obtained by the two methods are generally similar.

The older method, carried out not just for two goods as in our example but for all of GDP, involves the calculation of what Statistics Canada calls a fixed-weight GDP price index. The newer method involves the calculation of what is called an implicit chain price index. Each of these price indexes is what economists call a **GDP deflator**, a measure of the price level of goods and services included in GDP. The reason for the term *deflator* is that the price index is used to deflate nominal GDP in order to get real GDP, as the following formula shows:

GDP deflator a measure of the price level of goods and services included in GDP

$$\text{Real GDP} = \frac{\text{Nominal GDP}}{\text{GDP deflator}} \times 100.$$

[7]The change was announced in Statistics Canada, *The Daily*, 4 May 2001, http://www.statcan.ca/Daily/English/010504/p010504.htm.

> **RECAP**
>
> **NOMINAL GDP VERSUS REAL GDP**
>
> Nominal GDP is calculated using current-year prices. Real GDP, also called constant-dollar GDP, is GDP adjusted for inflation; it may be thought of as measuring the volume of production. Comparisons of economic activity at different times should always be done using real GDP, not nominal GDP.

5.5 REAL GDP IS INAPPROPRIATE AS THE SOLE ECONOMIC GOAL

Financial commentators in the news media frequently talk as if the maximum possible growth of GDP is the single appropriate goal for economic policy. Even some politicians talk this way.

Statisticians engaged in GDP accounting, however, emphasize that real GDP is not a magic number showing the level of society's well-being. Real GDP provides a measure of marketed output (and the market value of public services) that fits with the measure of employment in the *Labour Force Survey*. Such a measure is important for a number of reasons, one of which is that it provides data on something people care about—the goods and services they receive from market transactions or from the public sector. But people care about many other things as well. Because GDP is only intended to measure the market value of some things that people care about, most economists would argue that maximizing real GDP is not always the right goal for economic policy-makers.

The issue of the appropriate goals for economic policy-makers is by its very nature a normative one. Any two reasonable people with the same understanding of positive economics may differ about appropriate goals for economic policy-makers because the two of them have different values. Nevertheless, in Canada there is considerable agreement among economists on the normative economics of why maximizing growth of real GDP should not be the sole goal. To understand why, it is useful to consider two general issues: (1) shortcomings of using total GDP as a measure of the benefits people derive from the output of the economy, and (2) shortcomings of common proposals to increase GDP at the expense of other things that people value.

THE GDP TOTAL AND THE BENEFITS OF FINAL GOODS AND SERVICES

Real GDP has some shortcomings as an indicator of benefits that the average person or household derives from the output of the economy. These are not shortcomings of the way GDP is measured, but of the way some analysts interpret it.

A widely understood shortcoming of total real GDP is that the benefits people derive from economic output depend on what is available to them as individuals or households. Benefits are not primarily related to a total that would increase if the population increased while the amounts available per individual or household were held constant. This shortcoming is readily remedied by dividing GDP by the population to get GDP per capita (as we noted in Chapter 4).

A related shortcoming is that the benefits people derive from economic output depend upon the distribution of income among individuals, households, or other groups. For example, GDP per capita tells little about the benefits received by average households if a relatively small number of rich households control most of the GDP. Fortunately, data on the distribution of income among different groups is available from Statistics Canada publications like *Income Trends in Canada*.

A third shortcoming is that GDP is a measure of goods and services produced by the residents of a country. An associated concept, **gross national income (GNI)**, measures the market value of goods and services produced by factors of production owned by the residents of a country. For example, the output of a U.S.-owned auto plant is included in Canadian GDP. But while the wages paid to the auto-workers would be included in Canadian GNI, the profits of the plant would not be included. They would be included in U.S. GNI. Partly due to the high degree of foreign ownership of corporations operating in Canada, Canadian GNI has been less than Canadian GDP. (Over the period 1992–2007, for example, Canadian GNI averaged 97.5 percent of Canadian GDP.) That is, Canada had negative net foreign investment income—the value of profits, dividends, and interest flowing to foreign residents from Canadian production exceeded the value of the opposite flow. Statistics Canada now gives the GDP concept prominence over the GNI concept, but statistics on GNI are still collected and published.

Finally, "gross" concepts like GDP or GNI include the value of investment devoted to replacing capital goods that have worn out or become obsolete. While such investment is important, its growth is not necessarily related to the growth of the benefits that people derive from economic output. Thus, net measures, such as net domestic product and net national income, may be better indicators of economic performance than indicators like GDP or GNI. Net national income also has the merit of being free of the third shortcoming listed above.

gross national income (GNI) the market value of goods and services produced by factors of production owned by the residents of a country; formerly known as GNP

QUESTIONABLE PROPOSALS FOR INCREASING GDP

Over the years, there have been various proposals to increase GDP wholly or partly at the expense of other things that people value. To be able to evaluate such proposals properly, it is useful to know that GDP is only intended to measure the market value of goods and services.

Non-working time

Most Canadian workers (and workers in other industrialized countries as well) spend many fewer hours at paid employment than did Canadian workers of 100 or more years ago. In those times, industrial workers frequently worked 12 hours a day. Today, a workweek of 40 hours or less is typical in Canada. Indeed, in some European countries a workweek of 35 hours or less has become the norm. The increased non-working time available to workers today as compared to decades ago is something most workers value highly. A proposal to increase the length of the standard workweek in Canada could raise Canadian GDP. But longer hours would not necessarily make the average Canadian employee better off.

Part of the reason employees would not be better off is that they would have less time for rest and relaxation. But during off-work hours, women and men engage in a variety of activities, not just those purely for leisure. They prepare home-cooked meals, engage in volunteer activities, and so on. Longer working hours mean less time for those activities as well.

Environmental quality and resource depletion

Environmental regulations sometimes reduce the level or growth rate of GDP. But clean air, rivers, and lakes, for example, are things most Canadians value highly. To make the case for relaxing regulations designed to maintain air or water quality, it is not enough to prove that their removal would lead to an increase in GDP. Proposals regarding environmental regulation and deregulation need to be assessed by comparing costs and benefits (see Chapter 1 on the *cost–benefit principle*). Placing a dollar value on intangibles, like having a clean lake to swim in, may be difficult. But the fact that the benefits are difficult to measure does not mean that they are unimportant.

COST–
BENEFIT

Proposals to relax environmental regulations regarding exploitation of non-renewable or finite natural resources raise a special issue. At any point in time, a country has non-renewable resources of given value. They are a stock, a form of wealth. Increasing the production and sale of the natural resource will increase GDP, a flow, but the value of the stock will tend to decline.

Quality of daily life and working life

What makes a particular town or city an attractive place in which to live? Many people value such things as minimal traffic congestion, lack of noise pollution, and a low crime rate. Thus, citizens of a suburban area may be justified in opposing the construction of a new shopping centre if it would have a negative effect on their quality of life—even though the new centre may increase GDP.

Similarly, what makes a particular establishment an attractive place to work? Most employees value such things as procedural fairness in job evaluation, task assignment, and dismissals. They value scheduled breaks that allow time for relaxation with co-workers and they appreciate restrictions on involuntary overtime. They appreciate not being worked to their physical limit or beyond. Employment laws and collective agreements have evolved to deal with workplace issues like these. Sometimes, proposals to weaken employment laws or restrict unions are based on the argument that they will increase GDP. Even if a particular proposal would increase GDP, employees would rightly be concerned about the possible impact on the quality of their working lives, and might reasonably oppose it.

5.6 BUT REAL GDP PER CAPITA IS RELATED TO LIVING STANDARDS

Most economists would agree, then, that looking at the effects of a proposed policy only on the growth of real GDP is not a sufficient normative basis on which to evaluate a policy. Sound policy evaluation requires considering additional measures. Nevertheless, real GDP per person *does* tend to be positively associated with many things people value, including more and better goods and services, better health and life expectancies, and better education. Next we discuss some of the ways in which a higher real GDP per capita is associated with a higher standard of living.

AVAILABILITY OF GOODS AND SERVICES

Obviously, citizens of a country with a high real GDP per capita are likely to possess more and better goods and services (after all, that is what GDP measures). On average, people in high per capita GDP countries enjoy larger, better-constructed, and more comfortable homes, higher-quality food and clothing, a greater variety of entertainment opportunities, better access to transportation, better communications and sanitation, and other advantages. While it is easy to take a high standard of material consumption for granted if you have it, the majority of people in the world attach great importance to achieving material prosperity.

HEALTH AND EDUCATION

Beyond an abundance of consumer goods and services, a high GDP per capita brings other more basic advantages. Table 5.5 shows the differences among countries at different levels of real GDP per capita with regard to some important indicators of living standards, including life expectancy, infant mortality rates, births attended by skilled health personnel, and educational opportunity. The columns

A child born in one of the least developed countries has a 15 percent chance of dying before reaching the age of 5.

TABLE 5.5
GDP and Basic Indicators of Living Standards

Indicator	Canada	OECD countries	All developing countries	Least developed countries
GDP per person (U.S. dollars)	$33 375	$29 197	$5282	$1499
Life expectancy at birth (years)	79.8	77.8	65.5	52.7
Infant mortality rate (per 1000 births)	5	9	57	97
Probability at birth of surviving to age 65 (male)	84.9	80.5	62.6	44.3
Probability at birth of surviving to age 65 (female)	91	89.2	70.3	49.9
Births attended by skilled health personnel (percentage)	98	95	60	35
Secondary enrollment rate (as percentage of age group)	95.2	87	53	27
Female secondary age group enrollment (as percentage of male rate)	99	98	93	81

SOURCE: Statistics are from the United Nations, *Human Development Report 2007/2008*, available at http://www.undp.org/. For indicators not reported in the *Human Development Report 2007/2008* statistics from earlier issues of the *Human Development Report* were used. Note that while various indicators of living standards tend to improve with increases in GDP per person, a given percentage increase in real GDP per person may yield a smaller improvement in indicators of living standards at very high levels of real GDP per person than at low levels.

www.undp.org
**Human Development
Report**

provide data for (1) Canada; (2) countries belonging to the Organization for Economic Cooperation and Development (OECD), a group of mainly high-income countries; (3) all developing countries; and (4) the least developed countries. As the first row of Table 5.5 shows, GDP per capita in Canada and other OECD countries is several times that of the average developing country and over 19 times that of the least developed countries.

How do these large differences in GDP per capita relate to other indicators of living standards? Table 5.5 shows that on the most basic measures of human welfare, the developing countries fare much worse than the OECD countries. A child born in one of the least developed countries has a 9.7 percent $(\frac{97}{1000})$ chance of dying before reaching the age of one, and a less than 50 percent probability of surviving to age 65. The corresponding figures for the OECD countries are 0.9 percent $(\frac{9}{1000})$ and about 84 percent, respectively. A child born in an OECD country has a life expectancy of about 78 years, compared to about 53 years for a child born in one of the least developed countries. Superior nutrition, sanitation, and medical services in the richer countries account for these large discrepancies in basic welfare. For example, in OECD countries 95 percent of births are attended by skilled health personnel compared with only 35 percent in the least developed countries.

On another important dimension of living standards, education rates, countries with high levels of GDP per capita also have the advantage. As Table 5.5 shows, the percentage of children of secondary-school age who are enrolled in school is about 87 percent in OECD countries, compared with about 27 percent in the least developed countries. Note also that in the high-income countries, female youths are almost as likely as male youths to be enrolled in secondary education, whereas in the least developed countries, female youths are only four-fifths as likely as males to be enrolled.

WHY NOT MAKE GDP PER CAPITA INTO A MEASURE OF WELL-BEING?

We have seen that while real GDP per capita is closely associated with many important indicators of living standards, it does not measure everything that people care about. So why not replace GDP with a broad measure of well-being? Wouldn't this put an end to questionable proposals for increasing GDP at the expense of other things people care about?

Arguments against replacing GDP include the following:

- The GDP accounts have many uses—budget forecasting, testing macroeconomic theories, making international comparisons, and so on. Most day-to-day users of the GDP accounts would not want to see them replaced by something else.

- In particular, as we have emphasized, output in the GDP accounts is closely related to employment in the *Labour Force Survey*. If, for example, the measure of output is expanded to include an estimate of the value created in the time a retiree spends on recreational gardening, then two problems arise. Treating gardening as employment in the *Labour Force Survey* would render meaningless current distinctions between being "Employed," "Unemployed," and "Not in the labour force" (categories discussed later in this chapter). On the other hand, excluding gardening time from the measure of employment while including the value of gardening in the output measure would create a problem for productivity measurement—there would be an output without any corresponding input measure.

- GDP is measured with a high degree of objectivity in accordance with United Nations guidelines. A broader measure of well-being would lack official international approval and would require a series of more subjective valuations of difficult-to-measure activities.

- GDP should co-exist with other measures, such as the *Total Work Accounts System* published by Statistics Canada, the *Human Development Index* of the United Nations, the *Index of Economic Well-Being* (the Osberg-Sharpe index) of the Centre for the Study of Living Standards, and the *Personal Security Index* of the Canadian Council on Social Development. It should not be replaced by them.

- If questionable proposals for increasing GDP at the expense of other things that people care about come from special interests concerned with personal gain, it is unclear that replacing GDP with a broader measure would achieve anything beyond a change in the tactics employed by special interests.

BOX 5.1   THE INDEX OF ECONOMIC WELL-BEING

Canadian economists Lars Osberg and Andrew Sharpe recently developed an index of economic well-being based upon four main components:

- effective per capita consumption flows—includes consumption of marketed goods and services, government services, household production, leisure and changes in life span, and subtracts "regrettable necessities" (activities, such as cleaning up after oil spills, which are measured in GDP but are not viewed by Osberg and Sharpe as adding to human satisfaction);

- societal accumulation of stocks of productive resources—includes, among other things, changes in the value of natural resource stocks and environmental costs;
- income distribution—the intensity of poverty and the inequality of income;
- economic security from job loss and unemployment, illness, family breakup, and poverty in old age.

The index of economic well-being has been calculated for the United States, the United Kingdom, Canada, Australia, Norway, and Sweden for the period 1980 to 2001. In every case, long-term growth in the index of economic well-being was less than growth in GDP per capita, although to different degrees in different countries.[8] However, GDP per capita remains an important component in the index of economic well-being. Furthermore, some events move *all* components of the index in the same direction, at the same time—in a typical recession, for example, consumption, accumulation, economic equality and economic security *all* fall.

RECAP

REAL GDP AND LIVING STANDARDS

Real GDP is an objective measure of the market value of goods and services. But economists generally agree that maximizing real GDP growth is not appropriate as the sole normative goal for economic policy. In the first place, maximizing real GDP growth per capita makes more sense than maximizing real GDP growth. Moreover, if a policy proposal promoted growth of real GDP per capita at the expense of other things that people care about, then the policy should be evaluated according to the cost–benefit principle.

Although maximizing real GDP growth may not be appropriate as the sole normative goal for economic policy, real per capita GDP is associated with many things that people value, including consumption of more and better goods and services, better health, longer life expectancy, and higher rates of educational attainment.

There are many arguments for not replacing GDP with a broad measure of economic well-being, one of which is that real GDP can be supplemented with other measures without being replaced by them.

5.7   THE UNEMPLOYMENT RATE

In assessing the level of economic activity in a country, economists look at a variety of statistics. Besides real GDP, economists intensely analyze labour force statistics. One labour force statistic is the level of employment, and we have emphasized the link between it and GDP. But the best-known labour force statistic is the unemployment rate. The unemployment rate is a sensitive indicator

---

[8]See Lars Osberg and Andrew Sharpe, "An Index of Economic Well-Being for Selected OECD Countries," *Review of Income and Wealth*, September 2002, pp. 291–316. The most recent data on the index can be found at http://www.csls.ca.

of conditions in the labour market. When the unemployment rate is low, jobs are secure and relatively easier to find. Low unemployment is often associated with improving wages and working conditions as well, as employers compete to attract and retain workers.

We will discuss unemployment further in Chapter 7. This section will explain key labour force statistics with particular emphasis on the unemployment rate.

MEASURING UNEMPLOYMENT

Each month, Statistics Canada conducts a *Labour Force Survey* of about 54 000 households. Each person in a household who is 15 years of age or older is placed in one of three categories:

1. *Employed.* A person is considered employed during the survey week if he or she did any paid work (even for a few hours) in the context of an employee–employer relationship or self-employment or did unpaid work contributing directly to the operation of the family farm or business. A person is also considered employed if he or she had a job but was not at work during the survey week due to illness, personal or family responsibilities, vacation, or a labour dispute.

2. *Unemployed.* In general, a person is unemployed if he or she did not work during the preceding week but was available and made some effort to find work (for example, by going to a job interview) in the past four weeks. Persons on temporary layoff and persons with a job to start at a definite date in the future, however, can be counted as unemployed even if they did not actively search (the idea being that a person in either of those two categories is unemployed but is not looking for a job because he or she already has one lined up). Incidentally, the requirement of being available for work means that full-time students currently attending school and seeking full-time work to begin later are not counted as unemployed.

3. *Not in the labour force.* A person is considered to be not in the labour force if he or she did not work in the past week and did not look for work in the past four weeks. In other words, people who are neither employed nor unemployed (in the sense of looking for work but not being able to find it) are "not in the labour force." Full-time students, unpaid homemakers, retirees, and people unable to work because of illness are examples of people who are not in the labour force.

Based on the results of the survey, Statistics Canada estimates how many people in the whole country fit into each of the three categories.

To find the unemployment rate, Statistics Canada must first calculate the size of the *labour force*. The **labour force** is defined as the total number of employed and unemployed people in the economy (the first two categories of respondents to the *Labour Force Survey*). The **unemployment rate** is then defined as the number of unemployed people divided by the labour force. Notice that people who are out of the labour force (because they are in school, have retired, or are disabled, for example) are not counted as unemployed and thus do not affect the unemployment rate. In general, a high rate of unemployment indicates that the GDP growth rate has been low.

Because the *Labour Force Survey* is used to determine the total number of unemployed Canadian residents, the total is *not* a measure of how many Canadian residents are drawing Employment Insurance (EI) benefits. In fact, the number of unemployed workers in any given month is not even approximately equal to the number drawing EI benefits. For example, in November 2007 the number of Canadians receiving regular EI benefits was 503 529, about 47 percent of the 1.08 million Canadians unemployed during that month.

labour force the total number of employed and unemployed people in the economy

unemployment rate the number of unemployed people divided by the labour force

Another useful statistic is the **participation rate**, sometimes called the labour force participation rate, which is the percentage of the working-age population in the labour force (that is, the percentage that is either employed or looking for work). The participation rate for women is calculated by dividing the number of women in the labour force by the number of women of working age (aged 15 and over). Similarly, the male participation rate is the male labour force divided by the male working-age population. As Figure 5.3 shows, the gender gap in participation rates has narrowed since 1976.

participation rate the labour force divided by the working-age population

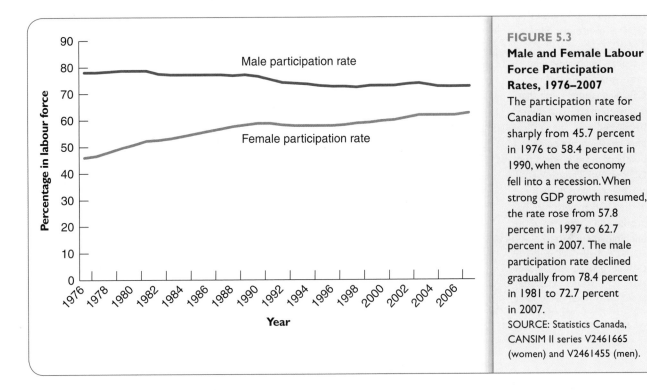

FIGURE 5.3

Male and Female Labour Force Participation Rates, 1976–2007
The participation rate for Canadian women increased sharply from 45.7 percent in 1976 to 58.4 percent in 1990, when the economy fell into a recession. When strong GDP growth resumed, the rate rose from 57.8 percent in 1997 to 62.7 percent in 2007. The male participation rate declined gradually from 78.4 percent in 1981 to 72.7 percent in 2007.
SOURCE: Statistics Canada, CANSIM II series V2461665 (women) and V2461455 (men).

Table 5.6 illustrates the calculation of key labour force statistics, using data from the *Labour Force Survey* for February 2008. In that month, 5.8 percent of the labour force was unemployed. The participation rate was 67.8 percent; that is, about two out of every three Canadian residents 15 years of age or older had a paid job or were looking for work.

TABLE 5.6
Canadian Labour Force Data, February 2008 (in thousands)

Employed	17 102.2
Plus:	
Unemployed	1056.6
Equals: Labour force	18 158.9
Plus:	
Not in the labour force	8615.9
Equals:	
Working-age (15+) population	26 774.8

Unemployment rate = unemployed/labour force = 1056.6/18 158.9 = 5.8%
Labour force participation rate = 18 158.9/26 774.8 = 67.8%

SOURCE: Adapted from Statistics Canada, *Labour Force Survey*, March 2008.

Figure 5.4 shows the Canadian unemployment rate since 1960. It shows, among other things, that the unemployment rate tends to increase sharply when GDP undergoes a sharp slowdown.

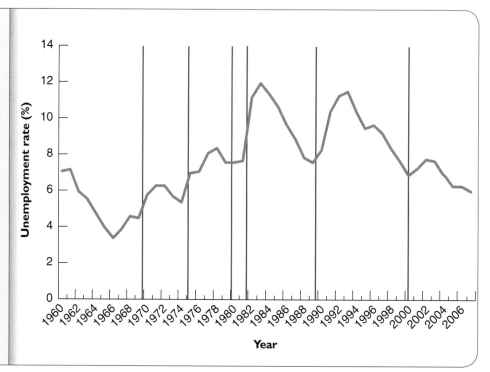

FIGURE 5.4

Canada's Unemployment Rate and Pronounced GDP Slowdowns Since 1960

Canada's unemployment rate—the fraction of the Canadian labour force that is unemployed—is shown by the red line. The vertical blue lines indicate starting points of periods when the GDP growth rate slowed sharply. A sharp decline in the GDP growth rate produces a sharp rise in the unemployment rate. SOURCE: Statistics Canada CANSIM II Series v2062815 and Historical Statistics of Canada Series D127 (total labour force).

THE COSTS OF UNEMPLOYMENT

Unemployment imposes *economic, psychological,* and *social* costs on a country. From an *economic* perspective, the main cost of unemployment is the output that is lost because the workforce is not fully utilized. Much of the burden of the reduced output is borne by the unemployed themselves, whose incomes fall when they are not working and whose skills may deteriorate from lack of use. However, society at large also bears part of the economic cost of unemployment. For example, workers who become unemployed are liable to stop paying income taxes and start receiving government support payments, such as employment insurance benefits. This net drain on the government's budget is a cost to all taxpayers.

The *psychological* costs of unemployment are felt primarily by unemployed workers and their families. Studies show that lengthy periods of unemployment can lead to a loss of self-esteem, feelings of loss of control over one's life, depression, and even suicidal behaviour.[9] The unemployed worker's family is likely to feel increased psychological stress, compounded by the economic difficulties created by the loss of income.

The *social* costs of unemployment are a result of the economic and psychological effects. People who have been unemployed for a while tend not only to face severe financial difficulties but also to feel anger, frustration, and despair. Not surprisingly, increases in unemployment tend to be associated with increases in crime, domestic violence, alcoholism, drug abuse, and other social problems. The

[9]For a survey of the literature on the psychological effects of unemployment, see William Darity, Jr., and Arthur H. Goldsmith, "Social Psychology, Unemployment and Macroeconomics," *Journal of Economic Perspectives,* #10, Winter 1996, pp. 121–140.

costs created by these problems are borne not only by the unemployed but by society in general, as more public resources must be spent to counteract these problems.

SUPPLEMENTARY MEASURES OF UNEMPLOYMENT

Canada's official unemployment rate is measured with a high level of sophistication in accordance with guidelines established by the International Labour Organization. But the official rate has been criticized, primarily for ignoring *discouraged workers* and *involuntary part-time workers*.

Discouraged workers are people who say they would like to have a job but have not made an effort to find one in the past four weeks because they believe no jobs are available to them. Because they have not engaged in a job search in the past four weeks, they are counted in the *Labour Force Survey* as being not in the labour force.

Involuntary part-time workers are people who say they would like to work full-time but are only able to find part-time work. Because they have jobs, they are counted as employed rather than unemployed.

Statistics Canada has responded to criticisms of the official unemployment rate by publishing several supplementary unemployment rate measures. Figure 5.5 shows Canada's official unemployment rate together with two of the supplementary unemployment rate measures. It also shows the official U.S. unemployment rate.

Notice that the unemployment rate that adjusts the official unemployment rate for the underutilization of labour associated with involuntary part-time workers (represented by the green line) is higher than the official Canadian rate (red line). The percentage point gap between this supplementary measure and the official unemployment rate tends to be higher when the official rate itself is high. But movements in this expanded measure are similar to movements in the official rate.

discouraged workers people who say they would like to have a job but have not made an effort to find one in the past four weeks

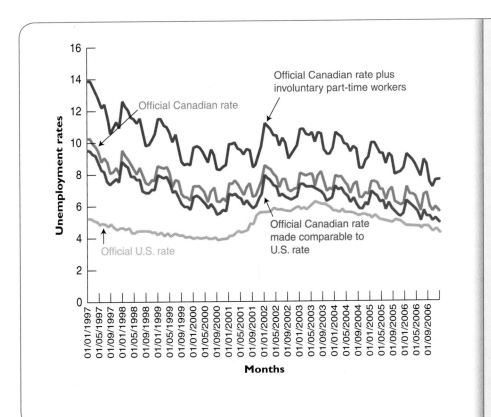

FIGURE 5.5

Official Canadian U.S. and Supplementary Canadian Unemployment Rates, Monthly, 1997–2006
Canada's official unemployment rate (red line) is shown together with two supplementary unemployment rate measures (green and blue lines). The supplementary rates tend to move in tune with the official Canadian rate. The official U.S. unemployment rate (orange line) is included for comparison.
SOURCE: Statistics Canada, *Labour Force Historical Review CD-ROM*, Catalogue no. 71F0004XCB. The U.S. rate is published by the U.S. Bureau of Labor Statistics.

Statistics Canada also adjusts the official rate to judge what Canada's unemployment rate would be if it were calculated according to U.S. labour force definitions (blue line). Like the other supplementary measures shown in Figure 5.5, it tends to move with the official Canadian rate. The Canadian rate adjusted to U.S. labour force definitions is an appropriate one for Canada–U.S. unemployment rate comparisons. It was 4.1 percentage points higher than the official U.S. unemployment rate (orange line) in 1997, when Canadian unemployment still reflected the "Great Slump" of 1990–1996 (the severe Canadian recession of 1990–1992 followed by a sluggish recovery of Canadian GDP growth). By December 2006, however, the gap between this supplementary rate and the official U.S. rate had been reduced to 0.6 percentage points.

While the various supplementary unemployment rate measures have their uses, the official unemployment rate is the best single indicator of Canadian labour-market conditions. A high official unemployment rate tends to be bad news even for those people who are employed, since raises and promotions are harder to come by in a "slack" labour market. We will discuss the causes and cures of unemployment at some length later.

SUMMARY

5.1 The basic indicator of an economy's output is *gross domestic product (GDP)*. It can be measured as the market value of the final goods and services produced in a country during a given period. Expressing output in terms of market values allows economists to aggregate the millions of goods and services produced in a modern economy.

5.1 Only *final goods and services* (which include *capital goods*) are counted in GDP, since they are the only goods and services that directly benefit final users. *Intermediate goods and services*, which are used up in the production of final goods and services, are not counted in GDP, nor are sales of existing assets, such as a 20-year-old house. Summing the value added by each firm in the production process is one of three methods of determining the value of final goods and services.

5.2 GDP can also be expressed as the sum of four types of expenditure: *consumption, private-sector investment, government purchases,* and *net exports*. These four types of expenditure correspond to the spending of households, firms, the government, and the foreign sector, respectively.

5.3 A third method of expressing GDP is in terms of income earned from domestic production. Income-based GDP can be broadly divided into labour income and capital income.

5.4 To compare levels of GDP over time, economists must eliminate the effects of inflation. They do so by measuring the market value of goods and services in terms of the prices in a base year. GDP measured in this way is called *real GDP,* while GDP measured in terms of current-year prices is called *nominal GDP*. Real GDP should always be used in making comparisons of economic activity over time.

5.5 Real GDP per person is not intended to be a measure of economic well-being. With a few exceptions, notably government purchases of goods and services (which are included in GDP at their cost of production), GDP includes only those goods and services sold in markets. It does not take into account such matters as time available to people, the value of unpaid or volunteer services, the quality of the environment, quality of life indicators such as the crime rate, or the degree of economic inequality.

5.6 Real GDP per capita is associated with living standards, however. Countries with a high real GDP per person not only enjoy high-quality consumption of goods and services, they also tend to have higher life expectancies, low rates of infant and child mortality, and high rates of school enrollment and literacy.

5.7 The unemployment rate, perhaps the best-known indicator of the state of the labour market, is based on the *Labour Force Survey*. The survey classifies all respondents aged 15 and over as employed, unemployed, or not in the labour force. The *labour force* is the sum of employed and unemployed workers—roughly speaking, people who have a job or are looking for one. The *unemployment rate* is calculated as the number of unemployed workers divided by the labour force. The *participation rate* is calculated as the labour force divided by the working-age population.

5.7 The costs of unemployment include the economic cost of lost output, the psychological costs borne by unemployed workers and their families, and the social costs associated with problems like increased crime and violence. Critics of the official unemployment rate argue that it understates "true" unemployment by excluding *discouraged workers* and *involuntary part-time workers*.

KEY TERMS

capital consumption allowances (117)
capital good (109)
consumption (111)
discouraged workers (131)
final goods or services (108)
GDP deflator (121)

government purchases (114)
gross domestic product (GDP) (106)
gross national income (GNI) (123)
intermediate goods or services (108)
labour force (128)
net exports (114)

nominal GDP (120)
participation rate (129)
private-sector investment (112)
real GDP (120)
unemployment rate (128)
value added (109)

REVIEW QUESTIONS

1. Why do economists use market values when calculating GDP? What is the economic rationale for giving high-value items more weight in GDP than low-value items?

2. Give examples of each of the four types of aggregate expenditure. Which of the four represents the largest share of GDP in Canada? Can an expenditure component be negative? Explain.

3. Al's Shoeshine Stand shined 1000 pairs of shoes last year and 1200 pairs this year. Al charged $4 for a shine last year and $5 this year. If last year is taken as the base year, find Al's contribution to both nominal GDP and real GDP in both years. Which measure would be better to use if you were trying to measure the change in Al's productivity over the past year? Why?

4. Why is maximization of real GDP inappropriate as a sole goal for economic policy?

5. True or false, and explain: A high participation rate in an economy implies a low unemployment rate.

PROBLEMS

1. How would each of the following transactions affect the GDP of Canada?
   a. The Canadian government pays $1 billion in salaries for government workers.
   b. The Canadian government pays $1 billion to Employment Insurance beneficiaries.
   c. The Canadian government pays a Canadian firm $1 billion for constructing an airport.
   d. The Canadian government pays $1 billion in interest to holders of Canadian government bonds.
   e. The Canadian government pays $1 billion to a U.S. firm for military aircraft.

2. Intelligence Incorporated produces 100 computer chips and sells them for $200 each to Bell Computers. Using the chips and other labour and materials, Bell produces 100 personal computers. Bell sells the computers, bundled with software that Bell licenses from Macrosoft at $50 per computer, to PC Charlie's for $800 each. PC Charlie's sells the computers to the public for $1000 each. Calculate the total contribution to GDP using the value-added method. Do you get the same answer by summing up the market values of final goods and services?

3. For each of the following transactions, state the effect both on Canadian GDP and on the four components of aggregate expenditure.
   a. Your mother-in-law buys a new car produced in Canada.
   b. Your mother-in-law buys a new car imported from Sweden.
   c. Your mother-in-law's car rental business buys a new car produced in Canada.
   d. Your mother-in-law's car rental business buys a new car imported from Sweden.

4. Here are some data for an economy. Find its GDP. Explain your calculation.

Consumption expenditures	$600
Exports	75
Government purchases of goods and services	200
Construction of new homes and apartments	100
Sales of existing homes and apartments	200
Imports	50
Beginning-of-year inventory stocks	100
End-of-year inventory stocks	125
Business fixed investment	100
Government payments to retirees	100
Household purchases of durable goods	150

5. The nation of Potchatoonie produces hockey pucks, cases of root beer, and back rubs. Here are data on prices and quantities of the three goods in the years 2004 and 2009.

Year	Pucks		Root beer		Back rubs	
	Quantity	Price	Quantity	Price	Quantity	Price
2004	100	$5	300	$20	100	$20
2009	125	$7	250	$20	110	$25

Assume that 2004 is the base year. Find nominal GDP and real GDP for both years.

6. The standard assumption is that the GDP deflator will rise over time and be used to reduce (or deflate) nominal GDP to real GDP of a lower dollar amount. But the implicit chain price index form of the GDP deflator dropped from 100 in the first quarter of 1997 to 99.1 by the fourth quarter of 1998. Nominal GDP increased from $870 billion in the first quarter of 1997 to approximately $928.3 billion in the fourth quarter of 1998. Use the GDP "deflator" to calculate real GDP for the fourth quarter of 1998.

7. The government is considering a policy to reduce air pollution by restricting the use of "dirty" fuels by factories. In deciding whether to implement the policy, how, if at all, should the likely effects of the policy on real GDP be taken into account? Discuss.

8. Here is a hypothetical report from a not-very-efficient survey taker: "There were 65 people in the houses I visited, 10 of them children under 15 and 10 retired; 25 people had full-time jobs, and 5 had part-time jobs. There were 5 full-time homemakers, 5 full-time students aged 15 and over, and 2 people who were ill and cannot work. The remaining people did not have jobs but all said they would like one. One of these people had not looked actively for work for 3 months, however."

Find the labour force, the unemployment rate, and the participation rate implied by the survey taker's report.

9. Ellen is downloading labour market data for the most recent month, but her connection is slow and so far this is all she has been able to get:

Unemployment rate	5.0%
Participation rate	62.5%
Not in the labour force	60 million

Find the labour force, the working-age population, the number of employed workers, and the number of unemployed workers for this high-population country.

ANSWERS TO IN-CHAPTER EXERCISES

5.1 In the text, GDP was calculated to be $64 million. If in addition Orchardia produces 5 million peaches at $0.30 each, GDP is increased by $1.5 million to $65.5 million.

5.2 The sale of stock represents a transfer of ownership of part of the assets of Benson Buggywhip, not the production of new goods or services. Hence the stock sale itself does not contribute to GDP. However, the broker's commission of $100 (2 percent of the stock sale proceeds) represents payment for a current service and is counted in GDP.

5.3 As in Example 5.4, the market value of domestic production is 1 000 000 autos multiplied by $15 000 per auto, or $15 billion.

Also as in Example 5.4, consumption is $10.5 billion and government purchases are $0.75 billion. However, because 25 000 of the autos that are purchased are imported rather than domestic, the domestic producers have unsold inventories at the end of the year of 50 000 (rather than 25 000 as in Example 5.4). Thus inventory investment is 50 000 autos times $15 000, or $0.75 billion, and total investment (autos purchased by businesses plus inventory investment) is $3.75 billion. Since exports and imports are equal (both are 25 000 autos), net exports (equal to exports minus imports) are zero. Notice that since we subtract imports to get net exports, it is unnecessary also to subtract imports from consumption. Consumption is defined as total purchases by households, not just purchases of domestically produced goods.

Total expenditure is $C + I + G + NX$ = $10.5 billion + $3.75 billion ÷ $0.75 billion + 0 = $15 billion, the same as the market value of production.

5.4 Real GDP in the year 2008 equals the quantities of pizzas and calzones produced in the year 2008, valued at the market prices that prevailed in the base year 2002. So real GDP in 2008 = (30 pizzas × $10/pizza) + (30 calzones × $5/calzone) = $450.

Real GDP in 2002 equals the quantities of pizzas and calzones produced in 2002, valued at 2002 prices, which is $175. Notice that since 2002 is the base year, real GDP and nominal GDP are the same for that year.

The real GDP in the year 2008 is $450/$175, or about 2.6 times what it was in 2002. Hence the expansion of real GDP lies between the threefold increase in pizza production and the doubling in calzone production that occurred between 2002 and 2008.

Chapter 6 Measuring the Price Level and Inflation

Your grandparents probably remember being able to buy comic books and chocolate sundaes for 25 cents. Today, the same two items might cost $4 or $5. You might conclude from this fact that kids were much better off in "the good old days." But were they really? Without more information we can't tell, because although the prices of comic books and sundaes have gone up, so have allowances. The real question is whether young people's amounts of spending money have increased as much as or more than the prices of the things they want to buy. If so, then they are no worse off today than their grandparents were as youngsters in the days when chocolate bars cost a nickel. In general, our purchasing power increases and we are better off if our income goes up at a faster rate than the overall price level does—that is, if the growth rate of our income exceeds the inflation rate.

An important benefit of studying macroeconomics is learning about the implications of inflation in order to compare changes in economic conditions over time. In this chapter, a continuation of our study of the construction and interpretation of economic data, we will see how inflation is measured and how dollar amounts, such as the price of a comic book or the hourly wage we receive, can be "adjusted" to eliminate the effects of inflation. Quantities that are measured in dollars, or other currency units, and then adjusted for inflation are called real quantities (recall, for example, the concept of real GDP in the last chapter). By working with real quantities, economists can compare real incomes, real wages, or real interest rates.

More important than the implications that inflation has for economic measurement is the impact that it has on the economy. Inflation has consequences for economic growth and income distribution, and the nature of these consequences depends on its level, its rate of change, and whether or not it is anticipated.

THE CONSUMER PRICE INDEX: MEASURING THE PRICE LEVEL

The **price level** is the overall level of prices at a point in time as measured by a price index. The basic tool economists use to measure the price level in the Canadian economy is the **consumer price index**, or CPI for short. The CPI for any period measures the cost in that period of a standard set, or basket, of goods and services *relative* to the cost of the same basket of goods and services in a fixed year, called the *base year*.

price level the overall level of prices at a point in time as measured by a price index such as the CPI

To illustrate how the CPI is constructed, suppose Statistics Canada has designated 2002 as the base year. (In fact, currently 2002 is the base year but it will change in the future.) Assume for the sake of simplicity that in 2002 a typical Canadian family's monthly household budget consisted of spending on just three items: rent on a two-bedroom apartment, hamburgers, and movie tickets. In reality, of course, families purchase hundreds of different items each month, but the basic principles of constructing the CPI are the same no matter how many items are included. Suppose, too, that the family's average monthly expenditures in 2002, the base year, were as shown in Table 6.1.

consumer price index (CPI) for any period, measures the cost in that period of a standard basket of goods and services relative to the cost of the same basket of goods and services in a fixed year, called the base year

TABLE 6.1

Monthly Household Budget of the Typical Family in 2002 (base year)

Item	Cost
Rent, two-bedroom apartment	$500
Hamburgers (60 at $2 each)	120
Movie tickets (10 at $6 each)	60
Total Expenditure	$680

Now let's fast-forward to the year 2009. Over that period, the prices of various goods and services are likely to have changed; some will have risen and some fallen. Let's suppose that by the year 2009 the rent that our family pays for the two-bedroom apartment has risen to $630. Hamburgers now cost $2.50 each, and the price of movie tickets has risen to $7 each. So, in general, prices have been rising.

By how much did the family's cost of living increase between 2002 and 2009? Table 6.2 shows that if the typical family wanted to consume the *same basket of goods and services* in the year 2009 as in the year 2002, it would have

TABLE 6.2

Cost of Reproducing the 2002 (base year) Basket of Goods and Services in Year 2009

Item	Cost (in 2009)	Cost (in 2002)
Rent, two-bedroom apartment	$630	$500
Hamburgers (60 at $2.50 each)	150	120
Movie tickets (10 at $7 each)	70	60
Total Expenditure	$850	$680

www.statcan.ca
Statistics Canada—CPI

to spend $850 per month, or $170 more than the $680 per month spent in 2002. In other words, to live the same way in the year 2009 as in the year 2002, the family would have to spend 25 percent more ($170/$680) each month. So, in this example, the cost of living for the typical family rose 25 percent between 2002 and 2009.

Statistics Canada calculates the official consumer price index (CPI) using essentially the same method. The first step in deriving the CPI is to pick a base year and determine the basket of goods and services that were consumed by the typical family during that year. Statistics Canada determines the basket using information obtained from family expenditure surveys. Let's call the basket of goods and services that results the *base-year basket*. Then, each month interviewers operating out of the regional offices of Statistics Canada gather tens of thousands of price quotations on over 600 goods and services. The CPI in any given year is computed using this formula:

$$\text{CPI} = \frac{\text{Cost of base-year basket of goods and services in current year}}{\text{Cost of base-year basket of goods and services in base year}} \times 100.$$

Returning to the example of the typical family that consumes three goods, we can calculate the CPI in the year 2009 as

$$\text{CPI in year 2009} = \frac{\$850}{\$680} \times 100 = 125.$$

In other words, in this example the cost of living in the year 2009 is 25 percent higher than it was in 2002, the base year. Notice that the base-year CPI is always equal to 100. The CPI for a given period (such as a month or year) measures the cost of living in that period *relative* to what it was in the base year.

EXAMPLE 6.1   Measuring the typical family's cost of living

Suppose that in addition to the three goods and services the typical family consumed in 2002, they also bought four sweaters at $30 each. In the year 2009 the same sweaters cost $50 each. The prices of the other goods and services in 2002 and 2009 were the same as in Table 6.2. Find the change in the family's cost of living between 2002 and 2009.

In the example in the text, the cost of the base-year (2002) basket was $680. Adding four sweaters at $30 each raises the cost of the base-year basket to $800. What does this same basket (including the four sweaters) cost in 2009? The cost of the apartment, the hamburgers, and the movie tickets is $850, as before. Adding the cost of the four sweaters at $50 each raises the total cost of the basket to $1050. The CPI equals the cost of the basket in 2009 divided by the cost of the basket in 2002 (the base year) multiplied by 100, or ($1050/$800) × 100 = 131. We conclude that the family's cost of living rose 31 percent between 2002 and 2009.

EXERCISE 6.1   **Returning to the three-good example in Tables 6.1 and 6.2, find the year 2009 CPI if the rent on the apartment falls from $500 in 2002 to $400 in 2009. The prices for hamburgers and movie tickets in the two years remain the same as in the two tables.**

---

price index a measure of the average price of a given class of goods or services relative to the price of the same goods and services in a base year

The CPI is not itself the price of a specific good or service; it is a *price index*. A **price index** measures the average price of a class of goods or services relative to the price of those same goods or services in a base year. The CPI is an especially well-known price index, one of many that economists use to assess economic trends. For example, because manufacturers tend to pass on increases in the prices of raw materials to their customers, economists use Statistics Canada's *Raw Materials Price Index* (which includes goods not produced in Canada) to forecast changes in the prices of Canadian manufactured goods. Other price indexes supplied by Statistics Canada include the *Industrial Product Price Index* (which measures the prices that producers in Canada receive as their goods leave their production facilities) and the price indexes of the national accounts. One of the price indexes of the national accounts, the *GDP deflator* we mentioned in Chapter 5, is particularly important because it measures the price level of all the goods and services making up GDP.

The CPI captures the change in prices affecting average households. Suppose you were to construct a price index to measure changes in the prices facing Canadian university students over the past decade. In general, how would you go about constructing such an index? Why might changes in a price index for university student expenditures differ from changes in the CPI?

EXERCISE 6.2

6.2   INFLATION

The CPI provides a measure of the average *level* of prices relative to prices in the base year. *Inflation,* in contrast, is a measure of how fast the average price level is *changing* over time. The **rate of inflation** is defined as the annual percentage rate of change in the price level, typically as measured by the CPI. For example, the Canadian CPI had a value of 110.2 in February 2007 and a value of 112.2 in February 2008. The inflation rate between February 2007 and February 2008 is the percentage increase in the price level, or 100 times the increase in the price level (112.2 − 110.2 = 2.0) divided by the initial price level (110.2), which is equal to 1.8 percent.

rate of inflation the annual percentage rate of change in the price level as measured, for example, by the CPI

Calculating inflation rates: 1972–1976

EXAMPLE 6.2

The CPIs for the years 1972 through 1976 are shown below. Find the rates of inflation between 1972 and 1973, 1973 and 1974, 1974 and 1975, and 1975 and 1976.

Year	CPI
1972	21.9
1973	23.6
1974	26.2
1975	29.0
1976	31.1

The inflation rate between 1972 and 1973 is the percentage increase in the price level between those years, or

$$\frac{(23.6 - 21.9)}{21.9} = \frac{1.7}{21.9} = 0.0776 = 7.8 \text{ percent.}$$

Do the calculations to confirm that inflation during each of the next three years was 11, 10.7, and 7.2 percent, respectively. During the 1970s, inflation rates were much higher than the 1 to 3 percent annual inflation rates that have prevailed in recent years.

EXERCISE 6.3

Below are CPIs for the years 1929 through 1933. Find the rates of inflation between 1929 and 1930, 1930 and 1931, 1931 and 1932, and 1932 and 1933.

Year	CPI
1929	9.2
1930	9.1
1931	8.2
1932	7.5
1933	7.1

How did inflation rates in the 1930s differ from those of the 1970s?

deflation a situation in which the prices of most goods and services are falling over time so that inflation is negative

The results of the calculations for Exercise 6.3 include some examples of *negative* inflation rates. A situation in which the prices of most goods and services are falling over time so that inflation is negative is called **deflation**. The early 1930s was the last time Canada experienced significant deflation. Japan experienced relatively mild deflation beginning in the late 1990s; in February 2008 Japan achieved a decade-high inflation rate of one percent, perhaps signalling the country's long hoped-for escape from a decade of deflation.

6.3   ADJUSTING FOR INFLATION

The CPI is an extremely useful tool. Not only does it allow us to measure changes in the *cost of living* (in terms of changes in the price of a fixed basket of goods and services), it can also be used to adjust economic data to eliminate the effects of inflation. In this section, we will see how the CPI can be used to convert quantities measured at current dollar values into real terms, a process called *deflating*. We will also see that the CPI can be used to convert real quantities into current-dollar terms, a procedure called *indexing*. Both procedures are useful not only to economists but to anyone who needs to adjust payments, accounting measures, or other economic quantities for the effects of inflation.

DEFLATING A NOMINAL QUANTITY WITH THE CPI

nominal quantity a quantity that is measured in terms of its current dollar value

An important use of the CPI is to adjust **nominal quantities**—quantities measured at their current dollar values—for the effects of inflation. To illustrate, consider a Canadian family with a total income of $50 000 in 2002 and $55 000 in the year 2007. Did the family experience an increase in purchasing power over the ten-year period?

Without any more information than this, we might be tempted to say yes. After all, the family's income has risen by 10 percent over the period. But prices might also have been rising, as fast or faster than the family's income. In fact, the CPI for Canada rose from 100 in 2002 to 111.5 for 2007. This means that prices rose by 11.5 percent. Since the family's income rose by only 10 percent, the family's purchasing power has declined.

real quantity a quantity that is measured in constant dollar terms

We can make a more precise comparison of the family's purchasing power in 2002 and 2007 by calculating its income in those years in *real terms*. In general, a **real quantity** is one that is measured in base-year dollars, also known as *constant dollars*. To convert a nominal quantity to a real quantity, we must divide the nominal quantity by a price index for the period, as shown in Table 6.3. The calculations in the table show that in *real* or purchasing power terms, the family's income actually *decreased* by $673, or by about 1.3 percent of the initial real income of $50 000, between 2002 and 2007.

The problem for this family is that though its income has been rising in nominal (dollar) terms, it has not kept up with inflation. Dividing a nominal quantity

TABLE 6.3

Comparing the Real Values of a Family's Income in 2002 and 2007

Year	Nominal family income	CPI	Real family income =Nominal family income/CPI
2002	$50 000	100	$50 000
2007	$55 000	111.5	$100 \times \left(\dfrac{\$55\ 000}{111.5} \right) = \$49\ 327$

by a price index to express the quantity in real terms is called **deflating** the nominal quantity. (Be careful not to confuse the idea of deflating a nominal quantity with deflation, or negative inflation. The two concepts are different.)

Dividing a nominal quantity by the current value of a price index to measure it in real or purchasing power terms is a very useful tool. It can be used to eliminate the effects of inflation from comparisons of any nominal quantity—workers' wages, healthcare expenditures, components of federal or provincial budgets—over time. Why does this method work? In general, if you know both how many dollars you have spent on a given item and the item's price, you can figure out how many of the items you bought (by dividing your expenditures by the price). For example, if you spent $100 on hamburgers last month and hamburgers cost $2.50 each, you can determine that you purchased 40 hamburgers. Similarly, if you divide a family's dollar income or expenditures by a price index, which is a measure of the average price of its purchased goods and services, you will obtain a measure of the real quantity of purchased goods and services. Such real quantities are sometimes referred to as *inflation-adjusted* quantities.

Clearly, in comparing wages or earnings at two different points in time, we must adjust for changes in the price level. Doing so yields the **real wage**—the wage measured in terms of real purchasing power. The real wage for any given period is calculated by dividing the nominal (dollar) wage by the CPI for that period.

deflating (a nominal quantity) the process of dividing a nominal quantity by a price index (such as the CPI) to express the quantity in real terms

real wage the wage paid to workers measured in terms of real purchasing power

Real wages of Canadian hourly paid employees

EXAMPLE 6.3

Hourly paid employees (as distinguished from salaried employees) constituted about half of all Canadian employees in 2006. Statistics Canada reports that the average hourly paid employee earned $16.67 per hour in 2002 and $18.02 per hour in 2006. Determine what happened to the real wages of these employees between these two years.

To find the real wage in 2002 and 2006, we need to know that the CPI was 100 in 2002, the base year, and 109.1 in 2006. In the base year of 2002 the nominal wage equalled $16.67 and, by definition, the real wage was also $16.67. Deflating the 2006 nominal wage of $18.02 by the 2006 CPI, we find that the real wage in 2006 was only $16.52. In real or purchasing power terms, we find that the real hourly wage of paid employees fell between 2002 and 2006 even though the nominal or dollar wage increased by about 8 percent.

Figure 6.1 shows nominal wages and real wages for Canadian hourly paid employees for the period 1983–2006. Notice the dramatic difference between the two trends. Looking only at nominal wages, one might conclude that hourly paid employees were much better paid in 2006 than in 1983. But once wages are adjusted for inflation, we see that in terms of buying power the wages of hourly paid employees have stagnated at least since 1983. This example illustrates the crucial importance of adjusting for inflation when comparing dollar values over time.

FIGURE 6.1

Nominal and Real Wages of Hourly Paid Employees in Canada, 1983–2006

Although nominal wages of hourly paid employees have risen in Canada over the past two decades, real wages have stagnated. Notice that the real wage and the nominal wage are equal in 2002, the base year.

SOURCE: Adapted from Statistics Canada, CANSIM II series v256149 (nominal wage, old series), v1809109 (nominal wage, new series), and v41693271 (CPI). The figure shows the new series for the years 1991–2006. For earlier years, the old series is scaled up to give the same value as the new series for 1991.

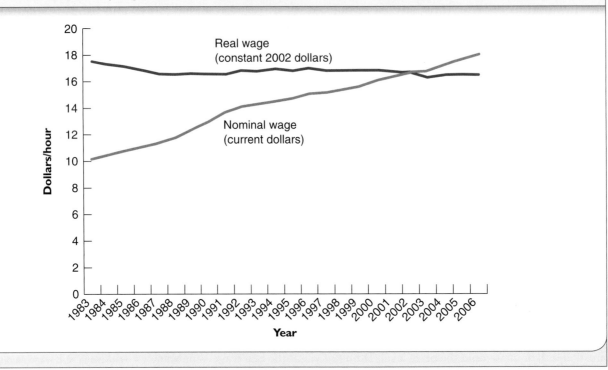

EXERCISE 6.4

From 1995 to 2003 the minimum wage in Ontario was fixed at $6.85. The Ontario CPI was 86.8 in 1995 and 102.7 in 2003. In real terms, by how much did the Ontario minimum wage decline between 1995 and 2003?

DEFLATING BY THE CPI VERSUS DEFLATING BY THE GDP DEFLATOR

The CPI is commonly used to deflate nominal wages and incomes. But the CPI is not the only general price index. In particular, the GDP deflator (discussed in Chapter 5) is a price index for all the goods and services making up GDP, and it can be used to do more than just deflate GDP. For example, while the nominal wage deflated by CPI gives a good measure of the real wage from the standpoint of workers, some economists think that the nominal wage divided by the GDP deflator provides a better measure of the real wage from the standpoint of employers.

Why would it make any difference whether one uses the CPI or the GDP deflator? First, the two can differ because the CPI includes import prices, whereas import prices are excluded from the GDP deflator (since imports are subtracted from exports in calculating GDP). Second, the CPI includes only the prices of consumer goods and services, while the GDP deflator also includes the prices of producer and intermediate goods. The third major difference is that the CPI compares the price of a fixed basket of goods and services today with the price of the same basket in the base year, whereas the composition of the goods and services used to compute the GDP deflator changes regularly.

INDEXING TO MAINTAIN BUYING POWER

The consumer price index can also be used to convert real quantities to nominal quantities. Suppose, for example, that in the year 2002 a married couple with children are divorced and they reach a settlement whereby the husband agrees to pay the wife spousal support of $1000 per month (in addition to child support payments) for five years. Suppose too that the agreement specifies that the spousal support payments should increase to prevent inflation from eroding their purchasing power.

The nominal or dollar amount the husband should pay the wife in the year 2007 to maintain the purchasing power of the spousal support payments depends on how much prices rose between 2002 and 2007. The CPI rose from 100 in 2002 to 111.5 in 2007, or by about 11.5 percent. For the spousal support payments to "keep up with inflation," they would be $1115 per month in 2007. In general, to keep purchasing power constant, the dollar benefit must be increased each year by the percentage increase in the CPI.

The practice of increasing a nominal quantity according to changes in a price index is called **indexing**. As we will see later in this chapter, indexing is used to some degree in Canada, particularly by the public sector.

> *indexing* the practice of increasing a nominal quantity each period by an amount equal to the percentage increase in a specified price index; indexing prevents the purchasing power of the nominal quantity from being eroded by inflation

---

RECAP ⤴

METHODS TO ADJUST FOR INFLATION

Deflating To correct a nominal quantity, such as a family's dollar income, for changes in the price level, divide it by a price index such as the CPI. This process, called *deflating* the nominal quantity, expresses the nominal quantity in terms of real purchasing power. If nominal quantities from two different years are deflated by a price index with the same base year, the purchasing power of the two deflated quantities can be compared.

Indexing To ensure that a nominal payment, such as a social insurance benefit, represents a constant level of real purchasing power, increase the nominal quantity each year by a percentage equal to the rate of inflation for that year.

6.4 NOMINAL VERSUS REAL INTEREST RATES

We have seen how to adjust nominal family income for inflation to get real family income and how to adjust nominal wages or salaries to get real wages or salaries. Our next task is to explain how to adjust nominal interest rates to get real interest rates. We will also introduce the hypothesis, known as the *Fisher effect*, that high inflation rates will tend to produce high nominal interest rates.

The **nominal interest rate** is the type of interest rate you are apt to see reported in the financial pages of a newspaper or posted on a sign in your bank branch. It can be thought of as the price paid per dollar borrowed per year. If you borrow $1000 now and in a year's time you repay the principal of $1000 plus interest of $100, then your nominal interest rate is 10 percent (the interest payment divided by the principal, all multiplied by 100 for expression as a percentage). Looked at from the standpoint of a lender, the nominal interest rate is the annual percentage increase in the nominal, or current dollar, value of an asset. The **real interest rate**, like the real wage rate, is something we calculate given the inflation rate and the relevant nominal rate.

> *nominal interest rate* the type of interest rate you usually encounter in everyday life—the price paid per dollar borrowed per year

> *real interest rate* the nominal interest rate minus the inflation rate

More precisely, we can calculate the real interest rate for any financial asset, from a savings account to a government bond, by subtracting the rate of inflation from the market or nominal interest rate on that asset.[1] So if the nominal interest rate on short-term government bonds equals 6 percent and the inflation rate equals 3 percent, then the real interest rate on short-term government bonds is 3 percent. Or if the nominal interest rate on outstanding credit card debt (an asset from the perspective of the lender) is 17 percent and the inflation rate equals 3 percent, then the real rate of interest for credit-card borrowing is 14 percent.

We can write this definition of the real interest rate in mathematical terms:

$$r = i - \pi$$

where r = the real interest rate,
i = the nominal, or market, interest rate,
π = the inflation rate.

EXAMPLE 6.4	**Real interest rates in recent decades**

Following are interest rates on short-term Canadian federal government bonds for selected years since 1970. Ignoring the impact of taxation, in which of these years did the financial investors who bought government bonds get the best deal? The worst deal?

Financial investors and lenders do best when the real (not the nominal) interest rate is high, since the real interest rate measures the increase in their purchasing power.

Year	Nominal interest rate (%)	Inflation rate (%)	Real interest rate (%)
1970	6.0	3.4	2.6
1975	7.4	10.9	−3.5
1980	12.7	10.1	2.6
1981	17.8	12.4	5.4
1987	8.2	4.4	3.8
1990	12.8	4.8	8.0
1995	7.0	2.2	4.8
2000	5.5	2.7	2.8
2003	2.9	2.8	0.1
2007	4.1	2.2	1.9

We can calculate the real interest rate for each year by subtracting the inflation rate from the nominal interest rate. The results, as shown in the column above headed "Real interest rate (%)," are 2.6 percent for 1970, −3.5 percent for 1975, 2.6 percent for 1980, 5.4 percent for 1981, 3.8 percent for 1987, 8.0 percent for 1990, 4.8 percent for 1995, 2.8 percent for 2000, 0.1 percent for 2003, and 1.9 percent for 2007.

For purchasers of government bonds, then, the best of these years was 1990, when they enjoyed a real return of 8.0 percent, a higher real return than associated with the whopping 17.8 percent nominal interest rate of 1981. The

[1]An alternative way of calculating the real interest rate takes into account not just the change in the purchasing power of the loan, but also the change in the purchasing power of the interest payments.

worst year was 1975, when their real return was actually negative. In other words, despite receiving 7.4 percent nominal interest, financial investors ended up losing buying power in 1975, as the inflation rate exceeded the interest rate on their investments.

Figure 6.2 shows the real interest rate in Canada since 1962 as measured by the nominal interest rate paid on the federal government's short-term bonds minus the inflation rate. Note that real interest rates were negative for several years in the 1970s but were high during the 1980s and reached a peak in 1990. They declined after the early 1990s, but until 2001 they still tended to be somewhat higher than during the 1960s. Over the period shown, the inflation rate was always positive so the nominal rate always exceeded the real rate. In 1994, when the inflation rate fell to nearly zero, the nominal and real interest rates were nearly the same. If the inflation rate had actually dropped below zero (that is, if there had been deflation), then the real interest rate would have exceeded the nominal rate.

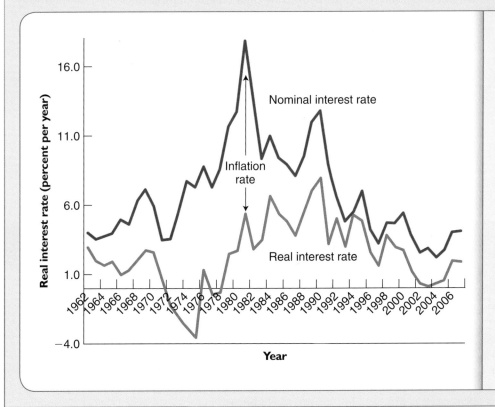

FIGURE 6.2

Real and Nominal Interest Rates in Canada, 1962–2007

The real interest rate (red line) is the nominal interest rate (blue line) minus the rate of CPI inflation. Real interest rates rose sharply during the 1980s, especially at the end of the decade. They declined after the early 1990s but until the slowdown of 2001, they still tended to be somewhat higher than during the 1960s. SOURCE: Adapted from the Statistics Canada, CANSIM II series v122531 (3 month Government of Canada treasury bill yields) and v41693271 (CPI).

The discussion above deals with real and nominal returns before taxation. But suppose that a financial investor pays a 40 percent rate of income tax on nominal interest earnings (and has no access to tax breaks like the Registered Retirement Savings Program). Then if the nominal interest rate is, say, 6 percent, the after-tax nominal interest rate will be 3.6 percent. The after-tax real interest rate will equal the after-tax nominal interest rate minus the inflation rate. If, for example, the inflation rate happens to equal the after-tax nominal interest rate, then the after-tax real interest rate will be zero.

Given these assumptions and definitions, examine the after-tax real returns in 1980 and 2007 using the interest rate and inflation rate data given in Example 6.4. The before-tax real returns, 2.6 percent in 1980 and 1.9 percent in 2007, are fairly similar. How do the after-tax real returns compare?

EXERCISE 6.5

ANTICIPATED INFLATION AND THE FISHER EFFECT

Economists generally assume that people are forward-looking. People take actions not just in response to past events but in the expectation of future events. To give a simple illustration, Canadian shopping malls regularly enjoy an upsurge in business during November and December due to Christmas shopping. The action of shopping during November and December comes before the event of Christmas on December 25.

People also take actions based upon expectations about uncertain economic outcomes, such as investors buying a company's shares in the hope the shares will go up in value. If expectations turn out to be correct, economists say that the outcome was *anticipated*. If the expectations prove wrong, outcomes are *unanticipated*.

So if the inflation rate for a given period fits with general expectations people had for it in the previous period, economists say that there has been **anticipated inflation**. If the inflation rate proves to be considerably higher or lower than generally expected, there has been **unanticipated inflation**.[2]

With the concepts of anticipated and unanticipated inflation, we can explain why nominal interest rates tend to be high when inflation rates are high and low when inflation rates are low.

Suppose inflation has recently been high, so borrowers and lenders anticipate that it will be high in the near future. We would expect lenders to raise their nominal interest rate so that their real rate of return will be unaffected. For their part, borrowers are willing to pay higher nominal interest rates when inflation is high, because they understand that the higher nominal interest rate only serves to compensate the lender for the loan being repaid in dollars of reduced real value—in real terms, their cost of borrowing is unaffected by an equal increase in the nominal interest rate and the inflation rate. Conversely, when inflation is low, lenders do not need to charge as high a nominal interest rate to ensure a given real return. Thus, nominal interest rates will be high when anticipated inflation is high and

anticipated inflation when the rate of inflation turns out to be roughly what most people had expected

unanticipated inflation when the rate of inflation turns out to be substantially different from what most people had expected

---

ECONOMIC Naturalist   6.1   Bad month to take out a mortgage

Why was September 1981 an incredibly bad month to take out a five-year mortgage? The answer might seem obvious from the average interest rate for five-year mortgages signed in Canada that month—an astounding 21.5 percent. That's about three times as high as the average five-year mortgage rate during 2008, for example.

But the 21.5 percent rate is a nominal one, and nominal rates tend to be high when inflation rates are high. In late August 1981, Statistics Canada had announced that inflation between July 1980 and July 1981 had been 12.9 percent. So a borrower taking out a mortgage in September 1981 would typically be doing so with the idea that inflation was running at an annual rate of about 12.9 percent. Subtracting 12.9 percent inflation from a 21.5 percent nominal rate yields a real interest rate of 8.6 percent.

It is true that a real interest rate of 8.6 percent on a five-year mortgage is no bargain by historical standards. The average rate over the 1981–2001 period was about 6.9 per-

cent. But real mortgage interest rates have been higher—for example, they hovered around 10 percent for most of 1994.

So why was September 1981 such a bad month to take out a five-year mortgage? Inflation rates dropped to about 4 percent within two years and stayed at about 4 percent through to September 1986. Those who borrowed at 21.5 percent interest knew that their nominal mortgage payments would be high but they expected that their nominal incomes would be growing in line with inflation of about 12.9 percent. Instead, inflation rates declined and so did nominal income growth rates. While a 21.5 percent nominal rate corresponded to an 8.6 percent real interest rate in September 1981, for over half of the mortgage period (when inflation averaged 4 percent) it corresponded to a crippling 17.5 percent real rate.

In short, September 1981 was an incredibly bad month to take out a mortgage because borrowers failed to anticipate the sharp *disinflation* (fall in the inflation rate) that followed.

---

[2]Some economists use these terms differently. They define anticipated inflation as that part of any actual inflation rate that people anticipated and they define unanticipated inflation as the difference between the actual inflation rate that occurs and the inflation rate people had anticipated.

FIGURE 6.3

Inflation and Nominal Interest Rates in Canada, 1962–2007
The tendency for nominal interest rates to be high when the inflation rate is high and low when inflation is low is called the Fisher effect. Some evidence for the Fisher effect is shown in the figure. For example, nominal interest rates were considerably lower in the low-inflation 1960s and the 1996–2007 period than in the high-inflation, 1973–1982 period. SOURCE: Adapted from the Statistics Canada, CANSIM II series v122531 (3 month Government of Canada treasury bill yields) and v41693271 (CPI).

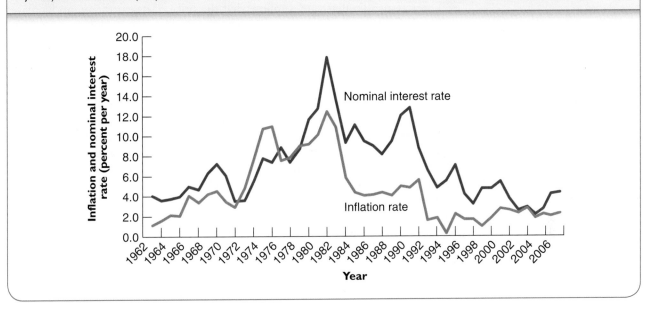

low when anticipated inflation is low. This tendency for nominal interest rates to follow inflation rates is called the **Fisher effect**, after the early twentieth-century American economist Irving Fisher who first pointed out the relationship.

Some evidence for the Fisher effect is shown in Figure 6.3. Nominal interest rates were much lower in the low-inflation 1960s than in the high-inflation 1973–1982 period. Nominal interest rates were also lower in the low-inflation years of 1992–2007 than they were in the moderate-inflation years of 1983–1991. But the relationship between nominal interest rates and the inflation rate is not exact.

Fisher effect the tendency for nominal interest rates to be high when inflation is high and low when inflation is low

6.5 TYPES OF PRICE CHANGES

Economists have developed precise terminology for describing different types of price changes. This terminology is essential for understanding analysis of the consequences of inflation.

THE PRICE LEVEL, RELATIVE PRICES, AND INFLATION

Economists distinguish carefully between the *price level* and the *relative price* of a good or service. The price level is a measure of the overall level of prices at a particular point in time as measured by a price index such as the CPI. Recall that the inflation rate is the percentage change in the price level from year to year. In contrast, a **relative price** is the price of a specific good or service *in comparison to* the prices of other goods and services. In Chapter 3 when we looked at price determination in specific markets using supply and demand diagrams, we were dealing with relative price determination. The diagrams were drawn under the assumption that all else was equal, including the general price level.

relative price the price of a specific good or service *in comparison* to the prices of other goods and services

How do we measure a relative price change when the price level also changes? For example, if the price of gasoline were to rise by 10 percent while the prices of other goods and services were rising on average by 3 percent, the relative price of gasoline would increase. But if gasoline prices rose by 3 percent while other prices rose by 10 percent, the relative price of gasoline would decrease. That is, gasoline would become cheaper relative to other goods and services, even though it would not become cheaper in absolute terms.

Why is the distinction between relative price changes and changes in the price level important? To illustrate, suppose that the price of gas at the pump increases by 20 percent because of a new tax to reduce carbon emissions from gasoline consumption, but the overall price level is unaffected. Some people might demand that the government do something about this "inflation." But while the increase in gas prices hits the wallets of gasoline consumers, is it an example of inflation? In this example, the overall price level is unaffected so inflation is not an issue. What upsets some gasoline consumers is the change in the relative price of gasoline, particularly compared to the price of labour (wages). By increasing the cost of using gasoline, the increase in the relative price of gasoline makes driving a car more expensive.

In general, changes in relative prices are not the same as a rise in the overall price level. Increases in the prices of some goods could well be counterbalanced by decreases in the prices of other goods, in which case the price level and the inflation rate would be largely unaffected. Conversely, in theory inflation can exist without changes in relative prices. Imagine, for example, that all prices in the economy, including wages and salaries, go up exactly 5 percent each year. The inflation rate is 5 percent, but relative prices are not changing. Indeed, because wages (the price of labour) and other sources of income are increasing by 5 percent per year, people's ability to buy goods and services is unaffected by the inflation.

One reason to distinguish between increases in the average price level (inflation) and increases in the relative prices of specific goods is that the appropriate responses to the two issues may be quite different. To counteract high inflation in an economy that is expanding too rapidly, it may be appropriate (as we will see) for the government to make changes in macroeconomic policies, such as monetary or fiscal policies. But it would not be appropriate for the government to make changes in its macroeconomic policies in response to an increase in gasoline prices caused by the imposition of a carbon tax.

EXAMPLE 6.5	**How to calculate changes in relative prices**

Suppose the value of the CPI is 120 in the year 2015, 132 in 2016, and 140 in 2017. Assume also that the price of oil increases 8 percent between 2015 and 2016 and another 8 percent between 2016 and 2017. What is happening to the price level, the inflation rate, and the relative price of oil?

The price level can be measured by the CPI. Since the CPI is higher in 2016 than in 2015 and higher still in 2017 than in 2016, the price level is rising throughout the period. The inflation rate is the percentage increase in the CPI. Since the CPI increases by 10 percent between 2015 and 2016, the inflation rate between those years is 10 percent. However, the CPI increases only about 6 percent between 2016 and 2017 ($140 \div 132 = 1.06$), so the inflation rate decreases to about 6 percent between those years. The decline in the inflation rate implies that although the price level is still rising, it is doing so at a slower pace than the year before.

The price of oil rises 8 percent between 2015 and 2016. But because the general inflation over that period is 10 percent, the relative price of oil—that is, its price relative to all other goods and services—falls by about 2 percent (8 percent − 10 percent = −2 percent). Between 2016 and 2017 the price of oil rises by another 8 percent, while the general inflation rate is about 6 percent. Hence the relative price of oil rises between 2016 and 2017 by about 2 percent (8 percent − 6 percent).

TERMINOLOGY USED TO DESCRIBE OVERALL PRICE CHANGE

The CPI measures the level of overall prices and the inflation rate is typically calculated by the percentage change in the CPI. But the price level and the inflation rate are not the only terms economists use to describe overall price change in the economy. In debates about monetary policy, for example, additional specialized terms are employed.

Figure 6.4 uses hypothetical data to show how change in the CPI is related to the CPI inflation rate and to several specialized terms for describing overall price changes. The blue line shows the value of the CPI in periods from 0 to 12. You can think of the periods as corresponding to calendar years. The red line shows the inflation rate. For any period, it is calculated as

$$100 \times \frac{(\text{CPI current period} - \text{CPI previous period})}{\text{CPI previous period}}.$$

The beige boxes show the specialized terminology used to describe overall price changes in the periods associated with the boxes.

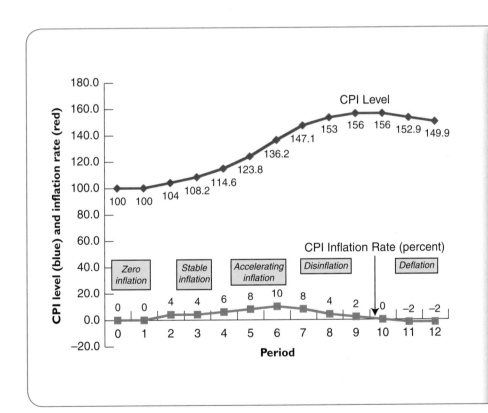

FIGURE 6.4

The Terminology of Price Change Illustrated
The CPI is shown by the blue line. The CPI inflation rate (red line), is the percentage change in the CPI. When the CPI stays the same from one period to the next, we have *zero inflation*. When it rises but at a constant rate, we have *stable inflation*. The CPI rising at a rate that increases from one period to the next indicates *accelerating inflation*. When it rises but at a rate that decreases from one period to the next, we have *disinflation*. And when the CPI falls from one period to the next, we have *deflation*.

In periods 0 and 1, the CPI is 100. Because the CPI undergoes no change between periods 0 and 1, we calculate an inflation rate of 0 percent for period 1. Economists use the term **zero inflation** to describe a situation like this when the CPI does not change from one period to the next. (Note that we have arbitrarily assumed a value of 0 for the inflation rate in period 0.) In Canadian history, zero inflation prevailed during the period 1926–1930 when the CPI held quite stable at a level of about 9.1 (2002 base year) and the inflation rate fluctuated around 0 (see Figure 4.4 for data on the Canadian inflation rate for the period 1915–2007).

zero inflation when the price level stays roughly constant from one year to the next

stable inflation when the inflation rate stays roughly constant from one year to the next

The CPI rises to 104 and 108.2 in periods 2 and 3 respectively. The inflation rate is the same 4 percent in each period. When the CPI rises at a constant rate, we have **stable inflation** or, more precisely, stable positive inflation. Even if the CPI rises by a roughly constant rate (say, 4 percent followed by 5 percent followed by 4 percent), economists tend to say there is stable inflation. For example, the period from 1992 to 2007 when the annual inflation rate averaged less than 2 percent was one of stable inflation.

accelerating inflation when the inflation rate rises from one year to the next

From period 3 to period 6, the CPI rises from 108.2 all the way to 136.2. Each period-to-period increase is proportionately larger than the one before it. The inflation rate goes up from 4 percent to 6 percent to 8 percent to 10 percent. When the CPI rises at a rate that increases from one period to the next—in other words, when the inflation rate is rising—we have **accelerating inflation**. Canada experienced accelerating inflation during the period 1971–1975 (when the inflation rate rose from about 3 percent to about 11 percent) and again during the period 1976–1981. Accelerating inflation is often unanticipated.

disinflation when the inflation rate falls from one year to the next

From periods 6 to 10 the CPI increases from 136.2 to 156. But it increases at a decreasing rate. The inflation rate falls from 10 percent all the way to 0 percent. When the inflation rate is falling, but the price level does not drop, we have **disinflation**. Canada experienced disinflation during the recessions of the early 1980s and 1990s. Between 1981 and 1984, for example, the inflation rate dropped from over 12 percent to just over 4 percent. Like accelerating inflation, disinflation is often unanticipated.

Finally, from period 10 to period 12 the CPI drops from 156 to 149.9. The inflation rate turns negative, as it did in Canada during the Great Depression of the 1930s. When the CPI falls from one period to the next, we have negative inflation or *deflation*. In periods 11 and 12 the deflation rate is −2 percent.

EXERCISE 6.6

Flip back to Figure 4.4. Practise using the terms *zero inflation*, *stable inflation*, *accelerating inflation*, *disinflation*, and *deflation* to describe how the inflation rate behaved in different periods of Canadian economic history.

Describing the intensity of inflation

It is useful to have terms not just to describe the rate of change of inflation, but also to describe its intensity. If you read research published by the Bank of Canada, for example, you will encounter terms such as those shown in italics in the following sentence: "In the case of Canada, there is evidence that uncertainty about long-run inflation fell considerably between the *high-inflation* period of the 1970s and early 1980s and the subsequent *moderate-inflation* period, and decreased still further in the *low-inflation* period that has been evident since the early 1990s."[3]

low inflation typically means inflation between 1 and 3 percent per year

Canadian economists have generally described annual inflation in the 1 to 3 percent range that Canada has experienced since 1992 as **low inflation**. Inflation in the range of roughly 3 to 6 percent, as Canada experienced between 1983 and 1991, is often described as **moderate inflation**. Canada's inflation in the 1974–1982 period, when the inflation rate continually exceeded 6 percent, has been described as **high inflation**.

moderate inflation typically means inflation between 3 and 6 percent per year

high inflation typically means inflation greater than 6 percent per year

Hyperinflation is used to describe very, very high inflation. While there is no official threshold above which high inflation becomes hyperinflation, inflation rates exceeding 500 percent per year would surely qualify. Several European countries experienced episodes of hyperinflation in the wake of the First and Second World Wars. In the past few decades, episodes of hyperinflation have occurred in several Latin American countries (including Argentina, Bolivia, Brazil, and Peru), in Israel, and in some "transition" economies, including Russia and Yugoslavia (Serbia and Montenegro).

hyperinflation typically means inflation greater than 500 percent per year

[3]Gerald Stuber, "Implications of Uncertainty about Long-Run Inflation and the Price Level," Working Paper 2001-16, October 2001, http://www.bankofcanada.ca/en/res/wp01-16.htm. (Italics added.)

An article in a November 2001 issue of *The Economist* **contained the following paragraph:**

> Everybody agrees that high inflation damages economic growth, but there is a dispute about the optimal rate of inflation. The European Central Bank has an inflation target of 0–2% and the Bank of England's is 2.5%... But some say that economies work better with a bit more inflation, say 3–4%. Their argument is that during a severe downturn such inflation makes it easier to cut real wages and to push real interest rates below zero, thereby helping recovery.[4]

What term would be used to describe the intensity of inflation associated with the inflation targets of the European Central Bank and the Bank of England (also a central bank)? What term would be used to describe the intensity of inflation favoured by those who say economies work better with a "bit more inflation"?

6.6 THE ECONOMIC CONSEQUENCES OF VARIOUS TYPES OF INFLATION

Previous sections of this chapter have dealt with the distinction between inflation and relative price changes. We have also introduced several terms (zero inflation, stable inflation, accelerating inflation, disinflation and deflation) for describing what is happening to the inflation rate. We have explained that both increases in the inflation rate (accelerating inflation) and decreases in the inflation rate (disinflation) are often unanticipated. And we have mentioned some adjectives economists use to describe the intensity of inflation (low, moderate, high, and hyper). We are now in a position to consider the economic *consequences* of various types of inflation. The *sources* of inflation rate change are analyzed in Chapter 11.

As you can now imagine, it is difficult to speak exactly about the consequences of anything so general as "inflation." The consequences of anticipated inflation differ from those of unanticipated inflation. Low inflation may have different consequences than moderate inflation. The consequences of disinflation must be distinguished from those of deflation. Hyperinflation constitutes a category all of its own. For these reasons, we will discuss specific consequences of various types of inflation. Take note that some consequences relate to income distribution, while others relate to economic growth.

UNANTICIPATED INFLATION AND INCOME DISTRIBUTION

One of the most widely accepted statements about inflation is that unanticipated changes in the inflation rate can have consequences for the distribution of income.

Consider a group of unionized workers who have signed a contract setting their wages for the next three years in nominal terms. The inflation rate has been 4 percent in recent years. Expecting inflation to continue along at 4 percent, the employer and representatives of the workers negotiate wages accordingly, providing nominal wage increases of 6 percent per year, and real wage increases of 2 percent per year, for each year of the contract.

But then suppose that, to everyone's surprise, there is disinflation and the inflation rate falls to 1 percent for the duration of the contract. The nominal wage increases of 6 percent per year will continue but the inflation-adjusted or real wages of the workers will be higher than before. In the first year, for example, real wages will increase by 5 percent instead of 2 percent. They will be 3 percentage points higher than anyone expected when the contract was negotiated. All else

[4]"The New Bogey," *The Economist*, 25 November 2001.

being equal, income will shift from the employer to the employees. Workers will benefit at the expense of the employer provided, of course, the employer does not resort to layoffs or get driven out of business.

The opposite type of situation would occur if, instead of unexpectedly shifting from 4 percent down to 1 percent, the inflation rate unexpectedly rose, say to 6 percent, for the rest of the contract. Then the workers, who had been expecting real wages to increase by 2 percent per year, would instead be getting no real wage increases at all. With nominal wage increases just equal to the inflation rate, their real wages would stagnate, and income would shift to the employer. Of course, depending on the availability of jobs, some workers might quit and seek higher real wages elsewhere.

It is to prevent unexpected changes in the rate of inflation from having an impact on real wages that union contracts are sometimes indexed to the CPI.[5] Indexing can help prevent unanticipated shifts in income between employers and employees as a consequence of unanticipated changes in the rate of inflation. So although unanticipated changes in inflation *can* have consequences for the distribution of income between employers and employees, such consequences are sometimes avoided by the indexing of wages.

Unanticipated changes in the inflation rate can also have consequences for the distribution of income between borrowers (debtors) and lenders (creditors). One illustration of this was provided by Economic Naturalist 6.1, which dealt with why September 1981 was a bad month to take out a mortgage. In general, unexpectedly high inflation rates help borrowers at the expense of lenders, because borrowers are able to repay their loans in less-valuable dollars. Unexpectedly low inflation rates, on the other hand, help lenders and hurt borrowers by forcing borrowers to repay in dollars that are worth more than expected when the loan was made.

Loan contracts, like union wage contracts, can in principle be indexed to the rate of inflation. In practice, full indexing of loans to the CPI is not common in Canada, though the practice is frequently observed in countries with high inflation rates. Even in Canada, however, variable-rate mortgage loans are widespread. To the extent that nominal mortgage interest rates reflect changes in the rate of inflation, variable rate mortgages provide a form of indexing.

ANTICIPATED INFLATION AND INCOME DISTRIBUTION

Economists tend to assume that if people anticipate changes in inflation they will design contracts to prevent inflation from eroding their incomes. As prices of goods and services go up, incomes go up as well, even without indexing. With anticipated inflation, employees and employers are expected to set wages with the inflation rate in mind, just as borrowers and lenders set interest rates in accordance with their expectations about inflation. But many noneconomists tend to be concerned that moderate or high inflation, even if anticipated, would lead to a substantial erosion of their living standards. Are such concerns justified?

Historically, senior citizens on public pensions have been concerned about inflation. Before the early 1970s, public pensions in Canada were not fully indexed to the rate of inflation. When inflation rates picked up in the early 1970s, however, the government of the late Pierre Elliott Trudeau did index public pensions, and they have remained indexed to the CPI ever since.

Historically, as well, the income tax system was not fully indexed for inflation, and this meant that inflation could erode the after-tax disposable incomes of taxpayers. Taxpayers would get bumped into tax brackets with higher marginal income tax rates and the value of credits or exemptions would be

[5]Paul Jenkins and Brian O'Reilly, "Monetary Policy and the Economic Well-Being of Canadians," *Review of Economic and Social Progress*, 2001, p. 101, cite evidence that the proportion of Canadian wage settlements with indexing clauses dropped from over 23 percent during 1978–1990 to under 11 percent during 1996–2000.

eroded. Around the time the Trudeau government indexed public pensions, how-ever, it also indexed the federal income tax system. The Brian Mulroney govern-ment elected in the 1980s removed full indexing of the income tax system as part of a campaign to reduce federal government deficits. But then in 2000 the Jean Chrétien government, facing large federal budget surpluses, moved to restore the indexing first implemented in the Trudeau years.

In short, both public pensions and the basic features of the federal income tax system are now fully indexed for inflation. On the other hand, private company pensions are a significant source of income for some people, and they are seldom indexed to inflation, at least explicitly. Economists would point out that although anticipated inflation may in special cases result in the erosion of living standards, the income lost by one group is largely gained by another—it does not just go up in smoke. For example, if program spending in some area is eroded by inflation, then program spending in some other area can be increased or, for example, taxes can be cut.

Finally, it is simplistic to just blame inflation when government spending fails to match increases in inflation or when government taxation is higher in real terms when inflation is higher, just as it is simplistic to regard erosion of the mini-mum wage by inflation as something caused by inflation alone (recall Exercise 6.4). When inflation is anticipated and governments fail to increase nominal pro-gram spending to offset the impact of inflation, then the decline in the real value of program spending is more the result of a government spending decision than it is the result of inflation. Similarly, when the Mulroney government removed full indexing of the tax system in the 1980s, it did so with an understanding that par-tial removal of indexing would increase government revenues. At most, inflation can help to cloak such decisions.

LOW INFLATION, MODERATE INFLATION, AND ECONOMIC GROWTH

Which is better for economic growth—low inflation or moderate inflation? The question evokes considerable controversy among economists. Here we will simply sketch some of the arguments.

On one side of the debate are economists, such as the ones with the Bank of Canada, who argue that low inflation, perhaps even zero inflation, is optimal for economic growth. A key argument of theirs is that inflation interferes with the information conveyed by price changes. In an economy with negligible infla-tion, the supplier of a product will recognize an increase in its price as a relative price increase signaling the profitability of bringing more of the product to mar-ket. Conversely, demanders will interpret the price increase as a relative price increase signaling that they should economize on their use of the product. But in the presence of inflation, not all price changes represent relative price changes. Participants in a market need to know not only the price of the product sold in the market but also what is happening to the prices of other goods and services. With inflation, then, the signals that are transmitted through the price system

price signal distortion hypothesis the claim that any substantial amount of change in the price level will make it difficult for market participants to interpret the extent to which price changes involve relative price changes

may become more difficult to interpret, much in the way that static, or "noise," makes a radio message harder to interpret. According to this **price signal distortion hypothesis**, even moderate inflation creates "noise" in the price system, and thereby reduces economic efficiency.

A second argument for little or no inflation is that inflation interferes with the long-term planning of households and firms. Suppose that you want to enjoy a certain standard of living when you retire. How much of your income do you need to save? That depends on what the goods and services you plan to buy will cost 30 or 40 years from now, assuming such goods and services would still be available then. Planning for retirement would be simplest if you knew that the future price level would be pretty much the same as the price level today.

A related argument is that when inflation is negligible and expected to stay negligible, people will tend to sign relatively long-term contracts involving interest rates, wages, and so on. They will avoid wasting time with frequent renegotiation of contracts and the economy will be more efficient as a consequence. By contrast, when inflation is higher and more volatile, people will generally judge long-term contracts as being too risky, and so will endure the time and trouble associated with short-term contracts.

On the other side of the debate are economists who favour moderate inflation over low or zero inflation.[6] Some of these economists argue that low or zero inflation can produce lower economic growth than moderate inflation because low inflation hampers flexibility of real wages. The argument is known as the **downward nominal wage rigidity hypothesis**, and is often attributed to the Nobel Prize-winning economist James Tobin. It states that adjustment generally requires that a decline in the demand for labour in a particular industry results in a reduction in real wages for workers in the industry. Labour demand and supply are discussed in detail in *Principles of Microeconomics*. If the inflation rate is a few percentage points or higher, then the appropriate real wage cuts can typically be achieved without nominal wage cuts. For example, if nominal wages go up by 1 percent, and inflation is 4 percent, then real wages will have fallen by 3 percent. If the inflation rate is zero, however, then a 3 percent cut in real wages requires a 3 percent cut in nominal wages. But workers tend to regard nominal wage cuts as unfair in most situations, so zero or low inflation tends to impair real wage flexibility and hence economic adjustment.

downward nominal wage rigidity hypothesis the claim that low levels of inflation will reduce efficiency because real wage cuts will then typically require nominal wage cuts, which will be resisted

A second argument for moderate inflation is that in fighting past recessions central banks have sometimes had to cut their official interest rates, or key policy rates, by several percentage points. (Details about how central banks use their official interest rates are provided in later chapters.) If the official rate is already very low in line with low inflation (recall the Fisher effect), then macroeconomic policy will be deprived of a key policy lever. In the economics literature, this is known as the **zero bound on nominal interest rates hypothesis**, and it is often credited to Lawrence Summers, an academic economist who served as U.S. Treasury Secretary in the Clinton Administration. One illustration is provided by Japan, where the inflation rate was approximately zero and the official rate of the central bank was only half a percentage point when the economy slipped into recession in 1997. A nominal interest rate cannot be negative, so Japan's official interest rate could not be reduced by even half a percentage point to offset the slump. In early 2008, as the U.S. financial crisis (associated with the collapse of the housing boom) intensified, concerns were raised by some U.S. economists about whether the U.S. central bank would be able to cut interest rates enough to cope with the crisis.

zero bound on nominal interest rates hypothesis the claim that because interest rates cannot go below zero, a central bank may be unable to stimulate the economy with rate cuts if the official interest rate is low to begin with

A third argument for moderate inflation is that a rapidly growing economy will naturally tend to produce moderate (not just low) inflation from time to time,

---

[6]Critics of zero or low inflation dominate, for example, among the contributors to Lars Osberg and Pierre Fortin, eds., *Hard Money, Hard Times,* (Toronto: Lorimer, 1998).

such as when the inflation rate picks up because of oil price increases or sales tax increases. If the government tolerates moderate inflation, as the government of Ireland did in 2000, then the economy may continue to grow at a healthy pace. If the government tries to keep the inflation rate more strictly under control, as was the case in Canada and the United States in 2000, then the growth rate will slow, and the economy may even be thrown into recession.

DISINFLATION AND ECONOMIC GROWTH

Economists generally agree that the process of getting from high or moderate inflation to low inflation can be very costly in terms of economic growth. In principle, a transition to a lower rate of inflation could be brought about in various ways, such as through an *incomes policy* (a government-initiated attempt to curb inflation by controlling the growth of labour and capital income).[7] But in recent times, disinflation has typically been the product of central bank policy. A central bank tries to produce disinflation by raising its official interest rate. In later chapters we will explain the process by which an increase in the official interest rate can increase interest rates in general and ultimately reduce the growth of overall spending and reduce both economic growth and the rate of inflation. Here it is perhaps sufficient to mention that the two biggest recessions in postwar Canadian economic history, the recessions of the early 1980s and the early 1990s, were both associated with attempts by the Bank of Canada to produce disinflation.

DEFLATION AND ECONOMIC GROWTH

Some columnists for the business sections of newspapers write about the importance of the central bank preserving the purchasing power of the currency. They can make it sound almost like the typical family keeps its life savings in a piggybank and that the value of the money in the piggybank will just go down and down if prices are allowed to rise.

Well, suppose families really did keep their life savings in the form of cash in piggybanks, and that the value of those life savings was the only proper concern of central bankers. Why should central bankers just aim for price stability to preserve the value of money? Why not increase the value of money by bringing about deflation (falling prices)?

To illustrate, suppose that you had $12 706 of Canadian money in a piggybank in 1929. Between 1929 and 1933 the level of the Canadian CPI (2002 base) actually fell from 9.2 to 7.1, a fall of about 23 percent or about 6 percent per year. To buy a basket of goods that cost about $12 960 in 1929 would cost only $10 000 in 1933. The extra $2960 or so is a windfall for the piggybank owner corresponding to a real rate of interest of about 6 percent per year.

While the years 1929–1933 might have been great years for anyone whose standard of living was based upon Canadian money stored in a piggybank, they were the worst years of the Great Depression, as discussed in Chapter 4. Canadian GDP dropped sharply from 1930 to 1933 and the unemployment rate reached a painfully high level never approached before or since.

Deflation has been associated with weak or negative economic growth for some of the same reasons disinflation has, but there are other reasons as well. One of them is suggested by the piggybank example—investors who can earn, say, a tax-free annual return of 6 percent just by holding cash may be reluctant to make their money available for the private-sector investment (in plant and equipment, office buildings, shopping malls, and so on) that would spur employment

---

[7]Incomes policies can be compulsory or voluntary and they may involve controls on prices as well as on income. Canada had a compulsory incomes policy (wage-and-price controls) during the 1975–1978 period when the *Anti-Inflation Act* was in effect.

and productivity increases in the economy. For this and other reasons, very few economists would view deflation as a sensible goal for economic policy.

HYPERINFLATION AND ECONOMIC GROWTH

One of the most widely accepted findings of research on inflation is that hyperinflation impairs the efficiency of an economy, often severely. Hence, countries experiencing hyperinflation tend to experience lower growth than economies that are comparable on other dimensions.

One reason that hyperinflation is associated with lower economic growth is that it greatly increases the costs of making economic transactions. As an extreme case, think of a shopper needing a wheelbarrow just to transport to the grocery store the cash needed to buy a loaf of bread.[8] Two of these *transactions costs* are known as *shoe-leather costs* and *menu costs*.

Shoe-leather costs become an issue because of the time and resources used up as people attempt to minimize the losses they incur from the rapidly falling value of money. The shoe leather worn out in the extra running around symbolizes this category of transactions costs although few people still wear shoes with leather soles. Businesses may have to issue paycheques by the day rather than by the week or month. People may visit the bank two or three times a day so as to keep as much of their money as possible in inflation-indexed accounts, if they are available, and as little as possible in rapidly depreciating cash. Or, as soon as they are paid, people may rush off to exchange the local currency for a stable, widely used international currency.

Menu costs become an issue because of the frequency with which prices must be changed. The cost to a restaurant of printing up a new set of menus with new prices symbolizes this category of costs. Under hyperinflation, annual or quarterly price adjustment is impractical—businesses must change their prices by the day, perhaps even by the hour.

Incidentally, while shoe-leather and menu costs become a serious issue with hyperinflations, they also exist in other situations. Shoe-leather costs would be minimized in a state of rapidly falling prices, but rapidly falling prices have negative side effects of a more serious nature, as noted above. Menu costs are increased, not just by rising prices, but by falling prices as well. In any case, most economists interpret the evidence as suggesting that these transaction costs are trivial at the rates of inflation observed throughout most of Canadian history.[9] Annual inflation rates in Canada, it is important to remember, have never reached 20 percent, let alone the 5000 percent or more observed in several hyperinflations.

HIGH, ACCELERATING INFLATION AND ECONOMIC GROWTH

Canadian advocates of high and accelerating inflation are few and far between. On the face of it, this might seem odd because Canada's years of high and accelerating inflation in the 1970s were characterized by relatively strong economic growth. Canadian inflation during the period 1971–1981 averaged over 8 percent,

---

[8]You may wonder how countries could ever allow themselves to fall into a state of hyperinflation. One common path is for a country to experience economic collapse as a result of war. The government needs revenue but is reluctant or unable to raise the funds through taxation. So it issues extra currency to pay for its purchases. With too much currency chasing too few goods and services, prices soar. People try to hoard goods and this contributes to accelerating inflation. The government then needs even more currency to pay for its purchases so it issues even more currency, and eventually the process spins out of control.

[9]Furthermore, technological improvements such as Internet banking, computerized cash registers, and Web-based price lists have worked to reduce the shoe-leather and menu costs of any given rate of inflation.

but the annual real per capita GDP growth rate for the whole period averaged a healthy 2.7 percent.[10]

By contrast, for the period 1982–1992 inflation averaged under 5 percent through years of disinflation followed by stable inflation and then disinflation again. Real per capita GDP growth for the 1982–1992 period averaged under 1 percent.

High inflation may or may not harm economic growth directly. One problem with high and accelerating inflation, however, is that it typically means that the future inflation rate is difficult to predict and income is thereby arbitrarily redistributed between employers and employees, borrowers and lenders, and so on. Another problem is that if high and accelerating inflation persists it may eventually transform into hyperinflation.

But perhaps the most serious problem with high and accelerating inflation is political. Because of widely held concerns about redistribution and the risk of hyperinflation, many economists have concluded that high and accelerating inflation will likely create a political consensus in favour of clamping down on inflation, typically through disinflation induced by central bank policies.[11] In turn, such disinflation will mean a recession, a sharp drop in economic growth.

It is true that political pressure could take the form of dealing with high and accelerating inflation by means other than a costly disinflation. The upsurge in Canadian inflation during the early 1970s, for example, led at first not to a costly disinflation but to a brief experiment with wage-and-price controls (which helped to reduce inflation, at least temporarily, but had other problems). Still, the conclusion holds that in many societies high and accelerating inflation carries the substantial risk of creating a political consensus in favour of costly disinflation.

EXERCISE 6.8

The Economist **article quoted in Exercise 6.7 also contained the following paragraph:**

> **First, it swells the real burden of debt, causing bankruptcies and bank failures. Second, expectations that prices will be lower tomorrow may encourage households to postpone their spending. Weaker demand may then push prices even lower. Third, workers are often reluctant to accept a pay cut in nominal terms, so that when prices are falling the real wage bill goes up. The only way to cut costs is to lay off more workers, which may deepen a recession. Last, but by no means least, interest rates cannot go below zero, so [it] makes real interest rates painfully high—as Japan has discovered.[12]**

What is "it"—zero inflation, deflation, or accelerating inflation? Explain.

RECAP ↑

THE ECONOMIC CONSEQUENCES OF VARIOUS TYPES OF INFLATION

Changes in relative prices (such as the price of bread) should be distinguished from inflation, which is a change in the overall level of prices. The distinction is important because remedies for undesired changes in relative prices and for inflation are different.

---

[10]On the lack of solid international evidence for the view that high inflation harms economic growth, see Jonathan Temple, "The New Growth Evidence," *Journal of Economic Literature*, March 1999, pp. 112–156.

[11]For international evidence that the public dislikes high inflation, see Rafael Di Tella, Robert MacCulloch, and Andrew Oswald, "Preferences over Inflation and Unemployment: Evidence from Surveys of Happiness," *American Economic Review*, March 2001, pp. 335–341.

[12]"The New Bogey," *The Economist*, 25 November 2001.

It is difficult to draw conclusions about the consequences of anything so general as "inflation." Instead we have examined the consequences of various types of inflation for income distribution and economic growth.

- If inflation is anticipated, it will generally not have major impacts on income distribution, even if indexing is uncommon.
- If inflation is unanticipated (as is often the case for disinflation or accelerating inflation), then it can have major impacts on income distribution, but only in the absence of indexing.
- Deflation has been associated with slow or negative economic growth.
- There is controversy over whether a policy of aiming for low inflation is superior to a policy of tolerating moderate inflation as a means of supporting economic growth.
- High, accelerating inflation can generate political support for a costly disinflation to get inflation back under control.
- Hyperinflation has typically been associated with low or negative economic growth and has often led to economic collapse.

SUMMARY

6.1 The basic tool for measuring inflation is the *consumer price index,* or CPI. The CPI measures the cost of purchasing a fixed basket of goods and services in any period relative to the cost of the same basket of goods and services in a base year. The *inflation rate* is the annual percentage rate of change in the price level as measured by a *price index* such as the CPI.

6.3 A *nominal quantity* is a quantity that is measured in terms of its current dollar value. Dividing a nominal quantity, such as a family's income or a worker's wage in dollars, by a price index such as the CPI expresses that quantity in terms of real purchasing power. This procedure is called *deflating* the nominal quantity. If nominal quantities from two different years are deflated by a common price index, the purchasing power of the two quantities can be compared. To ensure that a nominal payment, such as a Canada Pension Plan benefit, represents a constant level of real purchasing power, the nominal payment should be increased each year by a percentage equal to the inflation rate. This method of adjusting nominal payments to maintain their purchasing power is called *indexing.*

6.4 The *real interest rate* is equal to the *nominal,* or *market, interest rate* minus the inflation rate. When inflation is unexpectedly high, the real interest rate is lower than anticipated, which hurts lenders but benefits borrowers. When inflation is unexpectedly low, lenders benefit and borrowers are hurt.

To obtain a given real rate of return, lenders must charge a high nominal interest rate when inflation is high and a low nominal interest rate when inflation is low. The tendency for nominal interest rates to be high when inflation is high and low when inflation is low is called the *Fisher effect.*

6.5 It is important to distinguish between increases in the *relative prices* for specific goods and services and increases in the general price level. The distinction is important because the appropriate response to a change in relative prices differs from the appropriate response to inflation.

6.5 Economists employ precise terminology to describe the various types of inflation. Inflation can be *anticipated* or *unanticipated.* Distinctions are drawn between *zero inflation, stable inflation, accelerating inflation, disinflation,* and *deflation.* The intensity of inflation can be described by terms such as *low inflation, moderate inflation, high inflation,* and *hyperinflation.*

6.6 The various types of inflation have different consequences for income distribution and economic growth. It is almost universally accepted that macroeconomic policy should aim at avoiding the extremes of hyperinflation (which Canada has never experienced) and deflation (which Canada experienced during the Great Depression). It is widely accepted that macroeconomic policy should avoid high and accelerating inflation.

KEY TERMS

accelerating inflation (150)
anticipated inflation (146)
consumer price index (CPI) (137)
deflating (a nominal quantity) (141)

deflation (140)
disinflation (150)
downward nominal wage rigidity
   hypothesis (154)

Fisher effect (147)
high inflation (150)
hyperinflation (150)
indexing (143)

low inflation (150)
moderate inflation (150)
nominal interest rate (143)
nominal quantity (140)
price index (138)
price level (137)

price signal distortion hypothesis (154)
rate of inflation (139)
real interest rate (143)
real quantity (140)
real wage (141)
relative price (147)

stable inflation (150)
unanticipated inflation (146)
zero bound on nominal interest rates
     hypothesis (154)
zero inflation (149)

REVIEW QUESTIONS

1. Explain why changes in the cost of living for any particular individual or family may differ from changes in the CPI.

2. What is the difference between the *price level* and the *rate of inflation* in an economy?

3. Why is it important to adjust for inflation when comparing nominal quantities (for example, workers' average wages) at different points in time? What is the basic method for adjusting for inflation?

4. Describe how indexing might be used to guarantee that the purchasing power of the wage agreed to in a multiyear collective agreement will not be eroded by inflation.

5. "It's true that unanticipated inflation redistributes wealth from creditors to debtors, for example. But what one side of the bargain loses, the other side gains. So from the perspective of society as a whole, there is no real cost." Do you agree? Discuss.

6. How does deflation affect the real return on holding cash? How does positive inflation act as a tax on criminal gangs holding large quantities of cash to avoid detection by the authorities rather than keeping their money in interest-bearing bank accounts?

7. True or false, and explain: If both the potential lender and the potential borrower correctly anticipate the rate of inflation, inflation will not redistribute wealth from the creditor to the debtor.

8. Discuss the different consequences that deflation, high inflation, and hyperinflation have for economic growth.

PROBLEMS

1. In the city of Pizzaville, government survey takers determine that typical family expenditures each month in the year designated as the base year are as follows:

   20 pizzas at $10 each
   Rent of apartment, $600 per month
   Gasoline and car maintenance, $100
   Phone service (basic service plus 10 long-distance calls), $50

   In the year following the base year, the survey takers determine that pizzas have risen to $11 each, apartment rent is $640, gasoline and maintenance has risen to $120, and phone service has dropped in price to $40.
   a. Find the CPI in the subsequent year and the rate of inflation between the base year and the subsequent year.
   b. The family's nominal income rose by 5 percent between the base year and the subsequent year. Is the family worse off or better off in terms of what its income is able to buy?

2. Here are values of the Canadian CPI for each year over the period 1998–2007. For each year beginning with 1998, calculate the rate of inflation from the previous year. How would you characterize inflation rates over the 1998–2007 period?

1998	91.3
1999	92.9
2000	95.4
2001	97.8
2002	100.0
2003	102.8
2004	104.7
2005	107.0
2006	109.1
2007	111.5

3. An article in *The Economist* reports that agricultural prices have been rising worldwide and that the proportion of the consumer price index taken up by food is much higher in developing countries such as China and India than in developed countries such as the United States.[13]

   Suppose that the share of food in the consumer price index of Canada, China, India, and the United States is as shown in the table below. Suppose also that all four countries are hit by an agricultural price shock that sends the price of food up 10 percent. What impact will this price shock have on the overall price index in each of the four countries, all else being equal? Insert your answers in the blank cells of the column titled "Predicted Increase in CPI."

Country	Share of Food in CPI (%)[14]	Predicted Increase in CPI
Canada	17	
China	33	
India	46	
United States	14	

4. Suppose a study found that the real entry-level wage for graduates of a certain university declined by 8 percent between 2000 and 2007. The nominal entry-level wage in 2007 was $12.00 per hour. Assuming that the findings are correct, what was the nominal entry-level wage in 2000? Use the CPI data from Problem 2.

5. Here is the income tax schedule for a hypothetical country. It is expressed in nominal terms, for the year 2009:

Family income	Taxes due (percent of income)
≤ $20 000	10
$20 001–$30 000	12
$30 001–$50 000	15
$50 001–$80 000	20
>$80 000	25

The legislature wants to ensure that families with a given real income are not pushed up into higher tax brackets by inflation. The CPI is 175 in 2008 and 185 in 2009. How should the income tax schedule above be adjusted for the year 2009 to meet the legislature's goal?

6. In 2003, based upon the Survey of Household Spending of 2001, Statistics Canada announced the following weights for the major spending categories tracked by the CPI:[15]

Food	16.3%
Shelter	28.5%
Household operations and furnishings	10.7%
Clothing and footwear	5.8%
Transportation	18.8%
Health and personal care	4.5%
Recreation, education, and reading	12.1%
Alcoholic beverages and tobacco products	3.2%

Employ the weights given above and suppose that 2002 is the base year with a CPI equal to 100. Suppose also that since 2001 the price of food has increased by 5 percent; the price of housing has increased by 10 percent; and the price of recreation, education, and reading has increased by 20 percent. All other prices are unchanged. Find the CPI for the current year (2009).

[13]See "Rising food prices; the agonies of agflation," *The Economist,* 25 August 2007, http://www.economist.com/finance/displaystory.cfm?story_id=9707029 (May 2008).
[14]Sources: Share of food in CPI for China, India, and United States from "Rising food prices; the agonies of agflation," and share of food in CPI for Canada from Statistics Canada, "Weighting Diagram of the Consumer Price Index; 2005 basket at April 2007 Prices, Canada, provinces, Whitehorse and Yellowknife," http://www.statcan.ca/english/freepub/62-001-XIE/2007005/appendix1.htm (May 2008).
[15]Adapted from the Statistics Canada Web site, http://www.statcan.ca/english/sdds/document/2301_D12_T9_V1_B.pdf They do not add up to 100 percent because of rounding.

ANSWERS TO IN-CHAPTER EXERCISES

6.1 The cost of the family's basket in 2002 remains at $680, as in Table 6.1. If the rent on the apartment falls to $400 in 2009, the cost of reproducing the 2002 basket of goods and services in 2009 is $620 ($400 for rent + $150 for hamburgers + $70 for movie tickets). The CPI for 2009 is accordingly $620/$680, or 0.912. So in this example, the cost of living has fallen nearly 9 percent between 2002 and 2009.

6.2 To construct a price index for university student expenditures, you would need to determine the basket of goods and services purchased in the base year. The university student price index in each period would then be defined as the cost of the basket in that period relative to the cost in the base year. To the extent that the mix of purchases of university students differs from that of average households, the university student price index would differ from the CPI. For example, if in the base year university students spent a higher share of their budgets than the average Canadian household on goods and services that have risen relatively rapidly in price (such as tuition fees for post-secondary education), then the inflation rate experienced by university students would be higher than the CPI inflation rate.

6.3 The percentage changes in the CPI in each year from the previous year are as follows:

1930	$-1.1 \text{ percent} = 100 \times \dfrac{(9.1 - 9.2)}{9.2}$
1931	-9.9 percent
1932	-8.5 percent
1933	-5.4 percent

Negative inflation is called deflation. The experience of the 1930s, when prices were falling, contrasts sharply with the 1970s, during which prices rose rapidly.

6.4 Deflating the unchanged $6.85 minimum wage by the 1995 CPI value of 86.8 gives a real minimum wage for 1995 of $7.89 in 2002 dollars. Deflating by the 2003 CPI of 102.7 gives a real minimum wage for 2003 of $6.67 in 2002 dollars. The decline in the real value of the minimum wage over the 1995–2003 period is therefore equal to approximately 15.5 percent.

6.5 The nominal interest rate in 1980 is 12.7 percent. The after-tax return to the financial investor receiving that interest rate and paying a 40 percent tax rate is 7.6 percent. Subtracting inflation of 10.1 percent yields a negative after-tax real return of 2.5 percent. The nominal interest rate in 2007 is 4.1 percent. The after-tax return to the financial investor is 2.5 percent. Subtracting inflation of 2.2 percent yields an after-tax real return of 0.3 percent.

So although pre-tax real returns were lower in 2007 than in 1980, in our hypothetical example after tax real returns in 2007 were 2.8 percentage points greater than after-tax returns in 2007. All else being equal, then, a high rate of inflation can interact with the tax system to reduce the real after-tax returns available to financial investors.

6.6 No answer given.

6.7 The European Central Bank and the Bank of England aim for *low inflation*. Those who say economies work better with a "bit more inflation" are advocates of *moderate inflation*.

6.8 The paragraph is about *deflation*. The references to "when prices are falling" and to "expectations that prices will be lower tomorrow" are clearly references to deflation, which involves a falling price level. Zero inflation can cause some of the same economic problems that deflation causes. But zero inflation means the price level stays constant—it neither rises nor falls.

PART 3

The Economy in the Short Run

Short-term fluctuations around the long-run average of an economy's growth can be unpleasant. In particular, periods of low or negative economic growth, known as *recessions,* can create significant economic hardship and dissatisfaction for the general population. For example, during the severe recessions of the early 1980s and early 1990s, and even during the slowdown of 2000–2001, large numbers of Canadians lost their jobs, and many their homes also, when they were not able to make mortgage payments. In Part 3 of this text we will explore the causes of these short-term fluctuations in key economic variables including output, unemployment, and inflation, and we will discuss options for stabilizing the economy that are available to government policy-makers.

Chapter 7 provides some necessary background for this study of short-term fluctuations by describing key characteristics and reviewing the historical record of fluctuations in the Canadian economy. In Chapters 8 through 11 we develop a framework for the analysis of short-term fluctuations and of the alternative policy responses. Chapter 8 shows how changes in overall spending

in the economy may lead to short-run fluctuations in output and employment. The chapter also explains how changes in fiscal policy, or policies related to government spending and taxation, can be used to stabilize spending and output. Chapter 9 focuses on monetary policy, a second tool for stabilizing output and employment. Chapter 10 introduces a model that allows us to consider the causes and consequences of changes in the overall price level of the economy. Chapter 11 incorporates inflation into the analysis, discussing both the sources of inflation and the policies that can be used to control it.

Chapters 12 and 13 extend the analysis of Chapters 8 through 11. In the first place, Chapter 12 considers the relationship between exchange rate changes and short-term fluctuations in the economy and also the factors determining exchange rates. Then Chapter 13 goes further into the role played by money, the banking system, and central banks in the economy. It supplements the preceding chapters on monetary policy and exchange rates and provides a bridge to the chapters dealing with long-run economic issues that follow in Part 4.

Chapter 7

Short-Term Economic Fluctuations: An Introduction

How would you respond to the following situation? In the very year that you plan to graduate from university and get a full-time job, the economy goes into a serious recession and the unemployment rate soars.[1] Employers have many applicants for every job vacancy and they prefer qualified applicants with years of work experience over applicants such as you who have just graduated from university.

Some new graduates will stick with their original plan. Typically, they will succeed in finding suitable employment but it will take months and months of job search instead of the weeks that it would normally take. Other graduates will quickly settle for low-paying jobs for which they are considerably over-qualified. Yet another approach is to apply the *cost–benefit principle* and decide to postpone job hunting until the economy picks up. Some graduates will realize that, because they will not land the high-paying, suitable job they planned for, there will be a low opportunity cost associated with taking a few months to travel the world. So they will pack their bags and go. Other graduates will calculate that there will be a low opportunity cost in spending an extra year at university or college. Indeed, during Canada's last major recession, many universities and colleges saw a jump in enrolment due to students deciding that their time would be better spent in acquiring more education rather than in a frustrating job search in a high-unemployment labour market. For most, especially those who acquired postgraduate degrees and then access to top-notch jobs, this proved to be a wise decision.

While new graduates will revise their job search plans in various ways during a serious recession, they will tend to take a common political response to the situation; that is, in the first federal election that follows they will likely vote against

---

[1]This, incidentally, is the type of scenario some economists were forecasting for the U.S. economy as of the spring of 2008. See, for example, Dean Baker, "Economy Loses 83,000 Jobs, Unemployment Jumps to 5.1 Percent," *Job Bytes,* Center for Economy and Policy Research, 4 April 2008, http://www.cepr.net/index.php/data-bytes/jobs-bytes/ (May 2008).

the party that presided over the recession. In the federal election of 1993 that followed the last major recession in Canada, the governing party was reduced from a majority status to just two seats in the House of Commons.

This chapter provides insight into, among other things, the economic downturns that force complex decisions on graduating students and often create problems for governing political parties. It is the first of several chapters with a common theme.

In this part of the book we study short-term fluctuations in economic activity, commonly known as *recessions* and *expansions*. We will start, in this chapter, with some background on the history and characteristics of these economic ups and downs. However, the main focus of this part is the causes of short-term fluctuations, as well as the available *policy responses*. Because the analysis of short-term economic fluctuations can become complex and even controversial, we will proceed in a step-by-step fashion. In Chapter 8 we introduce a basic model of booms and recessions, which we will refer to as the *basic Keynesian model* in honour of its principal originator, the British economist John Maynard Keynes. The basic Keynesian model focuses on the components of aggregate spending, such as consumption spending by households and investment spending by firms, and the effects of changes in spending on total real GDP. The basic Keynesian model is a useful starting point. We will build upon it in the later chapters of Part 3.

7.1 RECESSIONS AND EXPANSIONS

As background to the study of short-term economic fluctuations, let's review the historic record of the fluctuations in the Canadian economy. Figure 7.1 shows the path of real GDP in Canada since 1926. As you can see, the growth path of real GDP is not always smooth; the bumps and wiggles correspond to short periods of faster or slower growth.

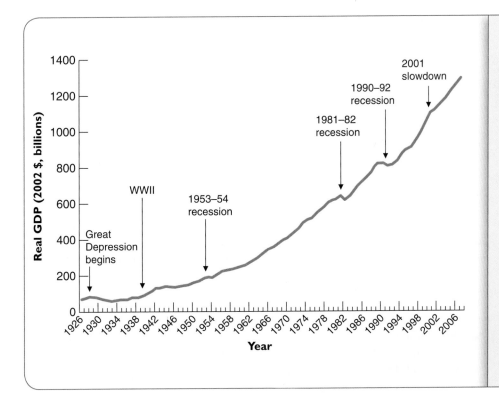

FIGURE 7.1

Fluctuations in Canadian Real GDP, 1926–2007

Real GDP has not grown smoothly but has undergone speedups (expansions or booms) and serious slowdowns (recessions or depressions). The most dramatic fluctuations are indicated. Note the contraction from 1929 to 1933 (the first phase of the Great Depression), the boom in 1939–1945 (WWII), and the recessions of the early 1980s and the early 1990s.
SOURCE: Adapted from the Statistics Canada CANSIM database, series v1992259, and from *HSC*, Catalogue 11-516, July 29, 1999, Series F55.

"Please stand by for a series of tones. The first indicates the official end of the recession, the second indicates prosperity, and the third the return of the recession."

recession (or contraction) a period in which the economy is growing at a rate significantly below normal

A period in which the economy is growing at a rate significantly below normal is called a **recession**, or a *contraction*. An extremely severe or protracted recession is called a **depression**. You should be able to pick out the Great Depression in Figure 7.1, particularly the sharp initial decline between 1929 and 1933. But you can also see that the Canadian economy experienced serious recessions in the early 1980s and during 1990–1992.

depression a particularly severe or protracted recession

A popular definition of a recession, one that is often cited by the media, is a period during which real GDP falls for at least two consecutive quarters. This definition is not a bad rule of thumb, as real GDP usually does fall during recessions. However, many economists would argue that periods in which real GDP growth is well below normal, though not actually negative, should be counted as recessions. The "two-consecutive-quarters" rule does not classify such slow-growth episodes as recessions.

Table 7.1 lists the beginning and ending dates of Canadian recessions during the 1947–2007 period, as well as the *duration* (length, in months) of each. The table also gives the highest unemployment rate associated with each recession and the percentage change in real GDP for the longer recessions. (Ignore the last column of the table for now.) The beginning of a recession is called the **peak**, because it represents the high point of economic activity prior to a downturn. The end of a recession, which marks the low point of economic activity prior to a recovery, is called the **trough**.

peak the beginning of a recession, the high point of economic activity prior to a downturn

trough the end of a recession, the low point of economic activity prior to a recovery

Table 7.1 shows what is probably the most widely accepted dating of Canadian recessions covering the period since 1947. It does not include the economic slowdown of 2000–2001 because that slowdown was not sufficiently pronounced in Canada to warrant being termed a "recession." As in Figure 7.1, the severity of the early 1980s and the early 1990s recessions stands out. The 1990–1992 recession featured a milder drop in GDP than the very sharp 1981–1982 recession but the one in 1990–1992 lasted several months longer. Indeed, at 24 months long, it was by far the longest recession since 1947.

expansion a period in which the economy is growing at a rate significantly above normal

The opposite of a recession is an **expansion**, a period in which the economy is growing at a rate that is significantly *above* normal. Canada has experienced three

TABLE 7.1
Canada Recessions 1947–2007

Peak date (start)	Trough date (end)	Approximate duration (months)	Highest unemployment rate (%)	Percentage change in annual real GDP	Duration of subsequent expansion (months)
Sept. 1947	Mar. 1948	6	2.8 (1949)	—	11
Feb. 1949	Jul. 1949	6	3.6 (1950)	—	11
Jun. 1951	Dec. 1951	6	2.9 (1952)	—	16
Apr. 1953	Apr. 1954	12	4.6 (1954)	−1.2 (1953–54)	36
Apr. 1957	Jan. 1958	9	7.0 (1958)	—	25
Feb. 1960	Mar. 1961	13	7.1 (1961)	2.8 (1960–61)	108
Mar. 1970	Jun. 1970	3	6.2 (1971)	—	55
Jan. 1975	Mar. 1975	3	7.0 (1976)	—	59
Feb. 1980	Jun. 1980	4	7.6 (1981)	—	13
Jul. 1981	Oct. 1982	15	11.9 (1983)	−2.9 (1981–82)	90
Apr. 1990	Apr. 1992	24	11.4 (1993)	−1.9 (1990–91)	108+

NOTES: Highest unemployment rate is the annual rate for the year shown in parentheses—the trough year or the subsequent year, whichever is higher. The percentage change in annual real GDP is measured from the peak year to the following year (as shown in parentheses) for those recessions that lasted 12 months or longer. The 2.8 percent annual real GDP growth associated with the 1960–1961 recession is not a typo. The very high real GDP growth numbers for "good years" in the 1950s and 1960s meant that 2.8 percent real GDP growth amounted to a marked slowdown in economic growth.

SOURCES: Adapted from CANSIM series v646957, v646954, and v646937. Peak and trough dates are from P.Cross, "Alternative Measures of Business Cycles in Canada: 1947–1992," *Canadian Economic Observer,* February 1996, appendix.

long expansions in the period since 1947: from 1961 to 1970, from 1982 to 1990, and from 1992 extending into this decade. A particularly strong and protracted phase of an expansion is called a **boom**. The 1997–2000 phase of Canada's most recent long expansion exhibited the characteristics of a boom. In 2007 much of the Canadian economy was in a boom, although with a weakness in manufacturing connected with the strong Canadian dollar.

boom a particularly strong and protracted phase of an expansion

Figure 7.2 presents another way of showing fluctuations in Canadian economic growth. It depicts year-to-year fluctuations in the growth of real GDP per capita during the 1927–2007 period and thus shows sharper fluctuations than does Figure 7.1, which depicted the level of real GDP. Observe that the Canadian economy produced very low growth rates of real GDP per capita during two long historical periods, the years 1919–1939 and the years 1980–1996, when the economy went through severe economic downturns.

Recessions in the United States invariably have an impact upon certain Canadian industries and usually have a major impact on the Canadian economy as a whole. The most widely accepted dating of U.S. recessions is that determined by the National Bureau of Economic Research. Go to the National Bureau of Economic Research Web site (at the time of writing the most relevant pages on the site are http://www.nber.org/cycles/recessions.html and http://www.nber.org/cycles.html) and find out how much time has elapsed since the last U.S. business cycle peak or trough. Is the U.S. economy currently in recession or expansion? How much time has elapsed since the last peak or trough?

EXERCISE 7.1

FIGURE 7.2

Canada's Real GDP Per Capita Growth Rate, 1927–2007

Growth of real GDP per capita (jagged red line) averaged 2.3 percent (grey line) over the 1927–2007 period. During some periods, the real GDP per capita growth rate has differed substantially from its long-term average. The economy registered negative average growth (−1.1 percent) during the Great Depression years of 1929 to 1938, sluggish average growth (1.2 percent) between 1980 and 1996, an amazingly strong pace (9.1 percent) during the WWII years of 1940 to 1944, a rapid pace from 1962 to 1979, and a moderate pace from 1997 to 2007.

SOURCE: Adapted from Statistics Canada CANSIM II Series v24661119 (Employment), v466668 (Population), and v41707175 (Real GDP), and from *Historical Statistics of Canada*, D129, A1, and F55.

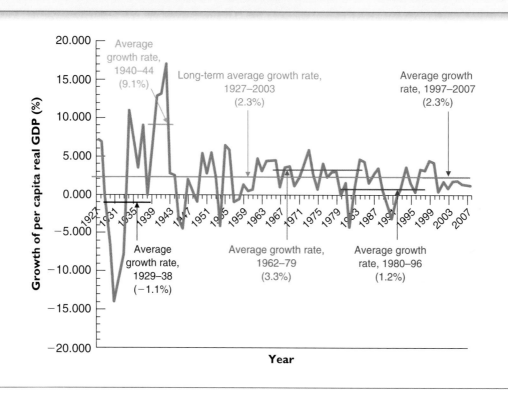

7.2 CHARACTERISTICS OF SHORT-TERM FLUCTUATIONS

Although Figure 7.1 and Table 7.1 show only twentieth and twenty-first-century data, periods of expansion and recession have been a feature of industrial economies since at least the late eighteenth century. Karl Marx and Friedrich Engels referred to these fluctuations, which they called "commercial crises," in their Communist Manifesto (1848). In Canada, economists have been studying short-term fluctuations for decades. The traditional term for these fluctuations is *business cycles*, and they are still often referred to as *cyclical fluctuations*. Neither term is very accurate though, since as Figure 7.1 shows, economic fluctuations are not "cyclical" at all in the sense that they recur at predictable intervals, but instead are quite *irregular in their length and severity*. This irregularity makes the dates of peaks and troughs extremely hard to predict, despite the fact that professional forecasters have devoted a great deal of effort and brainpower to the task.

Expansions and recessions usually are not limited to a few industries or regions but are *felt throughout the economy*. Indeed, the largest fluctuations may have a global impact. For instance, the Great Depression of the 1930s affected nearly all the world's economies, and the 1981–1982 recession, which originated primarily with the high interest rate policies of the United States, triggered not

Recessions are very difficult to forecast.

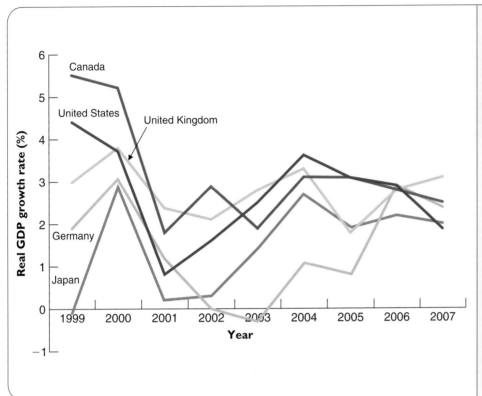

FIGURE 7.3
Real GDP Growth in Five Major Countries, 1999–2007
Annual growth rates for five major industrialized countries show that all the countries except for Japan enjoyed strong real GDP growth in 1999 and 2000. In 2001 each of these economies experienced an economic slowdown. By 2002 most of them had recovered, and by 2004 all of them had.
SOURCE: International Monetary Fund, *World Economic Outlook Database*, October 2007, http://www.imf.org/external/pubs/ft/weo/2007/02/weodata/index.aspx. Data for 2007 is based in part upon a forecast.

only recessions in other countries but also a foreign debt crisis affecting a wide range of developing countries. When East Asia suffered a major slowdown in the late 1990s, the effects of that slowdown spilled over into many other regions (including Canada, particularly British Columbia).

Even relatively moderate recessions may strike a number of countries simultaneously. Figure 7.3, which shows the growth rates of real GDP over the period 1999–2007 for Canada, Germany, Japan, the United Kingdom, and the United States, illustrates this point. You can see that—except for Japan, which had been suffering special problems related to deflation—all these countries experienced relatively strong growth rates in 1999 and 2000. The 2001 recession lowered the growth rates in all of the countries, with some recovery apparent by 2002 in all of the economies except Germany, which recovered in 2003.

Unemployment is a key indicator of short-term economic fluctuations. The unemployment rate typically rises sharply during recessions and recovers (although more slowly) during expansions. Figure 5.4 showed the Canadian unemployment rate since 1960. You should be able to identify the recessions that began in 1981 and 1990, for example, by noting the sharp increases in the unemployment rate that began in those years. As we will explain shortly, the part of unemployment that is associated with recessions is called *cyclical unemployment*. Beyond this increase in unemployment, labour market conditions become less favourable to workers during recessions. For example, real wages grow more slowly or even decline, and workers are less likely to receive promotions or bonuses during a recession than during expansionary periods.

Like unemployment, *inflation* follows a typical pattern in recessions and expansions, though it is not so sharply defined. Figure 7.4 shows the Canadian inflation rate since 1960; in the figure, vertical blue lines show the approximate starting dates of periods of recession. Recessions tend to be followed soon after by a decline in the rate of inflation, as indicated by the declines in the inflation rate after the recessions beginning in 1970, 1975, 1981, and 1990. Furthermore, some recessions have been

Unemployment among construction workers rises substantially during recessions.

FIGURE 7.4

Canadian Recessions and Disinflation, 1960–2007

The red line shows the CPI inflation rate and the blue lines indicate when recessions (and the economic downturn of 2000–2001) began. Note that the inflation rate fell after the recessions beginning in 1970, 1975, 1981, and 1990. The fall in the inflation rate after 1975 is partly due to the Anti-Inflation Act, which imposed wage and price controls during 1975–1978. The fall in the inflation rate after the recession beginning in 1990 was delayed due to the introduction of the GST (which increased consumer prices) and to sharply higher energy prices associated with the Gulf War.

SOURCE: Adapted from the Statistics Canada CANSIM database, series 41690973.

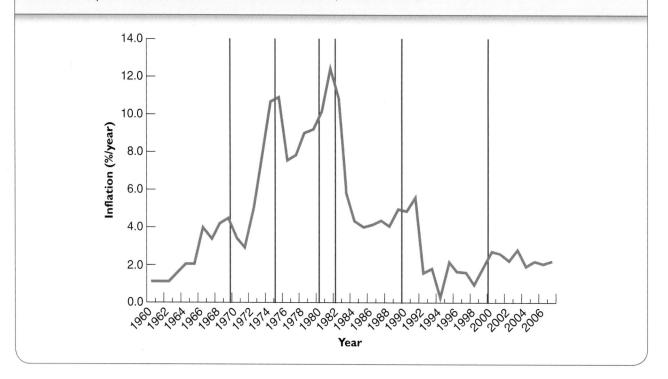

preceded by increases in inflation, as Figure 7.4 also shows. The behaviour of inflation during expansions and recessions will be discussed more fully in Chapter 11.

Generally, industries that produce *durable goods*, such as cars, houses, and capital equipment, are more affected than others by recessions and booms. In contrast, industries that provide *services* and *non-durable goods* like food are much less sensitive to short-term fluctuations. Thus an automobile worker or a construction worker is far more likely to lose his or her job in a recession than a hairstylist or a baker is.

RECAP

RECESSIONS, BOOMS, AND THEIR CHARACTERISTICS

- A recession is a period in which output is growing more slowly than normal. An expansion is a period in which output is growing more quickly than normal.
- The beginning of a recession is called the peak, and its end (which corresponds to the beginning of the subsequent expansion) is called the trough.
- The sharpest recession in the history of Canada was the initial phase of the Great Depression in 1929–1933. Severe recessions also occurred in the early 1980s and during 1990–1992.
- Short-term economic fluctuations are irregular in length and severity and thus are difficult to predict.

- Expansions and recessions have widespread (and sometimes global) impacts, affecting most regions and industries.
- Unemployment rises sharply during a recession and falls, usually more slowly, during an expansion.
- Recessions tend to be followed by a decline in inflation and are sometimes preceded by an increase in inflation.
- Durable goods industries are more affected by expansions and recessions than other industries. Services and non-durable goods industries are less sensitive to ups and downs in the economy.

7.3 MEASURING FLUCTUATIONS: OUTPUT GAPS AND CYCLICAL UNEMPLOYMENT

If policy-makers are to respond appropriately to recessions and expansions, and economists are to study them, knowing whether a particular economic fluctuation is "big" or "small" is essential. Intuitively, a "big" recession or expansion is one in which output and the unemployment rate deviate significantly from their normal or trend levels. In this section we will attempt to be more precise about this idea, in preparation for our analysis of the causes and cures of short-run fluctuations. Specifically, we will introduce the concept of the *output gap*, which measures how far output is from its normal level at a particular time, and we will analyze the idea of *cyclical unemployment*, or the deviation of unemployment from its normal level. Finally, we will examine how these two concepts are related.

POTENTIAL OUTPUT AND THE OUTPUT GAP

The concept of *potential output* is a useful starting point for thinking about the measurement of expansions and recessions. **Potential output**, also called *potential GDP* or *full-employment output*, is the amount of output (real GDP) that an economy can produce when using its resources, such as capital and labour, at normal rates. Potential output is not a fixed number but grows over time, reflecting increases in both the amounts of available capital and labour and their productivity. We will discuss the sources of growth in potential output (the economy's productive capacity) at some length in Chapter 14. We will use the symbol Y^* to signify the economy's potential output at a given point in time.

A recession, as we have seen, is a period in which the economy is growing significantly below its normal rate. What causes this slow growth? Logically, there are two possibilities. First, a recession could be a period in which actual output equals potential output, but potential output itself is growing very slowly. Severe soil erosion, for example, would reduce the rate of growth in an agricultural economy, and a decline in the rate of technological innovation might reduce the rate of potential output growth in an industrial economy. Similarly, new technologies, increased capital investment, or a surge in immigration that swells the labour force could produce unusually brisk growth in potential output, and thus an economic boom.

The usual explanation for short-term economic fluctuations, however, is that *actual output does not always equal potential output*. For example, potential output may be growing normally, but for some reason the economy's capital and labour resources may not be fully utilized, so actual output falls below potential output (a recession). Alternatively, capital and labour may be working harder than usual, so actual output expands beyond potential output (a boom). In either of these scenarios, policy-makers face a new problem: how to return actual output to potential. In the next four chapters we will discuss policies for *stabilizing* the economy, that is, bringing actual output into line with potential output.

potential output (or potential GDP or full-employment output) the amount of output (real GDP) that an economy can produce when using its resources, such as capital and labour, at normal rates

output gap (or Y*–Y) the difference between the economy's potential output and its actual output at a point in time

recessionary gap a positive output gap, which occurs when potential output exceeds actual output

expansionary gap a negative output gap, which occurs when actual output is higher than potential output

At any point in time, the difference between potential output and actual output is called the **output gap**. Recalling that Y^* is the symbol for potential output and that Y stands for actual output (real GDP), we can express the output gap as Y^*-Y. A positive output gap—when actual output is below potential and resources are not being fully utilized—is called a **recessionary gap**. A negative output gap—when actual output is above potential and resources are being utilized at above-normal rates—is referred to as an **expansionary gap**. You might find this method of defining the output gap, though it is the most common one, to at first seem counterintuitive. A recessionary gap is positive, not negative, and an expansionary gap is negative, not positive. If you find this to be contrary to what your perception tells you should be the case, note that here the terms "positive" and "negative" refer only to the sign, not to normative ideas about good and bad. For instance, even expansionary gaps, also known as inflationary gaps, are generally regarded as bad by macroeconomic policy authorities. The usual goal is an output gap of zero—that is, an output gap which is neither positive nor negative in sign.

ECONOMIC *Naturalist* 7.1 From "bubble economy" to "lost decade"

The Japanese economy from the late 1980s to the present provides an excellent example of how the distinction between *potential* and *actual* output of an economy illuminates the performance of that economy.

As shown in Figure 7.5, during the latter half of the 1980s the Japanese economy experienced an unsustainable boom with a large expansionary gap that persisted for about three years. Since the so-called "bubble economy" period of the late 1980s, however, growth in both actual and potential output has slowed significantly. According to the International Monetary Fund, growth of Japan's *potential* output fell from 3.6 percent per year in the 1980s to about 2.2 percent per year since then due to slower population growth and other factors. But since the early 1990s *actual* output has only grown at 1.5 percent a year, considerably less than the potential growth rate.

With growth of actual output typically lagging behind growth of potential output, Japan has had recessionary gaps in many years since the early 1990s. The economic period from 1993 to 2002 has been called the "lost decade" in that country. As of 2007, a small recessionary gap has persisted despite improved economic growth since 2003 (See Figure 7.3). The Japanese example illustrates that although recessionary gaps are usually regarded as short-term economic fluctuations, in extreme cases they can persist for at least a decade.

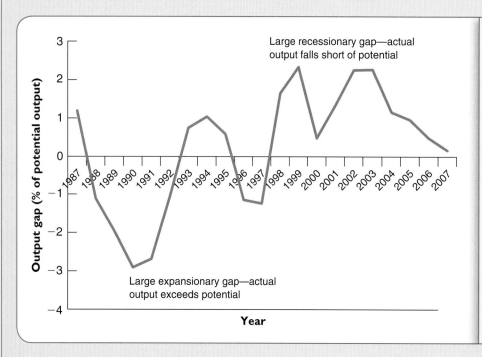

FIGURE 7.5

Output Gap for Japan, 1987–2007

The red line shows Japan's output gap as estimated by the International Monetary Fund. From the late 1980s to the early 1990s, during what has come to be known as the "bubble economy" period, Japan experienced a large expansionary gap. Since 1992 the economy has spent most years mired in recession, with especially large recessionary gaps in 1998, 1999, 2002, and 2003. SOURCE: Same as for Figure 7.3.

How do output gaps arise? Why doesn't the economy always produce at its potential? Is there anything policy-makers can do about output gaps? These are fundamental questions we will return to frequently in subsequent chapters.

THE OUTPUT GAP AND UNEMPLOYMENT

EFFICIENCY

Recessions typically arise because actual output falls below potential, and they bring bad times. Output falls (or at least grows more slowly), implying reduced living standards. Moreover, recessionary output gaps can be extremely embarrassing for policy-makers because they imply that the economy has the *capacity* to produce more but for some reason is not fully utilizing available resources. Recessionary gaps are *inefficient* in that they unnecessarily reduce the total economic "pie," making the typical person worse off.

An important indicator of the low utilization of resources during recessions is the unemployment rate. For instance, in 1989–92 the unemployment rate in Toronto went from 4 percent to 11.5 percent. In general, a high unemployment rate means that labour resources are not being fully utilized, so output has fallen below potential (a recessionary gap). By the same logic, an unusually low unemployment rate implies that labour is being utilized at a rate greater than normal, so actual output exceeds potential output (an expansionary gap).

As a starting point it is useful to think of unemployment as being of four broad types—*frictional, structural, seasonal,* and *cyclical*. We will see shortly that it is also useful to group frictional, structural, and seasonal unemployment together and to contrast them with cyclical unemployment.

Even when jobs are plentiful, some workers with skills in demand where they live will be counted among the unemployed because they are looking for work for a short time before they find it. Days or weeks may go by before, say, a university graduate is able to find suitable work. Short-term unemployment that is associated with the process of matching workers with jobs is called **frictional unemployment**. A certain amount of frictional unemployment is required to allow for good matching of workers with available jobs. So frictional unemployment is economically the least costly of the four broad types of unemployment.

frictional unemployment the short-term unemployment associated with the process of matching workers with jobs

Some unemployment occurs because of mismatch—workers are in the wrong place, or do not have the right skills for available jobs. This is usually labelled **structural unemployment** , because it occurs when the structure of demand does not match up with the structure of supply—workers are unable to fill available jobs because they lack the skills or do not live where jobs are available. Perceptions of the extent of structural unemployment are influenced by examples such as Newfoundland outports devastated by the closure of the cod fishery. But the population of such villages makes up a tiny percentage of the Canadian population. Surveys of the labour force as a whole have found that in some years job vacancies in Canada have amounted to 1 percent of the labour force or less.[2]

structural unemployment unemployment that occurs when workers are unable to fill available jobs because they lack the skills, or do not live where jobs are available

Canada is a country that experiences climatic extremes. **Seasonal unemployment** results when some jobs come and go with the seasons. This month-to-month variation in employment has predicable patterns (for example, retail stores increase their hiring in November, just in time for the Christmas sales rush, and then usually lay off workers in January). In the past, seasonal variation in employment was much greater in Canada than it is now—in part because sectors such as agriculture that are heavily influenced by the weather are much smaller than they used to be, and in part because sectors like construction have developed effective ways of dealing with the weather. Nevertheless, some impacts of the weather are unavoidable—sunbathing will just never be much fun on a Canadian beach in February—so industries such as tourism remain heavily affected by the seasons.

seasonal unemployment unemployment associated with the seasons and/or weather

[2]For a full discussion, see Lars Osberg and Zhengxi Lin, "How Much of Canada's Unemployment is 'Structural'?" *Canadian Public Policy*, July 2000, pp. S141–S158.

cyclical unemployment the extra unemployment brought about by periods of recession

natural rate of unemployment (or u*) the part of the total unemployment rate that is attributable to frictional, structural and seasonal unemployment; equivalently, the unemployment rate that prevails when cyclical unemployment is zero, so the economy has neither a recessionary nor an expansionary output gap

The fourth type of unemployment increases during recessions (that is, periods of substantially reduced output growth) and is called **cyclical unemployment**. This type of unemployment is also referred to as "demand-deficient" unemployment. The sharp peaks in unemployment that were shown in Figure 5.4 reflect the cyclical unemployment that occurs during recessions. Increases in cyclical unemployment are associated with significant declines in real GDP growth and are therefore quite costly economically.

The natural rate of unemployment is defined as the unemployment that is left when cyclical unemployment is subtracted from total unemployment. It refers to the part of unemployment that is attributable to frictional, structural, and seasonal unemployment. Because the total of frictional, structural, and seasonal unemployment is difficult to measure, however, the **natural rate of unemployment** is typically calculated as the unemployment rate that prevails when the economy has neither a recessionary nor an expansionary gap.

Some economists have used *full-employment rate of unemployment* to describe what we term the natural rate of unemployment, and other economists use *non-accelerating inflation rate of unemployment* (or *NAIRU*). But "natural rate of unemployment" is much more commonly used these days than "full-employment rate of unemployment," and it is simpler than "non-accelerating inflation rate of unemployment."

It is worth mentioning that the adjective "natural" in the natural rate of unemployment may give the false impression that nothing can be done to reduce frictional, structural, and seasonal unemployment. But many things are both "natural" and changeable—such as the number of deaths from malaria. Economists recognize

---

ECONOMIC *Naturalist* | 7.2 | Soaring incarceration rates and the natural rate of unemployment

The percentage of the adult population locked up in prison or in jail, expressed in terms of prisoners to 1000 adults, is known as the incarceration rate. The United States has by far the highest incarceration rate among developed countries. The U.S. incarceration rate doubled between 1985 and 1998, and since then it has continued to grow, reaching 10 in 1000 adults (or 1 in 100) in 2008. By comparison, the latest rate for Canada is 0.82 per 1000 adults, or one-tenth the U.S. rate.[3] About 90 percent of those incarcerated in the United States are men. These numbers are so dramatic they prompted two leading labour economists, Lawrence Katz of Harvard University and Alan Krueger of Princeton University, to look at the possible impact of the rising incarceration rate on the decline in the natural rate of unemployment among U.S. males since 1985.[4]

Prisoners are counted in neither the numerator (unemployed) nor the denominator (labour force = employed + unemployed) of the unemployment rate. Yet those in jail or prison are likely to have been unemployed prior to arrest and imprisonment. They are disproportionately high-

school dropouts under 35 years or age, and like others in that demographic category, they do not have characteristics sought by most employers. That is, when not in prison, they are prone to structural unemployment, a key component of the natural rate of unemployment.

What happens to the natural rate of unemployment when hundreds of thousands of men prone to structural unemployment are locked up behind bars? According to the calculations of Katz and Krueger, a plausible estimate is that the rising incarceration rate for U.S. males had reduced the natural unemployment rate for U.S. males by 0.3 percentage points from 1985 to 1998.

The example of the impact of rising incarceration rates on the natural rate of unemployment for U.S. males illustrates that the natural rate of unemployment depends on social factors. Also, since a substantial fraction of the incarcerated were convicted of drug-related offences that would not be labelled criminal activity in some other countries, the rising incarceration rate in the United States illustrates that policies that reduce the natural rate of unemployment are not always "good" ones.

---

[3]See Statistics Canada, "Adult correctional services, average counts of offenders in provincial, territorial and federal programs," CANSIM series v21536802.

[4]For a detailed analysis of factors affecting the natural rate of unemployment in the United States, see Lawrence Katz and Alan Krueger, "The High-Pressure U.S. Labor Market of the 1990s," *Brookings Papers on Economic Activity*, 1, 1999 pp. 1–88.

that the amount of frictional, structural, and seasonal unemployment depends upon institutions, structural policies, technology, and other factors. Such factors explain, for example, why natural rates of unemployment vary considerably among countries. Therefore, just as economists recognize that the rate of death from malaria in many developing countries could be substantially reduced by bed nets, medicines, and so on, they also recognize that the natural rate of unemployment in many countries could be lowered by measures such as structural policies.

We will denote the natural rate of unemployment as u^*. Cyclical unemployment, which is the difference between the total unemployment rate and the natural unemployment rate, can thus be expressed as $u - u^*$, where u is the actual unemployment rate and u^* denotes the natural rate of unemployment. Broadly speaking, when the economy experiences a recessionary gap, the actual unemployment rate exceeds the natural unemployment rate, so cyclical unemployment $u - u^*$ is positive. When the economy experiences an expansionary gap, in contrast, the actual unemployment rate is lower than the natural rate, so cyclical unemployment is negative. This corresponds to a situation in which labour is being used more intensively than normal, so actual unemployment has dipped below its usual frictional, structural, and seasonal levels.

OKUN'S LAW

What is the relationship between an output gap and the amount of cyclical unemployment in the economy? We have already observed that by definition, cyclical unemployment is positive when the economy has a recessionary gap, negative when there is an expansionary gap, and zero when there is no output gap. A more quantitative relationship between cyclical unemployment and the output gap is given by a rule of thumb called *Okun's law*, after Arthur Okun, one of U.S. President John F. Kennedy's chief economic advisers. According to **Okun's law**, each extra percentage point of cyclical unemployment is associated with about a 2-percentage-point increase in the output gap, measured in relation to potential output.[5] So, for example, if cyclical unemployment increases from 1 to 2 percent of the labour force, the recessionary gap will increase from 2 to 4 percent of potential GDP. Given an estimate of the natural rate of unemployment, Okun's law can be used to infer the value of the output gap. Conversely, given an estimate of the output gap, Okun's law can be used to infer the natural rate of unemployment, as is done in Example 7.1.

Okun's law states that each extra percentage point of cyclical unemployment is associated with about a 2-percentage-point increase in the output gap, measured in relation to potential output

Okun's law and Canada's output gap in 1994	**EXAMPLE 7.1**

In 1994, Canada was still suffering from a double-digit unemployment rate as the economy slowly recovered from the 1990–1992 recession. A debate arose about the magnitude of Canada's output gap. The Canadian Centre for Policy Alternatives (CCPA) claimed the output gap was $109 billion. Human Resources Development Canada, the federal department most responsible for the administration of the employment insurance program, had a lower "estimate" of the output gap—$77 billion. And the Department of Finance estimated that the output gap was "only" $45 billion. Even Finance's output gap estimate, however, was higher than the IMF's output gap estimate of $37 billion. These four output gap estimates, from smallest to largest, are shown in column 2 of the table below. We will use them to show that Okun's law can be used to calculate an approximate value of the natural rate of unemployment estimate implied by an output gap estimate.

---

[5]Mathematically, Okun's law can be expressed as $(Y^* - Y)/Y^* = 2\,(u - u^*)$. Okun's law as stated above is widely believed to apply to Canada and the United States today. However, the relationship between unemployment and output varies from country to country and from one historical period to another. When Arthur Okun first formulated his law in the 1960s, he suggested that each extra percentage point of U.S. unemployment was associated with about a 3-percentage-point increase in the output gap.

1. Source	2. Output gap (1994 $, billions)	3. Actual GDP (1994 $, billions)	4. Potential GDP (1994 $, billions)	5. Percentage output gap	6. $u - u^*$ (percentage points)	7. Unemployment rate, u (%)	8. Implied natural rate of unemployment, u^* (%)
IMF	37	773	810	4.6	2.3	10.3	8.0
Finance	45	773	818	5.5	2.8	10.3	7.5
HRDC	77	773	850	9.1	4.5	10.3	5.8
CCPA	109	773	882	12.4	6.2	10.3	4.1

SOURCES: The IMF output gap estimate is derived from Figure 7.5. The Finance, HRDC, and CCPA output gap estimates are from Linda McQuaig, *The Cult of Impotence* (Toronto: Penguin, 1998), p. 92. Adapted from the Statistics Canada CANSIM database http://cansim2.statcan.ca, series v646937.

Column 4 of the table gives the potential GDP estimate formed by adding the output gap estimate from column 2 to actual GDP from column 3. The entries for column 5 are derived by dividing the output gap estimates from column 2 by the corresponding potential GDP estimates from column 4 and multiplying by 100 to get the output gap as a percentage of GDP. Okun's law tells us that the percentage output gap is double the percentage-point gap between the actual unemployment rate and the natural rate. In other words, the gap between the actual and natural unemployment rates is half the percentage output gap. So entries in column 6 are derived by dividing the corresponding entries in column 5 by two. Subtracting the column 6 entries from the column 7 entries gives us the corresponding column 8 entries.

Column 8 indicates the natural rate of unemployment estimates that can be inferred by Okun's law from the output gap estimates in column 2. The lower the output gap estimate, the higher the implied natural rate of unemployment. Notice that the highest natural rate of unemployment estimate is almost double the lowest one, which points to the difficulty of accurately estimating the natural rate of unemployment. Different economists come up with different estimates for the natural rate of unemployment for the same country in the same year.

It should be noted that even the lowest estimate of the output gap in column 2, $37 billion, points to the large size of the output losses resulting from recessions. In 1994, Canada had a population of about 29 million people. Hence the output loss per person in that year, according to the lowest estimate in column 2, equalled the output gap of $37 billion divided by 29 million people, or about $1276—more than $5100 for a family of four in 1994 dollars or about $6635 in 2007 dollars. This calculation implies that output gaps and cyclical unemployment have significant costs.[6]

RECAP

OUTPUT GAPS, CYCLICAL UNEMPLOYMENT, AND OKUN'S LAW

Potential output is the amount of output (real GDP) that an economy can produce when using its resources, such as capital and labour, at normal rates. The *output gap* $Y^* - Y$ is the difference between potential output Y^*

[6]The output losses for 1994 are just a fraction of the output losses associated with the recession that began in 1990. For a discussion of the cumulative output losses associated with the 1990–1992 recession and the subsequent slow recovery, see Pierre Fortin, "The Great Canadian Slump," *Canadian Journal of Economics*, November 1996, pp. 761–787. The cumulative output loss by 1996 was estimated to be $400 billion.

and actual output Y. When actual output is below potential, the resulting output gap is called a *recessionary gap*. When actual output is above potential, the difference is called an *expansionary gap*.

The *natural rate of unemployment u^** is the sum of the frictional, structural, and seasonal unemployment rates. It is the rate of unemployment that is observed when the economy is operating at a normal level, with no output gap.

Cyclical unemployment $u - u^*$ is the difference between the actual unemployment rate u and the natural rate of unemployment u^*. Cyclical unemployment is positive when there is a recessionary gap, negative when there is an expansionary gap, and zero when there is no output gap.

Okun's law relates cyclical unemployment and the output gap. According to this rule of thumb, each percentage point increase in cyclical unemployment is associated with about a 2 percentage-point increase in the output gap, measured in relation to potential output.

7.4 WHY DO SHORT-TERM FLUCTUATIONS OCCUR? A PREVIEW AND A PARABLE

What causes periods of slowdown and expansion? In the previous section we discussed two possible reasons. First, growth in potential output itself may slow down or speed up, reflecting changes in the growth rates of available capital and labour and in the pace of technological progress. Second, even if potential output is growing normally, actual output may be higher or lower than potential output; that is, expansionary or recessionary output gaps may develop. We have not yet addressed the question of how output gaps can arise or what policy-makers should do in response. The causes and cures of output gaps will be a major topic of the next four chapters. Here is a brief preview of the main conclusions of those chapters:

1. In a world in which prices are adjusted immediately to balance the quantities supplied and demanded for all goods and services, output gaps might not exist.[7] However, for many goods and services, the assumption that prices will adjust immediately is not realistic. Instead, many firms adjust the prices of their output only periodically. In particular, rather than changing prices with every variation in demand, firms tend to adjust to changes in demand in the short run by varying the quantity of output they produce and sell. This type of behaviour is known as "meeting the demand" at a preset price.

2. Because in the short-run firms tend to meet the demand for their output at preset prices, changes in the amount that customers decide to spend will affect output. When total spending is low for some reason, output may fall below potential output; conversely, when spending is high, output may rise above

[7]Although macroeconomists argue that inflexibility of prices may be named as a *sufficient* condition to explain short-term economic fluctuations, many Keynesian macroeconomists would argue that it is not a *necessary* condition. It would be an example of the *fallacy of composition* to suppose that because price flexibility eliminates output gaps in micro markets, such as the ice cream market, it would therefore also necessarily eliminate gaps between aggregate demand and aggregate supply at the macro level of the economy. Indeed, many Keynesian economists would argue that downward price flexibility can worsen a recession, as evidenced by the many economies, including Canada's, that experienced deflation without economic recovery during the Great Depression of the 1930s. Recall that in Chapter 6 we noted that deflation, a downward price flexibility at the macro level of the economy, typically has a negative impact on economic growth and that central banks around the world therefore work to avoid deflation.

potential output. In other words, *changes in economy-wide spending are the primary cause of output gaps*. Thus, government policies can help to eliminate output gaps by influencing total spending. For example, the government can affect total spending directly simply by changing its own level of purchases.

3. Although firms tend to meet demand in the short run, they will not be willing to do so indefinitely. If customer demand continues to differ from potential output, firms will eventually adjust their prices so as to eliminate output gaps. If demand exceeds potential output (an expansionary gap), firms will raise their prices aggressively, spurring inflation. If demand falls below potential output (a recessionary gap), firms will raise their prices less aggressively or even cut prices, reducing inflation.

4. Eventually price changes by firms and adjustments to wages may work to eliminate output gaps and bring production back into line with the economy's potential output. This process of adjustment can be slow, however, so that in practice policy-makers such as central bankers often take action to speed up the elimination of output gaps.

These ideas will become clearer as we proceed through the next chapters. Before plunging into the details of the analysis, let's consider an example that, while it does not necessarily hold true for the overall economy, illustrates the links between spending and output.

Al's ice cream store produces gourmet ice cream on the premises and sells it directly to the public. What determines the amount of ice cream that Al produces on a daily basis? The productive capacity, or potential output, of the shop is one important factor. Specifically, Al's potential output of ice cream depends on the amount of capital (number of ice cream makers) and labour (number of workers) that he employs and on the productivity of that capital and labour.

The main source of day-to-day variations in Al's ice cream production is fluctuations in the demand for ice cream by the public. Some of these fluctuations in spending occur predictably over the course of the day (more demand in the afternoon than in the morning, for example), the week (more demand on weekends), or the year (more demand in the summer). Other changes in demand are less regular—more demand on a hot day than on a cool one, or on a day when a parade is passing by the store. Some changes in demand are hard for Al to interpret: For example, a surge in demand for rocky road ice cream on one particular Tuesday could reflect a permanent change in consumer tastes, or it might just be a random, one-time event.

How should Al react to these ebbs and flows in the demand for ice cream? The basic supply and demand model that we introduced in Chapter 3, if applied to the market for ice cream, would predict that the price of ice cream should change with every change in the demand for ice cream. For example, prices should rise just after the movie theatre next door to Al's shop lets out on Friday night, and should fall on unusually cold, blustery days, when most people would prefer hot chocolate to an ice cream cone. Indeed, taken literally, the supply and demand model of Chapter 3 predicts that ice cream prices should change almost moment to moment. Imagine Al standing in front of his shop like an auctioneer, calling out prices in an effort to determine how many people are willing to buy at each price!

Of course, we do not expect to see this behaviour by an ice cream store owner. Price setting by auction does in fact occur in some markets, such as the market for grain or the stock market, but it is not the normal procedure in most retail markets, such as the market for ice cream. Why this difference? The basic reason is that sometimes the economic benefits of hiring an auctioneer and setting up an auction exceed the costs of doing so, and sometimes they do not. In the market for grain, for example, many buyers and sellers gather together in the same place at the same time to transact large volumes of standardized goods (bushels of grain). In that kind of situation, an auction is an efficient way to determine prices and balance the quantities supplied and demanded. In an ice cream store, by contrast, customers come in by twos and threes at random times throughout the day. Some want shakes, some cones, and some sodas. With small numbers of customers and a low sales volume at any given time, the *costs* involved in selling ice cream by auction are much greater than the *benefits* of allowing prices to vary with demand. One consideration in judging the size of potential benefits from varying prices is that vendors can lose customers if they engage in "price gouging," raising prices in a way that customers interpret as being unfair (see Economic Naturalist 7.3).

COST–BENEFIT

So how does Al the ice cream store manager deal with changes in the demand for ice cream? Observation suggests that he begins by setting prices based on the best information he has about the demand for his product and the costs of production. Perhaps he prints up a menu or makes a sign announcing the prices. Then, over a period of time, he will keep his prices fixed and serve as many customers as want to buy (up to the point where he runs out of ice cream or room in the store at these prices). This behaviour is what we call "meeting the demand" at preset prices, and it implies that *in the short run*, the amount of ice cream Al produces and sells is determined by the demand for his products.

However, with the passage of time the situation is quite different. Suppose, for example, that Al's ice cream earns a city-wide reputation for its freshness and flavour. Day after day Al observes long lines in his store. His ice cream maker is overtaxed, as are his employees and his table space. There can no longer be any doubt that at current prices, the quantity of ice cream the public wants to consume exceeds what Al is able and willing to supply on a normal basis (his potential output in the short run). What will Al do?

One possibility is that Al could respond by raising his prices. At higher prices, Al will earn higher profits, and the higher prices will bring the quantity of ice cream demanded closer to Al's normal production capacity. Hiring more employees and expanding the store are other actions Al could take in response to such a situation. Such actions would result in an increase in Al's normal production capacity—a higher level of potential output. (Greater production capacity for quality ice cream could also arise if Al's obvious success spawns imitators.)

This example illustrates in a simple way the links between spending and output—except, of course, that we must think of this story as applying to the whole economy, not to a single business. The key point is that changes in demand produce a series of responses from producers as time passes. At first, producers will typically choose not to change their prices but rather to meet demand at preset prices. Thus, Al's ice cream store enjoys a boom on an unusually hot day, when the demand for ice cream is strong, while an unseasonably cold day brings an ice cream recession. But with the passage of time, prices can adjust. Eventually firms may add plant and equipment and hire additional workers. (And the workers themselves may demand wage increases.)

In Chapters 8 and 9 we develop a short-run model for examining the situation where firms meet demand at preset prices. Chapters 10 and 11 present more complex models based upon a longer time frame.

ECONOMIC *Naturalist*	7.3	Why did the Coca-Cola Company test a vending machine that "knows" when the weather is hot?

According to *The New York Times* (28 October 1999) the Coca-Cola Company quietly tested a pop vending machine that included a temperature sensor. Why would Coca-Cola want a vending machine that "knows" when the weather is hot?

When the weather is hot, the demand for refreshing soft drinks rises, increasing their market-clearing price. To take advantage of this variation in consumer demand, the vending machines that Coca-Cola tested were equipped with a computer chip that gave them the capability to raise pop prices automatically when the temperature climbed. The company's chairman and chief executive, M. Douglas Ivester, described in an interview how the desire for a cold drink increases during a sports championship final held in the summer heat. "So it is fair that it should be more expensive," Mr. Ivester was quoted as saying. "The machine will simply make this process automatic." Company officials suggested numerous other ways in which vending machine prices could be made dependent on demand. For example, machines could be programmed to reduce prices during off-peak hours or at low-traffic machines.

In traditional vending machines, cold drinks are priced in a way analogous to the way Al prices his ice cream: a price is set, and demand is met at the preset price, until the machine runs out of pop. The weather-sensitive vending machine illustrates how technology may change pricing practices in the future. Indeed, increased computing power and access to the Internet have already allowed some firms, such as airline companies, to change prices almost continuously in response to variations in demand.

On the other hand, Coca-Cola's experiments with "smart" vending machines also illustrate the barriers to fully flexible pricing in practice. First, the new vending machines are more costly than the standard model. In deciding whether to use them, the company must decide whether the extra revenues from variable pricing justify the extra cost of the machines. Second, in early tests many consumers reacted negatively to the new machines, complaining that they take unfair advantage of thirsty customers. In practice, customer complaints and concerns about "fairness" make companies less willing to vary prices sensitively with changing demand.

SUMMARY

7.1 Real GDP does not grow smoothly. Periods in which the economy is growing at a rate significantly below normal are called *recessions;* periods in which the economy is growing at a rate significantly above normal are called *expansions*. A severe or protracted recession, like the long decline that occurred between 1929 and 1933, is called a *depression*, while a particularly strong expansion is called a *boom*.

7.1 The beginning of a recession is called the *peak*, because it represents the high point of economic activity prior to a downturn. The end of a recession, which marks the low point of economic activity prior to a recovery, is called the *trough*. Since the Second World War, Canadian recessions have been shorter on average than booms.

7.2 Short-term economic fluctuations are irregular in length and severity and are thus hard to forecast. Expansions and recessions are typically felt throughout the economy and may even be global in scope. Unemployment rises sharply during recessions (the phenomenon of cyclical unemployment), while inflation tends to fall during or shortly after a recession. Durable goods industries tend to be particularly sensitive to recessions and booms, while services and non-durable goods industries are less sensitive.

7.3 *Potential output*, also called potential GDP or full-employment output, is the amount of output (real GDP) that an economy can produce when it is using its resources, such as capital and labour, at normal rates. The difference between potential output and actual output is the *output gap*. When output is below potential, the gap is called a *recessionary gap;* when output is above potential, the difference is called an *expansionary gap*. Recessions can occur because potential output is growing unusually slowly, but typically occur because actual output is below potential.

7.3 The *natural rate of unemployment* is the part of the total unemployment rate that is attributable to *frictional, structural,* and *seasonal unemployment*. Equivalently, the natural rate of unemployment is the rate of unemployment that exists when the output gap is zero. *Cyclical unemployment*, the part of unemployment that is associated with recessions and expansions, equals the total unemployment rate less the natural unemployment rate. Cyclical unemployment is related to the output gap by *Okun's law*, which states that each extra percentage point of cyclical unemployment is associated with about a 2-percentage-point increase in the output gap, measured in relation to potential output.

7.4 In the following chapters our study of recessions and expansions will focus on the role of economy-wide spending. Changes in economy-wide spending produce a series of responses from producers as time passes. At first, producers will typically choose not to change their prices but rather to meet demand at preset prices. With the passage of time, however, prices can adjust. Eventually firms may add to their plant and equipment and hire additional workers.

KEY TERMS

boom (167)
cyclical unemployment (174)
depression (166)
expansion (166)
expansionary gap (172)
frictional unemployment (173)
natural rate of unemployment
(or u^*) (174)

Okun's law (175)
ouput gap (or $Y^* - Y$) (172)
peak (166)
potential output (or potential GDP or
full-employment output
or Y^*) (171)

recession (or contraction) (166)
recessionary gap (172)
seasonal unemployment (173)
structural unemployment (173)
trough (166)

REVIEW QUESTIONS

1. Define *recession* and *expansion*. What are the beginning and ending points of a recession called? In postwar Canada, which have been longer on average, recessions or expansions?

2. Why is the traditional term *business cycles* a misnomer? How does your answer relate to the ease or difficulty of forecasting peaks and troughs?

3. Which firm is likely to see its profits reduced the most in a recession: an automobile producer, a manufacturer of boots and shoes, or a barbershop? Which is likely to see its profits reduced by the least? Explain.

4. List four broad types of unemployment and their causes. Which of these types is the least costly economically?

5. How is each of the following likely to be affected by a recession: the natural unemployment rate, the cyclical unemployment rate, the inflation rate?

6. Define *potential output*. Is it possible for an economy to produce an amount greater than potential output? Explain.

7. True or false, and explain: When output equals potential output, the unemployment rate is zero.

8. If the natural rate of unemployment is 5 percent, what is the overall rate of unemployment if output is 2 percent below potential output? What if output is 2 percent above potential output?

PROBLEMS

1. Given below are data on real GDP and estimates of potential GDP for Canada prepared by the IMF. For each year, calculate the output gap as a percentage of potential GDP, and state whether the gap is a recessionary gap or an expansionary gap, according to the IMF. Also, calculate the year-to-year growth rates of real GDP.

Year	Real GDP (1997 $, billions)	Potential GDP (1997 $, billions)
2001	1032	981
2002	1053	1011
2003	1086	1140
2004	1113	1113
2005	1155	1132
2006	1201	1177

2. Back in 2000, the Canadian unemployment rate averaged 6.8 percent and current dollar GDP reached $1056 billion (or $1.056 trillion). Pierre Fortin, a leading Canadian macroeconomist affiliated with the Université du Québec à Montréal, had estimated Canada's natural rate of unemployment for 2000 as being 5.3 percent. By contrast, one could infer an estimate of a natural rate of unemployment of about 7 percent from official Bank of Canada statements, such as the Bank's claim that the Canadian economy was operating with an expansionary gap for most of 2000 (when the actual unemployment rate was around 6.8 percent in most months).

Using Okun's law, what would be the potential GDP number for 2000 corresponding to a natural unemployment rate of 5.3 percent? What would be the dollar value of the recessionary gap? Also, what would be the potential GDP number corresponding to a natural rate of 7 percent? What would be the dollar value of the expansionary gap?

3. Using Okun's law, fill in the four pieces of missing data in the following table. That is, replace (1), (2), (3), and (4) with correct data.

Year	Real GDP	Potential GDP	Natural unemployment rate (%)	Actual unemployment rate (%)
2006	7840	8000	(1)	6
2007	8100	(2)	5	5
2008	(3)	8200	4.5	4
2009	8415	8250	5	(4)

ANSWERS TO IN-CHAPTER EXERCISES

7.1 The answer depends on current data.

Chapter 8 Spending and Output in the Short Run

When one of the authors of this book was a small boy, he used to spend some time every summer with his grandparents, who lived a few hours from his home. A favourite activity of his during these visits was to spend a summer evening on the front porch with his grandmother, listening to her stories. For some reason Grandma's recounting of her own life was particularly fascinating to her grandson.

The early years of Grandma's marriage covered the worst part of the Great Depression. In one of her reminiscences she remarked that at that time, in the mid-1930s, it had been a satisfaction to her to be able to buy her children a new pair of shoes every year. In the small town where she and her family lived, many children had to wear their shoes until they fell apart, and a few unlucky boys and girls went to school barefoot. Her grandson thought this was scandalous: "Why didn't their parents just buy them new shoes?" he demanded.

"They couldn't," said Grandma. "They didn't have the money. Most of the fathers had lost their jobs because of the Depression."

"What kind of jobs did they have?"

"They worked in the shoe factories, which had to close down."

"Why did the factories close down?"

"Because," Grandma explained, "nobody had any money to buy shoes."

The grandson was only 6 or 7 years old at the time, but even he could see that there was something badly wrong with Grandma's logic. On the one side were boarded-up shoe factories and shoe workers with no jobs; on the other, children without shoes. Why couldn't the shoe factories just open and produce the shoes the children so badly needed? He made his point quite firmly, but Grandma just shrugged and said it didn't work that way.

The story of the closed-down shoe factories illustrates in a microcosm the cost to society of a recessionary gap. In an economy with a recessionary gap, available resources that could in principle be used to produce valuable goods and services are instead allowed to lie fallow. This waste of resources lowers the economy's output and standard of living, compared to its potential.

Grandma's account also suggests how such an unfortunate situation might come about. Suppose factory owners and other producers, being reluctant to accumulate unsold goods on their shelves, produce just enough output to satisfy the demand for their products. And suppose that for some reason the public's willingness or ability to spend declines. If spending declines, factories will respond by cutting their production (because they don't want to produce goods they can't sell) and by laying off workers who are no longer needed. And because the workers who are laid off will lose most of their income—a particularly serious loss in the 1930s, in the days before government-sponsored employment insurance—they must reduce their own spending. As their spending declines, factories will reduce their production again, laying off more workers, who in turn reduce their spending, and so on, in a vicious circle. In this scenario, the problem is not a lack of productive capacity—the factories have not lost their ability to produce—but rather *insufficient spending* to support the normal level of production.

The idea that a decline in aggregate spending may cause output to fall below potential output was one of the key insights of John Maynard Keynes (1883–1946), a British economist whose name headed many "most influential economists of the past century" lists published in 2000. The goal of this chapter is to develop a model of how recessions and expansions may arise from fluctuations in aggregate spending, along the lines first suggested by Keynes. This model, which we call the *basic Keynesian model,* is also known as the *Keynesian cross,* after the diagram that is used to illustrate the theory. In the body of the chapter we will emphasize a numerical and graphical approach to the basic Keynesian model. The appendix to this chapter provides a more general algebraic analysis.

We will begin with a brief discussion of the key assumption of the basic Keynesian model. We will then turn to the important concept of total, or aggregate, *planned spending* in the economy. We will show how, in the short run, planned spending helps to determine the level of output, which can be greater than or less than potential output. In other words, depending on the level of spending, the economy may develop an output gap. "Too little" spending leads to a recessionary output gap, while "too much" creates an expansionary output gap.

An implication of the basic Keynesian model is that government policies that affect the level of spending can be used to reduce or eliminate output gaps. Policies used in this way are called *stabilization policies.* Keynes himself argued for the active use of fiscal policy—policy relating to government spending and taxes—to eliminate output gaps and stabilize the economy. In the latter part of this chapter we will show why Keynes thought fiscal policy could help to stabilize the economy, and we will discuss the usefulness of fiscal policy as a stabilization tool.

As we foreshadowed in Chapter 7, the basic Keynesian model is a somewhat simplified model of the economy. It is geared towards showing how an economy suffering from a recessionary gap can raise actual output to the level of potential output. And it is a static model in two respects. First, it treats prices as fixed—firms do not adjust their prices but instead meet the demand forthcoming at preset prices. In other words, a situation of zero inflation is assumed. Second, it treats the level of potential output as fixed. That is, the model deals only with that part of real-world growth that comes about from increasing actual output to its potential level. This means, for example, that fiscal policy is assumed to impact only on actual output and not on potential output, and that the impact of private-sector investment on potential output is ignored.

Nevertheless, the basic Keynesian model is a useful one for understanding macroeconomic commentary in the news media. It is also a key building block of current theories of short-run economic fluctuations and stabilization policies. In subsequent chapters we will extend the basic Keynesian model to incorporate inflation and other important features of the economy.

John Maynard Keynes
(1883–1946)

8.1 THE KEYNESIAN MODEL'S CRUCIAL ASSUMPTION: FIRMS MEET DEMAND AT PRESET PRICES

The basic Keynesian model is built on a key assumption, highlighted in Box 8.1. This assumption is that firms do not continuously change their prices as supply and demand conditions change; rather, over short periods, firms tend to keep their prices fixed and *meet the demand* that is forthcoming at those prices. As we will see, the assumption that firms vary their production in order to meet demand at preset prices implies that fluctuations in spending will have powerful effects on the nation's real GDP.

BOX 8.1   KEY ASSUMPTION OF THE BASIC KEYNESIAN MODEL

In the short run, firms meet the demand for their products at preset prices.

Firms do not respond to every change in the demand for their products by changing their prices. Instead, they typically set a price for some period, and then *meet the demand* at that price. By meeting the demand, we mean that firms produce just enough to satisfy their customers at the prices that have been set.

The assumption that over short periods of time firms will meet the demand for their products at preset prices is generally realistic. Think of the stores where you shop: the price of a pair of jeans does not fluctuate with the number of customers who enter the store or the latest news about the price of denim. Instead, the store posts a price and sells jeans to any customer who wants to buy at that price, at least until the store runs out of stock. Similarly, the corner pizza restaurant may leave the price of its large pizza unchanged for months or longer, allowing its pizza production to be determined by the number of customers who want to buy at the preset price.

Firms like these do not change their prices frequently because doing so would be costly. Economists refer to the costs of changing prices as **menu costs**. In the case of the pizza restaurant, the menu cost is literally just that—the cost of printing up a new menu when prices change. Similarly, the clothing store faces the cost of re-marking all its merchandise if the manager changes prices. But menu costs may also include other kinds of costs, including, for example, the cost of doing a market survey to determine what price to charge and the cost of informing customers about price changes.

menu costs the costs of changing prices

Menu costs will not prevent firms from changing their prices indefinitely. As we saw in Chapter 7 in the case of Al's ice cream store, too great an imbalance between demand and supply, as reflected by a difference between sales and potential output, will eventually lead to a change in price. If no one is buying jeans, for example, at some point the clothing store will mark down its jeans prices. Or if the pizza restaurant becomes the local hot spot, with a line of customers stretching out the door, eventually the manager will raise the price of a large pizza. Like other economic decisions, the decision to change prices reflects a *cost–benefit comparison*: prices should be changed if the benefit of doing so—the fact that sales will be brought more nearly into line with the firm's normal production capacity—outweighs the menu costs associated with making the change. As we have stressed, the basic Keynesian model developed in this chapter ignores the fact that prices will eventually adjust, and should therefore be interpreted as applying to the short run.

COST–BENEFIT

8.2   PLANNED AGGREGATE EXPENDITURE

planned aggregate expenditure (PAE) total planned spending on final goods and services

In the Keynesian theory discussed in this chapter, output at each point in time is determined by the amount that people want to spend—what economists call *planned aggregate expenditure.* Specifically, **planned aggregate expenditure** (*PAE*) is total planned spending on final goods and services. Sometimes in economics total planned spending is called total desired spending.

The four components of total, or aggregate, spending on final goods and services were introduced in Chapter 5:

1. *Consumer expenditure,* or simply *consumption* (*C*), is spending by households on final goods and services. Examples of consumer expenditure are spending on food, clothes, and entertainment, and on consumer durable goods like automobiles and furniture.

2. *Private-sector investment* (*I*) is spending by firms on new capital goods, such as office buildings, factories, and equipment. Spending on new houses and apartment buildings (residential investment) and changes in inventories (inventory investment) are also included. Recall from Chapter 5 that *I* refers to newly created goods, *not* purchases of financial assets like stocks and bonds.

3. *Government purchases (G)* refers to spending by governments (federal, provincial, and municipal) on goods and services. Examples of government purchases include new schools and hospitals, roads, computers, office supplies, military equipment, and the services of public-sector employees, such as teachers, nurses, government office workers, police, and armed forces personnel. Recall from Chapter 5 that government transfer payments, such as Canada Pension Plan and employment insurance benefits, and interest on the public debt are not included in government purchases.

4. *Net exports* (*NX*) equals exports minus imports. Exports are sales of domestically produced goods and services to foreigners; imports are purchases by domestic residents of goods and services produced abroad. Net exports represent the net demand for domestic goods by foreigners.

Together these four types of spending—by households, firms, the government, and the rest of the world—sum to total, or aggregate, spending.

PLANNED SPENDING VERSUS ACTUAL SPENDING

In the Keynesian model, output is determined by planned aggregate expenditure, or planned spending for short. Could *planned* spending ever differ from *actual* spending? The answer is yes. The most important case is that of a firm that sells either less or more of its product than expected. As was noted in Chapter 5, additions to the stocks of goods sitting in a firm's warehouse are treated in the GDP accounts as inventory investment by the firm. In effect, the GDP accounts are based on the assumption that the firm buys its unsold inventory from itself. The inventory is then counted as part of the firm's investment spending.[1]

Suppose, then, that a firm's actual sales are less than expected so that part of what it had planned to sell remains in the warehouse. In this case, the firm's actual investment, including the unexpected increases in its inventory, is greater than its planned investment, which did not include added inventory. Suppose we agree to let I^p equal the firm's planned investment, including planned inventory investment. A firm that sells less of its output than planned, and therefore adds more to its inventory than planned, will find that its actual investment (including unplanned inventory investment) exceeds its planned investment so that $I > I^p$.

[1]For the purposes of measuring GDP, treating unsold output as being purchased by its producer has the virtue of ensuring that actual production and actual expenditure are equal.

What about a firm that sells more of its output than expected? In that case, the firm will add less to its inventory than it planned, so actual investment will be less than planned investment, or $I < I^p$. Example 8.1 gives a numerical illustration.

Actual and planned investment   EXAMPLE 8.1

The Fly-by-Night Kite Company produces $5 000 000 worth of kites during the year. It expects sales of $4 800 000 for the year, leaving $200 000 worth of kites to be stored in the warehouse for future sale. During the year, Fly-by-Night adds $1 000 000 in new production equipment as part of an expansion plan. Find Fly-by-Night's actual investment I and its planned investment I^p if actual kite sales turn out to be $4 600 000. What if sales are $4 800 000? What if they are $5 000 000?

Fly-by-Night's planned investment I^p equals its purchases of new production equipment ($1 000 000) plus its planned additions to inventory ($200 000), for a total of $1 200 000 in planned investment. The company's planned investment does not depend on how much it actually sells.

If Fly-by-Night sells only $4 600 000 worth of kites, it will add $400 000 in kites to its inventory instead of the $200 000 worth originally planned. In this case, actual investment equals the $1 000 000 in new equipment plus the $400 000 in inventory investment, so $I = \$1\ 400\ 000$. We see that when the firm sells less output than planned, actual investment exceeds planned investment ($I > I^p$).

If Fly-by-Night has $4 800 000 in sales, then it will add $200 000 in kites to inventory, just as planned. In this case, actual and planned investment are the same: $I = I^p = \$1\ 200\ 000$.

Finally, if Fly-by-Night sells $5 000 000 worth of kites, it will have no output to add to inventory. Its inventory investment will be zero, and its total actual investment (including the new equipment) will equal $1 000 000, which is less than its planned investment of $1 200 000 ($I < I^p$).

Because firms that are meeting the demand for their product or service at preset prices cannot control how much they sell, their actual investment (including inventory investment) may well differ from their planned investment. However, for households, the government, and foreign purchasers, we may reasonably assume that actual spending and planned spending are the same. Thus, from now on we will assume that for consumption, government purchases, and net exports, actual spending equals planned spending.

With these assumptions, we can define planned aggregate expenditure by the equation:

$$PAE = C + I^p + G + NX. \tag{8.1}$$

Equation 8.1 says that planned aggregate expenditure is the sum of planned spending by households, firms, governments, and foreigners. We use a superscript p to distinguish planned investment spending by firms, I^p, from actual private-sector investment spending, I. However, because planned spending equals actual spending for households, the government, and foreigners, we do not need to use superscripts for consumption, government purchases, or net exports.

HEY BIG SPENDER! CONSUMER SPENDING AND THE ECONOMY

The largest component of planned aggregate expenditure—about 56 percent of Canadian GDP in recent years—is consumption spending, or C. What determines how much people plan to spend on consumer goods and services in a given period?

While many factors may be relevant, a particularly important determinant of the amount people plan to consume is their after-tax, or *personal disposable,* income. All else being equal, households and individuals with higher disposable incomes will consume more than those with lower disposable incomes. Keynes himself stressed the importance of disposable income in determining household consumption decisions, claiming a "psychological law" that people would tie their spending closely to their incomes.

Disposable income of the private sector is the total production of the economy, *Y,* less net taxes (taxes minus transfers, including both government transfer payments—like Canada Pension Plan benefits—and interest on the public debt). Disposable income corresponds more or less to personal income as defined by Statistics Canada. So, all else being equal, we can assume that consumption spending (C) increases as *disposable income* (*Y* − *T*) increases. As already mentioned, other factors may also affect consumption, such as the real interest rate. For now we will ignore those other factors, returning to some of them later.

An equation that captures the link between consumption and disposable income is:

$$C = \overline{C} + c(Y - T). \tag{8.2}$$

This equation, which we will dissect in a moment, is known as a *consumption function.* A **consumption function** relates consumption spending to its determinants, such as disposable income.

consumption function the relationship between consumption spending and its determinants, such as disposable (after-tax) income

Let's look at this consumption function, Equation 8.2, more carefully. The right side of the equation contains two terms, $\overline{C}$ and $c(Y - T)$. The first term, $\overline{C}$, is a constant term in the equation that is intended to capture factors *other than disposable income* that affect consumption. For example, suppose consumers were to become more optimistic about the future so that they desire to consume more and save less at any given level of their current disposable incomes. An increase in desired consumption at any given level of disposable income would be represented in the consumption function, Equation 8.2, as an increase in the term $\overline{C}$.

We can imagine other factors that may affect the term $\overline{C}$ in the consumption function. For example, suppose there is a boom in the stock market or a sharp increase in house prices, making consumers feel wealthier and thus more inclined to spend, for a given level of current disposable income. This effect could be captured by assuming that $\overline{C}$ increases. Likewise, a fall in house prices or stock prices that made consumers feel poorer and less inclined to spend would be represented by a decrease in $\overline{C}$. Economists refer to the effect of changes in asset prices on household wealth and thus their consumption spending as the **wealth effect** of changes in asset prices.

wealth effect the tendency of changes in asset prices to affect households' wealth and thus their spending on consumption goods and services

The second term on the right side of Equation 8.2, $c(Y - T)$, reflects the effect of disposable income *Y* − *T* on consumption. The parameter *c*, a fixed number, is called the *marginal propensity to consume.* The **marginal propensity to consume,** or **MPC,** is the amount by which consumption rises when current disposable income rises by $1. Presumably, if people receive an extra dollar of income, they will consume part of the dollar and save the rest. In other words, their consumption will increase but by less than the full dollar of extra income. Thus we assume that the marginal propensity to consume is greater than 0 (an increase in income leads to an increase in consumption), but less than 1 (the increase in consumption will be less than the full increase in income). These assumptions can be written symbolically as $0 < c < 1$.

marginal propensity to consume (MPC) the amount by which consumption rises when disposable income rises by $1; we assume that $0 < MPC < 1$

It is important to recognize that the marginal propensity to consume will generally differ from the *average propensity to consume.* The **average propensity to consume,** or **APC,** is calculated by dividing consumption by disposable income. Whereas the marginal propensity to consume is the change in consumption brought about by a change in disposable income, the average propensity to consume is the proportion of all disposable income that is devoted to consumption.

average propensity to consume (APC) consumption divided by disposable income

The average–marginal distinction that is important for understanding the output decisions of firms (see Chapter 1), is also important for understanding the consumption function. For our present purposes, it is the marginal propensity to consume that is the most relevant concept, not the average propensity to consume.

Figure 8.1 shows a hypothetical consumption function, with consumption spending (C) on the vertical axis and disposable income (Y − T) on the horizontal axis. The intercept of the consumption function on the vertical axis equals the constant term $\overline{C}$, and the slope of the consumption function equals the marginal propensity to consume c.

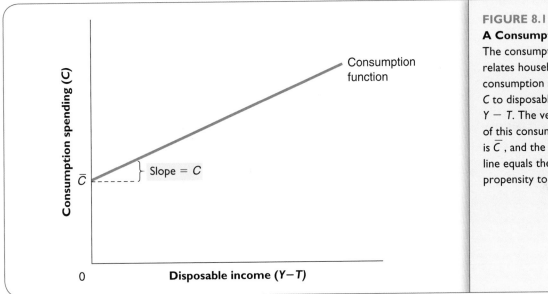

FIGURE 8.1

A Consumption Function
The consumption function relates households' consumption spending C to disposable income Y − T. The vertical intercept of this consumption function is $\overline{C}$, and the slope of the line equals the marginal propensity to consume, c.

To see how this consumption function fits reality, compare Figure 8.1 to Figure 8.2, which shows the relationship between aggregate real consumption expenditures and real personal disposable income in Canada for the period 1981 through 2007. In Figure 8.2, a scatter plot, each point on the graph corresponds to a year between 1981 and 2007 (selected years are indicated in the figure). The position of each point is determined by the combination of consumption and personal disposable income associated with that year. As you can see, higher disposable income implies higher consumption.

PLANNED AGGREGATE EXPENDITURE AND OUTPUT

Thinking back to Grandma's reminiscences, recall that an important element of her story involved the links among production, income, and spending. As the shoe factories in Grandma's town reduced production, the incomes of both factory workers and factory owners fell. Workers' incomes fell as the number of hours of work per week were reduced (a common practice during the Depression), as workers were laid off, or as wages were cut. Factory owners' income fell as profits declined. Reduced incomes, in turn, forced both workers and factory owners to curtail their spending—which led to still lower production and further reductions in income. This vicious circle led the economy further and further into recession.

The logic of Grandma's story has two key elements: (1) declines in production (which imply declines in the income received by producers) lead to reduced spending; and (2) reductions in spending lead to declines in production and income. In this section we look at the first part of the story, the effects of production and income on spending. We return later in this chapter to the effects of spending on production and income.

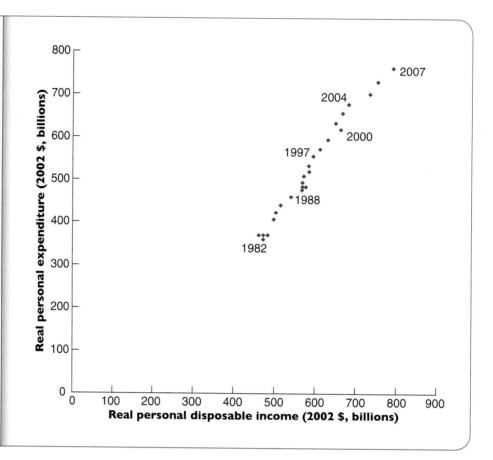

FIGURE 8.2

The Canadian Consumption Function, 1981–2007

Each point on this figure represents a combination of aggregate real personal expenditure and aggregate real personal disposable income for a specific year between 1981 and 2007. Note the strong positive relationship between personal expenditure (consumption) and personal disposable income.
SOURCE: Adapted from the Statistics Canada CANSIM series v1997738, v1992229, v691566, and v3840566.

Why do changes in production and income affect planned aggregate spending? The consumption function, which relates consumption to disposable income, is the basic source of this relationship. Because consumption spending C is a large part of planned aggregate spending, and because consumption depends on output Y, aggregate spending as a whole depends on output. Example 8.2 illustrates this relationship numerically.

EXAMPLE 8.2

Linking planned aggregate expenditure to output

In a particular economy, the consumption function is:

$$C = 620 + 0.8 (Y - T),$$

so that the intercept term in the consumption function $\overline{C}$, equals 620, and the marginal propensity to consume c equals 0.8. Also, suppose that we are given that planned private-sector investment spending $I^p = 220$, government purchases $G = 300$, net exports $NX = 20$, and net taxes $T = 250$.

Write a numerical equation linking planned aggregate expenditure PAE to output Y. How does planned spending change when output, and hence income, change?

Recall the definition of planned aggregate expenditure, Equation 8.1:

$$PAE = C + I^p + G + NX.$$

To find a numerical equation for planned aggregate expenditure, we need to find numerical expressions for each of its four components. The first component of spending, consumption, is defined by the consumption function, $C = 620 + 0.8 (Y - T)$. Since net taxes $T = 250$, we can substitute for T to write the consumption function as $C = 620 + 0.8(Y - 250)$. Now plug this expression for C into the definition of planned aggregate expenditure above to get

$$PAE = [620 + 0.8\,(Y - 250)] + I^p + G + NX,$$

where we have just replaced C by its value as determined by the consumption function. Similarly, we can substitute the given numerical values of planned private-sector investment I^p, government purchases G, and net exports NX into the definition of planned aggregate expenditure to get

$$PAE = [620 + 0.8\,(Y - 250)] + 220 + 300 + 20.$$

To simplify this equation, first note that $0.8(Y - 250) = 0.8Y - 200$, then add all the terms that don't depend on output Y. The result is

$$PAE = (620 - 200 + 220 + 300 + 20) + 0.8Y$$
$$= 960 + 0.8Y.$$

The final expression shows the relationship between planned aggregate expenditure and output in this numerical example. Note that, according to this equation, a \$1 increase in Y leads to an increase in PAE of $(0.8)\,(\$1)$, or 80 cents. The reason for this is that the marginal propensity to consume, c, in this example is 0.8. Hence a \$1 increase in income raises consumption spending by 80 cents. Since consumption is a component of total planned spending, total spending rises by 80 cents as well.

The solution to Example 8.2 illustrates a general point: planned aggregate expenditure can be divided into two parts, a part that depends on output (Y) and a part that is independent of output. The portion of planned aggregate expenditure that is independent of output is called **autonomous expenditure**. In Example 8.2, autonomous expenditure is the constant term in the equation for planned aggregate expenditure, or 960. This portion of planned spending, being a fixed number, does not vary when output varies. By contrast, the portion of planned aggregate expenditure that depends on output (Y) is called **induced expenditure**. In Example 8.2, induced expenditure equals $0.8Y$, the second term in the expression for planned aggregate expenditure. Note that the numerical value of induced expenditure depends, by definition, on the numerical value taken by output. Autonomous expenditure and induced expenditure together equal planned aggregate expenditure.

autonomous expenditure the portion of planned aggregate expenditure that is independent of output

induced expenditure the portion of planned aggregate expenditure that depends on output Y

RECAP

PLANNED AGGREGATE EXPENDTURE

Planned aggregate expenditure (PAE) is total planned spending on final goods and services. The four components of planned aggregate expenditure are consumer expenditure (C), planned private-sector investment (I^p), government purchases (G), and net exports (NX). Planned investment differs from actual investment when firms' sales are different from what they expected so that additions to inventory (a component of investment) are different from what firms anticipated.

The largest component of planned aggregate expenditure is consumer expenditure, or simply consumption. Consumption depends on disposable income ($Y - T$). The slope of the consumption function equals the marginal propensity to consume c. The *marginal propensity to consume*, a number between 0 and 1, is the amount by which consumption rises when disposable income rises by \$1.

Increases in output, which imply increases in income, cause consumption to rise. As consumption is part of planned aggregate expenditure, planned aggregate expenditure depends on output as well. The portion of planned aggregate expenditure that depends on output, and hence is determined within the model, is called *induced expenditure*. The portion of planned aggregate expenditure determined outside the model is *autonomous expenditure*.

SHORT-RUN EQUILIBRIUM OUTPUT

Now that we have defined planned aggregate expenditure and seen how it is related to output, the next task is to determine what output will be. Recall the assumption of the basic Keynesian model: that in the short run, producers leave prices at preset levels and simply meet the demand at those prices. In other words, during the short-run period in which prices are preset, firms produce an amount that is equal to planned aggregate expenditure. Accordingly, we define **short-run equilibrium output** as the level of output at which output Y equals planned aggregate expenditure PAE:

$$Y = PAE. \tag{8.3}$$

Short-run equilibrium output is the level of output that prevails during the period in which prices are predetermined.

We can find the short-run equilibrium output for the economy described in Example 8.2 using Table 8.1. Column 1 in the table gives some possible values for short-run equilibrium output. To find the correct one, we must compare each to the value of planned aggregate expenditure at that output level. Column 2 shows the value of planned spending corresponding to the values of output in column 1. Recall that in Example 8.2, planned spending is determined by the equation

$$PAE = 960 + 0.8Y.$$

Because consumption rises with output, planned aggregate expenditure (which includes consumption) rises also. But if you compare columns 1 and 2, you will see that when output rises by 200, planned spending rises by only 160. That is, because the marginal propensity to consume in this economy is 0.8, each dollar in added income raises consumption and planned aggregate expenditure by 80 cents.

short-run equilibrium output the level of output at which output Y equals planned aggregate expenditure; the level of output that prevails during the period in which prices are predetermined

---

TABLE 8.1
Numerical Determination of Short-Run Equilibrium Output

(1) Output Y	(2) Planned aggregate expenditure PAE = 960 + 0.8Y	(3) Y − PAE	(4) Y = PAE?
4000	4160	−160	No
4200	4320	−120	No
4400	4480	−80	No
4600	4640	−40	No
4800	4800	0	Yes
5000	4960	40	No
5200	5120	80	No

Again, short-run equilibrium output is the level of output at which $Y = PAE$, or equivalently, $Y - PAE = 0$. Looking at Table 8.1, we can see that there is only one level of output that satisfies that condition, $Y = 4800$. At that level, output and planned aggregate expenditure are precisely equal, so the producers are just meeting the demand.

In this economy, what would happen if output happened to differ from its equilibrium value of 4800? Suppose, for example, that output were 4000. Looking at column 2 of Table 8.1, we can see that when output is 4000, planned aggregate expenditure equals $960 + 0.8(4000)$, or 4160. Thus if output is 4000, firms are not producing enough to meet the demand. They will find that as sales exceed the amounts they are producing, their inventories of finished goods are being depleted by 160 per year, and that actual private-sector investment is less than planned private-sector investment. Under the assumption that firms are committed to meeting their customers' demand, firms will respond by expanding their production.

Would expanding production to 4160, the level of planned aggregate expenditure firms faced when output was 4000, be enough? The answer is no, because of induced expenditure. That is, as firms expand their output, aggregate income (wages and profits) rises with it, which in turn leads to higher levels of consumption. Indeed, if output expands to 4160, planned aggregate expenditure will increase as well, to $960 + 0.8(4160)$, or 4288. So an output level of 4160 will still be insufficient to meet demand. As Table 8.1 shows, output will not be sufficient to meet planned aggregate expenditure until it expands to its short-run equilibrium value of 4800.

What if output were initially greater than its equilibrium value—say, 5000? From Table 8.1 we can see that when output equals 5000, planned aggregate expenditure equals only 4960—less than what firms are producing. So at an output level of 5000, firms will not sell all they produce and will find that their merchandise is piling up on store shelves and in warehouses (actual investment is greater than planned investment). In response, firms will cut their production runs and lay off personnel (who would then cut their spending). As Table 8.1 shows, firms will have to reduce production to its equilibrium value of 4800 before output just matches planned aggregate expenditure.

EXERCISE 8.1

Construct a table like Table 8.1 for an economy like the one we have been working with, assuming that the consumption function is $C = 820 + 0.7(Y - T)$ and that $I^P = 600$, $G = 600$, $NX = 200$, and $T = 600$.

What is short-run equilibrium output in this economy? (*Hint:* Try using values for output above 5000.)

Short-run equilibrium output can also be determined graphically, as Example 8.3 shows.

Finding short-run equilibrium output (graphical approach)

EXAMPLE 8.3

Using a graphical approach, find short-run equilibrium output for the economy described in Example 8.2.

Figure 8.3 shows the graphical determination of short-run equilibrium output for the economy described in Example 8.2. Output Y is plotted on the horizontal axis and planned aggregate expenditure PAE on the vertical axis. The figure contains two lines, one of which is a 45° line extending from the origin. In general, a 45° line from the origin includes the points at which the variable on the vertical axis equals the variable on the horizontal axis. In this case, the 45° line represents the equation $Y = PAE$. Recall that short-run equilibrium output must satisfy the condition $Y = PAE$. So we know that the value of short-run equilibrium output must lie somewhere on the $Y = PAE$ line.

FIGURE 8.3

Determination of Short-Run Equilibrium Output (Keynesian Cross)

The 45° line represents the short-run equilibrium condition $Y = PAE$. The line $PAE = 960 + 0.8Y$, referred to as the expenditure line, shows the relationship of planned aggregate expenditure to output. Short-run equilibrium output (4800) is determined at the intersection of the two lines, point E. This and subsequent Keynesian cross diagrams in this textbook are not drawn to scale.

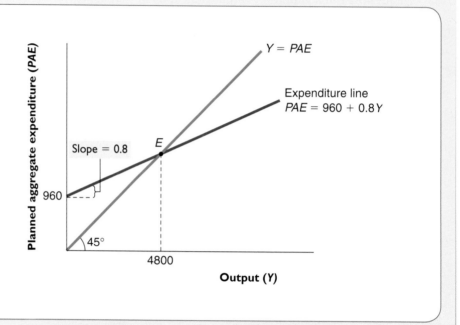

The second line in Figure 8.3, less steep than the 45° line, shows the relationship between planned aggregate expenditure PAE and output Y. Because it summarizes how total expenditure depends on output, we will call this line the *expenditure line*. In this example, we know that the relationship between planned aggregate expenditure and output (the equation for the expenditure line) is

$$PAE = 960 + 0.8Y.$$

According to this equation, when $Y = 0$, the value of PAE is 960. Thus 960 is the intercept of the expenditure line, as shown in Figure 8.3. The slope of the line relating aggregate demand to output is 0.8, the value of the coefficient of output in the equation $PAE = 960 + 0.8Y$. Where does the number 0.8 come from? (*Hint:* What determines by how much aggregate spending increases when output rises by a dollar?)

Only one point in Figure 8.3 is consistent with both the definition of short-run equilibrium output $Y = PAE$ and the given relationship between planned aggregate expenditure and output, $PAE = 960 + 0.8Y$. That point is the intersection of the two lines, point E. At point E, short-run equilibrium output equals 4800, which is the same value that we obtained using Table 8.1. Notice that at points to the right of E, output exceeds planned aggregate expenditure. Hence, to the right of point E, firms will be producing more than they can sell and will tend to reduce their production. Similarly, to the left of point E, planned aggregate expenditure exceeds output. In that region, firms will not be producing enough to meet demand and will tend to increase their production. Only at point E, where output equals 4800, will firms be producing enough to just satisfy planned spending on goods and services.

The diagram in Figure 8.3 is often called the *Keynesian cross*, after its characteristic shape. The Keynesian cross shows graphically how short-run equilibrium output is determined in a world in which producers meet demand at predetermined prices.

EXERCISE 8.2 **Use a Keynesian cross diagram to show graphically the determination of short-run equilibrium output for the economy described in Exercise 8.1. What are the intercept and the slope of the expenditure line?**

PLANNED SPENDING AND THE OUTPUT GAP

We are now ready to use the basic Keynesian model to show how insufficient planned aggregate expenditure can lead to a recession. To illustrate this idea, we will continue to work with the economy introduced in Example 8.2. We have shown that in this economy, short-run equilibrium output equals 4800. Let's now make the additional assumption that potential output in this economy also equals 4800, or $Y^* = 4800$. In other words, we will assume that at first, actual output equals potential output so that there is no output gap. Starting from this position of full employment, Example 8.4 shows how a fall in planned aggregate expenditure can lead to a recession.

A fall in planned spending leads to a recession

EXAMPLE 8.4

For the economy introduced in Example 8.2, we have found that short-run equilibrium output Y equals 4800. Assume also that potential output Y^* equals 4800, so that the output gap $Y^* - Y$ equals zero.

Suppose, though, that consumers become more pessimistic about the future, so that they begin to spend less at every level of current disposable income. We can capture this change by assuming that $\overline{C}$, the constant term in the consumption function, falls to a lower level. To be specific, suppose that $\overline{C}$, falls by 10 units, which in turn implies a decline in autonomous expenditure of 10 units. What is the effect of this reduction in planned spending on the economy?

We can see the effects of the decline in consumer spending on the economy using the Keynesian cross diagram. Figure 8.4 shows the original short-run equilibrium point of the model (E), at the intersection of the 45° line, along which $Y = PAE$, and the original expenditure line, representing the equation $PAE = 960 + 0.8Y$. As before, the initial value of short-run equilibrium output is 4800, which we have now assumed also corresponds to potential output Y^*. But what happens when $\overline{C}$ declines by 10, reducing autonomous expenditure by 10 as well?

Originally, autonomous expenditure in this economy was 960, so a decline of 10 units causes it to fall to 950. Instead of the economy's planned spending being described by the equation $PAE = 960 + 0.8Y$, as initially, it is now given by $PAE = 950 + 0.8Y$. What does this change imply for the graph in Figure 8.4? Since the intercept of the expenditure line (equal to autonomous expenditure) has decreased from 960 to 950, the effect of the decline in consumer spending will be to shift the expenditure line down in parallel fashion, by 10 units. Figure 8.4 indicates

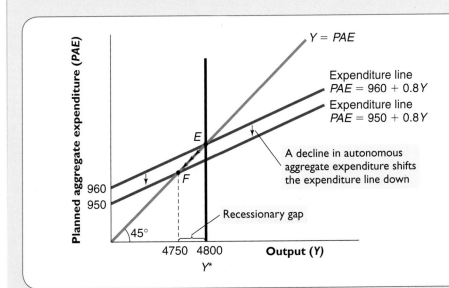

FIGURE 8.4

A Decline in Planned Spending Leads to a Recession

A decline in consumers' willingness to spend at any current level of disposable income reduces planned autonomous expenditure and shifts the expenditure line down. The short-run equilibrium point drops from E to F, reducing output and opening up a recessionary gap.

this downward shift in the expenditure line. The new short-run equilibrium point is at point *F*, where the new, lower expenditure line intersects the 45° line.

Point *F* is to the left of the original equilibrium point *E*, so we can see that output and spending have fallen from their initial levels. Since output at point *F* is lower than potential output, 4800, we see that the fall in consumer spending has resulted in a recessionary gap in the economy. More generally, starting from a situation of full employment (where output equals potential output), any decline in autonomous expenditure leads to a recession.

Numerically, how large is the recessionary gap in Figure 8.4? To answer this question, we can use Table 8.2, which is in the same form as Table 8.1. The key difference is that in Table 8.2 planned aggregate expenditure is given by $PAE = 950 + 0.8Y$, rather than by $PAE = 960 + 0.8Y$, as in Table 8.1.

TABLE 8.2
Determination of Short-Run Equilibrium Output after a Fall in Spending

(1) Output Y	(2) Planned aggregate expenditure $PAE = 950 + 0.8Y$	(3) Y − PAE	(4) Y = PAE?
4600	4630	− 30	No
4650	4670	− 20	No
4700	4710	− 10	No
4750	4750	0	Yes
4800	4790	10	No
4850	4830	20	No
4900	4870	30	No
4950	4910	40	No
5000	4950	50	No

As in Table 8.1, the first column of the table shows alternative possible values of output *Y*, and the second column shows the levels of planned aggregate expenditure *PAE* implied by each value of output in the first column. Notice that 4800, the value of short-run equilibrium output found in Table 8.1, is no longer an equilibrium; when output is 4800, planned spending is 4790, so output and planned spending are not equal. As the table shows, following the decline in planned aggregate expenditure, short-run equilibrium output is 4750, the only value of output for which $Y = PAE$. Thus a drop of 10 units in autonomous expenditure has led to a 50-unit decline in short-run equilibrium output. If full-employment output is 4800, then the recessionary gap shown in Figure 8.4 is $4800 - 4750 = 50$ units.

EXERCISE 8.3

In the economy described in Example 8.4, we found a recessionary gap of 50, relative to potential output of 4800. Suppose that in this economy, the natural rate of unemployment *u** is 5 percent. If the relationship between the recessionary gap and cyclical unemployment follows Okun's law (as described in Chapter 7), what will be the actual unemployment rate after the recessionary gap appears?

"These are hard times for retailers, so we should show them our support in every way we can."

Example 8.4 showed that a decline in autonomous expenditure, arising from a decreased willingness of consumers to spend, causes short-run equilibrium output to fall and opens up a recessionary gap. The same conclusion applies to declines in autonomous expenditure arising from other sources. Suppose, for example, that firms become disillusioned with new technologies and cut back their planned investment in new equipment. Another possibility—one which the U.S. faced in 2007–08 (for details, see Economic Naturalist 13.1 on page 350)—is that firms are suddenly unable to borrow the funds they need to invest. In terms of the model, this reluctance or inability to invest can be interpreted as a decline in planned investment spending, I^p. Under our assumption that planned investment spending is given and does not depend on output, planned investment is part of autonomous expenditure. So a decline in planned investment spending depresses autonomous expenditure and output, in precisely the same way that a decline in the autonomous part of consumption spending does. Similar conclusions apply to declines in other components of autonomous expenditure, such as government purchases and net exports, as we will see in later applications.

Repeat the analysis of Example 8.4, except assume that consumers become *more* rather than less confident about the future. As a result, $\overline{C}$ rises by 10 units, which in turn raises autonomous expenditure by 10 units. Show graphically that this increase in consumers' willingness to spend leads to an expansionary output gap. Find the numerical value of the expansionary output gap.

EXERCISE 8.4

THE INCOME-EXPENDITURE MULTIPLIER

Note that in Example 8.4, although the initial decline in consumer spending (as measured by the fall in $\overline{C}$) was only 10 units, short-run equilibrium output fell by 50 units. The reason the impact on output and planned aggregate expenditure was greater than the initial change in spending is the "vicious circle" effect suggested by Grandma's reminiscences about the Great Depression. Specifically, a fall in consumer spending not only decreases planned aggregate expenditure, it also reduces the incomes of workers and owners in the industries that produce consumer goods. As their incomes fall, these workers and capital owners reduce their spending, which reduces the output and incomes of *other* producers in the economy. And these reductions in income lead to still further cuts in spending. Ultimately, these successive rounds of declines in spending and income may lead to a decrease in planned aggregate expenditure that is significantly greater than the change in spending that started the process.

The idea that a change in spending may lead to a substantially larger change in short-run equilibrium output is an important feature of the basic Keynesian model. In Example 8.4 we considered the effects of a decrease in spending, but an increase in spending produces the same effect in reverse. For example, if desired consumption had *increased* rather than decreased by 10, it would have set off successive rounds of increases in income and spending, culminating in a final increase of 50 in short-run equilibrium output. The same type of effect also applies to changes in other components of autonomous expenditure. For example, in this hypothetical economy, an increase of 10 in desired investment spending ($\overline{I}$), in government purchases ($\overline{G}$), or in net exports ($\overline{NX}$) would increase short-run equilibrium output by 50.

income-expenditure multiplier the effect of a one-unit increase in autonomous expenditure on short-run equilibrium output

The effect on short-run equilibrium output of a one-unit increase in autonomous expenditure is called the **income-expenditure multiplier**, or the *multiplier* for short. In the economy of Example 8.4 the multiplier is 5. That is, each \$1 increase in autonomous expenditure leads to a \$5 increase in short-run equilibrium output, and each \$1 decrease in autonomous expenditure implies a \$5 decrease in short-run equilibrium output. Appendix 8B provides more details on the multiplier in the basic Keynesian model, including a formula ($1/(1 - c)$) that allows us to calculate the value of the multiplier under specific assumptions about the economy.

We stress that, because our basic Keynesian model omits some important features of an actual economy, it tends to yield unrealistically high values of the multiplier. Indeed, virtually no one believes that the multiplier in the Canadian economy is as high as 5. Real-world estimates typically put the multiplier at less than 2. Later we will discuss why our basic Keynesian model tends to overstate the value of the multiplier. Nevertheless, the idea that changes in planned aggregate expenditure can have important effects on short-run equilibrium output remains a central tenet of Keynesian economics and a major factor in modern policy-making.

RECAP

FINDING SHORT-RUN EQUILIBRIUM OUTPUT

Short-run equilibrium output is the level of output at which output equals planned aggregate expenditure; or in symbols, $Y = PAE$. For a specific example economy, short-run equilibrium output can be solved for numerically, as in Table 8.1, or graphically.

The graphical solution is based on a diagram called the Keynesian cross. The Keynesian cross diagram includes two lines: a 45° line that captures the condition $Y = PAE$ and the expenditure line, which shows the relationship of planned aggregate expenditure to output. Short-run equilibrium output is determined at the intersection of the two lines. If short-run equilibrium output differs from potential output, an output gap exists.

Increases in autonomous expenditure shift the expenditure line upward, increasing short-run equilibrium output, and decreases in autonomous expenditure induce declines in short-run equilibrium output. Decreases in autonomous expenditure that drive actual output below potential output are a possible source of recessions.

Generally, a one-unit increase in autonomous expenditure leads to a larger increase in short-run equilibrium output, a result of the *income-expenditure multiplier*. The multiplier arises because a given initial increase in spending raises the incomes of producers, which leads them to spend more, raising the incomes and spending of other producers, and so on.

8.3 STABILIZING PLANNED SPENDING: THE ROLE OF FISCAL POLICY

According to the basic Keynesian model, inadequate spending is an important cause of recessions. To fight recessions, policy-makers must find ways to increase aggregate expenditure. Policies that are used to affect planned spending, with the objective of eliminating output gaps, are called **stabilization policies.**

Policy actions intended to increase planned spending and output are called **expansionary policies**; expansionary policy actions are normally taken when the economy is in recession. It is also possible, as we have seen, for the economy to be "overheated," with output greater than potential output (an expansionary gap). The risk of an expansionary gap, as we will see in more detail later, is that it may lead to an increase in inflation. To offset an expansionary gap, policy-makers will try to reduce spending and output. **Contractionary policies** are policy actions intended to reduce planned spending and output.

The two major types of stabilization policy, *monetary policy* and *fiscal policy,* were introduced in Chapter 4. Recall that monetary policy refers to central bank decisions about interest rates, while fiscal policy refers to decisions about the government's budget—how much the government spends and how much tax revenue it collects. In the remainder of this chapter we will focus on fiscal policy (monetary policy will be discussed in Chapters 9, 10, and 11). Specifically, we will consider how fiscal policy works in the basic Keynesian model, looking first at the effects of changes in government purchases of goods and services and then at changes in tax collections. We will conclude the chapter with a discussion of some practical issues that arise in the application of fiscal policy.

stabilization policies
government policies that are used to affect planned aggregate expenditure, with the objective of eliminating output gaps

expansionary policies
government policy actions intended to increase planned spending and output

contractionary policies
government policy actions designed to reduce planned spending and output

GOVERNMENT PURCHASES AND PLANNED SPENDING

Decisions about government spending represent one of the two main components of fiscal policy, the other being decisions about the level and type of taxes. As was mentioned earlier, Keynes himself felt that changes in government purchases were probably the most effective tool for reducing or eliminating output gaps. His basic argument was straightforward: Government purchases of goods and services are a component of planned aggregate expenditure, so planned spending is directly affected by changes in government purchases. If output gaps are caused by too much or too little total spending, then the government can help to guide the economy toward full employment by changing its own level of spending. Keynes's views seemed to be vindicated by the events of the 1930s, notably the fact that the Depression did not finally end until governments of several countries greatly increased their spending (especially military spending) in connection with the Second World War.

Example 8.5 shows how increased government purchases of goods and services can help to eliminate a recessionary gap. (The effects of government spending on transfer programs, such as employment insurance benefits, are a bit different. We will return to that case shortly.)

EXAMPLE 8.5 **An increase in the government's purchases eliminates a recessionary gap**

In Example 8.4, we found that a drop of 10 units in consumer spending creates a recessionary gap of 50 units. How can the government eliminate the output gap and restore full employment by changing its purchases of goods and services G?

In Example 8.4, we found that planned aggregate expenditure was initially given by the equation $PAE = 960 + 0.8Y$, so that autonomous expenditure equalled 960. The 10-unit drop in $\overline{C}$ implied a 10-unit drop in autonomous expenditure, to 950. Because the multiplier in that sample economy equalled 5, this 10-unit decline in autonomous expenditure resulted in turn in a 50-unit decline in short-run equilibrium output.

To offset the effects of the consumption decline, the government would have to restore autonomous expenditure to its original value, 960. Under our assumption that government purchases are simply given and do not depend on output, government purchases are part of autonomous expenditure, and changes in government purchases change autonomous expenditure one for one. Thus, to increase autonomous expenditure from 950 to 960, the government should simply increase its purchases by 10 units (for example, by increasing spending on military defence or road construction). According to the basic Keynesian model, this increase in government purchases should return autonomous expenditure and hence output to their original levels.

The effect of the increase in government purchases is shown graphically in Figure 8.5. After the 10-unit decline in the autonomous component of consumption spending $\overline{C}$, the economy is at point F, with a 50-unit recessionary gap. A 10-unit increase in government purchases raises autonomous expenditure by

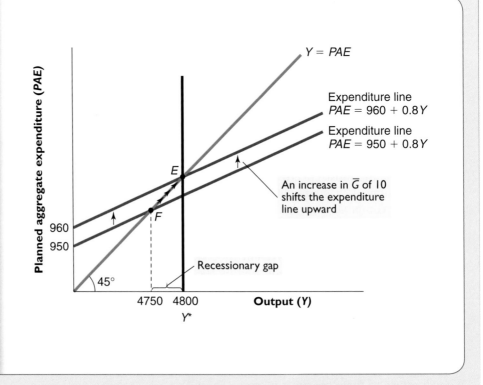

FIGURE 8.5

An Increase in Government Purchases Eliminates a Recessionary Gap
After a 10-unit decline in the autonomous part of consumer spending $\overline{C}$, the economy is at point F, with a recessionary gap of 50. A 10-unit increase in government purchases raises autonomous expenditure by 10 units, shifting the expenditure line back to its original position and raising the equilibrium point from F to E. At point E, where output equals potential output ($Y = Y^* = 4800$), the output gap has been eliminated.

10 units, raising the intercept of the expenditure line by 10 units and causing the expenditure line to shift upward in parallel fashion. The economy returns to point E, where short-run equilibrium output equals potential output ($Y = Y^* = 4800$) and the output gap has been eliminated.

In Exercise 8.4, you considered the case in which consumers become more rather than less confident, leading to an expansionary output gap. Discuss how a change in government purchases could be used to eliminate this output gap. Show your analysis graphically.

EXERCISE 8.5

We should point out that in our model a 10-unit increase in private-sector investment, say, or a 10-unit increase in net exports would have exactly the same impact on the recessionary gap as a 10-unit increase in government purchases.

Economic Naturalist boxes 8.1 and 8.2 illustrate the application of fiscal policy in actual economies. Economic Naturalist 8.2 illustrates the idea that a reduction in government purchases could be offset by an increase in net exports.

ECONOMIC *Naturalist* 8.1   The Second World War and the end of Canada's Great Depression

During the 1930s Canada's unemployment rate averaged about 13 percent, with a peak of 19.3 percent in 1933. Although there was some recovery in the late 1930s, the rate still stood at 11.4 percent in 1939. The Great Depression of the 1930s has passed into historical infamy due to the depth and length of its economic downturn, and the social and political turmoil which it produced.

With the wisdom of hindsight, today's economists recognize that the "balanced budget" economic orthodoxy of the time contributed to the severity of The Great Depression. A stock market crash in 1929 and a crisis in the banking system (see Economic Naturalist 13.1 on page 350) started the downturn. But when tax revenue declined because incomes and sales had fallen, governments tried to avoid deficits and cut their spending, which worsened the situation by depressing Planned Aggregate Expenditure even more.

When war with Nazi Germany came in 1939, Canadian government purchases increased dramatically. They went up from 10 percent of GDP in 1939 to 15 percent in 1940. By 1942 government purchases constituted about 35 percent of GDP (far higher, incidentally, than their roughly 20 percent share of Canadian GDP in recent years).

As government purchases increased, Canada's unemployment rate declined sharply. It plummeted from 11.4 percent in 1939 to 2.7 percent in 1942.

This historical experience helped convince many Canadian economists of the real-world relevance of Keynes's explanation of how government purchases could eliminate a recessionary gap and sharply reduce the unemployment rate.

ECONOMIC *Naturalist* 8.2   Saved by the net exports

With his February 1995 budget, Finance Minister Paul Martin launched the federal government of Canada on a budget deficit reduction crusade that featured major government spending cutbacks. Most provinces followed suit. As a result, government purchases declined from about 22 percent of Canadian GDP in 1994 to 20 percent in 1997. (Government transfer payments, which we will analyze below, also declined as a percentage of GDP.)

Why did the Canadian economy continue to recover from the recession of the early 1990s despite the cutbacks in government purchases? One explanation suggested by our basic Keynesian model is that although the cutbacks acted to slow or stall the economic recovery, they were offset by booming net exports. Both the boom in the U.S. economy (which created demand for Canadian exports) and the weak Canadian dollar (which made Canadian exports relatively cheaper and imports relatively more expensive) contributed to a net export surge during 1994–1997. Canadian net exports had been slightly negative during the 1989–1993 period. But during 1994–1997 net exports surged, averaging about 2 percent of GDP.

"Your Majesty, my voyage will not only forge a new route to the spices of the East but also create over three thousand new jobs."

TAXES, TRANSFERS, AND AGGREGATE SPENDING

Besides making decisions about government purchases of goods and services, fiscal policy-makers also determine the level of tax collections (or, more generally, government revenue) and government transfer payments. Interest on the public debt is a significant transfer from the government to households but it is largely determined by the stock of outstanding public debt and by market interest rates, rather than by current decisions of fiscal policy-makers. For the sake of simplicity, we will assume that it is constant.

Unlike changes in government purchases, changes in taxes or transfer payments do not affect planned spending directly. Instead they work indirectly by changing disposable income in the household sector. Specifically, either a tax cut or an increase in government transfer payments increases disposable income in the household sector, which according to the consumption function should encourage households to spend more on consumer goods and services. In short, changes in taxes and transfer payments affect planned spending only to the extent that they change the level of spending by the household sector. Example 8.6 shows the effect of a tax cut (or an equal-size increase in transfer payments) on spending and output.

EXAMPLE 8.6	Using a tax cut to close a recessionary gap

In Example 8.4, we found that in our hypothetical economy, an initial drop in consumer spending of 10 units creates a recessionary gap of 50. Example 8.5 showed that this recessionary gap could be eliminated by a 10-unit increase in government purchases. Suppose that, instead of increasing government purchases, fiscal policy-makers decided to stabilize planned spending by changing the level of tax collections. By how much should they change taxes to eliminate the output gap?

A common first guess at the answer to this problem is that policy-makers should cut taxes by 10, but that guess is not correct. Let's see why.

The source of the recessionary gap in Example 8.4 is the assumption that households have reduced their consumption spending by 10 units at each level of output Y. To eliminate this recessionary gap, the change in taxes must induce households to increase their consumption spending by 10 units at each output level. However, if net taxes T are cut by 10 units, raising disposable income $Y - T$ by 10 units, consumption at each level of output Y will increase by only 8 units. The reason is that the marginal propensity to consume out of disposable income is 0.8, so consumption spending increases by only 0.8 times the amount of the tax cut. (The rest of the tax cut is saved.)

To raise consumption spending by 10 units, fiscal policy-makers must cut taxes by 12.5 units, reducing $\overline{T} = 250$ to $\overline{T} = 237.5$. Because $0.8(12.5) = 10$, a tax cut of 12.5 will spur households to increase their consumption by 10 units at each level of output. That increase will just offset the 10-unit decrease in autonomous consumption $\overline{C}$, restoring the economy to full employment.

Note that since T refers to *net taxes,* or taxes less transfers, the same result could be obtained by increasing transfer payments by 12.5 units. Because households spend 0.8 times any increase in transfer payments they receive, this policy would also raise consumption spending by 10 units at any level of output.

Graphically, the effect of the tax cut is identical to the effect of the increase in government purchases, shown in Figure 8.5. Because it leads to a 10-unit increase in consumption at any level of output, the tax cut shifts the expenditure line up by 10 units. Equilibrium is attained at point E in Figure 8.5, where output again equals potential output.

In a particular economy, a 20-unit increase in planned investment moved the economy from an initial situation with no output gap to a situation with an expansionary gap. Describe two ways in which fiscal policy could be used to offset this expansionary gap. Assume the marginal propensity to consume equals 0.5.

EXERCISE 8.6

RECAP

FISCAL POLICY AND PLANNED SPENDING

Stabilization policies are policies used to affect planned spending with the objective of eliminating output gaps. *Expansionary polices* are designed to increase planned spending and output and thereby eliminate a recessionary gap. *Contractionary polices* are designed to decrease planned spending and output and thereby eliminate an expansionary gap.

Fiscal policy includes two methods for affecting planned spending: changes in government purchases and changes in taxes or transfer payments. An increase in government purchases increases autonomous expenditure by an equal amount. A reduction in taxes or an increase in transfer payments increases autonomous expenditure by an amount equal to the marginal propensity to consume times the reduction in taxes or increase in transfer payments. The ultimate effect of a fiscal policy change on short-run equilibrium output equals the change in autonomous expenditure times the multiplier.

Accordingly, if the economy is in recession, an increase in government purchases, a cut in taxes, or an increase in transfer payments can be used to stimulate spending and eliminate the recessionary gap.

8.4 FISCAL POLICY AS A STABILIZATION TOOL: SIX QUALIFICATIONS

We have shown that the basic Keynesian model provides insights into the impact of fiscal policy on an economy suffering from a recessionary gap. But our discussion has overlooked many fiscal policy issues. Six warrant special mention.

First, fiscal policy may affect potential output as well as planned spending. In the examples in this chapter we assumed that changes in government purchases, taxes, and transfer payments change planned aggregate expenditure without affecting the supply side of the economy, as represented by potential output. But this assumption is often not correct. On the spending side, for example, investments in public capital, such as roads, airports, and schools, can play a major role in the growth of potential output. On the other side of the ledger, tax and transfer programs may well affect the incentives, and thus the economic behaviour, of households and firms. For example, a tax break on new investment may encourage firms to increase their rate of capital formation. An increase in investment will in turn affect potential output. Many other examples could be given of how taxes and transfer payments affect economic behaviour and thus potential output. In judging alternative fiscal policies, therefore, it is necessary to consider their impact on both actual and potential GDP.

Incidentally, the mainstream economics view that fiscal policy may have some effect on potential GDP is quite distinct from *supply-side economics*, the view that cuts in taxes will produce such large increases in potential GDP (the supply side of the economy) that total tax revenue will increase. Mainstream economists have long insisted that there is no convincing statistical evidence that tax cuts are capable of producing such large increases in potential GDP.

A second issue about fiscal policy is that it affects more than just actual and potential GDP. Changes in government spending and taxation often have consequences that extend beyond GDP to the distribution of income, economic security (the extent to which people are protected by a social safety net), environmental protection, leisure time, and other matters discussed in Chapter 5. For example, changes in taxes typically have consequences for the distribution of income. Changes in transfer payments change both the distribution of income and the degree of economic security. So in judging alternative fiscal policies, it is necessary not just to consider their impact on actual GDP and potential GDP, as mentioned above, but also to consider their impact on matters that extend beyond GDP.

A third issue is that fiscal policy-makers generally want to avoid large and persistent budget deficits. Recall from Chapter 4 that the government budget deficit is the excess of government expenditure over government revenue. The budget deficit, which is a flow, adds to the stock of government debt (just as water flowing into a bath will fill the tub and continued personal borrowing leads to a larger stock of personal debt). If the deficit is large and persistent, the government debt will grow more rapidly than GDP, and the government debt to GDP ratio will rise. Debt becomes a problem when it gets too large to repay compared to income. So if a country develops an especially high government debt to GDP ratio, lenders get nervous and governments may need to pay especially high interest rates on government borrowing (to compensate lenders for the risk of default).

Canada has never reached the point where the federal government has had to pay such high interest rates, but in the early 1990s Canada had one of the highest government debt to GDP ratios among the G7 countries. Since the mid-1990s a central objective of Canadian fiscal policy has been to reduce the government debt to GDP ratio. Indeed, even though by 2004 Canada had the second lowest government debt to GDP ratios among the G7 countries, the 2004 federal budget announced the objective of continuing to reduce the federal government debt to GDP ratio—from about 40 percent to 25 percent over the next ten years.

A fourth issue is that decisions to change levels of government spending and taxation to stabilize planned spending, known as **discretionary fiscal policy**, take time to formulate and implement, meaning that in some situations governments may not be able to eliminate output gaps quickly. For example, when the party controlling the U.S. presidency does not also control both the House of Representatives and the Senate, a proposal to change fiscal policy may have to go through a long legislative process. If discretionary fiscal policy takes a long time to formulate and implement it may not function to stabilize planned aggregate expenditure during short recessions; it may only function properly during prolonged episodes of recession. On the other hand, in a parliamentary system with a majority government, as has typically been the case in Canada, it is sometimes possible for the government to change fiscal policy in a matter of weeks. The federal government required little time to release the October 2000 mini-budget in advance of the November 2000 federal election.

A fifth issue about fiscal policy (and also monetary policy) is that, given the inevitable delay between economic events and the reporting of them, there is typically a *recognition lag* between the onset of an economic slowdown or recession and the realization by the fiscal authorities that a discretionary fiscal response may be appropriate.

The sixth issue is that fiscal policy need not take the form of discretionary fiscal policy; fiscal policy can also involve **automatic stabilizers**, provisions in the law that imply *automatic* increases in government spending or decreases in taxes when GDP declines (or even when GDP grows much more slowly than normal). For example, income tax collections fall (because taxable incomes fall) when GDP declines, while employment insurance payments and social assistance payments increase (as more people qualify for income support due to rising unemployment)—all without any explicit action from the federal or provincial governments. These automatic changes in government spending and tax collections help to increase planned aggregate expenditure during recessions and reduce it during expansions, thereby stabilizing the economy (as shown in Problem 10 at the end of this chapter). Note that because automatic stabilizers move the budget balance in the direction of a deficit during recessions and in the direction of a surplus during expansions, the cumulative impact of automatic stabilizers is that surpluses tend to offset deficits. That is, the working of automatic stabilizers does not result in a long-term rise in the government debt–GDP ratio (or even in the stock of debt itself).

Economists tend to support allowing automatic stabilizers to operate and to be critical of any balanced budget legislation that would force governments to override automatic stabilizers and actively cut spending or increase taxation in recessions in order to avoid deficits. Some economists tend to be unenthusiastic about discretionary fiscal policy as a means for dealing with anything but the most stubborn recessions, suggesting instead that planned aggregate expenditure be stabilized by monetary policy so that decisions about government spending and taxation can focus on, say, raising potential output, changing the distribution of income, or improving health and education outcomes. The role of monetary policy in stabilizing planned aggregate expenditure is the subject of the next chapter. Other economists argue that monetary policy may need to be supplemented by discretionary fiscal policy in certain situations, such as during the Canadian and U.S. slowdowns of 2001.

discretionary fiscal policy
changes in government spending and taxation deliberately made to stabilize planned aggregate expenditure

automatic stabilizers
provisions in the law that imply automatic increases in government spending or decreases in taxes when real output declines

8.5   MORE ON IMPORTS, TAXES, AND THE MULTIPLIER

In our presentation of the basic Keynesian model we have made the simplifying assumptions that both net exports and net taxes are fixed. These are convenient assumptions, and we will continue to hold them for most of our analysis in later chapters of Part 3. In this section, however, we will briefly examine a number of more realistic assumptions about net exports and net taxes and the effect these have on the income-expenditure multiplier. In a more realistic situation, the income-expenditure multiplier is impacted not only by the marginal propensity to consume but also by the *marginal propensity to import* and the *economy-wide marginal tax rate*.

First consider net exports, the difference between the value of exports and the value of imports. Canadian goods and services that are exported have a value that is relatively independent of Canadian income, but the total value of goods and services that are imported tends to increase as Canadian income increases. This is because our consumption of all goods and services, whether domestically produced or imported, tends to increase when our incomes increase.

marginal propensity to import the amount by which imports rise when income rises by $1

The **marginal propensity to import** is the amount by which imports rise when income rises by $1. Earlier, when we assumed that net exports were fixed, we assumed that the marginal propensity to import was zero. More realistically, however, the marginal propensity to import is greater than zero but less than one.

How is the multiplier changed when the marginal propensity to import is greater than zero rather than equal to zero? Suppose that exports from Canada increase, for instance, because of increased demand for Canadian resources from China and India. This will increase both output and income in Canada and result in increased consumption expenditure. But because the marginal propensity to import is positive, part of the increased consumption expenditure will be spent on imports. Spending on imports does not directly boost production, jobs, and spending in Canada. The income-expenditure multiplier will therefore be smaller than in the case when the marginal propensity to import was zero. The larger the marginal propensity to import is, the smaller the income-expenditure multiplier will be.

Next, let us reconsider the assumption that net taxes are fixed. This amounts to assuming that as incomes rise the amount of taxes collected by government will stay the same. But income taxes, as the term itself suggests, are income related and will increase with increases in income and expenditure, as will the amount of sales taxes paid. In general, as income goes up so will taxes paid and collected.

economy-wide marginal tax rate the amount by which taxes rise when income rises by $1

The **economy-wide marginal tax rate** is the amount by which taxes rise when income rises by $1. When we assumed that net taxes were fixed, we assumed that the economy-wide marginal tax rate was zero. A more realistic assumption is that this marginal tax rate is greater than zero but less than one.

What are the implications of a positive economy-wide marginal tax rate for the multiplier? Suppose, again, that exports from Canada increase because of increased demand for Canadian resources from China and India. This will increase output and income in Canada. But part of the increase in income will now go to paying extra taxes, so the increase in consumption expenditure and the consequent boost to production, spending, and jobs in Canada will be less than in the case in which the economy-wide marginal income tax rate was zero. (Note that we are following our usual practice of assuming that all else is equal; e.g., we are assuming that despite the increase in tax revenues, government expenditure will stay the same.) The larger the economy-wide marginal tax rate is, the smaller the income-expenditure multiplier will be.

Figure 8.6 illustrates the implications of recognizing a positive marginal propensity to import and a positive economy-wide marginal tax rate for our basic Keynesian model. Panel (a) of Figure 8.6 is very similar to Figure 8.5, which was used to illustrate how an increase in government purchases could be used to eliminate a recessionary gap. At the original equilibrium point **C**, actual output is 4750 and potential output is 4800, which implies a recessionary gap of 50 units. The marginal propensity to import and the economy-wide marginal income tax rate are both zero. The income-expenditure multiplier is 5. An increase

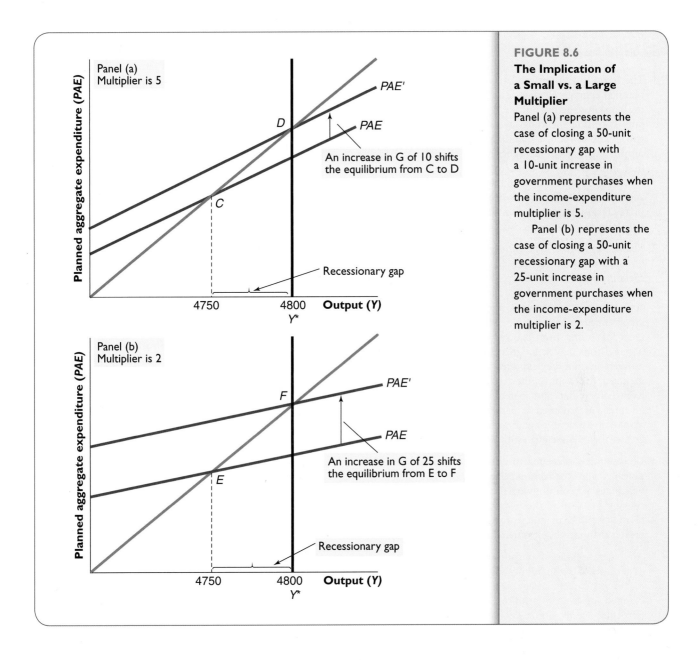

FIGURE 8.6

The Implication of a Small vs. a Large Multiplier

Panel (a) represents the case of closing a 50-unit recessionary gap with a 10-unit increase in government purchases when the income-expenditure multiplier is 5.

Panel (b) represents the case of closing a 50-unit recessionary gap with a 25-unit increase in government purchases when the income-expenditure multiplier is 2.

of 10 units in government purchases raises planned aggregate expenditure by enough to close the recessionary gap and bring the economy to the equilibrium point **D**.

Panel (b) of Figure 8.6 illustrates a situation in which, at the original equilibrium point **E**, actual output is 4750 and potential output is 4800, implying a recessionary gap of 50 units as in panel (a). In this case, however, the marginal propensity to import and the economy-wide marginal tax rate are both positive, resulting in a smaller income-expenditure multiplier than the multiplier of 5 underlying panel (a). Panel (b) shows a multiplier of 2, which means that a 25-unit increase in government purchases raises planned aggregate expenditure by enough to close the recessionary gap and bring the economy to the equilibrium point **F**.

In short, the income-expenditure multiplier is smaller when the marginal propensity to import and/or the economy-wide marginal tax rate are positive than it is when they are zero. A smaller multiplier means it takes a larger increase in autonomous expenditure to close any given output gap.

SUMMARY

8.1 The basic Keynesian model shows how fluctuations in planned aggregate expenditure, or total planned spending, can cause actual output to differ from potential output. Too little spending leads to a recessionary output gap, while too much spending creates an expansionary output gap. This model relies on the crucial assumption that firms do not respond to every change in demand by changing prices. Instead they typically set a price for some period, then meet the demand forthcoming at that price. Firms do not change prices continually because changing prices entails costs, called *menu costs*.

8.2 *Planned aggregate expenditure* is total planned spending on final goods and services. The four components of total spending are consumption, private-sector investment, government purchases, and net exports. Planned and actual consumption, government purchases, and net exports are assumed to be the same. Actual private-sector investment may differ from planned private-sector investment, because firms may sell a greater or lesser amount of their production than they expected. If firms sell less than they expected, for example, they are forced to add more goods to inventory than anticipated. And because additions to inventory are counted as part of investment, in this case actual investment (including inventory investment) is greater than planned investment.

8.2 Consumption is related to disposable income by a relationship called the *consumption function*. The amount by which desired consumption rises when disposable income rises by $1 is called the *marginal propensity to consume* (*MPC*, or *c*). The marginal propensity to consume is always greater than zero but less than one (that is, $0 < c < 1$).

8.2 An increase in real output raises planned aggregate expenditure, since higher output (and equivalently, higher income) encourages households to consume more. Planned aggregate expenditure can be broken down into two components, autonomous expenditure and induced expenditure. *Autonomous expenditure* is the portion of planned spending that is independent of output. *Induced expenditure* is the portion of spending that depends on output.

8.2 At predetermined prices, *short-run equilibrium output* is the level of output that equals planned spending. Short-run equilibrium can be determined numerically by a table that compares alternative values of output and the planned spending implied by each level of output. Short-run equilibrium can be determined graphically in a Keynesian cross diagram, drawn with planned aggregate expenditure on the vertical axis and output on the horizontal axis. The Keynesian cross contains two lines: an expenditure line, which relates planned aggregate expenditure to output, and a 45° line, which represents the condition that short-run equilibrium output equals planned aggregate expenditure.

Short-run equilibrium output is determined at the point at which these two lines intersect.

8.2 Changes in autonomous expenditure will lead to changes in short-run equilibrium output. In particular, if the economy is initially at full employment, a fall in autonomous expenditure will create a recessionary gap and a rise in autonomous expenditure will create an expansionary gap. The amount by which a one-unit increase in autonomous expenditure raises short-run equilibrium output is called the *income-expenditure multiplier*. An increase in autonomous expenditure not only raises spending directly, it also raises the incomes of producers, who in turn increase their spending, and so on. Hence the multiplier is greater than one; that is, a one dollar increase in autonomous expenditure raises short-run equilibrium output by more than one dollar.

8.3 To eliminate output gaps and restore full employment, the government employs *stabilization policies*. The two major types of stabilization policy are monetary policy and fiscal policy. Stabilization polices work by changing planned aggregate expenditure, and thus short-run equilibrium output. For example, an increase in government purchases raises planned aggregate expenditure, so it can be used to reduce or eliminate a recessionary gap. Similarly, a cut in taxes or an increase in transfer payments increases the public's disposable income, raising consumption and planned aggregate expenditure. Higher planned aggregate expenditure, in turn, raises short-run equilibrium output.

8.4 There is more to fiscal policy than understanding the magnitude of changes in government purchases, taxes or transfer payments required to close a particular output gap. Fiscal policy may affect potential output, as well as planned spending. Fiscal policy may also affect matters that extend beyond either actual or potential GDP levels, such as the distribution of income or the level of economic security. And fiscal policy must take into account the fact that large and persistent deficits would create an ever-rising government debt–GDP ratio. It is important to distinguish between discretionary fiscal policy and fiscal policy involving automatic stabilizers. Discretionary fiscal policy refers to deliberate decisions to change levels of spending and taxation to stabilize planned spending. Automatic stabilizers are provisions in the law that imply automatic increases in government spending or reductions in taxes when output declines.

8.5 The income-expenditure multiplier is smaller when the marginal propensity to import and/or the economy-wide marginal tax rate are positive than it is when they are zero. The smaller the multiplier is, the larger the increase in autonomous expenditure will need to be in order to close any given output gap.

KEY TERMS

average propensity to consume
  (*APC*) (188)
automatic stabilizers (205)
autonomous expenditure (191)
consumption function (188)
contractionary policies (199)
discretionary fiscal policy (205)

economy-wide marginal tax rate (206)
expansionary policies (199)
income-expenditure multiplier (198)
induced expenditure (191)
marginal propensity to consume
  (*MPC*) (188)
marginal propensity to import (206)

menu costs (185)
planned aggregate expenditure (186)
short-run equilibrium output (192)
stabilization policies (199)
wealth effect (188)

REVIEW QUESTIONS

1. What is the key assumption of the basic Keynesian model? Explain why this assumption is needed if one is to accept the view that aggregate spending is a driving force behind short-term economic fluctuations.

2. Give an example of a good or service whose price changes very frequently and one whose price changes relatively infrequently. What accounts for the difference?

3. Define *planned aggregate expenditure* and list its components. Why does planned aggregate expenditure change when output changes?

4. Explain how planned spending and actual spending can differ. Illustrate with an example.

5. Sketch a graph of the consumption function, labelling the axes of the graph. Discuss the economic meaning of (a) a movement from left to right along the graph of the consumption function and of (b) a parallel upward shift of the consumption function.

6. Sketch the Keynesian cross diagram. Explain in words the economic significance of the two lines graphed in the diagram. Given only this diagram, how could you determine autonomous expenditure, induced expenditure, the marginal propensity to consume, and short-run equilibrium output?

7. Define the *income-expenditure multiplier*. In economic terms, why is the multiplier greater than one?

8. The government is considering two alternative policies, one involving increased government purchases of 50, the other involving a tax cut of 50. Which policy will stimulate planned aggregate expenditure by more? Why?

9. Discuss six reasons why the use of fiscal policy to stabilize the economy is more complex than suggested by the basic Keynesian model.

10. How does the size of the income–expenditure multiplier affect the use of government purchases to close a recessionary gap?

PROBLEMS

1. Acme Manufacturing is producing $4 000 000 worth of goods this year and is expecting to sell its entire production. It is also planning to purchase $1 500 000 in new equipment during the year. At the beginning of the year the company has $500 000 in inventory in its warehouse. Find actual investment and planned investment if:
   a. Acme actually sells $3 850 000 worth of goods.
   b. Acme actually sells $4 000 000 worth of goods.
   c. Acme actually sells $4 200 000 worth of goods.
   Assuming that Acme's situation is similar to that of other firms, in which of these three cases is output equal to short-run equilibrium output?

2. Data on before-tax income, taxes paid, and consumption spending for the Simpson family in various years are given below.

Before-tax income ($)	Taxes paid ($)	Consumption spending ($)
25 000	3000	20 000
27 000	3500	21 350
28 000	3700	22 070
30 000	4000	23 600

a. Graph the Simpsons' consumption function, and find their household's marginal propensity to consume.
b. How much would you expect the Simpsons to consume if their income was $32 000 and they paid taxes of $5000?
c. Homer Simpson wins a lottery prize. As a result, the Simpson family increases its consumption by $1000 at each level of after-tax income. ("Income" does not include the prize money.) How does this change affect the graph of their consumption function? How does it affect their marginal propensity to consume?

3. An economy is described by the following equations:

$$C = 1800 + 0.6(Y - T),$$
$$I^p = \bar{I} = 900,$$
$$G = \bar{G} = 1500,$$
$$NX = \overline{NX} = 100,$$
$$T = \bar{T} = 1500,$$
$$Y^* = 9000.$$

a. Find a numerical equation linking planned aggregate expenditure to output.
b. Find autonomous expenditure and induced expenditure.

4. For the economy described in Problem 3:
a. Construct a table like Table 8.1 to find short-run equilibrium output. Consider possible values for short-run equilibrium output ranging from 8200 to 9000.
b. Show the determination of short-run equilibrium output for this economy using the Keynesian cross diagram.
c. What is the output gap for this economy? If the natural rate of unemployment is 4 percent, what is the actual unemployment rate for this economy (use Okun's law)?

5. For the economy described in Problem 3, find the effect on short-run equilibrium output of each of the following changes, taken one at a time:
a. An increase in government purchases from 1500 to 1600.
b. A decrease in net taxes from 1500 to 1400 (leaving government purchases at their original value).
c. A decrease in planned investment spending from 900 to 800.
Assume each of these changes is a change in autonomous expenditure. Take as given that the multiplier for this economy is 2.5. If you have studied Appendix B in this chapter, show why this is so.

6. For the following economy, find autonomous expenditure, the multiplier, short-run equilibrium output, and the output gap. By how much would autonomous expenditure have to change to eliminate the output gap?

$$C = 3000 + 0.5(Y - T),$$
$$I^p = \bar{I} = 1500,$$
$$G = \bar{G} = 2500,$$
$$NX = \overline{NX} = 200,$$
$$T = \bar{T} = 2000,$$
$$Y^* = 12\ 000.$$

7. An economy has zero net exports ($\overline{NX} = 0$). Otherwise, it is identical to the economy described in Problem 6.
a. Find short-run equilibrium output.
b. Economic recovery abroad increases the demand for the country's exports; as a result, $\overline{NX}$ rises to 100. What happens to short-run equilibrium output?
c. Repeat part (b), but this time assume that foreign economies are slowing, reducing the demand for the country's exports so that $\overline{NX} = -100$. (A negative value of net exports means that exports are less than imports.)
d. How do your results help to explain the tendency of recessions and expansions to spread across countries?

8. (More difficult.) In a particular economy, planned private-sector investment spending is given by the equation

$$I^p = 300 + 0.1Y.$$

This equation captures the idea that when real GDP rises, firms find it more profitable to make capital investments. Specifically, in this economy, when real GDP rises by a dollar, planned investment spending rises by 10 cents. All the other equations describing this economy are the same as in Problem 6. Find autonomous expenditure, the multiplier, short-run equilibrium output, and the output gap. (Be careful: the multiplier is no longer given by the formula $1/(1 - c)$. You will need to calculate directly the effect of a change in autonomous expenditure on short-run equilibrium output.) By how much would autonomous expenditure have to change to eliminate any output gap?

9. An economy is described by the following equations:

$$C = 40 + 0.8(Y - T),$$
$$I^p = \overline{I} = 70,$$
$$G = \overline{G} = 120,$$
$$NX = \overline{NX} = 10$$
$$T = \overline{T} = 150.$$

    a. Potential output Y^* equals 580. By how much would government purchases have to change to eliminate any output gap? By how much would taxes have to change? Show the effects of these fiscal policy changes in a Keynesian cross diagram.

    b. Repeat part (a), assuming that $Y^* = 630$.

10. (More difficult.) This problem illustrates the workings of automatic stabilizers. Suppose that the components of planned spending in an economy take their usual forms: $C = \overline{C} + c(Y - T)$, $I^p = \overline{I}$, $G = \overline{G}$, and $NX = \overline{NX}$. However, suppose that, realistically, net taxes are not fixed but depend on income as discussed in section 8.5. Specifically, we assume

$$T = tY,$$

where t (a number between 0 and 1) is the fraction of income paid in taxes (the economy-wide marginal tax rate). As we will see in this problem, a tax system of this sort serves as an automatic stabilizer, because taxes collected automatically fall when incomes fall.

    a. Find an algebraic expression for short-run equilibrium output in this economy.

    b. Find an algebraic expression for the multiplier, that is, the amount that output changes when autonomous expenditure changes by one unit. Compare the expression you found to the formula for the multiplier when net taxes are fixed. Show that making net taxes proportional to income reduces the multiplier.

    c. Explain how reducing the size of the multiplier helps to stabilize the economy, holding constant fluctuations in the components of autonomous expenditure.

    d. Suppose $\overline{C} = 500$, $\overline{I} = 1500$, $\overline{G} = 2000$, $\overline{NX} = 0$, $c = 0.8$, and $t = 0.25$. Calculate numerical values for short-run equilibrium output and the multiplier.

11. (More difficult.) This problem illustrates how much smaller the multiplier can get when both net taxes and net exports depend on income. Let X = exports and M = imports. Assume that the import function is of the form $M = \overline{M} + mY$, where m is a number between 0 and 1. Assume that exports, like private-sector investment and government purchases, are independent of income. Now suppose, as in Problem 10, that $\overline{C} = 500$, $\overline{I} = 1500$, $\overline{G} = 2000$, $c = 0.8$, and $t = 0.25$. But also suppose that $\overline{X} = 5000$, $\overline{M} = 1000$, and $m = 0.4$. Calculate numerical values for short-run equilibrium output and the multiplier.

ANSWERS TO IN-CHAPTER EXERCISES

8.1   First we need to find an equation that relates planned aggregate expenditure (PAE) to output. We start with the definition of planned aggregate expenditure and substitute the numerical values given in the problem:

$$PAE = C + I^p + G + NX$$
$$= [\overline{C} + c(Y - T)] + I^p + G + NX$$
$$= [820 + 0.7(Y - 600)] + 600 + 600 + 200$$
$$= 1800 + 0.7Y.$$

Using this relationship we construct a table analogous to Table 8.1. Some trial and error is necessary to find an appropriate range of guesses for output (column 1).

Determination of Short-Run Equilibrium Output

(1) Output Y	(2) Planned aggregate expenditure PAE = 1800 + 0.7Y	(3) Y − PAE	(4) Y = PAE?
5000	5300	−300	No
5200	5440	−240	No
5400	5580	−180	No
5600	5720	−120	No
5800	5860	−60	No
6000	6000	0	Yes
6200	6140	60	No
6400	6280	120	No
6600	6420	180	No

Short-run equilibrium output equals 6000, as that is the only level of output that satisfies the condition $Y = PAE$.

8.2 The graph below (not drawn to scale) shows the determination of short-run equilibrium output, $Y = 6000$. The intercept of the expenditure line is 1800, and its slope is 0.7. Notice that the intercept equals autonomous expenditure and the slope equals the marginal propensity to consume.

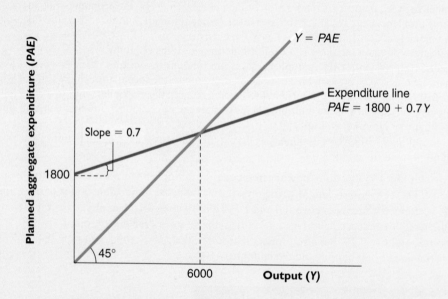

8.3 This problem is an application of Okun's law, introduced in Chapter 7. The recessionary gap in this example is 50/4800, or about 1.04 percent of potential output. By Okun's law, cyclical unemployment is one-half the percentage size of the output gap, or 0.52 percent. As the natural rate of unemployment is 5 percent, the total unemployment rate after the recessionary gap appears will be approximately 5.52 percent.

8.4 This exercise is just the reverse of Example 8.4. An increase in $\overline{C}$ of 10 units raises autonomous expenditure and hence the intercept of the expenditure line by 10 units. The expenditure line shifts up, in parallel fashion, by 10 units, leading to an increase in output and an expansionary output gap. As output falls by 50 units in Example 8.4, it rises by 50 units, to 4850, in the case analyzed here. To verify that short-run equilibrium output equals 4850, note that an increase of 10 units in autonomous expenditure implies that PAE rises from $960 + 0.8Y$ to $970 + 0.8Y$. When $Y = 4850$, then $PAE = 970 + 0.8(4850) = 4850$, so that we have $Y = PAE$.

8.5   In Exercise 8.4 we saw that a 10-unit increase in $\overline{C}$ increases autonomous expenditure and hence the intercept of the expenditure line by 10 units. The expenditure line shifts upward, in parallel fashion, by 10 units, leading to an expansionary output gap. To offset this gap, the government should reduce its purchases by 10 units, returning autonomous expenditure to its original level. The expenditure line shifts back down to its original position, restoring output to its initial full-employment level. The graph is just the reverse of Figure 8.5, with the expenditure line being shifted up by the increase in consumption and down by the offsetting reduction in government purchases.

8.6   The 20-unit increase in planned investment is a 20-unit increase in autonomous expenditure, which will lead to an even greater increase in short-run equilibrium output. To offset the 20-unit increase in autonomous expenditure by means of fiscal policy, the government can reduce its purchases by 20 units. Alternatively, it could raise taxes (or cut transfers) to reduce consumption spending. Since the $MPC = 0.5$, to reduce consumption spending by 20 units at each level of output, the government will need to increase taxes (or reduce transfers) by 40 units. At each level of output, a 40-unit tax increase will reduce disposable income by 40 units and cause consumers to reduce their spending by $0.5 \times 40 = 20$ units, as needed to eliminate the expansionary output gap.

An Algebraic Solution of the Basic Keynesian Model

This chapter has shown how to solve the basic Keynesian model numerically and graphically, using the Keynesian cross diagram. In this appendix we will show how to find a more general algebraic solution for short-run equilibrium output in the basic Keynesian model. This solution has the advantage of showing clearly the links between short-run equilibrium output, the multiplier, and autonomous expenditure. The general method can also be applied when we make changes to the basic Keynesian model, as we will see in following chapters.

The model we will work with is the same one presented in the main part of the chapter. Start with the definition of planned aggregate expenditure, Equation 8.1:

$$PAE = C + I^p + G + NX. \tag{8.1}$$

Equation 8.1 says that planned aggregate expenditure is the sum of the four types of planned spending: consumption spending by households C; planned investment spending by firms I^p; government purchases G; and net exports purchased by foreigners NX.

The first component of planned aggregate expenditure, consumption spending, is determined by the *consumption function,* Equation 8.2:

$$C = \overline{C} + c(Y - T). \tag{8.2}$$

The consumption function says that consumption spending increases when disposable (after-tax) income $Y - T$ increases. Each dollar increase in disposable income raises consumption spending by c dollars, where c, known as the *marginal propensity to consume,* is a number between 0 and 1. Other factors affecting consumption spending are captured by the term $\overline{C}$. For example, a boom in the stock market that leads consumers to spend more at each level of disposable income (a *wealth effect*) would be represented as an increase in $\overline{C}$.

As in the body of the chapter, we assume that planned private-sector investment, government purchases, net exports, and net tax collections are simply given numbers. A variable whose value is fixed and given from outside the model is called an *exogenous* variable; so in other words, we are assuming that planned private-sector investment, government purchases, net exports, and net tax collections are exogenous variables. Using an overbar to denote the given value of an exogenous variable, we can write this assumption as

$$I^p = \overline{I} \qquad \text{Planned private-sector investment,}$$
$$G = \overline{G} \qquad \text{Government purchases,}$$
$$NX = \overline{NX} \qquad \text{Net exports,}$$
$$T = \overline{T} \qquad \text{Net taxes (taxes less transfers).}$$

So for example, $\overline{I}$ is the given value of planned private-sector investment spending, as determined outside the model. In our examples we will set $\overline{I}$ and the other exogenous variables equal to some particular number.

Our goal is to solve algebraically for *short-run equilibrium output,* the level of output that prevails during the period in which prices are predetermined. The first step is to relate planned aggregate expenditure *PAE* to output *Y*. Starting with the definition of planned aggregate expenditure (Equation 8.1), use the consumption function (Equation 8.2) to substitute for consumption spending *C* and replace I^p, *G*, *NX*, and *T* with their exogenous values. With these substitutions, planned aggregate expenditure can be written as

$$PAE = \overline{C} + c(Y - \overline{T})] + \overline{I} + \overline{G} + \overline{NX}.$$

Rearranging this equation to separate the terms that do and do not depend on output *Y*, we get

$$PAE = [\overline{C} - c\overline{T} + \overline{I} + \overline{G} + \overline{NX}] + cY. \qquad (8A.1)$$

Equation 8A.1 is an important equation, because it shows the relationship between planned aggregate expenditure *PAE* and output *Y*. The bracketed term on the right side of the equation represents *autonomous expenditure,* the part of planned spending that does not depend on output. The term *cY* represents *induced expenditure,* the part of planned spending that does depend on output. Equation 8A.1 is also the equation that describes the *expenditure line* in the Keynesian cross diagram; it shows that the intercept of the expenditure line equals autonomous expenditure and the slope of the expenditure line equals the marginal propensity to consume.

We can illustrate how Equation 8A.1 works numerically by using Example 8.2 in the text. That example assumed the following numerical values: $\overline{C} = 620$, $\overline{I} = 220$, $\overline{G} = 300$, $\overline{NX} = 20$, $\overline{T} = 250$, and $c = 0.8$. Plugging these values into Equation 8A.1 and simplifying, we get

$$PAE = 960 + 0.8Y,$$

which is the same answer we found in Example 8.2. Autonomous expenditure in this example equals 960, and induced expenditure equals $0.8Y$.

The second step in solving for short-run equilibrium output begins with the definition of short-run equilibrium output (Equation 8.3)

$$Y = PAE.$$

Remember that short-run equilibrium output is the value of output at which output equals planned aggregate expenditure. Using Equation 8A.1 above to substitute for *PAE* in the definition of short-run equilibrium output, we get

$$Y = [\overline{C} - c\overline{T} + \overline{I} + \overline{G} + \overline{NX}] + cY.$$

The value of *Y* that solves this equation is the value of short-run equilibrium output. To solve for *Y*, group all terms involving *Y* on the left side of the equation:

$$Y - cY = [\overline{C} - c\overline{T} + \overline{I} + \overline{G} + \overline{NX}]$$

or

$$Y(1 - c) = [\overline{C} - c\overline{T} + \overline{I} + \overline{G} + \overline{NX}].$$

Dividing both sides of the equation by $(1 - c)$ gives

$$Y = \left(\frac{1}{1 - c}\right)[\overline{C} - c\overline{T} + \overline{I} + \overline{G} + NX]. \qquad (8A.2)$$

Equation 8A.2 gives short-run equilibrium output for our model economy in terms of the exogenous values $\overline{C}, \overline{I}, \overline{G}, \overline{NX}$, and $\overline{T}$, and the marginal propensity to consume, c. We can use this formula to solve for short-run equilibrium output in specific numerical examples. For example, suppose that we once again plug in the numerical values assumed in Example 8.2: $\overline{C} = 620, \overline{I} = 220, \overline{G} = 300, \overline{NX} = 20, \overline{T} = 250$, and $c = 0.8$. We get

$$Y = \left(\frac{1}{1 - 0.8}\right)[620 - 0.8(250) + 220 + 300 + 20] = \frac{1}{0.2}(960) = 5(960) = 4800,$$

which is the same answer we found more laboriously using Table 8.1.

EXERCISE 8A.1

Use Equation 8A.2 to find short-run equilibrium output for the economy described in Exercise 8.1. What are the intercept and the slope of the expenditure line?

Equation 8A.2 shows clearly the relationship between autonomous expenditure and short-run equilibrium output. Autonomous expenditure is the first term on the right side of Equation 8A.1, equal to $\overline{C} - c\overline{T} + \overline{I} + \overline{G} + \overline{NX}$. The equation shows that a one-unit increase in autonomous expenditure increases short-run equilibrium output by $1/(1 - c)$ units. In other words, we can see from Equation 8A.2 that the *multiplier* for this model equals $1/(1 - c)$. Further discussion of the multiplier is given in Appendix 8B.

ANSWER TO IN-APPENDIX EXERCISE

8A.1 The equation describing short-run equilibrium output is

$$Y = \left(\frac{1}{1 - c}\right)(\overline{C} - c\overline{T} + \overline{I} + \overline{G} + NX). \qquad (8A.2)$$

Using data from Exercise 8.1, set $\overline{C} = 820, c = 0.7, \overline{I} = 600, \overline{G} = 600, \overline{NX} = 200$, and $\overline{T} = 600$. Plugging these values into Equation (8A.2) we get

$$Y = \left(\frac{1}{1 - 0.7}\right)[820 - 0.7(600) + 600 + 600 + 200] = 3.33 \times 1800 = 6000,$$

which is the same result obtained in Exercise 8.1. The intercept of the expenditure line is 1800 and the slope is 0.7.

The Multiplier in the Basic Keynesian Model

This appendix builds on Example 8.4 in the text to give a more complete explanation of the *income-expenditure multiplier* in the basic Keynesian model. In Example 8.4, we saw that a drop in autonomous expenditure of 10 units caused a decline in short-run equilibrium output of 50 units, five times as great as the initial change in spending. Hence the multiplier in this example is 5.

To see why this multiplier effect occurs, note that the initial decrease of 10 in consumer spending (more precisely, in the constant term of the consumption function, $\overline{C}$) in Example 8.4 has two effects. First, the fall in consumer spending directly reduces planned aggregate expenditure by 10 units. Second, the fall in spending also reduces by 10 units the incomes of producers (workers and firm owners) of consumer goods. Under the assumption of Example 8.4 that the marginal propensity to consume is 0.8, the producers of consumer goods will therefore reduce *their* consumption spending by 8, or 0.8 times their income loss of 10. This reduction in spending cuts the income of *other* producers by 8 units, leading them to reduce their spending by 6.4, or 0.8 times their income loss of 8. These income reductions of 6.4 lead still other producers to cut their spending by 5.12, or 0.8 times 6.4, and so on. In principle this process continues indefinitely, although after many rounds of spending and income reductions the effects become quite small.

When all these "rounds" of income and spending reductions are added, the *total* effect on planned spending of the initial reduction of 10 in consumer spending is

$$10 + 8 + 6.4 + 5.12 + \cdots.$$

The three dots indicate that the series of reductions continues indefinitely. The total effect of the initial decrease in consumption can also be written as

$$10[1 + 0.8 + (0.8)^2 + (0.8)^3 + \cdots].$$

This expression highlights the fact that the spending that takes place in each round is 0.8 times the spending in the previous round (0.8), because that is the marginal propensity to consume out of the income generated by the previous round of spending.

A useful algebraic relationship, which applies to any number x greater than 0 but less than 1, is

$$1 + x + x^2 + x^3 + \cdots = \frac{1}{1 - x}.$$

If we set $x = 0.8$, this formula implies that the total effect of the decline in consumption spending on aggregate demand and output is

$$10\left(\frac{1}{1 - 0.8}\right) = 10\left(\frac{1}{0.2}\right) = 10 \times 5 = 50.$$

This answer is consistent with our earlier calculation, which showed that short-run equilibrium output fell by 50 units, from 4800 to 4750.

By a similar analysis we can also find a general algebraic expression for the multiplier in the basic Keynesian model. Recalling that c is the marginal propensity to consume out of disposable income, we know that a 1-unit increase in autonomous expenditure raises spending and income by 1 unit in the first round; by $c \times 1 = c$ units in the second round; by $c \times c = c^2$ units in the second round; by $c \times c^2 = c^3$ units in the third round; and so on. Thus the total effect on short-run equilibrium output of a 1-unit increase in autonomous expenditure is given by

$$1 + c + c^2 + c^3 + \cdots.$$

Applying the algebraic formula given above, and recalling that $0 < c < 1$, we can rewrite this expression as $1/(1 - c)$. Thus, in a basic Keynesian model with a marginal propensity to consume of c, the multiplier equals $1/(1 - c)$, the same result found in Appendix 8A. Note that if $c = 0.8$, then $1/(1 - c) = 1/(1 - 0.8) = 5$, which is the same value of the multiplier we found numerically above.

EXERCISE 8B.1

Recent research reported in the *New England Journal of Medicine* indicates that many adults gain body weight if their close friends do. Within a group of friends, if one person gains weight others in the group are likely to "respond" by gaining an amount of weight that is proportional to the first person's initial weight gain. The first person will then gain more weight in response to the weight gain of the others, and so on. That is, any initial weight gains are subject to a multiplier response that results from social interactions among friends. The economist Gary Becker has called this multiplier response a "social multiplier."[1] This situation is analogous to the income-expenditure multiplier in macroeconomics.

Suppose that you gain 0.6 kilograms of body weight for every kilogram your best friend gains and your best friend gains 0.6 kilograms for each kilogram that you gain.

a. What is the "social multiplier"—that is, what will be your combined weight increase for an autonomous 1-unit increase in the body weight of either of you?

b. If your best friend gains 10 kilograms due to some autonomous change (such as a decline in the price of calories or an increase in the price of

[1]Gary Becker, "Social Causes of the Obesity 'Epidemic'," *The Becker–Posner Blog*, 5 August 2007, http://www.becker-posner-blog.com/archives/2007/08/social_causes_o.html (May 2008).

calorie-burning activities), how much will the two of you eventually gain in total, all else being equal?

c. Approximately how much will each of you, individually, eventually gain in the scenario of (b), where your friend initially gains 10 kilograms?

ANSWER TO IN-APPENDIX EXERCISE

8B.1 a. A 1-unit increase in your friend's body weight in the first round will cause a .6-unit increase in your body weight in the second round. In the third round, your friend will add .6 times .6 units of body weight. The total weight gain of the two of you will be $1 + .6 + .6^2 + .6^3 + \cdots$. In other words, it will be $1/(1 - .6) = 1/.4 = 2.5$. So the social multiplier for weight gain in this example is 2.5.

b. If your best friend undergoes an initial increase of 10 kilograms, your combined weight will go up by 10 kilograms times the multiplier: 10 kilograms $\times$ 2.5 = 25 kilograms.

c. Your friend's weight will go up by about 16 (that is, $10 + 3.6 + 1.30 + 0.47 + 0.17 + \cdots$) kilograms and your weight will go up by about 9 (that is, $6.00 + 2.16 + 0.78 + 0.28 + 0.10 + \cdots$) kilograms.

Chapter 9

Stabilizing the Economy: The Role of the Central Bank

Central bank decisions about monetary policy, and especially about the level of interest rates, are subject to intense scrutiny by financial market participants and commentators. In Canada, for example, the business sections of major newspapers speculate intensely about potential Bank of Canada interest rate announcements. Interest rate hikes cause bond prices to drop and can trigger declines in stock prices. When interest rates are cut, the Canadian dollar loses value on the foreign exchange markets. These changes have consequences for financial investors, which is why the business pages pay so much attention to this topic. But interest rate changes also have consequences for the economy as a whole, and that is our main concern as macroeconomists.

In this chapter we examine the workings of monetary policy, one of the two major types of *stabilization policy*. (The other type, fiscal policy, was discussed in Chapter 8.) As we saw in Chapter 8, stabilization policies are government policies that are meant to influence planned aggregate expenditure, with the goal of eliminating output gaps. Both types of stabilization policy are important and have been useful at various times. Under normal circumstances, however, monetary policy is used more actively than fiscal policy to help stabilize the economy.

We begin with a brief discussion of the Bank of Canada, the institution with primary responsibility for monetary policy in Canada. Then we will examine in detail how the Bank of Canada changes interest rates and how those interest rate changes affect the economy.

9.1 THE BANK OF CANADA

As you will recall, the Bank of Canada is Canada's central bank. It is Canada's counterpart to the Federal Reserve in the United States, the European Central Bank, the Bank of England, the Bank of Japan, and so on. The Bank of Canada is responsible for monetary policy and it uses interest rates to achieve its monetary policy objective.

Unlike commercial banks, which in Canada are often called chartered banks, the objective of the Bank of Canada is not profit maximization. The Bank of Canada Act, through which the Bank was established in 1935, indicated that the institution should pursue several objectives including economic growth, exchange rate stability, low unemployment, and low inflation.

In fact, the Bank does not strictly follow the Bank of Canada Act. For example, although the Canadian dollar appreciated sharply against the U.S. dollar from 2003 to 2007, the Bank did not try to control this appreciation and thereby stabilize the exchange rate. The strong Canadian dollar had consequences for Canada's manufacturing exports and hence manufacturing jobs. In 2007, trade union representatives argued that the strong dollar was the main cause of over 250 000 manufacturing job losses during the 2004 to 2007 period, and they accused the Bank of ignoring its mandate. The Bank of Canada has claimed that its sole policy objective, at least since the early 1990s, is to keep the inflation rate low. More precisely, the Bank has signed multi-year agreements with the Government of Canada which specify that the Bank of Canada is to keep inflation as close as possible to 2 percent, and to keep annual inflation within a 1 to 3 percent range.

Like the Department of Finance, which is the government institution with the greatest responsibility for fiscal policy, the Bank of Canada is based in Ottawa. In contrast to the Department of Finance, which works closely with the government of the day, the Bank of Canada is similar to most central banks in that it possesses a substantial degree of independence from the government. The Bank is headed by a governor who is selected for a seven-year term.

The key policy instrument that the Bank of Canada employs to achieve its monetary objective of low inflation is control over interest rates. As you will learn in greater detail later in this chapter, lower real interest rates promote more spending in the economy and hence lead to higher levels of inflation. Conversely, higher real interest rates promote less spending in the economy and result in lower inflation. To achieve its monetary policy objectives, the Bank of Canada makes regularly scheduled announcements about interest rate changes. Eight times a year the Bank of Canada announces whether it will increase, decrease, or leave unchanged its interest rate target.

The Bank of Canada and central banking will be discussed in further detail in Chapter 13, in connection with the topic of money and banking.

> **RECAP**
>
> **THE BANK OF CANADA**
>
> The Bank of Canada is Canada's central bank. Through interest rate changes it works to achieve its monetary-policy objective of low inflation. It raises its interest rate target in response to higher inflation and cuts its interest rate target in response to lower inflation.

9.2 THE MODERN CENTRAL BANKING THEORY OF INTEREST RATE DETERMINATION

The **modern central banking theory** of interest rate determination maintains that the central bank influences market interest rates directly by changing its key policy rate. When the central bank changes the key policy rate, commercial banks respond by changing their market interest rates. The modern central banking theory is the official view of many central banks, including the Bank of Canada.

modern central banking theory the view that the central bank changes its official interest rate directly and commercial banks respond by changing market interest rates

**www.bankofcanada.ca
Bank of Canada**

prime business rate the interest rate that commercial banks charge to their least risky business borrowers; also called the prime rate

overnight rate target the interest rate that the Bank of Canada wants to prevail in the financial market where major Canadian institutions borrow and lend funds to settle daily transactions with one another

overnight rate the market interest rate that financial institutions charge each other for overnight loans

Large Value Transfer System (LVTS) an electronic wire system overseen by the Bank of Canada that allows major financial institutions operating in Canada to send large payments back and forth to each other

settlement balances accounts held at the Bank of Canada by financial institutions for the purpose of settling their net payment obligations to one another

operating band a term used by the Bank of Canada to describe the range of possible overnight interest rates: from 0.25 percentage points below the overnight rate target to 0.25 percentage points above the target

bank rate the interest rate that the Bank of Canada charges commercial banks for overnight loans, it corresponds to the upper limit of the Bank of Canada's operating band for the overnight rate; for decades, it was the Bank's official interest rate

According to the Bank of Canada, its main tool for monetary policy is its key policy rate (also called the official interest rate). When the Bank changes the key policy rate, "this sends a clear signal about the direction in which it wants short-term interest rates to go. These changes usually lead to moves in the prime rate at commercial banks, which serves as a benchmark for many of their loans."[1]

The essence of the theory is that the central bank, the Bank of Canada, changes its official interest rate and in response commercial banks change the market interest rates (particularly short-term ones) they charge customers, starting with the **prime business rate,** the rate commercial banks charge to their least risky business borrowers. In every month since February 1996 changes in the Bank of Canada's key policy rate have produced changes of the same amount in the prime business rate.

While the essence of the theory is straightforward, interest rate targeting by the central bank does involve a bit more than just announcing targets. In the Canadian case, starting in December 2000, the Bank of Canada introduced a system of eight pre-specified dates each year for announcing any changes to its key policy rate, which is now the **overnight rate target** (sometimes called the target for the overnight rate). Simply by announcing a change in the overnight rate target the Bank is able to alter the range in which the *overnight rate* will move. But the Bank takes additional actions—borrowing and lending operations—to ensure that the overnight rate stays very close to the target that the Bank has announced for it.

The **overnight rate** is a market interest rate that large financial institutions (mainly commercial banks) charge one another for overnight loans. The participants in the overnight market are generally financial institutions such as banks. The banks participate in a national system for the clearing and settlement of cheques and electronic funds transfers, the most important component of which is the **Large Value Transfer System (LVTS).** The LVTS, which now carries more than $140 billion in payments each day, is an electronic wire system that lets financial institutions send large payments to each other with certainty that these payments will settle. Certainty of settlement is guaranteed because net payment obligations are settled from account balances, known as **settlement balances,** held by all LVTS participants at the Bank of Canada. The Bank holds collateral from LTVS participants, and would use it if ever a participating institution could not meet its net payment obligations. As a central bank, the Bank of Canada can supply whatever balances the system may require. In any case, if at the end of the working day one bank has a surplus of funds it will lend them, overnight, to another bank that is short of funds. The borrowing bank will pay the lending bank the overnight rate and their net LVTS positions will be covered.

The Bank of Canada makes sure that the overnight rate stays within an **operating band** of 0.5 percentage points of its overnight rate target (see Figure 9.1). The lower limit of the operating band is 0.25 percentage points below the overnight rate target. The lower limit is a rate (sometimes called the *bankers deposit rate*) at which the Bank of Canada will pay interest on overnight funds deposited at the Bank by commercial banks unable to obtain a better rate from other commercial banks. The upper limit of the operating band, which is called the **bank rate,** is 0.25 percentage points above the overnight rate target. If a commercial bank is not able to borrow overnight funds from another commercial bank at a rate below the upper limit, then the Bank of Canada will lend money overnight to the commercial bank at the upper limit. By standing ready to borrow funds at the lower limit of the operating band and to lend funds at the upper limit, the Bank of Canada is able to keep the overnight rate within the operating band.

---

[1]Bank of Canada, "Target for the Overnight Rate," http://www.bankofcanada.ca/en/backgrounders/bg-p9.html.

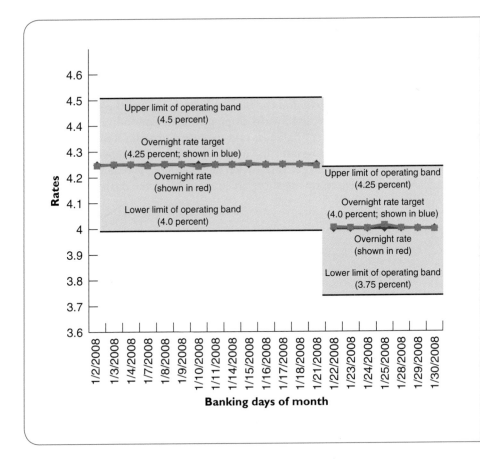

FIGURE 9.1

A Downward Shift of the Operating Band for the Overnight Rate, January 2008

The target for the overnight rate (shown in blue) can change at pre-specified dates, as it did on January 22, 2008, when the Bank of Canada lowered it from 4.25 to 4 percent. A lowering of the overnight rate target means that the operating band (shown in beige) shifts downward. The actual overnight rate (shown in red) need not be exactly the same as the overnight rate target, but it is very close. When the Bank of Canada changes the overnight rate target, it is usually by 0.25 percentage points, as shown here.

But, as is suggested by the closeness of the overnight rate to the overnight target for the days of January 2008 shown in Figure 9.1, the Bank of Canada does not just aim to keep the overnight rate within the operating band—it aims to keep the overnight rate very close to the overnight rate target. In January 2008, for example, the overnight rate only differed from the overnight rate target by more than one basis point (one hundredth of a percentage point) for a single day; that is, on January 2, 2008, when it differed by 0.014 percentage points.

How is the overnight rate kept so close to the overnight rate target? The Bank manages the overnight rate by monitoring the overnight loans market on a daily basis and taking appropriate actions.[2] When the overnight rate is exceeding the overnight rate target, it is because the amount that participants wish to borrow is greater than the amount that other members are willing to lend at that overnight rate target. When this is the case, settlement balances are said to be in deficit. This situation leads the Bank to buy Government of Canada bonds from market participants with an agreement, called a **special purchase and resale agreement (SPRA)**, to sell them back at a predetermined price the next business day. The bonds serve as collateral for the Bank of Canada loans, provide liquidity to the market, and bring settlement balances up to zero. Conversely, if overnight funds are trading below the overnight rate target, the Bank of Canada will sell Government of Canada bonds to market participants, with the agreement, called a **sale and repurchase agreement (SRA)**, to buy them back the next business day. The bond sales by the Bank of Canada soak up liquidity in the market and bring settlement balances down to zero.

special purchase and resale agreement (SPRA) a financial transaction, used to reinforce the overnight rate target, in which the Bank of Canada buys Government of Canada bonds in the overnight market with an agreement to sell them back the next business day; SPRAs are initiated by the Bank when overnight funds are trading above the target rate

sale and repurchase agreement (SRA) a financial transaction, used to reinforce the overnight rate target, in which the Bank of Canada sells Government of Canada bonds in the overnight market with an agreement to buy them back the next business day; SRAs are initiated by the Bank when overnight funds are trading below the target rate

[2]For further details on the approach to monetary policy implementation adopted by the Bank of Canada beginning in February 1999, see Donna Howard, "A Primer on the Implementation of Monetary Policy in the LVTS Environment," *Bank of Canada*, December 2001, http://www.bankofcanada.ca/en/lvts/lvts_primer_2007.pdf.

Figure 9.2 provides a graphical representation of the process. The vertical line of the figure measures interest rates and the horizontal axis measures settlement balances in the overnight market. When settlement balances are negative (with the market as a whole in an overdraft situation, as shown by the values on the horizontal line left of 0) the overnight rate exceeds the overnight rate target. When settlement balances are positive and the market is in a surplus, the overnight rate is lower than the target. The downward-sloping dashed line indicates a negative relationship between settlement balances and the overnight rate. For convenience, a straight-line relationship is assumed. The Bank of Canada keeps the overnight rate extremely close to the target rate by keeping settlement balances extremely close to zero, as represented by the short green segment of the dashed line.

FIGURE 9.2

Precise Control of the Overnight Rate

If settlement balances are negative, the overnight rate is higher than the overnight rate target. If settlement balances are positive, the overnight rate is lower than the target. The downward-sloping dashed line indicates a negative relationship between settlement balances and the overnight rate. The Bank of Canada keeps the overnight rate extremely close to the target rate by keeping settlement balances extremely close to zero, as represented by the short green segment of the dashed line.
SOURCE: Derived in part from Marc Lavoie, "Monetary base endogeneity and the new procedures of asset-based North American monetary systems," PowerPoint presentation, http://aix1.uottawa.ca/~robinson/Lavoie/Presentations/en/DR12.ppt.

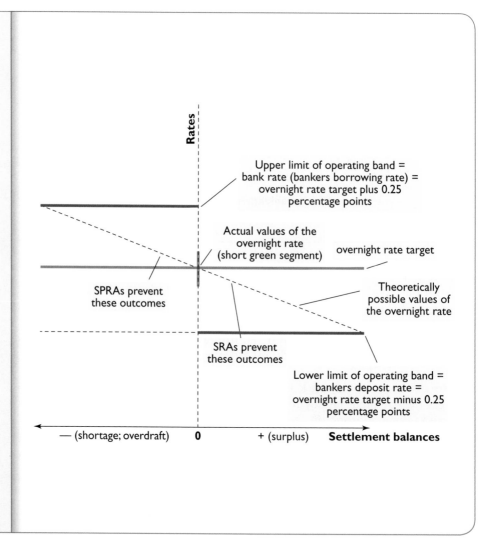

We have mentioned that the Bank of Canada's key policy rate or official interest rate is the overnight rate target. But for decades its official rate was something called the *bank rate*. The replacement of the bank rate by the overnight rate target as the official rate has led to a "frequently asked question" posed and answered on the Bank of Canada Web site: What happened to the bank rate?

In fact, not much has really changed. The bank rate still exists. Its ups and downs over the period 1996–2008 are shown in Figure 9.3. Under the Bank of Canada's current policies, the bank rate is always 0.25 percentage points above the overnight rate target. In other words, when the Bank of Canada changes the overnight rate target, it also changes the bank rate at the same time, and by an equal amount. On January 21, 2008, for example, the overnight rate target stood at 4.25 percent and the bank rate stood at 4.5 percent. The next morning the Bank of Canada announced it had cut the overnight rate target by 0.25 percentage points to 4 percent. At the same time the bank rate was cut by 0.25 percentage points to 4.25 percent.

Why is there a 0.25-percentage-point gap between the overnight rate target and the bank rate? As explained above, the overnight rate target is the average interest rate that the Bank of Canada wants to see in the market for overnight loans among large financial institutions (mainly commercial banks). The overnight rate target is the middle of a 0.5-percentage-point-wide operating band for these overnight loans. The **bank rate** is the upper limit of the operating band (see Figure 9.1), 0.25 percentage points above the overnight rate target. It is the rate of interest the Bank charges commercial banks for overnight loans.

Why does the Bank of Canada now emphasize the overnight rate target rather than the bank rate? One reason is that it does not want to be criticized for having an official interest rate that is too high relative to the official rate in the United States. The overnight rate target of the Bank of Canada corresponds closely to the intended federal funds rate pursued by the Federal Reserve, the central bank of the United States. Just as the overnight rate target is the average interest rate that the Bank of Canada wants to see in the market for overnight loans among Canada's chartered banks, the intended federal funds rate is the interest rate that the Federal Reserve wants to see U.S. banks charge each other for overnight loans.

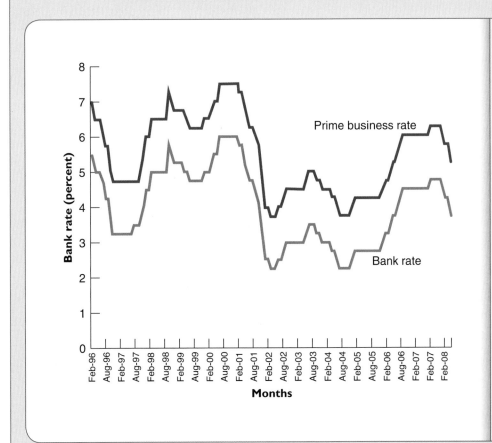

FIGURE 9.3

The Bank Rate and the Prime Business Rate, February 1996–March 2008

The bank rate is the rate of interest that the Bank of Canada charges on overnight loans to commercial banks (and other financial institutions). For decades it was the official rate of the Bank of Canada. Since February 1996, the prime business rate charged by banks to their best customers has been 1.5 percentage points above the bank rate (and 1.75 percentage points above the overnight rate target). SOURCE: Statistics Canada, CANSIM series v122495 (prime business rate) and v122530 (bank rate).

RECAP

THE MODERN CENTRAL BANKING THEORY OF INTEREST RATE DETERMINATION

The modern central banking theory claims that when the central bank changes its key policy rate (also called its official interest rate), commercial banks respond by changing market interest rates. In Canada, the key policy rate used to be the bank rate but is now the overnight rate target. The Bank of Canada monitors the overnight rate on a daily basis and takes whatever actions are necessary to keep the overnight rate very close to the overnight rate target.

9.3 CAN THE BANK OF CANADA CONTROL THE REAL INTEREST RATE?

The modern central banking theory claims that a central bank, such as the Bank of Canada, has the power to control the economy's *nominal* interest rate. But many important decisions, such as the decisions to consume and invest, depend on the *real* rate of interest. To affect those decisions, a central bank like the Bank of Canada must exert some control over the real interest rate.

Most economists believe that the Bank of Canada can control the real interest rate, at least for some period. To see why, recall the definition of the real interest rate from Chapter 6:

$$r = i - \pi.$$

That is, the real interest rate r equals the nominal interest rate i minus the rate of inflation π. As we have seen, the Bank of Canada can control the nominal interest rate quite precisely. Furthermore, inflation appears to change relatively slowly in response to changes in policy or economic conditions, for reasons we discuss in Chapter 11. Because inflation tends to adjust slowly, action by the Bank of Canada to change the nominal interest rate causes the real interest rate to change by about the same amount. (Additional discussion of interest rates is provided in Chapter 12, where we mention real interest rate determination in an open economy with flexible exchange rates.)

In discussing the Bank of Canada's control over interest rates, we should also recognize that in reality there are many thousands of interest rates in the economy, not just one. Because interest rates tend to move together (allowing us to speak of "the" interest rate), an action by the Bank of Canada to change the overnight rate generally causes other interest rates to change in the same direction. However, the tendency of other interest rates (such as the long-term government bond rate or the rate on bonds issued by corporations) to move in the same direction as the overnight rate is only a tendency, not an exact relationship. In practice, then, the Bank of Canada's control of other interest rates, particularly long-term ones, is somewhat less precise than its control of the overnight rate—a fact that complicates the Bank of Canada's policy-making.

RECAP

THE CENTRAL BANK AND THE NOMINAL INTEREST RATE

The modern central banking theory claims that the central bank is able to control the nominal interest rate. And because inflation is slow to adjust, in the short run central banks like the Bank of Canada can control the real interest rate (equal to the nominal interest rate minus the inflation rate) as well as the nominal interest rate.

In macroeconomics, we typically assume that interest rates move together, allowing us to speak of "the" interest rate. This simplification abstracts from the fact that central banks generally have better control over short-term interest rates than over long-term ones.

9.4 THE EFFECTS OF BANK OF CANADA ACTIONS ON THE ECONOMY

Now that we have seen how the Bank of Canada can influence interest rates (both nominal and real), we can turn to the question of how monetary policy can be used to eliminate output gaps and stabilize the economy. The basic idea is relatively straightforward; planned aggregate expenditure (as we will see) depends on the real interest rate. Specifically, a lower real interest rate encourages higher spending by households and firms, while a higher real interest rate reduces spending. By adjusting the real interest rate, the Bank of Canada can move planned aggregate expenditure in the desired direction. Assuming that firms produce just enough to meet the demand for their output, the stabilization of planned aggregate expenditure leads to stabilization of aggregate output and employment as well. In this section we will first explain how planned aggregate expenditure is related to the real interest rate. Then we will show how the Bank of Canada can use changes in the real interest rate to fight a recession or inflation.

PLANNED AGGREGATE EXPENDITURE AND THE REAL INTEREST RATE

In Chapter 8 we saw how planned spending is affected by changes in real output Y. Changes in output affect the household sector's disposable income, which in turn influences consumption spending, a relationship captured by the consumption function.

A second variable that has potentially important effects on aggregate expenditure is the real interest rate r. The real interest rate influences the behaviour of both households and firms.

For households, the empirical evidence suggests that a higher real interest rate reduces consumption spending. This idea makes sense; think, for example, about people's willingness to buy consumer durables, such as automobiles or furniture. Consumer durables, which are part of consumption spending, are often financed by borrowing from a bank, credit union, or other financial intermediary. When the real interest rate rises, the monthly finance charges associated with the purchase of a car or a piano are higher, and people become less willing or able to make the purchase. Thus a higher real interest rate reduces people's willingness to spend on consumer goods, assuming disposable income and other factors that affect consumption remain constant.

Besides reducing consumption spending, a higher real interest rate may also discourage firms from making capital investments. For example, upgrading a computer system may be profitable for a manufacturing firm when the cost of the system can be financed by borrowing at a real interest rate of 3 percent. However, if the real interest rate rises to 6 percent, doubling the cost of funds to the firm, the same upgrade may not be profitable and the firm may choose not to invest.[3]

When the real interest rate rises, financing a new car becomes more expensive and fewer cars are purchased.

[3]Even if non-residential business fixed capital formation is relatively insensitive to interest rate changes, as some empirical evidence suggests, overall private-sector investment will tend to be fairly responsive to interest rate changes because of the interest-rate sensitivity of the residential investment component of private-sector investment.

We conclude that *both consumption spending and planned private-sector investment spending decline when the real interest rate increases.* Conversely, a fall in the real interest rate tends to stimulate consumption and investment spending, by reducing financing costs. Example 9.1 is a numerical illustration of how planned aggregate expenditure can be related to the real interest rate and output.

EXAMPLE 9.1   **Planned aggregate expenditure and the real interest rate**

In a hypothetical version of the Canadian economy, the components of planned spending are given by

$$C = 640 + 0.8(Y - T) - 400r,$$
$$I^p = 250 - 600r,$$
$$G = 300,$$
$$NX = 20,$$
$$T = 250.$$

Find the relationship of planned aggregate expenditure to the real interest rate r and output Y in this economy. Find autonomous expenditure and induced expenditure.

This example is similar to Example 8.2, except that now the real interest rate r is allowed to affect both consumption and planned private-sector investment. For example, the final term in the equation describing consumption, $-400r$, implies that a 1 percent (0.01) increase in the real interest rate, from 4 percent to 5 percent, for example, reduces consumption spending by $400(0.01) = 4$ units. Similarly, the final term in the equation for planned private-sector investment tells us that in this example, a 1 percent increase in the real interest rate lowers planned private-sector investment by $600(0.01) = 6$ units. Thus the overall effect of a 1 percent increase in the real interest rate is to lower planned aggregate expenditure by 10 units, the sum of the effects on consumption and private-sector investment. As in the earlier examples, disposable income $(Y - T)$ is assumed to affect consumption spending through a marginal propensity to consume of 0.8 (see the first equation), and government purchases G, net exports NX, and taxes T are assumed to be fixed numbers.

To find a numerical equation that describes the relationship of planned aggregate expenditure *(PAE)* to output, we can begin as in Chapter 8 with the general definition of planned aggregate expenditure:

$$PAE = C + I^p + G + NX.$$

Substituting for the four components of expenditure, using the equations describing each type of spending above, we get

$$PAE = [640 + 0.8(Y - 250) - 400r] + [250 - 600r] + 300 + 20.$$

The first term in brackets on the right side of this equation is the expression for consumption, using the fact that taxes $T = 250$; the second bracketed term is planned private-sector investment; and the last two terms correspond to the given numerical values of government purchases and net exports. If we simplify this equation and group together the terms that do not depend on output Y and the terms that do depend on output, we get

$$PAE = [(640 - 0.8 \times 250 - 400r) + (250 - 600r) + 300 + 20] + 0.8Y,$$

or, simplifying further,

$$PAE = [1010 - 1000r] + 0.8Y.$$

In the equation above, the term in brackets is *autonomous expenditure,* the portion of planned aggregate expenditure that does not depend on output. *Notice that in this example autonomous expenditure depends on the real interest rate r.* Induced expenditure, the portion of planned aggregate expenditure that does depend on output, equals $0.8Y$ in this example.

The real interest rate and short-run equilibrium output   **EXAMPLE 9.2**

In the economy described in Example 9.1, the real interest rate r is set by the Bank of Canada to equal 0.05 (5 percent). Find short-run equilibrium output.

We found in Example 9.1 that, in this economy, planned aggregate expenditure is given by Equation 9.1. We are given that the Bank of Canada sets the real interest rate at 5 percent. Setting $r = 0.05$ in Equation 9.1 gives

$$PAE = [1010 - 1000 \times (0.05)] + 0.8Y.$$

Simplifying, we get

$$PAE = 960 + 0.8Y.$$

So, when the real interest rate is 5 percent, autonomous expenditure is 960 and induced expenditure is $0.8Y$. Short-run equilibrium output is the level of output that equals planned aggregate spending. To find short-run equilibrium output, we could now apply the tabular method used in Chapter 8, comparing alternative values of output with the planned aggregate expenditure at that level of output. Short-run equilibrium output would be determined as the value of output such that output just equals spending, or

$$Y = PAE.$$

However, conveniently, when we compare this example with Example 8.2 in the last chapter, we see that the equation for planned aggregate expenditure, $PAE = 960 + 0.8Y$, is identical to what we found there. Thus Table 8.1, which we used to solve Example 8.2, applies to this example as well, and we get the same answer for short-run equilibrium output, which is $Y = 4800$.

Short-run equilibrium output can also be found graphically, using the Keynesian cross diagram from Chapter 8. Again, since the equation for planned aggregate output is the same as in Example 8.2, Figure 8.3 applies equally well here.

For the economy described in Example 9.2, suppose the Bank of Canada sets the real interest rate at 3 percent rather than at 5 percent. Find short-run equilibrium output.   **EXERCISE 9.1**

THE BANK OF CANADA FIGHTS A RECESSION

We have seen that the Bank of Canada can control the real interest rate and that the real interest rate in turn affects planned aggregate expenditure and short-run equilibrium output. Putting these two results together, we can see how Bank of Canada policies can help to stabilize planned aggregate expenditure and output.

Suppose the economy faces a recessionary gap—a situation in which real output is below potential output and planned aggregate expenditure is "too low."

To fight a recessionary gap, the Bank of Canada should reduce the real interest rate, stimulating consumption and private-sector investment spending. According to the theory we have developed, this increase in planned aggregate expenditure will increase output, restoring the economy to full employment. Example 9.3 illustrates this point by extending Example 9.2.

EXAMPLE 9.3	The Bank of Canada fights a recession

For the economy described in Example 9.2, suppose potential output Y^* equals 5000.[4] As before, the Bank of Canada has set the real interest rate equal to 5 percent. At that real interest rate, what is the output gap? What should the Bank of Canada do to eliminate the output gap and restore full employment? You are given that the multiplier in this economy is 5. (Recall from Chapter 8 that real-world income-expenditure multipliers are typically less than 2; we employ 5 here for ease of calculation.)

In Example 9.2 we showed that with the real interest rate at 5 percent, short-run equilibrium output for this economy is 4800. Potential output is 5000, so the output gap ($Y^* - Y$) equals $5000 - 4800 = 200$. Because actual output is below potential, this economy faces a recessionary gap.

To fight the recession, the Bank of Canada should lower the real interest rate, raising aggregate expenditure until output reaches 5000, the full-employment level. That is, the Bank of Canada's objective is to increase output by 200. Because the multiplier equals 5, to increase output by 200 the Bank of Canada must increase autonomous expenditure by $200/5 = 40$ units. By how much should the Bank of Canada reduce the real interest rate to increase autonomous expenditure by 40 units? Autonomous expenditure in this economy is $[1010 - 1000r]$, as you can see from Equation 9.1, so that each percentage point reduction in r increases autonomous expenditure by $1000 \times (0.01) = 10$ units. To increase autonomous expenditure by 40, then, the Bank of Canada should lower the real interest rate by 4 percentage points, from 5 percent to 1 percent.

In summary, to eliminate the recessionary gap of 200, the Bank of Canada should lower the real interest rate from 5 percent to 1 percent. Notice that the Bank of Canada's decrease in the real interest rate increases short-run equilibrium output, as economic logic suggests.

The Bank of Canada's recession-fighting policy is shown graphically in Figure 9.4. The reduction in the real interest rate raises planned spending at each level of output, shifting the expenditure line upward. When the real interest rate equals 1 percent, the expenditure line intersects the $Y = PAE$ line at $Y = 5000$, so that output and potential output are equal. A reduction in interest rates by the Bank of Canada, made with the intention of reducing a recessionary gap in this way, is an example of an *expansionary* monetary policy—or, less formally, a *monetary easing*.

EXERCISE 9.2	**Continuing Example 9.3, suppose that potential output is 4850 rather than 5000. By how much should the Bank of Canada cut the real interest rate to restore full employment? You may take as given that the multiplier is 5.**

THE BANK OF CANADA PREVENTS INFLATION

To this point we have focused on the problem of stabilizing output, without considering inflation. In Chapter 11 we will see how ongoing inflation can be incorporated

[4]For the sake of simplicity, we are assuming that potential output can be precisely estimated. Recall from Chapter 7, however, that potential output is difficult and controversial to estimate and is never known with full certainty, as will be emphasized later in this chapter and again in Chapter 11.

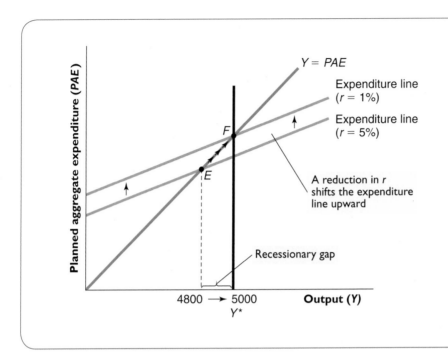

FIGURE 9.4

The Bank of Canada Fights a Recession
When the real interest rate is 5 percent, the expenditure line intersects the $Y=PAE$ line at point E. At that point output is 4800, below the economy's potential output of 5000 (a recessionary gap of 200). If the Bank of Canada reduces the real interest rate to 1 percent, stimulating consumption and investment spending, the expenditure line will shift upward. At the new point of intersection F, output will equal potential output at 5000.

into our analysis. For now we will simply note that one important cause of inflation is an expansionary output gap—a situation in which aggregate expenditure, and hence actual output, exceeds potential output. When an expansionary gap exists, firms find that the demand for their output exceeds their normal rate of production. Although firms may be content to meet the excess demand at previously determined prices for some time, if it persists they will ultimately raise their prices, which means inflation.

Because an expansionary gap stimulates inflation, central banks tend to move to eliminate expansionary gaps as well as recessionary gaps. The procedure for getting rid of an expansionary gap, a situation in which output is "too high" relative to potential output, is the reverse of that for fighting a recessionary gap, a situation in which output is "too low." As we have seen, the cure for a recessionary gap is to reduce the real interest rate, an action that stimulates planned spending and increases output. The cure for an expansionary gap is to *raise* the real interest rate, which reduces consumption and planned private-sector investment by raising the cost of borrowing. The resulting fall in planned spending leads in turn to a decline in output and to a reduction in inflationary pressures.

The Bank of Canada prevents inflation   **EXAMPLE 9.4**

For the economy studied in Examples 9.2 and 9.3, assume that potential output is 4600 rather than 5000. At the initial real interest rate of 5 percent, short-run equilibrium output is 4800, so this economy has an expansionary gap of 200. How should the Bank of Canada change the real interest rate to eliminate this gap?

In Example 9.3 we were told that the income-expenditure multiplier in this economy is 5. Thus, to reduce total output by 200, the Bank of Canada needs to reduce autonomous expenditure by 200/5 = 40 units. From Equation 9.1, we know that autonomous expenditure in this economy is [1010 − 1000r], so that each percentage point (0.01) increase in the real interest rate lowers autonomous expenditure by 10 units (1000 × 0.01). We conclude that to eliminate the inflationary gap, the Bank of Canada should raise the real interest rate by 4 percentage points (0.04), from 5 percent to 9 percent. The higher real interest rate will reduce planned aggregate expenditure and output to the level of potential output, 4600, thus eliminating inflationary pressures.

The effects of the Bank of Canada's anti-inflation policy are shown in Figure 9.5. With the real interest rate at 5 percent, the expenditure line intersects the $Y = PAE$ line at point E in the figure, where output equals 4800. To reduce planned aggregate expenditure and output, the Bank of Canada raises the real interest rate to 9 percent. The higher real interest rate reduces consumption and private-sector investment spending, moving the expenditure line downward. At the new equilibrium point G, actual output equals potential output at 4600. The Bank of Canada's policy of raising the real interest rate has eliminated the expansionary output gap, and with it, the threat of inflation.

FIGURE 9.5

The Bank of Canada Prevents Inflation

When the real interest rate is 5 percent, the expenditure line intersects the $Y = PAE$ line at point E, where short-run equilibrium output equals 4800. If potential output is 4600, an expansionary output gap of 200 exists. If the Bank of Canada raises the real interest rate to 9 percent, reducing planned aggregate expenditure, the expenditure line shifts downward. At the new intersection point G, actual output equals potential output at 4600, and the expansionary gap is eliminated.

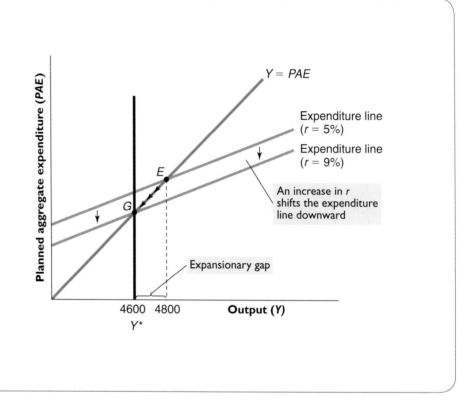

"Interest rates gyrated wildly today, on rumors that the Federal Reserve Board would be replaced by the cast of 'Saturday Night Live.'"

OUR KEYNESIAN CROSS MODEL OF MONETARY POLICY COMPARED TO THE BANK OF CANADA'S EXPLANATION

In introducing the Keynesian cross (or basic Keynesian) model, we mentioned that it is highly simplified. In this chapter we have indicated that, despite being highly simplified, the Keynesian cross model is of considerable relevance to understanding real-world monetary policy. This raises the question of how our Keynesian cross model compares to other explanations of real-world monetary policy. For example, how does the simple Keynesian cross model developed in this chapter compare with the explanation of monetary policy provided by the Bank of Canada?

Figure 9.6 depicts the Bank of Canada's view of how its monetary policy actions impact upon the economy. A monetary policy action could be either an increase or a decrease in the overnight rate target. An increase in the overnight rate target, for example, would quickly cause market interest rates to rise and the exchange rate to appreciate. The Canadian dollar would appreciate because Canadian interest rates would rise relative to rates in the United States and other countries, leading to increased demand for Canadian dollars by investors who would need them to purchase Canadian financial assets, particularly bonds. (A full discussion of exchange rate determination will be provided in Chapter 12.)

FIGURE 9.6

The Bank of Canada's View of Monetary Policy
The diagram illustrates that monetary policy actions in the form of changes in the overnight rate target produce changes in market interest rates and the exchange rate that ultimately affect aggregate expenditure growth (either increasing or reducing it) and the rate of inflation.
SOURCE: Adapted from www.bankofcanada.ca/en/monetary_mod/mechanism/index.html.

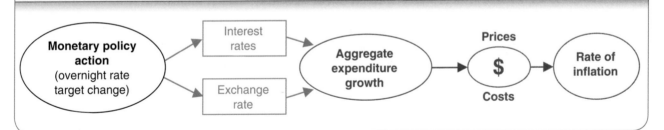

Higher market interest rates would gradually slow the growth of consumer spending and private-sector investment and would hence slow the growth of aggregate expenditure (spending). The stronger exchange rate would also gradually slow the growth of aggregate expenditure—by reducing the growth of net exports. That is, a stronger Canadian dollar would slow the growth of Canadian exports and stimulate the growth of imports.

The slower growth of aggregate expenditure would translate into slower growth of production (output) and employment. Finally, slower growth would eventually tend to reduce price and cost increases and result in a lower rate of inflation.

This explanation has much in common with the Keynesian cross explanation underlying Figure 9.5. The basic process is that the Bank of Canada increases the overnight rate target, the higher overnight rate results in higher market interest rates in general, aggregate expenditure is weakened, and inflationary pressure is reduced. Conversely, Figure 9.6 could be used to discuss a decrease in the overnight rate target and the explanation would have much in common with the explanation underlying Figure 9.4.

EXERCISE 9.3

Based upon Figure 9.6 and the discussion above, describe how the Bank of Canada would view the impact of a decrease in the overnight rate target. That is, describe how a decrease in the overnight rate target would impact on market interest rates, the exchange rate, and the inflation rate.

There are a few noteworthy differences between the Keynesian cross model of Figures 9.4 and 9.5 and the Bank of Canada explanation we have illustrated with Figure 9.6. First, the Bank of Canada explanation emphasizes that changes in the overnight rate target also produce changes in the exchange rate and hence in net exports. Our Keynesian cross model could be modified to recognize the impact that interest rates have on net exports. Rather than assume that net exports are fixed, we could assume that a rise in the interest rate will decrease net exports and that a fall in the interest rate will increase net exports. Our model would then be more realistic but the basic result would be the same—an increase in the overnight rate target would lead to a reduction in planned aggregate expenditure.

Second, the Bank of Canada explanation deals with changes in the growth rates of consumer and private-sector investment spending, net exports, aggregate expenditure, and output. Our Keynesian cross model, however, is based upon the assumption that potential output is fixed for the period of analysis. Hence in the Keynesian cross model, aggregate expenditure and the level of output go up or down relative to a fixed level. In applying the Keynesian cross model to real-world situations, we typically assume that a decrease in the level of aggregate expenditure in the model corresponds to a decrease in the growth rate of aggregate expenditure in the real world. Similarly we assume that an increase in the level of aggregate expenditure in the model corresponds to an increase in the growth rate of aggregate expenditure in the real world. But the assumption that potential output is fixed is a genuine limitation of the Keynesian cross model that students should recognize. Real-world analysis is typically not about output going up or down relative to a fixed level but about the growth of output increasing or declining relative to the current trend.

Third, the Bank of Canada explanation deals with changes in the rate of inflation. Interest rate increases, for example, will tend eventually to decrease the rate of inflation. On the other hand, while the Keynesian cross model can be used to talk about eliminating an expansionary (inflationary) gap and thereby preventing the emergence of inflation, the truth is that the Keynesian cross model does not incorporate inflation explicitly. In fact, as explained back in Chapter 8, an underlying assumption of the model is that in the short-run firms meet the demand for their products at preset prices—in other words, zero inflation (see Figure 6.4) is assumed. To consider the more general case where the economy starts from a non-zero rate of inflation, we have to move to the analysis of Chapters 10 and 11.

RECAP ↑

THE EFFECTS OF BANK OF CANADA ACTIONS ON THE ECONOMY

An increase in the real interest rate reduces both consumption spending and planned private-sector investment spending. Through its control of the real interest rate, the Bank of Canada is thus able to influence planned aggregate expenditure and short-run equilibrium output.

To fight a recession (a recessionary gap), the Bank of Canada should lower the real interest rate, stimulating planned aggregate expenditure and output. Conversely, to fight inflation (an expansionary output gap), the Bank of Canada should raise the real interest rate.

Although the Keynesian cross model employed in this chapter is highly simplified, it allows for an analysis of monetary policy that has much in common with the Bank of Canada's explanation. One limitation of the Keynesian cross model is the assumption that in the short run firms meet the demand for their products at preset prices, but this limitation will be overcome with the models of Chapters 10 and 11.

9.5 MONETARY POLICY-MAKING AND REAL-WORLD UNCERTAINTY

In this chapter we used a simplified model to explain the basic economics underlying monetary policy. We worked through a number of examples showing the calculation of the real interest rate that is needed to restore output to its full-employment level. While those examples are useful in understanding how monetary policy works, as with our analysis of fiscal policy in Chapter 8, they overstate the precision of monetary policy-making. The real-world economy is highly complex and knowledge of its workings quite imperfect. For example, though we assumed in our analysis that the Bank of Canada knows the exact value of potential output, in reality potential output can be estimated only approximately (and many economists believe that the Bank of Canada is prone to underestimating potential output). As a result, at any given time the Bank of Canada has only a rough idea of the size of the output gap. Similarly, Bank of Canada policy-makers have only an approximate idea of the effect of a given change in the real interest rate on planned aggregate expenditure, or the length of time before that effect will occur. Because of these uncertainties, the Bank of Canada tends to proceed cautiously. Bank of Canada policy-makers avoid large changes in interest rates, and rarely raise or lower the overnight rate target more than 0.25 percentage points (from 3.25 to 3.00 percent, for example) at any one time.

ECONOMIC *Naturalist* **9.2** Why did the Bank of Canada cut the overnight rate target nine times in 2001?

For the first three weeks of January 2001, the overnight rate target of the Bank of Canada stood at 5.75 percent. Then on January 23 it was cut to 5.5 percent, the first of nine cuts that would take the overnight rate target to 2.25 percent by the end of the year. Why did the Bank of Canada cut the overnight rate target 3.5 percentage points during 2001?

In the last quarter of 2000, real GDP growth in Canada slowed dramatically, following a slowdown of real GDP growth in the United States, Canada's largest trading partner. For several previous quarters real GDP growth in Canada had averaged over 4 percent but in the last quarter of 2000 it dropped to 1.6 percent.

One factor in Canada's growth slowdown was the negative impact on Canadian net exports from the United States' growth slowdown. But another factor was the Bank of Canada's own series of increases in the overnight rate target, which raised the target by 1.25 percentage points

between November 1999 and May 2000. The increases had been instituted because the Bank had feared (incorrectly perhaps) that otherwise Canada's actual economic growth rate would have exceeded its potential and triggered an upsurge in inflation.

There were indications that Canada's growth slowdown in the last quarter of 2000 might not just be a temporary one but could turn into a recession. For example, machinery and equipment investment by business fell by a full 7 percent that quarter. In addition, the Toronto Stock Exchange 300 index fell by about 20 percent from August to December 2000 and, as mentioned above, growth had declined in the United States.

Reacting to signals that the Canadian economy might be headed for a recession, the Bank of Canada began to make cuts to the overnight rate target in January 2001. The rate cuts were intended as a pre-emptive strike against recessionary forces. In announcing the fifth of those rate cuts, the

Bank of Canada declared in July 2001 that, "Today's rate cut brings the total reduction in interest rates by the Bank this year to 1½ percentage points. This cumulative reduction will underpin domestic economic growth in the face of weaker-than-anticipated economic conditions outside North America and continuing uncertainty about the timing and strength of the recovery in investment in the United States. The Bank continues to expect that the pace of growth in Canada will increase in the second half of 2001."[5]

But signs of the recovery in the latter half of 2001 that had been anticipated by the Bank (and most Bay Street economists) failed to materialize. So the Bank continued to make cuts to the overnight rate target in the second half of 2001.

This episode of nine cuts in the overnight rate target in one year illustrates that monetary policy is made under conditions of less than perfect knowledge. There is always uncertainty about the economy's potential output, uncertainty about the rate of future economic growth in the absence of interest rate changes, and uncertainty about the exact impact of interest rate changes upon growth.

ECONOMIC *Naturalist* 9.3 — Why did the Bank of Canada raise the overnight rate target 2.5 percentage points in the period from 2004 to 2007?

As noted in Economic Naturalist 9.2, the Bank of Canada cut the overnight rate target by a large amount, in several stages, to combat the economic slowdown of 2000–2001. The overnight rate was kept low in 2002, 2003, and into the second half of 2004 as the economy recovered. Other short-term nominal interest rates, which move more or less in tandem with the overnight rate target, were low as well. Indeed, real short-term interest rates were close to zero in the 2002–2004 period (as shown in Figure 6.2).

By the second half of 2004, inflation was running at about 2.3 percent, somewhat above the 2 percent that the Bank of Canada regards as consistent with its objective of maintaining a low inflation rate. The Bank began to judge that the recessionary gap would soon be eliminated and that the economy was on the verge of entering an expansionary gap situation. If an expansionary gap situation did arise the inflation rate would be expected to rise as well.

The Bank of Canada's judgment that action was required in order to prevent an inflation increase was based on the unemployment rate (we have seen in Chapter 7 that the unemployment rate is linked to the output gap through Okun's law). The unemployment rate had dropped to a low of 6.7 percent at the peak of the economic boom in June 2000, a level that the Bank of Canada viewed as less than or equal to the natural rate of unemployment. After the economic slowdown of late 2000 and 2001, the unemployment rate had reached a high of 7.9 percent in September 2003. But then the unemployment rate began to plummet as the economic recovery took hold. By the end of September 2004 the unemployment rate was down to 7 percent. The Bank of Canada feared that unless it began to raise the overnight target, thereby raising real interest rates and slowing the growth of spending, an expansionary (that is, inflationary) gap would develop and the inflation rate would rise.

The shrinking output gap, however, was not the only factor causing the Bank of Canada to worry about an upsurge in the inflation rate. The Bank was also concerned with already high and still rising energy prices. One indicator of energy prices is the price of gasoline and, as Figure 9.7 indicates, from 2002 the price of gasoline rose sharply relative to price levels in general as measured by the CPI. Energy price increases tend, all else being equal, to generate increases in the CPI unless offsetting events or deliberate countermeasures take place. (For further explanation, see Chapters 10 and 11.)

On September 8, 2004, the Bank of Canada announced that it was raising the overnight rate target by 0.25 percentage points, from 2 to 2.25 percent. The press release announcing the interest rate hike stated that "Looking forward, the Bank expects aggregate demand to grow at, or marginally above, the rate of growth of production capacity. With the economy operating close to its capacity, monetary stimulus needs to be reduced to avoid a buildup of inflationary pressures. In this context, the Bank decided to raise its target for the overnight rate."[6]

As the unemployment rate continued to fall in 2005 and 2006 (see Figure 4.3), and as energy prices continued

---

[5]For this and any other quotations from Bank of Canada interest rate announcements, see the Bank's press release for the day of the announcement under the press releases page at www.bankofcanada.ca.
[6]Bank of Canada, "Press Release, 8 September 2004," http://bankofcanada.ca/en/fixed-dates/2004/rate_080904.html (May 2008).

to rise at a rapid rate (see Figure 9.7), the Bank of Canada continued to raise the overnight target. By July 10, 2007, the Bank of Canada had raised the overnight rate target to 4.5 percent, a level 2.5 percentage points higher than the rate of three years earlier. (For the exact path of the interest rate hikes, just subtract 0.25 percentage points from the *bank rate* line shown in Figure 9.3.)

In announcing the interest rate hike on July 10, 2007, however, the Bank of Canada noted that there were some risks connected with its inflation projection—namely, the uncertainty associated with the assessment that the overnight rate should be raised in order to prevent inflation rate increases. It stated, "The main downside risks are related to the higher Canadian dollar and the ongoing adjustment in the U.S. housing sector."[7] From 2003 to 2007, the Canadian dollar had appreciated rapidly against the U.S. dollar, as can be seen in Figure 4.6. A stronger Canadian dollar tends to reduce inflation directly by reducing import prices, which are included in the CPI. It also tends to reduce inflation indirectly by reducing the growth of net exports, an important component of planned aggregate expenditure,

thereby reducing the growth of actual output relative to potential output. (For more on the dollar and exchange rates, see Chapter 12.) The adjustment in the U.S. housing sector refers to a collapse in U.S. housing construction after the dissolving of speculative price bubbles in many U.S. housing markets. (An important subcomponent of the investment aspect of planned aggregate expenditure in the U.S., the housing sector corresponds to the "residential structures" line in Table 5.2.) This adjustment threatened to trigger a recession in the United States, and a U.S. recession would impact Canada by reducing U.S. imports from Canada. (Recall the discussion of the marginal propensity to import from section 8.5.)

By December of 2007, the period of repeated hikes in the Bank of Canada's overnight rate target had come to an end. The Bank announced what would be the first of a series of overnight rate target decreases. These were designed not just to offset the threat of a U.S. recession, but were intended to help the Canadian economy cope with the impact of a global financial crisis that followed the collapse of the U.S. housing bubble.

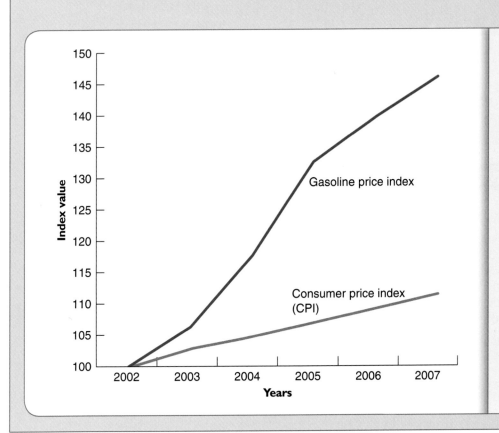

FIGURE 9.7

The Gasoline Price Explosion, 2002–2007
A key concern of the Bank of Canada in the 2004–2007 period was that high and rising energy prices would contribute to a more rapid increase in the overall price level. One indicator of energy prices is the gasoline price index component of the CPI. Over the 2002–2007 period shown, the CPI rose from 100 to 111.5, but the gasoline price index rose from 100 to 146.1.
SOURCE: Statistics Canada, CANSIM series v41693434 (gasoline) and v41693271 (CPI).

[7]Bank of Canada, "Press Release, 10 July 2007" http://bankofcanada.ca/en/fixed-dates/2007/rate_100707.html (May 2008).

SUMMARY

9.1 Monetary policy is one of two major types of stabilization policy, the other being fiscal policy. Monetary policy influences the state of the economy by changing interest rates.

9.1 The Bank of Canada is Canada's central bank. It uses interest rate changes to achieve its monetary policy objective of low inflation.

9.2 According to the *modern central banking theory*, the Bank of Canada changes market interest rates by changing its official interest rate, the *overnight rate target*. The Bank takes whatever actions are necessary to keep the overnight loans rate close to the overnight rate target. The overnight rate is a reference point for other market interest rates (particularly short-term interest rates) charged by commercial banks.

9.3 The Bank of Canada can control the real interest rate as well as the nominal interest rate. The real interest rate equals the nominal interest rate minus the inflation rate. Because the inflation rate adjusts relatively slowly,

the Bank of Canada can change the real interest rate by changing the nominal interest rate.

9.4 The Bank of Canada's actions affect the economy because changes in the real interest rate affect planned aggregate expenditure. Specifically, an increase in the real interest rate raises the cost of borrowing, reducing consumption and planned private-sector investment. Thus, by increasing the real interest rate, the Bank of Canada can reduce planned aggregate expenditure and short-run equilibrium output. Conversely, by reducing the real interest rate, the Bank of Canada can stimulate planned aggregate expenditure and raise short-run equilibrium output. To eliminate a recessionary output gap, the Bank of Canada will lower the real interest rate. To eliminate an expansionary output gap, the Bank of Canada will raise the real interest rate.

9.5 In practice, a central bank's information about the level of potential output and the size and speed of the effects of its actions is imprecise. Thus, monetary policy-making must attempt to cope with real-world uncertainty.

KEY TERMS

bank rate (222)
Large Value Transfer System
    (LVTS) (222)
modern central banking theory (221)
operating band (222)

overnight rate (222)
overnight rate target (222)
prime business rate (222)
sale and repurchase agreement
    (SRA) (223)

settlement balances (222)
special purchase and resale agreement
    (SPRA) (223)

REVIEW QUESTIONS

1. Is the Bank of Canada a chartered bank, a commercial bank, or a central bank?

2. What is the main policy objective of the Bank of Canada?

3. Describe the modern central banking theory of how the Bank of Canada manages the overnight rate to change interest rates in the economy.

4. You hear a news report that employment growth is lower than expected. How do you expect that report to affect market interest rates? Explain. (*Hint:* Assume that Bank of Canada policy-makers have access to the same data that you do.)

5. How does the real interest rate affect planned aggregate expenditure in the Keynesian cross model underlying Figures 9.4 and 9.5? How does the explanation associated with Figures 9.4 and 9.5 compare with the Bank of Canada explanation associated with Figure 9.6?

6. The Bank of Canada faces a recessionary gap. How would you expect it to respond? Explain step by step how its policy change is likely to affect the economy.

7. Discuss why the analysis of Figures 9.4 and 9.5 overstates the precision with which monetary policy can be used to eliminate output gaps.

PROBLEMS

1. Suppose that the Bank of Canada cuts the overnight rate target from, say, 4 percent to 3.75 percent. How would the bank rate change? By how much would you expect the prime business rate to change? (*Hint*: Figure 9.3 shows that the prime business rate has been 1.5 percentage points above the bank rate in every month since February 1996.)

2. An economy is described by the following equations:

$$C = 2600 + 0.8(Y - T) - 10\,000r,$$
$$I^p = 2000 - 10\,000r,$$
$$G = \bar{G} = 1800.$$

Net exports are zero, net taxes T are fixed at 3000, and the real interest rate r, expressed as a decimal is 0.10 (that is, 10 percent). Find a numerical equation relating planned aggregate expenditure to output. Using a table or other method, solve for short-run equilibrium output. Show your result graphically using the Keynesian cross diagram.

3. For the economy described in Problem 2:
   a. Potential output Y^* equals 12 000. What real interest rate should the Bank of Canada set to bring the economy to full employment?
   b. Repeat part (a) for $Y^* = 9000$.

4. Here is another set of equations describing an economy:

$$C = 14\,400 + 0.5(Y - T) - 40\,000r,$$
$$I^p = 8000 - 20\,000r,$$
$$G = 7000,$$
$$NX = -1800,$$
$$T = 8000,$$
$$Y^* = 40\,000.$$

   a. Find a numerical equation relating planned aggregate expenditure to output and to the real interest rate.
   b. At what value should the Bank of Canada set the real interest rate to eliminate any output gap? (*Hint*: Set output Y equal to the value of potential output given above in the equation you found in part a. Then solve for the real interest rate that also sets planned aggregate expenditure equal to potential output.)

5. The Bank of Canada publishes overviews of its monetary policy every quarter. From the Bank of Canada Web site (http://www.bankofcanada.ca), obtain a copy of the latest of these overviews (called *Monetary Policy Report* or *Monetary Policy Report Update*). In the period covered by the overview, did the Bank of Canada raise interest rates, cut them, or leave them unchanged? What principal developments in the economy did the Bank of Canada say were responsible for its monetary policy stance during the period?

ANSWERS TO IN-CHAPTER EXERCISES

9.1 If $r = 0.03$, then consumption is $C = 640 + 0.8(Y - 250) - 400(0.03) = 428 + 0.8Y$, and planned private-sector investment is $I^p = 250 - 600(0.03) = 232$. Planned aggregate expenditure is given by

$$PAE = C + I^p + G + NX$$
$$= (428 + 0.8Y) + 232 + 300 + 20$$
$$= 980 + 0.8Y.$$

To find short-run equilibrium output, one approach would be to construct a table by trial and error, as shown below.

Determination of short-run equilibrium output

(1) Output Y	(2) Planned aggregate expenditure PAE = 980 + 0.8Y	(3) Y − PAE	(4) Y = PAE
4500	4580	−80	No
4600	4660	−60	No
4700	4740	−40	No
4800	4820	−20	No
4900	4900	0	Yes
5000	4980	20	No
5100	5060	40	No
5200	5140	60	No
5300	5220	80	No
5400	5300	100	No
5500	5380	120	No

Short-run equilibrium output equals 4900, as that is the only level of output that satisfies the condition $Y = PAE$.

The answer can be obtained more quickly by simply setting $Y = PAE$ and solving for short-run equilibrium output Y. Remembering that $PAE = 980 + 0.8Y$ and substitution for PAE, we get

$$Y = 980 + 0.8Y$$
$$Y(1 - 0.8) = 980$$
$$Y = 5 \times 980 = 4900.$$

So lowering the real interest rate from 5 percent to 3 percent increases short-run equilibrium output from 4800 (as found in Example 9.2) to 4900.

If you have read Appendix 8B on the income-expenditure multiplier, there is yet another way to find the answer. Using Appendix 8B we can determine that the multiplier in this model is 5, since $1/(1 - c) = 1/(1 - 0.8) = 5$. Each percentage point reduction in the real interest rate increases consumption by 4 units and planned private-sector investment by 6 units, for a total impact on planned spending of 10 units per percentage point reduction. Reducing the real interest rate by 2 percentage points, from 5 percent to 3 percent, thus increases autonomous expenditure by 20 units. Because the multiplier is 5, an increase of 20 in autonomous expenditure raises short-run equilibrium output by $20 \times 5 = 100$ units, from the value of 4800 we found in Example 9.2 to the new value of 4900.

9.2   When the real interest rate is 5 percent, output is 4800. Each percentage point reduction in the real interest rate increases autonomous expenditure by 10 units. Since the multiplier in this model is 5, to raise output by 50 units the real interest rate should be cut by 1 percentage point, from 5 percent to 4 percent. Increasing output by 50 units, to 4850, eliminates the output gap.

9.3   Compare your answer to the Bank of Canada's explanation (at http://www.bankofcanada.ca/) about keeping the inflation rate from moving below the target range.

Appendix 9A

Monetary Policy in the Basic Keynesian Model

This appendix extends the algebraic analysis of the basic Keynesian model that was presented in Appendix 8A to include the role of monetary policy. The main difference from Appendix 8A is that in this analysis the real interest rate is allowed to affect planned spending. We will simply assume that the Bank of Canada can set the real interest rate r at any level it chooses.

The real interest rate affects consumption and planned private-sector investment. To capture these effects, we will modify the equations for those two components of spending as follows:

$$C = \bar{C} + c(Y - T) - ar,$$
$$I^p = \bar{I} - br.$$

The first equation is the consumption function with an additional term, equal to $-ar$. Think of a as a fixed number, greater than zero, that measures the strength of the interest rate effect on consumption. Thus the term $-ar$ captures the idea that when the real interest rate r rises, consumption declines by a times the increase in the interest rate. Likewise, the second equation adds the term $-br$ to the equation for planned private-sector investment spending. The parameter b is a fixed positive number that measures how strongly changes in the real interest rate affect planned private-sector investment; for example, if the real interest rate r rises, planned private-sector investment is assumed to decline by b times the increase in the real interest rate. We continue to assume that government purchases, taxes, and net exports are exogenous variables, so that $G = \bar{G}$, $T = \bar{T}$, and $NX = \overline{NX}$.

To solve for short-run equilibrium output, we start as usual by finding the relationship of planned aggregate expenditure to output. The definition of planned aggregate expenditure is

$$PAE = C + I^p + G + NX.$$

Substituting the modified equations for consumption and planned private-sector investment into this definition, along with the exogenous values of government spending, net exports, and taxes, we get

$$PAE = [\bar{C} + c(Y - \bar{T}) - ar] + [\bar{I} - br] + \bar{G} + \overline{NX}.$$

The first term in brackets on the right side describes the behavior of consumption, and the second bracketed term describes planned private-sector investment. Rearranging this equation in order to group together terms that depend on the real interest rate and terms that depend on output, we find

$$PAE = [\overline{C} - c\overline{T} + \overline{I} + \overline{G} + \overline{NX}] - (a + b)r + cY.$$

This equation is similar to Equation 8A.1, in the first appendix to Chapter 8, except that it has an extra term, $-(a + b)r$, on the right side. This extra term captures the idea that an increase in the real interest rate reduces consumption and planned private-sector investment, lowering planned spending. Notice that the term $-(a + b)r$ is part of autonomous expenditure, since it does not depend on output. Since autonomous expenditure determines the intercept of the expenditure line in the Keynesian cross diagram, changes in the real interest rate will shift the expenditure line up (if the real interest rate decreases) or down (if the real interest rate increases).

To find short-run equilibrium output, we uses the definition of short-run equilibrium output to set $Y = PAE$ and solve for Y:

$$Y = PAE$$
$$= [\overline{C} - c\overline{T} + \overline{I} + \overline{G} + \overline{NX}] - (a + b)r + cY$$
$$Y(1 - c) = [\overline{C} - c\overline{T} + \overline{I} + \overline{G} + \overline{NX}] - (a + b)r$$
$$Y = \left(\frac{1}{1 - c}\right)[(\overline{C} - c\overline{T} + \overline{I} + \overline{G} + \overline{NX}) - (a + b)r]. \qquad (9A.1)$$

Equation 9A.1 shows that short-run equilibrium output once again equals the multiplier, $1/(1 - c)$, times autonomous expenditure, $\overline{C} - c\overline{T} + \overline{I} + \overline{G} + \overline{NX} - (a + b)r$. Autonomous expenditure in turn depends on the real interest rate r. The equation also shows that the impact of a change in the real interest rate on short-run equilibrium output depends on two factors: (1) the effect of a change in the real interest rate on consumption and planned private-sector investment, which depends on the magnitude of $(a + b)$; and (2) the size of the multiplier, $1/(1 - c)$, which relates changes in autonomous expenditure to changes in short-run equilibrium output. The larger the effect of the real interest rate on planned spending, and the larger the multiplier, the more powerful will be the effect of a given change in the real interest rate on short-run equilibrium output.

To check Equation 9A.1, we can use it to resolve Example 9.2. In that example we are given $\overline{C} = 640$, $\overline{I} = 250$, $\overline{G} = 300$, $\overline{NX} = 20$, $\overline{T} = 250$, $c = 0.8$, $a = 400$, and $b = 600$. The real interest rate set by the Bank of Canada is 5 percent, or 0.05. Substituting these values into Equation 9A.1 and solving, we obtain

$$Y = \left(\frac{1}{1 - 0.8}\right)[640 - 0.8 \times 250 + 250 + 300 + 20 - (400 + 600) \times 0.05]$$
$$= 5 \times 960 = 4800.$$

This is the same result we found in Example 9.2.

Chapter **10** The Aggregate Demand–Aggregate Supply Model

CHAPTER OUTLINE

First-year students taking this course today are typically about 19 years old, which means that they were born when the Canadian inflation rate last went above 3 percent for a full year (the inflation rate in 1991 was 5.6 percent). For Canada's current generation of students, rapid inflation—a rapid general increase in the price level—is something they may have read about or heard about, but it is also something they have never experienced. For the ten years from 1998 to 2007, Canada's inflation rate averaged 2.1 percent per year.

Someone taking economics for the first time forty or fifty years ago would have had much the same life experience. Between 1952 and 1965, the Canadian inflation rate averaged 1.4 percent—so the undergraduates of the 1960s had much the same personal experience of inflation as the undergraduates of today. Economics textbooks of the 1960s rarely talked about inflation. Inflation was simply not the focus of much economic analysis, since there had been so little of it. All that changed dramatically in the 1970s. Inflation in Canada averaged 3.9 percent per year from 1966 to 1972 and then accelerated, averaging 9.6 percent per year from 1973 to 1982. Other industrialized countries experienced a similar pattern.

Economists had to react—their models said very little about changes in the general level of prices, but suddenly the cup of coffee that used to cost a dime cost a quarter. Before much longer it was fifty cents and still rising. Of course, if the price of coffee had been the only price that was increasing, consumers could just have switched to drinking other beverages—but most prices were increasing at roughly the same rate, so switching was not a solution. The problem was that the purchasing power of a dollar was shrinking as the price level rose.

As we discussed in Chapters 8 and 9, the Keynesian cross model (also called the basic Keynesian model) typically assumes that the price level stays constant for the period of analysis. Though the assumption of a constant price level had never been completely realistic, for many years it was not a bad approximation. In Canada, for example, the price level as measured by the consumer price index

(2002 = 100) stood at 9.2 when the Great Depression began in 1929 and did not exceed 9.2 again until 1946, the year of Keynes's death.

There were some increases in the price level just after the Second World War (e.g., during the Korean War) but during most of the 1950s and 1960s it stayed pretty constant. The same basket of goods that could be purchased for $16.90 in 1952 would have cost $17.60 in 1957 and had only crept up in price to $20 by 1965. But by the 1970s, assuming a constant price level did not fit well with the experience of most countries, including Canada.

Economists, including economics textbook authors, therefore became open to a new model to supplement the Keynesian cross model of output determination and to provide an explanation of price level determination. The *aggregate demand–aggregate supply model* we present in this chapter was the first to achieve widespread acceptance as an answer to that need. The **aggregate demand–aggregate supply model** shows how economic factors and policies can simultaneously affect the overall price level as well as real output.

Notice that the aggregate demand–aggregate supply model deals with changes in the overall *price level* of the economy. In order to discuss *general* movements in prices, economists have to average all the prices of a typical *market basket* of goods. In this chapter we will be focusing on the *consumer price index*. In 1964, the consumer price index for Canada was 16.4 and in 1965 it was 16.8—but by 1992 it was 84 and in 2007 it was 112. This means that Canadian consumers could buy the same basket of typical consumer goods for $19.52 in 1964 and $20 in 1965, but it would take $100 in 1992 and $133 in 2007 to buy the same basket of goods.

Earlier, we talked about the *annual inflation rate*—which is calculated from data on the price level. If it cost $19.52 to buy a basket of goods in 1964 and $20 to buy the same basket in 1965, then the *percentage change* in prices is 2.5 percent [= (20 − 19.52)/19.52]. The news media often tend to focus on the inflation rate but the price level and the inflation rate are as different as the speed of a car and its rate of acceleration. As long as a car is going forward, its speed will be greater than zero—but braking or stepping on the gas will cause the car to decelerate or accelerate. Similarly, as long as the price level is rising, the inflation rate will be a positive number. If the economy slows down, and the price level is increasing at a slower rate than before, then the inflation rate goes down (but it is still a positive number). Only if the price level actually declines—which in modern economies seldom happens, even in recessions—will the inflation rate be negative.

In the 1970s, economists focused on the importance of the *price level,* largely because the general level of prices directly determines the purchasing power of money. We will do the same in this chapter.

Of course, the rapid rise in the price level was not the only factor that made economists receptive to a new macroeconomic model. In the mid-1970s a number of countries, including the United States and Japan, experienced recessions at the same time as they experienced large increases in their price levels. The combination of recession with a sharply rising price level was dubbed "stagflation."

However, stagflation was difficult to explain with the Keynesian cross model. Recall that in our analysis of Chapters 8 and 9 the Keynesian cross model was characterized either by a recessionary gap with actual output below potential output or by an expansionary gap with actual output above potential output and pressure for the price level to rise. The model did not recognize the possibility of a recessionary gap co-existing with a rising price level. Both because of the everrising price level and because of the puzzling phenomenon of stagflation, by the 1970s more and more economists had recognized that the Keynesian cross model needed to be supplemented.

Later in this chapter we will examine a Phillips curve model that deals directly with the inflation rate rather than just the overall price level. And Chapter 11 deals with another model that focuses on the inflation rate. But for now we will

aggregate demand–aggregate supply model a model of real output and overall price level determination

focus on an aggregate demand–aggregate supply model that deals with determining the price level and real output.

10.1 THE THREE COMPONENTS OF THE AGGREGATE DEMAND–AGGREGATE SUPPLY MODEL

The aggregate demand–aggregate supply (*AD–AS*) model that will be developed in this chapter has three central components: a long-run aggregate supply curve, a short-run aggregate supply curve, and an aggregate demand curve. Each of the curves is related to material covered earlier in the textbook. The long-run aggregate supply curve is related to the concept of potential output introduced in Chapter 7. The short-run aggregate supply curve is related to a key assumption underpinning Chapters 8 and 9: in the short run, firms meet demand at existing prices. Later in this chapter we will consider an alternative, upward–sloping version of the short-run aggregate supply curve. The aggregate demand curve is derived from the planned aggregate expenditure curve of Chapters 8 and 9.

In this section, we will discuss the economic rationale for each of these three curves. In the following section, the three curves will be combined to form the *AD–AS* model and we will analyze short-run and long-run equilibrium in the context of the model.

LONG-RUN AGGREGATE SUPPLY

When we discussed the determinants of the economy's potential output, we mentioned *real inputs* (like labour, capital, and human skills) and the *productivity* with which those inputs are combined in order to produce *real output*. We did not emphasize the money units in which inputs and outputs are measured because these do not affect potential output. Potential output, as first discussed in Chapter 7, is the amount of output (real GDP) that an economy can produce when using its resources, most notably capital and labour, at normal rates. Potential output depends, then, on the amounts of capital, labour, and other inputs, and upon factors that determine the productivity of inputs, such as education levels and technological knowledge—but it is not affected by the general price level. If all the dollar bills (and bank accounts and contracts) in Canada were suddenly multiplied by ten, there would be an extra zero in all contracts and bank accounts and on all dollar bills, but no one in Canada would be able to produce any more or less than before. The **long-run aggregate supply (*LRAS*) curve**, or the relationship between the overall price level of the economy and the economy's potential output, is therefore a vertical line.

The representation of the long-run aggregate supply curve as a vertical line in Figure 10.1 says that the economy's potential output (Y^*) during a given period is independent of the price level during that period. That is, the vertical *LRAS* curve means that neither increases nor decreases in the CPI will have any effect on potential output.

Remember that when the overall price level rises, which it does as we move up a vertical *LRAS* curve, industries then not only receive higher prices for their output but also must pay higher prices for their inputs. This means that *for the economy as a whole* higher prices have a different impact than for a given perfectly competitive industry. To generalize from the case of a perfectly competitive industry to the economy as a whole would be an example of the *fallacy of composition*.

If input prices did not go up, then rising prices for output would produce an upward-sloping industry supply curve—but when *all* prices are going up, each firm finds that it is no better off, so there is a vertical long-run supply curve for the economy as a whole, even assuming that the economy is composed entirely of perfectly competitive industries.

long-run aggregate supply (LRAS) curve a relationship between potential output and the overall price level; the vertical LRAS curve indicates that potential output is independent of the overall price level

FIGURE 10.1

The Long-Run Aggregate Supply Curve
Drawing the long-run aggregate supply (*LRAS*) curve as a vertical line represents the idea that the economy's potential output (*Y**) during a given period is independent of the price level during that period. If we think of the price level as being represented by the consumer price index (*CPI*), the vertical *LRAS* curve means that neither increases nor decreases in the *CPI* will have any effect on potential output.

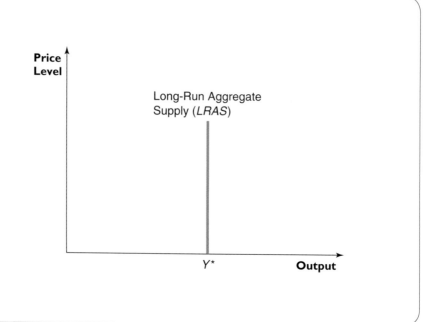

To fully understand the *LRAS* curve, we must not just understand movements along the curve (that is, that changes in the price level do not affect potential output), we must also understand the factors that cause the curve to shift. *LRAS* curve shifts are caused by the factors that cause potential output to change.

A rightward shift of the *LRAS* curve, as shown in panel a) of Figure 10.2, signifies an increase in potential output caused by such factors as a rise in the size of the capital stock, an increase in the size of the labour force, or improvements in technology. In modern developed economies, the normal pattern is for potential output to increase from one year to the next.

FIGURE 10.2

Shifts of the *LRAS* Curve
LRAS curve shifts are caused by the factors that cause potential output to change. A rightward shift of the *LRAS* curve is (panel a) an increase in potential output and would be caused by a factor such as improvement in technology. A leftward shift of the *LRAS* curve is (panel b), a decrease in potential output. This is rare in modern developed economies and could be caused by a factor such as destruction of the capital stock due to war.

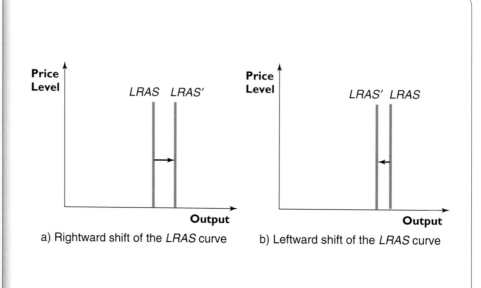

A leftward shift of the *LRAS* curve, as shown in panel b), signifies a decrease in potential output. Decreases in potential output could be caused by such factors as destruction of the capital stock due to war or natural disasters, reduction of agricultural capacity due to poor weather, and depletion of natural resources.

In practice, in peacetime it is rare for developed economies, which are typically composed of a diverse collection of industries, to experience decreases in potential output. For example, in 2003 the potential output of the Canadian economy increased somewhat even though Canada was struck by a unusually severe string of disasters—the Canadian beef industry was devastated due to one reported case of "mad cow" disease, the British Columbia forestry industry lost capacity due to massive forest fires, Ontario was struck by an unprecedented power outage, the Toronto tourism industry was temporarily stopped in its tracks by the SARS outbreak, and both Nova Scotia and Prince Edward Island experienced extensive hurricane damage.

SHORT-RUN AGGREGATE SUPPLY

The *short-run aggregate supply curve* in Figure 10.3 is drawn as a horizontal line. The **short-run aggregate supply (SRAS) curve** represents the idea, previously discussed in connection with the Keynesian cross model, that in the short run, firms supply the output that their customers demand at the prices that they have posted. This version of the curve is sometimes called the Keynesian SRAS curve.

short-run aggregate supply (SRAS) curve a relationship between real output and the overall price level in the short run; the horizontal *SRAS* curve indicates that firms in the short run meet demand, on average, at existing prices

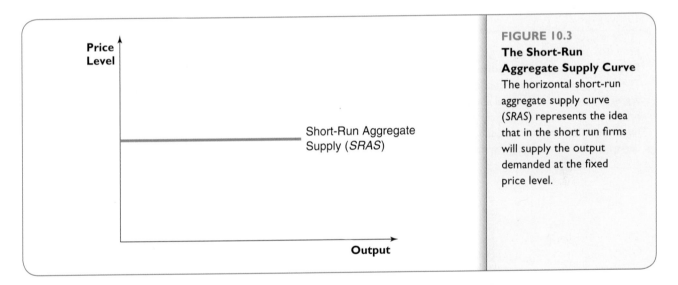

FIGURE 10.3
The Short-Run Aggregate Supply Curve
The horizontal short-run aggregate supply curve (*SRAS*) represents the idea that in the short run firms will supply the output demanded at the fixed price level.

The horizontal *SRAS* curve of Figure 10.3 will shift in the short run whenever firm costs (such as input prices) change.[1] If costs fall for firms in general, the *SRAS* curve will shift downward, as depicted in panel a) of Figure 10.4. For example, in a computer-intensive economy, if the price of computers (a widely-used input) was reduced, the *SRAS* curve would shift downward.

If costs rise for firms in general, the *SRAS* curve will shift upwards, as depicted in panel b) of Figure 10.4. For example, in an oil-based economy, if a rise in the price of oil were to occur, the *SRAS* would shift upward.

---

[1]The crucial part of Figure 10.3 is that it is horizontal *over the relevant range of outputs*. Very large deviations in output would be likely to force immediate changes in the price level—such as would occur if output were to be cut in half (which would likely produce price cuts), or if output were to increase dramatically above potential output (which would likely only occur in the context of higher prices). However, for fluctuations in output of the size actually observed in recent business cycles, Figure 10.3 is defensible.

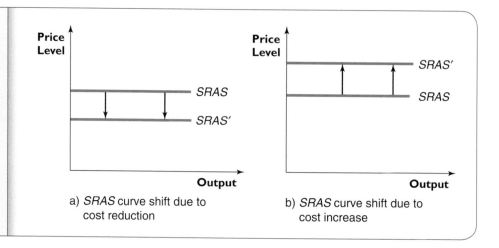

FIGURE 10.4

Shifts of the *SRAS* Curve

Shifts of the *SRAS* curve occur in the short run whenever costs change in the same direction for firms in general. Panel a) represents a *SRAS* curve shift due to cost reduction. Panel b) represents a *SRAS* curve shift due to a cost increase.

a) *SRAS* curve shift due to cost reduction

b) *SRAS* curve shift due to cost increase

AGGREGATE DEMAND

aggregate demand curve a relationship between overall spending in the economy and the aggregate price level

An important part of the cause of the rise in the general price level during the 1970s was an increase in the price of oil starting after 1973. Economists began to ask what effect this might have on aggregate demand. The **aggregate demand curve** shows the amount of planned aggregate expenditure (and output) at various price levels, as illustrated in the two panels of Figure 10.5.

FIGURE 10.5

Planned Aggregate Expenditure (*PAE*) and Aggregate Demand

The two panels show the relationship between the planned aggregate expenditure curve (introduced in Chapter 8) and the aggregate demand curve. Panel a) represents the idea that the price level is a factor causing shifts in the *PAE* curve: A lower price level (P′) causes the *PAE* curve to move upwards compared to the *PAE* associated with the pre-existing price level P. A higher price level would cause the *PAE* curve to shift down. In panel b) the two price levels P and P′ underpinning the two *PAE* curves in panel a) are plotted against their respective short-run equilibrium output levels Y and Y′.

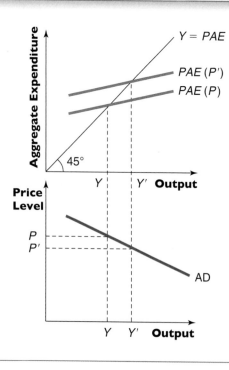

a) Changes in the price level shift planned aggregate expenditure and change real output

b) The aggregate demand schedule shows aggregate output for different price levels

The aggregate expenditure curve was introduced in Chapter 8. Panel a) of Figure 10.5 represents the idea that the price level is a factor causing shifts in the aggregate expenditure curve. A lower price level (P') causes the planned aggregate expenditure curve to shift upwards compared to the planned aggregate expenditure associated with the pre-existing price level P. A higher price level causes the planned aggregate expenditure curve to shift down.

In panel b) the two price levels P and P' underpinning the two planned aggregate expenditure curves in panel a) are plotted against their respective short-run equilibrium output levels Y and Y'. The downward-sloping aggregate demand shown in panel b) of Figure 10.5, then, represents the idea that the price level and output are inversely related.[2]

Historically, two major explanations that have been provided for an inverse relationship between the price level and output, as depicted by a downward-sloping aggregate demand curve, are the *real-balances effect* and the *foreign trade effect*.

The **real-balances effect** is the idea that consumption is positively related to wealth, and that wealth is negatively related to the price level (i.e., that wealth decreases when the price level rises). Why would this be true? Recall that one component of wealth is the money held by households and businesses. When the price level rises, the real value of a given stock of money falls. If you had $10 000 in cash and the price level rose by 20 percent, you would be worse off, because the purchasing power of your savings has fallen. In real terms, the value of your cash would have fallen by $2000—if so, you might feel less affluent and less willing to consume. Conversely, when the price level falls, the real value of a given stock of money rises. Since we saw earlier that consumption is a large component of planned aggregate expenditure, anything that influences consumer spending is potentially important—but the empirical question is whether many people actually hold large enough money balances to produce an appreciable impact.

The **foreign trade effect** is based on the assumption that the foreign exchange rate will remain unchanged as the price level changes.[3] (Obviously, this assumption is most reasonable if—as was the case in Canada from 1962 to 1971—the foreign exchange rate is fixed by the central bank at a particular level.) When this assumption is true, then an increase in the price level makes domestic goods and services more expensive relative to foreign goods and services, and tends to result in reduced demand for domestic goods and services. Similarly, a decrease in the price level makes locally produced goods cheaper and produces increased demand for domestic goods and services. As a result, a rise in the price level will reduce net exports (one of the four major components of planned aggregate expenditure) whereas a fall in the price level will increase net exports.

In panel b) of Figure 10.5 we show how, if nothing else were to change, a different price level might affect the level of aggregate demand—that is, we trace out movements *along* a given *AD* curve (which may be caused by any combination of the *real-balances effect* and the *foreign trade effect*).

real-balances effect the hypothesis that overall wealth in the economy will be inversely related to the overall price level, and therefore that aggregate demand and the price level will be inversely related

foreign trade effect the hypothesis that net exports will be inversely related to the overall price level, and therefore that aggregate demand and the price level will be inversely related

[2]The downward slope of the aggregate demand curve is *not* based on the same logic that underlies the demand curve for a particular product—i.e., that when prices are higher, people can't afford to buy more goods, and that when prices are lower, people can afford to buy more goods. If the prices of goods and services in general go up (as shown by movement up the aggregate demand curve), then the incomes of the people who produce those goods and services will tend to go up in the same proportion. If the prices of goods and services in general go down, then the incomes of the people who produce those goods and services will tend to go down proportionally. To assume that the logic that underpins the downward-sloping demand curve for a particular product also underpins the aggregate demand curve is another example of the *fallacy of composition*.

[3]In Chapter 12 we will consider the topic of exchange rate determination. We will present the argument that if the price level in a country rises relative to the price level in other countries, then a flexible exchange rate will tend to depreciate to offset the rise in the price level. The foreign trade effect used to explain the aggregate demand curve assumes that the adjustment of exchange rates to price level changes is either slow or incomplete.

However, the *AD* curve may also shift its location if the amount of planned expenditure *at a given price level* changes. Panel a) of Figure 10.6 shows a rightward shift of the *AD* curve, which might be caused by increases in autonomous consumption, autonomous private-sector investment, or net exports. It can also be caused by expansionary monetary policy (interest rate cuts) or expansionary fiscal policy (government expenditure increases or tax cuts).

FIGURE 10.6

Shifts of the *AD* curve
Panel a) depicts a rightward shift of the *AD* curve. A rightward shift of the *AD* curve can be caused by such factors as increases in autonomous expenditure and expansionary monetary or fiscal policy. A leftward shift of the *AD* curve, as depicted in panel b) can be caused by such factors as decreases in autonomous expenditure and contractionary monetary or fiscal policy.

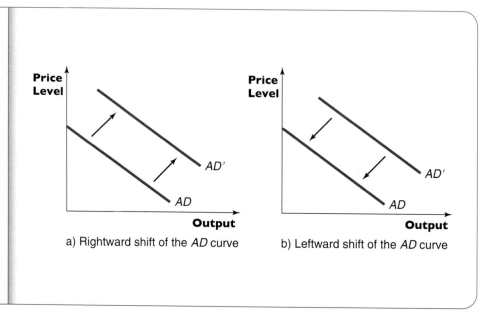

a) Rightward shift of the *AD* curve

b) Leftward shift of the *AD* curve

A leftward shift of the *AD* curve, as depicted in panel b) of Figure 10.6, can be caused by decreases in autonomous consumption, autonomous private-sector investment, or net exports. It can also be caused by contractionary monetary policy (interest rate hikes) or contractionary fiscal policy (government expenditure cuts or tax increases).

In other words, *shifts* in the aggregate demand curve of this chapter are explained by the same factors that explained the shift of the aggregate expenditure curve in Chapters 8 and 9.

RECAP

THE THREE COMPONENTS OF THE AGGREGATE DEMAND–AGGREGATE SUPPLY MODEL

The *AD–AS* model is represented graphically with the overall price level on the vertical axis and real output on the horizontal axis. The model has three central components: a long-run aggregate supply curve, a short-run aggregate supply curve, and an aggregate demand curve.

The long-run aggregate supply (*LRAS*) curve is drawn as a vertical line at potential output. It represents the assumption that the potential output of the economy is independent of the overall price level. Potential output depends on the amounts of capital, labour, and other inputs, and on factors that determine the productivity of inputs, such as education levels and technological knowledge. Thus, for example, an increase in capital will cause the *LRAS* curve to shift to the right and a reduction in capital (due to a war, say) will cause the *LRAS* curve to shift to the left.

The Keynesian short-run aggregate supply curve (*SRAS*) is drawn as a horizontal line. This represents the idea that in the short run, firms will supply the output demanded at their already posted prices. General increases in the costs of firms will cause firms to revise their posted prices and the *SRAS* curve will shift upwards. General decreases in the costs of firms will cause the *SRAS* curve to shift downwards.

The aggregate demand (*AD*) curve is derived from the planned aggregate expenditure curve of Chapters 8 and 9. Two major explanations have been provided for an inverse relationship between the price level and output, as depicted by the downward-sloping aggregate demand curve: the real-balances effect and the foreign trade effect. Increases in autonomous aggregate expenditure or expansionary monetary and fiscal policies cause the *AD* curve to shift to the right. Decreases in autonomous aggregate expenditure or contractionary monetary and fiscal policies cause the *AD* curve to shift to the left.

10.2 SHORT-RUN AND LONG-RUN EQUILIBRIUM IN THE *AD–AS* MODEL

In the short run, actual output is determined by the intersection of the *SRAS* and *AD* curves. If the *SRAS* and *AD* curves intersect at an output level to the left of the *LRAS* curve, actual output falls below potential output and there is a recessionary gap. Panel a) of Figure 10.7 shows how a recessionary gap is represented in the *AD–AS* model with a horizontal, or Keynesian, *SRAS* curve.

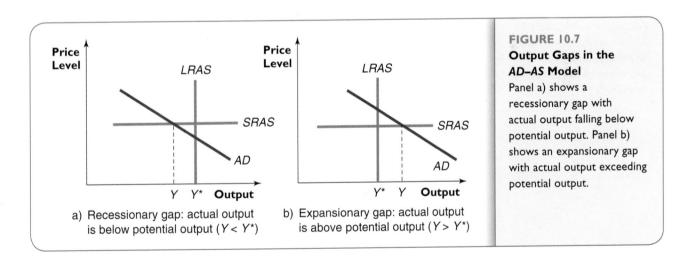

FIGURE 10.7

Output Gaps in the AD–AS Model

Panel a) shows a recessionary gap with actual output falling below potential output. Panel b) shows an expansionary gap with actual output exceeding potential output.

a) Recessionary gap: actual output is below potential output ($Y < Y^*$)

b) Expansionary gap: actual output is above potential output ($Y > Y^*$)

If the *SRAS* and *AD* curves intersect at an output level to the right of the *LRAS* curve, actual output exceeds potential output and there is an expansionary gap. Panel b) of Figure 10.7 shows an expansionary gap.

Both panels of Figure 10.7 show short-run equilibrium points. They are not, however, long-run equilibrium points. Long-run equilibrium occurs in the *AD–AS* model where the *SRAS* and *AD* curves intersect along the *LRAS* curve.

What brings about long-run equilibrium in the *AD–AS* model?

Let's look first at what happens when aggregate demand (*AD*) produces an output level that is greater than the long-run aggregate supply (*LRAS*) of the economy. As in the Keynesian cross model of Chapters 8 and 9, an expansionary gap will create pressure for the price level to rise. In the *AD–AS* model, the rise in the price level is shown by an upward shift in the *SRAS* curve. In other words, if the *SRAS* and *AD* curves intersect to the right of potential output, there will be pressure for the price level to rise, and the *SRAS* curve will shift upward. When the *SRAS* curve shifts upward enough so that it intersects with the *AD* curve at potential output, there is no longer any pressure for the price level to rise. The model is then in long-run equilibrium.

In panel a) of Figure 10.8, the model is initially at a short-run equilibrium point *A* determined by the intersection of *AD* and *SRAS*. At point *A* there is an expansionary gap, so in the long run, *SRAS* shifts upward to *SRAS'*. Long-run equilibrium is shown by point *B*, where *AD* and *SRAS'* intersect the *LRAS* curve.

FIGURE 10.8

Automatic Elimination of Output Gaps in the AD–AS Model

In panel a) the economy is initially experiencing an expansionary gap at point *A*. In the long run *SRAS* will shift to *SRAS'* and the economy will return to potential output but with a higher price level as shown by point *B*. In panel b) the economy is initially experiencing a recessionary gap at point *C*. In the long run *SRAS* will shift to *SRAS'* and the economy will return to potential output but with a lower price level as shown by point *D*.

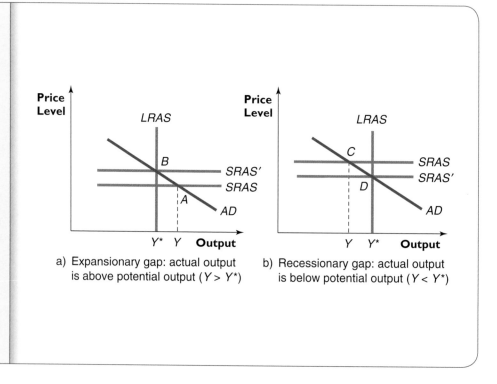

a) Expansionary gap: actual output is above potential output ($Y > Y^*$)

b) Recessionary gap: actual output is below potential output ($Y < Y^*$)

If, on the other hand, the *AD* curve intersects the *SRAS* curve to the left of the *LRAS* curve, actual output is less than potential output and the economy is experiencing a recessionary gap. In this case, there will be pressure for the price level to drop and for the *SRAS* curve to shift down. When the *SRAS* curve shifts down enough to intersect with the *AD* curve at potential output, there is no longer any pressure for the price level to fall. The model is then in long-run equilibrium.

In panel b) of Figure 10.8, the model is initially at a short-run equilibrium point *C* determined by the intersection of *AD* and *SRAS*. At point *C*, there is a recessionary gap, so in the long run, *SRAS* shifts downward to *SRAS'*. Long-run equilibrium is shown by point *D*, where *AD* and *SRAS'* intersect the *LRAS* curve.

It is at this point that there is controversy among economists. The *AD–AS* model is one of a self-correcting economy. In the short run, actual output can deviate from potential output, but in the long run, the price level adjusts to bring actual output into line with potential output. How long do we have to wait for this long-run result? The model does not specify how long it will take for price level adjustments to eliminate output gaps. It is possible for output gaps, particularly recessionary gaps, to last for years, if monetary or fiscal policies are not used to eliminate them. During the Great Depression of the 1930s, Keynes argued that without government intervention output gaps would persist, and that there was a strong case for using macroeconomic policy to close the recessionary output gap.

EXAMPLE 10.1

Let us consider a numerical example of short-run output and price determination in the *AD–AS* model. Suppose that the *SRAS* curve is horizontal at a price level of 100. We can represent the *SRAS* curve by the equation Price Level = 100. Suppose also that the *AD* curve can be represented by Price Level = 200 − .02 × Y, where Y represents real output. The short-run equilibrium requires that *SRAS* equals *AD*. So set 100 = 200 − .02 × Y. That is, .02 × Y = 100, which implies that actual output is equal to 5000. The equilibrium price level, of course, is 100.

Suppose that, as in Example 10.1, the *SRAS* curve is horizontal at a price level of 100, but that the *AD* curve shifts to the right and can be represented by the equation Price Level = 220 − .02 × Y. What will be the new short-run equilibrium values for real output and the price level?

EXAMPLE 10.2

Let us consider a numerical example of long-run output and price determination in the *AD–AS* model. Suppose the *LRAS* is vertical at 5000. That is, Y = 5000. As in Example 10.1, the *AD* curve is presented by Price Level = 200 − .02 × Y. In the long run, equilibrium requires that the *AD* equal potential output. So substituting Y = 5000 into the *AD* curve equation yields Price Level = 200 − .02 × 5000 = 200 − 100 = 100.

Suppose that the economy is initially in long-run equilibrium with the *LRAS* curve vertical at a real output of 5000, the *SRAS* curve is horizontal at a price level of 100, and the *AD* curve is given by Price Level = 200 − .02 × Y. Then the *AD* curve shifts rightward to 220 − .02 × Y. What will be the new long-run equilibrium price level and real output?

RECAP ↑

SHORT-RUN AND LONG-RUN EQUILIBRIUM IN THE *AD–AS* MODEL

In the short run, actual output in the *AD–AS* model is determined by the intersection of the *SRAS* and *AD* curves. If the *SRAS* and *AD* curves intersect at an output level to the left of the *LRAS* curve, actual output falls below potential output and there is a recessionary gap. If the *SRAS* and *AD* curves intersect at an output level to the right of the *LRAS* curve, actual output exceeds potential output and there is an expansionary gap.

The *AD–AS* model is one of a self-correcting economy. In the long run, the price level adjusts to bring actual output into line with potential output—the price level falls to eliminate a recessionary gap or it rises to eliminate an expansionary gap.

10.3   THE *AD–AS* MODEL IN ACTION

Having developed the *AD–AS* model, we can now apply it to policy issues. In this section, we will first explain how macroeconomic policy can be used to close output gaps in the *AD–AS* model and then we will consider how the *AD–AS* model can be used to explain stagflation.

USING MACROECONOMIC POLICY TO CLOSE OUTPUT GAPS IN THE *AD–AS* MODEL

How can macroeconomic policy be used to close output gaps in the *AD–AS* model? Let us first consider an economy operating with a recessionary gap. In panel a) of Figure 10.9, the economy is experiencing a short-run equilibrium *A* where actual output is below potential output. The use of expansionary monetary policy (interest rate cuts) and/or fiscal policy (government expenditure increases and/or tax cuts) shifts the *AD* curve to *AD'* and results in a new equilibrium point *B* at which the recessionary gap has been eliminated.

FIGURE 10.9

Using Macro Policy to Close Output Gaps in the *AD–AS* Model

In panel a) the economy is initially experiencing a recessionary gap. Expansionary macroeconomic policy could be used to shift *AD* rightward to *AD'* and eliminate the recessionary gap. In panel b) the economy is initially experiencing an expansionary gap. Contractionary macroeconomic policy could be used to shift *AD* leftward to *AD'* and eliminate the expansionary gap.

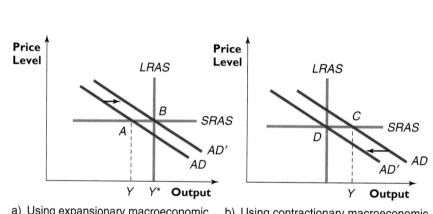

a) Using expansionary macroeconomic policy to close a recessionary gap

b) Using contractionary macroeconomic policy to close an expansionary gap

The opposite case occurs when the economy is experiencing an expansionary gap. In panel b) of Figure 10.9, the economy is experiencing a short-run equilibrium *C*, where actual output exceeds potential output. The use of contractionary monetary policy (interest rate hikes) and/or fiscal policy (government expenditure cuts and/or tax increases) shifts the *AD* curve to *AD'* and results in a new equilibrium point *D* at which expansionary gap has been eliminated.

Figure 10.9, of course, makes it look easy—as would be the case if the macroeconomic policy authorities had precise knowledge of the current state of the economy and how the economy responds to macroeconomic policy. However, recall from Chapter 9 that in practice, macroeconomic policy may not work out so smoothly. If, for example, the potential output of the economy were underestimated, an attempt to eliminate an expansionary gap might go too far, and end up creating a recession.

EXAMPLE 10.3

Suppose that *AD* is given by Price Level = 210 − .02 × Y and *SRAS* is given by Price Level = 100. Potential output is equal to 5000. How large will the expansionary gap be? If the macroeconomic policy authorities can change the intercept of the *AD* equation, to what value should they change it to eliminate the expansionary gap?

To find the short-run equilibrium output, set *AD* equal to *SRAS*, which gives 210 − .02 × Y = 100 or .02 × Y = 110 or Y = 5500. That is, actual output of 5500 exceeds potential output of 5000 for an expansionary gap of 500. From Example 10.1, we know that for *SRAS* given by Price Level = 100, *AD* given by *AD* = 200 − .02 × Y will give actual output of 5000, which would eliminate the expansionary gap.

Suppose that, as in Example 10.3, *AD* is given by Price Level = 210 − .02 × Y, *SRAS* is given by Price Level = 100, and potential output is equal to 5000. The macroeconomic policy authorities wish to eliminate the expansionary gap but their knowledge of the economy is less than perfect, and they engineer a shift of the *AD* curve to Price Level = 190 − .02 × Y. What will be the short-run consequence of this shift of the *AD* curve?

USING THE *AD–AS* MODEL TO EXPLAIN STAGFLATION

As mentioned in the introduction to this chapter, the *AD–AS* model gained acceptance in part because it provided an explanation for the phenomenon of **stagflation**—a recessionary gap combined with a rising price level. Stagflation arises in the context of the *AD–AS* model when some external factor causes the *SRAS* curve to shift upward. Such an external factor is termed an adverse price shock.

stagflation the combination of a recessionary gap and a rising price level

The external factor could be an increase in oil prices (because the increase in prices of the 1970s followed shortly after the oil price shock of 1973, this example is not just hypothetical). We will consider the case in which the increase in oil prices shifts the *SRAS* curve upward but does not affect the position of the *LRAS* curve.

Suppose the economy is initially in a state of long-run equilibrium, with the *SRAS* curve intersecting the *AD* curve at potential output, as shown by point *A* in Figure 10.10. When energy prices rise and firms revise their posted prices to reflect their higher level of input costs, the *SRAS* curve shifts upwards to *SRAS'*. As a result, the economy will move to a short-run equilibrium point *B*. Compared with point *A*, point *B* features a lower level of output and a higher price level—i.e., stagflation.

In the *AD–AS* model, however, stagflation will not persist if the self-correcting mechanism of the economy is allowed to work. That is, in the long run, the *AD–AS* model predicts that the recessionary gap will cause the *SRAS* curve to shift down, and actual output will return to potential output. In terms of Figure 10.10, in the long run the economy will return to the old equilibrium point *A*.[4]

---

[4]Some students may be asking, if the country really is self-sufficient in oil, and the recessionary gap is caused by the surge in inflation caused by the increase in the price level set off by increased oil prices, why doesn't the government step in and fix oil prices, keeping the economy at potential output? During the 1970s, Canada's federal government did control oil prices somewhat under the National Energy Program—to the detriment (and intense resentment) of oil-exporting Alberta. Oil prices were later allowed to rise to motivate both greater production and less domestic consumption in the longer run—that is, to increase Canada's net energy exports.

FIGURE 10.10

Stagflation in the AD–AS Model

Suppose that the economy is initially in a state of long-run equilibrium with the *SRAS* curve intersecting the *AD* curve at potential output, as shown by point A. If the *SRAS* curve shifts upwards to *SRAS'* because of an adverse price shock, the economy will move to a short-run equilibrium point B. Compared with point A, point B features a lower level of output and a higher price level. This amounts to stagflation.

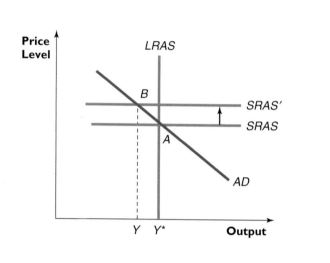

ECONOMIC Naturalist 10.1   The collapse of oil prices in the latter half of the 1980s

The *AD–AS* model became popular in the late 1970s and early 1980s, because economists had to find an explanation for "stagflation"—the simultaneous combination of rising prices and depressed economic activity. However, the rise of oil prices in the 1970s prompted two economic responses. First, the high price of oil triggered intensified oil exploration that resulted in the discovery of new oil fields and increased oil production. Second, the high price of oil prompted consumers of oil to conserve. The combination of increased supply and reduced demand caused the price of oil to drop. In international markets, the price of a barrel of crude oil plummeted (measured in 2007 U.S. dollars) from U.S. $90 in 1980 to a mere U.S. $26 in 1988, as shown in Figure 10.11.

Just about anyone can understand how lower crude oil prices translated into lower gasoline prices at the pump. But what macroeconomic impact did the collapse of oil prices have?

Using our *AD–AS* model, with the economy initially in a position of long-run equilibrium, and assuming that the decrease in the price of oil just shifts the *SRAS* curve downwards without asffecting the position of the *LRAS* curve, the macroeconomic impact would be as shown by Figure 10.12.

In Figure 10.12, the economy is initially in long-run equilibrium at point A. The drop in oil prices causes the *SRAS'*

curve shift to shift downwards to *SRAS'*. The economy will move to a short-run equilibrium point B. Compared with point A, point B features a higher level of output (Y instead of Y*) and a lower price level (P' instead of P).

But at point B there is an expansionary gap. There will be pressure for the price level to return to P. As the price level returns to P, output returns to Y*.

According to our *AD–AS* model, then, the short-run impact of a drop in oil prices is positive. Output goes up and the price level goes down. But there is no long-run macroeconomic impact. In the long run, the price level and output both return to the levels they registered before the oil price drop.

Although the *AD–AS* model predicted that a collapse of oil prices would result in a drop in the aggregate price level, this did not happen. In the late 1980s, the rate of inflation declined in most countries, but the aggregate price level did not drop (i.e., the inflation rate declined, but remained greater than zero—it did not become negative, as a decline in the price level would require). The aggregate price level just rose more slowly than in the 1970s. As a consequence, economists looked again at their macro models—as we will see in Chapter 11.

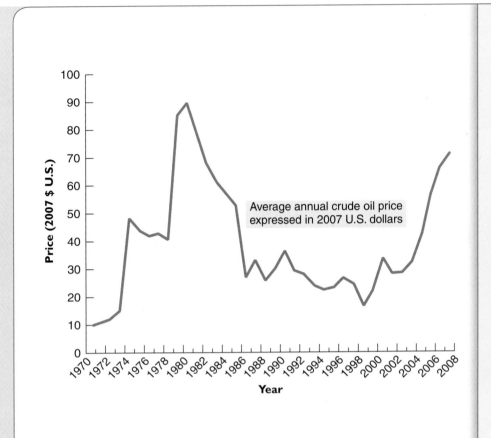

FIGURE 10.11

Crude Oil Prices, 1970–2007

Crude oil prices rose dramatically in the 1970s, reaching a peak of almost US $90 in 1980 (expressed in 2007 dollars). But crude oil prices then fell dramatically in the 1980s, reaching US $26 in 1988. The drop in oil prices during the 1980s was what economists call a favourable aggregate price shock.

Oil prices rose sharply again after 2002, reaching US $71 in 2007.
SOURCE: Adapted from International Monetary Fund, *International Financial Statistics*, 2006, and the United States Consumer Price Index, Bureau of Labor Statistics.

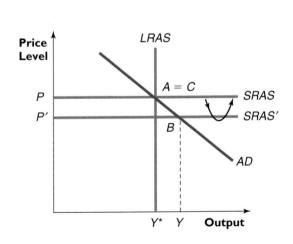

FIGURE 10.12

A Favourable Oil Price Shock in the *AD–AS* Model

Suppose that the economy is initially in a state of long-run equilibrium with the *SRAS* curve intersecting the *AD* curve at potential output and price level *P*, as shown by point *A*. If the *SRAS* curve shifts downwards to *SRAS′* because of a favourable oil price shock, the economy will move to a short-run equilibrium point *B*. Compared with point *A*, point *B* features a higher level of output (*Y*) and a lower price level (*P′* instead of *P*). But the expansionary gap associated with point *B* will cause the price level to return to *P*.

THE *AD–AS* MODEL IN ACTION

In the *AD–AS* model, macroeconomic policy can be used to speed up the return to long-run equilibrium. Expansionary macroeconomic policy can be used to eliminate a recessionary gap and contractionary macroeconomic policy can be used to eliminate an expansionary gap.

The *AD–AS* model can also be used to explain stagflation. Suppose the economy experiences an adverse price shock, causing the *SRAS* curve to shift upwards. The new short-run equilibrium will then feature both a higher price level and a lower level of real output.

10.4   AN ALTERNATIVE VERSION OF THE *AD–AS* MODEL

In the previous sections of this chapter, we have presented an *AD–AS* model in which the short-run aggregate supply (*SRAS*) curve is drawn as a horizontal line to indicate that in the short run, firms will supply the output that their customers demand at the prices the firms have posted.

Some economists, however, present an alternative version of the *AD–AS* model in which the *SRAS* curve is upward sloping, as shown in Figure 10.13. The alternative version of the *AD–AS* model also has a different explanation of what causes the *SRAS* curve to shift in response to output gaps.

According to the alternative version of the *AD–AS* model, the upward-sloping *SRAS* curve represents how the aggregate quantity of output supplied by firms will increase with a rise in the price level (or decrease with a fall in the price level). Suppose that firms face a price level that is 2 percent higher than before because the output prices of firms are 2 percent higher. Will firms increase their output? It depends on what happens to their input prices (that is, their costs). If input prices such as wages also increased by 2 percent, firms would not have a profit incentive to increase output. But if wages did not increase immediately when prices increased, the firms could increase their profits by expanding output.

FIGURE 10.13

An Upward-Sloping *SRAS* Curve

An alternative version of the *AD–AS* model features an upward-sloping *SRAS* curve. The assumption behind the upward slope is that when the price level rises, input prices lag behind, which provides firms with a profit incentive to expand output in the short run. Conversely, when the price level falls, input prices again lag behind, which provides firms with a profit incentive to contract output in the short run.

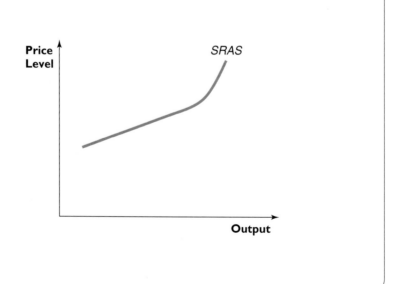

The upward-sloping *SRAS* curve, then, represents the assumption that wages lag behind output prices and that this lag gives firms a profit incentive to raise output when the price level rises (and to lower output when the price level falls).

What difference does it make if the *SRAS* curve is upward-sloping? Panel a) of Figure 10.14 shows the alternative version of the *AD–AS* model for the case when an economy initially operating at potential output is subjected to an *increase* in aggregate demand. At the initial equilibrium point *A*, *AD* = *SRAS* = *LRAS*. A rightward shift of *AD* to *AD′* produces a short-run equilibrium *B* with both a higher price level (*P′* instead of *P*) and a higher output level (*Y′* instead of *Y**). In the long run, the *SRAS* curve shifts leftward to *SRAS′* and the economy moves to point *C* where output has returned to *Y** and the price level has increased even further, from *P′* to *P″*. In terms of results, the only difference with the *AD–AS* model presented earlier in this chapter is that in this case the price level rises even in the short run.

Panel b) of Figure 10.14 shows the alternative version of the *AD–AS* model for the opposite case when an economy initially operating at potential output is subjected to a decrease in aggregate demand. The initial equilibrium point is *D*, but a leftward shift of *AD* to *AD′* produces a short-run equilibrium *E* with both a lower price level (*P′* instead of *P*) and a lower output level (*Y′* instead of *Y″*). The leftward shift in *AD* produces a recessionary gap. In the long run, the *SRAS* curve shifts rightward to *SRAS* and the economy moves to point *F*, where output has returned to *Y** and the price level has fallen even further, from *P′* to *P″*. In terms of results, the difference from the *AD–AS* model presented earlier in this chapter is that the price level falls even in the short run.

In less abstract terms, if there was a sharply increased demand for Canadian resource exports to Asia, this initial change would be represented in terms of a rightward shift of the *AD* curve in an *AD–AS* model. The full analysis in terms of our *AD–AS* model with an upward-sloping *AS* curve would be as is shown in panel a) of Figure 10.14.

FIGURE 10.14

An Alternative Version of the *AD–AS* Model in Action

In panel a) the economy is initially in long-run equilibrium at point *A* with price level *P* and output equal to potential output *Y**. A shift of *AD* rightward to *AD′* moves the economy to point *B* in the short run. Output rises to *Y* and the price level rises to *P′*. In the long run, the *SRAS* curve shifts leftward to *SRAS′* and the economy moves to point *C*.

In panel b) the economy is initially in long-run equilibrium at point *D* with price level *P* and output equal to *Y**. A shift of *AD* leftward to *AD′* moves the economy to point *E* in the short run. Output falls to *Y* and the price level falls to *P′*. In the long run, the *SRAS* curve shifts rightward to *SRAS′* and the economy moves to point *F*.

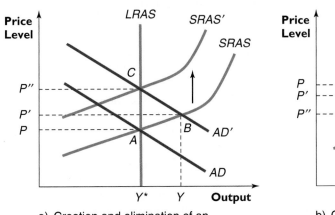

a) Creation and elimination of an expansionary gap

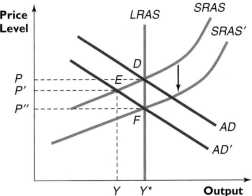

b) Creation and elimination of a recessionary gap

If there was sharply reduced demand for Canadian lumber exports to the United States because of a collapse in U.S. housing markets, this initial change would be represented in terms of a leftward shift of the *AD* curve in an *AD–AS* model. The full analysis of this event with an upward-sloping AS curve would be as shown in panel b) of Figure 10.14.

Note that panel b) predicts that the price level will fall in the short run, and fall even further in the long run. But in reality this is unlikely as the price level in Canada, as measured by the CPI, has not fallen on an annual basis during the lifetime of the typical reader of this textbook.

> **RECAP**
>
> **AN ALTERNATIVE VERSION OF THE *AD–AS* MODEL**
>
> In one version of the *AD–AS* model, the *SRAS* curve is upward sloping, not horizontal. The *SRAS* curve would be upward sloping if the overall level of wages adjusted more slowly than the rate of the overall price level adjustment.
>
> If the *SRAS* curve is upward sloping and the economy is initially operating at potential output, a rightward shift of the *AD* curve produces a short-run equilibrium with both a higher price level and a higher level of output. In the long run the *SRAS* curve experiences a leftward shift, which produces an even higher price level but actual output matches potential output.
>
> Conversely, given the same initial conditions for the model, a leftward shift of the *AD* curve would result in both a lower price level and a lower level of output in the short run. The model predicts an even lower price level and a return of actual output to the level of potential output, in the long run.

10.5 THE EXPECTATIONS-AUGMENTED PHILLIPS CURVE MODEL AS A SUPPLEMENT TO THE *AD–AS* MODEL

The *AD–AS* model arose to explain *stagflation*—a phenomenon not easily handled by the Keynesian cross model. The key merit of the *AD–AS* model compared with the Keynesian cross model is that both the price level and the output level are directly represented. However, progress in economics proceeds in steps, and over time it became apparent that the *AD–AS* model was only partially satisfactory.

In the first place, as the discussion at the start of the chapter implicitly recognized, for most purposes it is the inflation rate—the rate of *change* of the price level—that interests most people. And although the *AD–AS* model gives the impression that the price level and nominal wages decline during recessions, in most recessions the price level and nominal wages continue to rise, *just at a slower rate*—disinflation. The rate of inflation typically declines during a recession, but the price *level* does not actually fall. Deflation does not occur.

One way to deal with the problem that the *AD–AS* model does not deal directly with the rate of inflation is to supplement the model with a model of the Phillips curve. The *Phillips curve* is named after A. W. Phillips, an economist who used British data to link unemployment rates to inflation in a famous paper published in 1958.[5] Phillips found that unemployment rates and wage inflation rates were inversely related. Studies were conducted for other countries in the 1960s, and they usually linked the overall inflation rate to the unemployment rate.

---

[5]You can learn more about A. W. Phillips and the Phillips curve at: http://cepa.newschool.edu/het/profiles/phillips.htm.

Today the term **Phillips curve** is typically used to indicate a statistical relationship between the inflation rate and the unemployment rate. Panel a) of Figure 10.15 shows a Phillips curve for Canadian data from the 1960s—during the 1960s many economists estimated the inflation/unemployment relationship and thought of it as representing a "trade-off" in economic policy.

Phillips curve a term that typically refers to a statistical relationship between the inflation rate and the unemployment rate

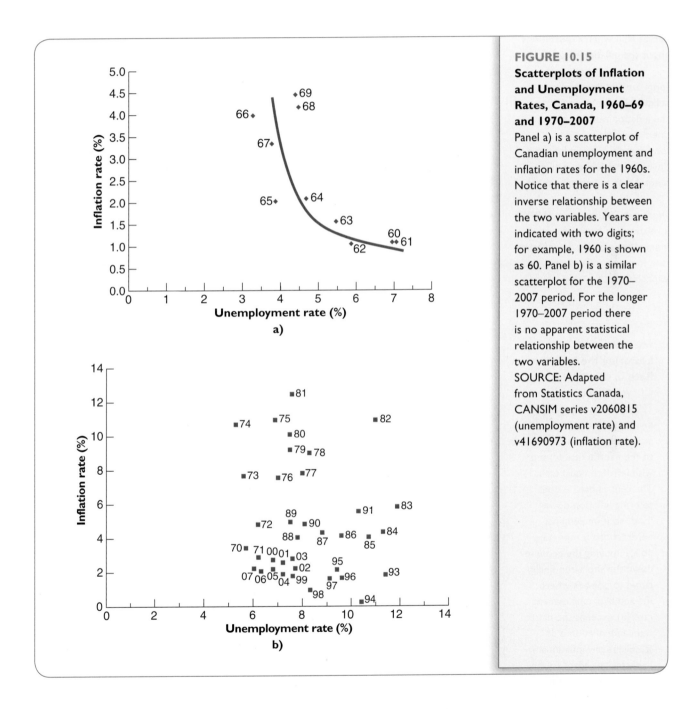

FIGURE 10.15

Scatterplots of Inflation and Unemployment Rates, Canada, 1960–69 and 1970–2007

Panel a) is a scatterplot of Canadian unemployment and inflation rates for the 1960s. Notice that there is a clear inverse relationship between the two variables. Years are indicated with two digits; for example, 1960 is shown as 60. Panel b) is a similar scatterplot for the 1970–2007 period. For the longer 1970–2007 period there is no apparent statistical relationship between the two variables.
SOURCE: Adapted from Statistics Canada, CANSIM series v2060815 (unemployment rate) and v41690973 (inflation rate).

But in more recent decades, the inverse relationship between inflation and unemployment rates observed in the 1960s has broken down. Panel b) of Figure 10.15 shows a scatterplot of annual inflation rates and unemployment rates for Canada between 1970 and 2007. Note that there is no obvious way to fit a curve through the scatterplot of data points.

expectations-augmented Phillips curve model distinguishes between a short-run Phillips curve and a long-run Phillips curve and argues that short-run Phillips curves shift when expectations about the inflation rate change

long-run Phillips curve a relationship between the inflation rate and the unemployment rate in the long run; the vertical long-run Phillips curve is drawn at the natural rate of unemployment

short-run Phillips curve (SRPC) a relationship between actual unemployment and the inflation rate for given inflationary expectations

Why did the simple Phillips curve model of the relationship between inflation and unemployment work well in say, the 1960s but not in, say, the 1980s? One possible explanation is because of changing expectations of inflation. Recall that at the start of this chapter we noted that the Canadian inflation rate between 1952 and 1965 was on average 1.4 percent. On this basis, it was reasonable for Canadians in the mid-1960s to expect little inflation. But between 1973 and 1982, Canada's inflation rate averaged 9.6 percent—so expecting little change in prices was, by the early 1980s, becoming pretty unreasonable. The *expectations-augmented Phillips curve model* has become widely used as an explanation for why the Phillips curve estimated for the 1960s does not fit the data for later decades. The **expectations-augmented Phillips curve model** distinguishes between a *short-run Phillips curve* and a *long-run Phillips curve* and argues that short-run Phillips curves shift when expectations about the inflation rate change. Figure 10.16 provides a graphical representation of the model.

A key assumption of the model is that there is a vertical long-run Phillips curve at the natural rate of unemployment. In other words, the **long-run Phillips curve** represents the hypothesis that the natural rate of unemployment is independent of changes in the inflation rate.

According to the expectations-augmented Phillips curve model, at any point in time, people have some set of expectations about future inflation. The **short-run Phillips curve (SRPC)** shows an inverse relationship between the inflation rate and the unemployment rate *given* expectations about inflation. But if people

---

FIGURE 10.16

Lowering the Inflation Rate in the Phillips Curve Model

The economy is initially in equilibrium at point A with actual unemployment equal to the natural rate u* and with inflation equal to π. The central bank wishes to bring inflation down to π′ so it implements contractionary monetary policy, moving the economy down the short-run Phillips curve to point B, where the actual unemployment rate (u) exceeds the natural rate, and inflation is at π′. Eventually inflationary expectations adapt to the new environment, and the short-run Phillips curve shifts to move the equilibrium to C, where inflation equals π′ and the unemployment rate has returned to the natural rate.

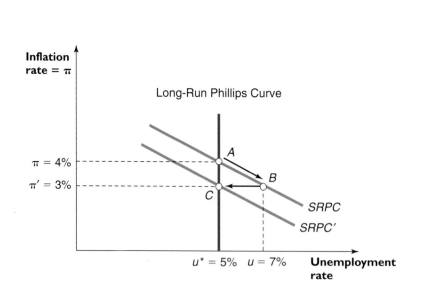

expect some change in the rate of inflation, the short-run Phillips curve will shift. If people had expected inflation to be low and they change to expecting inflation to be high, the short-run Phillips curve shifts up. A change in inflationary expectations may occur because actual experience has changed—that is, because inflation has picked up recently, or perhaps because something happens (like an oil embargo) that people have good reason to believe will produce an increase in inflation. Either way, the short-run Phillips curve shifts up when people expect inflation to increase.

Conversely, if people had expected inflation to be high and they change to expecting inflation to be low (say, because inflation has declined in recent months), the short-run Phillips curve shifts down.

What determines expectations of inflation? According to the Phillips curve model, people have *adaptive expectations* about inflation. **Adaptive expectations of inflation** means that people adapt their expectations about the future rate of inflation based upon their recent experience with inflation. If inflation has been high, people expect inflation to be high in the future. If inflation has been low, they expect inflation to be low in the future.

adaptive expectations of inflation a method of forming expectations about the inflation rate that involves looking to past experience, especially recent past experience

How is this model used to explain the scatterplot of inflation and unemployment rates in panel b) of Figure 10.15? The idea is that the scatterplot fits several different short-run Phillips curves rather than a single one. For example, given the fact that inflation had been very low between 1952 and 1965, one might think that if people expected that low inflation to continue, there would be one short-run Phillips curve for the 1960s. Since inflation accelerated during the 1970s, and people's expectations of inflation changed, there would be a different short-run Phillips curve for the 1970s and the 1980s (i.e., a shift up in the short-run Phillips curve). During the 1990s, expectations changed again, and as a result the short-run Phillips curve shifted again (downward).

As a hypothetical example, suppose that, initially, the economy is at point *A* in Figure 10.16—which is drawn to represent the idea that the economy is at the natural rate of unemployment (estimated to be 5 percent) and the inflation rate is 4 percent.[6] Suppose also that the central bank wishes to reduce the inflation rate to 3 percent. The central bank will take action—that is, raise interest rates—to create a recessionary gap. When there is a recessionary gap, the actual unemployment rate will be above the natural rate. The recessionary gap and the higher actual unemployment rate will produce a lower inflation rate. So in the short run, the economy will have moved from point *A* to point *B* with a higher rate of unemployment (the cost of the policy of reducing the inflation rate) and a lower rate of inflation (the goal of the policy). In the hypothetical example of Figure 10.16, the actual unemployment rate has increased from 5 percent to 7 percent and the inflation rate has been reduced from 4 percent to 3 percent. In the short run, the economy moves along the short-run Phillips curve (*SRPC*).

But at point *B*, people in the economy are experiencing a lower rate of inflation than before. If they have adaptive expectations, they will come to expect lower inflation, and the short-run Phillips curve will shift downward. If the central bank succeeds in creating a recessionary gap just large enough to realize its inflation target of 3 percent, then the short-run Phillips curve will shift to *SRPC'*.

Notice that the expectations-augmented Phillips curve model is, like the *AD–AS* model, a model of a self-correcting economy. In the short run, the actual unemployment rate can be above or below the natural rate of unemployment. But in the long run, the actual unemployment rate will return to the natural rate of unemployment.

[6]Figure 10.16 embodies the assumption that, at the natural rate of unemployment, the economy is operating with actual output equal to potential output.

RECAP

THE EXPECTATIONS-AUGMENTED PHILLIPS CURVE MODEL AS A SUPPLEMENT TO THE *AD–AS* MODEL

The expectations-augmented Phillips curve model is used to supplement the *AD–AS* model because the *AD–AS* model does not deal directly with the rate of inflation. The Phillips curve model is represented graphically with the inflation rate on the vertical axis and the unemployment rate on the horizontal axis. The short-run Phillips curve shows a trade-off between the inflation rate and the actual unemployment rate. But the long-run Phillips curve is drawn vertically at the natural rate of unemployment. The expectations-augmented Phillips curve model is, like the *AD–AS* one, a model of a self-correcting economy. One implication of the expectations-augmented Phillips curve model is that if a central bank wishes to achieve a lower rate of inflation it will have to bring about an actual rate of unemployment higher than the natural rate for some period of time.

10.6 CONCLUSION

One approach to dealing with the limitations of the Keynesian cross model is to supplement it with the *AD–AS* model and the expectations-augmented Phillips curve model. In the next chapter, however, we will build on this approach and address more directly the idea that it is the *rate of change of prices* (i.e., inflation) that is the focus of economic policy, not the *level* of prices, and the fact that the central bank changes monetary policy in response to changes in inflation.

When the *AD–AS* model was becoming popular in the 1970s, prices were increasing so rapidly that the idea of an actual decline in prices (that is, negative inflation, also called deflation) was too irrelevant to be worth bothering about. However, as very low inflation became entrenched in the 1990s, this possibility ceased to be remote. (For example, consumer prices in Japan fell in 1995 and from 1998 to 2006.) A crucial issue then became the claim of the *AD–AS* model that a decline in the price level would provide a self-correcting mechanism for the elimination of a recessionary gap. The idea behind the *AD–AS* model is that the decline in the price level will boost aggregate demand (because of real balances and foreign trade effects) and thereby raise actual output—but does this actually happen?

There appear to be strong reasons to doubt that it does. For example, Canada has not experienced a sustained fall in the price level since the Great Depression of the 1930s, but the fall in the price level during the Depression did not seem to boost aggregate demand. Similarly, the recessionary gap in Japan has persisted to 2007 despite the decline in consumer prices there for almost a decade.

When prices start to fall, consumers and businesses may start to postpone their purchases, on the expectation that whatever they could buy today will be even cheaper tomorrow. If they do that, then aggregate demand will fall—worsening the deflationary gap.

Central banks are thus opposed to deflation as a matter of policy. Typically they would like to keep the inflation rate low or moderate, but they do not want the price level to fall (for reasons that were mentioned in the discussion of inflation in Chapter 6). In Canada, the mid-point of the Bank of Canada's inflation target range is 2 percent and the lower bound is 1 percent—which means that the Bank of Canada aims to have the price level rise by 2 percent a year on average and to never increase it by less than 1 percent a year. The Bank of Canada is so convinced that the self-correcting mechanism of the *AD–AS* model would not do the job that they are unwilling to accept even a short period of deflation—so the Bank changes its setting of interest rates to try to keep Canada's inflation rate in the 1 percent to 3 percent range.

To understand the implications of this, we have to develop a third macroeconomic model. This macroeconomic model, the subject of Chapter 11, relates real output not to the price level but to the inflation rate.

SUMMARY

10.1 The aggregate demand-aggregate supply (AD–AS) model was developed to supplement the Keynesian cross model. The AD–AS model is designed to analyze how shifts in aggregate demand and supply can affect not just output but also the overall price level. Thus, the model is represented graphically with the overall price level on the vertical axis and real output on the horizontal axis. The AD–AS model has three central components: a long-run aggregate supply curve, a short-run aggregate supply curve, and an aggregate demand curve.

10.1 The long-run aggregate supply (LRAS) curve is drawn as a vertical line at potential output. It represents the assumption that the potential output of the economy is independent of the overall price level. Potential output depends on the amounts of capital, labour, and other inputs, and upon factors determining the productivity of inputs.

10.1 The Keynesian short-run aggregate supply curve (SRAS) is drawn as a horizontal line. This represents the idea that in the short run, firms will supply the output demanded at their posted prices. General changes in the costs of firms will cause firms to revise their posted prices and the SRAS curve to shift.

10.1 Two major explanations have been provided for an inverse relationship between the price level and output, as depicted by the downward-sloping aggregate demand (AD) curve: the "real balances" effect and the foreign trade effect. Changes in autonomous aggregate expenditure or in monetary and fiscal policies cause the AD curve to shift.

10.2 In the short run, actual output is determined by the intersection of the SRAS and AD curves, and recessionary or expansionary gaps can result. In the long run, the price level adjusts to bring actual output into line with potential output. Macroeconomic policy, however, can be used to speed up the return to long-run equilibrium.

10.3 The AD–AS model can be used to explain stagflation. Suppose the economy experiences an adverse price shock, causing the SRAS curve to shift upwards. The new short-run equilibrium will then feature both a higher price level and a lower level of real output.

10.4 One version of the AD–AS model features an upward-sloping SRAS curve. In this alternative version of the model, shifts in AD will produce price–level changes even in the short run.

10.5 The expectations-augmented Phillips curve model, which is used to supplement the AD–AS model, is represented graphically with the inflation rate on the vertical axis and the unemployment rate on the horizontal axis. The short-run Phillips curve shows a trade-off between the inflation rate and the actual unemployment rate, but the long-run Phillips curve is drawn vertically at the natural rate of unemployment.

10.6 As the Canadian economy moved from approximately 10 percent inflation in the early 1980s to roughly 2 percent inflation in the 1990s, the possibility (and the consequences) of negative inflation (that is, deflation—an actual fall in average prices) had to be seriously considered. Partly as a result, the macroeconomic model considered in Chapter 11 was developed.

KEY TERMS

adaptive expectations of inflation (263)
aggregate demand curve (248)
aggregate demand–aggregate supply model (244)
expectations-augmented Phillips curve model (262)

foreign trade effect (249)
long-run aggregate supply (LRAS) curve (245)
long-run Phillips curve (262)
Phillips curve (261)

real-balances effect (249)
short-run aggregate supply (SRAS) curve (247)
short-run Phillips curve (SRPC) (262)
stagflation (255)

REVIEW QUESTIONS

1. What does stagflation mean? Why is it difficult to explain stagflation with a Keynesian cross diagram?

2. "If a rise in the price of a good causes firms in an industry to produce more of the good, then a rise in the overall price level must produce higher output for the economy as a whole." What is the term for the logical fallacy committed in this quotation? According to the hypothesis of a vertical long-run aggregate supply curve, what impact does a rise in the overall price level have on potential output?

3. What type of firm behaviour would justify a horizontal short-run aggregate supply curve?

4. True or false, and explain: The downward-sloping aggregate demand curve is explained by the law of demand.

5. Given that the AD–AS model is one of a self-correcting economy, how could the AD–AS model be used to justify expansionary macroeconomic policy to eliminate a recessionary gap?

6. How can stagflation be explained with an AD–AS model?

7. Is the rationale for an upward-sloping SRAS curve the same as the rationale for an upward-sloping industry supply curve in microeconomics? Explain

8. What does the short-run Phillips curve indicate?

9. According to the expectations-augmented Phillips curve model, does a central bank face a trade-off if it wishes to lower the inflation rate? Explain.

PROBLEMS

1. Suppose you had $1000 in cash in a base year and the price level increased by 10 percent. What would happen to the real value of your cash?

2. (More difficult.) "The multiplier for an increase in autonomous aggregate expenditure in the basic Keynesian model equals the multiplier for the AD–AS model in the short run. In the long run, the multiplier for the AD–AS model equals the short-run multiplier if the shift in AD is just large enough to close a recessionary gap. But the long-run multiplier for the AD–AS model equals zero if the economy is initially operating at potential output." Explain using diagrams.

3. For each of the following events, state whether the impact would be to shift the aggregate demand curve, the short-run aggregate supply curve, or both curves. Also state in which direction the curves would shift.
   a. Increased demand by Japan for Canadian lumber.
   b. An increase in the Bank of Canada's overnight rate target.
   c. An increase in the GST.
   d. A sharp drop in world oil prices.
   e. A sharp appreciation of the Canadian dollar.

4. Suppose that an economy is initially at long-run equilibrium, with the SRAS curve intersecting the AD curve at potential output. Use an AD–AS diagram to show the impact on the price level and real output of an autonomous increase in consumption spending. Distinguish between the short-run impact and the long-run impact.

5. Suppose policy-makers are faced with an economy with an actual rate of unemployment above the natural rate. Use the expectations-augmented Phillips curve model to analyze two alternatives: a) policy-makers implement expansionary macroeconomic policy to move the actual rate to the natural rate; and b) policy-makers allow the economy to self-correct.

6. Assume that the price level is initially equal to 100. Is there a difference between a 2 percentage point drop in the price level and a 2 percentage point drop in the inflation rate? Explain.

ANSWERS TO IN-CHAPTER EXERCISES

10.1 For the new short-run equilibrium, AD must equal SRAS. So $100 = 220 - .02Y$. That is, $.02Y = 120$, which implies that real output is equal to 6000.

10.2 In long-run equilibrium, AD must equal potential output. So substituting $Y = 5000$ into the AD curve equation yields Price Level $= 220 - .02 \times 5000 = 220 - 100 = 120$. The SRAS curve will shift up and will be horizontal at a price level of 120.

10.3 For the new short-run equilibrium, AD must equal SRAS. So $100 = 190 - .02Y$. That is, $.02Y = 90$, which implies that real output is equal to 4500. The short-run consequence of the macroeconomic policy authorities shifting the AD too far to the left would be a recessionary gap of 500.

Chapter 11 Inflation and Output

On October 6, 1979, the policy-making committee of the U.S. Federal Reserve held a highly unusual, and unusually secretive, Saturday meeting. However unnoticed this meeting may have been at the time, in retrospect it marked a turning point in the post-Second World War economic history of the United States and of many other countries, including Canada.

When Paul Volcker called the meeting, what most concerned him was the rate of inflation in the United States. In 1979, it averaged 11.3 percent (reflecting, among other things, the doubling of oil prices following the overthrow of the Shah of Iran). While Volcker's plan to deal with this was couched in technical details, in essence he proposed a dramatic increase in interest rates. Everyone in the room at the October 6 meeting of the policy-making committee knew that raising interest rates would cause aggregate demand to fall, with a cost in terms of a recession, lost output, and lost jobs. But when a vote was called, every hand went up.

The "Volcker disinflation," as it was called, did succeed in bringing down the U.S. rate of inflation. By 1983, the United States had achieved an inflation rate of less than 4 percent. On the other hand, the U.S. economy went through a severe recession. The impact was also global, and many indebted developing countries were more affected than the United States itself. Following Mexico's default on foreign debt payments in 1982, the "Third World debt crisis" became a stock phrase used to describe the situation in which many developing countries had become unable to service their debts to foreign lenders (such as Canada's largest banks). The debt crisis had several causes, but the Volcker disinflation contributed to it by producing higher real interest rates. The higher real interest rates meant higher interest payments on the debt.

In Canada, partly because the Bank of Canada under Governor Gerald Bouey followed Volcker's lead and also because of the spillover from the slowdown in U.S. economic growth, the economy went into a recession (as discussed in Chapter 7) and Canada's unemployment rate soared to over 11 percent. As in the United States, however, the inflation rate was reduced from about 11 percent to the 4 percent range.

© Dennis Brack/Black Star Publishing/PictureQuest

Paul Volcker's "shock treatment" created a turning point in post-Second World War economic history.

The wide-ranging impact of the Volcker disinflation illustrates the need for having a framework for understanding inflation and the policies used to control it. In Chapters 8 and 9 we made the assumption that firms are willing to meet the demand for their products at preset prices. When firms simply produce what is demanded, the level of planned aggregate expenditure determines the country's real GDP. If planned aggregate expenditure is lower than potential output, a recessionary output gap develops, and if expenditure exceeds potential output the economy experiences an expansionary gap. As we saw in Chapters 8 and 9, policy-makers can attempt to eliminate output gaps by taking actions that affect the level of autonomous expenditure, such as changing the level of government spending or taxes (fiscal policy) or changing the real interest rate (monetary policy).

The basic Keynesian model is useful for understanding the role of spending in the short-run determination of output, but, as we noted in Chapter 9, it is too simplified for some purposes. The main shortcoming of the basic Keynesian model is that it does not explain the behaviour of inflation. Although firms may meet demand at preset prices for a time, as assumed in the basic Keynesian model, prices do *not* remain fixed indefinitely. Indeed, sometimes they may rise quite rapidly, as we saw in Chapter 6. In this chapter we will extend the basic Keynesian model to allow for ongoing inflation. As we will show, the extended model can be conveniently represented by a new diagram, called the *aggregate demand–inflation adjustment diagram*. Using this extended analysis, we will be able to show how macroeconomic policies affect inflation as well as output, illustrating in the process the difficult trade-offs policy-makers sometimes face. We will emphasize numerical and graphical analysis of output and inflation in the body of the chapter. The appendix at the end of the chapter presents a more general algebraic treatment.

11.1   INFLATION, SPENDING, AND OUTPUT: THE AGGREGATE DEMAND (ADI) CURVE

aggregate demand (ADI) curve short for aggregate demand/inflation curve, shows the relationship between short-run equilibrium output Y and the rate of inflation π; the name of the curve reflects the fact that short-run equilibrium output is determined by, and equals, total planned spending in the economy; increases in inflation reduce planned spending and short-run equilibrium output, so the aggregate demand (ADI) curve is downward-sloping

To begin incorporating inflation into the model, our first step is to introduce a new relationship, called the *aggregate demand/inflation curve*, or *aggregate demand curve* for short.[1] The **aggregate demand (ADI) curve**, which is shown graphically in Figure 11.1, is based on the relationship between short-run equilibrium output Y and the rate of inflation, denoted π. The name of the curve reflects that, as we have seen, short-run equilibrium output is determined by the total planned spending, or demand, in the economy. Indeed, by definition short-run equilibrium output *equals* planned aggregate expenditure, so we could just as well say that the ADI curve shows the relationship between inflation and spending.

It is important to distinguish the ADI curve from both the expenditure line, introduced as part of the Keynesian cross diagram in Chapter 8, and from the aggregate demand (AD) curve, which you might be familiar with from the AD–AS analysis of Chapter 10. The upward-sloping expenditure line of the Keynesian cross diagram shows the relationship between planned aggregate expenditure and output. The AD curve of the AD–AS analysis of Chapter 10 shows the relationship between short-run equilibrium output and the price level. But the ADI curve shows the relationship between short-run equilibrium output (which equals planned spending) and the inflation rate. The ADI curve represents a modification of the AD curve. Because we want

[1]The graphical analysis used in this chapter was initially developed by Ben Bernanke, now chairman of the U.S. Federal Reserve, and it closely follows the approach recommended by David Romer in his work "Keynesian Macroeconomics Without the LM Curve," *Journal of Economic Perspectives*, Spring 2000, pp. 149–170. It is similar to the approach followed by Stanford University economist John Taylor in textbooks and articles, including his "Teaching Modern Macroeconomics at the Principles Level," *American Economic Review*, May 2000, pp. 90–94. It provides a strong foundation for students who go on to study the short-run analysis in intermediate macroeconomics textbooks such as that of Charles Jones, *Macroeconomics*, (New York: Norton, 2008).

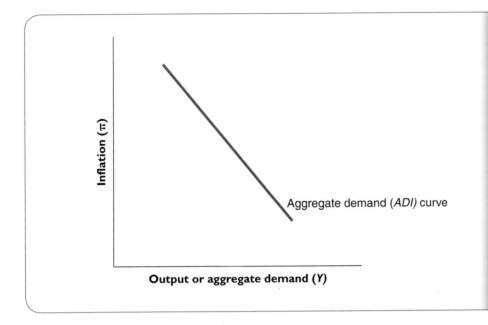

FIGURE 11.1

The Aggregate Demand (*ADI*) Curve
The aggregate demand curve *ADI* shows the relationship between aggregate demand and inflation. Because short-run equilibrium output equals aggregate demand, the *ADI* curve also shows the relationship between short-run equilibrium output and inflation. The downward slope of the *ADI* curve implies that an increase in inflation reduces aggregate demand.

to incorporate the very important influence of the central bank's monetary policy on aggregate demand and because the Bank of Canada reacts to changes in the *inflation rate* and not to changes in the *price level*, Figure 11.1 graphs the relationship between aggregate demand and the inflation rate.

We will see shortly that, all else being equal, *an increase in the rate of inflation tends to reduce both aggregate demand and short-run equilibrium output*. Therefore, in a diagram showing inflation π on the vertical axis and output Y on the horizontal axis, the aggregate demand curve is downward sloping. Note that we refer to the *ADI* "curve," even though the relationship is drawn as a straight line in Figure 11.1. Although the *ADI* curve happens to be a straight line in the examples presented in this chapter, in general the *ADI* curve can be either straight or curved.

Why does higher inflation lead to a lower level of aggregate demand? As we will see next, one important reason is the central bank's response to increases in inflation.

INFLATION, THE BANK OF CANADA, AND AGGREGATE DEMAND

One of the primary responsibilities of the Bank of Canada, or of any central bank, is to control the rate of inflation. For example, in recent years the Bank of Canada has tried to keep inflation in Canada in the range of 1 to 3 percent. By keeping inflation in this low range, the Bank of Canada tries to avoid the costs that high inflation imposes on the economy (although, as mentioned in Chapter 6, some economists argue that the Bank of Canada could also avoid the costs of high inflation by keeping inflation moderate—in, say, the 3 to 6 percent range—instead of keeping it low).

What can the Bank of Canada do to keep inflation low and stable? As we have already mentioned, one situation that is likely to lead to increased inflation is an expansionary output gap, in which aggregate demand exceeds potential output. When aggregate demand exceeds potential output firms must produce at above-normal capacity to meet the demands of their customers. Like Al's ice cream store described in Chapter 7, firms may be willing to do so for a time, but eventually they will raise their prices, contributing to inflation. To control inflation, then, the Bank of Canada needs to dampen aggregate demand when it threatens to exceed potential output.

How can the Bank of Canada restrain aggregate demand? As we saw in Chapter 9, the Bank of Canada can reduce private spending, and hence aggregate demand, by raising the real interest rate. This behaviour by the Bank of Canada underlies the link between inflation and aggregate demand that is summarized by the aggregate demand curve. When inflation is high, the Bank of Canada responds by raising the real interest rate. The increase in the real interest rate reduces consumption and private-sector investment spending and hence aggregate demand. Because higher inflation leads, through the Bank of Canada's actions, to a reduction in aggregate demand, the aggregate demand (*ADI*) curve is downward sloping, as Figure 11.1 shows. We can summarize this chain of reasoning symbolically as follows:

$$\pi \uparrow \Rightarrow r \uparrow \Rightarrow \text{autonomous expenditure} \downarrow \Rightarrow Y \downarrow \qquad (ADI \text{ curve})$$

where, recall, π is inflation, r is the real interest rate, and Y is output.

The downward slope of the aggregate demand curve, therefore, depends critically on the Bank of Canada setting high real interest rates when the inflation rate is high and low real interest rates when the inflation rate is low. Economists find it convenient to summarize this type of central bank behaviour in terms of a *policy reaction function*. In general, a **policy reaction function** describes how the action a policy-maker takes depends on the state of the economy. Here the policy-maker's action is the central bank's choice of the real interest rate, and the state of the economy is given by the inflation rate.

Table 11.1 presents a policy reaction function that assumes the Bank of Canada reacts only to inflation. According to the hypothetical policy reaction function given in the table, the higher the rate of inflation, the higher the real interest rate set by the Bank of Canada. This relationship is consistent with the idea that the Bank of Canada responds to an expansionary gap (which threatens to lead to increased inflation) by raising the real interest rate. Figure 11.2 shows a graph of this policy reaction function. The vertical axis of the graph shows the real interest rate chosen by the Bank of Canada; the horizontal axis shows the rate of inflation. The upward slope of the policy reaction function captures the idea that the Bank of Canada reacts to increases in inflation by raising the real interest rate.

policy reaction function describes how the action a policy-maker takes depends on the state of the economy

TABLE 11.1
A Hypothetical Policy Reaction Function for the Bank of Canada

Rate of Inflation (π)	Real interest rate set by Bank of Canada (r)
0.00 (= 0%/year)	0.02 (= 2%)
0.01	0.03
0.02	0.04
0.03	0.05
0.04	0.06

What determines the shape of the Bank of Canada's policy reaction function? A key consideration is how aggressively the Bank plans to pursue its inflation target. To illustrate, suppose that the Bank of Canada's policy reaction function were flatter (less steep) than the policy reaction function in Figure 11.2, implying that the Bank changes the real interest rate rather modestly in response to increases or decreases in inflation. In that case we would conclude that the Bank of Canada does not intend to be as aggressive in its attempts to offset movements

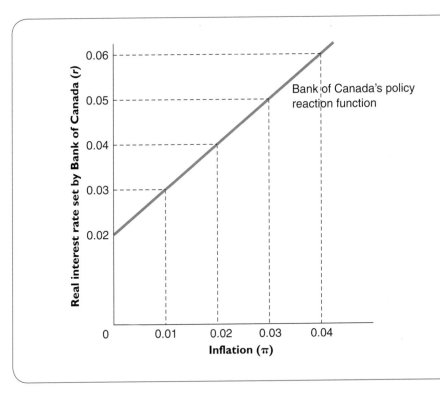

FIGURE 11.2

An Example of a Bank of Canada Policy Reaction Function
This example of a policy reaction function for the Bank of Canada shows the real interest rate the Bank of Canada sets in response to any given value of the inflation rate. The upward slope captures the idea that the Bank of Canada raises the real interest rate when inflation rises. The numerical values in the figure are from Table 11.1.

of inflation away from the target level. This would roughly correspond to the Bank of Canada adopting a broader inflation-control target range, say, from 0 to 4 percent instead of from 1 to 3 percent, but with the same medium-term target of 2 percent. In contrast, if the reaction function slopes more steeply upward so that a given change in inflation elicits a larger adjustment of the real interest rate by the Bank of Canada, we would say that the Bank plans to be more aggressive in responding to changes in inflation. (As we will see later in this chapter, the adoption of a different inflation target would be shown by a shift of the Bank of Canada's policy reaction function.)

SHIFTS OF THE AGGREGATE DEMAND CURVE

The downward slope of the aggregate demand, or *ADI,* curve shown in Figure 11.1 reflects the fact that, *all other factors held constant,* a higher level of inflation will lead to lower planned spending and lower short-run equilibrium output. Again, the reason higher inflation reduces planned spending is that the Bank of Canada tends to react to increases in inflation by raising the real interest rate, which in turn reduces consumption and planned private-sector investment, two important components of planned aggregate expenditure.

However, although our main focus in this chapter is on the relationship between inflation and aggregate demand, inflation is not the only thing that can affect aggregate demand. Even if inflation is held constant, planned spending and short-run equilibrium output can change for other reasons. Graphically, we represent the impact of these other factors as causing the *ADI* curve to shift. Specifically, for a given level of inflation, if there is a change in the economy that *increases* short-run equilibrium output, the *ADI* curve will shift to the *right*. If, on the other hand, the change *reduces* short-run equilibrium output at any given level of inflation, the *ADI* curve will shift to the *left*. Two sorts of changes can shift the aggregate demand *ADI* curve: (1) changes in spending caused by factors other than output or interest rates, which we will refer to as *autonomous* changes in spending; and (2) changes in the Bank of Canada's monetary policy, as reflected in a shift in the Bank of Canada's policy reaction function.

Changes in Spending

We have seen that planned aggregate expenditure depends both on income (through the consumption function) and on the real interest rate (which affects both consumption and planned investment). However, many factors, whose causes lie outside macroeconomics, can cause changes in the economy. (If, for example, there is a war the government will have to spend more on armaments—this change in government spending can be seen as a change in *fiscal policy*.) Even at given levels of output and the real interest rate, changes in fiscal policy will affect the level of government purchases and change aggregate demand. As well, changes in consumer confidence can affect consumption spending, new technological opportunities may lead firms to increase their planned investment, or an increased willingness of foreigners to purchase domestic goods may raise net exports. We will refer to changes in planned spending that are not caused by changes in output or the real interest rate as *autonomous* changes in spending.

For a given inflation rate (and thus for a given real interest rate set by the Bank of Canada), an exogenous increase in spending raises short-run equilibrium output, for the reasons we have discussed in earlier chapters. Because it increases output at each level of inflation, *an exogenous increase in spending shifts the ADI curve to the right*. This result is illustrated graphically in Figure 11.3. Imagine, for example, that there is a rise in the stock market because of optimism about new technologies and that this increase in wealth makes consumers more willing to spend. Or suppose that suddenly foreign consumers decide that Canadian beer is the best beer on the planet, and beer exports increase dramatically.[2] Then, for each level of inflation, aggregate spending and short-run equilibrium output will be higher, a change which is shown as a shift of the *ADI* curve to the right, from *ADI* to *ADI'*.

Similarly, at a given inflation rate, an exogenous decline in spending—for example, a fall in government purchases resulting from a more restrictive fiscal policy, or a decline in consumer spending caused by a collapse in stock

FIGURE 11.3

Effect of an Increase in Exogenous Spending

The *ADI* curve is seen both *before* (*ADI*) and *after* (*ADI'*) an increase in exogenous spending—specifically, an increase in consumption spending resulting from a rise in the stock market. If the inflation rate and the real interest rate set by the Bank of Canada are held constant, an increase in exogenous spending raises short-run equilibrium output. As a result, the *ADI* curve will shift to the right, from *ADI* to *ADI'*.

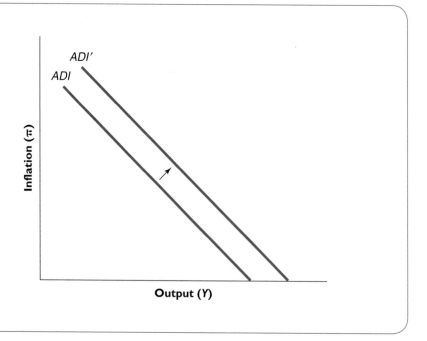

[2]Actually, the impact on aggregate demand of a surge in beer exports would have a far smaller effect on aggregate demand (*ADI*) than a surge in stock prices—but the point both examples have in common is that there is a change in spending for reasons unrelated to inflation or real interest rates.

prices—will cause short-run equilibrium output to fall. We conclude that *an exogenous decrease in spending shifts the ADI curve to the left.*

Determine how the following events would affect the *ADI* curve:

a. Due to widespread concerns about future weakness in the economy, businesses reduce their spending on new capital.

b. The federal government reduces sales taxes (as was done when the GST was cut by one percentage point on July 1, 2006, and by another percentage point on January 1, 2008).

EXERCISE 11.1

Changes in the Bank of Canada's Policy Reaction Function

Recall that the Bank of Canada's policy reaction function describes how the Bank of Canada sets the real interest rate at each level of inflation. This relationship is built into the *ADI* curve—indeed, it accounts for the curve's downward slope. As long as the Bank of Canada sets the real interest rate according to this reaction function, its adjustments in the real rate will not cause the *ADI* curve to shift.

However, on occasion the Bank of Canada may choose to be "tighter" or "easier" than normal, given the rate of inflation. For example, if inflation is too high and has stubbornly refused to decrease, the Bank of Canada might choose a tighter monetary policy, setting the real interest rate higher than normal given the rate of inflation. This change of policy can be interpreted as an upward shift in the Bank of Canada's policy reaction function, as shown in Figure 11.4(a). A decision by the Bank of Canada to set the real interest rate at a higher level for each given rate of inflation reduces planned expenditure, and thus short-run equilibrium output at each rate of inflation also. Why might the Bank of Canada do this? The objective of such a change in policy is to reduce the long-run target level of inflation. An important example of such a shift in the policy reaction function occurred in 1988 when the Bank of Canada lowered its target rate of inflation. Because an upward shift of the Bank of Canada's policy reaction function—a tightening of monetary policy—decreases aggregate demand and output at any given rate of inflation, the *ADI* curve shifts to the left [Figure 11.4(b)].

Similarly, if the economy is experiencing an unusually severe and stubborn recession, the Bank of Canada may choose to stimulate the economy by setting the real interest rate lower than normal, given the rate of inflation. This change in policy can be interpreted as a downward shift of the Bank of Canada's policy

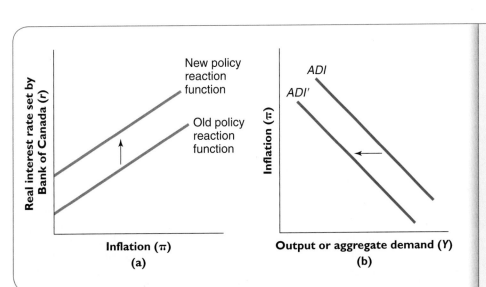

FIGURE 11.4

A Tightening of Monetary Policy

A tightening of monetary policy implies that, at any given inflation rate, the Bank of Canada sets a higher value of real interest rate than normal. Graphically, this change corresponds to an upward movement in the Bank of Canada's policy reaction function [part (a)]. A tightening of monetary policy shifts the *ADI* curve to the left [part (b)].

reaction function. Given the rate of inflation, a lower-than-normal setting of the real interest rate will increase aggregate demand and output. Therefore a downward shift of the Bank of Canada's policy reaction function—an easing of monetary policy—causes the *ADI* curve to shift to the right.

Note that the terms "tightening" and "easing" are generally used more broadly than they are used here. In general, any lowering of interest rates by the Bank of Canada, even down an existing policy reaction function, would be termed easing, and any raising of interest rates by the Bank, even up an existing policy reaction function, would be termed tightening.

MOVEMENTS ALONG THE *ADI* CURVE VERSUS SHIFTS OF THE *ADI* CURVE

Let's end this section by reviewing and summarizing the important distinction between *movements along* the *ADI* curve and *shifts of* the *ADI* curve.

The downward slope of the *ADI* curve captures the inverse relationship between inflation, on the one hand, and short-run equilibrium output, on the other. As we have seen, a rise in the inflation rate leads the Bank of Canada to raise the real interest rate, according to its policy reaction function. The higher real interest rate, in turn, depresses aggregate demand and short-run equilibrium output. The downward slope of the *ADI* curve embodies this relationship among inflation, spending, and output. Thus, changes in the inflation rate and the resulting changes in the real interest rate and short-run equilibrium output are represented by *movements along* the *ADI* curve. In particular, as long as the Bank of Canada sets the real interest rate in accordance with a fixed policy reaction function, changes in the real interest rate will *not* shift the *ADI* curve.

However, any factor that changes the short-run equilibrium level of output *at a given level of inflation* will shift the *ADI* curve—to the right if short-run equilibrium output increases, or to the left if short-run equilibrium output decreases. We have identified two reasons for a shift in the *ADI* curve: autonomous changes in spending (that is, changes in government, business, consumer or foreign trade spending unrelated to output or the real interest rate) and changes in the Bank of Canada's policy reaction function. An autonomous increase in spending or a rightward shift of the Bank of Canada's policy reaction function increases short-run equilibrium output at every level of inflation, thus shifting the *ADI* curve to the right. An autonomous decline in spending or a leftward shift in the Bank of Canada's policy reaction function decreases short-run equilibrium output at every level of inflation, shifting the *ADI* curve to the left.

EXERCISE 11.2

What is the difference, if any, between the following?

a. A leftward shift in the Bank of Canada's policy reaction function.

b. A response by the Bank of Canada to higher inflation, for a given policy reaction function.

How does each scenario affect the *ADI* curve?

RECAP

THE AGGREGATE DEMAND (ADI) CURVE

- The *ADI* curve shows the relationship between aggregate demand (equal to short-run equilibrium output) and inflation. Higher inflation leads the Bank of Canada to raise the real interest rate, which reduces aggregate demand and short-run equilibrium output. Therefore the *ADI* curve slopes downward.

- An increase in autonomous aggregate demand raises short-run equilibrium output at each value of inflation and so shifts the *ADI* curve to the right. Conversely, a decrease in autonomous aggregate demand shifts the *ADI* curve to the left.

- An easing of monetary policy, as reflected by a downward shift in the Bank of Canada's policy reaction function, shifts the *ADI* curve to the right. A tightening of monetary policy, as reflected by an upward shift in the Bank of Canada's policy reaction function, shifts the *ADI* curve to the left.

- Changes in inflation correspond to movements *along* the *ADI* curve; they do not shift the *ADI* curve.

11.2 INFLATION AND AGGREGATE SUPPLY

Until this point in the chapter we have focused on how changes in inflation affect aggregate demand and short-run equilibrium output, a relationship captured by the *ADI* curve. But we have not yet discussed how inflation itself is determined. In the rest of the chapter we will examine the main factors that determine the inflation rate in modern industrial economies, as well as the options that policy-makers have to control inflation. In doing so we will introduce a useful diagram for analyzing the behaviour of output and inflation called the *aggregate demand–inflation adjustment diagram*.

The laws of physics say that a body will tend to keep moving with a constant speed and direction unless it is acted upon by some outside force, a tendency referred to as *inertia*. Applying this concept to economics, many observers have noted that inflation seems to be inertial in the sense that it tends to remain roughly constant as long as the economy is not mired in recession (when the inflation rate would tend to fall), nor operating at significantly above capacity (when the inflation rate would tend to rise) and there are no external shocks to the price level. In the first part of this section we will discuss why inflation behaves in this way.

However, just as a physical object will change speed if it is acted on by outside forces, various economic forces can change the rate of inflation. Later in this section we will discuss three factors that can cause the inflation rate to change. The first is the presence of an *output gap*: inflation tends to rise when there is an expansionary output gap and to fall when there is a recessionary output gap. The second factor that can affect the inflation rate is a shock that directly affects prices, which we will refer to as an *inflation shock*. An example would be a large increase in the price of imported oil that raises the price of gasoline, heating oil, and other fuels, as well as of goods made with oil or services using oil. Finally, the third factor that directly affects the inflation rate is a *shock to potential output*, or a sharp change in the level of potential output. An extreme example of a negative shock to potential output would be a natural disaster that destroyed a significant portion of a country's factories and businesses. A major technological breakthrough reducing costs in a wide range of businesses would be an example of a positive shock to potential output. Together, inflationary shocks and shocks to potential output are known as *aggregate supply shocks*.

INFLATION INERTIA

In low-inflation industrial economies like that of Canada since the early 1990s, inflation tends to change relatively slowly from year to year, a phenomenon that is sometimes referred to as *inflation inertia*. If the rate of inflation in one year is 1.5 percent, it may be 2 percent or even 3 percent in the next year. But unless the country experiences a very unusual economic shock, inflation is unlikely to rise to 6 or 8 percent or fall to −2 percent in the following year. This relatively sluggish behaviour contrasts sharply with the behaviour of economic variables such as stock or commodity prices, which can change rapidly from day to day. For example, oil prices might well rise by 20 percent over the course of a year and then fall 20 percent over the next year. Yet, since 1992 the Canadian inflation rate has generally remained in the range of 1 to 3 percent per year.

Why does inflation tend to adjust relatively slowly in modern industrial economies? To answer this question we must consider two closely related factors that play an important role in determining the inflation rate: the behaviour of the public's *inflation expectations* and the existence of *long-term wage and price contracts*.

First, consider the public's expectations about inflation. In negotiating future wages and prices, both buyers and sellers take into account the rate of inflation they expect will prevail in the next few years. As a result, today's *expectations* of future inflation, in and of themselves, may help to determine the future inflation rate. Suppose, for example, that office worker Fred and his boss Colleen agree that Fred's performance this past year justifies an increase of 2 percent in his real wage for next year. What nominal wage increase should they agree on? If Fred believes that inflation is likely to be 3 percent over the next year, he will ask for a 5 percent increase in his nominal wage to obtain a 2 percent increase in his real wage. If Colleen agrees that inflation is likely to be 3 percent, she should be willing to go along with a 5 percent nominal increase, knowing that it implies only a 2 percent increase in Fred's real wage. Thus the rate at which Fred and Colleen *expect* prices to rise affects the rate at which at least one price—Fred's nominal wage—*actually* rises.

A similar dynamic affects the contracts for production inputs other than labour. For example, if Colleen is negotiating with her office supply company, the prices she will agree to pay for next year's deliveries of copy paper and staples will depend on what she expects the inflation rate to be. If Colleen anticipates that the price of office supplies will not change relative to the prices of other goods and services and that the general inflation rate will be 3 percent, then she should be willing to agree to a 3 percent increase in the price of office supplies. On the other hand, if she expects the general inflation rate to be 6 percent, then she will agree to pay 6 percent more for copy paper and staples next year, knowing that a nominal increase of 6 percent implies no change in the real, or relative, price of office supplies.

Economy-wide, then, the higher the expected rate of inflation, the more nominal wages and the cost of other inputs will rise. But if wages and other costs of production grow rapidly in response to expected inflation, firms will have to raise their prices rapidly as well to cover their costs. Thus a low rate of expected inflation tends to lead to a low rate of actual inflation, a moderate rate of expected inflation tends to produce a moderate rate of actual inflation, and a high rate of expected inflation tends to contribute to a high rate of actual inflation.

EXERCISE II.3 **Assume that employers and workers both agree that real wages should rise by 2 percent next year and intend to sign collective agreements that have that effect.**

   a. If the inflation rate is expected to be 2 percent next year, what will happen to nominal wages next year?

   b. If inflation is expected to be 4 percent next year, rather than 2 percent, what will happen to nominal wages next year?

   c. Use your answers from parts (a) and (b) to explain how an increase in expected inflation will tend to affect the following year's actual rate of inflation.

The conclusion that actual inflation is partially determined by expected inflation raises the question of what determines inflation expectations. To a great extent, people's expectations are influenced by their recent experience. If inflation has been low and stable for some time, people are likely to expect it to continue to be low. But if inflation has recently been high, people will expect it to continue to be high. If inflation has been unpredictable, alternating between low and high levels, the public's expectations will likewise tend to be volatile, rising or falling with news or rumours about economic conditions or economic policy.

Figure 11.5 illustrates schematically how low and stable inflation may tend to be self-perpetuating. As the figure shows, if inflation has been low for some time, people will continue to expect low inflation. Increases in nominal wages and other production costs will thus tend to be small. If firms raise prices only by enough to cover costs, then actual inflation will be low, as expected. This low actual rate will in turn promote low expected inflation, perpetuating the "virtuous circle." The same logic applies in an economy with high inflation (and also, of course, in an economy with moderate inflation). A high inflation rate implies high expected inflation, which in turn contributes to a high rate of actual inflation, and so on in a "vicious circle." This role of inflation expectations in the determination of wage and price increases helps to explain why inflation often seems to adjust slowly.

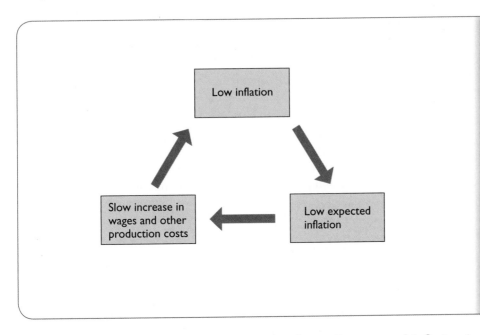

FIGURE 11.5

A "Virtuous Circle" of Low Inflation and Low Expected Inflation
Low inflation leads people to expect low inflation in the future. As a result, they agree to accept small increases in wages and the prices of the goods and services they supply, which keeps inflation—and expected inflation—low. In a similar way, high inflation leads people to expect high inflation, which in turn tends to produce high inflation.

The role of inflation expectations in the slow adjustment of inflation is strengthened by a second key element, the existence of *long-term wage and price contracts*. Union wage contracts, for example, often extend for three years into the future. Likewise, contracts that set the prices manufacturing firms pay for parts and raw materials often cover a few years. Long-term contracts serve to "build in" wage and price increases that depend on inflation expectations at the time the contracts were signed.

To summarize, in the absence of external shocks inflation tends to remain relatively stable over time, at least in low-inflation industrial economies like Canada's. In other words, inflation is *inertial* (or as some economists put it, "sticky"). Inflation tends to be inertial for two main reasons. The first is the behaviour of people's expectations of inflation. All else being equal, a low or moderate inflation rate leads people to expect low or moderate inflation in the future, which results in reduced pressure for wage and price increases. Similarly, a high inflation rate leads people to expect high inflation in the future, resulting in more rapid increases in wages and prices. The effects of expectations are reinforced by the existence of long-term wage and price contracts, which is the second reason inflation tends to be stable over time. Long-term contracts tend to build in the effects of people's inflation expectations.

Although the rate of inflation is inertial, it does, of course, change over time. We next discuss a key factor that causes the inflation rate to change.

THE OUTPUT GAP AND INFLATION

An important factor that influences the rate of inflation is the output gap, or the difference between potential output and actual output ($Y^* - Y$). We have seen that, in the short run, firms will meet the demand for their output at previously determined prices. For example, Al's ice cream shop will serve ice cream to any customer who comes into the shop, at the prices posted behind the counter. The level of output that is determined by aggregate demand at preset prices is called short-run equilibrium output.

At a particular time, the level of short-run equilibrium output may happen to equal the economy's long-run productive capacity, or potential output. But, as we have seen, that is not necessarily the case. Output may exceed potential output, giving rise to an expansionary gap, or it may fall short of potential output, producing a recessionary gap. Let's consider what happens to inflation in each of these three possible cases: no output gap, an expansionary gap, and a recessionary gap.

If actual output equals potential output, then by definition there is no output gap. When the output gap is zero, firms are satisfied in the sense that their sales equal their normal production rates. As a result, firms have no incentive either to reduce or increase their prices *relative* to the prices of other goods and services. However, the fact that firms are satisfied with their sales does *not* imply that inflation—the rate of change in the overall price level—is zero.

To see why, let's go back to the idea of inflation inertia. Suppose that inflation has recently been steady at 2 percent per year so that the public has come to expect an inflation rate of 2 percent per year. If the public's inflation expectations are reflected in the wage and price increases agreed to in long-term contracts, then firms will find their labour and materials costs are rising at 2 percent per year. To cover their costs, firms will need to raise their prices by 2 percent per year. Note that if all firms are raising their prices by 2 percent per year, the *relative* prices of various goods and services—say, the price of ice cream relative to the price of a taxi ride—will not change. Nevertheless, the economy-wide rate of inflation equals 2 percent, the same as in previous years. We conclude that, *if the output gap is zero, the rate of inflation will tend to remain the same.*

Suppose instead that an expansionary gap exists so that most firms' sales exceed their normal production rates. As we might expect in situations in which the quantity demanded exceeds the quantity firms desire to supply, firms will respond by trying to increase their relative prices. To do so, they will increase their prices by *more* than the increase in their costs. If all firms behave this way, then the general price level will begin to rise more rapidly than before. Thus, *when an expansionary gap exists, the rate of inflation will tend to increase.* This is why economists sometimes refer to an expansionary gap as an inflationary gap.

Finally, if a recessionary gap exists, firms will be selling less than their capacity to produce, and they will have an incentive to cut their relative prices so they can sell more. In this case, firms will raise their prices less than needed to cover fully their increases in costs, as determined by the existing inflation rate. As a result, *when a recessionary gap exists, the rate of inflation will tend to decrease.* These important results are summarized in Box 11.1. (Note that the real-world behaviour of inflation in response to output gaps may not be as precise as suggested by Box 11.1. For example, the inflation rate may be slow to decline in response to a recessionary output gap. As well, potential output, as mentioned in Chapter 7, cannot be measured with the same precision as actual output—credible estimates of potential output can differ by tens of billions of dollars. So "no output gap" can only mean that actual and potential output are roughly equal, not that they are exactly equal.)

BOX 11.1 | THE OUTPUT GAP AND INFLATION

Relationship of output to potential output	Behaviour of inflation
1. No output gap: $Y = Y^*$	Inflation remains unchanged
2. Expansionary gap: $Y > Y^*$	Inflation rises: $\pi \uparrow$
3. Recessionary gap: $Y < Y^*$	Inflation falls: $\pi \downarrow$

Spending changes and inflation

EXAMPLE 11.1

In Chapters 8 and 9 we saw that changes in spending can create expansionary or recessionary gaps. Therefore, based on the discussion above, we can conclude that changes in spending also lead to changes in the rate of inflation. If the economy is currently operating at potential output, what will be the effect on inflation of a fall in consumer confidence that makes consumers less willing to spend at each level of disposable income?

A decrease in exogenous consumption spending, C, for a given level of inflation, output, and real interest rates, reduces aggregate expenditures and short-run equilibrium output. If the economy was originally operating at potential output, the reduction in consumption will cause a recessionary gap, since actual output, Y, will now be less than potential output, Y^*. As indicated above, when $Y < Y^*$, the rate of inflation will tend to fall because firms' sales fall short of normal production rates, leading them to slow down the rate at which they increase their prices.

Suppose that firms become optimistic about the future and decide to increase their investment in new capital. What effect will this have on the rate of inflation, assuming that the economy is currently operating at potential output?

EXERCISE 11.4

THE AGGREGATE DEMAND–INFLATION ADJUSTMENT DIAGRAM

The adjustment of inflation in response to an output gap can be shown conveniently in a diagram. Figure 11.6, drawn with inflation π on the vertical axis and real output Y on the horizontal axis, is an example of an *aggregate demand–inflation adjustment diagram*, or *ADI–IA diagram* for short. The diagram has three elements, one of which is the downward-sloping *ADI* curve, introduced earlier in the chapter. Recall that the *ADI* curve shows how planned aggregate spending, and hence short-run equilibrium output, depend on the inflation rate. The second element is a vertical line marking the economy's potential output Y^*. Because potential output represents the economy's long-run productive capacity, we will refer to this vertical line as the **long-run aggregate supply line**, or *LRAS* line. The third element in Figure 11.6, and a new one, is the *inflation adjustment line*, labelled *IA* in the diagram. The **inflation adjustment line** is a horizontal line that shows the current rate of inflation in the economy, which in the figure is labelled π. We can think of the current rate of inflation as having been determined

long-run aggregate supply (LRAS) line a vertical line showing the economy's potential output Y^*

inflation adjustment (IA) line a horizontal line showing the current rate of inflation, as determined by past expectations and pricing decisions

FIGURE 11.6

The Aggregate Demand—Inflation Adjustment (ADI–IA) Diagram

This diagram has three elements: the *ADI* curve, which shows how short-run equilibrium output depends on inflation; the vertical long-run aggregate supply line (*LRAS*), which marks the economy's potential output; and the horizontal inflation adjustment line (*IA*), which shows the current value of inflation (π). Short-run equilibrium output, which is equal to *Y* here, is determined by the intersection of the *ADI* curve and the *IA* line (point *A*). Because actual output *Y* is less than potential output *Y**, this economy has a recessionary gap.

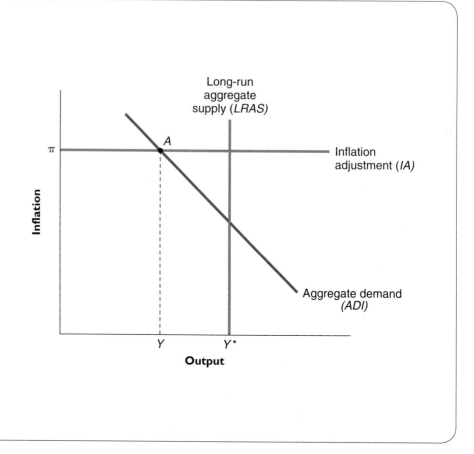

short-run equilibrium a situation in which inflation equals the value determined by past expectations and pricing decisions, and output equals the level of short-run equilibrium output that is consistent with that inflation rate; graphically, short-run equilibrium occurs at the intersection of the *ADI* curve and the *IA* line

by past expectations of inflation and past pricing decisions. The inflation adjustment line is horizontal because, in the short run, producers supply whatever output is demanded at preset prices.

The *ADI–IA* diagram can be used to determine the level of output prevailing at any particular time. As we have seen, the inflation rate at any moment is given directly by the position of the *IA* line; for example, current inflation equals π in Figure 11.6. To find the current level of output, recall that the *ADI* curve shows the level of short-run equilibrium output at any given rate of inflation. Since the inflation rate in this economy is π, we can infer from Figure 11.6 that short-run equilibrium output must equal *Y*, which corresponds to the intersection of the *ADI* curve and the *IA* line (point *A* in the figure). Notice that in Figure 11.6, short-run equilibrium output *Y* is less than potential output *Y**, so there is a recessionary gap in this economy.

The intersection of the *ADI* curve and the *IA* line (point *A* in Figure 11.6) is referred to as the point of *short-run equilibrium* in this economy. When the economy is in **short-run equilibrium**, inflation equals the value determined by past expectations and past pricing decisions, and output equals the level of short-run equilibrium output that is consistent with that inflation rate.

Although the economy may be in short-run equilibrium at point *A* in Figure 11.6, it will not remain there. The reason is that at point *A* the economy is experiencing a recessionary gap (output is less than potential output, as indicated by the *LRAS* line). As we have just seen, when a recessionary gap exists firms are not selling as much as they would like to and so they slow down the rate at which they increase their prices. With prices increasing more slowly, the inflation rate declines. According to the central bank policy reaction function that underlies the *ADI* curve, the central bank responds to declines in the inflation rate with interest rate cuts that stimulate consumption and private-sector investment spending.

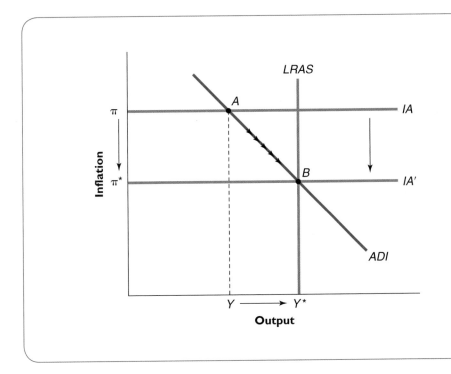

FIGURE 11.7

The Adjustment of Inflation When a Recessionary Gap Exists
At the initial short-run equilibrium point A, a recessionary gap exists, putting downward pressure on inflation. As inflation falls gradually, the IA line moves downward until it reaches IA' and actual output equals potential output (point B). Once the recessionary gap has been eliminated, inflation stabilizes at π*, and the economy settles into long-run equilibrium at the intersection of ADI, LRAS, and IA' (point B).

The adjustment of inflation in response to a recessionary gap is shown graphically in Figure 11.7. As inflation declines, the IA line moves downward, from IA to IA'. Because of inflation inertia (caused by the slow adjustment of the public's inflation expectations and the existence of long-term contracts), inflation adjusts downward only gradually. However, as long as a recessionary gap exists, inflation will continue to fall, and the IA line will move downward until it intersects the ADI curve at point B in the figure. At that point, actual output equals potential output, and the recessionary gap has been eliminated. Because there is no further pressure on inflation at point B, the inflation rate stabilizes at the lower level. A situation like that represented by point B in Figure 11.7, in which the inflation rate is stable and actual output equals potential output, is referred to as a **long-run equilibrium** of the economy. Long-run equilibrium occurs when the ADI curve, the IA line, and the LRAS line all intersect at a single point. At long-run equilibrium, the *equilibrium principle* applies, so that the economy is performing efficiently.

Figure 11.7 illustrates the important point that when a recessionary gap exists, inflation will tend to fall. It also shows that as inflation declines, short-run equilibrium output rises, increasing gradually from Y to Y* as the short-run equilibrium point moves down the ADI curve. The source of this increase in output is the behaviour of the Bank of Canada, which lowers the real interest rate as inflation falls, stimulating aggregate demand. As output rises, cyclical unemployment, which by Okun's law is proportional to the output gap, also declines. This process of falling inflation, falling real interest rates, rising output, and falling unemployment continues until the economy reaches full employment at point B in Figure 11.7, the economy's long-run equilibrium point.

What happens if, instead of a recessionary gap, the economy has an expansionary gap, with output greater than potential output? An expansionary gap would cause the rate of inflation to *rise* as firms respond to high demand by raising their prices more rapidly than their costs are rising. In graphical terms, an expansionary gap would cause the IA line to move upward over time. Inflation and the IA line would continue to rise until the economy reached long-run equilibrium, with actual output equal to potential output. This process is illustrated in Figure 11.8. Initially, the economy is in short-run equilibrium at point A, where

long-run equilibrium a situation in which actual output equals potential output and the inflation rate is stable; graphically, long-run equilibrium occurs when the ADI curve, the IA line, and the LRAS line all intersect at a single point

EQUILIBRIUM

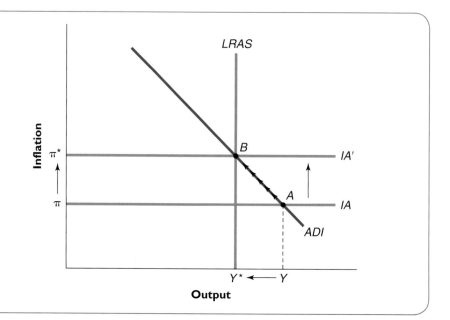

FIGURE 11.8

The Adjustment of Inflation When an Expansionary Gap Exists

At the initial short-run equilibrium point A, an expansionary gap exists. Inflation rises gradually (the IA line moves upward), and output falls. The process continues until the economy reaches long-run equilibrium at point B, where inflation stabilizes and the output gap is eliminated.

$Y > Y^*$ (an expansionary gap). The expansionary gap causes inflation to rise over time; graphically, the inflation adjustment line moves upward, from IA to IA'. As the IA line rises, short-run equilibrium output falls, the result of the Bank of Canada's tendency to increase the real interest rate when inflation rises. Eventually the IA line intersects the ADI curve and LRAS line at point B, where the economy reaches long-run equilibrium, with no output gap and stable inflation.

A SELF-CORRECTING ECONOMIC MODEL

Our analysis of Figures 11.7 and 11.8 makes an important general point: If the policy reaction function of the central bank is stable, the ADI–IA model is *self-correcting* in the long run.[3] In other words, given enough time, output gaps tend to disappear as a result of a mechanism built into the model. Inflation rate changes trigger Bank of Canada interest rate changes via the Bank of Canada's given policy reaction function. Hence expansionary output gaps tend to be eliminated by rising inflation, while recessionary output gaps tend to be eliminated by falling inflation.

This result differs somewhat from the basic Keynesian model, which does not include a self-correcting mechanism. The difference in results is explained by two facts. First, the basic Keynesian model concentrates on the short-run period, during which prices do not adjust; it does not take into account the changes in the inflation rate that occur over a longer period. Second, the basic Keynesian model does not incorporate the Bank of Canada's policy reaction function.

Does the self-correcting character of our economic model rule out the need for active manipulation of monetary policy (that is, shifting of the central bank's policy reaction function) or fiscal policy? The answer to this question depends crucially on the speed with which the self-correction process takes place. If self-correction takes place very slowly so that actual output differs from potential output for protracted periods, then active use of monetary and fiscal policies will help to stabilize output. (Recall that many economists, as mentioned in Chapters 8 and 9, believe that policy-makers should generally give active monetary policy a try before resorting to active fiscal policy.) But if self-correction is rapid, then the

---

[3]Note that it is the model incorporating the central bank reaction function that is self-correcting, not the market economy itself.

case for active stabilization policies is weaker. Indeed, if the economy returns to full employment quickly, then attempts by policy-makers to influence aggregate demand would cause actual output to "overshoot" potential output.

The speed with which a particular economy eliminates an output gap depends on a variety of factors. However, a reasonable conclusion is that the greater the initial output gap, the longer it will take for the gap to be eliminated. This observation suggests that active stabilization policies are required to remedy large gaps—such as when the unemployment rate is high. The Canadian economy, for example, recovered very slowly from the 1990–1992 recession.

RECAP ↑

ADI–IA AND THE SELF-CORRECTING MECHANISM

The economy is in *short-run equilibrium* when inflation equals the value determined by past expectations and pricing decisions, and when output equals the level of short-run equilibrium output that is consistent with that inflation rate. Graphically, short-run equilibrium occurs at the intersection of the *ADI* curve and the *IA* line.

The economy is in *long-run equilibrium* when actual output equals potential output (there is no output gap) and the inflation rate is stable. Graphically, long-run equilibrium occurs when the *ADI* curve, the *IA* line, and the *LRAS* line intersect at a common point.

Inflation adjusts gradually and, in conjunction with the Bank of Canada's policy reaction function, this adjustment brings the economy into long-run equilibrium. Hence expansionary output gaps are eliminated by rising inflation (which triggers interest rate increases by the Bank of Canada), while recessionary output gaps are eliminated by falling inflation (which triggers interest rate cuts by the Bank).

The more rapid the self-correction process, the less need there is for active stabilization policies to eliminate output gaps. In practice, attempts to eliminate output gaps through shifting the *ADI* curve are more likely to be helpful when the output gap is large than when it is small.

11.3 SOURCES OF CHANGE IN INFLATION

We have seen that inflation can rise or fall in response to an output gap. But what creates the output gaps that give rise to changes in inflation? And are there other factors besides output gaps that can affect the inflation rate? In this section we use the *ADI–IA* diagram to explore the ultimate sources of inflation rate changes. We first discuss how excessive growth in aggregate demand can spur inflation, then turn to factors operating through the supply side of the economy.

EXCESSIVE AGGREGATE DEMAND

One important source of inflation in practice is excessive aggregate demand, otherwise known as "demand–pull inflation," or, in more colloquial terms, "too much spending chasing too few goods." Example 11.2 illustrates.

Military buildups and inflation

EXAMPLE 11.2

Wars and military buildups are sometimes associated with increased inflation. Explain why, using the *ADI–IA* diagram. Can the central bank do anything to prevent the increase in inflation that may be caused by a military buildup?

actual output falls below potential output. So even after real GDP growth has picked up again, it may take some years of relatively faster growth (at rates that exceed the continuing expansion of potential output) before the recessionary gap is fully closed.

For example, the Canadian economy entered a recession in 1990 when real GDP growth fell to 0.3 percent. The economy sank deeper into recession in 1991 when real GDP fell by −1.9 percent, and it was still in recession during much of 1992 when the real GDP growth rate was 0.9 percent. By 1993, the real GDP growth rate was 2.3 percent and the economy was no longer in recession. But a recessionary gap still persisted for most of the 1990s (at least according to the International Monetary Fund).

Indeed, since potential output is growing all the time (thanks to population growth and technological advances), a recessionary gap can open up even when no recession has taken place. If real GDP continued to grow, but at an unusually slow rate that was less than the ongoing growth of potential output, then a recessionary gap would gradually emerge between actual and potential output. Once again, a sustained period of faster-than-normal growth would be required to close the gap.

The *ADI–IA* model of this chapter shares another limitation with the basic Keynesian model of Chapters 8 and 9. Both models have assumed, for the sake of simplicity, that net exports are autonomous. Thus, the models assume that interest rate changes do not produce changes in net exports. But, as we noted in Chapter 9, when the Bank of Canada changes the overnight rate target it tends to produce changes in the exchange rate and hence in net exports. When the overnight rate target goes down, the exchange rate tends to depreciate—the Canadian dollar becomes weaker—and net exports increase. When the overnight rate target goes up, the exchange rate tends to appreciate—the Canadian dollar becomes stronger—and net exports increase.

Like the Keynesian cross model, the *ADI–IA* model can be modified to recognize the impact that interest rates have on net exports. The basic result, however, would be the same—an increase in the overnight rate target would lead to a reduction in aggregate demand; a decrease in the overnight rate target would lead to an increase in aggregate demand. We will discuss exports, imports and exchange rates further in Chapter 12.

www.imf.org
International Monetary
Fund

RECAP

LIMITATIONS OF THE AGGREGATE DEMAND– AGGREGATE SUPPLY MODEL

A few of the limitations of our *ADI–IA* model relate to the *LRAS* curve. Because potential output cannot be precisely estimated, it might be better to think of *LRAS* not as a thin vertical line but as a thick line or band. Also, above some high threshold level the *LRAS* might bend upward to the left, and below some low threshold level it might bend downward to the left.

Another limitation of the *ADI–IA* model is its assumption that potential output is fixed. In the real world, potential output continues to expand during a recession as the economy stagnates. To close the recessionary gap, it is not sufficient to bring actual output back to the level of potential output prevailing before the recession. It is necessary to bring actual output to the economy's current level of potential output, which has kept growing from year to year.

The *ADI–IA* model of this chapter assumed, for the sake of simplicity, that net exports are autonomous. But the model can be modified to recognize the impact that interest rates have on net exports via their impact on exchange rates.

SUMMARY

11.1 This chapter extended the basic Keynesian model to include inflation. First, we showed how planned spending and short-run equilibrium output are related to inflation, a relationship that is summarized by the aggregate demand curve. Second, we discussed how inflation itself is determined. In the short run, inflation is determined by past expectations and pricing decisions, but in the long run inflation adjusts in a way that promotes the elimination of output gaps.

11.1 The *aggregate demand (ADI) curve* shows the relationship between aggregate demand and inflation. Because short-run equilibrium output is equal to planned spending, the aggregate demand curve also relates short-run equilibrium output to inflation. Since increases in inflation reduce both planned spending and short-run equilibrium output, the aggregate demand curve is downward-sloping in a diagram with inflation on the vertical axis and output on the horizontal axis.

11.1 The inverse relationship of inflation and short-run equilibrium output is the result of the behaviour of the Bank of Canada. To keep inflation low and stable, the Bank of Canada reacts to rising inflation by increasing the real interest rate. A higher real interest rate reduces consumption and planned private-sector investment, lowering planned aggregate expenditure and thus short-run equilibrium output.

11.1 For a given value of inflation, an autonomous increase in spending (that is, an increase in spending at given levels of output and the real interest rate) raises short-run equilibrium output, shifting the *ADI* curve to the right. The *ADI* curve can also be shifted by a change in the Bank of Canada's policy reaction function. If the Bank of Canada gets "tougher," choosing a higher real interest rate at each level of inflation, the aggregate demand curve will shift to the left. If the Bank of Canada gets "easier," setting a lower real interest rate at each level of inflation, the *ADI* curve will shift to the right.

11.2 In industrial economies like Canada's, inflation tends to be inertial, or slow to adjust to changes in the economy. This inertial behaviour reflects the fact that inflation depends in part on people's expectations of future inflation, which in turn depend on their recent experience with inflation. Long-term wage and price contracts tend to "build in" the effects of people's expectations for multiyear periods.

11.2 Although inflation is inertial, it does change over time in response to output gaps. An expansionary gap tends to raise the inflation rate, because firms raise their prices more quickly when they are facing demand that exceeds their normal productive capacity. A recessionary gap tends to reduce the inflation rate, as firms become more reluctant to raise their prices. The *inflation adjustment (IA) line* is a horizontal line that shows the current rate of inflation, as determined by past expectations and pricing decisions.

11.2 The economy is in *short-run equilibrium* when inflation equals the value determined by past expectations and pricing decisions, and output equals the level of short-run equilibrium output that is consistent with that inflation rate. Graphically, short-run equilibrium occurs at the intersection of the *ADI* curve and the *IA* line. If an output gap exists, however, the inflation rate will adjust in a way that promotes the elimination of the gap. Graphically, the *IA* line moves upward or downward as needed to restore output to its full-employment level. When the inflation rate is stable and actual output equals potential output, the economy is in *long-run equilibrium*. Graphically, long-run equilibrium corresponds to the common intersection point of the *ADI* curve, the *IA* line, and the long-run aggregate supply (*LRAS*) line, a vertical line that marks the economy's potential output.

11.2 If an economic model tends to move toward long-run equilibrium as a result of factors incorporated into the model, it is said to be self-correcting. The more rapid the self-correction process, the smaller the need for active fiscal policies (or shifts in the central bank's policy reaction function) to eliminate output gaps. In practice, the larger the output gap, the stronger the case for implementing active monetary or fiscal policies.

11.3 One source of rising inflation is excessive spending, which leads to expansionary output gaps. Aggregate supply shocks are another source. *Aggregate supply shocks* include both *inflation shocks*—sudden changes in the normal behaviour of inflation, created, for example, by a rise in the price of imported oil—and shocks to potential output. Adverse supply shocks both lower output and increase inflation, creating a difficult dilemma for policy-makers.

11.4 To reduce inflation, policy-makers typically must shift the aggregate demand curve to the left—for example, through "tight" monetary policy. In the short run, the main effects of a reduction in aggregate demand are reduced output and higher unemployment, as the economy experiences a recessionary gap. These costs of *disinflation* must be balanced against the benefits of a lower rate of inflation.

11.5 The *ADI–IA* model of this chapter has a number of possible limitations. The range of actual output levels corresponding to the situation of "no output gap" may be wide. The *LRAS* curve may not be vertical above a high threshold level of inflation or below a low threshold. In the *ADI–IA* model, potential output is fixed in the "long run" during which a recessionary gap will tend to be eliminated by a self-correcting process, but in the real world potential output will be expanding noticeably while the correcting process is taking place. Finally, for the sake of simplicity, we have ignored that in the real world interest rate changes will tend to produce exchange rate adjustments having consequences for the level of net exports.

KEY TERMS

aggregate demand (*ADI*) curve (268)
aggregate supply shock (288)
inflation adjustment (*IA*) line (279)

inflation shock (286)
long-run aggregate supply
   (*LRAS*) line (279)

long-run equilibrium (281)
policy reaction function (270)
short-run equilibrium (280)

REVIEW QUESTIONS

1. What two variables are related by the aggregate demand (*ADI*) curve? Give an economic explanation of the slope of the curve.

2. State how each of the following affects the *ADI* curve, and explain.
   a. An increase in government purchases.
   b. A cut in taxes.
   c. A decline in planned investment spending by firms.
   d. A decision by the Bank of Canada to lower the real interest rate at each level of inflation.

3. Recent years have seen sharp increases in oil and grain prices. Why does the overall rate of inflation tend to adjust more slowly than prices of commodities, such as oil or grain?

4. Discuss the relationship between output gaps and inflation. How is this relationship captured in the aggregate demand–inflation adjustment diagram?

5. Sketch an aggregate demand–inflation adjustment diagram depicting an economy away from long-run

equilibrium. Indicate the economy's short-run equilibrium point. Discuss how the economy reaches long-run equilibrium over a period of time. Illustrate the process in your diagram.

6. True or false, and explain: The existence of a central bank policy reaction function makes active use of stabilization policy unnecessary.

7. What factors led to increased inflation in Canada during 1973–1974 and 1980–1981?

8. Why does an adverse inflation shock pose a particularly difficult dilemma for policy-makers?

9. How does a very tight monetary policy, like that conducted by the Bank of Canada in the late 1980s and early 1990s, affect output, inflation, and the real interest rate in the short run? In the long run?

10. Summarize three criticisms of the thin vertical *LRAS* curve.

PROBLEMS

1. We saw in Chapter 9 that short-run equilibrium output falls when the Bank of Canada raises the real interest rate. Suppose the relationship between short-run equilibrium output Y and the real interest rate r set by the Bank of Canada is given by

$$Y = 1000 - 1000r.$$

Suppose also that the Bank of Canada's reaction function is the one shown in Table 11.1. For whole-number inflation rates between zero and 4 percent, find the real interest rate set by the Bank of Canada and the resulting short-run equilibrium output. Graph the aggregate demand curve numerically.

2. For the economy in Problem 1, suppose that potential output $Y^* = 960$. From the policy reaction function in Table 11.1, what can you infer about the Bank of Canada's objective for the inflation rate in the long term?

3. An economy's aggregate demand curve (the relationship between short-run equilibrium output and inflation) is described by the equation

$$Y = 13\ 000 - 20\ 000\pi.$$

Initially, the inflation rate is 4 percent, or $\pi = 0.04$. Potential output Y^* equals 12 000.
   a. Find inflation and output in short-run equilibrium.
   b. Find inflation and output in long-run equilibrium.

Show your work.

4. (More difficult.) This problem asks you to trace out the adjustment of inflation when the economy starts off with an output gap.
   a. Suppose that the economy's aggregate demand curve is

   $$Y = 1000 - 1000\pi,$$

   where Y is short-run equilibrium output and π is the inflation rate, measured as a decimal. Potential output Y^* equals 950, and the initial inflation rate is 10 percent ($\pi = 0.10$). Find output and inflation for this economy in short-run equilibrium and in long-run equilibrium.
   b. Suppose that, each quarter, inflation adjusts according to the following rule:

   This quarter's inflation = Last quarter's inflation − 0.0004 × Last quarter's output gap.

   Starting from the initial value of 10 percent for inflation, find the value of inflation for each of the next four quarters. Does inflation come close to its long-run value?

5. For each of the following, use an *ADI–IA* diagram to show the short-run and long-run effects on output and inflation. Assume the economy starts in long-run equilibrium.
   a. An increase in autonomous consumption.
   b. A reduction in taxes.
   c. An easing of monetary policy by the Bank of Canada (a downward shift in the policy reaction function).
   d. A sharp drop in oil prices.
   e. A war that raises government purchases.

6. Suppose that a permanent increase in oil prices both creates an inflationary shock and reduces potential output. Use an *ADI–IA* diagram to show the effects of the oil price increase on output and inflation in the short run and the long run, assuming that there is no policy response. What happens if the Bank of Canada responds to the oil price increase by tightening monetary policy?

ANSWERS TO IN-CHAPTER EXERCISES

11.1 a. At the current level of inflation, output, and the real interest rate, an exogenous reduction in business spending on new capital will reduce planned investment, causing a decline in overall aggregate expenditures, and a reduction in short-run equilibrium output. Because output has fallen for a given level of inflation, the decrease in business spending leads to a leftward shift in the *ADI* curve.
   b. At the current level of inflation, output, and the real interest rate, a reduction in federal sales taxes increases consumers' disposable income ($Y - T$), which leads to an exogenous increase in consumption at all income levels. The upward shift in the consumption function increases overall aggregate expenditures and leads to an increase in short-run equilibrium output. Because output has increased for a given level of inflation, the reduction in income taxes leads to a rightward shift in the *ADI* curve.

11.2 a. A leftward shift in the Bank of Canada's policy reaction function means that the Bank of Canada is raising the real interest rate associated with a given level of inflation. An increase in the real interest rate causes both consumption and planned private-sector investment spending to fall, reducing overall aggregate expenditures and short-run equilibrium output. Thus, a shift in the Bank of Canada's policy reaction function causes the output level to fall for a given level of inflation, resulting in a leftward shift in the *ADI* curve.
   b. The Bank of Canada's policy reaction function illustrates that the Bank of Canada responds to rising inflation rates by raising the real interest rate (a move *along* the policy reaction function), which causes a reduction in overall aggregate expenditures and short-run equilibrium output. However, in this case the Bank of Canada's response to higher inflation causes a *move along* a given *ADI* curve.

       Note that while the two actions appear to be similar, there is a key difference. In the first case the Bank of Canada is changing its policy rule for a *given inflation rate,* while in the second case the Bank of Canada is responding to a *changing inflation rate.* Changes in aggregate spending for a given inflation rate shift the *ADI* curve, while changes in aggregate spending resulting from Bank of Canada policy responses to a rise or fall in inflation lead to moves along a given *ADI* curve.

11.3 a. If inflation is expected to be 2 percent next year and workers are expecting a 2 percent increase in their real wages, then they will expect, and ask for, a 4 percent increase in their nominal wages.

b. If inflation is expected to be 4 percent next year, rather than 2 percent, workers will expect, and ask for, a 6 percent increase in their nominal wages.

c. If wage costs rise, firms will need to increase the prices of their goods and services to cover their increased costs, leading to an increase in inflation. In part b, when expected inflation was 4 percent, firms will be faced with larger increases in nominal wages than in part a, when expected inflation was only 2 percent. Thus, we can expect firms to raise prices by more when expected inflation is 4 percent than when expected inflation is 2 percent. From this example, we can conclude that increased inflationary expectations lead to higher inflation.

11.4 An increase in spending on new capital by firms for a given level of inflation, output, and the real interest rate increases aggregate expenditures and short-run equilibrium output. Since the economy was originally operating at potential output, the increase in investment spending will lead to an expansionary gap; actual output, Y, will now be greater than potential output, Y^*. When $Y > Y^*$, the rate of inflation will tend to rise.

11.5 The effects will be the opposite of those illustrated in Figure 11.9. Beginning in a long-run equilibrium with output equal to potential output and stable inflation (that is, where the ADI curve intersects both the IA and $LRAS$ lines, the fall in consumption spending will initially lead to a leftward shift in the ADI curve and the economy moves to a new, lower, short-run equilibrium output level at the same inflation rate. The shift in ADI creates a recessionary gap, since Y is now less than Y^*. The immediate effect of the decrease in consumption spending is only to reduce output. However, over time inflation will fall because of the recessionary gap. As inflation falls the IA line will shift downward. The Bank of Canada responds to the fall in inflation by reducing real interest rates, leading to an increase in aggregate expenditure and output, a move down along the new ADI curve. When inflation has fallen enough (and real interest rates have fallen enough) to eliminate the output gap, the economy will be back in long-run equilibrium where output equals potential output, but the inflation rate will be lower than before the fall in consumption spending.

11.6 A decrease in oil prices is an example of a "favourable" inflation shock and the economic effects of such a shock are the reverse of those illustrated in Figure 11.10. In this case, starting from a long-run equilibrium where output equals potential output, a favourable inflation shock reduces current inflation, causing the IA line to shift downward. The downward shift in the IA curve leads to a short-run equilibrium with lower inflation and higher output, creating an expansionary gap. If the Bank of Canada does nothing, eventually the IA will begin to shift upward and the economy will return to its original inflation and output levels. However, the Bank of Canada may instead choose to tighten its monetary policy by shifting up its policy reaction function, raising the current real interest rate, shifting the ADI curve to the left and restoring equilibrium at potential GDP, but at the new, lower inflation rate.

11.7

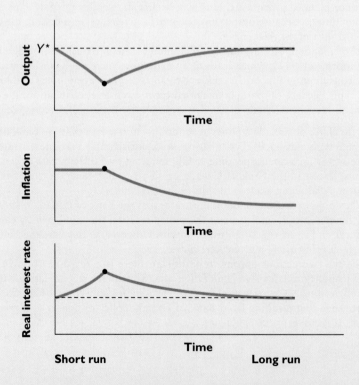

The Algebra of the *ADI–IA* Model

In this appendix we will derive the aggregate demand (*ADI*) curve algebraically. Then we will show how together the *ADI* and the inflation adjustment line determine the short-run and long-run equilibrium points of the economy.

THE *ADI* CURVE

In the appendix to Chapter 9, Equation 9A.1 showed that short-run equilibrium output depends on both exogenous components of expenditure and the real interest rate:

$$Y = \left(\frac{1}{1-c}\right)[\overline{C} - c\overline{T} + \overline{I} + \overline{G} + \overline{NX} - (a+b)r],$$

where $1/(1-c)$ is the multiplier, $\overline{C} - c\overline{T} + \overline{I} + \overline{G} + \overline{NX}$ is the exogenous component of planned spending, the term in brackets is autonomous expenditure, and a and b and are positive numbers that measure the effect of changes in the real interest rate on consumption and planned private-sector investment, respectively.

The *ADI* curve incorporates the behaviour of the Bank of Canada, as described by its policy reaction function. According to its policy reaction function, when inflation rises, the Bank of Canada raises the real interest rate. Thus the Bank of Canada's policy reaction function can be written as an equation relating the real interest rate r to inflation π:

$$r = \overline{r} + g\pi, \tag{11A.1}$$

where $\overline{r}$, and g are positive constants chosen by Bank of Canada officials. This equation states that when inflation π rises by 1 percentage point—say from 2 to 3 percent per year—the Bank of Canada responds by raising the real interest rate by g percentage points. So, for example, if $g = 0.5$, an increase in inflation from 2 to 3 percent would lead the Bank of Canada to raise the real interest rate by 0.5 percentage points. The intercept term $\overline{r}$, tells us at what level the Bank of Canada would set the real interest rate if inflation happened to be zero (so that the term $g\pi$ dropped out of the equation).

We can combine the equation for short-run equilibrium output with the equation for the policy reaction function by substituting the right-hand side of Equation 11A.1 for the real interest rate r in the above-mentioned Equation 9A.1:

$$Y = \left(\frac{1}{1-c}\right)[\overline{C} - c\overline{T} + \overline{I} + \overline{G} + \overline{NX} - (a + b)(\overline{r} + g\pi)]. \quad (11A.2)$$

This equation, which is the general algebraic expression for the *ADI* curve, summarizes the link between inflation and short-run equilibrium output, as shown graphically in Figure 11.1. Equation 11A.2 implies that an increase in inflation π reduces short-run equilibrium output Y, so that the *ADI* curve is downward sloping.

For a numerical illustration of this equation, we can assume that $\overline{C} = 640$, $\overline{T} = 250$, $\overline{I} = 250$, $\overline{G} = 300$, $\overline{NX} = 20$, $c = 0.8$, $a = 400$, and $b = 600$. To derive the *ADI* curve, we also need the parameters for the Bank of Canada's policy reaction function. Table 11.1 related the Bank of Canada's choice of the real interest rate to the inflation rate. To express the relationship in the table in the form of an equation, note that when inflation π equals zero, the real interest rate r equals 2 percent. Therefore the constant term in the Bank of Canada's policy reaction function, $\overline{r}$, equals 2 percent, or 0.02. Second, Table 11.1 shows that the real interest rate rises one point for each point that inflation rises; therefore the slope of the reaction function, g, equals 1.0. Substituting these numerical values into Equation 11A.2 and simplifying, we get the following numerical equation for the *ADI* curve:

$$Y = 5[640 - 0.8(250) + 250 + 300 + 20 - (400 + 600)(0.02 + \pi)]$$
$$= 4950 - 5000\pi. \quad (11A.3)$$

Note that, in this equation, higher values of inflation imply lower values of short-run equilibrium output.

SHIFTS OF THE *ADI* CURVE

Recall that exogenous changes in spending in the Bank of Canada's policy reaction function will shift the *ADI* curve. These results follow directly from Equation 11A.2. First, the equation shows that, for a given rate of inflation π, an increase in exogenous spending, $\overline{C} - c\overline{T} + \overline{I} + \overline{G} + \overline{NX}$, will raise short-run equilibrium output Y. Thus an increase in exogenous spending shifts the *ADI* curve to the right; conversely, a decrease in exogenous spending shifts the *ADI* curve to the left.

A shift in the Bank of Canada's policy reaction can be captured by a change in the intercept term $\overline{r}$ in Equation 11A.1. For example, suppose the Bank of Canada tightens monetary policy by setting the real interest rate 1 percent higher than before at every level of inflation. Such a change is equivalent to raising the intercept term in the policy reaction function $\overline{r}$, by 0.01. If you look at Equation 11A.2, you will see that with the level of inflation held constant, an increase in $\overline{r}$, reduces short-run equilibrium output. Thus a tightening of monetary policy shifts the *ADI* curve to the left; conversely, an easing of monetary policy (represented by a decline in $\overline{r}$,) shifts the *ADI* curve to the right.

EXERCISE I IA.I

a. **For the economy described above, find an algebraic equation for the *ADI* curve after an exogenous increase in spending (say, in planned private-sector investment) of 10 units.**

b. **For the economy described above, find an algebraic equation for the *ADI* curve after a tightening of monetary policy which involves setting the real interest rate 1 percent higher at each level of inflation.**

SHORT-RUN EQUILIBRIUM

Recall that in short-run equilibrium, inflation is equal to its previously determined value, and the *IA* line is horizontal at that value. At that level of inflation, the level of output in short-run equilibrium is given by the aggregate demand curve, Equation 11A.2. For instance, in the economy of Equation 11A.3, suppose the current value of inflation is 3 percent. The value of short-run equilibrium output is therefore

$$Y = 4950 - 5000\pi = 4950 - 5000(0.03) = 4800.$$

LONG-RUN EQUILIBRIUM

Recall that in long-run equilibrium, actual output Y equals potential output Y^*. Thus, in long-run equilibrium, the inflation rate can be obtained from the equation for the *ADI* curve by substituting Y^* for Y. To illustrate, let's write the equation for the *ADI* curve in the economy in Example 11.1 once again:

$$Y = 4950 - 5000\pi.$$

Suppose, in addition, that $Y^* = 4900$. Substituting this value for Y in the aggregate demand equation yields

$$4900 = 4950 - 5000\pi.$$

Solving for the inflation rate π, we get

$$\pi = 0.01 = 1\%.$$

When this economy is in long-run equilibrium, then, the inflation rate will be 1 percent. If we start from the value of inflation in short-run equilibrium, 3 percent, we can see that the inflation adjustment line must shift downward until inflation reaches 1 percent before long-run equilibrium can be achieved.

ANSWER TO IN-APPENDIX EXERCISE 11A.1

11A   The algebraic solutions for the *ADI* curves in each case, obtained by substituting the numerical values into the formula, are given below.
a. $Y = 5000 - 5000\pi$.
b. $Y = 4900 - 5000\pi$.

Chapter 12 Exchange Rates and the Open Economy

Two tourists visiting London many years ago were commiserating over their problems understanding English currency. "Pounds, shillings, tuppence, thruppence, bob, and quid, it's driving me crazy," said the first tourist. "This morning it took me twenty minutes to figure out how much to pay the taxi driver."

The second tourist was more upbeat. "Actually," he said, "since I adopted my new system, I haven't had any problems at all."

The first tourist looked interested. "What's your new system?"

"Well," replied the second, "now, whenever I take a taxi, I just give the driver all the English money I have. And would you believe it, I have got the fare exactly right every time!"

Dealing with unfamiliar currencies—and translating the value of foreign money into one's domestic currency—is a problem every international traveller faces.[1] The traveller's problem is complicated by the fact that *exchange rates*—the rates at which one country's money trades for another—may change unpredictably. Thus the number of British pounds, Russian rubles, Japanese yen, or U.S. dollars that a Canadian dollar can buy may vary over time, sometimes quite a lot.

The economic consequences of variable exchange rates are much broader than their impact on travel and tourism, however. For example, the competitiveness of Canadian exports depends in part on the prices of Canadian goods in terms of foreign currencies, which in turn depend on the exchange rate between the Canadian dollar and those currencies. Likewise, the prices Canadians pay for imported goods depend in part on the value of the dollar relative to the currencies of the countries that produce those goods. Exchange rates also affect the value of financial investments made across national borders. For countries that are heavily dependent on trade and international capital flows—the majority of the world's nations—fluctuations in the exchange rate may have a significant economic impact.

---

[1]However, British money today is less complicated than suggested by this introductory story. In 1971, the British switched to a decimal monetary system, under which each pound is worth 100 pence. At that time, the traditional British system, under which a pound equalled 20 shillings and each shilling equalled 12 pence, was abandoned.

This chapter discusses exchange rates and the role they play in open economies. We will start by distinguishing between the *nominal exchange rate*—the rate at which one national currency trades for another—and the *real exchange rate*—the rate at which one country's goods trade for another's. We will show how exchange rates affect the prices of exports and imports, and thus the pattern of trade.

Next we will turn to the question of how exchange rates are determined. Exchange rates may be divided into two broad categories, flexible and fixed. The value of a *flexible* exchange rate is determined freely in the market for national currencies, known as the *foreign exchange market*. Flexible exchange rates vary continually with changes in the supply of and demand for national currencies. In contrast, the value of a *fixed* exchange rate is set by the government at a constant level. Many large industrial countries, including Canada, have a flexible exchange rate. We will see that, in that case, a country's monetary policy plays a particularly important role in determining the exchange rate. Furthermore, in an open economy with a flexible exchange rate, the exchange rate becomes a tool of monetary policy, in much the same way as the real interest rate.

Although many large industrial countries have a flexible exchange rate, other economies fix their exchange rates, so we will consider the case of fixed exchange rates as well. We will explain first how a country's government (usually, its central bank) goes about maintaining a fixed exchange rate at the officially determined level. Though fixing the exchange rate generally reduces day-to-day fluctuations in the value of a nation's currency, we will see that, at times, a fixed exchange rate can become severely unstable, with potentially serious economic consequences. We will then discuss the relative merits of fixed and flexible exchange rates, and we will close the chapter by summarizing the effect of the exchange rate on the economy.

12.1   EXCHANGE RATES

Trade *between* nations usually involves dealing in different currencies. So, for example, if a Canadian resident wants to purchase an automobile manufactured in South Korea, she (or more likely, the automobile dealer) must first trade dollars for the Korean currency, called the won. The Korean car manufacturer is then paid in won. Similarly, an American who wants to purchase shares in a Canadian company (a Canadian financial asset) must first trade his U.S. dollars for Canadian dollars and then use the Canadian dollars to purchase the shares.

NOMINAL EXCHANGE RATES

Because international transactions generally require that one currency be traded for another, the relative values of different currencies are an important factor in international economic relations. The rate at which two currencies can be traded for each other is called the **nominal exchange rate**, or more simply the *exchange rate,* between the two currencies. For example, if one Canadian dollar can be exchanged for 100 Japanese yen, the nominal exchange rate between the Canadian and Japanese currencies is 100 yen/dollar. For a decade beginning in 1991, Argentina set the value of its currency so that it traded one-for-one with the U.S. dollar. That is, the nominal exchange rate between the Argentine peso and the U.S. dollar was 1 Argentine peso/U.S. dollar. Each country has many nominal exchange rates, one corresponding to each currency against which its own currency is traded. Thus the Canadian dollar's value can be quoted in terms of British pounds, Swedish kronor, Israeli shekels, Russian rubles, or dozens of other currencies. Table 12.1 gives exchange rates between the dollar and five other important currencies as of noon in Toronto on April 15, 2008.

nominal exchange rate the rate at which two currencies can be traded for each other

TABLE 12.1
Nominal Exchange Rates for the Canadian Dollar

Country	Foreign currency/dollar	Dollar/foreign currency
United States (dollar)	0.982	1.018
United Kingdom (pound)	0.500	1.998
Japan (yen)	99.500	0.010
Switzerland (Swiss franc)	0.984	1.016
Euro zone countries (euro)	0.622	1.609

*rates current as of April 15, 2008 at noon EST.
SOURCE: http://www.bankofcanada.ca/fmd/exchange.html.

As Table 12.1 shows, exchange rates can be expressed either as the amount of foreign currency needed to purchase one Canadian dollar (left column) or as the number of dollars needed to purchase one unit of the foreign currency (right column). These two ways of expressing the exchange rate are equivalent: Each is the reciprocal of the other. For example, on April 15, 2008, the Canadian–U.S. exchange rate could have been expressed either as 0.982 U.S. dollars per Canadian dollar or as 1.018 Canadian dollars per U.S. dollar, where 1.018 = 1/0.982.

EXAMPLE 12.1　　　**Nominal exchange rates**

Based on Table 12.1, find the exchange rate between the U.S. and British currencies. Express the exchange rate in both pounds per U.S. dollar and U.S. dollars per pound.

From Table 12.1, we see that 0.500 British pounds will buy a Canadian dollar, and that 0.982 U.S. dollars will buy a Canadian dollar. Therefore 0.500 British pounds and 0.982 U.S. dollars are equal in value:

$$0.500 \text{ pounds} = 0.982 \text{ U.S. dollars.}$$

Dividing both sides of this equation by 0.982, we get

$$0.509 \text{ pounds} = 1 \text{ U.S. dollar.}$$

In other words, the British–U.S. exchange rate can be expressed as 0.509 pounds per U.S. dollar. Alternatively, the exchange rate can be expressed as 1/0.509 = 1.965 U.S. dollars per pound.

EXERCISE 12.1　　　**From the business section of the newspaper or an online source (try the Bank of Canada Web site, www.bankofcanada.ca), find recent quotations of the value of the Canadian dollar against the British pound, the U.S. dollar, and the Japanese yen. Based on these data, find the exchange rate (a) between the pound and the U.S. dollar and (b) between the U.S. dollar and the yen. Express the exchange rates you derive in two ways (e.g., both as pounds per U.S. dollar and as U.S. dollars per pound).**

Figure 12.1 shows the nominal exchange rate for the Canadian dollar for 1971 to March 2008, relative to the U.S. dollar. You can see from Figure 12.1 that the Canadian dollar's value has fluctuated over time, sometimes increasing

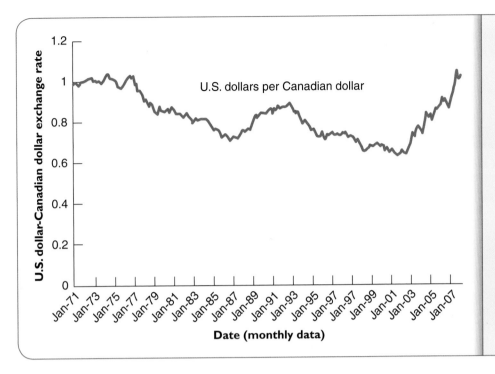

FIGURE 12.1

Canada's Nominal Exchange Rate, January 1971–March 2008
The figure expresses the value of the Canadian dollar relative to the U.S. dollar from 1971 to March 2008. The declining value of the Canadian dollar from the early 1990s until 2002 was a source of controversy in Canada. More recently, the sharply appreciating value of the Canadian dollar has been controversial.
SOURCE: Pacific Exchange Rate Service, http://fx.sauder.ubc.ca/.

(as in the periods 1986–1992 and 2003–2008) and sometimes decreasing (as in 1992–2002). An increase in the value of a currency relative to another currency is known as an **appreciation;** a decline in the value of a currency relative to another currency is called a **depreciation.** So we can say that the Canadian dollar appreciated in 1986–1992 and in 2003–2008, and depreciated in 1992–2002. We will discuss the reasons a currency may appreciate or depreciate later in this chapter.

In this chapter we will use the symbol e to stand for a country's nominal exchange rate. Although the exchange rate can be expressed either as foreign currency units per unit of domestic currency, or vice versa, as we saw in Table 12.1,

appreciation an increase in the value of a currency relative to another currency

depreciation a decrease in the value of a currency relative to another currency

"On the foreign-exchange markets today, the dollar fell against all major currencies and the doughnut."

let's agree to define *e* as *the number of units of the foreign currency that the domestic currency will buy.* For example, if we treat Canada as the "home" or "domestic" country and the United States as the "foreign" country, *e* will be defined as the number of U.S. dollars that one Canadian dollar will buy (e.g., 0.98 U.S. dollars per Canadian dollar). Defining the nominal exchange rate this way implies that an *increase* in *e* corresponds to an *appreciation,* or a strengthening, of the home currency, while a *decrease* in *e* implies a *depreciation,* or weakening, of the home currency.

FLEXIBLE VERSUS FIXED EXCHANGE RATES

As we saw in Figure 12.1, the exchange rate between the Canadian dollar and the U.S. dollar isn't constant, but rather varies continually. Indeed, changes in the value of the Canadian dollar occur daily, hourly, even minute by minute. Such fluctuations in the value of a currency are normal for countries like Canada, which have a *flexible* or *floating exchange rate.* The value of a **flexible exchange rate** is not officially fixed but varies according to the supply of and demand for the currency in the **foreign exchange market**—the market on which currencies of various nations are traded for one another. We will discuss the factors that determine the supply of and demand for currencies shortly.

Some countries do not allow their currency values to vary with market conditions but instead maintain a *fixed exchange rate.* The value of a **fixed exchange rate** is set by official government policy. (A government that establishes a fixed exchange rate typically determines the exchange rate's value independently, but sometimes exchange rates are set according to an agreement among a number of governments.) Some economies fix their exchange rates in terms of the U.S. dollar (Hong Kong, for example), but there are other possibilities. Some French-speaking African countries traditionally fixed the value of their currencies in terms of the French franc. Under the gold standard, which many countries used until its collapse during the Great Depression, currency values were fixed in terms of ounces of gold. In the past decade or so, fifteen countries of the European Union have fixed their exchange rates to a new currency, the euro. In the next part of the chapter we will focus on flexible exchange rates, but we will return later to the case of fixed rates. We will also discuss the costs and benefits of each type of exchange rate.

THE REAL EXCHANGE RATE

The nominal exchange rate tells us the price of the domestic currency in terms of a foreign currency. As we will see in this section, the *real exchange rate* tells us the price of the average domestic *good or service* in terms of the average foreign *good or service.* We will also see that a country's real exchange rate has important implications for its ability to sell its exports abroad.

To provide background for discussing the real exchange rate, imagine you are in charge of purchasing for a Canadian corporation that is planning to acquire a large number of new trucks. The company's transportation specialist has identified two models, one Japanese made and one Canadian made, that meet the necessary specifications. Since the two models are essentially equivalent, the company will buy the one with the lower price. However, since the trucks are priced in the currencies of the countries of manufacture, the price comparison is not so straightforward. Your job is to determine which of the two models is cheaper.

To complete your assignment you will need three pieces of information: the nominal exchange rate between the Canadian dollar and the yen and the prices of the two models in terms of the currencies of their countries of manufacture. Example 12.2 shows how you can use this information to determine which model is cheaper.

flexible exchange rate an exchange rate whose value is not officially fixed but varies according to the supply of and demand for the currency in the foreign exchange market

foreign exchange market the market on which currencies of various nations are traded for one another

fixed exchange rate an exchange rate whose value is set by official government policy

Comparing prices expressed in different currencies

EXAMPLE 12.2

A Canadian-made truck costs $24 000, and a similar Japanese-made truck costs 1 875 000 yen. If the nominal exchange rate happens to be 75 yen per dollar, which truck is the better buy?

To make this price comparison, we must measure the prices of both trucks in terms of the same currency. To make the comparison in dollars, we first convert the Japanese truck's price into dollars. The price in terms of Japanese yen is ¥1 875 000 (the symbol ¥ means "yen"), and we are told that ¥75 = $1. To find the dollar price of the truck, then, we observe that for any good or service,

Price in yen = Price in dollars × Value of dollar in terms of yen.

Note that the value of a dollar in terms of yen is just the yen–dollar exchange rate. Making this substitution and solving, we get

$$\text{Price in dollars} = \frac{\text{Price in yen}}{\text{Yen–dollar exchange rate}}$$

$$= \frac{¥1\,875\,000}{¥75/\$1} = \$25\,000.$$

Notice that the yen symbol appears in both the numerator and the denominator of the ratio, so it cancels out. Our conclusion is that the Canadian truck is cheaper than the Japanese truck at $24 000 or $1000 less than the price of the Japanese truck, $25 000. The Canadian truck is the better deal.

Continuing Example 12.2, compare the prices of the Japanese and Canadian trucks by expressing both prices in terms of yen.

In Example 12.2, the fact that the Canadian truck was cheaper implied that your firm would choose it over the Japanese-made truck. In general, a country's ability to compete in international markets depends in part on the prices of its goods and services *relative* to the prices of foreign goods and services, when the prices are measured in a common currency. In the hypothetical example of the Japanese and Canadian trucks, the price of the domestic (Canadian) good relative to the price of the foreign (Japanese) good is $24 000/$25 000, or 0.96. So the Canadian truck is 4 percent cheaper than the Japanese truck, putting the Japanese product at a competitive disadvantage.

More generally, economists ask whether *on average* the goods and services produced by a particular country are expensive relative to the goods and services produced by other countries. This question can be answered by the country's *real exchange rate*. Specifically, a country's **real exchange rate** is the price of the average domestic good or service *relative* to the price of the average foreign good or service, when prices are expressed in terms of a common currency.

To obtain a formula for the real exchange rate, recall that e equals the nominal exchange rate (the number of units of foreign currency per dollar) and that P equals the domestic price level, as measured, for example, by the consumer price index. We will use P as a measure of the price of the "average" domestic good or service. Similarly, let P^f equal the foreign price level. We will use P^f as the measure of the price of the "average" foreign good or service.

The real exchange rate equals the price of the average domestic good or service relative to the price of the average foreign good or service. It would not be correct, however, to define the real exchange rate as the ratio P/P^f, because the two price levels are expressed in different currencies. As we saw in Example 12.2,

real exchange rate the price of the average domestic good or service *relative* to the price of the average foreign good or service, when prices are expressed in terms of a common currency

to convert foreign prices into Canadian dollars we must divide the foreign price by the exchange rate. By this rule, the price in dollars of the average foreign good or service equals P^f/e. Now we can write the real exchange rate as

$$\text{Real exchange rate} = \frac{\text{Price of domestic good}}{\text{Price of foreign good, in dollars}}$$

$$= \frac{P}{P^f/e}.$$

To simplify this expression, multiply the numerator and denominator by e to get

$$\text{Real exchange rate} = \frac{eP}{P^f}, \tag{12.1}$$

which is the formula for the real exchange rate.[2]

To check this formula, let's use it to re-solve the truck example, Example 12.2. (For this exercise, we imagine that trucks are the only good produced by Canada and Japan, so the real exchange rate becomes just the price of Canadian trucks relative to Japanese trucks.) In that example, the nominal exchange rate e was ¥75/$1, the domestic price P (of a truck) was $24 000, and the foreign price P^f was ¥1 875 000. Applying Equation 12.1, we get

$$\text{Real exchange rate (for trucks)} = \frac{(¥75/\$1) \times \$24\,000}{¥1\,875\,000}$$

$$= \frac{¥1\,800\,000}{¥1\,875\,000}$$

$$= 0.96$$

which is the same answer we got earlier.

The real exchange rate, an overall measure of the cost of domestic goods relative to foreign goods, is an important economic variable. When the real exchange rate rises, domestic goods become more expensive relative to foreign goods (when priced in the same currency). An increase in the real exchange rate implies that domestic producers will have greater difficulty exporting to other countries (domestic goods have become "overpriced"), while foreign goods will sell well in the home country (because imported goods have become cheaper relative to goods produced at home). Since a higher real exchange rate tends to reduce exports and increase imports, we conclude that *net exports will tend to decrease when the real exchange rate increases.* Conversely, if the real exchange rate declines, then the home country will find it easier to export (because its goods are priced lower relative to those of foreign competitors), while domestic residents will buy few imports (because imports have become more expensive relative to domestic goods). Thus *net exports will tend to increase when the real exchange rate decreases.*

Equation 12.1 also shows that the real exchange rate tends to move in the same direction as the nominal exchange rate e (since e appears in the numerator of the

[2]Because both P and P^f are indexes, the real exchange rate for an economy is necessarily an index. The most frequently analyzed real exchange rate for the Canadian dollar is the U.S. dollar/Canadian dollar real exchange rate, and it is usually set equal to 1.0 for 1973. Back in 1973 the U.S. and Canadian dollars traded at par, meaning it cost one U.S. dollar to buy a Canadian dollar or that e was equal to 1.0. For the real exchange rate to equal 1.0 when e is equal to 1.0, the ratio of P and P^f must also be set to equal 1.0. Some economists set the ratio of the Canadian CPI to equal the U.S. CPI, whereas other economists set the ratio of the Canadian GDP deflator to equal the U.S. GDP deflator.

formula for the real exchange rate). To the extent that real and nominal exchange rates move in the same direction, we can conclude that net exports will be hurt by a high nominal exchange rate and helped by a low nominal exchange rate.

ECONOMIC Naturalist 12.1 Does a strong currency imply a strong economy?

Politicians and the public sometimes take pride in the fact that their national currency is "strong," meaning that its value in terms of other currencies is high or rising. Likewise, policy-makers sometimes view a depreciating ("weak") currency as a sign of economic failure. Does a strong currency necessarily imply a strong economy?

There are times, such as in 2006 in Canada, when the national currency is strong, real GDP growth is substantial, and the unemployment rate is low by historical standards. But contrary to popular opinion, there is no simple connection between the strength of a country's currency and the strength of its economy. For example, Figure 12.1 shows that the value of the Canadian dollar relative to the U.S. dollar was greater in the year 1992 than in the year 2000, though Canadian economic performance was considerably better in 2000 than in 1992, a period of deep recession and rising unemployment.

One reason a strong currency does not necessarily imply a strong economy is that an appreciating currency (an increase in e) tends to raise the real exchange rate (equal to eP/P^f), which may hurt a country's net exports. For example, if the Canadian dollar strengthens against the yen (that is, if a dollar buys more yen than before), Japanese goods will become cheaper in terms of dollars. The result may be that Canadians prefer to buy Japanese goods rather than goods produced at home. Likewise, a stronger dollar implies that each yen buys fewer dollars, so exported Canadian goods become more expensive to Japanese consumers. As Canadian goods become more expensive in terms of yen, the willingness of Japanese consumers to buy Canadian exports declines. A strong dollar may therefore imply lower sales and profits for Canadian industries that export, as well as for Canadian industries (like automobile manufacturers) that compete with foreign exporters for a share of the domestic Canadian market.

RECAP

EXCHANGE RATES

- The *nominal exchange rate* between two currencies is the rate at which the currencies can be traded for each other. More precisely, the nominal exchange rate e for any given country is the number of units of foreign currency that can be bought for one unit of the domestic currency.

- An *appreciation* is an increase in the value of a currency relative to other currencies (a rise in e); a *depreciation* is a decline in a currency's value (a fall in e).

- An exchange rate can be either *flexible*, meaning that it varies freely according to supply and demand for the currency in the foreign exchange market, or *fixed*, meaning that its value is fixed by official government policy.

- The *real exchange rate* is the price of the average domestic good or service *relative* to the price of the average foreign good or service, when prices are expressed in terms of a common currency. A useful formula for the real exchange rate is eP/P^f, where e is the nominal exchange rate, P is the domestic price level, and P^f is the foreign price level.

- An increase in the real exchange rate implies that domestic goods are becoming more expensive relative to foreign goods, which tends to reduce exports and stimulate imports. Conversely, a decline in the real exchange rate tends to increase net exports.

12.2 DETERMINATION OF FLEXIBLE EXCHANGE RATES

Countries that have flexible exchange rates, such as Canada, see the international values of their currencies change continually. What determines the value of the nominal exchange rate at any point in time? In this section we will try to answer this basic economic question. Again, our focus for the moment is on flexible exchange rates, whose values are determined by the foreign exchange market. Later in the chapter we discuss the case of fixed exchange rates.

A SIMPLE THEORY OF EXCHANGE RATES: PURCHASING POWER PARITY (PPP)

The most basic theory of how nominal exchange rates are determined is called *purchasing power parity*, or PPP. To understand this theory, we must first discuss a fundamental economic concept called *the law of one price*. The **law of one price** states that if transportation costs are relatively small, the price of an internationally traded commodity will be the same in all locations. For example, if transportation costs are not too large the price of a tonne of wheat ought to be the same in Bombay, India, and Sydney, Australia. Suppose that were not the case—that the price of wheat in Sydney were only half the price in Bombay. In that case grain merchants would have a strong incentive to buy wheat in Sydney and ship it to Bombay, where it could be sold at double the price of purchase. As wheat left Sydney, reducing the local supply, the price of wheat in Sydney would rise, while the inflow of wheat into Bombay would reduce the price in Bombay. According to the *equilibrium principle* (Chapter 3), the international market for wheat would return to equilibrium only when unexploited opportunities to profit had been eliminated—specifically, only when the prices of wheat in Sydney and in Bombay became equal or nearly equal (with the difference being less than the cost of transporting wheat from Australia to India).

law of one price if transportation costs are relatively small, the price of an internationally traded commodity will be the same in all locations

EQUILIBRIUM

If the law of one price were to hold for all goods and services (which is not a realistic assumption, as we will see shortly), then the value of the nominal exchange rate would be determined, as Example 12.3 illustrates.

EXAMPLE 12.3	How many Indian rupees equal one Australian dollar? (1)

Suppose that a tonne of wheat costs 475 Australian dollars in Sydney and 17 575 rupees in Bombay. If the law of one price holds for wheat, what is the nominal exchange rate between Australia and India?

Because the market value of a tonne of wheat must be the same in both locations, we know that the Australian price of wheat must equal the Indian price of wheat so that

475 Australian dollars = 17 575 Indian rupees.

Dividing by 475, we get

1 Australian dollar = 37 Indian rupees.

So the nominal exchange rate between Australia and India should be 37 rupees per Australian dollar.

EXERCISE 12.3

The price of gold is U.S.$930/ounce in New York and 5580 kronor/ounce in Stockholm, Sweden. If the law of one price holds for gold, what is the nominal exchange rate between the U.S. dollar and the Swedish krona?

Example 12.3 and Exercise 12.3 illustrate the application of the purchasing power parity theory. According to the **purchasing power parity** (PPP) theory, nominal exchange rates are determined as necessary for the law of one price to hold.

A particularly useful prediction of the PPP theory is that in the long run, the *currencies of countries that experience relatively high inflation will tend to depreciate against the currencies of countries that experience relatively low inflation.* To see why, we will extend the analysis in Example 12.4.

purchasing power parity (PPP) the theory that nominal exchange rates are determined as necessary for the law of one price to hold

How many Indian rupees equal one Australian dollar? (2)

EXAMPLE 12.4

Suppose India experiences very high inflation so that the price of a tonne of wheat in Bombay rises from 17 575 to 35 150 rupees. Australia has no inflation, so the price of wheat in Sydney remains unchanged at 475 Australian dollars. If the law of one price holds for wheat, what will happen to the nominal exchange rate between Australia and India?

As in Example 12.3, we know that the market value of a tonne of wheat must be the same in both locations. Therefore,

475 Australian dollars = 35 150 rupees.

Equivalently,

1 Australian dollar = 74 rupees.

The nominal exchange rate is now 74 rupees/Australian dollar. Before India's inflation, the nominal exchange rate was 37 rupees/Australian dollar (Example 12.3). So in this example, inflation has caused the rupee to depreciate against the Australian dollar. Conversely, Australia, with no inflation, has seen its currency appreciate against the rupee.

This link between inflation and depreciation makes economic sense. Inflation implies that a nation's currency is losing purchasing power in the domestic market. Analogously, exchange rate depreciation implies that the nation's currency is losing purchasing power in international markets.

Figure 12.2 shows annual rates of inflation and nominal exchange rate depreciation for the 10 largest South American countries from 1995 to 2001, a period during which several of these countries experienced high inflation. Inflation is measured as the annual rate of change in the country's consumer price index; depreciation is measured relative to the U.S. dollar. As you can see, inflation varied greatly among South American countries during the period. For example, Argentina's inflation rate was essentially the same as that of the United States, while Venezuela had inflation of 37 percent per year and Ecuador's inflation was 45 percent per year.

Figure 12.2 shows that, as the PPP theory implies, countries with the highest inflation during the 1995–2001 period tended to experience the most rapid depreciation of their currencies.

SHORTCOMINGS OF THE PPP THEORY

Empirical studies have found that the PPP theory is useful for predicting some of the change in nominal exchange rates over the relatively long run. However, the theory is less successful in predicting short-run movements in exchange rates,

FIGURE 12.2

Inflation and Currency Depreciation in South America, 1995–2001

The annual rates of inflation and nominal exchange-rate depreciation (relative to the U.S. dollar) in 10 South American countries varied considerably during 1995–2001. High inflation was associated with rapid depreciation of the nominal exchange rate.

SOURCE: International Monetary Fund, *International Financial Statistics*, and authors' calculations.

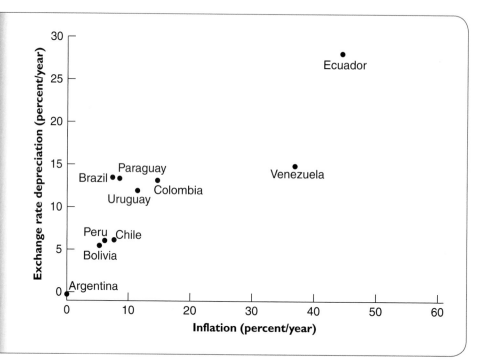

except where very high inflation causes rapid depreciation of a country's exchange rate, as shown in Figure 12.2.

A particularly dramatic failure of the PPP theory occurred in Canada beginning in the 1990s. As Figure 12.1 indicates, between 1992 and 2002 the value of the Canadian dollar fell nearly 30 percent relative to the U.S. dollar. This strong depreciation could be explained by PPP theory only if inflation were considerably higher in Canada than in the U.S. In fact, inflation was slightly lower in Canada than in the United States throughout the period.

Another example is the recent behaviour of the Brazilian real, one of the currencies shown in Figure 12.2. Over the 2004–2007 period, Brazilian inflation exceeded U.S. inflation by about 2 percentage points per year; inflation in Brazil averaged 5.3 percent compared to 3 percent in the United States. But over this same period, the Brazilian real appreciated strongly against the U.S. dollar, moving from 2.85 reais per U.S. dollar in January 2004 to 1.79 reais per U.S. dollar in December 2007.

Why does the PPP theory work less than perfectly at best, and less well in the short run (say, under a decade) than in the long run? Recall that this theory relies on the law of one price, which says that the price of an internationally traded commodity must be the same in all locations. The law of one price works well for goods such as wheat or gold, which are standardized commodities that are traded widely. However, *not all goods and services are traded internationally,* and *not all goods are standardized commodities.*

Many goods and services are not traded internationally, because the assumption underlying the law of one price—that transportation costs are relatively small—does not hold for them. For example, for Indians to export haircuts to Australia, they would need to transport an Indian barber to Australia every time a Sydney resident desired a trim. Because transportation costs prevent haircuts from being traded internationally, the law of one price does not apply to them. Thus, even if the price of haircuts in Australia were double the price of haircuts in India, market forces would not necessarily influence prices toward equality in the short run. (Over the long run, some Indian barbers might emigrate to Australia.) Other examples of non-traded goods and services are agricultural land, buildings, heavy construction materials (whose value is low relative to their transportation costs), and highly perishable foods. In addition, some products use non-traded goods and services as inputs: A McDonald's hamburger served in Moscow has both a tradable component (frozen hamburger patties) and a non-tradable component (the labour of counter workers). In general, the greater the share of non-traded goods and services in a nation's output, the less precisely the PPP theory will apply to the country's exchange rate.[3]

www.economist.com/
markets/bigmac/index.cfm

The second reason the law of one price and the PPP theory sometimes fails to apply is that not all internationally traded goods and services are perfectly standardized commodities, like grain or gold. For example, Canadian-made automobiles and Japanese-made automobiles are not identical; they differ in styling, horsepower, reliability, and other features. As a result, some people strongly prefer one nation's cars to the other's. Thus if Japanese cars cost 10 percent more than Canadian cars, Canadian automobile exports will not necessarily flood the Japanese market, since many Japanese will still prefer Japanese-made cars even at a 10-percent premium. Of course, there are limits to how far prices can diverge before people will switch to the cheaper product. But the law of one price, and hence the PPP theory, will not apply exactly to non-standardized goods.

To summarize, the PPP theory often works reasonably well as an explanation of exchange rate behaviour over the long run, though it is not perfect. Because transportation costs limit international trade in many goods and services, and because not all goods that are traded are standardized commodities, the law of one price (on which the PPP theory is based) works only imperfectly. In the short run, except when inflation rate differences between countries are very large, PPP theory has severe shortcomings. To understand the short-run movements of exchange rates, we need to incorporate some additional factors. In the next section we will study a supply and demand framework for the determination of exchange rates.

THE DETERMINATION OF THE EXCHANGE RATE: A SUPPLY AND DEMAND ANALYSIS

Although the PPP theory helps to explain the long-run behaviour of the exchange rate, supply and demand analysis is more useful for studying its short-run behaviour. As we will see, Canadian dollars are demanded in the foreign exchange market by foreigners who seek to purchase Canadian goods and assets, and are supplied by Canadian residents who need foreign currencies to buy foreign goods and assets. The equilibrium exchange rate is the value of the dollar that equates the number of dollars supplied and demanded in the foreign exchange market. In this section we will discuss the factors that affect the supply of and demand for dollars, and thus the Canadian exchange rate.

The Supply of Canadian Dollars

Anyone who holds Canadian dollars is a potential supplier of them to the foreign exchange market. In practice, however, the principal suppliers of dollars to the foreign exchange market are Canadian households and firms. Why would a Canadian household or firm want to supply dollars in exchange for foreign currency? There are two major reasons. First, a Canadian household or firm may need foreign currency *to purchase foreign goods or services*. For example, a Canadian electronics retailer may need U.S. dollars to purchase U.S. computers, or a Canadian tourist may need U.S. dollars to make purchases in New York. Second, a Canadian household or firm may need foreign currency *to purchase foreign assets*. For example, a Canadian mutual fund may wish to acquire stocks issued

---

[3]Trade barriers, such as tariffs and quotas, also increase the costs associated with shipping goods from one country to another. Thus trade barriers reduce the applicability of the law of one price in much the same way that physical transportation costs do.

by U.S. companies, or an individual Canadian saver may want to purchase U.S. government bonds. Because U.S. assets are priced in U.S. dollars, the Canadian household or firm will need to trade Canadian dollars for U.S. dollars to acquire these assets.

The supply of Canadian dollars to the foreign exchange market is illustrated in Figure 12.3. We will focus on the market in which Canadian dollars are traded for U.S. dollars, but bear in mind that similar markets exist for every other pair of traded currencies. The vertical axis of the figure shows the Canadian–U.S. exchange rate as measured by the number of U.S. dollars that can be purchased with each Canadian dollar. The horizontal axis shows the number of Canadian dollars being traded in the U.S. dollar–Canadian dollar market.

FIGURE 12.3

The Supply and Demand for Canadian Dollars in the U.S. Dollar–Canadian Dollar Market

The supply of Canadian dollars to the foreign exchange market is upward sloping, because an increase in the number of U.S. dollars offered for each Canadian dollar makes U.S. goods, services, and assets more attractive to Canadian buyers. Similarly, the demand for Canadian dollars is downward sloping, because holders of U.S. dollars will be less willing to buy Canadian dollars the more expensive they are in terms of U.S. dollars. The equilibrium exchange rate e^* equates the quantities of Canadian dollars supplied and demanded.

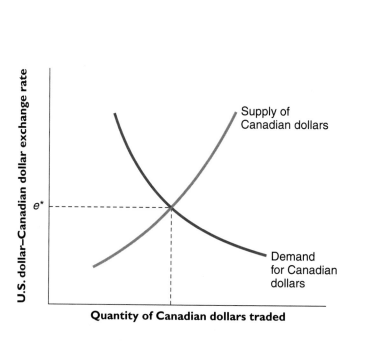

Note that the supply curve for Canadian dollars is upward-sloping. In other words, the more U.S. dollars each Canadian dollar can buy, the more Canadian dollars people are willing to supply to the foreign exchange market. Why? At given prices for U.S. goods, services, and assets, the more U.S. dollars a Canadian dollar can buy, the cheaper those goods, services, and assets will be in Canadian-dollar terms. For example, if a wooden hockey stick costs $30 in the U.S., and a Canadian dollar can buy 0.75 U.S. dollars, the Canadian-dollar price of the hockey stick will be $40. However, if a Canadian dollar can buy one U.S. dollar, then the Canadian-dollar price of the same hockey stick will be $30. Assuming that lower Canadian-dollar prices will induce Canadians to increase their expenditures on U.S. goods, services, and assets, a higher U.S. dollar–Canadian dollar exchange rate will increase the supply of dollars to the foreign exchange market. Thus the supply curve for dollars is upward sloping.

The Demand for Canadian Dollars

In the U.S. dollar–Canadian dollar foreign exchange market, demanders of Canadian dollars are those who wish to acquire Canadian dollars in exchange for U.S. dollars. Most demanders of Canadian dollars in the U.S. dollar–Canadian dollar market are U.S. households and firms, although anyone who happens to hold U.S. dollars is free to trade them for Canadian dollars. Why demand dollars? The reasons for acquiring Canadian dollars are analogous to those for acquiring U.S. dollars. First, households and firms that hold U.S. dollars will demand Canadian dollars *so that they can purchase Canadian goods and services*. For example, a U.S. firm that wants to license Canadian-produced software needs Canadian dollars to pay the required fees, and a U.S. student studying in a Canadian university must pay tuition in Canadian dollars. The firm or the student can acquire the necessary Canadian dollars only by offering U.S. dollars in exchange. Second, households and firms demand Canadian dollars *in order to purchase Canadian assets*. The purchase of Toronto real estate by a U.S. company or the acquisition of Bombardier stock by a U.S. pension fund are two examples.

The demand for dollars is represented by the downward-sloping curve in Figure 12.3. The curve slopes downward because the more U.S. dollars a U.S. citizen must pay to acquire a Canadian dollar, the less attractive Canadian goods, services, and assets will be. Hence, the demand for dollars will be low when Canadian dollars are expensive in terms of U.S. dollars and high when Canadian dollars are cheap in terms of U.S. dollars.

The Equilibrium Value of the Canadian Dollar

As mentioned earlier, Canada maintains a flexible, or floating, exchange rate, which means that the value of the Canadian dollar is determined by the forces of supply and demand in the foreign exchange market. In Figure 12.3 the equilibrium value of the dollar is e^*, the U.S. dollar–Canadian dollar exchange rate at which the quantity of dollars supplied equals the quantity of dollars demanded. The equilibrium value of the exchange rate is also called the **fundamental value of the exchange rate**. In general, the equilibrium value of the dollar is not constant but changes with shifts in the supply of and demand for dollars in the foreign exchange market.

fundamental value of the exchange rate (or equilibrium exchange rate) the exchange rate that equates the quantities of the currency supplied and demanded in the foreign exchange market

CHANGES IN THE SUPPLY OF CANADIAN DOLLARS

Recall that people supply Canadian dollars to the U.S. dollar–Canadian dollar foreign exchange market in order to purchase U.S. goods, services, and assets. Factors that affect the desire of Canadian households and firms to acquire U.S. goods, services, and assets will therefore affect the supply of Canadian dollars to the foreign exchange market. Some factors that will *increase* the supply of Canadian dollars, shifting the supply curve for Canadian dollars to the right, include:

- An increased preference for U.S. goods. For example, suppose that U.S. firms produce some popular new consumer electronics, such as MP3 players. To acquire the U.S. dollars needed to buy these goods, Canadian importers will increase their supply of Canadian dollars to the foreign exchange market.

- An increase in Canadian real GDP. An increase in Canadian real GDP will raise the incomes of Canadians, allowing them to consume more goods and services (recall the consumption function, introduced in Chapter 8). Some part of this increase in consumption will take the form of goods imported from the U.S. (recall the discussion of the marginal propensity to import in Chapter 8). To buy more U.S. goods, Canadians will supply more Canadian dollars to acquire the necessary U.S. dollars.

- An increase in the real interest rate on U.S. assets. Recall that Canadian households and firms acquire U.S. dollars in order to purchase U.S. assets as well as goods and services. Other factors such as risk held constant, the higher the real interest rate paid by U.S. assets, the more U.S. assets Canadians will choose to hold. To purchase additional U.S. assets, Canadians households and firms will supply more Canadian dollars to the foreign exchange market.

Conversely, reduced demand for U.S. goods, a lower Canadian GDP, or a lower real interest rate on U.S. assets will *reduce* the number of U.S. dollars Canadians need, in turn reducing their supply of dollars to the foreign exchange market and shifting the supply curve for dollars to the left. Of course, any shift in the supply curve for dollars will affect the equilibrium exchange rate, as Example 12.5 shows.

EXAMPLE 12.5	Hockey sticks, the U.S. dollar, and the Canadian dollar

Suppose U.S.–based firms come to dominate the hockey stick market with sticks of increased quality relative to those produced in Canada. All else being equal, how will this change affect the relative value of the U.S. dollar and the Canadian dollar?

FIGURE 12.4

An Increase in the Supply of Canadian Dollars Lowers the Value of the Canadian Dollar
Increased Canadian demand for U.S. hockey sticks forces Canadians to supply more Canadian dollars to the foreign exchange market to acquire the U.S. dollars they need to buy the sticks. The supply curve for Canadian dollars shifts from S to S′, lowering the value of the Canadian dollar in terms of the U.S. dollar. The fundamental value of the exchange rate falls from e* to e*′.

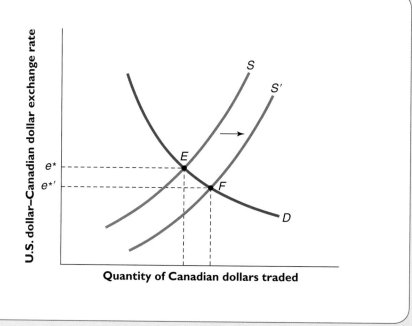

The increased quality of U.S. hockey sticks will increase the demand for the sticks in Canada. To acquire the U.S. dollars necessary to buy more U.S. hockey sticks, Canadian importers will supply more Canadian dollars to the foreign exchange market. As Figure 12.4 shows, the increased supply of dollars will reduce the value of the dollar. In other words, a Canadian dollar will buy fewer U.S. dollars than it did before. At the same time, the U.S. dollar will increase in value: a given number of U.S. dollars will buy more Canadian dollars than it did before.

EXERCISE 12.4   **Canada goes into a recession, and real GDP falls. All else being equal, how is this economic weakness likely to affect the value of the Canadian dollar?**

CHANGES IN THE DEMAND FOR CANADIAN DOLLARS

The factors that can cause a change in the demand for dollars in the foreign exchange market, and thus a shift of the dollar demand curve, are analogous to the factors that affect the supply of dollars. Factors that will *increase* the demand for dollars include:

- An increased preference for Canadian goods. For example, U.S. executives might decide to buy more Bombardier planes. To buy the Canadian aircraft, U.S. firms would demand more Canadian dollars on the foreign exchange market.

- An increase in real GDP abroad, which implies higher incomes abroad, and thus more demand for imports from Canada.

- An increase in the real interest rate on Canadian assets, which would make those assets more attractive to foreign savers. To acquire Canadian assets, U.S. savers would demand more Canadian dollars.

MONETARY POLICY AND THE FLEXIBLE EXCHANGE RATE

Of the many factors that could influence a country's exchange rate, among the most important is the monetary policy of the country's central bank. As we mentioned in earlier chapters, monetary policy affects the exchange rate primarily through its effect on the real interest rate.

Suppose the Bank of Canada is concerned about inflation and raises real interest rates in response. The effects of this policy change on the value of the Canadian dollar are shown in Figure 12.5. Before the policy change, the equilibrium value of the exchange rate is e^*, at the intersection of supply curve S and the demand curve D (point E in the figure). The increase in the Canadian real interest rate, r, makes Canadian assets more attractive to foreign financial investors. The increased willingness of foreign investors to buy Canadian assets increases the demand for dollars, shifting the demand curve rightward from D to D' and the equilibrium point from E to F. As a result of this increase in demand, the equilibrium value of the dollar rises from e^* to $e^{*\prime}$.

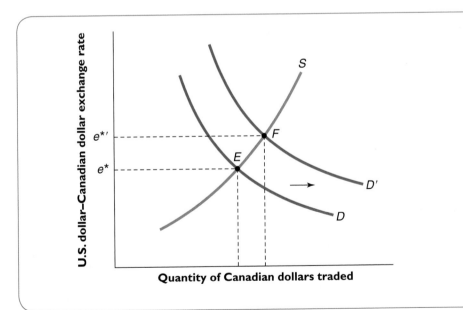

FIGURE 12.5

An Increase in the Real Interest Rate Strengthens the Canadian Dollar
When the Bank of Canada raises the real interest rate, it increases the demand for Canadian assets by foreign investors. An increased demand for Canadian assets in turn increases the demand for Canadian dollars. The demand curve shifts from D to D', leading the exchange rate to appreciate from e^* to $e^{*\prime}$.

In short, an increase in the real interest rate engineered by the Bank of Canada raises the demand for Canadian dollars, causing the Canadian dollar to appreciate. By similar logic, a reduction of the real interest rate by the Bank of Canada would weaken the demand for the Canadian dollar, causing it to depreciate.

In an economic model with fixed net exports, monetary policy affects aggregate demand solely through the real interest rate. For example, by raising the real interest rate, a tight monetary policy reduces consumption and private-sector investment spending. However, the real interest rate affects the exchange rate so the exchange rate serves as another channel for monetary policy, one that reinforces the effects of the real interest rate.

To illustrate, suppose that policy-makers are concerned about inflation and decide to restrain aggregate demand. To do so, they increase the real interest rate, reducing consumption and private-sector investment spending. But, as Figure 12.5 shows, the higher real interest rate also increases the demand for Canadian dollars, causing the dollar to appreciate. The stronger dollar, in turn, further reduces aggregate demand. Why? As we saw in discussing the real exchange rate, a stronger dollar reduces the cost of imported goods, increasing imports. It also makes Canadian exports more costly to foreign buyers, which tends to reduce exports. Recall that net exports—or exports minus imports—is one of the four components of aggregate demand. Thus, by reducing exports and increasing imports, a stronger dollar (more precisely, a higher real exchange rate) reduces aggregate demand.

In sum, when the exchange rate is flexible, a higher real interest rate reduces net exports (through a stronger dollar) as well as consumption and private-sector investment spending (through a higher real interest rate). Conversely, a lower real interest rate weakens the dollar and stimulates net exports, reinforcing the effect of the lower real interest rate on consumption and private-sector investment spending. Thus, relative to the case of a closed economy that we emphasized earlier, *monetary policy is more effective in an open economy with a flexible exchange rate.*

It is widely recognized that real interest rates (particularly long-term ones) in small open economies like Canada's will be influenced by foreign interest rates. It is worth noting that a flexible exchange rate is typically seen as increasing the power of the central bank in a small open economy like Canada's to maintain a real interest rate different from the real foreign interest rate—say, the U.S. rate. When the central bank of a small open economy raises the domestic real interest rate, for example, the net capital inflow (a concept discussed further in Chapter 17) will tend to increase and push up the value of the domestic currency. But as the value of the domestic currency rises, investors will start judging both that the currency is above its normal level and that it will eventually depreciate. The higher domestic real interest rate will be seen as a premium associated with the risk of currency depreciation, and this perception will slow net capital inflow and hence slow the return of the real interest rate back toward its original level.[4]

RECAP

DETERMINING THE EXCHANGE RATE

- The most basic theory of nominal exchange rate determination, *purchasing power parity (PPP),* is based on the law of one price. The *law of one price* states that if transportation costs are relatively small, the price of an internationally traded commodity must be the same in all locations. According to the PPP theory, the nominal exchange rate between two currencies can be found by setting the price of a traded commodity in one currency equal to the price of the same commodity expressed in the second currency.

---

[4]In the early 1990s when the Canadian dollar was exceptionally strong relative to the U.S. dollar, the real interest rate on Canadian long-term government bonds exceeded the rate on comparable U.S. bonds by about 2 percentage points for a few years.

- A useful prediction of the PPP theory is that the currencies of countries with relatively high inflation will tend to depreciate against the currencies of countries that experience relatively low inflation. However, the fact that many goods and services are non-traded, and that not all traded goods are standardized, reduces the applicability of the law of one price, and hence of the PPP theory. Thus the theory has severe shortcomings for short-run analysis.

- Supply and demand analysis is a useful tool for studying the short-run determination of the exchange rate. Canadian households and firms supply Canadian dollars to the foreign exchange market to acquire foreign currencies, which they need to purchase foreign goods, services, and assets. Foreigners demand Canadian dollars in the foreign exchange market to purchase Canadian goods, services, and assets. The equilibrium exchange rate, also called the *fundamental value of the exchange rate,* equates the quantities of dollars supplied and demanded in the foreign exchange market.

- An increased preference for foreign goods, an increase in Canadian real GDP, or an increase in the real interest rate on foreign assets will increase the supply of dollars on the foreign exchange market, lowering the value of the dollar. An increased preference for Canadian goods by foreigners, an increase in real GDP abroad, or an increase in the real interest rate on Canadian assets will increase the demand for dollars, raising the value of the dollar.

- If the Bank of Canada raises the real interest rate, it will tend to increase the demand for Canadian dollars and thereby strengthen the Canadian dollar. A stronger dollar reinforces the effects of tight monetary policy on aggregate spending by reducing net exports, a component of aggregate demand. Conversely, if the Bank of Canada lowers the real interest rate, it will tend to weaken the Canadian dollar.

12.3 FIXED EXCHANGE RATES

So far we have focused on the case of flexible exchange rates, the relevant case for many industrial countries like Canada. However, the alternative approach, fixing the exchange rate, has been quite important historically and is still used in many countries, especially small or developing nations. In this section we will see how our conclusions change when the nominal exchange rate is fixed rather than flexible. One important difference is that when a country maintains a fixed exchange rate, its ability to use monetary policy as a stabilization tool is greatly reduced.

HOW TO FIX AN EXCHANGE RATE

In contrast to a flexible exchange rate, whose value is determined solely by supply and demand in the foreign exchange market, the value of a fixed exchange rate is determined by the government (in practice, usually the finance ministry or treasury department, with the cooperation of the central bank). Today, the value of a fixed exchange rate is usually set in terms of a major currency (for instance, Hong Kong pegs its currency to the U.S. dollar), or relative to a "basket" of currencies, typically those of the country's trading partners. Historically, currency values were often fixed in terms of gold or other precious metals, but in recent decades precious metals have rarely, if ever, been used for that purpose.

Once an exchange rate has been fixed, the government usually attempts to keep it unchanged for some time.[5] However, sometimes economic circumstances force the government to change the value of the exchange rate. A reduction in the official value of a currency is called a **devaluation**; an increase in the official value is called a **revaluation**. The devaluation of a fixed exchange rate is analogous to the depreciation of a flexible exchange rate; both involve a reduction in the currency's value. Conversely, a revaluation is analogous to an appreciation.

The supply and demand diagram we used to study flexible exchange rates can be adapted to analyze fixed exchange rates. Let's consider the case of a country called Latinia, whose currency is called the peso. Figure 12.6 shows the supply of and demand for the Latinian peso in the foreign exchange market. Pesos are *supplied* to the foreign exchange market by Latinian households and firms who want to acquire foreign currencies to purchase foreign goods and assets. Pesos are *demanded* by holders of foreign currencies who need pesos to purchase Latinian goods and assets. Figure 12.6 shows that the quantities of pesos supplied and demanded in the foreign exchange market are equal when a peso equals 0.1 U.S. dollars (10 pesos to the U.S. dollar). Hence 0.1 U.S. dollars per peso is the *fundamental value* of the peso. If Latinia had a flexible-exchange-rate system, the peso would trade at 10 pesos to the U.S. dollar in the foreign exchange market.

devaluation a reduction in the official value of a currency (in a fixed-exchange-rate system)

revaluation an increase in the official value of a currency (in a fixed-exchange-rate system)

FIGURE 12.6

An Overvalued Exchange Rate

The peso's official value (0.125 U.S. dollars) is shown as greater than its fundamental value (0.10 U.S. dollars), as determined by supply and demand in the foreign exchange market. Thus the peso is overvalued. To maintain the fixed value, the government must purchase pesos in the quantity *AB* each period.

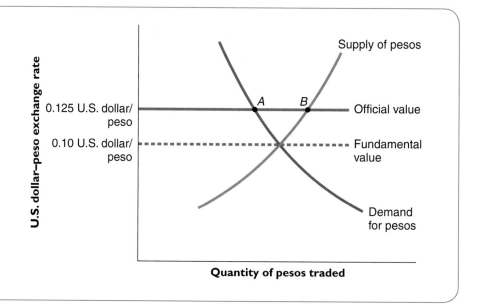

But let's suppose that Latinia has a fixed exchange rate and that the government has decreed the value of the Latinian peso to be 8 pesos to the U.S. dollar, or 0.125 U.S. dollars per peso. This official value of the peso, 0.125 U.S. dollars, is indicated by the solid horizontal line in Figure 12.6. Notice that it is greater than the fundamental value, corresponding to the intersection of the supply and demand curves. When the officially fixed value of an exchange rate is greater than its fundamental value, the exchange rate is said to be **overvalued**. The official

overvalued exchange rate an exchange rate that has an officially fixed value greater than its fundamental value

---

[5]There are exceptions to this statement. Some countries employ a *crawling peg* system, under which the exchange rate is fixed at a value that changes in a preannounced way over time. For example, the government may announce that the value of the fixed exchange rate will fall 2 percent each year. Other countries use a *target zone* system, in which the exchange rate is allowed to deviate by a small amount from its fixed value. To focus on the key issues, we will assume that the exchange rate is fixed at a single value for a protracted period.

value of an exchange rate can also be lower than its fundamental value, in which case the exchange rate is said to be **undervalued**.

In this example, Latinia's commitment to hold the peso at 8 to the U.S. dollar is inconsistent with the fundamental value of 10 to the U.S. dollar, as determined by supply and demand in the foreign exchange market (the Latinian peso is over-valued). How could the Latinian government deal with this inconsistency? There are several possibilities. First, Latinia could simply devalue its currency, from 0.125 U.S. dollars per peso to 0.10 U.S. dollars per peso, which would bring the peso's official value into line with its fundamental value. As we will see, devaluation is often the ultimate result of an overvaluation of a currency. However, a country with a fixed exchange rate will be reluctant to change the official value of its exchange rate every time the fundamental value changes. If a country must continually adjust its exchange rate to market conditions, it might as well switch to a flexible exchange rate.

As a second alternative, Latinia could try to maintain its overvalued exchange rate by restricting international transactions. Imposing quotas on imports and prohib-iting domestic households and firms from acquiring foreign assets would effectively reduce the supply of pesos to the foreign exchange market, raising the fundamental value of the currency. An even more extreme action would be to prohibit Latinians from exchanging the peso for other currencies without government approval, a policy that would effectively allow the government to determine directly the supply of pesos to the foreign exchange market. Such measures might help to maintain the official value of the peso. However, restrictions on trade and capital flows are costly to the economy, because they reduce the gains from specialization and trade and deny domestic households and firms access to foreign capital markets.

The third and most widely used approach to maintaining an overvalued exchange rate is for the government to become a demander of its own currency in the foreign exchange market. Figure 12.6 shows that at the official exchange rate of 0.125 U.S. dollars per peso, the private-sector supply of pesos (point *B*) exceeds the private-sector demand for pesos (point *A*). To keep the peso from falling below its official value, in each period the Latinian government could purchase a quantity of pesos in the foreign exchange market equal to the length of the line segment *AB* in Figure 12.6. If the government followed this strategy, then at the official exchange rate of 0.125 U.S. dollars per peso, the total demand for pesos (private demand at point *A* plus government demand *AB*) would equal the private supply of pesos (point *B*). This situation is analogous to government attempts to keep the price of a commodity, like grain or milk, above its market level. To maintain an official price of grain that is above the market-clearing price, the government must stand ready to purchase the excess supply of grain forthcoming at the official price. In the same way, to keep the "price" of its cur-rency above the market-clearing level, the government must buy the excess pesos supplied at the official price.

To be able to purchase its own currency and maintain an overvalued exchange rate, the government (usually the central bank) must hold foreign currency assets, called **international reserves**, or simply *reserves*. For example, the Latinian central bank may hold U.S.-dollar deposits in banks or U.S. government debt, which it can trade for pesos in the foreign exchange market as needed. In the situation shown in Figure 12.6, to keep the peso at its official value, in each period the Lati-nian central bank will have to spend an amount of international reserves equal to the length of the line segment *AB*.

Because a country with an overvalued exchange rate must use part of its reserves to support the value of its currency in each period, over time its available reserves will decline. The net decline in a country's stock of international reserves over a year is called its **balance-of-payments deficit**. Conversely, if a country experiences a net increase in its international reserves over the year, the increase is called its **balance-of-payments surplus**.

undervalued exchange rate
an exchange rate that has an officially fixed value less than its fundamental value

international reserves
foreign currency assets held by a government for the purpose of purchasing the domestic currency in the foreign exchange market

balance-of-payments deficit
the net decline in a country's stock of international reserves over a year

balance-of-payments surplus
the net increase in a country's stock of international reserves over a year

EXAMPLE 12.6	Latinia's balance-of-payments deficit

The demand for and supply of Latinian pesos in the foreign exchange market are

$$\text{Demand} = 25\,000 - 50\,000e,$$
$$\text{Supply} = 17\,600 + 24\,000e,$$

where the Latinian exchange rate e is measured in U.S. dollars per peso. Officially, the value of the peso is 0.125 U.S. dollars. Find the fundamental value of the peso and the Latinian balance-of-payments deficit, measured in both pesos and U.S. dollars.

To find the fundamental value of the peso, equate the demand and supply for pesos:

$$25\,000 - 50\,000e = 17\,600 + 24\,000e.$$

Solving for e, we get

$$7400 = 74\,000e$$
$$e = 0.10.$$

So the fundamental value of the exchange rate is 0.10 U.S. dollars per peso, as in Figure 12.6.

At the official exchange rate, 0.125 U.S. dollars/peso, the demand for pesos is $25\,000 - 50\,000(0.125) = 18\,750$, and the supply of pesos is $17\,600 + 24\,000(0.125) = 20\,600$. Thus the quantity of pesos supplied to the foreign exchange market exceeds the quantity of pesos demanded by $20\,600 - 18\,750 = 1850$ pesos. To maintain the fixed rate, the Latinian government must purchase 1850 pesos per period, which is the Latinian balance-of-payments deficit. Since pesos are purchased at the official rate of 8 pesos to the U.S. dollar, the balance-of-payments deficit in U.S. dollars is (1850 pesos) × (0.125 U.S. dollars/peso) = $(1850/8) = $231.25.

EXERCISE 12.5 **Repeat Example 12.6 under the assumption that the fixed value of the peso is 0.15 U.S. dollars/peso. What do you conclude about the relationship between the degree of currency overvaluation and the resulting balance-of-payments deficit?**

Although a government can maintain an overvalued exchange rate for a time by offering to buy back its own currency at the official price, there is a limit to this strategy, since no government's stock of international reserves is infinite. Unless the demand and supply situation for pesos happens to change in a favourable way, the government will eventually run out of reserves, and the fixed exchange rate will collapse. The collapse of a fixed exchange rate can be quite sudden and dramatic.

EXERCISE 12.6 **Diagram a case in which a fixed exchange rate is *undervalued* rather than overvalued. Show that, to maintain the fixed exchange rate, the central bank must use domestic currency to purchase foreign currency in the foreign exchange market. With an undervalued exchange rate, is the country's central bank in danger of running out of international reserves? (*Hint:* Keep in mind that a central bank is always free to print more of its own currency.)**

MONETARY POLICY AND THE FIXED EXCHANGE RATE

We have seen that there is no really satisfactory way of maintaining a fixed exchange rate above its fundamental value for an extended period. A central bank can maintain an overvalued exchange rate for a time by using international reserves to buy up the excess supply of its currency in the foreign exchange market. But a country's international reserves are limited and may eventually be exhausted by the attempt to keep the exchange rate artificially high.

An alternative to trying to maintain an overvalued exchange rate is to take actions that increase the fundamental value of the exchange rate. If the exchange rate's fundamental value can be raised enough to equal its official value, then the overvaluation problem will be eliminated. The most effective way to change the exchange rate's fundamental value is through monetary policy. As we saw earlier in the chapter, a monetary policy that raises the real interest rate will increase the demand for the domestic currency, as domestic assets become more attractive to foreign financial investors. Increased demand for the currency will in turn raise its fundamental value.

The use of monetary policy to support a fixed exchange rate is shown in Figure 12.7. At first, the demand for and supply of the Latinian peso in the foreign exchange market are given by the curves *D* and *S,* so the fundamental value of the peso equals 0.10 U.S. dollars per peso—less than the official value of 0.125 U.S. dollars per peso. Just as before, the peso is overvalued. This time, however, the Latinian central bank uses monetary policy to eliminate the overvaluation problem. To do so, the central bank increases the domestic real interest rate, making Latinian assets more attractive to foreign financial investors and raising the

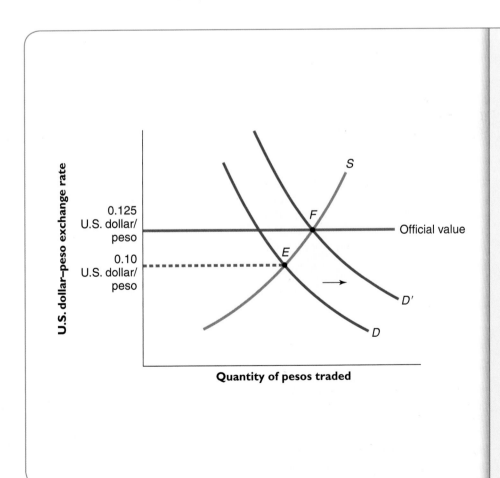

FIGURE 12.7

An Increase in the Real Interest Rate Eliminates an Overvaluation
With the demand for the peso given by *D* and the supply given by *S,* equilibrium occurs at point *E* and the fundamental value of the peso equals 0.10 U.S. dollars per peso—below the official value of 0.125 U.S. dollars per peso. The central bank can eliminate the overvaluation of the peso by raising the domestic real interest rate, making domestic assets more attractive to foreign financial investors. The resulting increase in demand for the peso, from *D* to *D',* raises the peso's fundamental value to 0.125 U.S. dollars per peso, the official value. The peso is no longer overvalued.

demand for pesos from D to D'. After this increase in the demand for pesos, the fundamental value of the peso equals the officially fixed value, as can be seen in Figure 12.7. Because the peso is no longer overvalued, it can be maintained at its fixed value without loss of international reserves or fear of "speculative attack" (see below). Conversely, a reduction of the real interest rate by the central bank could be used to remedy an undervaluation, in which the official exchange rate is below the fundamental value.

Although monetary policy can be used to keep the fundamental value of the exchange rate equal to the official value, using monetary policy in this way has some drawbacks. In particular, *if monetary policy is used to set the fundamental value of the exchange rate equal to the official value, it is no longer available for stabilizing the domestic economy.* Suppose, for example, that the Latinian economy were suffering a recession due to insufficient aggregate demand at the same time that its exchange rate is overvalued. The Latinian central bank could lower the real interest rate to increase spending and output, or it could raise the real interest rate to eliminate overvaluation of the exchange rate, *but it cannot do both.* Hence, if Latinian officials decide to maintain the fixed exchange rate, they must give up any hope of fighting the recession using monetary policy. The fact that a fixed exchange rate limits or eliminates the use of monetary policy for the purpose of stabilizing aggregate demand is one of the most important features of a fixed-exchange-rate system.

"It's just a flesh wound. I got it defending the dollar."

speculative attack a massive selling of domestic currency assets by financial investors

The conflict monetary policy-makers face, between stabilizing the exchange rate and stabilizing the domestic economy, is most severe when the exchange rate is under a *speculative attack*. A **speculative attack** involves massive selling of domestic currency assets by both domestic and foreign financial investors. A speculative attack lowers the fundamental value of the exchange rate still further, by increasing the supply of the currency in the foreign exchange market.

To stop a speculative attack, the central bank must raise the fundamental value of the currency a great deal, which requires a large increase in the real interest rate. (In a famous episode in 1992, the Swedish central bank responded to an attack on its currency by raising the short-term interest rate to 500 percent!) However, because the increase in the real interest rate that is necessary to stop a speculative attack reduces aggregate demand, it can cause a severe economic slowdown. Economic Naturalist 12.2 describes a real-world example of this phenomenon.

www.riksbank.com
Swedish Central Bank

ECONOMIC *Naturalist*   12.2   What were the causes and consequences of the East Asian crisis of 1997–1998?

During the past three decades the countries of East Asia have enjoyed impressive economic growth and stability. But the "East Asian miracle" seemed to end in 1997, when a wave of speculative attacks hit the region's currencies. Thailand, which had kept a constant value for its currency in terms of the U.S. dollar for more than a decade, was the first to come under attack, but the crisis spread to other countries, including South Korea, Indonesia, and Malaysia. Each of these countries was ultimately forced to devalue its currency. What caused this crisis, and what were its consequences?

Because of the impressive economic record of the East Asian countries, the Asian currency crisis was not expected by most policy-makers, economists, and financial investors. With the benefit of hindsight, however, we can identify some of its causative factors.

One is that the U.S. dollar strengthened from mid-1995 to 1997, particularly against the Japanese yen, and this caused the East Asian currencies pegged to it to strengthen, and their trade deficits to widen. If an economy with a fixed exchange rate is running large trade deficits, currency traders often judge that the currency is overvalued. So larger trade deficits triggered speculation against certain East Asian currencies, particularly the Thai baht. Thailand used its foreign currency reserves to defend the baht, but eventually it was forced to devalue. Then panic struck currency markets. Financial investors became increasingly fearful of other devaluations in the region, speculative attacks intensified, and several other East Asian economies were eventually forced to devalue.

Many of the countries forced to devalue had abandoned controls of international capital flows in the early 1990s. But China and Vietnam, which had never abandoned capital controls, were able to withstand the speculative attacks. Also, both China and Hong Kong were aided in withstanding attacks by their massive holdings of foreign currency reserves.[6]

The International Monetary Fund (IMF) provided emergency loans to several East Asian countries (see Box 12.1), but some economists believe that the conditions attached to the loans worsened the situation. In an attempt to raise the fundamental values of their exchange rates and stave off additional devaluation, several of the countries increased their real interest rates sharply, at IMF urging. However, the rise in real interest rates depressed aggregate demand, contributing to sharp declines in output and rising unemployment.

Fortunately, by 1999 most East Asian economies had begun to recover. Still, the crisis impressed the potential dangers of fixed exchange rates quite sharply in the minds of policy-makers in developing countries.

BOX 12.1   THE INTERNATIONAL MONETARY FUND

The International Monetary Fund (IMF) was established after the Second World War. An international agency, the IMF is controlled by a 24-member executive board. Eight executive board members represent individual countries (China, France, Germany, Japan, Russia, Saudi Arabia, the United Kingdom, and the United States); the other 16 members each represent a group of countries. A managing director oversees the IMF's operations and its approximately 2600 employees.

[6]For further analysis of the East Asian currency crisis, see Brian MacLean, ed., "The Transformation of International Economic Policy Debate, 1997–98," in *Out of Control: Canada in an Unstable Financial World* (Lorimer: Toronto, 1999), pp. 67–94.

The original purpose of the IMF was to help manage the system of fixed exchange rates, called the Bretton Woods system, put in place after the war. Under Bretton Woods, the IMF's principal role was to lend international reserves to member countries who needed them so that those countries could maintain their exchange rates at the official values. However, by 1973, the United States, the United Kingdom, Germany, and most other industrial nations had abandoned fixed exchange rates for flexible rates, leaving the IMF to find a new mission. Since 1973 the IMF has been involved primarily in lending to developing countries. It lent heavily to Mexico when that country experienced speculative attacks in 1994, and it made loans to East Asian countries during the 1997–1998 crisis. Other countries that received large IMF loans in recent years include Russia and Brazil.

The IMF's performance in recent crises has been controversial. Many observers credit the IMF with helping Mexico, the East Asian nations, and others to recover quickly from the effects of speculative attacks and contend that the IMF plays a vital role in maintaining international economic stability. However, some critics have charged that the IMF has required recipients of its loans to follow economic policies—such as tight monetary policies and fiscal cutbacks—that have turned out to be ill-advised. In particular, some believe that the IMF's policies were aimed at keeping Wall Street investors happy, rather than at providing economic stability. They have claimed that the IMF's loans help foreign financial investors and the richest people in the countries receiving loans, rather than the average person.

The IMF has also come into conflict with the World Bank, a separate international institution that was set up at about the same time as the IMF. The World Bank, whose mission is to provide long-term loans to help poor nations develop their economies, has complained that IMF interventions in poor countries interfered with World Bank programs and objectives. In 2000, a report commissioned by the U.S. Congress recommended reducing the IMF's powers (as well as, incidentally, those of the World Bank).

A strategy followed by many developing countries over the past several years has been to accumulate massive foreign exchange reserves in order to be able to prevent currency crises and thereby avoid the need to call on the IMF for loans. As a consequence, the IMF loan portfolio (that is, credit outstanding) shrank from U.S. $117 billion in late 2003 to just $16 billion in early 2008. In 2008 the IMF itself was running deficits and was forced to make major cuts to its staff.

RECAP

FIXED EXCHANGE RATES

- The value of a fixed exchange rate is set by the government. The official value of a fixed exchange rate may differ from its fundamental value, as determined by supply and demand in the foreign exchange market. An exchange rate whose officially fixed value exceeds its fundamental value is *overvalued;* an exchange rate whose officially fixed value is below its fundamental value is *undervalued.*

- For an overvalued exchange rate, the quantity of the currency supplied to the foreign exchange market at the official exchange rate exceeds the quantity demanded. The government can maintain an overvalued exchange rate for a time by using its *international reserves* (foreign currency assets) to purchase the excess supply of its currency. The net decline in a country's stock of international reserves during the year is its *balance-of-payments deficit.*

- Because a country's international reserves are limited, it cannot maintain an overvalued exchange rate indefinitely. Moreover, if financial investors fear an impending devaluation of the exchange rate, they may launch a *speculative attack,* selling domestic currency assets and supplying large amounts of the country's currency to the foreign exchange market—an action that exhausts the country's reserves even more quickly.

- By raising the real interest rate, a central bank raises the demand for the currency and hence its fundamental value. By raising a currency's fundamental value to its official value, tight monetary policies can eliminate the problem of overvaluation and stabilize the exchange rate. However, if monetary policy is used to set the fundamental value of the exchange rate, it is no longer available for stabilizing the domestic economy.

12.4 SHOULD EXCHANGE RATES BE FIXED OR FLEXIBLE?

Should countries adopt fixed or flexible exchange rates? In briefly comparing the two systems, we will focus on two major issues: (1) the effects of the exchange rate system on monetary policy and (2) the effects of the exchange rate system on trade and economic integration.

On the issue of monetary policy, we have seen that the type of exchange rate a country has strongly affects the central bank's ability to use monetary policy to stabilize the economy. A flexible exchange rate actually strengthens the impact of monetary policy on aggregate demand. But a fixed exchange rate prevents policymakers from using monetary policy to stabilize the economy, because they must instead use it to keep the exchange rate's fundamental value at its official value (or else risk speculative attack).

In large economies like those of the United States and Japan, and also in medium-sized developed economies like Canada and Australia, giving up the power to stabilize the domestic economy via monetary policy makes little economic sense. Thus, for such economies there is a very strong case for employing a flexible exchange rate. However, in very small economies, giving up this power may have benefits that exceed the costs. The benefits may be particularly large for small developing economies that have a history of very high and damaging rates of inflation. A fixed exchange rate may help such economies achieve low or moderate rates of inflation.

The second important issue is the effect of the exchange rate on trade and economic integration. Proponents of fixed exchange rates argue that fixed rates promote international trade and cross-border economic cooperation by reducing uncertainty about future exchange rates. For example, a firm that is considering building up its export business knows that its potential profits will depend on the future value of its own country's currency relative to the currencies of the countries to which it exports. Under a flexible-exchange-rate regime, the value of the home currency fluctuates with changes in supply and demand and is therefore difficult to predict far in advance. Such uncertainty may make the firm reluctant to expand its export business. Supporters of fixed exchange rates argue that if the exchange rate is officially fixed, uncertainty about the future exchange rate is reduced or eliminated.

One problem with this argument, which has been underscored by episodes like the East Asian crisis, is that fixed exchange rates are not guaranteed to remain fixed forever. Although they do not fluctuate from day to day as flexible rates do, a speculative attack on a fixed exchange rate may lead suddenly and unpredictably to a large devaluation. Thus, a firm that is trying to forecast the exchange rate 10 years into the future may face as much uncertainty if the exchange rate is fixed as if it is flexible.

The potential instability of fixed exchange rates caused by speculative attacks has led some countries to try a more radical solution to the problem of uncertainty about exchange rates: the adoption of a common currency. Economic Naturalist 12.3 describes an important instance of this strategy.

ECONOMIC Naturalist   12.3   Why have 15 European countries adopted a common currency?

Effective January 1, 1999, eleven Western European nations, including France, Germany, and Italy, adopted for some purposes a new currency called the euro, irrevocably fixed the exchange rates between their currencies, and transferred key functions from their central banks to the European Central Bank (ECB). A twelfth country, Greece, joined this arrangement in 2001, and in January 2002 the various countries began to call in their domestic currencies and replace them with euro currency. Since then, Cyprus, Malta, and Slovenia have also adopted the euro. Why have these nations adopted a common currency?

For some decades the nations of Western Europe have worked to increase economic cooperation and trade among themselves. European leaders believed that a unified and integrated European economy would be more productive and perhaps more competitive with the North American economy than a fragmented one. As part of this effort, these countries established fixed exchange rates under the auspices of a system called the European Monetary System (EMS). Unfortunately, the EMS did not prove stable. Numerous devaluations of the various currencies occurred, and in 1992 severe speculative attacks forced several nations, including Great Britain, to abandon the fixed-exchange-rate system.

In December 1991, in Maastricht in the Netherlands, the member countries of the European Community (EC)

adopted a treaty popularly known as the Maastricht Treaty. One of the major provisions of the Treaty, which took effect in November 1993, was that member countries would strive to adopt a common currency. This common currency, known as the euro, was formally adopted on January 1, 1999. The advent of the euro means that Europeans will no longer have to change currencies when trading with other European countries, much as Canadians from different provinces can trade with each other without worrying that a "Nova Scotia dollar" will change in value relative to a "British Columbia dollar." The euro should help to promote European trade and cooperation while eliminating the problem of speculative attacks on the currencies of individual countries.

Because Western Europe now has a single currency, it also must have a common monetary policy. The EC members agreed that European monetary policy would be put under the control of a new European Central Bank (ECB), a multinational institution located in Frankfurt, Germany. One potential problem with having a single monetary policy for 15 different countries is that different countries may face different economic conditions, so a single monetary policy cannot respond to all of them. What can the ECB do, for example, if Italy is suffering from a recession (which requires an easing of monetary policy) while Germany is worried about inflation (which requires a tightening)?

ECONOMIC Naturalist   12.4   Why has China stopped pegging the yuan to the U.S. dollar?

From mid-1995 to mid-2005 the Chinese yuan (also known as the renminbi) was pegged to the U.S. dollar. Although this practice was often criticized by U.S. politicians who wished for a stronger yuan in order to prevent rising Chinese trade surpluses with the United States, to many Chinese politicians and economists the fixed exchange rate seemed to be a key component in the package of policies that consistently produced very high real GDP growth rates for China. Why then, in mid-2005, did the Chinese government finally allow the yuan to appreciate against the

U.S. dollar, as shown by the upward slope of the red line in Figure 12.8?

One explanation emphasizes the impact of a depreciating exchange rate on the growth of aggregate demand in China. Since about 2002–2003, the United States dollar has been depreciating against almost all other major currencies. When it was pegged to the U.S. dollar, the yuan also depreciated against other major currencies. For example, the red line of Figure 12.8 shows the appreciation of the euro against the yuan, and thus against the U.S. dollar to which the yuan was pegged, beginning in 2002. This gave a strong stimulus to China's net exports and hence to aggregate demand growth in China. But the aggregate demand growth of China, according to this explanation, was already sufficient without depreciation of the yuan. The depreciating yuan caused actual GDP growth to exceed potential GDP growth. And if actual GDP growth exceeds potential GDP growth, the inflation rate tends to rise, as is explained in Chapter 11. So to combat rising inflation from excessive aggregate demand growth, the yuan was allowed to appreciate.

A related explanation, which has been advanced by *The Economist* newsweekly, is that China has recently allowed the yuan to appreciate in order to offset an increase in domestic inflation due to, among other things, a surge in the prices of imported foods, particularly grains and fuel. The argument is that a stronger yuan will act to reduce the prices of imports and thereby counteract the rise of domestic inflation as measured by the consumer price index. China's consumer price index includes the prices of imports consumed by households, as does the Canadian consumer price index, explained in Chapter 6.

A final explanation for allowing the appreciation is that China wished to stem the excessive growth of the country's official foreign exchange reserves. Some economists believe that the yuan became increasingly undervalued during much of the period it was pegged to the U.S. dollar. As discussed earlier in this chapter, if a country with a fixed exchange rate has an undervalued currency, it can expect to accumulate foreign exchange reserves. Conversely, if it revalues its currency or allows the currency to appreciate, the accumulation of foreign exchange reserves should be slowed or stopped as a result. Official foreign exchange reserves are desirable, up to a point, because they allow a country to defend its exchange rate against speculative attacks, and China's exchange rate, while not pegged to the U.S. dollar, is still pegged to a basket of major currencies. But as of March 2008, China's foreign exchange reserves stood at a massive total of U.S.$1.7 trillion, a total $700 billion greater than that of Japan, the country with the second largest official foreign exchange reserves. The bulk of China's foreign exchange reserves, as with the majority of those from most countries, are held in the form of U.S. dollar, short-term government bonds. And as the U.S. dollar began to depreciate against most other currencies, many economists have pointed to the risk China faces by holding so much of its wealth in U.S. dollars.

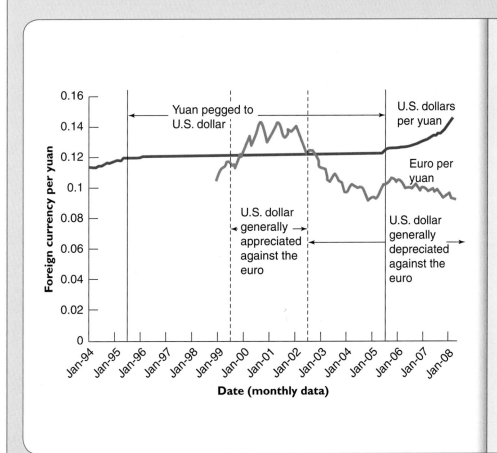

FIGURE 12.8

The Chinese Yuan, January 1994–April 2008
From mid-1995 to mid-2005, the Chinese yuan was pegged to the U.S. dollar at about 0.1208 U.S. dollars per yuan (or about 8.3 yuan per dollar). During this period, however, the yuan fluctuated very substantially against other currencies. The yuan, for example, appreciated against the euro from the inception of the euro until the latter half of 2002. Since mid-2005 the yuan has appreciated against the U.S. dollar by about 18 percent, but it has depreciated against the euro. SOURCE: Monthly average exchange rate data from the Pacific Exchange Rate Service, http://fx.sauder.ubc.ca/.

www.ecb.int
European Central Bank

12.5   THE IMPACT OF MONETARY POLICY WITH A FLEXIBLE EXCHANGE RATE: A RESTATEMENT

This chapter has been primarily about the economic factors that determine fluctuations in flexible exchange rates and the economic policies necessary to maintain fixed exchange rates. To close the chapter, however, let us re-emphasize the point that changes in the exchange rate do have an important effect on the Canadian economy. In particular, exchange rate changes that result from monetary policy changes (increases or decreases in the key policy rate by the Bank of Canada) tend to intensify the impact of monetary policy.

Figure 12.9 shows how a reduction in real interest rates by the Bank of Canada results in a rise in GDP, through two channels. First, as we saw in Chapter 9, falling interest rates reduce the cost of borrowing for firms and households, which encourages private-sector investment spending (particularly residential investment) and consumer durables spending. Second, as this chapter shows, falling interest rates lower the return on Canadian assets, making them less attractive relative to foreign assets. This reduces the value of the Canadian dollar, raising exports and lowering imports. The increases in private-sector investment, consumption, and net exports pull up planned aggregate expenditure, causing GDP to rise. What would happen if the Bank of Canada engineered a rise in real interest rates?

FIGURE 12.9

Lower Interest Rates and a Lower Value of the Currency Raise GDP

Falling interest rates in Canada raise GDP both through a lower cost of borrowing, increasing private-sector investment and consumption, and through a fall in the real exchange rate, increasing net exports.

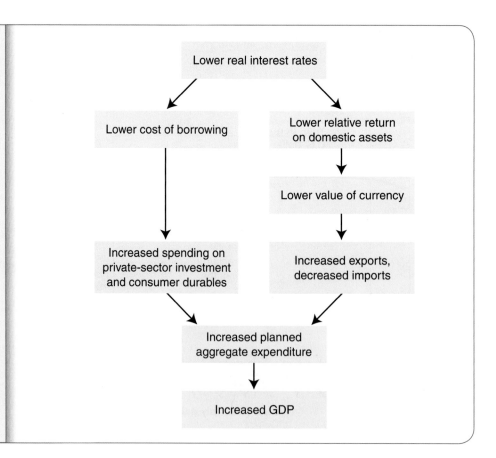

SUMMARY

12.1 The *nominal exchange rate* between two currencies is the rate at which the currencies can be traded for each other. A rise in the value of a currency relative to another currency is called an *appreciation;* a decline in the value of a currency is called a *depreciation.*

12.1 Exchange rates can be flexible or fixed. The value of a *flexible exchange rate* is determined by the supply of and demand for the currency in the *foreign exchange market,* the market on which currencies of various nations are traded for one another. The government sets the value of a *fixed exchange rate.*

12.1 The *real exchange rate* is the price of the average domestic good or service *relative* to the price of the average foreign good or service, when prices are expressed in terms of a common currency. An increase in the real exchange rate implies that domestic goods and services are becoming more expensive relative to foreign goods and services, which tends to reduce exports and increase imports. Conversely, a decline in the real exchange rate tends to increase net exports.

12.2 A basic theory of nominal exchange rate determination, the *purchasing power parity* (PPP) theory, is based on the law of one price. The *law of one price* states that if transportation costs are relatively small, the price of an internationally traded commodity must be the same in all locations. According to the PPP theory, we can find the nominal exchange rate between two currencies by setting the price of a commodity in one of the currencies equal to the price of the commodity in the second currency. The PPP theory correctly predicts that the currencies of countries that experience very high inflation will tend to depreciate. However, the fact that many goods and services are not traded internationally, and that not all traded goods are standardized, makes the PPP theory less useful for explaining other situations, particularly short-run changes in exchange rates.

12.2 Supply and demand analysis is a useful tool for studying the determination of exchange rates in the short run. The equilibrium exchange rate, also called the *fundamental value of the exchange rate,* equates the quantities of the currency supplied and demanded in the foreign exchange market. A currency is supplied by domestic residents who wish to acquire foreign currencies to purchase foreign goods, services, and assets. An increased preference for foreign goods, an increase in the domestic GDP, or an increase in the real interest rate on foreign assets will all increase the supply of a currency on the foreign exchange market and thus lower its value. A currency is demanded by foreigners who wish to purchase domestic goods, services, and assets. An increased preference for domestic goods by foreigners, an increase in real GDP abroad, or an increase in the domestic real interest rate will all increase the demand for the currency on the foreign exchange market and thus increase its value.

12.2 If the exchange rate is flexible, by raising the real interest rate the central bank will tend to increase the demand for the currency and cause it to appreciate. The stronger currency reinforces the effects of the tight monetary policy on aggregate demand by reducing net exports. Conversely, by lowering the real interest rate, the central bank weakens the currency, which in turn stimulates net exports.

12.3 The value of a fixed exchange rate is officially established by the government. A fixed exchange rate whose official value exceeds its fundamental value in the foreign exchange market is said to be *overvalued.* An exchange rate whose official value is below its fundamental value is *undervalued.* A reduction in the official value of a fixed exchange rate is called a *devaluation;* an increase in its official value is called a *revaluation.*

12.3 For an overvalued exchange rate, the quantity of the currency supplied at the official exchange rate exceeds the quantity demanded. To maintain the official rate, the country's central bank must use its *international reserves* (foreign currency assets) to purchase the excess supply of its currency in the foreign exchange market. Because a country's international reserves are limited, it cannot maintain an overvalued exchange rate indefinitely.

12.3 By raising the real interest rate and thereby raising the fundamental value of the exchange rate, a central bank can eliminate the problem of overvaluation. However, if monetary policy is used to set the fundamental value of the exchange rate equal to the official value, it is no longer available for stabilizing the domestic economy. Thus under fixed exchange rates, monetary policy has little or no power to affect domestic output and employment.

12.4 Because a fixed exchange rate implies that monetary policy can no longer be used for domestic stabilization, most large and medium-sized developed countries employ a flexible exchange rate. A fixed exchange rate may benefit a small country with a poor inflation record by forcing its central bank to follow the monetary policies of the country to which it has tied its rate. Advocates of fixed exchange rates argue that they increase trade and economic integration by making the exchange rate more predictable. However, the threat of speculative attacks greatly reduces the long-term predictability of a fixed exchange rate.

KEY TERMS

appreciation (305)
balance-of-payments deficit (321)
balance-of-payments surplus (321)
depreciation (305)

devaluation (320)
fixed exchange rate (306)
flexible exchange rate (306)
foreign exchange market (306)

fundamental value of the exchange
  rate (315)
international reserves (321)
law of one price (310)

nominal exchange rate (303)
overvalued exchange rate (320)
purchasing power parity (PPP) (311)

real exchange rate (307)
revaluation (320)

speculative attack (324)
undervalued exchange rate (321)

REVIEW QUESTIONS

1. Japanese yen trade at 100 yen/Canadian dollar and Mexican pesos trade at 10 pesos/Canadian dollar. What is the nominal exchange rate between the yen and the peso? Express in two ways.

2. Define *nominal exchange rate* and *real exchange rate*. How are the two concepts related? Which type of exchange rate most directly affects a country's ability to export its goods and services?

3. Would you expect the law of one price to apply to crude oil? To fresh milk? To taxi rides? Explain your answer in each case.

4. Why do Canadian households and firms supply dollars to the foreign exchange market? Why do foreigners demand dollars in the foreign exchange market?

5. Under a flexible exchange rate, how does a reduction of the real interest rate by the central bank affect the value of the exchange rate? Does this change in the exchange rate tend to weaken or strengthen the effect of the monetary ease on output and employment? Explain.

6. Define *overvalued exchange rate*. Discuss four ways in which government policy-makers can respond to an overvaluation. What are the drawbacks of each approach?

7. Contrast fixed and flexible exchange rates in terms of how they affect (a) the ability of monetary policy to stabilize domestic output and (b) the predictability of future exchange rates.

PROBLEMS

1. Using the data in Table 12.1, find the nominal exchange rate between the British pound and the Japanese yen. Express in two ways. How do your answers change if the pound appreciates by 10 percent against the dollar while the value of the yen against the dollar remains unchanged?

2. A British-made automobile is priced at £20 000 (20 000 British pounds). A comparable U.S.-made car costs U.S. $26 000. One pound trades for U.S. $2 in the foreign exchange market. Which country's cars are more competitively priced?

3. Between last year and this year, the CPI in Blueland rose from 100 to 110 and the CPI in Redland rose from 100 to 105. Blueland's currency unit, the blue, was worth $1 (Canadian) last year and is worth 90 cents (Canadian) this year. Redland's currency unit, the red, was worth 50 cents (Canadian) last year and is worth 45 cents (Canadian) this year.

    Find the percentage change from last year to this year in Blueland's *nominal* exchange rate with Redland and in Blueland's *real* exchange rate with Redland. (Treat Blueland as the home country.) Relative to Redland, do you expect Blueland's exports to be helped or hurt by these changes in exchange rates?

4. The demand for Canadian-made cars in Japan is given by

    Japanese demand = 10 000 − 0.001 (Price of Canadian cars in yen).

    Similarly, the demand for Japanese-made cars in Canada is

    Canadian demand = 30 000 − 0.2 (Price of Japanese cars in dollars).

    The domestic price of a Canadian-made car is $20 000, and the domestic price of a Japanese-made car is ¥2 500 000. From the perspective of Canada, find the real exchange rate in terms of cars and net exports of cars to Japan, if:
    a. The nominal exchange rate is 100 yen/dollar.
    b. The nominal exchange rate is 125 yen/dollar.
    How does an appreciation of the dollar affect Canadian net exports of automobiles (considering only the Japanese market)?

5. a. Suppose that gold is $1050/ounce in the United States and 8400 pesos/ounce in Mexico. What nominal exchange rate between U.S. dollars and Mexican pesos is implied by the PPP theory?

b. Mexico experiences inflation so that the price of gold rises to 12 600 pesos/ounce. Gold remains at $1050/ounce in the United States. According to the PPP theory, what happens to the exchange rate? What general principle does this example illustrate?

c. Gold is $1050/ounce in the United States and 12 600 pesos/ounce in Mexico. Crude oil (excluding taxes and transportation costs) is $70/barrel in the U.S. According to the PPP theory, what should a barrel of crude oil cost in Mexico?

d. Gold is $1050/ounce in the United States. The exchange rate between the United States and Canada is 0.95 U.S. dollars/Canadian dollar. How much does an ounce of gold cost in Canada?

6. How would each of the following be likely to affect the value of the dollar, all else being equal? Explain.

a. Canadian stocks are perceived as having become much riskier financial investments.

b. European computer firms switch from Canadian-produced software to software produced in India, Israel, and other nations.

c. As East Asian economies grow, international financial investors become aware of many new, high-return investment opportunities in the region.

d. The Canadian government imposes a large tariff on imported automobiles.

e. The Bank of Canada reports that it is less concerned about inflation and more concerned about an impending recession in Canada.

f. Canadian consumers increase their spending on imported goods.

7. The demand for and supply of shekels in the foreign exchange market is

$$Demand = 30\ 000 - 8000e,$$

$$Supply = 25\ 000 = 12\ 000e,$$

where the nominal exchange rate is expressed as Canadian dollars per shekel.

a. What is the fundamental value of the shekel?

b. The shekel is fixed at 0.30 Canadian dollars. Is the shekel overvalued, undervalued, or neither? Find the balance-of-payments deficit or surplus in both shekels and dollars. What happens to the country's international reserves over time?

c. Repeat part (b) for the case in which the shekel is fixed at 0.20 Canadian dollars.

8. Eastland's currency is called the eastmark, and Westland's currency is called the westmark. In the market in which eastmarks and westmarks are traded for each other, the supply of and demand for eastmarks is given by

$$Demand = 25\ 000 - 5000e + 50\ 000(r_E - r_W).$$

$$Supply = 18\ 500 + 8000e - 50\ 000(r_E - r_W).$$

The nominal exchange rate e is measured as westmarks per eastmark, and r_E and r_W are the real interest rates prevailing in Eastland and Westland, respectively.

a. Explain why it makes economic sense for the two real interest rates to appear in the demand and supply equations in the way they do.

b. Initially, $r_E = r_W = 0.10$, or 10 percent. Find the fundamental value of the eastmark.

c. The Westlandian central bank grows concerned about inflation and raises Westland's real interest rate to 12 percent. What happens to the fundamental value of the eastmark?

d. Assume that the exchange rate is flexible and that Eastland does not change its real interest rate following the increase in Westland's real interest rate. Is the action of the Westlandian central bank likely to increase or reduce aggregate demand in Eastland? Discuss.

e. Now suppose that the exchange rate is fixed at the value you found in part (b). After the action by the Westlandian central bank, what will the Eastlandian central bank have to do to keep its exchange rate from being overvalued? What effect will this action have on the Eastlandian economy?

f. In the context of this example, discuss the effect of fixed exchange rates on the ability of a country to run an independent monetary policy.

9. The following table provides, for each of the years from 1997 to 2005, the price levels for China and the United States, as well as the fixed nominal exchange rate of 0.12 U.S. dollars per Chinese yuan.

a. Find the real exchange rate for each of the years from 1997 to 2005.

b. Did the real exchange rate appreciate or depreciate?

Year	Price Level for China	Price Level for the United States	Exchange Rate: U.S. Dollars per yuan
1997	100.00	100.00	0.12
1998	99.20	101.55	0.12
1999	97.81	103.77	0.12
2000	98.20	107.27	0.12
2001	98.91	110.29	0.12
2002	98.16	112.05	0.12
2003	99.30	114.62	0.12
2004	103.17	117.68	0.12
2005	105.03	121.65	0.12

c. If the real exchange rate was an equilibrium exchange rate in 1997, and assuming that all relevant factors other than relative inflation rates held constant, would we predict that the yuan would be undervalued or overvalued in 2005?

d. All else being equal, what would be the predicted consequences of the change in the real exchange rate from 1997 to 2005 for China's net exports and official foreign exchange reserves?

e. The price level data in the table is for the consumer price index. Why might the GDP deflator give different conclusions about relative inflation in the two countries? (To answer this part of the question, it may be helpful to review Chapter 6.)

ANSWERS TO IN-CHAPTER EXERCISES

12.1 The answer depends on current data.

12.2 The dollar price of the Canadian truck is \$24 000, and each dollar is equal to 75 yen. Therefore the yen price of the Canadian truck is (75 yen/dollar) × (\$24 000), or 1 800 000 yen. The price of the Japanese truck is 1 875 000 yen. Thus the conclusion that the Japanese vehicle is more expensive does not depend on the currency in which the comparison is made.

12.3 Since the law of one price holds for gold, its price per ounce must be the same in New York and Stockholm:

$$\$930 = 5580 \text{ kronor}.$$

Dividing both sides by 930, we get

$$\$1 = 6 \text{ kronor}.$$

So the exchange rate is 6 kronor/dollar. (Incidentally, *Kronor* is the plural of *Krona*.)

12.4 A decline in Canadian GDP reduces consumer incomes and hence imports. As Canadians are purchasing fewer imports, they supply fewer dollars to the foreign exchange market, so the supply curve for dollars shifts to the left. Reduced supply raises the equilibrium value of the dollar.

12.5 At a fixed value for the peso of 0.15 dollars, the demand for the peso equals 25 000 − 50 000(0.15) = 17 500. The supply of the peso equals 17 600 + 24 000(0.15) = 21 200. The quantity supplied at the official rate exceeds the quantity demanded by 3700. Latinia will have to purchase 3700 pesos each period, so its balance-of-payments deficit will equal 3700 pesos, or 3700 × 0.15 = 555 dollars. This balance-of-payments deficit is larger than we found in Example 12.6. We conclude that the greater the degree of overvaluation, the larger the country's balance-of-payments deficit is likely to be.

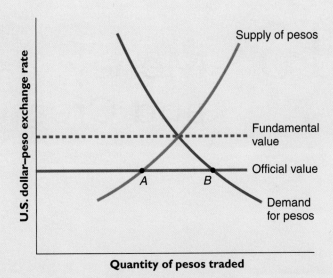

12.6 The figure above shows a situation in which the official value of the currency is *below* the fundamental value, as determined by the supply of and demand for the currency in the foreign exchange market, so the currency is undervalued. At the official value of the exchange rate, the quantity demanded of the domestic currency (point *B*) exceeds the quantity supplied (point *A*). To maintain the official value, the central bank must supply domestic currency to the foreign exchange market each period in the amount *AB*. In contrast to the case of an overvalued exchange rate, here the central bank is providing its own currency to the foreign exchange market and receiving foreign currency in return.

The central bank can print as much of its own currency as it likes, and so with an undervalued currency there is no danger of running out of international reserves. Indeed, the central bank's stock of international reserves increases in the amount *AB* each period, as it receives foreign currency in exchange for the domestic currency it supplies.

Chapter 13 Money: Its Uses and Creation

The Aztec, who dominated central Mexico until the coming of the Spanish in the sixteenth century, are perhaps best remembered today for their elaborate ceremonies that culminated in human sacrifice. But the Aztec Empire also had a sophisticated economic system, which included active trade not only in a wide variety of agricultural goods—such as corn, tomatoes, and peanuts—but also in manufactured items, including jewelry, sandals, cloaks, baskets, alcohol, and weapons. Slaves and captives, some designated for sacrifice, were also bought and sold. Trade was carried out in local markets, notably in the Aztec capital city located where Mexico City now stands, and over long distances, as far north as present-day Arizona, for example.[1]

Despite ample supplies of gold, the Aztec did not use metallic coins to carry out their market transactions, as most European peoples did, including settlers to Canada from Europe. Instead, they often used chocolate or, more specifically, cacao "beans" (the seeds of the cacao plant). Prices of goods or services were quoted in cacao beans, in much the same way that today we quote prices in terms of dollars. Cacao beans could also be used to purchase goods, to pay for a service, or to make change—for example, to balance a transaction when a good of greater value was traded for one of lesser value. For larger items, prices were quoted in terms of bags of approximately 24 000 cacao beans, although large purchases might actually be paid for with something easier to carry, such as woven cloaks.

Cacao beans were, for the Aztec, a form of money. In everyday language, people use the word *money* to mean "income" or "wealth," as in, "That job pays good money" or, "I wish I had as much money as she does." Economists, however, give a much more specific meaning to the term. To the economist, **money** is any asset that can be used as a means of payment for purchases and settling debts.

---

[1]See Jack Weatherford, *The History of Money: From Sandstone to Cyberspace*, (New York: Crown Publishers, 1997), for a discussion of the use of money in many economies from the ancients to the present day.

The cocoa beans of the Aztec, as well as the gold and silver coins used by Europeans, are examples of *commodity money*. **Commodity money** has intrinsic value; commodities that have emerged as money in different societies have typically been storable, easily transportable, and difficult to fake or counterfeit.

Contrast commodity money with *fiat money*. **Fiat money** has no intrinsic value or usefulness; its value arises from its widespread acceptance as a means of making purchases and settling debts. New France, the French colony that eventually developed into the province of Quebec, produced a unique form of fiat money. In the late 17th century, the colonial authorities came up with an innovative solution to the shortage of coinage—they issued playing cards with amounts written on the back, and used them to pay soldiers, who then used them for making purchases. Merchants accepted the cards for payments, and the authorities continued to issue new playing card money from time to time. In 1729, a new kind of card money made of ordinary white cardboard was issued. Its size varied by denomination and it was issued until the defeat of France in 1759. When New France came under British control, however, the card money was redeemed at only a fraction of its face value.

Currency and coins are common examples of money in the modern world. Both are fiat money—the currency is made of paper with no intrinsic value comparable to its face value, and although the coins have metallic content, the value of the metal bears no relation to the value of the coin.

A chequing account balance represents another asset that can be used in making payments (as when you write a cheque to pay for your weekly groceries) and so is also counted as money. In contrast, shares of stock, for example, cannot be used directly in most transactions. Stock must first be sold—that is, converted into cash or a chequing account deposit—before further transactions, such as buying your groceries, can be made.

In this chapter we discuss the role of money in modern economies: why it is important, and how it is measured. We explain in detail the riddle of how commercial banks create money, and also how central banks can change the reserves available to commercial banks and thereby change the money supply. Finally, we investigate the significance of the money supply for understanding hyperinflation.

money any asset that can be used as a means of payment for purchases and to settle debts

commodity money an asset with intrinsic value, such as a gold or silver coin, that is generally accepted as a means of payment for purchases and to settle debts

fiat money an asset with no intrinsic value, such as paper currency, that is generally accepted as a means of payment for purchases and to settle of debts

13.1 | MONEY AND ITS USES

Why do people use money? Money has three principal uses: a *medium of exchange*, a *unit of account*, and a *store of value*.

Money serves as a **medium of exchange** when it is used to purchase goods and services, such as when you pay cash for a newspaper or write a cheque to cover your utilities bill. This is perhaps money's most crucial function. Think about how complicated daily life would become if there were no money. Without money, all economic transactions would have to be in the form of **barter**, which is the direct trade of goods or services for other goods or services.

Barter is highly inefficient because it requires that both parties to a trade have something that the other party wants, a so-called "double coincidence of wants." For example, under a barter system, a musician could get her dinner only by finding someone willing to trade food for a musical performance. Finding such a match of needs, where both parties happen to want exactly what the other person has to offer, would be difficult to do on a regular basis. In a world with money, the musician's problem is considerably simpler. First, she must find someone who is willing to pay money for her musical performance. Then, with the money received, she can purchase the food and other goods and services that she needs. In a society that uses money, it is not necessary that the person who wants to hear music and the person who is willing to provide food to the musician be one and the same. In other words, there need not be a double coincidence of wants for trades of goods and services to take place.

medium of exchange an asset used in purchasing goods and services

barter the direct trade of goods or services for other goods or services

In a world without money, this violinist could eat only by finding someone willing to trade food for a musical performance.

By eliminating the problem of having to find a double coincidence of wants in order to trade, the use of money in a society permits individuals to specialize in producing particular goods or services, as opposed to having every family or village produce most of what it needs. Specialization greatly increases economic efficiency and material standards of living, as we discussed in Chapter 2 (*the principle of comparative advantage*). This usefulness of money in making transactions explains why financial investors hold money, even though money generally pays a low rate of return. Cash, for example, pays no interest at all, and the balances in chequing accounts usually pay a lower rate of interest than could be obtained in alternative financial investments.

COMPARATIVE
ADVANTAGE

unit of account a basic measure of economic value

Money's second function is as a *unit of account*. As a **unit of account**, money is the basic yardstick for measuring economic value. In Canada virtually all prices—including the price of labour (wages) and the prices of financial assets, such as shares of Bombardier stock—are expressed in dollars. Expressing economic values in a common unit of account allows for easy comparisons. For example, gasoline can be measured in litres and coal in tonnes, but to judge whether 500 litres of gasoline is economically more or less valuable than a tonne of coal, we express both values in dollar terms. The use of money as a unit of account is closely related to its use as a medium of exchange; because money is used to buy and sell things, it makes sense to express prices of all kinds in money terms.

store of value an asset that serves as a means of holding wealth

As a **store of value**, its third function, money is a way of holding wealth. For example, the miser who stuffs cash in his mattress or buries gold coins under the old oak tree at midnight is holding wealth in money form. Likewise, if you regularly keep a balance in your chequing account, you are holding part of your wealth in the form of money. Although money is usually the primary medium of exchange or unit of account in an economy, it is not the only store of value. There are numerous other ways of holding wealth, such as owning stocks, bonds, or real estate.

For most people, money is not a particularly good way to hold wealth, apart from its usefulness as a medium of exchange. Unlike government bonds and other types of financial assets, most forms of money pay no interest, and there is always the risk of cash being lost or stolen. However, cash has the advantage of being anonymous and difficult to trace, making it an attractive store of value for smugglers, drug dealers, and others who want their assets to stay out of the view of authorities.

MEASURING MONEY

How much money, defined as financial assets usable for making purchases, is there in the Canadian economy at any given time? This question is not simple to answer because in practice it is not easy to draw a clear distinction between those assets that should be counted as money and those that should not. Dollar bills are certainly a form of money, and a van Gogh painting certainly is not. However, brokerage firms now offer accounts that allow their owners to combine financial investments in stocks and bonds with cheque-writing and credit card privileges. Should the balances in these accounts, or some part of them, be counted as money? It is difficult to tell.

Statisticians and economists have skirted the problem of deciding what is or is not money by using several alternative definitions of it that vary in how broadly the concept of money is defined. Historically, considerable attention was paid to a relatively narrow definition called **M1**, that is, the sum of currency outside banks and the balances held in chequing accounts, known as demand deposits. It excluded the balances held in savings accounts, otherwise known as notice deposits.

M1 sum of currency outside banks and balances held in chequing accounts

At one time it was possible to draw a meaningful line between demand and notice deposits, and the commercial banks were required to hold different percentages of reserves against balances in each of these types of deposits. However, according to the Bank of Canada:

[F]inancial innovation and the removal of reserve requirements have made the distinction between demand and notice deposits artificial, and it has become increasingly difficult and arbitrary for financial institutions to allocate their deposit accounts between those two categories. Therefore, the reliability of the data needed to create these aggregates has eroded over time. Consequently, the Bank has eliminated the breakdown of demand and notice deposits in an upcoming revision to the reporting system and has ceased to construct and publish time series that rely on this distinction.[2]

Based upon this rationale, as of February 2007 the Bank of Canada ceased to construct or publish M1 statistics.

The Bank of Canada continues to publish statistics relating to a broader concept of money known as *M2*. As shown in Table 13.1, **M2** consists of currency outside banks, personal deposits, and non-personal demand and notice deposits. It is the most widely used measure of the money supply. The Bank also publishes statistics on M3 which, as shown in Table 13.1, is a much larger aggregate than M2. Notice that currency is a small fraction of either M2 or M3.

M2 all the assets in M1 plus some additional assets that are usable in making payments but at greater cost or inconvenience than currency or chequing accounts

TABLE 13.1

Major Components of M2 and M3, January 2008 (billions of dollars)

M2		**783.39**
Currency outside banks	48.66	
Non-personal demand and notice deposits	207.61	
Personal Deposits	528.67	
M3		**1204.03**
M2	783.39	
Non-personal term deposits plus foreign currency deposits	430.14	

SOURCE: *Bank of Canada Banking and Financial Statistics,* March 2008, Table E1.

NOTE: The major components do not add exactly to the M2 and M3 aggregates primarily due to minor Bank of Canada adjustments not shown. Non-personal notice deposits are deposits of businesses for which banks reserve the right to require notice before a withdrawal is made. This table of money supply measures is not exhaustive. Bank of Canada publications also make reference to other measures such as Gross M2+ and M2++.

RECAP ↑

MONEY: A SPECIAL FINANCIAL ASSET

Money is any asset that can be used in making purchases, such as currency or a chequing account. Money serves as a *medium of exchange* when it is used to purchase goods and services. The use of money as a medium of exchange eliminates the need for *barter* and the difficulties of finding a double coincidence of wants. Money also serves as a *unit of account* and a *store of value.*

The most widely used measure of the money supply is M2, which consists of currency outside banks, personal deposits, and non-personal demand and notice deposits.

[2]Bank of Canada, "Changes to Monetary Aggregates," http://boclab.com/en/rates/aggreg_note.html (June 2008).

13.2 COMMERCIAL BANKS AND THE CREATION OF MONEY

What determines the amount of money in the economy? If the economy's supply of money consisted entirely of currency, the answer would be simple: the supply of money would just be equal to the value of the currency created and circulated by the government. However, as we have seen, in modern economies the money supply consists not only of currency but also of deposit balances held by the public in commercial (that is, private) banks and other financial intermediaries.[3] The determination of the money supply in a modern economy thus depends in part on the behaviour of financial intermediaries and their depositors.

To see how the existence of financial intermediaries affects the money supply, we will use the example of a fictional economy. We assume, initially, that this economy has no financial intermediaries. To make trading easier and to eliminate the need for barter, the government directs the central bank to put into circulation a million identical paper notes, called guilders. The central bank prints the guilders and distributes them to the populace. At this point the money supply is a million guilders.

However, the citizens are unhappy with a money supply made up entirely of paper guilders, since the notes may be lost or stolen. In response to the demand for safekeeping of money, some entrepreneurs set up a system of commercial banks. At first, these banks are only storage vaults where people can deposit their guilders. When people need to make a payment they can either physically withdraw their guilders or, more conveniently, write a cheque on their account. Cheques give the banks permission to transfer guilders from the account of the person paying by cheque to the account of the person to whom the cheque is made out. With a system of payments based on cheques the paper guilders need never leave the banking system, although they flow from one bank to another as a depositor of one bank makes a payment to a depositor in another bank. Deposits do not pay interest in this economy; indeed, the banks can make a profit only by charging depositors fees in exchange for safeguarding their cash.

Let's suppose for now that people prefer bank deposits to cash and so deposit all of their guilders with the commercial banks. With all guilders in the vaults of banks, the balance sheet of all of the economy's commercial banks taken together is as shown in Table 13.2.

TABLE 13.2
Consolidated Balance Sheet of the Commercial Banks (Initial)

Assets		Liabilities	
Currency	1 000 000 guilders	Deposits	1 000 000 guilders

The *assets* of the commercial banking system of this fictional economy are the paper guilders sitting in the vaults of all the individual banks. The banking system's *liabilities* are the deposits of the banks' customers, since chequing account balances represent money owed by the banks to the depositors.

Cash or similar assets held by banks are called **bank reserves**. In this example, bank reserves, for all the banks taken together, equal 1 000 000 guilders—the

bank reserves cash or similar assets held by commercial banks for the purpose of meeting depositor withdrawals and payments

[3]In Canada the commercial banks are also known as chartered banks. The big five chartered banks (in order of value of their assets, 2005–2006) are the Royal Bank of Canada ($537 billion), Toronto-Dominion Bank ($365 billion), Bank of Nova Scotia ($314 billion), Canadian Imperial Bank of Commerce ($304 billion), and the Bank of Montreal ($298 billion).

currency listed on the asset side of the consolidated balance sheet. Banks hold reserves to meet depositors' demands for cash withdrawals or to pay cheques drawn on their depositors' accounts. In this example, the bank reserves of 1 000 000 guilders equal 100 percent of banks' deposits, which are also 1 000 000 guilders. A situation in which bank reserves equal 100 percent of bank deposits is called **100 percent reserve banking.**

100 percent reserve banking a situation in which banks' reserves equal 100 percent of their deposits

Bank reserves are held by banks in their vaults, rather than circulated among the public, and thus are *not* counted as part of the money supply. However, bank deposit balances, which can be used in making transactions, *are* counted as money. So, after the introduction of "safekeeper" banks in our fictional economy, the money supply, equal to the value of bank deposits, is 1 000 000 guilders, which is the same as it was prior to the introduction of banks.

After a while, to continue the story, the commercial bankers begin to realize that keeping 100 percent reserves against deposits is not necessary. True, a few guilders flow in and out of the typical bank as depositors receive payments or write cheques, but for the most part the stacks of paper guilders just sit there in the vaults, untouched and unused. It occurs to the bankers that they can meet the random inflow and outflow of guilders to their banks with reserves that are less than 100 percent of their deposits. After some observation, the bankers conclude that keeping reserves equal to only 10 percent of deposits is enough to meet the random ebb and flow of withdrawals and payments from their individual banks. The remaining 90 percent of deposits, the bankers realize, can be lent out to borrowers to earn interest.

So the bankers decide to keep reserves equal to 100 000 guilders, or 10 percent of their deposits. The other 900 000 guilders they lend out at interest to business owners who want to use the money to make improvements to their firms. After the loans are made, the balance sheet of all of the commercial banks taken together has changed, as shown in Table 13.3

TABLE 13.3
Consolidated Balance Sheet of the Commercial Banks after One Round of Loans

Assets		Liabilities	
Currency (= reserves)	100 000 guilders	Deposits	1 000 000 guilders
Loans to farmers	900 000 guilders		

After the loans are made, the banks' reserves of 100 000 guilders no longer equal 100 percent of the banks' deposits of 1 000 000 guilders. Instead, the **reserve-deposit ratio,** which is bank reserves divided by deposits, is now equal to 100 000/1 000 000, or 10 percent. A banking system in which banks hold fewer reserves than deposits so that the reserve-deposit ratio is less than 100 percent is called a **fractional-reserve banking system.**

reserve-deposit ratio bank reserves divided by deposits

Notice that 900 000 guilders have flowed out of the banking system (as loans to farmers) and are now in the hands of the public. But we have assumed that private citizens prefer bank deposits to cash for making transactions. So ultimately people will redeposit the 900 000 guilders in the banking system. After these deposits are made, the consolidated balance sheet of the commercial banks is as in Table 13.4.

fractional-reserve banking system a banking system in which bank reserves are less than deposits so that the reserve-deposit ratio is less than 100 percent

Notice that bank deposits, and hence the economy's money supply, now equal 1 900 000 guilders. In effect, the existence of the commercial banking system has permitted the creation of new money. These deposits, which are liabilities of the banks, are balanced by assets of 1 000 000 guilders in reserves and 900 000 guilders in loans owed to the banks.

TABLE 13.4

Consolidated Balance Sheet of the Commercial Banks after Guilders are Redeposited

Assets		Liabilities	
Currency (= reserves)	1 000 000 guilders	Deposits	1 900 000 guilders
Loans to farmers	900 000 guilders		

The story does not end here. On examining their balance sheets, the bankers are surprised to see that they once again have "too many" reserves. With deposits of 1 900 000 guilders and a 10 percent reserve-deposit ratio, they need only 190 000 guilders in reserve. But they have 1 000 000 guilders in reserve—810 000 too many. Since lending out their excess guilders is always more profitable than leaving them in the vault, the bankers proceed to make another 810 000 guilders in loans. Eventually these loaned-out guilders are redeposited in the banking system, after which the consolidated balance sheet of the banks is as shown in Table 13.5.

TABLE 13.5

Consolidated Balance Sheet of the Commercial Banks after Two Rounds of Loans and Redeposits

Assets		Liabilities	
Currency (= reserves)	1 000 000 guilders	Deposits	2 710 000 guilders
Loans to farmers	1 710 000 guilders		

Now the money supply has increased to 2 710 000 guilders, equal to the value of bank deposits. Despite the expansion of loans and deposits, however, the bankers find that their reserves of 1 000 000 guilders *still* exceed the desired level of 10 percent of deposits, which is 2 710 000 guilders. And so yet another round of lending will take place.

EXERCISE 13.1

Determine what the balance sheet of the banking system of our fictional economy will look like after a third round of lending to farmers and redeposits of guilders into the commercial banking system. What is the size of the money supply at that point?

The process of expansion of loans and deposits will only end when reserves equal 10 percent of bank deposits, because as long as reserves exceed 10 percent of deposits the banks will find it profitable to lend out the extra reserves. Since reserves at the end of every round equal 1 000 000 guilders, for the reserve-deposit ratio to equal 10 percent, total deposits must equal 10 000 000 guilders. Further, since the balance sheet must balance, with assets equal to liabilities, we also know that at the end of the process, loans must equal 9 000 000 guilders. If loans equal 9 000 000 guilders, then bank assets, the sum of loans and reserves (1 000 000 guilders), will equal 10 000 000 guilders, which is the same as bank liabilities (bank deposits). The final consolidated balance sheet is as shown in Table 13.6.

TABLE 13.6
Final Consolidated Balance Sheet of the Commercial Banks

Assets		Liabilities	
Currency (= reserves)	1 000 000 guilders	Deposits	10 000 000 guilders
Loans to farmers	9 000 000 guilders		

The money supply, which is equal to total deposits, is 10 000 000 guilders at the end of the process. We see that the existence of a fractional-reserve banking system has multiplied the money supply by a factor of 10, relative to the economy with no banks or the economy with 100 percent reserve banking. Put another way, with a 10 percent reserve-deposit ratio, each guilder deposited in the banking system can "support" 10 guilders worth of deposits.

To find the money supply in this example more directly, we observe that deposits will expand through additional rounds of lending as long as the ratio of bank reserves to bank deposits exceeds the reserve-deposit ratio desired by banks. When the actual ratio of bank reserves to deposits equals the desired reserve-deposit ratio, the expansion stops. Ultimately, deposits in the banking system satisfy the following relationship:

$$\frac{\text{Bank reserves}}{\text{Bank deposits}} = \text{Desired reserve-deposit ratio.}$$

This equation can be rewritten to solve for bank deposits:

$$\text{Bank deposits} = \frac{\text{Bank reserves}}{\text{Desired reserve-deposit ratio}} \qquad (13.1)$$

Since all the currency in our fictional economy flows into the banking system, bank reserves equal 1 000 000 guilders. The reserve-deposit ratio desired by banks is 0.10. Therefore, using Equation 13.1, we find that bank deposits equal (1 000 000 guilders)/0.10, or 10 million guilders, the same answer we found in the consolidated balance sheet of the banks, Table 13.6.

EXERCISE 13.2

Find deposits and the money supply if the banks' desired reserve-deposit ratio is 5 percent rather than 10 percent. What if the total amount of currency circulated by the central bank is 2 000 000 guilders and the desired reserve–deposit ratio remains at 10 percent?

THE MONEY SUPPLY WITH BOTH CURRENCY AND DEPOSITS

In our example we assumed that all money is held in the form of deposits in banks. In reality, of course, people keep only part of their money holdings in the form of bank accounts and hold the rest in the form of currency. Fortunately, allowing for the fact that people hold both currency and bank deposits does not greatly complicate the determination of the money supply, as Example 13.1 shows.

The money supply with both currency and deposits

EXAMPLE 13.1

Suppose that the citizens choose to hold a total of 500 000 guilders in the form of currency and to deposit the rest of their money in banks. Banks keep reserves equal to 10 percent of deposits. What is the money supply?

The money supply is the sum of currency in the hands of the public and bank deposits. Currency in the hands of the public is given as 500 000 guilders. What is the quantity of bank deposits? Since 500 000 of the 1 000 000 guilders issued by the central bank are being used by the public in the form of currency, only the remaining 500 000 guilders are available to serve as bank reserves. We know that deposits equal bank reserves divided by the reserve-deposit ratio, so deposits are 500 000 guilders/0.10 = 5 000 000 guilders. The total money supply is the sum of currency in the hands of the public (500 000 guilders) and bank deposits (5 000 000 guilders), or 5 500 000 guilders.

We can write a general relationship that captures the reasoning of Example 13.1. First, let's write out the assumption that the money supply equals currency plus bank deposits:

$$\text{Money supply} = \text{Currency held by the public} + \text{Bank deposits}.$$

We also know that bank deposits equal bank reserves divided by the reserve–deposit ratio that is desired by commercial banks (Equation 13.1). Using that relationship to substitute for bank deposits in the expression for the money supply, we get

$$\text{Money supply} = \text{Currency held by public} + \frac{\text{Bank reserves}}{\text{Desired reserve-deposit ratio}}. \quad (13.2)$$

We can use Equation 13.2 to confirm our answer to Example 13.1. In that example, currency held by the public is 500 000 guilders, bank reserves are 500 000 guilders, and the desired reserve-deposit ratio is 0.10. Plugging these values into Equation 13.2, we find that the money supply equals 500 000 + (500 000/0.10) = 5 500 000, the same answer we found before.

EXAMPLE 13.2   **The money supply at Christmas**

During the Christmas season people choose to hold unusually large amounts of currency for shopping. With no action by the central bank, how would this change in currency-holding affect the national money supply?

To illustrate with a numerical example, suppose that initially bank reserves are 500, the amount of currency held by the public is 500, and the desired reserve-deposit ratio in the banking system is 0.2. Inserting these values into Equation 13.2, we find that the money supply equals 500 + (500/0.2) = 3000.

Now suppose that, because of Christmas shopping needs, the public increases its currency holdings to 600 by withdrawing 100 from commercial banks. These withdrawals reduce bank reserves to 400. Using Equation 13.2 we find now that the money supply is 600 + (400/0.2) = 2600. So the public's increased holdings of currency have caused the money supply to drop, from 3000 to 2600. The reason for the drop is that with a reserve-deposit ratio of 20 percent, every dollar in the vaults of banks can "support" $5 of deposits and hence $5 of money supply. However, the same dollar in the hands of the public becomes $1 of currency, contributing only $1 to the total money supply. So when the public withdraws cash from the banks, the overall money supply declines significantly.

RECAP

COMMERCIAL BANKS AND THE CREATION OF MONEY

Part of the money supply consists of deposits in private commercial banks and other financial intermediaries. Hence the behaviour of financial intermediaries and their depositors helps to determine the money supply.

Cash or similar assets held by banks are called *bank reserves*. In modern economies, banks' reserves are less than their deposits, a situation called *fractional-reserve banking*. The ratio of bank reserves to deposits is called the *reserve-deposit ratio;* in a fractional-reserve banking system, this ratio is less than one.

The portion of deposits not held as reserves can be lent out by the banks to earn interest. Banks will continue to make loans and accept deposits as long as the reserve-deposit ratio exceeds its desired level. This process stops only when the actual and desired reserve-deposit ratios are equal. At that point, total bank deposits equal bank reserves divided by the desired reserve-deposit ratio, assuming that the money supply equals the currency held by the public plus bank deposits (see Equation 13.2).

13.3 CENTRAL BANKING

Central banks exist in most economies as government agencies responsible for the day-to-day administration of monetary policy. Unlike commercial banks, which are private businesses whose principal objective is to make a profit, central banks focus on promoting public goals such as low or moderate inflation, economic growth, and the smooth operation of financial markets. During recent decades, the central banks appearing most frequently in international financial news have been those of the G7 countries—the Bank of Canada, the Bank of England, the Banque de France, the German Bundesbank, the Bank of Italy, the Bank of Japan, and the U.S. Federal Reserve System. Since the European Central Bank became fully operative in early 1999, however, the central banks of France, Germany and Italy have appeared less frequently in the news, as many of their former functions have been assigned to the European Central Bank.

For participants in Canadian financial markets and for average Canadian citizens as well, the Bank of Canada is clearly the central bank with the most impact on their lives. But the decisions of the U.S. Federal Reserve also have a major impact on Canada, and the decisions of the European Central Bank are of some importance as well. To lay the groundwork for discussing how central banks—especially the Bank of Canada—carry out their responsibilities, we first briefly review the history and structure of the Bank of Canada, the U.S. Federal Reserve, and the European Central Bank.

THE HISTORY AND STRUCTURE OF THE BANK OF CANADA

The **Bank of Canada** opened its doors in March 1935, following the passage of the *Bank of Canada Act* in 1934. The preamble of the Act specified that the role of the Bank would be "to regulate credit and currency in the best interests of the economic life of the nation, to control and protect the external value of the national monetary unit and to mitigate by its influence fluctuations in the general level of production, trade, prices and employment, so far as may be possible within the scope of monetary action, and generally to promote the economic and financial welfare of Canada." Although the preamble of the Act has never been amended, the Bank of Canada now focuses monetary policy rather narrowly on the task of keeping Canada's rate of inflation low and stable.

Bank of Canada Canada's central bank

key policy rate the interest rate employed by the central bank as its major policy tool; the key policy rate for the Bank of Canada, which is also called its official interest rate, is the target for the overnight rate

Within the Bank of Canada, responsibility for monetary policy lies with the governing council, composed of the governor (currently Mark Carney, appointed in February 2008), the senior deputy governor, and four deputy governors. The governor, who is appointed for a term of seven years, is the Bank's chief executive officer. The governor, the senior deputy governor, 12 outside directors and the deputy minister of finance (who has no vote) constitute a board of directors charged with ensuring that the Bank is managed properly.

As was discussed in Chapter 9, monetary policy decisions typically involve changes to the Bank of Canada's official interest rate or **key policy rate**, the target for the overnight rate, that is one-quarter of a percentage point below the bank rate, which had been the Bank's official rate for several decades. Starting in December 2000, the Bank of Canada introduced a system of eight pre-specified dates each year for announcing any changes to the official rate. Under special circumstances, the Bank of Canada will change the official interest rate outside of the fixed dates, as it did in conjunction with the U.S. Federal Reserve on September 17, 2001, the day U.S. financial markets re-opened following the September 11 attacks on the World Trade Center in Manhattan, the home of Wall Street.

Besides monetary policy, the Bank of Canada is responsible for three other major functions: providing central banking services, issuing bank notes, and administering the federal debt. The central banking services function includes activities such as overseeing certain clearing and settlement systems (involving large-scale transactions among financial institutions), managing the federal government's bank accounts and foreign exchange reserves, and occasionally intervening in foreign exchange markets on behalf of the minister of finance to moderate fluctuations in the value of the Canadian dollar. With regard to bank notes, the Bank of Canada is responsible not only for issuing them, but also for preventing counterfeiting and ensuring that the supply of bank notes meets the public demand. Administering the federal debt means the Bank of Canada acts as the federal government's fiscal agent.

The Bank of Canada, like many other central banks, has been criticized for being largely outside of democratic control. It is certainly true that none of the members of either the governing council or the board of directors is elected. But defenders of existing practice note that the Bank of Canada is not completely independent of the elected government. The power of appointing directors to fill vacant seats on the Bank's board rests with the federal minister of finance (who is, of course, elected). The board of directors is responsible for appointing the governor, yet only subject to approval by the federal cabinet. The federal government has a say in the inflation-control targets that have been announced jointly by the Bank and the government every few years since 1991, and these targets make the Bank of Canada accountable to an explicit standard of performance. In addition, the minister of finance can issue a written directive to the governor specifying a change in policy in the case of a profound policy disagreement (in which case the governor would probably resign).

The Bank of Canada, which is based in Ottawa, has also been criticized for its lack of regional representation. Defenders of the Bank point out that it does have regional branch offices in Vancouver, Calgary, Toronto, Montreal and Halifax, and its 12 outside directors represent different regions across Canada. Compared to the U.S. Federal Reserve System, however, the Bank of Canada is highly centralized.

THE HISTORY AND STRUCTURE OF THE U.S. FEDERAL RESERVE SYSTEM

Federal Reserve System (the Fed) the central bank of the United States; also known as the Fed

The **Federal Reserve System** was created by the *Federal Reserve Act*, passed by the U.S. Congress in 1913. The *Federal Reserve Act* established a system of 12 regional Federal Reserve banks, each associated with a geographical area called a

Federal Reserve district. The regional Feds regularly assess economic conditions in their districts and report this information to national-level policy-makers.

At the national level, the leadership of the Federal Reserve System is provided by its board of governors, which, together with a large professional staff, is located in Washington, D.C. The board consists of seven governors, who are appointed by the president of the United States to 14-year terms. The president also appoints one of these board members to serve as chairman of the board of governors for a term of 4 years. The Fed chairman (currently Ben Bernanke, co-author of this textbook, who assumed office in February 2006) is the U.S. counterpart to the Bank of Canada governor.

Decisions about monetary policy are made by a 12-member committee called the Federal Open Market Committee (or FOMC). The FOMC consists of the seven Fed governors, the president of the Federal Reserve Bank of New York, and four of the presidents of the other regional Federal Reserve banks. The FOMC meets approximately eight times a year to determine monetary policy, changes in which are signalled by changes in the federal funds rate target, a target that corresponds to the Bank of Canada's target for the overnight rate. Unlike the Bank of Canada, the Fed does not have an explicit inflation rate target.

http://www.federalreserve
.gov/
Federal Reserve Board

THE HISTORY AND STRUCTURE OF THE EUROPEAN CENTRAL BANK

The **European Central Bank (ECB)** is one of the world's youngest central banks. It was established in June 1998, but became fully operative only at the beginning of 1999. That was when the euro was introduced, the exchange rates between the currencies of the initial 11 participating European Union member states were irrevocably fixed, and the central banks of member states transferred key functions to the ECB.

European Central Bank (ECB) the central bank of the euro zone countries

The highest decision-making body of the ECB is the governing council, which is composed of six members of the executive board plus the governors of all national central banks of the euro area. The executive board, members of which are appointed by common accord of the euro area governments, consists of the ECB president (a position corresponding to that of Bank of Canada governor or Federal Reserve chairman, filled since 2003 by Jean Claude Trichet), the ECB vice-president, and four other members.

www.ecb.int
European Central Bank

A distinction is made between the ECB and the Eurosystem. The ECB has headquarters in Frankfurt, Germany, with about 800 staff members. The Eurosystem consists of the ECB plus the national central banks of the euro area countries. In other words, in terms of U.S. central banking institutions, the ECB roughly corresponds to the board of governors and staff located in Washington, D.C., whereas the Eurosystem corresponds to the whole Federal Reserve System, including the 12 regional Federal Reserve banks.

The primary objective of the ECB's governing council is to maintain low and stable inflation in the euro area. The precise target is to keep the year-on-year increase in consumer prices below, but close to, 2 percent over the medium term (about two years). But the ECB is also concerned with avoiding deflation. Like the Bank of Canada's inflation control target, the ECB's target has been criticized for being too low.

Currently, the ECB's governing council convenes twice a month to decide on monetary policy, changes in which take the form of increases or reductions in the minimum bid rate, a target for overnight lending rates similar to the key policy rates of the Bank of Canada and the U.S. Fed. For example, on September 17, 2001, the Bank of Canada lowered its target for the overnight rate by half a percentage point to 3.5 percent, the U.S. Fed cut its target for the federal funds rate by half a percentage point to 3 percent, and the ECB cut the minimum bid rate by half a percentage point to 3.75 percent.

CHANGING RESERVES TO CHANGE THE MONEY SUPPLY

There are a variety of techniques that central banks use to affect the reserves of commercial banks. We will first explain how three of these techniques could be used to change commercial bank reserves and the money supply in our fictional economy. Then we will consider real-world complications that central banks face in changing the money supply.

Affecting the Supply of Bank Reserves: Changing Reserve Requirements

Recall that Equation 13.2 relates to a fictional economy where there is only one type of deposit and hence only one definition of the money supply: currency held by the public plus bank deposits. As Equation 13.2 shows, in such an economy, the money supply depends on just three factors: the amount of currency the public chooses to hold, the supply of bank reserves, and the reserve-deposit ratio maintained by commercial banks. For given quantities of currency held by the public and of reserves held by the banks, an increase in the reserve-deposit ratio reduces the money supply, as you can see from Equation 13.2. A higher reserve-deposit ratio implies that banks lend out a smaller share of their deposits in each of the rounds of lending and redeposit described earlier, limiting the overall expansion of loans and deposits.

Suppose that the central bank wished to change the supply of commercial bank reserves in order to change the money supply. Specifically, suppose that the commercial banks maintain a common 3 percent reserve-deposit ratio, and the central bank wants to contract the money supply. One technique the central bank could use is to force the commercial banks to raise their reserve-deposit ratio.

reserve requirements set by some central banks, the minimum values of the ratio of bank reserves to bank deposits that commercial banks are allowed to maintain; the Bank of Canada does not set reserve requirements

Legally required values of the reserve-deposit ratio set by a central bank are called **reserve requirements**. By raising required reserves to, say, 5 percent of deposits, the central bank could force commercial banks to raise their reserve-deposit ratio, at least until it reached 5 percent. As you can see from Equation 13.2, an increase in the reserve-deposit ratio lowers deposits and the money supply, all else being equal.

Note that raising reserve requirements above the desired reserve-deposit ratio of the commercial banks will tend to reduce the money supply, and similarly reducing reserve requirements from a "forced" high level like 5 percent of deposits back down to the desired 3 percent reserve-deposit ratio will tend to increase the money supply. But lowering reserve requirements below the banks' desired reserve-deposit ratio of 3 percent would have no effect—banks would simply hold more reserves than required.

Note also that while some central banks make use of reserve requirements, required reserves were abolished in Canada in the early 1990s.

Affecting the Supply of Bank Reserves: Open-Market Operations

Open-market operations occur when the central bank buys or sells financial assets and thereby increases or decreases commercial bank reserves. Suppose, for example, that the central bank buys financial assets, such as short-term government bonds, from the public. Such a purchase of government bonds from the public by the central bank is called an **open-market purchase**. Think of the central bank as paying for the bonds it acquires with newly printed money. Assuming that the public is already holding all the currency that it wants, people will deposit the cash they receive as payment for their bonds in commercial banks. Thus, the reserves of the commercial banking system will increase by an amount equal to the value of the bonds purchased by the central bank. For a given desired reserve-deposit ratio on the part of the banks, the increase in bank reserves will lead in turn, through the process of lending and redeposit of funds described in the previous section, to an expansion of bank deposits and the money supply, as summarized by Equation 13.2.

open-market purchase the purchase of government bonds from the public by the central bank for the purpose of increasing the supply of bank reserves

To reduce bank reserves and thus the money supply, the central bank reverses the procedure. It sells some of the government bonds that it holds (acquired in previous open-market purchases) to the public. The sale of government bonds by the central bank to the public is called an **open-market sale**. Assume that people pay for the bonds by writing cheques on their accounts with commercial banks. Then, when the central bank presents the cheques to the commercial banks for payment, reserves equal in value to the government bonds sold by the central bank are transferred from the commercial banks to the central bank. The central bank retires these reserves from circulation, lowering the supply of bank reserves and, hence, lowering the overall money supply, all else being equal.

open-market sale the sale by the central bank of government bonds for the purpose of reducing bank reserves

Together, open-market purchases and sales are called **open-market operations**. They are a widely used technique of central banking.

open-market operations open-market purchases and open-market sales

Increasing the money supply by open-market operations

EXAMPLE 13.3

In Shekellia, an economy with a financial system like the fictional one we have been analyzing, currency held by the public is 1000 shekels, bank reserves are 200 shekels, and the desired reserve-deposit ratio is 0.2. What is the money supply? How is the money supply affected if the central bank prints 100 shekels and uses this new currency to buy government bonds from the public? Assume that the public does not wish to change the amount of currency it holds.

As bank reserves are 200 shekels and the reserve-deposit ratio is 0.2, bank deposits must equal 200 shekels/0.2, or 1000 shekels. The money supply, equal to the sum of currency held by the public and bank deposits, is therefore 2000 shekels, a result you can confirm using Equation 13.2.

The open-market purchase puts 100 more shekels into the hands of the public. We assume that the public continues to want to hold 1000 shekels in currency, so people will deposit the additional 100 shekels in the commercial banking system, raising bank reserves from 200 to 300 shekels. As the desired reserve-deposit ratio is 0.2, multiple rounds of lending and redeposit will eventually raise the level of bank deposits to 300 shekels/0.2, or 1500 shekels. The money supply, equal to 1000 shekels held by the public plus bank deposits of 1500 shekels, equals 2500 shekels. So the open-market purchase of 100 shekels, by raising bank reserves by 100 shekels, has increased the money supply by 500 shekels. Again, you can confirm this result using Equation 13.2.

EXERCISE 13.3

Continuing Example 13.3, suppose that instead of an open-market purchase of 100 shekels, the central bank conducts an open-market sale of 50 shekels' worth of government bonds. What happens to bank reserves, bank deposits, and the money supply? Continue to assume that the public does not wish to change the amount of currency it holds and that the desired reserve-deposit ratio remains as before.

Affecting the Supply of Bank Reserves: Government Deposit Shifting

The government typically maintains deposits in accounts at both the central bank and the commercial banks. The central bank can increase or decrease commercial bank reserves by **government deposit shifting** between itself and the commercial banks.

Suppose that the central bank writes cheques on a government account at the central bank and deposits the cheques into government accounts at the commercial banks. Commercial bank reserves will be increased. For a given desired reserve-deposit ratio on the part of the commercial banks, the increase in bank reserves will lead to an increase in the money supply.

government deposit shifting the transfer of government deposits by the central bank between the government's account at the central bank and the government's accounts at commercial banks

banking panic a rush of withdrawals from the banking system made by depositors responding to news or rumours of impending bankruptcy of one or more banks

By shifting government deposits in the opposite direction—that is, by shifting government deposits from commercial banks to government accounts with itself—the central bank can decrease bank reserves. With no change in the desired reserve-deposit ratio, the commercial banks will contract their loans, and the money supply will decrease.

ECONOMIC *Naturalist* 🖋 13.1   The U.S. banking panic of 1930–1933 and the money supply

A **banking panic** occurs when depositors, spurred by news or rumours of the imminent bankruptcy of one or more banks, rush to try to withdraw their deposits from the banking system. One of the most dramatic banking panics in world history occurred in the United States during the early stages of the Great Depression, between 1930 and 1933. Although Canada also went through a severe economic downturn in the same period, the country was not gripped by a banking panic, apparently because Canadian banks were large institutions with national networks of branch offices that inspired confidence in Canadian depositors. The U.S. experience with banking panic, however, is of general relevance as it dramatically illustrates how the public demand for currency and the desired reserve-deposit ratio of banks affect the money supply.

The relevance of the U.S. experience of the 1930s to us today is expressed in the comment of Princeton University economist Paul Krugman regarding the U.S. housing and mortgage financial crisis of 2007–2008: "The financial crisis currently under way is basically an updated version of the wave of bank runs that swept the nation three generations ago."[4] In March 2008, fearing a repeat of the 1930s events he studied as an academic economist, Federal Reserve Chairman Ben Bernanke led a decisive move to rescue the near-bank Bear Stearns and have it merged with JP Morgan Chase. The move was made to prevent the possibility of an impending bankruptcy of Bear Stearns, due to losses on mortgage-backed securities, from setting off a chain reaction.

During the 1930–1933 period, approximately one-third of the banks in the United States were forced to close. This near-collapse of the banking system was probably an important reason why the Depression was so severe. With many fewer banks in operation it was very difficult for small businesses and consumers during the early 1930s to obtain credit. Another important effect of the banking panics was to greatly reduce the nation's money supply. Why should banking panic reduce the national money supply?

During a banking panic people are afraid to keep deposits in a bank because of the risk that the bank will go bankrupt and their money will be lost (this was prior to the introduction of federal deposit insurance). During the 1930–1933 period, many bank depositors withdrew their money from banks, holding currency instead. These withdrawals reduced bank reserves. Each extra dollar of currency held by the public adds one dollar to the money supply; but each extra dollar of bank reserves translates into several dollars of money supply, because in a fractional-reserve banking system each dollar of reserves can "support" several dollars in bank deposits. Thus the public's withdrawals from banks, which increased currency holdings by the public but reduced bank reserves by an equal amount, led to a net decrease in the total money supply (currency plus deposits).

In addition, fearing banking panics and the associated withdrawals by depositors, banks increased their reserve-deposit ratios, which reduced the quantity of deposits that could be supported by any given level of bank reserves. This change in reserve-deposit ratios also tended to reduce the money supply.

Data on currency holdings by the public, the reserve-deposit ratio, bank reserves, and the money supply for selected dates are shown in Table 13.7. Notice the increase over the period in the amount of currency held by the public and in the reserve-deposit ratio, as well as the decline in bank reserves after 1930. The last column shows that the U.S. money supply dropped by about one-third between December 1929 and December 1933.

Using Equation 13.2, we can see that increases in currency holdings by the public and increases in the reserve-deposit ratio both tend to reduce the money supply. These effects were so powerful in 1930–1933 that the U.S. money supply, shown in the fourth column of Table 13.7, dropped precipitously, even though currency holdings and bank reserves, taken separately, actually rose during the period.

[4]Paul Krugman, "Partying like It's 1929," *New York Times*, 21 March 2008.

TABLE 13.7
Key U.S. Monetary Statistics, 1929–1933

	Currency held by public	Reserve-deposit ratio	Bank reserves	Money supply
December 1929	3.85	0.075	3.15	45.9
December 1930	3.79	0.082	3.31	44.1
December 1931	4.59	0.095	3.11	37.3
December 1932	4.82	0.109	3.18	34.0
December 1933	4.85	0.133	3.45	30.8

NOTE: Data on currency, bank reserves, and the money supply are in billions of dollars.
SOURCE: Milton Friedman and Anna J. Schwartz, *A Monetary History of the United States, 1863–1960*, (Princeton, N.J.: Princeton University Press, 1963), Table A-1.

EXERCISE 13.4

Using the data from Table 13.7, confirm that the relationship between the money supply and its determinants is consistent with Equation 13.2. Would the money supply have fallen in 1931–1933 if the public had stopped withdrawing deposits after December 1930 so that currency held by the public had remained at its December 1930 level?

REAL WORLD LIMITS TO MONEY SUPPLY CONTROL

In the real world, commercial banks offer various categories of deposits (such as chequing accounts, savings accounts, term deposits, and so on) and members of the public hold deposits not just with commercial banks but also with other financial intermediaries (such as trust companies, credit unions, and caisses populaires in Canada). As a consequence, in the real world we cannot talk about "the" money supply, as if there were only one possible measure of it, but we must recognize that there are many alternative measures of the money supply. These measures differ widely not just in magnitude but also in their annual growth rates. In simplified examples, the money supply either increases or decreases. In a real-world economy like Canada, some measures of the money supply may increase at the same time that others are decreasing. How these measures of the money supply change depends directly upon decisions taken by depositors, borrowers, and lenders in response to changes in income, interest rates, and other economic variables, and only indirectly upon actions by the central bank, the issuer of currency.[5] Indeed, if you visit the Bank of Canada Web site you can find statements bluntly declaring that the "Bank of Canada can't directly increase or decrease the money supply at will." By this, the Bank means that it is not able to fine-tune money supply growth targets such as, for example, 5 percent give or take 0.5 percent. But if, very unrealistically speaking, the Bank wished to decimate the money supply and cause a depression, it could do so. It also has the power to create an astronomical expansion of the money supply and thereby create hyperinflation. These effects of the money supply will be discussed in the next section.

[5]Bruce Montador, "The Implementation of Monetary Policy in Canada," *Canadian Public Policy*, XXI, 1, March 1995, pp. 110–111, notes that: "central banks' views about money supply determination have for a long time been that the money stock is demand determined, and a function of income (and/or wealth) and interest rates."

13.4   THE SIGNIFICANCE OF MONEY SUPPLY

We opened this chapter on money with a discussion of the definition of money, its functions, and how it is measured. Then, expanding further on the topic of central banks that has been ongoing in Chapters 9 through 12, we saw how, besides the role they play in monetary and exchange rate policies, central banks also have an impact on the economy through their effect on money supply: how they create money, change its level through small increases in currency, and also how their ability to control it is limited.

Why is it important to understand how money is created and how the supply of it can, or cannot, be changed? Understanding how the money supply is changed, and the role of central banks in this, is important to an understanding of other economic theories. For example, many intermediate macroeconomics textbooks present a theory of interest rate determination based upon the idea of a money supply curve controlled by the central bank. The material presented in this chapter explains some of the methods that a central bank could use to change interest rates according to that theory.

We have already seen one example of how the money supply is critical to the economy. Economic Naturalist 13.1 detailed how a collapse in the money supply can be associated with a severe economic depression. An understanding of the money supply is also critical to understanding hyperinflation, the extremely high inflation discussed in Chapter 6. This is another clear example of the significance of money supply and the value of a correct understanding of its role. Although hyperinflation has never occurred in Canada, it has occurred in a large number of countries, invariably with dire economic consequences.

The most famous hyperinflation was that of Germany in 1922–1923, often illustrated in history textbooks with a picture of a woman feeding a furnace with banknotes so worthless it was more economical to burn them as fuel than it was to buy firewood with them. An article in *The Economist* described the German hyperinflation as follows: "Workers were paid twice a day, and given half-hour breaks to rush to the shops with their satchels, suitcases or wheelbarrow, to buy something, anything, before their paper money halved in value yet again. By mid-November [1923], when a new currency was issued, prices had added twelve noughts since the First World War began in 1914."[6]

One of eight hyperinflations that occurred between 1920 and 1947, the German experience of 1922–1923 meets a strict definition for hyperinflation as a situation in which monthly inflation exceeded 50 percent. There were no such hyperinflations between 1947 and the early 1980s, but these events, unfortunately, are not a thing of the past. According to the International Monetary Fund, if hyperinflation is defined as annual inflation exceeding 1000 percent, then, since the early 1980s, some 25 countries have suffered it: 5 Latin American countries, 17 Central and East European or countries of the former Soviet Union, and 3 African countries.[7]

All countries that suffered hyperinflations have one thing in common—during the period of hyperinflation they experienced extremely high rates of growth of their money supply. In fact, their rates of hyperinflation were often very close to their rates of money supply growth, something that can be explained by a well-known relationship in economics called the *quantity equation*.

---

[6]"German Hyperinflation: Loads of Money," *The Economist*, 23 December 1999.
[7]Sharmini Coorey et al., "Lessons from High Inflation Episodes for Stabilizing the Economy in Zimbabwe," IMF Working Paper, April 2007, http://www.imf.org/external/pubs/ft/wp/2007/wp0799.pdf (June 2008).

The **quantity equation** is an identity stating that money (M) times its *velocity* (V) equals the price level (P) times real output (Y). This results in the equation

$$M \times V = P \times Y. \tag{13.3}$$

The price level times real output equals nominal GDP, as discussed in Chapter 6. The **velocity of money**, also known as the rate of circulation of money, can be thought of as a measure of the speed at which money changes hands in the economy. But since the quantity equation is an identity, we can through substitution write

$$V = (P \times Y) / M = \text{Nominal GDP/Money Supply.} \tag{13.4}$$

The velocity of money differs according to which definition of money supply is employed—the broader the definition of the money supply is, the larger the denominator of the Nominal GDP/ Money Supply part of Equation 13.4 will be, and thus the smaller the velocity of money will be as a result.

When explaining hyperinflation, it is common to assume that V and Y are constant. But this is not strictly true; Y tends to fall during hyperinflation and V moves around somewhat. During hyperinflation, however, changes in M are so great relative to changes in Y and V that it is reasonable to assume that Y and V are constant throughout, which results in the expression

$$M \times \overline{V} = P \times \overline{Y} \tag{13.5}$$

where the bars over Y and V indicate that Y and V are assumed to be constant. If V and Y are constant, it can be derived mathematically from Equation 13.5 that

$$\% \text{ change in } M = \% \text{ change in } P. \tag{13.6}$$

In other words, the rate of growth of the money supply (% change in M) equals the rate of inflation (% change in P).

A word of caution is necessary here. Equation 13.6 has been shown to be an excellent theory of hyperinflation. There is also evidence that it applies reasonably well to countries with very high inflation, defined as annual inflation of over 100 percent per year.[8] It is not, however, a theory that can explain changes in the inflation rate for a country with low or moderate inflation, as is the case with Canada, the United States, the euro-area countries, Japan, or Britain. As Figure 13.1 shows, money supply growth in Canada has in recent years been a few times higher than the rate of inflation, and fluctuations of money supply growth and the inflation rate exhibit no perceptible link. Similarly, we noted in Chapter 12 that although the purchasing power parity theory of exchange rate determination is useful for explaining exchange rate movements over the long run between countries with very different inflation rates, it is not useful for explaining exchange rate movements between countries with moderate inflation. The theory supporting Equation 13.6 is similar to the purchasing power parity theory in that it is accurate for explaining special situations while at the same time it is irrelevant as an explanation of those that are more commonplace.[9]

quantity equation an amount of money times its velocity equals nominal GDP; $M \times V = P \times Y$

velocity of money a measure of the speed at which money changes hands in transactions involving final goods and services; $V = (P \times Y)/M$

[8]See Stanley Fischer et al., "Modern Hyper- and High Inflations," IMF Working Paper, November 2002, www.imf.org/external/pubs/ft/wp/2002/wp02197.pdf (June 2008).
[9]In early 2008, measures of broad money supply growth were rising in Britain, the euro area, Japan and the United States as economic growth was slowing. In the article "Broad Money Supply," *The Economist*, 8 May 2008, the following explanation was provided: "If money flowed around the economy at a stable rate, an annual increase much above 5% in a rich country would provide an early warning of inflation—too much cash would be chasing too few goods. . . . [i]n fact money-supply growth is an unreliable indicator, because its rate of circulation varies. In times of economic stress, as now, firms and households prefer to keep more of their wealth in cash or in liquid bank deposits. This helps explain why broad money has either picked up or stayed strong despite weaker economic growth."

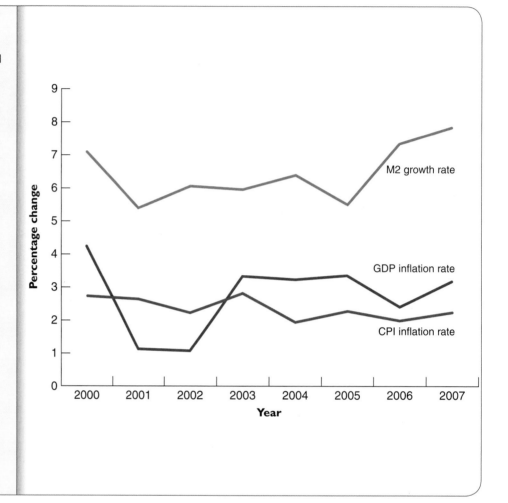

FIGURE 13.1

No Apparent Relationship: Inflation and Money Supply Growth; Canada, 2000–2007

Although hyperinflation is associated with high rates of money supply growth, in countries with low or moderate inflation, growth of the money supply (red line) is not a reliable predictor of changes in the rate of inflation (blue and green lines). In some of the years shown, for example, the M2 growth rate is from 2 to 4 times larger than the inflation rate, and a drop in the M2 growth rate from 2004 to 2005 is accompanied by slight rise rather than a drop in the inflation rate.

SOURCE: Adapted from CANSIM series v41552796 (M2 gross), v1997756 (GDP deflator), and v41690973 (CPI).

ECONOMIC *Naturalist* **13.2** | **Why did Zimbabwe's annual inflation rate exceed 66 212 percent in early 2008?**

According to Zimbabwe's official statistics, which may underestimate the severity of the situation, Zimbabwe's annual inflation rate had reached 66 212 percent by the end of 2007. And it was still rising. In 1980, one Zimbabwe dollar had been worth more than one U.S. dollar, but in early 2008 a $10-million note was not enough to purchase a kilogram of chicken.[10]

Zimbabwe's hyperinflation, as with other hyperinflations, was the direct result of massive growth in the money supply. Less than two years earlier, in 2006, the inflation rate was several hundred percent and the annual rate of growth of the money supply was also several hundred percent. Both the rate of growth of the money supply and the inflation rate soared afterwards.

Critics and defenders of the government of then President Robert Mugabe offer different explanations as to why the government resorted to printing money to pay its bills. Critics, for example, emphasize such factors as the loss of government revenue resulting from the collapse of agricultural production that followed Mugabe's controversial farm seizures in 2000. The situation, they say, was made worse by the supply shortages that arose when companies had to stop production of some goods as a result of price controls imposed by the government. Mugabe, on the other hand, blamed the situation on sanctions imposed by the West. Regardless of the reason for firing up the printing presses however, there is no denying that, by printing astronomical amounts of currency to finance its activities, the government created hyperinflation.

---

[10]"Zimbabwe's Inflation Rate Jumps to Record 66,212%," CBC news, 15 February 2008, http://www.cbc.ca/money/story/2008/02/15/zimbabwe.html (June 2008).

If rates of money growth of several hundred percent or more per year lead to hyperinflation, why do countries allow their money supplies to explode? Usually, extremely rapid rates of money growth are the result of governments accumulating large budget deficits that they cover by printing money rather than by selling bonds. Particularly in developing countries or in those suffering from war or political instability, governments sometimes find that they cannot raise sufficient taxes or borrow enough from the public to cover their expenditures. In this situation, if they have direct control over the central bank, they often yield to the temptation to print new money in order to pay their bills. If the resulting increase in the level of inflation is large enough, hyperinflation will follow.

RECAP ↑

THE SIGNIFICANCE OF MONEY SUPPLY

- All countries that suffer hyperinflations experience extremely high rates of growth of their money supply.

- *Velocity of money* measures the speed at which money circulates in payments for final goods and services; equivalently, it is equal to nominal GDP divided by the stock of money.

- The *quantity equation* states that money times velocity equals nominal GDP, or, in symbols, $M \times V = P \times Y$. If the velocity of money (V) and real GDP (Y) can be assumed to be constant, which is a reasonable assumption when analyzing hyperinflation, the quantity equation implies that a given percentage increase in the money supply leads to approximately the same percentage increase in the price level. In other words, the rate of growth of the money supply approximately equals the rate of hyperinflation.

- Although the *quantity equation* theory successfully explains hyperinflation, it cannot be applied to situations of low or moderate inflation as is the case in Canada. For such situations the models of Chapters 9, 10, and 11 are relevant instead.

SUMMARY

13.1 Money is any asset that can be used in making purchases, such as currency and chequing account balances. Money has three main functions. (1) It is a medium of exchange, which means that it can be used in transactions. (2) It is a unit of account, in that economic values are typically measured in units of money (e.g., dollars). And (3) it is a store of value, a means by which people can hold wealth. In practice, it is difficult to measure the money supply, since many assets have some money-like features. A relatively narrow measure of money is M1, which includes currency and chequing accounts at commercial banks. A broader measure of money, M2, includes all the assets in M1 plus additional assets that are somewhat less convenient to use in transactions. There are other measures of money as well, and the various measures differ substantially in magnitude.

13.2 Because bank deposits are part of the money supply, the behaviour of commercial banks and of bank depositors affects the amount of money in the economy. A key factor is the reserve-deposit ratio chosen by banks. Bank reserves are cash or similar assets held by commercial banks, for the purpose of meeting depositor withdrawals and payments. The reserve-deposit ratio is bank reserves divided by deposits in banks. Modern banking systems have reserve-deposit ratios far below 1, and are called fractional-reserve banking systems.

13.2 Commercial banks create money through multiple rounds of lending and accepting deposits. This process of lending and increasing deposits comes to an end when banks' reserve-deposit ratios equal their desired levels. At that point, bank deposits equal bank reserves divided by the desired reserve-deposit ratio. The money supply equals currency held by the public plus deposits in the banking system.

13.3 Central banks can affect the reserves available to commercial banks using techniques such as open-market operations, shifting government deposits, and, in some jurisdictions, changes in legal reserve requirements.

13.3 In a real-world economy, some measures of the money supply may increase at the same time that others are decreasing, and for reasons other than the actions of the central bank. Thus, precise control of the money supply may not be possible.

13.4 Hyperinflation is the direct result of massive growth of the money supply, as can be explained by the quantity equation.

KEY TERMS

Bank of Canada (345)
bank reserves (340)
banking panic (350)
barter (337)
commodity money (337)
European Central Bank (ECB) (347)
Federal Reserve System (the Fed) (346)
fiat money (337)
fractional-reserve banking system (341)

government deposit shifting (349)
key policy rate (346)
M1 (338)
M2 (339)
medium of exchange (337)
money (337)
100 percent reserve banking (341)
open-market operations (349)
open-market purchase (348)

open-market sale (349)
quantity equation (353)
reserve-deposit ratio (341)
reserve requirements (348)
store of value (338)
unit of account (338)
velocity of money (353)

REVIEW QUESTIONS

1. What is *money?* Why do people hold money even though it pays a lower return than other financial assets?

2. Suppose that the public switches from doing most of its shopping with currency to using cheques instead. If the central bank takes no action, what will happen to the national money supply? Explain.

3. Name the most commonly used measure of money supply in Canada and explain its components.

4. What techniques do central banks employ to change commercial bank reserves?

5. What is the quantity equation and how is it used to explain hyperinflation?

PROBLEMS

1. During the Second World War, an Allied soldier named Robert Radford spent several years in a large German prisoner-of-war camp. At times, more than 50 000 prisoners were held in the camp, with some freedom to move about within the compound. Radford later wrote an account of his experiences. He described how an economy developed in the camp, in which prisoners traded food, clothing, and other items. Services, such as barbering, were also exchanged.

Lacking paper money, the prisoners began to use cigarettes (provided monthly by the Red Cross) as money. Prices were quoted, and payments made, using cigarettes.

a. In Radford's POW camp, how did cigarettes fulfill the three functions of money?

b. Why do you think the prisoners used cigarettes as money, as opposed to other items of value such as squares of chocolate or pairs of boots?

c. Do you think a non-smoking prisoner would have been willing to accept cigarettes in exchange for a good or service in Radford's camp? Why or why not?

2. a. In an imaginary economy bank reserves are 100, the public holds 200 in currency, and the desired reserve-deposit ratio is 0.25. Find deposits and the money supply.

b. The money supply is 500, and currency held by the public equals bank reserves. The desired reserve-deposit ratio is 0.25. Find currency held by the public and bank reserves.

c. The money supply is 1250, of which 250 is currency held by the public. Bank reserves are 100. Find the desired reserve-deposit ratio.

3. When a central bank increases bank reserves by $1, the money supply rises by more than $1. The amount of extra money created when the central bank increases bank reserves by $1 is called the *money multiplier*.

a. Explain why the money multiplier is generally greater than 1. In what special case would it equal 1?

b. In an imaginary economy the initial money supply is $1000, of which $500 is currency held by the public. The desired reserve-deposit ratio is 0.2. Find the increase in money supply associated with increases in bank reserves of $1, $5, and $10. What is the money multiplier in this economy?

c. Find a general rule for calculating the money multiplier in such an economy.

d. Explain the difficulties that would arise in calculating a money multiplier for the Canadian economy. Do you think such a multiplier would stay constant from year to year?

4. Refer to Table 13.7. Suppose that the Fed had decided to set the U.S. money supply in December 1932 and in December 1933 at the same value as in December 1930. Assuming that the values of currency held by the public and the reserve-deposit ratio had remained as given in the table, by how much more should the Fed have increased bank reserves at each of those dates to accomplish that objective?

5. Suppose that inflation is running at an annual rate of 1000 percent, as it was in Zimbabwe in 2006.

a. Change in which economic variable would lie directly behind this inflation rate? Name and briefly explain the theory that applies to predicting the level of hyperinflation.

b. If the annual inflation rate is 1000 percent, in what range would you expect to find short-term nominal interest rates? Name and explain the theory that applies to predicting how inflation affects nominal interest rates. (*Hint:* see Chapter 6.)

c. If the annual inflation rate is 1000 percent, would you expect the market exchange rate to appreciate or depreciate against the U.S. dollar? Name and explain the theory that applies to predicting exchange rate changes between a country with very high inflation and one with low or moderate inflation. (*Hint:* see Chapter 12.)

ANSWERS TO IN-CHAPTER EXERCISES

13.1 Table 13.5 shows the balance sheet of banks after two rounds of lending and redeposits. At that point deposits are 2 710 000 guilders and reserves are 1 000 000 guilders. Since banks have a desired reserve–deposit ratio of 10 percent, they will keep 271 000 guilders (10 percent of deposits) as reserves and lend out the remaining 729 000 guilders. Loans to farmers are now 2 439 000 guilders. Eventually the 729 000 guilders lent to the farmers will be redeposited into the banks, giving the banks deposits of 3 439 000 guilders and reserves of 1 000 000 guilders. The balance sheet is as shown in the accompanying table.

Assets		Liabilities	
Currency (= reserves)	1 000 000 guilders	Deposits	3 439 000 guilders
Loans to farmers	2 439 000 guilders		

Notice that assets equal liabilities. The money supply equals deposits, or 3 439 000 guilders. *Currency held in the banks as reserves does not count in the money supply.*

13.2   Because the public holds no currency, the money supply equals bank deposits, which in turn equal bank reserves divided by the reserve–deposit ratio (Equation 13.1). If bank reserves are 1 000 000 and the reserve–deposit ratio is 0.05, then deposits equal 1 000 000/0.05 = 20 000 000 guilders, which is also the money supply. If bank reserves are 2 000 000 guilders and the reserve–deposit ratio is 0.10, then the money supply and deposits are again equal to 20 000 000 guilders, or 2 000 000/0.10.

13.3   If the central bank sells 50 shekels of government bonds in exchange for currency, the immediate effect is to reduce the amount of currency in the hands of the public by 50 shekels. To restore their currency holding to the desired level of 1000 shekels, the public will withdraw 50 shekels from commercial banks, reducing bank reserves from 200 shekels to 150 shekels. The desired reserve-deposit ratio is 0.2, so ultimately deposits must equal 150 shekels in reserves divided by 0.2, or 750 shekels. (Note that to contract deposits, the commercial banks will have to "call in" or not renew or replace maturing loans, reducing their loans outstanding.) The money supply equals 1000 shekels in currency held by the public plus 750 shekels in deposits, or 1750 shekels. Thus the open-market purchase has reduced the money supply from 2000 to 1750 shekels.

13.4   Verify directly for each date in Table 9.7 that

$$\text{Money supply} = \text{Currency} + \frac{\text{Bank reserves}}{\text{Desired reserve-deposit ratio}}$$

For example, for December 1929 we can check that 45.9 = 3.85 + 3.15/0.075.

   Suppose that the currency held by the public in December 1933 had been 3.79, as in December 1930, rather than 4.85, and that the difference (4.85 − 3.79 = 1.06) had been left in the banks. Then bank reserves in December 1933 would have been 3.45 + 1.06 = 4.51, and the money supply would have been 3.79 + 4.51/0.133 = 37.7. So the money supply would still have fallen between 1930 and 1933 if people had not increased their holdings of currency, but only by about half as much.

PART 4

The Economy in the Long Run

For millennia the great majority of the world's inhabitants eked out a spare existence by tilling the soil. Only a small proportion of the population lived above the level of subsistence, learned to read and write, or travelled more than a few miles from their birthplaces. Large cities grew up, serving as imperial capitals and centres of trade, but the great majority of urban populations lived in dire poverty, subject to malnutrition and disease.

Then, about three centuries ago, a fundamental change occurred. Spurred by technological advances and entrepreneurial innovations, a process of economic growth began that has transformed every aspect of how people live in most countries—from what we eat and wear to how we work and play. Economists recognize that this growth has been central to improvements in living standards and they have been intensely concerned with the important questions it raises. What is necessary to sustain economic growth and improvements in living standards? Why have

some countries enjoyed substantially greater growth than others?

The subject of Part 4 is the long-term behaviour of economies, including the factors that cause economies to grow. Chapter 14 begins by tackling directly the causes and consequences of economic growth. A key conclusion of the chapter is that improvements in average labour productivity are a key source of long-term improvements in living standards; hence, policies to improve living standards must be concerned with stimulating productivity growth. International trade theory and trade policy, including the issue of how trade relates to economic growth, are the topics of Chapter 15. Chapter 16 examines the process of saving and capital formation in Canada, which has an open economy connected to international capital markets. Capital formation plays an important role in raising average labour productivity. Finally, Chapter 17 extends the discussion of saving and capital formation, with particular emphasis on financial markets and international capital flows.

Chapter 14 Economic Growth, Productivity, and Living Standards

At the time of Canadian Confederation in 1867, doctors lacked effective treatments for a wide range of communicable diseases that are now quite treatable. Tuberculosis, typhoid fever, diphtheria, influenza, and pneumonia were once major killers. The shortcomings of healthcare in decades past were not limited to ineffective treatments for now-curable diseases. In addition, healthcare suffered because hospital administrators were slow to learn how much the health of medical patients depended on sanitary conditions and proper nursing care, a fact often illustrated with the story of Florence Nightingale (1820–1910). Nightingale became famous in mid-nineteenth-century England after implementing sanitary reforms at a military hospital that drastically reduced the mortality rates of patients. She then used statistical evidence on the effectiveness of those reforms to campaign for their widespread adoption. Recognizing that the lack of training of nurses left them incapable of contributing to the recovery of patients, she campaigned successfully to establish nursing as a profession. Nightingale-trained nurses eventually came to Canada, and in 1881 a nursing school based on a modification of the Nightingale system was started at the Toronto General Hospital.

Healthcare is just one aspect of ordinary life where extraordinary progress has been made since the time of Confederation. No doubt you can think of other enormous changes in the conditions average Canadians face, even over the past few decades.

Computer technologies and the Internet have changed the ways people work and study in just a few years, for example. Though these changes are due in large part to scientific advances, such discoveries *by themselves* usually have little effect on most people's lives. New scientific knowledge leads to widespread improvements in living standards only when it is incorporated into widely used goods and services or production processes. Better understanding of the human immune system, for example, has little impact unless it leads to new therapies or drugs. And a new drug will do little to help unless it is affordable to those who need to buy it or is available to them through public health care.

Most improvements in living standards are the result not just of scientific and technological advances but of an economic system that makes the benefits of those advances available to the average person.

In this chapter we will explore the sources of economic growth and rising living standards in the modern world. We will begin by reviewing the remarkable economic growth in the industrialized countries, as measured by real GDP per person. Since the mid-nineteenth century (and earlier in some cases), a radical transformation in living standards has occurred in these countries. What explains this transformation? Generally speaking, rising living standards over long periods require a *continuing increase in average labour productivity,* which depends on several factors, including the equipment with which workers perform their tasks, the skills workers bring to their jobs, the transportation and communications infrastructure, and the legal and social environment. We will analyze each of these factors and discuss its implications for government policies to promote growth. We will also discuss the costs of rapid economic growth and consider whether there may be limits to the amount of growth a society can or should achieve.

14.1 THE REMARKABLE RISE IN REAL GDP PER CAPITA: THE RECORD

The advances in healthcare and computing mentioned in the beginning of this chapter illustrate only a few of the impressive changes that have taken place in people's living standards over the past two centuries, particularly in industrialized countries like Canada. To study the factors that affect living standards systematically, however, we must go beyond anecdotes and adopt a specific indicator of living standards in a particular country and time.

In Chapter 5 we introduced the concept of real GDP as a basic measure of the level of economic activity in a country. Recall that, in essence, real GDP measures the volume of goods and services produced within a country's borders during a specific period, such as a quarter or a year. Consequently, real GDP *per person* provides a measure of the quantity of goods and services available to the typical resident of a country at a particular time.[1] Moreover, although maximizing growth of real GDP per person may not be an appropriate normative goal for economic policy, as we saw in Chapter 5, real GDP per person is positively related to a range of basic indicators of human development, such as life expectancy, infant health, and years of schooling. Lacking a better alternative, economists have focused on real GDP per person as a rough indicator of a country's living standard and stage of economic development.

Figure 4.2 showed the remarkable growth in real GDP per person that occurred in Canada between 1926 and 2007. For comparison, Table 14.1 shows real GDP per person in eight major countries in selected years from 1870 to 2007. Figure 14.1 displays the same data graphically for five of the eight countries.

The data in Table 14.1 and Figure 14.1 tell a dramatic story. For example, in Canada, real GDP per person grew more than 14 times larger between 1870 and 2007. In Japan, real GDP per person grew more than 31 times larger over the same period. Underlying these statistics is an amazingly rapid process of economic growth and transformation, through which in just a few generations relatively poor agrarian societies became highly industrialized economies—with average standards of living that could scarcely have been imagined in 1870. As

---

[1] If the income distribution is highly unequal, then real GDP per person considerably overstates the quantity of goods and services available to the typical resident.

TABLE 14.1

Real GDP per Person in Selected Countries, 1870–2007 (in 2000 U.S. Dollars)

Country	1870	1913	1950	1979	2007	Annual % change 1870–2007	Annual % change 1950–2007
Australia	5512	7236	9369	17 670	32 280	1.3	2.2
Canada	2328	5509	8906	19 882	32 722	1.9	2.3
France	2291	4484	6164	18 138	28 348	1.9	2.7
Germany	1152	2218	4785	17 222	27 146	2.3	3.1
Italy	2852	4018	5128	16 912	26 854	1.6	3
Japan	931	1763	2141	16 329	29 174	2.5	4.7
United Kingdom	3892	5976	8709	16 557	29 965	1.5	2.2
United States	2887	6852	12 110	22 835	39 850	1.9	2.1

SOURCES: Derived from Angus Maddison, *Phases of Capitalist Development*, (Oxford: Oxford University Press, reprinted 1988), Tables A2, B2–B4. Rebased to 2000 and updated to 2007 by the authors using OECD *Quarterly National Accounts* (real GDP), "Germany" refers to West Germany in 1950 and 1979.

Figure 14.1 shows, a significant part of this growth has occurred since 1950, particularly in Japan (although not since the early 1990s).

A note of caution is in order. The farther back in time we go, the less precise are historical estimates of real GDP. Most governments did not keep official GDP statistics until after the Second World War; production records from earlier periods are often incomplete or of questionable accuracy. Comparing economic output over a century or more is also problematic because many goods and services that are produced today were unavailable—indeed, inconceivable—in 1870. How many nineteenth-century horse-drawn wagons, for example, would be the economic equivalent of a modern luxury car or a jumbo jet? Despite the difficulty

FIGURE 14.1

Real GDP Per Person in Five Industralized Countries, 1870–2007
Economic growth has been especially rapid since the 1950s, particularly in Japan (until the early 1990s). U.S. per capita GDP in 2007 was higher than in the other countries due to its relatively high GDP per capita in 1870 and relatively rapid growth until, but not since, 1950.
SOURCES: Same as for Table 14.1.

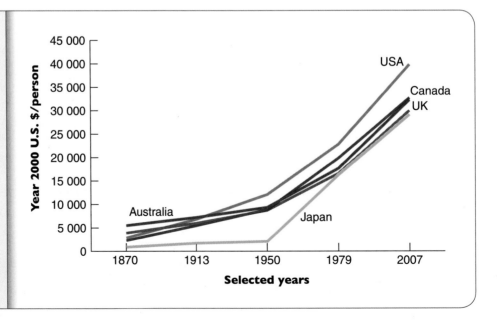

of making precise comparisons, however, we can say with certainty that the variety, quality, and quantity of available goods and services increased enormously in industrialized countries since the nineteenth century, a fact reflected in the data on real GDP per person.

14.2 WHY "SMALL" DIFFERENCES IN GROWTH RATES MATTER

The last two columns of Table 14.1 show the annual growth rates of real GDP per person, both for the entire 1870–2007 period and the more recent years, 1950–2007. At first glance these growth rates don't seem to differ much from country to country. For example, for the period 1870–2007, the highest growth rate is 2.5 percent (Japan) and the lowest is 1.3 percent (Australia). But consider the long-run effect of this seemingly "small" difference in annual growth rates. In 1870, in terms of output per person, Australia was by far the richest of the eight countries listed in Table 14.1, with a real GDP per person nearly six times that of Japan. Yet by 2007 Japan had pretty much caught up to Australia. This remarkable change in economic fortunes is the result of the apparently small difference between a 1.3 percent growth rate and a 2.5 percent growth rate, maintained over 137 years.

The fact that small differences in growth rates can have large long-run effects results from a general principle called the **power of compound growth**, a specific instance of which is the power of compound interest.

power of compound growth the fact that small differences in growth rates, maintained over long periods, will produce large differences in magnitude

Compound interest (1)   EXAMPLE 14.1

Suppose that in 1879 your great-great-grandfather deposited $10 in a savings account at 4 percent interest. Interest is compounded annually (so that interest paid at the end of each year receives interest itself in later years). Great-great-Grandpa's will specified that the account be turned over to his most direct descendant (you) in the year 2009. If you withdrew the funds in 2009, how much would the account be worth?[2]

The account was worth $10 in 1879; $10 \times 1.04 = \$10.40$ in 1880, $10 \times 1.04 \times 1.04 = \$10 \times (1.04)^2 = \$10.82$ in 1881; and so on. Since 130 years have elapsed between 1879, when the deposit was made, and the year 2009, when the account was closed, the value of the account in the year 2009 was $10 \times (1.04)^{130}$, or 10×1.04 to the 130th power. Using a calculator, you will find that $10 times 1.04 to the 130th power is $1638.08—a good return for a $10 deposit!

Compound interest is an arrangement in which interest is paid not only on the original deposit but on all previously accumulated interest and is distinguished from *simple interest*, in which interest is paid only on the original deposit. If your great-grandfather's account had been deposited at 4 percent simple interest, it would have accumulated only 40 cents each year (4 percent of the original $10 deposit), for a total value of $10 + (130 \times \$0.40) = \$52$ after 130 years.

compound interest the payment of interest not only on the original deposit but on all previously accumulated interest

Compound interest (2)   EXAMPLE 14.2

Refer to Example 14.1. What would your great-grandfather's $10 deposit have been worth after 130 years if the annual interest rate had been 2 percent? 6 percent?

[2]This, of course, is a hypothetical example. It assumes that the savings account pays the same rate of interest for 130 years and that the interest generated by the account is not subject to taxation.

At 2 percent interest the account would be worth $10 in 1879; $10 × 1.02 = $10.20 in 1880; $10 × (1.02) = $10.40 in 1881; and so on. In the year 2009 the value of the account would be $10 × $(1.02)^{130}$, or $131.22. If the interest rate were 6 percent, after 130 years the account would be worth $10 × $(1.06)^{130}$, or $19 487.79. Let's summarize the results of Examples 14.1 and 14.2.

Interest rate (%)	Value of $10 after 130 years
2	$131.22
4	$1638.08
6	$19 487.79

The power of compound interest is that even at relatively low rates of interest, a small sum, compounded over a long enough period, can greatly increase in value. A more subtle point, illustrated by this example, is that small differences in interest rates matter a lot—hence the phrase "the power of compound interest." The difference between a 2 percent and a 4 percent interest rate doesn't seem tremendous, but over a long period of time it implies large differences in the amount of interest accumulated on an account. The 4 percent interest rate is only twice as high, but after 130 years, it produced a balance more than 12 times as large.

As the term *power of compound growth* suggests, economic growth rates are similar to compound interest rates. Just as the value of a bank deposit grows each year at a rate equal to the interest rate, so the size of a nation's economy expands each year at the rate of economic growth. This analogy suggests that even a relatively modest rate of growth in output per person, 1 to 2 percent per year, will produce tremendous increases in average living standards over a long period. And relatively small *differences* in growth rates, as in the case of Australia versus Japan, will ultimately produce very different living standards if they persist for decades.

BOX 14.1 **THE RULE OF 72**

rule of 72 a rule of thumb stating that to find the number of years it takes a magnitude to double when it is growing at a constant rate, divide 72 by the growth rate

An often-used rule of thumb for examining differences in growth rates is known as the **rule of 72**. The rule states that to find how many years it takes for a magnitude to double when the magnitude is growing at a constant rate, divide 72 by the growth rate expressed in percentage terms. For example, if an economy's GDP per person is growing at 1 percent a year, it will take approximately 72 years for the economy's GDP per person to double. But if the economy's GDP per person is growing at the very high rate of 7.2 percent a year, it will only take about 10 years for GDP per person to double.

EXERCISE 14.1 **Suppose that real GDP per person in Canada had grown at 2.5 percent per year, as Japan's did, instead of the actual 1.9 percent per year, from 1870 to 2007. How much larger would real GDP per person have been in Canada in 2007?**

14.3 WHY NATIONS BECOME RICH: THE CRUCIAL ROLE OF AVERAGE LABOUR PRODUCTIVITY

What determines a nation's economic growth rate? To get some insight into this vital question, we find it useful to express real GDP per person as the product of two terms: average labour productivity and the share of the population that is working.

To do this, let Y equal total real output (as measured by real GDP, for example), N equal the number of employed workers, and POP equal the total population. Then real GDP per person can be written as Y/POP; average labour productivity, or output per employed worker, equals Y/N; and the share of the population that is working is N/POP. The relationship between these three variables is

$$\frac{Y}{POP} = \frac{Y}{N} \times \frac{N}{POP},$$

which, as you can see by cancelling out N on the right-hand side of the equation, always holds exactly. In words, this basic relationship is

Real GDP per person = Average labour productivity ×
Share of population employed.

This expression for real GDP per person tells us something very basic and intuitive: The quantity of goods and services produced per person depends on (1) how much each worker can produce and (2) how many people (as a fraction of the total population) are working. Furthermore, because real GDP per person equals average labour productivity times the share of the population that is employed, real GDP per person can *grow* only to the extent that there is *growth* in worker productivity and/or the fraction of the population that is employed.

Figures 14.2 and 14.3 show the Canadian figures for the three key variables in the relationship above for the period 1961–2007. Figure 14.2 shows both real GDP per person and real GDP per worker (average labour productivity) for

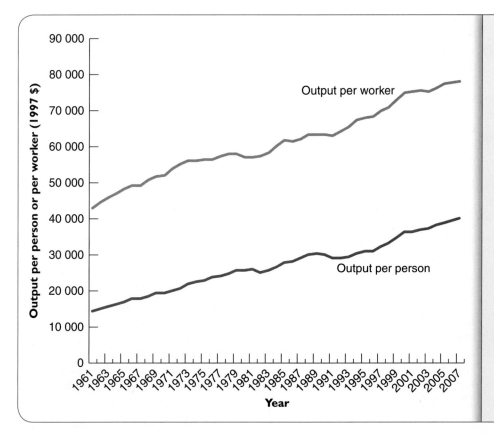

FIGURE 14.2

Output per Person and per Worker in the Canadian Economy, 1961–2007

Real output per person in Canada grew 182 percent between 1961 and 2007 while real output per worker (average labour productivity) grew by 82 percent.

SOURCE: Adapted from Statistics Canada, CANSIM II series v2461119 (employment), v466668 (population), and v1992259 (real GDP); and from *HSC* Catalogue 11-516, July 29, 1999, series D129, A1, and F55.

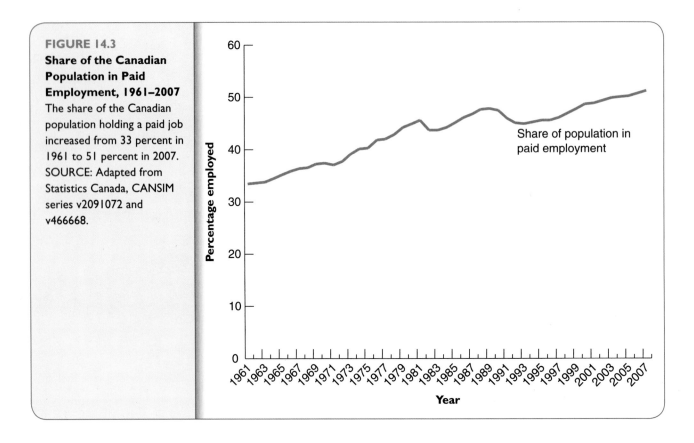

FIGURE 14.3

Share of the Canadian Population in Paid Employment, 1961–2007

The share of the Canadian population holding a paid job increased from 33 percent in 1961 to 51 percent in 2007. SOURCE: Adapted from Statistics Canada, CANSIM series v2091072 and v466668.

1961–2007. Figure 14.3 shows the portion of the entire Canadian population (not just the working-age population) that was employed for 1961–2007. Once again, we see that the expansion in output per person in Canada has been impressive. Between 1961 and 2007, real GDP per person in Canada grew by 182 percent. Thus in 2007, the average Canadian produced more than 2.8 times as many goods and services as in 1961. Figures 14.2 and 14.3 show that increases in both labour productivity and the share of the population holding a job contributed to this rise in living standards.

Let's look a bit more closely at these two contributing factors, beginning with the share of the population that is employed. As Figure 14.3 shows, between 1961 and 2007 the number of people employed in Canada rose from 33 to 51 percent of the entire population, a remarkable increase. The growing number of women working outside the home was the most important reason for this rise in employment.

Although the rising share of the Canadian population with jobs contributed significantly to the increase in real GDP per person during the past four decades, this trend almost certainly will not continue in the future. Women's participation in paid employment, for example, seems unlikely to continue rising at the same rate as in the past four decades.

What about the other factor that determines output per person: average labour productivity? As Figure 14.2 shows, between 1961 and 2007, average labour productivity in Canada increased by 82 percent, accounting for a sizable share of the overall increase in GDP per person. In other periods, the link between average labour productivity and output per person in Canada has often been even stronger, since in most earlier periods the share of the population holding jobs was more stable than it has been recently. (See Figure 4.2 for the behaviour of real GDP per person and average labour productivity in Canada over the period 1926–2007.)

This quick look at recent data supports a more general conclusion. *In the long run, increases in average labour productivity are important for increases in output per person.* To understand why economies grow, then, we must understand the reasons for increased labour productivity.

RECAP ↑

ECONOMIC GROWTH AND PRODUCTIVITY

Real GDP per person, a rough indicator of living standards, has grown dramatically in the industrialized countries. This growth reflects the *power of compound growth:* even a modest growth rate, if sustained over a long period of time, can lead to large increases in the size of the economy.

Output per person equals average labour productivity times the share of the population that is employed. Since 1961 the share of the Canadian population with jobs has risen significantly, but it is unlikely to continue to increase in future decades. In coming decades, increases in output per person and, hence, living standards will depend primarily upon increases in average labour productivity.

14.4 THE DETERMINANTS OF AVERAGE LABOUR PRODUCTIVITY

What determines the productivity of the average worker in a particular country at a particular time? Popular discussions of this issue often equate worker productivity with the willingness of workers of a given nationality to work hard. Everything else being equal, a culture that promotes hard work certainly tends to increase worker productivity. But intensity of effort cannot explain the huge differences in average labour productivity that we observe around the world. For example, average labour productivity in the United States is about 24 times what it is in Indonesia and 100 times what it is in Bangladesh, though there is little doubt that Indonesians and Bangladeshis work very hard.

In this section we will examine six factors that appear to account for the major differences in average labour productivity, both between countries and between generations. It should be noted that contributions to productivity differences made by three of these factors—human capital, physical capital, and natural resources (including land)—are much easier to quantify than the contributions made by the other three factors—technology, entrepreneurship, and the legal and political environment. Later in the chapter we will discuss how economic policies can influence these factors to spur productivity and growth.

HUMAN CAPITAL

To illustrate the factors that determine average labour productivity, we introduce two prototypical assembly line workers, Paris and Nicole.

Paris and Nicole on the assembly line

EXAMPLE 14.3

Paris and Nicole have jobs wrapping chocolate candies and placing them into boxes. Paris, a novice wrapper, can wrap only 100 candies/hour. Nicole, who has had on-the-job training, can wrap 300 candies/hour. Paris and Nicole each work 40 hours/week. Find average labour productivity, in terms of candies wrapped per week and candies wrapped per hour, (a) for Paris, (b) for Nicole, and (c) for Paris and Nicole as a team.

We have defined average labour productivity in general terms as output per worker. Note, though, that the measurement of average labour productivity depends on the time period that is specified. For example, the data presented in Figure 14.2 tell us how much the average worker produces *in a year*. In this example we are concerned with how much Paris and Nicole can produce *per hour* of work or *per week* of work. All of these ways of measuring labour productivity are valid, as long as we are clear about the time unit we are using.

Paris and Nicole's hourly productivities are given in the problem: Paris can wrap 100 candies/hour and Nicole can wrap 300. Paris's weekly productivity is (40 hours/week) × (100 candies wrapped/hour) = 4000 wrapped candies/week. Nicole's weekly productivity is (40 hours/week) × (300 candies wrapped/hour), or 12 000 candies/week.

Together Paris and Nicole can wrap 16 000 candies/week. As a team, their average weekly productivity is (16 000 candies wrapped)/(2 weeks of work), or 8000 candies/week. Their average hourly productivity as a team is (16 000 candies wrapped)/(80 hours of work) = 200 candies/hour. Notice that, taken as a team, the two women's productivity lies midway between their individual productivities.

Nicole is more productive than Paris because she has had on-the-job training, which has allowed her to develop her candy-wrapping skills to a higher level than Paris's. Because of her training, Nicole can produce more than Paris can in a given number of hours.

EXERCISE 14.2 **Suppose Nicole attends additional classes in candy wrapping and learns how to wrap 500 candies/hour. Find the output per week and output per hour for Paris and Nicole, both individually and as a team.**

Many economists would explain the difference in the two women's performance by saying that Nicole has more human capital than Paris. *Human capital* is often used as a catch-all term for the talents, education, training, and skills of workers. Workers with a large stock of human capital are more productive than workers with less training. For example, a secretary who knows how to use a word processing program will be able to type more letters than one who does not; an auto mechanic who is familiar with computerized diagnostic equipment will be able to fix engine problems that less well-trained mechanics could not.

COST–
BENEFIT

Education and training ("human capital") require the investment of time and money. For example, to learn how to use a word processing program, a secretary might need to attend a technical school at night. The cost of going to school includes not only the tuition paid but also the *opportunity cost* of the secretary's time spent attending class and studying. The benefit of the schooling is typically the increase in wages the secretary will tend to earn when the course has been completed. If the secretary follows the *cost–benefit principle*, he or she will choose to learn word processing if the benefits exceed the costs, including the opportunity costs. The higher wages and other benefits that typically accrue to workers with more human capital provide an incentive for acquiring additional education and training.

PHYSICAL CAPITAL

Workers' productivity depends not only on their skills and effort but also on the tools they have to work with. Even the most skilled surgeon cannot perform open-heart surgery without sophisticated equipment, and an expert computer programmer is of limited value without a computer. These examples illustrate the importance of *physical capital,* such as factories and machines. More and better capital allows workers to produce more efficiently, as Example 14.4 illustrates.

Paris and Nicole get automated   **EXAMPLE 14.4**

Refer to Example 14.3. Since that time, Paris and Nicole's boss has acquired an electric candy-wrapping machine, which is designed to be operated by one worker. Using this machine, an untrained worker can wrap 500 candies/hour. What are Paris and Nicole's hourly and weekly outputs now? Will the answer change if the boss gets a second machine? A third?

Suppose for the sake of simplicity that a candy-wrapping machine must be assigned to one worker only. (This assumption rules out sharing arrangements, in which one worker uses the machine on the day shift and another on the night shift.) If the boss buys just one machine, she will maximize output by assigning it to Paris. (Why? See Exercise 14.3.) Now Paris will be able to wrap 500 candies/hour, while Nicole can wrap only 300/hour. Paris's weekly output will be 20 000 wrapped candies (40 hours × 500 candies wrapped/hour). Nicole's weekly output is still 12 000 wrapped candies (40 hours × 300 candies wrapped/hour). Together they can now wrap 32 000 candies/week, or 16 000 candies/week each. On an hourly basis, average labour productivity for the two women taken together is 32 000 candies wrapped/80 hours of work, or 400 candies wrapped/hour—twice their average labour productivity before the boss bought the machine.

With two candy-wrapping machines available, both Paris and Nicole could use a machine. Each could wrap 500 candies/hour, for a total of 40 000 wrapped candies/week. Average labour productivity for both women taken together would be 20 000 wrapped candies/week, or 500 wrapped candies/hour.

What would happen if the boss purchased a third machine? With only two workers, a third machine would be useless: it would add nothing to either total output or average labour productivity.

Using the assumptions made in Examples 14.3 and 14.4, explain why the boss will maximize output by assigning the single available candy-wrapping machine to Paris rather than Nicole. (Hint: Use *the principle of increasing opportunity cost,* introduced in Chapter 2.)

EXERCISE 14.3

INCREASING
OPPORTUNITY
COST

The candy-wrapping machine is an example of a *capital good,* defined in Chapter 5 as a long-lived good which is itself produced and used to produce other goods and services. Capital goods include machines and equipment (such as computers, earthmovers, or assembly lines) as well as buildings (such as factories or office buildings).

Capital goods like the candy-wrapping machine enhance workers' productivity. Table 14.2 summarizes the results from Examples 14.3 and 14.4. For each number of machines the boss might acquire (column 1), Table 14.2 gives the total weekly output of Paris and Nicole taken together (column 2), the total number of hours worked by the two women (column 3), and average output per hour (column 4), equal to total weekly output divided by total weekly hours.

Table 14.2 demonstrates two important points about the effect of additional capital on output. First, for a given number of workers, adding more capital generally increases both total output and average labour productivity. For example, adding the first candy-wrapping machine increases weekly output (column 2) by 16 000 candies and average labour productivity (column 4) by 200 candies wrapped/hour.

TABLE 14.2

Capital, Output, and Productivity in the Candy-Wrapping Factory

(1) Number of machines (capital)	(2) Total number of candies wrapped each week (output)	(3) Total hours worked per week	(4) Candies wrapped per hour worked (productivity)
0	16 000	80	200
1	32 000	80	400
2	40 000	80	500
3	40 000	80	500

The second point illustrated by Table 14.2 is that, beyond some point, additional units of capital produce smaller and smaller benefits. In this particular example, the first machine adds 16 000 candies to total output, but the second machine adds only 8000. The third machine, which cannot be used since there are only two workers, does not increase output or productivity at all. The result, that additional units of a variable input eventually produce smaller and smaller benefits, illustrates a general principle of economics called the *law of diminishing returns*. When the variable input is capital, the general principle implies **diminishing returns to capital:** If the amount of labour and other inputs employed is held constant, then the amount an additional unit of capital adds to production eventually begins to decrease. In the case of the candy-wrapping factory, diminishing returns to capital are exhibited when the first candy-wrapping machine acquired adds more output than the second, which in turn adds more output than the third.

Table 14.2 illustrates the link between units of capital and output at the level of a factory, but a similar relationship between units of capital and output seems to exist at the level of the economy as a whole. First, increasing the amount of

diminishing returns to capital if the amount of labour and other inputs employed is held constant, then the greater the amount of capital already in use, the less an additional unit of capital will tend to add to production

FIGURE 14.4

Average Labour Productivity and Capital per Worker in 15 Countries, 1990

Countries with large amounts of capital per worker also tend to have high average labour productivity, as measured by real GDP per worker. SOURCE: Penn World Tables [http://pwt.econ.upenn.edu/]. Countries included are those listed in Table 14.1, plus all countries with populations of 40 million or more for which data are available.

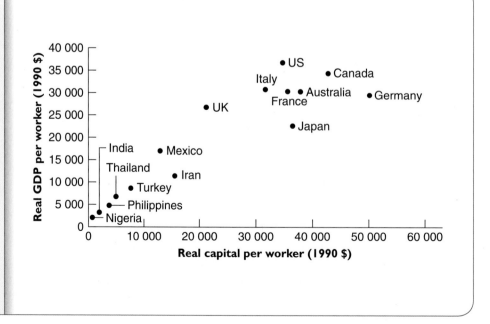

capital available to the workforce will tend to increase output and average labour productivity. The more adequately equipped workers are, the more productive they will be. Second, the degree to which productivity can be increased by an expanding stock of capital is limited. An economy in which the quantity of capital available to each worker is already very high will typically benefit less dramatically from any further expansion of the capital stock than an economy in which the quantity of capital per worker is low.

Is there empirical evidence that giving workers more capital makes them more productive? Figure 14.4 shows the relationship between average labour productivity and the amount of capital per worker in 15 major countries, including the eight industrialized countries listed in Table 14.1. The figure shows a strong relationship between the amounts of capital per worker and productivity.

BOX 14.2   CAPITAL, GROWTH, AND THE PPC

We have made the argument that if an economy increases its physical capital, all else being equal, we would then expect the output of the economy to increase in future periods because of a higher capital to labour ratio. This argument is often represented by a production possibilities curve (PPC) because the image of the curve in your mind's eye can help you to remember the argument.

The PPCs used in Chapter 2 illustrated concepts in addition to those associated with international trade. Points inside the PPC were inefficient, points on the curve were efficient, and points outside the curve were unattainable at the current time. In Figure 2.8, the PPCs were used to illustrate the idea that increases in productive resources, such as labour and physical capital or improvements in knowledge and technology, cause the PPC to shift outward, a shift corresponding to (potential) growth of the economy.

In Figure 2.8, the PPCs were drawn for an economy producing two goods: sugar cane and nuts. Figure 14.5 presents a more general case; it shows the output of physical capital goods along the vertical axis and the output of consumption goods along the horizontal axis.

FIGURE 14.5

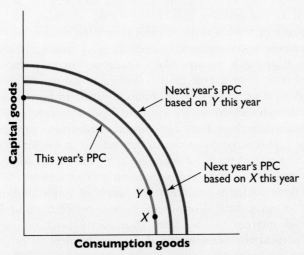

A few simplifying assumptions help explain the connection between physical capital accumulation (real investment) and economic growth. The first is that that all output can be divided into consumption goods and physical capital goods, as in Figure 14.5. Another assumption is that we have a closed economy, so that there will be a close match between the amount of physical capital produced in the economy and the amount of it employed. Labour, technology, and other factors affecting output are fixed.

The red curve in Figure 14.5 shows the PPC for the current period; that is, this year. Assume that our economy is currently operating at potential, producing a combination of consumption and capital goods shown by point X on the red curve.

Provided that X involves an output level of capital goods that is more than sufficient to offset the wearing out of the existing stock of capital goods, then next year the PPC will be further from the origin than is the red curve. The blue curve represents the PPC for next year if X is the output combination for this year.

If this year, instead of X, we had a output combination Y representing a larger addition to the stock of capital goods (that is, more investment), then next year we would have a PPC that is further from the origin than the blue curve is. The green curve in Figure 14.5 represents a PPC for next year if this year's output combination is as shown by the point Y.

In summary, economic growth arising from additions to physical capital can be represented by PPC curve shifts. Figure 14.5 illustrates the idea that shifting output from consumption to investment, that is, adding to the stock of physical capital in the current period causes the PPC in the future period to shift out more than it otherwise would.

LAND AND NATURAL RESOURCES

Besides capital goods, other inputs to production help to make workers more productive—among them are natural resources and land. An abundance of natural resources increases the productivity of workers in natural resource industries. The link between rich natural resources and labour productivity can be illustrated with data for Canada in the mid-1990s.[3] Annual output per worker in the natural resources sectors (essentially, the oil and gas industries) of Saskatchewan and Alberta was $360 000 and $290 000, respectively. These are many times higher than average output per worker for the Canadian economy as a whole (see Figure 14.2). The rich natural resource bases in these two provinces, not just high levels of capital intensity or worker skills, explain these high productivity levels.

Similarly, fertile land is essential to agriculture. A farmer can produce a much larger crop in a land-rich country like Canada or Australia than in a country where the soil is poor or arable land is limited in supply. With modern farm machinery and great expanses of land, today's Canadian farmers are so productive that even though they constitute less than 3 percent of the employed population, they provide enough of many agricultural commodities not only to feed the country but to export large quantities to the rest of the world. Of course, fertile farm land is most important to an economy at an early stage of economic development when most of the employed population is in agriculture.

Although there are limits to a country's supply of arable land, it is important to recognize that many natural resources, such as petroleum and metals, can be obtained through international markets. Thus, economies need not possess large quantities of natural resources within their own borders to achieve economic growth. Indeed, a number of economies have become rich without substantial natural resources of their own, including Japan, Hong Kong, Singapore, and Switzerland.

[3]David Sabourin and Danielle Zietsma, "Interprovincial Productivity Differences," *Canadian Economic Observer*, Statistics Canada, August 2001.

TECHNOLOGY

Besides human capital, physical capital, and natural resources, a country's ability to develop and apply new, more productive technologies helps to determine its productivity. Consider just one industry, transportation. Two centuries ago, even in the richest countries, the horse-drawn wagon was the primary means of transportation, a slow and costly method indeed. But in the nineteenth century, technological advances such as the steam engine supported the expansion of riverborne transportation and the development of national rail networks. In the twentieth century, the invention of the internal combustion engine and the development of aviation, supported by the construction of an extensive infrastructure of roads and airports, have produced increasingly rapid, cheap, and reliable transport. Technological change has clearly been a driving force in the transportation revolution.

New technologies can improve productivity in industries other than the one in which they are introduced. Once farmers could sell their produce only in their local communities, for example. Now rapid shipping and refrigerated transport allow farmers to sell their products internationally. With a broader market in which to sell, farmers can specialize in those products best suited to local land and weather conditions. Similarly, factories can obtain their raw materials wherever they are cheapest and most abundant, produce the goods they are most efficient at manufacturing, and sell their products wherever they will fetch the best price. Both these examples illustrate the *principle of comparative advantage*: overall productivity increases when producers concentrate on those activities at which they are relatively most efficient (see Chapter 2).

COMPARATIVE
ADVANTAGE

Numerous other technological developments have led to increased productivity, including advances in communication and medicine and the introduction of computer technology. All indications are that the Internet will have a major impact in many economies, not just in retailing but in many other sectors.

However, economic growth does not automatically follow from breakthroughs in basic science. To make the best use of new knowledge, an economy needs entrepreneurs who can implement scientific advances, as well as a legal and political environment that encourages the practical application of new knowledge.

A new kind of wrapping paper has been invented that makes candy-wrapping quicker and easier. The use of this paper increases the number of candies a person can wrap by hand by 200 per hour, and the number of candies a person can wrap by machine by 300 per hour. Using the data from Examples 14.3 and 14.4, construct a table like Table 14.2 that shows how this technological advance affects average labour productivity. Do diminishing returns to capital still hold?

EXERCISE 14.4

ENTREPRENEURSHIP

Increases in average labour productivity depend in part upon **entrepreneurship**, or innovative behaviour: that is, behaviour that results in new products, services, technological processes, or organizational innovations that are productivity enhancing. In a capitalist economy, much of entrepreneurial behaviour is associated with the owners and managers of capitalist enterprises. A classic example known throughout the world is that of Henry Ford, the American entrepreneur who developed mass production of automobiles. Mass production raised labour productivity and therefore lowered average costs enough to bring automobiles within reach of the average household. Another example, dating from the 1970s and 1980s, is of Japanese companies whose new just-in-time production methods greatly increased the efficiency of their manufacturing plants.

entrepreneurship behaviour that results in new products, services, technological processes, or organizational innovations that are productivity enhancing

www.greatlakes-seaway.com
St. Lawrence Seaway
System

But entrepreneurial behaviour is not exclusively limited to the owners or managers of capitalist enterprises. For example, Florence Nightingale exhibited entrepreneurial behaviour in campaigning to have nursing established as a profession in nineteenth-century England. The organizational innovation of replacing untrained servants with trained professionals greatly improved the efficiency of nursing in England's medical sector. Similarly, the politicians, civil servants, and others in Canada and the United States whose efforts resulted in the St. Lawrence Seaway project in the 1950s exhibited entrepreneurial behaviour. The system of locks and canals linking the Great Lakes with the Atlantic Ocean through the St. Lawrence River provided relatively low freight rates for bulk commodities, and facilitated the development of both resource industries and manufacturing industries in much of Canada and the United States.

Entrepreneurial behaviour, then, can take place in the for-profit sector, the non-profit sector, or the government sector. One common element is the exercise of creativity, typically combined with leadership skills, to produce new products, services, technological processes, or organizations. The other element is that these innovations serve to raise average labour productivity.

Like any form of creativity or leadership skills, entrepreneurship is difficult to teach (although some of the supporting knowledge can be learned in university). How, then, does a society encourage entrepreneurship? History suggests that the entrepreneurial spirit will always exist; the challenge is to channel that spirit into economically productive channels.

For example, to encourage entrepreneurship in the for-profit sector, economic policy-makers need to ensure that excessive regulations do not keep small businesses, some of which will eventually become big businesses, from getting off the ground. (Recent international surveys have ranked Canada as a country with relatively few barriers to establishing new businesses.) Sociological factors may play a role as well. Societies in which business and commerce are considered to be beneath the dignity of refined, educated people are less likely to produce successful entrepreneurs in the for-profit sector. Similarly, societies in which non-profit and government sectors are denigrated in favour of private business and the "free market" may suffer from a lack of entrepreneurial behaviour in those sectors.

THE LEGAL AND POLITICAL ENVIRONMENT

One of the key ways that government can foster productivity growth is to provide a legal and political environment that encourages people to behave in economically productive ways. The legal system should provide clear rules for determining who owns what resources (through a system of deeds and titles, for example) and how those resources can be used. Imagine living in a society in which a dictator, backed by the military and the police, could take whatever he wanted, and regularly did so. The incentive to invest in new enterprises or expand existing enterprises would be drastically impaired.

The political system can advance productivity growth by preventing extreme instability. Continuous civil unrest, terrorism, or guerrilla warfare are obviously detrimental to economic growth. Policies that promote social cohesion—that is, that reduce social conflicts between classes, ethnic groups, or linguistic communities—can contribute to economic growth by contributing to political stability.

At the same time, a political system that promotes the open exchange of ideas will speed the development of new technologies and products. For example, some economic historians have suggested that the decline of Spain as an economic power was due in part to the advent of the Spanish Inquisition, which permitted no dissent from religious orthodoxy. Because of the Inquisition's persecution of those whose theories about the natural world contradicted Church doctrine, Spanish science and technology languished, and Spain fell behind more tolerant nations such as the Netherlands.

A Bangladeshi worker who immigrates to Canada is likely to find that his average labour productivity is much higher in Canada than it was at home. This worker is, of course, the same person he was when he lived in Bangladesh. How can the simple act of moving to Canada increase the worker's productivity?

EXERCISE 14.5

> **RECAP** ↑
>
> ## DETERMINANTS OF AVERAGE LABOUR PRODUCTIVITY
>
> Key factors determining average labour productivity in a country include:
>
> - The skills and training of workers, called *human capital*.
> - The quantity and quality of *physical capital*: machines, equipment, and buildings.
> - The availability of land and other *natural resources*.
> - The sophistication of the *technologies* applied in production.
> - *Entrepreneurship*.
> - The broad *legal and political environment*.

BOX 14.3   PRODUCTION FUNCTIONS

Economists often use a mathematical expression called a *production function* to describe the relationship between the amounts of inputs and outputs. In its general form, a production function is written as

$$Y = f(K, L, M, A)$$

where

Y = the amount of output or real GDP,

K = the amount of physical capital,

L = the amount of labour, adjusted for the level of human capital,

M = the amount of available land and other natural resources,

A = the level of technology and other factors, such as the effectiveness of management and the social and legal environment,

$f(\ )$ is some unspecified functional form.

In practice, there are a number of specific functional forms that are used to calculate the level of output. One simple but famous one that involves only Y, K, and L is

$$Y = K^{1/2}L^{1/2} = \sqrt{KL}.$$

For example, if $K = 25$ and $L = 100$, $Y = \sqrt{25 \times 100} = \sqrt{2{,}500} = 50$. This simple production function has two notable properties. First, if all the inputs K and L double, output also will double; that is, if $K = 50$ and $L = 200$, $Y = \sqrt{50 \times 200} = \sqrt{10{,}000} = 100$. Secondly, it exhibits diminishing returns to capital (as well as diminishing returns to labour), so that if we hold the level of labour constant and keep adding more capital, output will rise by smaller and smaller increments. Thus, if L remains equal to 100 and K rises from 25 to 26, output rises from 50 to $\sqrt{26 \times 100} = 50.99$, or by 0.99 unit. If K rises by one more unit to 27, output rises to $\sqrt{27 \times 100} = 51.96$, or by only 0.97 unit.

14.5 THE PRODUCTIVITY SLOWDOWN

WORLDWIDE SLOWDOWN—AND RECOVERY?

During the 1950s and 1960s most of the major industrialized countries saw rapid growth in real GDP and average labour productivity. In the 1970s, however, productivity growth began to slow around the world. Slower growth in real GDP and in average living standards followed.

The slowdown in the growth of labour productivity is documented in Table 14.3, which gives data for six of the eight industrialized countries included in Table 14.1. Note the sharp decline in productivity growth in all six countries during 1973–1979 compared with 1960–1973. Japan's case was particularly striking: its productivity growth rate fell from 7.6 percent per year in 1960–1973 to 2.7 percent in 1973–1979. In Canada, annual productivity growth fell from 2.1 percent before 1973 to just 0.8 percent per year during 1973–1979. During the period 1979–1992, when inflation fighting was a high priority in most countries, productivity growth generally continued at a slow pace.

TABLE 14.3
Average Labour Productivity Growth Rates in Selected Countries, 1960–2006

Country	Percentage growth, annual rates			
	1960–1973	1973–1979	1979–1992	1993–2006
Canada	2.1	0.8	0.7	1.4
France	4.6	2.6	2.1	1.2
Germany	4.0	2.6	1.4	1.3
Japan	7.6	2.7	2.8	1.4
United Kingdom	2.8	1.3	1.7	2.2
United States	2.3	0.6	0.9	1.9

SOURCE: Growth rates of real GDP per employed person ("Labour productivity per person employed" in OECD terminology), OECD, U.S. Bureau of Labor Statistics, and Statistics Canada.

The sudden decline in worldwide productivity growth around 1973 puzzles economists and policy-makers alike. What might have caused it? In the 1970s and 1980s many economists thought that the fourfold increase in oil prices that followed the Arab–Israeli war (1973) might have caused the slowdown. However, when oil prices (relative to the prices of other goods) returned to pre-1973 levels, productivity growth did not. Thus oil prices are no longer thought to have played a critical role in the slowdown.

One view of the slowdown in productivity growth since 1973 has been called the *technological depletion hypothesis*.[4] According to the **technological depletion hypothesis,** the high rates of productivity growth in the 1950s and 1960s reflected an unusual period of "catch-up" after the Depression and the Second World War. Although scientific and technical advances (many of which arose from military research during the Second World War) continued to be made during the 1930s and 1940s, depression and war hindered their application to civilian use. During the 1950s and 1960s, the backlog of technological breakthroughs was applied commercially, producing high rates of productivity growth at first and then a

technological depletion hypothesis the theory that the productivity slowdown after 1973 was due to the depletion of the backlog of technological advances made but not implemented during the 1930s and the Second World War

[4]See, for example, William Nordhaus, "Economic Policy in the Face of Declining Productivity Growth," *European Economic Review,* May/June 1982, pp. 131–158.

sharp decline in new technological opportunities. Once the catch-up period was over, productivity growth slowed. According to this hypothesis, then, the slow-down in productivity growth since the 1970s reflects a dearth of technological opportunities in the immediate postwar period. From this perspective, the 1950s and 1960s were the exception, and the period since the 1970s instead represents a return to more normal rates of productivity growth.

Although the rate of productivity growth since the early 1970s has gener-ally been low, in recent years there have been signs of a possible recovery in productivity growth in the English-speaking countries of Canada, the United Kingdom, and the United States, as shown by their productivity growth rates for 1993–2006. One hypothesis for this has been that the English-speaking countries have been first to capitalize on a technological revolution sparked by advances in information technology, including personal computers, computer software, and the Internet. A competing explanation is a variation of the above-mentioned *tech-nological depletion hypothesis*, namely, that because countries such as Canada and the United States lagged in implementation of new technologies during the inflation-fighting 1979–1992 period, much of which was spent in recession, they had a backlog to draw from in the post-1992 period.[5]

PRODUCTIVITY SLOWDOWN AND REAL WAGE STAGNATION

We have seen that in the 1970s labour productivity growth began to slow in many countries, including Canada, followed by slower growth in average living stan-dards. What happened to real wages in Canada during this period of productivity growth slowdown?

Over most of the twentieth century, real wages in Canada grew in line with labour productivity growth. So you might expect that during the period of pro-ductivity growth slowdown in Canada, real wage growth would have slowed in line with slower productivity growth. But, as shown in Figure 14.6, average real hourly wages in Canada stagnated from the late 1970s to 1996. Real wages did not just grow slowly—they did not grow at all.

Canada's experience of real wage stagnation during the 1977–1996 period, despite 1 percent annual labour productivity growth, illustrates an important point. Although labour productivity growth largely determines real wage growth over long periods, such as a century, other factors can substantially affect real wage growth over shorter periods. Real wage growth may then diverge from labour productivity growth.

How can we explain the stagnation of real wages from the late 1970s to 1996? It cannot be because the human capital of Canadian workers failed to improve. The average educational credentials of the Canadian workforce increased very substantially over the final quarter of the twentieth century.

Part of the explanation goes back to the income-based GDP measure intro-duced in Chapter 5. Recall that income-based GDP can be divided into two parts—labour income, which comes from wages, and capital income, which comes mainly from profits, dividends, and interest.

[5]In comparing the performance of countries in different periods, it is important to be aware of the statistical phenomenon of regression toward the mean, an early example of which is the finding, by Francis Galton (1822–1911), that the sons of especially tall fathers tend to be taller than the mean (i.e., average) but not as tall as their fathers. In general, when outcomes have a random component, those that have especially high outcomes relative to the mean in one period will tend, on average, to have outcomes closer to the mean in the next period. For example, countries that have especially high growth rates relative to the mean in one period will tend, on average, to have growth rates closer to the mean in the next period, and countries with especially low growth rates in one period will also tend to have growth rates closer to the mean in the next period. For a lively discussion of regression toward the mean in the analysis of income distribution statistics, see Paul Krugman, "The Rich, the Right and the Facts," *American Prospect*, 30 November 2002.

FIGURE 14.6

Average Real Hourly Wage in Canada, 1914–2007

Real hourly wages in Canada increased fivefold between 1914 and 1977. From 1978 to 1996 real wages stagnated. Growth in real wages since 1997 has been positive but modest.

SOURCES: Adapted from the CANSIM series v2415197 (wages) for 1997–2007), v717706 (wages) for 1961–1996, and v41693271 (CPI 2002=100); and from *HSC*, series E198 (wage index) for 1914–1960.

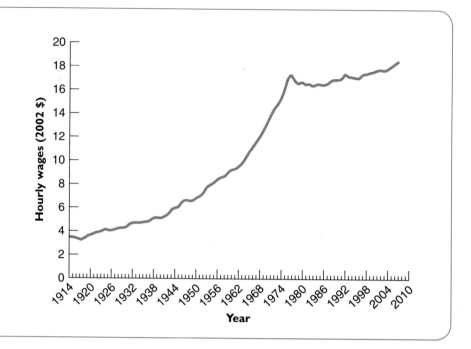

As Figure 14.7 illustrates, labour income as a share of Canadian GDP rose from the early 1960s to the early 1970s. But it declined from 57 percent of GDP in 1976 to 51 percent in 1996. When labour's share of GDP falls, hourly wages tend to stagnate.

One hypothesis states that labour's share of GDP fell because the bargaining power of labour deteriorated. Possible explanations as to why the bargaining

FIGURE 14.7

The Labour Income Share, Canada, 1961–2007

The share of labour income in Canadian GDP (red line) rose during the 1960s and early 1970s to a peak of 57 percent in 1976. There has been a downward trend in the share of labour income since 1976. In recent years, the share of labour income in GDP has hovered around 51 percent. The decline since the late 1970s is related to the stagnation of real wages. Note that the vertical axis is abbreviated.

SOURCE: Adapted from the Statistics Canada, CANSIM database, http://cansim2. statcan.ca, series v498076 (labour income), and v498074 (GDP).

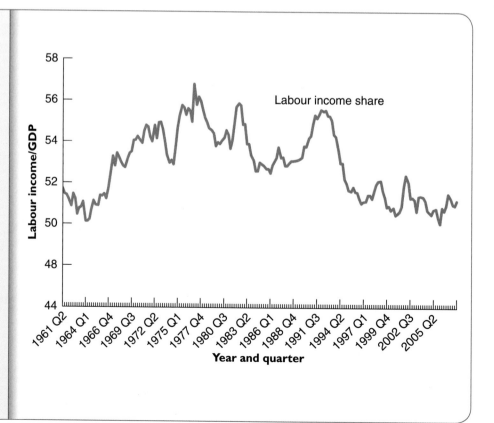

power of labour deteriorated include the high unemployment rates of the 1980s and the first half of the 1990s. Since 1996, the downward trend of the labour income share seems to have ended, productivity growth has improved somewhat, and real wages have grown, although slowly. Even with relatively low unemployment rates, labour's bargaining power is increasingly constrained by global competition.

RECAP ↑

THE PRODUCTIVITY SLOWDOWN

Beginning in the 1970s, the industrial world experienced a slowdown in average labour productivity growth. According to the technological depletion hypothesis, the slower growth in productivity beginning in the 1970s reflected a return to a normal rate of productivity growth following the abnormally high productivity growth of the 1950s and 1960s. In recent years, however, there have been signs of a modest recovery in productivity growth.

From the late 1970s to 1996, a period of productivity growth slowdown in Canada, the growth of real wages stagnated. During the same period, the share of labour income (wages) in GDP fell by several percentage points. One hypothesis is that real wages stagnated because the bargaining power of labour was weak during the 1980s and the first half of the 1990s due to high unemployment rates.

14.6 TWO POSSIBLE OPPORTUNITY COSTS OF ECONOMIC GROWTH: CONSUMPTION AND LEISURE

Both this chapter and Chapter 5 emphasized the positive effects of economic growth on the average person's living standard. But even if we accept for the moment the idea that increased output per person is always desirable, maximization of the economic growth rate is a questionable economic goal. If the economy is already operating at or near capacity, then increasing the growth rate will require devoting more resources to investment as opposed to consumption, or increasing hours of work at the expense of leisure. In an economy operating at or near capacity, then, there are opportunity costs associated with increased investment and increased hours of work.

We know that by expanding the capital stock through investment, we can increase future productivity and output. But, to increase the capital stock, a society may have to divert resources that could otherwise be used to increase the supply of consumer goods. For example, to add more robot-operated assembly lines, a society must employ more of its skilled technicians in building industrial robots and fewer in designing video games. To build new factories, more carpenters and lumber must be assigned to factory construction and less to making furniture for homes. In short, a higher rate of investment in new capital would require fewer resources devoted to consumer goods—a real economic cost. (Alternatively, a higher rate of investment would require borrowing from abroad, which also has a real economic cost.)

Consumption sacrificed to capital formation is not the only cost of achieving higher growth. In Canada in the nineteenth and early twentieth centuries, before the rise of industrial unions, periods of rapid economic growth were often times in which many people worked extremely long hours at dangerous and unpleasant jobs. While those workers helped to build the economy that Canadians enjoy today, the costs were great in terms of reduced leisure time and, in some cases, workers' health and safety. Many developing countries today are purchasing rapid economic growth at least partly at the same costs as Canada experienced in decades past.

COST–
BENEFIT

The fact that, in an economy operating at capacity, a higher living standard tomorrow must typically be purchased at the cost of current sacrifices is an example of the *scarcity problem*: having more of one good thing usually means having less of another. Because achieving higher economic growth imposes real economic costs, we know from the *cost–benefit* principle that a rational approach to the normative issue of whether higher growth should be pursued involves weighing benefits and costs.

14.7   PROMOTING ECONOMIC GROWTH

If a society decides to try to raise its rate of economic growth, what are some of the measures that policy-makers might take to achieve this objective? We have mentioned a few broad considerations in our discussions of entrepreneurship and

---

ECONOMIC *Naturalist*   14.1   Why do almost all countries provide free public education?

All industrial countries provide their citizens free public education through high school, and most subsidize college and other post-secondary schools. Why?

Canadians are so used to the idea of free public education that this question may seem odd. But why should the government provide free education when it does not provide even more-essential goods and services for free? Furthermore, educational services can be, and indeed commonly are, supplied and demanded in the private market, without the aid of the government.

An important argument for free or at least subsidized education is that the private demand curve for educational services does not include all the social benefits of education. For example, the democratic political system relies on an educated citizenry to operate effectively—a factor that an individual demander of educational services has little reason to consider. From a narrower economic perspective, we

Why do almost all countries provide free public education?

might argue that individuals do not capture the full economic returns from their schooling. For example, people with high human capital, and thus high earnings, pay more taxes—funds that can be used to finance government services and aid the less fortunate. Because of income taxation, the private benefit to acquiring human capital is less than the social benefit, and the demand for education in the private market may be less than optimal from society's viewpoint. Similarly, educated people are more likely than others to contribute to technological development, and hence to general productivity growth, which may benefit many other people besides themselves. Finally, another argument for public support of education is that poor people who would like to invest in human capital may not be able to do so because of insufficient income.[6]

---

[6]For a more complete discussion of the external benefits associated with higher levels of education, see Barbara Wolfe and Robert Haveman, "Accounting for the Social and Non-Market Benefits of Education," in John Helliwell, ed., *The Contribution of Human and Social Capital to Sustained Economic Growth and Well Being*, (Ottawa: HRDC and OECD, 2001), pp. 220–250.

the legal and political environment. Here are some additional suggestions, based on our discussion of the factors that contribute to growth in average labour productivity and, thus, output per person.

POLICIES TO INCREASE HUMAN CAPITAL

Because skilled and well-educated workers are more productive than unskilled labour, governments in most countries try to increase the human capital of their citizens by supporting education and training programs. In Canada, provincial governments provide public education through high school and grant extensive support to post-secondary schools, including technical schools, colleges, and universities. To a lesser degree than some European countries, Canada also funds job training and supports retraining for workers whose skills no longer match available jobs.

POLICIES THAT PROMOTE INVESTMENT IN CAPITAL GOODS

Average labour productivity increases when workers can utilize a sizable and modern capital stock. One way that public policies can support the creation of new capital is to encourage a high rate of business investment (or, more precisely, what Statistics Canada calls non-residential business fixed capital formation). But how to encourage such investment is a controversial issue.

For example, some provincial governments have cut corporate income tax rates in recent years for the stated purpose of stimulating business investment. But there is some debate about whether corporate income tax cuts by provinces will actually stimulate investment at the national level or mainly just encourage some firms to relocate from higher-tax provinces to lower-tax ones. And questions have been raised about whether an investment tax credit to corporations, based upon new investment in plant and equipment in Canada, might have been more effective in stimulating new investment than income tax cuts awarded to corporations whether or not they expand their investment.

The federal government provides major tax breaks for Registered Retirement Savings Plans (RRSPs) for the stated purpose of encouraging personal saving. There is some doubt about whether tax breaks are even effective as a means of encouraging personal saving. More important, the empirical evidence (as we shall see in Chapter 16) suggests that the level of personal saving in Canada is not closely linked to the level of business investment.

In addition to encouraging business investment, public policies can contribute directly to capital formation through public investment, or the creation of government-owned capital. Public investment includes the building of roads, bridges, airports, dams, and so on, as explained in Chapter 5. As mentioned previously, the construction of the St. Lawrence Seaway, carried out in the 1950s by a federal Crown corporation (in conjunction with a U.S. counterpart), is often cited as an example of especially successful public investment. Today, the Internet, which received crucial public-sector funding in its early stages, is having a similar effect.

POLICIES THAT SUPPORT RESEARCH AND DEVELOPMENT

Productivity is enhanced by technological progress, which in turn requires investment in research and development (R&D). In many industries, private firms have adequate incentive to conduct research and development activities. There is no need, for example, for the government to finance research for developing a better underarm deodorant. But some types of knowledge, particularly basic scientific knowledge, may have widespread economic benefits that cannot be captured by a single private firm. The developers of the silicon computer chip, for example, were instrumental in creating huge new industries, yet they received only a small portion of the profits flowing from their inventions. Because society in general, rather than the individual inventors, may receive much of the benefit from basic research, government may need to support basic research, as it does through agencies such as the National Research Council of Canada and through support for research conducted at universities across the country. The federal government encourages applied research by the same institutions that conduct basic research, and it provides generous tax incentives to support the R&D activity of the private sector. Despite these generous tax incentives, the Canadian ratio of private-sector R&D investment to GDP is low compared to the ratios of other advanced economies, possibly because of the high degree of foreign ownership of Canadian industry. R&D tends to be conducted in head offices, and foreign ownership typically means that head offices are located abroad rather than in Canada.

The federal government also influences research and development by its laws regarding patent protection. Advocates of strong patent protection assert that if companies can patent their discoveries for long periods of time, they can charge high monopoly prices that result in large profits, and the lure of these large profits will encourage more R&D. Critics argue that long periods of patent protection encourage companies to engage in copycat R&D designed simply to get around the patents of other companies; for example, drug companies come up with second and third cures for the same disease. Critics also emphasize that high prices may hinder use of the inventions resulting from R&D (as when the high prices of patented AIDS drugs kept them out of reach of millions whose lives might have been saved by them).

www.nrc-cnrc.gc.ca
National Research Council of Canada

14.8 LIMITS TO GROWTH

Earlier in this chapter we saw that even relatively low rates of economic growth, if sustained for a long period, will produce huge increases in the size of the economy. This fact raises the question of whether economic growth can continue indefinitely without depleting natural resources and causing massive damage to the global environment. Does the basic truth that we live in a finite world of finite resources imply that, ultimately, economic growth must come to an end?

The question is a complex one that requires expertise extending beyond economics. But economics can shed some light. On the one hand, most economists would agree that not all of the problems created by economic growth can be dealt with effectively through the market or through domestic politics. Probably most important, global environmental problems, such as the possibility of climate change or the ongoing destruction of rainforests, are a particular challenge for existing economic and political institutions. Environmental quality is not bought and sold in markets and thus will not automatically reach its optimal level through market processes (recall the *equilibrium principle*). Nor can local or national governments effectively address problems that are global in scope. Unless international mechanisms are established for dealing with global environmental problems, these problems may become worse as economic growth continues.

EQUILIBRIUM

On the other hand, economists have long raised doubts about pessimistic arguments that economic growth must come to an end. In particular, economists were quick to point out flaws in an influential 1972 book, *The Limits to Growth*.[7]

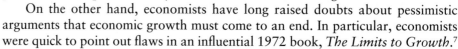
[7]Donella H. Meadows, Dennis L. Meadows, Jørgen Randers, and William W. Behrens, III, *The Limits to Growth*, (New York: New American Library, 1972).

This book reported the results of computer simulations that suggested that unless population growth and economic expansion were halted, the world would soon run out of natural resources, drinkable water, and breathable air.

One problem with the "limits to growth thesis," whether in its original form or in recent restatements, lies in its underlying concept of economic growth. It assumes implicitly that economic growth will always take the form of more of what we have now: more smoky factories, more polluting cars, more fast-food restaurants. If that were indeed the case, then surely there would be limits to the growth the planet can sustain. But growth in real GDP does not necessarily take such a form. Increases in real GDP can also arise from new or higher-quality products and services, such as an expanded number of TV channels, higher-quality and more efficient vehicles, and environmentally benign human services (like education or childcare). Thus, economic growth need not take the form of more and more of the same old stuff; it can mean newer, better, and perhaps cleaner and more efficient goods and services. If technological progress saves resources, GDP growth may mean reduced environmental impact.

A second problem with the limits to growth conclusion is that it overlooks the fact that increased wealth and productivity expand society's capacity to take measures to safeguard the environment. In fact, some of the most polluted countries in the world are not the richest but rather those that are in a relatively early stage of industrialization. At this stage, countries tend to devote the bulk of their resources to basic needs—food, shelter, and healthcare—and continued industrial expansion. In more economically developed countries, extra income is available to support environmental protection both at home and, through targeted foreign aid, in developing countries. (Whether the extra income is actually used for environmental protection at home and abroad, of course, depends upon the efforts of environmental activists and other political forces.)

A third problem with the limits to growth thesis is that it ignores the issue of how market participants will respond to temporary resource shortages (situations when demand outstrips supply). During the oil-supply disruptions of the 1970s, for example, newspapers were filled with headlines about the energy crisis and the imminent depletion of world oil supplies. But reduced oil supplies led to an increase in prices that changed the behaviour of both demanders and suppliers. Consumers insulated their homes, purchased more energy-efficient cars and appliances, and switched to alternative sources of energy. Suppliers engaged in a hunt for new reserves, opening up new sources in Latin America, China, and the North Sea. For a wide range of minerals and other natural resources, not just for oil, shortages will trigger price changes that induce suppliers and demanders to deal with the problem. Simply extrapolating current economic trends into the future ignores how market participants recognize shortages and tend to make the necessary corrections.[8]

In short, economic growth does give rise to environmental problems, and those environmental problems requiring international political solutions may be particularly difficult to solve. But not all concerns about limits to growth are equally valid. Economics can help with the task of sorting out which concerns deserve attention and which are not well founded.

---

[8]That said, some economists now believe that world oil production may be at or near a peak. See, for example, Paul Krugman, "Running Out of Planet to Exploit," *New York Times*, 21 April 2008, http://www.nytimes.com/2008/04/21/opinion/21krugman.html (June 2008).

SUMMARY

14.2 Over the past two centuries the industrialized nations saw enormous improvements in living standards, as reflected in large increases in real GDP per person. Because of the power of *compound growth*, relatively small differences in growth rates, if continued over long periods, can produce large differences in real GDP per person and average living standards. Thus, the rate of long-term economic growth is an economic variable of critical importance.

14.3 Real GDP per person is the product of average labour productivity (real GDP per employed worker) and the share of the population that is employed. Growth in real GDP per person can occur only through growth in average labour productivity, in the share of the population that is working, or both. Since 1960, increases in the share of the Canadian population holding a job contributed significantly to rising real GDP per person. Over the last four decades, the growth in real GDP per person came roughly half from increases in the employment–population ratio, and half from growth in average labour productivity. In future years, however, higher labour productivity will be the main source of continuing improvements in real GDP per capita.

14.4 Among the factors that determine labour productivity are the talents, education, training, and skills of workers, or human capital; the quantity and quality of the physical capital that workers use; the availability of land and other natural resources; the application of technology to the production and distribution of goods and services; entrepreneurship; and the broad political and legal environment.

14.5 Since the 1970s the industrial world has experienced a slowdown in productivity growth. Some economists have suggested that the exploitation of a backlog of technological opportunities following the Great Depression and the Second World War led to unusually high growth rates in the 1950s and 1960s, a view called the *technological depletion hypothesis*. In this view, the slower growth in productivity since about 1970 in fact reflects a return to a more normal rate of growth.

14.6 Economic growth has costs as well as benefits. If the economy is already operating at or near capacity, then increasing the growth rate may require devoting more resources to investment as opposed to consumption or increasing hours of work at the expense of leisure. Thus more economic growth is not necessarily better; whether increased economic growth is desirable depends on whether the benefits of growth outweigh the costs.

14.7 Government can stimulate economic growth by adopting policies that: encourage the creation of human capital; promote investment, including public investment in infrastructure; support research and development, particularly in the basic sciences; and provide a legal and political framework that supports innovations in economic activity.

14.8 Are there limits to growth? The question is a complex one that requires expertise beyond economics. But economics can shed some light. On the one hand, economic growth does give rise to environmental problems, and those environmental problems requiring international political solutions may be particularly difficult to solve. On the other hand, not all concerns about limits to growth are equally valid. Economic growth can take the form of cleaner and more-efficient goods and services. Higher productivity expands a society's capacity to take measures to safeguard the environment. And for a variety of natural resources, shortages will trigger price changes that induce suppliers and demanders to deal with the problem. Economics can help with the task of sorting out which concerns about limits to growth deserve the most attention.

KEY TERMS

compound interest (363)
diminishing returns to capital (370)

entrepreneurship (373)
power of compound growth (363)

rule of 72 (364)
technological depletion hypothesis (376)

REVIEW QUESTIONS

1. What has happened to real GDP per person in the industrialized countries over the past century? What implications does this have for the average person?

2. Why do economists consider growth in average labour productivity to be the key factor in determining long-run living standards?

3. What is *human capital*? Why is it economically important? How is new human capital created?

4. You have employed five workers of varying physical strength to dig a ditch. Workers without shovels have zero productivity in ditchdigging. How should you assign shovels to workers if you don't have enough

shovels to go around? How should you assign any additional shovels that you obtain? Using this example, discuss (a) the relationship between the availability of physical capital and average labour productivity and (b) the concept of diminishing returns to capital.

5. Discuss how entrepreneurship can enhance average labour productivity.

6. What major contributions can the government make to the goal of increasing average labour productivity?

7. Discuss one explanation that has been offered for the slowdown in productivity growth observed in industrial countries since the early 1970s.

8. Discuss the following statement: "Because the environment is fragile and natural resources are finite, ultimately economic growth must come to an end."

PROBLEMS

1. Richland's real GDP per person is $10 000, and Poorland's real GDP per person is $5000. However, Richland's real GDP per person is growing at 1 percent per year and Poorland's is growing at 3 percent per year. Compare real GDP per person in the two countries after ten years and after twenty years. Approximately how many years will it take Poorland to catch up to Richland? Using the rule of 72, calculate how many years it will take for real GDP per person to double in both Richland and Poorland.

2. Refer to Table 14.3 for growth rates of average labour productivity over the periods 1960–1973, 1973–1979, 1979–1992, and 1993–2006. Suppose that the growth of average labour productivity in Canada had continued at its 1960–1973 rate until 2006. Proportionally, how much higher would Canadian average labour productivity in 2006 have been, compared to its actual value? (*Note:* You do not need to know the actual values of average labour productivity in any year to solve this problem.) Does your answer shed light on why economists consider the post-1973 productivity slowdown to be an important issue?

3. Between 1961 and 2007, the rising share of the Canadian population in paid employment contributed to rising GDP per person. But suppose that the share of the Canadian population in paid employment had remained constant between 1961 and 2007. What would Canadian GDP per person have been in 2007? Make use of the relevant data from the following table:

Year	GDP per capita	Average labour productivity	Share of population employed
1961	$13 044	$39 290	33.2%
2007	$39 736	$77 688	51.1%

4. Here are approximate data for Canada and Japan on the ratio of employment to population in 1979 and 2007:

	1979	2007
Canada	0.45	0.54
Japan	0.47	0.58

Using data from Table 14.1 on real GDP per person, find average labour productivity for each country in 1979 and in 2007. How much of the increase in output per person in each country over the 1979–2007 period is due to increased labour productivity? To increased employment relative to population?

5. Joanne has just completed high school and is trying to determine whether to go to college for two years or go directly to work. Her objective is to maximize the savings she will have in the bank five years from now. If she goes directly to work, she will earn $20 000 per year for each of the next five years. If she goes to college, for each of the next two years she will earn nothing; indeed, she will have to borrow $6000 each year to cover tuition and books. This loan must be repaid in full three years after graduation. If she graduates from college, in each of the subsequent three years

her wages will be $38 000 per year. Joanne's total living expenses and taxes, excluding tuition and books, equal $15 000 per year.

    a. Suppose for simplicity that Joanne can borrow and lend at 0 percent interest. On purely economic grounds, should she go to college or work?

    b. Does your answer to part (a) change if she can earn $23 000 per year with only a high school degree?

    c. Does your answer to part (a) change if Joanne's tuition and books cost $8000 per year?

    d. (More difficult.) Suppose that the interest rate at which Joanne can borrow and lend is 10 percent per year, but other data are as in part (a). Savings are deposited at the end of the year they are earned and receive (compound) interest at the end of each subsequent year. Similarly, the loans are taken out at the end of the year in which they are needed, and interest does not accrue until the end of the subsequent year. Now that the interest rate has risen, should Joanne go to college or go to work?

6. The Good'n'Fresh Grocery Store has two checkout lanes and four employees. Employees are equally skilled, and all are able either to operate a register (checkers) or bag groceries (baggers). The store owner assigns one checker and one bagger to each lane. A lane with a checker and a bagger can check out 40 customers per hour. A lane with a checker only can check out 25 customers per hour.

    a. In terms of customers checked out per hour, what is total output and average labour productivity for the Good'n'Fresh Grocery Store?

    b. The owner adds a third checkout lane and register. Assuming that no employees are added, what is the best way to reallocate the workers to tasks? What is total output and average labour productivity (in terms of customers checked out per hour) now?

    c. Repeat part (b) for the addition of a fourth checkout lane, and a fifth. Do you observe diminishing returns to capital in this example?

7. Harrison, Carla, and Fred are housepainters. Harrison and Carla can paint 30 square metres per hour using a standard paintbrush, and Fred can paint 24 square metres per hour. Any of the three can paint 60 square metres per hour using a roller.

    a. Assume Harrison, Carla, and Fred have only paintbrushes at their disposal. What is the average labour productivity, in terms of square metres per painter-hour, for the three painters taken as a team? Assume that the three painters always work the same number of hours.

    b. Repeat part (a) for the cases in which the team has one, two, three, or four rollers available. Are there diminishing returns to capital?

    c. An improvement in paint quality increases the area that can be covered per hour (by either brushes or rollers) by 20 percent. How does this technological improvement affect your answers to part (b)? Are there diminishing returns to capital? Does the technological improvement increase or reduce the economic value of an additional roller?

8. Hester's Hatchery raises fish. At the end of the current season she has 1000 fish in the hatchery. She can harvest any number of fish that she wishes, selling them to restaurants for $5 apiece. Because fish reproduce, for every fish that she leaves in the hatchery this year she will have two fish at the end of next year. The price of a fish is expected to be $5 next year as well. Hester relies entirely on income from current fish sales to support herself.

    a. How many fish should Hester harvest if she wants to maximize the growth of her stock of fish from this season to next season?

    b. Do you think maximizing the growth of her fish stock is an economically sound strategy for Hester? Why or why not? Relate to the text discussion on the costs of economic growth.

    c. How many fish should Hester harvest if she wants to maximize her current income? Do you think this is a good strategy?

    d. Explain why Hester is unlikely to harvest either all or none of her fish, but instead will harvest some and leave the rest to reproduce.

9. "For advances in basic science to translate into improvements in standards of living, they must be supported by favourable economic conditions." True or false, and discuss. Use concrete examples where possible to illustrate your arguments.

ANSWERS TO IN-CHAPTER EXERCISES

14.1 If Canada had grown at the Japanese rate for the period 1870–2007, real GDP per person in 2007 would have been $2328 \times (1.025)^{137} = \$68\ 573$. Actual GDP per person in Canada in 2007 was \$32 722 (in 2000 U.S. dollars), so at the higher rate of growth output per person would have been \$68 573/\$32 722 = 2.1 times higher.

14.2 As before, Paris can wrap 4000 candies/week, or 100 candies/hour. Nicole can wrap 500 candies/hour, and working 40 hours weekly she can wrap 20 000 candies/week. Together Paris and Nicole can wrap 24 000 candies/week. Since they work a total of °80 hours between them, their output per hour as a team is 24 000 candies wrapped/80 hours = 300 candies wrapped/hour, midway between their hourly productivities as individuals.

14.3 Because Nicole can wrap 300 candies/hour by hand, the benefit of giving Nicole the machine is $500 - 300 = 200$ additional candies wrapped/hour. Because Paris wraps only 100 candies/hour by hand, the benefit of giving Paris the machine is 400 additional candies wrapped/hour. So the benefit of giving the machine to Paris is greater than of giving it to Nicole. Equivalently, if the machine goes to Nicole, then Paris and Nicole between them can wrap 500 + 100 = 600 candies/hour, but if Paris uses the machine the team can wrap 300 + 500 = 800 candies/hour. So output is increased by letting Paris use the machine.

14.4 Now, working by hand, Paris can wrap 300 candies/hour and Nicole can wrap 500 candies/hour. With a machine, either Paris or Nicole can wrap 800 candies/hour. As in Exercise 14.3, the benefit of giving a machine to Paris (500 candies/hour) exceeds the benefit of giving a machine to Nicole (300 candies/hour), so if only one machine is available, Paris should use it.

The table analogous to Table 14.2 now looks like this:

Relationship of Capital, Output, and Productivity in the Candy-Wrapping Factory

Number of machines (K)	Candies wrapped per week (Y)	Total hours worked (N)	Average hourly labor productivity (Y/N)
0	32 000	80	400
1	52 000	80	650
2	64 000	80	800
3	64 000	80	800

Comparing this table with Table 14.2, you can see that technological advance has increased labour productivity for any value of K, the number of machines available.

Adding one machine increases output by 20 000 candies wrapped/week, adding the second machine increases output by 12 000 candies wrapped/week, and adding the third machine does not increase output at all (because there is no worker available to use it). So diminishing returns to capital still hold after the technological improvement.

14.5 Although the individual worker is the same person he was in Bangladesh, by coming to Canada he gains the benefit of factors that enhance average labour productivity in this country compared with his homeland. These include factors such as more and better capital to work with, more natural resources per person, and more advanced technologies.

Chapter 15 International Trade and Trade Policy

Under the headline "Sudbury Goes Boom, Windsor Goes Bust," a *Toronto Star* business story of May 2008 tells how two Canadian cities have had opposite experiences in the past several years.[1] In Sudbury, population and incomes have been growing; the unemployment rate of 5.7 percent is at its lowest level since the 1960s. As the business reporter puts it, "Revellers crowd the nightclubs. Shoppers vie for elbow room in malls on weekends. Builders can't keep up." On the other hand, Windsor has lost 10 000 manufacturing jobs in the past six years and housing starts have plunged; the unemployment rate of 8.3 percent is one of the highest in the country. In the reporter's breathless prose, "Factories are lifeless. Stores keep shutting down. Cheques bounce. Movers are busy. Worry is everywhere."

Developments in international trade explain the contrasting situations of Sudbury and Windsor. Sudbury is a hub for mining, particularly for nickel and copper; Windsor has, historically, depended on the auto industry.

Sudbury's economy struggled when nickel prices hovered around U.S.$3 per pound for many years. But nickel prices were in the $13 range on international commodity exchanges in mid-2008. Miners at Vale Inco are doing especially well because of a "nickel bonus" (incentives tied to company profits and the nickel price) negotiated by their United Steelworkers Union in 1985 when nickel prices were depressed. The *Toronto Star* article states that soaring nickel prices in the past few years can be traced to a surging worldwide demand for commodities as China and other Asian countries are hungry for copper and nickel, key elements in stainless steel and other products ranging from batteries to computers.

When the Canadian auto industry boomed in the late 1990s, thanks in part to the international competitive advantage provided by the low value of the Canadian dollar, Windsor thrived. Even in 2005 Windsor produced 360 000 vehicles, 1 000 000 engines, and 885 000 transmissions. But Ford reduced its engine operations, and by

[1]Tony Van Alphen, "Sudbury Goes Boom, Windsor Goes Bust," *Toronto Star*, 17 May 2008, http://www.thestar.com/article/426845. See also Tony Van Alphen, "Windsor is Falling Apart," *Toronto Star*, 17 May 2008, http://www.thestar.com/article/426770; Tony Van Alphen, "Sudbury Booms on Soaring Metal Prices," *Toronto Star*, 18 May 2008; and CAW Local 200, "What the Auto Industry Means to Windsor," http://www.cawlocal200.org/.

May 2008 the Canadian Auto Workers Union had to negotiate a closeout agreement for its members at the General Motors Windsor transmission plant after the company announced the plant would close in 2010. The massive 47 percent appreciation of the Canadian dollar between 2002 and 2007 sharply reduced the international competitiveness of Canada's auto industry. The automakers demanded cost reductions from their suppliers and, as the business reporter states, "companies in China—one of the drivers of Sudbury's boom—South Korea and the U.S. are producing some of the parts and tooling, putting operations like Kasko [producer of auto machinery for Chrysler] in Windsor out of business."

The impact of shifts in international trade are more visible in cities such as Sudbury and Windsor than they would be in larger, more diversified cities such as Toronto, Montreal, and Vancouver, or in the broader economy. But the impact of trade and changes in it is pervasive. It has been estimated, for example, that one in five paid jobs in Canada is directly linked to international trade.[2]

This chapter addresses international trade and trade policy as well as their effects on the broader economy. We begin by presenting statistics on Canada's position in the international trading system. The second section of the chapter provides a supply and demand perspective on winners and losers from trade. The third section provides background on the institutions of trade policy. In the final section we conduct a quick review, especially as it relates to Chapter 8, of our treatment of international trade from a short-run, macroeconomic perspective.

15.1 CANADA IN THE INTERNATIONAL TRADING SYSTEM

Before we consider international trade theory and institutions, let us first examine some basic facts about Canada's place in the international trading system from a statistical perspective. As Figure 4.5 showed, trade is very important to modern-day Canada. In some recent years, exports and imports have each amounted to over 40 percent of Canadian GDP.[3]

To put Canada's reliance upon international trade in context, view Figure 15.1, which compares Canada's trade dependence to that of the other G7 countries (the United States, Japan, Germany, France, United Kingdom, and Italy) and to Australia. In Figure 15.1, trade dependence is measured by the value, expressed relative to GDP, of an economy's combined exports and imports. Of the high-income countries shown, Germany has the highest ratio of trade to GDP and Canada has the second highest.[4]

This characteristic of Canada being highly dependent on trade is a long standing one. Indeed, the great Canadian economic historian Harold Innis (1894–1952) analyzed Canada's economic development by focusing on a succession of leading exports: furs, fish, forestry products, grain, and oil and natural gas. Innis's *staples thesis* maintained that these natural resource exports, or staples, had a pervasive impact, not just on the Canadian economy, but on society and politics as well, because the staples affected everything from Canada's patterns of settlement to Canada's international relations. Although the importance of trade to the Canadian economy has not diminished, there have been major changes in Canada's trading partners and in the composition of Canada's exports since the days of Innis.

---

[2]See http://www.international.gc.ca/trade-agreements-accords-commerciaux/matters-important/index.aspx?lang=en.

[3]Recall, however, that what counts as a component of GDP is the value of net exports—that is, exports *minus* imports.

[4]The definition of trade underlying Figure 15.1 is *merchandise trade*. Merchandise trade refers to exports and imports of goods rather than to exports and imports of goods *and* services, the broader definition of trade employed in Figure 4.5. Because data on trade in goods tends to be more reliable than data on trade in services, the merchandise trade definition is often used for international comparisons of trade dependence.

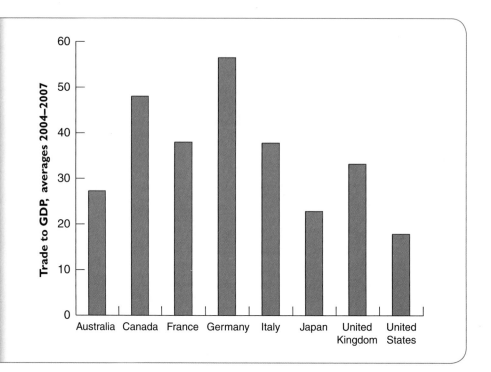

FIGURE 15.1

Trade to GDP Ratios for Selected Countries, 2004–2007 Averages

Canada and Germany are more heavily dependent on international trade than many other high-income countries. Each bar on the graph indicates the ratio of that country's combined merchandise exports and imports to its GDP. SOURCES: Adapted from export and import data provided by the OECD and current GDP data from the IMF *World Economic Outlook Database,* April 2008.

From the time of Confederation in 1867 until World War II, Canada had two major trading partners, the United Kingdom and the United States. But after World War II, the share of trade with the United States in all of Canada's trade began a dramatic upward rise. And the share of trade with the United Kingdom began an equally dramatic decline. Figure 15.2 shows this trend by focusing on the export side of Canada's trade.

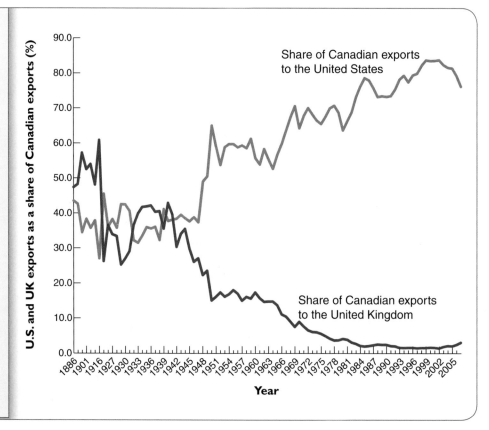

FIGURE 15.2

Canadian Exports to the United States and the United Kingdom, 1886–2007

Until the mid 1940s, the United States and the United Kingdom were of roughly equal importance as trading partners of Canada. The figure shows that since the late 1940s the United States has become the destination for the bulk of Canada's exports and the United Kingdom has become a minor export destination. SOURCES: Adapted from CANSIM series v191334 (exports to U.S.), v191335 (exports to UK), and v191490 (total exports), and from *HSC* series G402, G401, G393, G390, and G389.

In recent years, about 80 percent of Canada's exports have been destined for the United States compared with less than 2 percent for the United Kingdom. The rise in the share of Canada's trade with the United States has worried those who value Canada's independence, and for a period in the 1970s and early 1980s the Canadian government sought to boost the share of Canada's trade with Europe.

Today, Canada's other leading trading partners are Japan, China, and the United Kingdom, as shown in Figure 15.3, but their importance pales in comparison to that of the United States. Japan had become an important trading

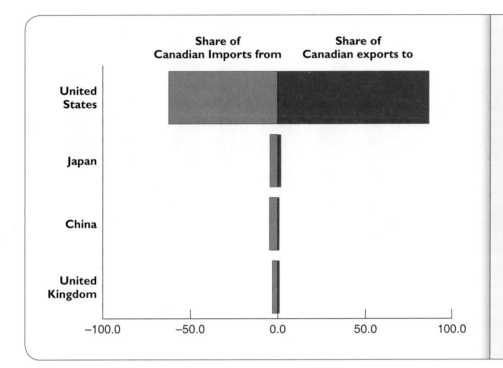

FIGURE 15.3

Canada's Four Major Trading Partners, 2005–2007

The United States is Canada's most important trading partner by far as measured by either the share of Canadian imports from it (red bar) or by the share of Canadian exports destined to (blue bar) it. If the blue bar for a country is larger than the red bar, then Canada runs a trade surplus with that country.

SOURCE: Adapted from Department of Foreign Affairs and International Trade, http://www.dfait-maeci.gc.ca/eet/merchandise-trade-en.asp.

partner for Canada by the 1980s. The major development in Canada's trade pattern in the past several years has been the rise of China as a source of imports, which will not surprise you if you have ever shopped at a "dollar" store and noticed where most of the goods are made. China, which accounted for only 1 percent of Canada's imports in 1989, accounted for 9.4 percent of Canada's imports by 2007.

Figure 15.4 shows the pattern of Canada's exports and imports by broad categories of merchandise trade. In the past few years, natural resource exports have surged. Although the value of Canada's combined exports of industrial products, machinery and equipment, and automotive products ($243 billion) was double the value of Canadian exports of agricultural and fishing products, energy products, and forestry products ($124 billion) in 2003, by 2007 the value of industrial-type exports had dropped to $187 billion, while the value of resource-type exports had risen to $155 billion.

Like many other countries, in the early stages of its development Canada relied upon tariffs (taxes on imported goods) as an important source of government revenue and as a means of providing protection to domestic industries. Over the decades, however, other sources of government revenue—income, payroll, and sales taxes—have gained in relative importance and Canada has become more open to imports.

One indication of this is provided by Figure 15.5, which shows the evolution of Canada's average tariff rate—that is, the ratio of tariff revenue (also called

FIGURE 15.4

Canada's Exports and Imports by Major Product Category, Average 2003–2007

Canada's top export in 2007 was machinery and equipment but natural resource exports are still an important component of Canadian trade, and they have surged in the past few years.

SOURCE: Adapted from Statistics Canada CANSIM database, http://cansim2.statcan.ca, Tables 228-0002 and 228-0003.

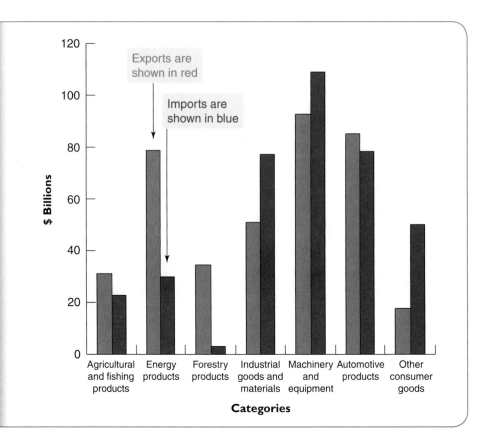

FIGURE 15.5

Average Tariff Rates for Canada, 1868–2006

Average tariff rates for Canada were high during the early stages of Canada's development, reaching a peak of 22 percent in 1888. Since the early 1950s, Canada's average has shown a sharp downward trend, and it dropped below 1 percent by 1996. The average tariff rate measures the ratio of tariff revenues to the value of imports.

SOURCE: Adapted from Statistics Canada CANSIM database, http://cansim2.statcan.ca, series v690200 (customs imports duties) and *HSC* series G485.

import duties or custom duties) to the value of imports. Canada's average tariff rate, which peaked at 22 percent in 1888, had dropped below 1 percent by 1996. A high tariff rate was associated with the implementation in 1879 of the National Policy to protect domestic manufacturing, a policy that was maintained for most years until the late 1930s. Since the early 1950s, Canada's average tariff rate has shown a sharp downward trend, associated in part with the establishment of the General Agreement on Tariffs and Trade (GATT) and the various multilateral rounds of tariff reductions negotiated under the GATT (which we will examine further in section 15.3).

RECAP ↑

CANADA IN THE INTERNATIONAL TRADING SYSTEM

- International trade is very important to the Canadian economy. Canada has the second highest trade to GDP ratio among the G7 countries.
- In recent decades Canada's reliance upon trade with the United States has increased. Now the U.S. share of Canada's exports is about 80 percent.
- Natural resource exports are still an important component of Canada's international trade and they have surged in the past few years. But machinery and equipment has been Canada's largest export category by value.
- Canada's average tariff rate, which peaked at 22 percent in 1888, has remained below 1 percent since 1996.

15.2 A SUPPLY AND DEMAND PERSPECTIVE ON TRADE

We study international trade theory to arrive at an awareness of what goes on in the real world of international trade. The international trade theory we considered in Chapter 2 in connection with the concept of comparative advantage provides a starting point for understanding the real world of trade. Although there were some qualifications, a series of figures culminating in Figure 2.12 showed that the logic that prompts individuals to specialize and to exchange is also the rationale that leads nations to specialize and trade with each other. Each trading partner can benefit from this, even though one may have an absolute advantage in each good. All else being equal, the output of an **open economy**, one that trades with other economies, should be greater than that of a **closed economy**, one that does not trade with others. The larger the difference between the trading partners' opportunity costs, the greater the benefits of trade tend to be.

The international trade theory behind Figure 2.12 helps us to understand, for example, why a country such as Canada would reduce trade barriers over time, as is indicated by the declining average tariff rates shown in Figure 15.5. The theory behind Figure 2.12 suggests that reducing trade barriers was in Canada's interest. But why has it taken Canada so many decades to reduce tariffs? Why do many countries continue to maintain tariffs that are much higher than Canada's? If it is possible for each partner to benefit from trade, why has Canada had a long-standing trade dispute with the United States over exports of softwood lumber?

open economy an economy that trades with other countries

closed economy an economy that does not trade with the rest of the world; also known as an autarky

In order to answer questions such as these, it is helpful to learn some additional trade theory. In certain situations some of the assumptions behind the international trade theory of Chapter 2 may not hold, so we have to qualify the conclusions of that chapter. But even if the international trade theory of Chapter 2 applies reasonably well in a given situation, there are still reasons for some groups to oppose freer trade.

In this section, we will develop a supply and demand model of international trade. With the aid of this model, we will see that opening up trade with other countries will generally create winners and losers, even if freer trade increases total output.

In Figure 15.6 we see supply and demand for wine, one commodity in the markets for wine and lumber in the hypothetical economy we'll call Beaverland.

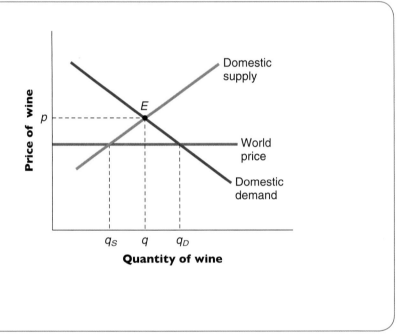

FIGURE 15.6

The Market for Wine in Beaverland

If Beaverland is closed to international trade, the equilibrium price and quantity of wine are determined by the intersection of the domestic supply and demand curves at point E. But if Beaverland is open to trade, the domestic price of wine must equal the world price. At that price, citizens will demand q_D wine, but domestic producers will supply only q_S wine. Thus $q_D - q_S$ wine must be imported from abroad.

As usual, the price is shown on the vertical axis and the quantity on the horizontal axis. For now, think of the price of wine as being measured in terms of lumber rather than in terms of dollars (in other words, we measure the price of wine *relative* to the price of the other good in the economy). As usual, the upward-sloping curve in Figure 15.6 is the supply curve of wine, in this case for wine produced in Beaverland, and the downward-sloping curve is the demand curve for wine by Beaverland residents. The supply curve for wine in Beaverland reflects the opportunity cost of supplying wine (see Chapter 3 for a general explanation). Specifically, at any level of wine production, the relative price at which Beaverland firms are willing to supply an additional bottle of wine equals their opportunity cost of doing so. The demand curve, which tells us the number of bottles of wine Beaverland residents will purchase at each relative price, reflects the preferences and buying power of Beaverland residents.

If the Beaverland economy is closed to international trade, then market equilibrium occurs where the domestic supply and demand curves intersect, at point E in Figure 15.6. The equilibrium price will be p, and the equilibrium quantity will be q. We will ignore transportation and other trading costs.

If Beaverland opens its market to trade, however, the relevant price for wine becomes the **world price** of wine, the price at which wine is traded internationally. The world price for wine is determined by worldwide supply and demand. If we assume that Beaverland's wine market is too small to affect the world price for wine very much, the world price can be treated as fixed, and represented by a horizontal line in the figure. Figure 15.6 shows the world price for wine as being lower than Beaverland's closed-economy price.

If Beaverland residents are free to buy and sell wine on the international market, then the market price of wine in Beaverland must be the same as the world price. (The typical buyer in Beaverland will not pay a price above the world price, and the typical seller will not accept a price below the world price.) Figure 15.6 shows that at the world price, Beaverland consumers and firms demand q_D of wine but Beaverland wine producers will supply only q_S of wine. The difference between the two quantities, $q_D - q_S$, is the amount of wine that Beaverland must import from abroad. Figure 15.6 illustrates a general conclusion: *If the price of a good or service in a closed economy is greater than the world price, and that economy opens itself to trade, the economy will tend to become a net importer of that good or service.*

A different outcome occurs in Beaverland's lumber market shown in Figure 15.7.[5] The price of lumber (measured relative to the price of wine) is shown on the vertical axis, and the quantity of lumber on the horizontal axis. The downward-sloping demand curve in the figure shows how much lumber Beaverland purchasers want to buy at each relative price, and the upward-sloping supply curve how much lumber Beaverland producers are willing to supply at each relative price. If Beaverland's economy is closed to trade with the rest of the world, then equilibrium in the market for lumber will occur at point E, where the domestic demand and supply curves intersect. The quantity produced will be q and the price p.

world price the price at which a good or service is traded on international markets

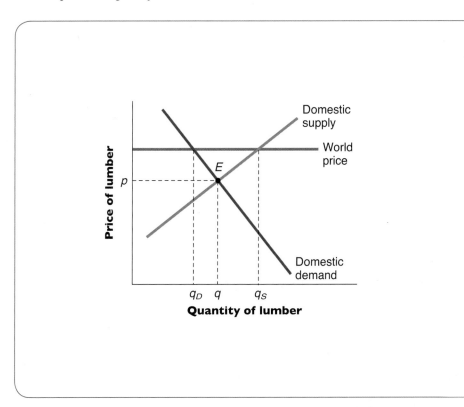

FIGURE 15.7

The Market for Lumber in Beaverland

With no international trade, the equilibrium price and quantity of lumber in Beaverland are determined by the intersection of the domestic supply and demand curves (point E). But if the country opens to trade, the domestic price of lumber must equal the world price. At the higher world price, Beaverland residents will demand the quantity of lumber q_D, less than the amount supplied by Beaverland producers, q_S. The excess lumber supplied by Beaverland producers, $q_S - q_D$, is exported.

[5]In this example, the terms "buyers," "purchasers," and "consumers" are synonyms. For wine purchasers, the buyers are uisually final consumers and for lumber purchases, the buyers are usually builders, and not final consumers. In any case, "consumers," as used here, does not necessarily mean final consumers.

Now imagine that Beaverland opens its lumber market to international trade. As in the case of wine, if free trade in lumber is permitted, then the prevailing price for lumber in Beaverland must be the same as the world price. Unlike the case of wine, however, the world price of lumber as shown in Figure 15.7 is *higher* than the domestic equilibrium price. How do we know that the world price of lumber will be higher than the domestic price? Recall that the price of lumber is measured relative to the price of wine, and vice versa. If the price of wine relative to the price of lumber is higher in Beaverland than in the world market, then the price of lumber relative to the price of wine must be lower, as each price is the reciprocal of the other. More generally, as we saw in Chapter 2, when two people or two countries trade with each other neither can have a comparative advantage in *every* good and service. Thus, in an example with only two goods, if non-Beaverland producers have a comparative advantage in wine, reflected in the lower cost of wine relative to lumber in the world market, then Beaverland producers must have a comparative advantage in lumber. By definition, this comparative advantage implies that the opportunity cost of lumber in terms of wine must be lower in Beaverland than in the rest of the world.

Figure 15.7 shows that at the world price for lumber, Beaverland producers are willing to supply q_S lumber, while Beaverland buyers want to purchase a smaller amount, q_D. The difference between domestic production and domestic purchases, $q_S - q_D$, is exported to the world market. The general conclusion of Figure 15.7 is this: *If the price of a good or service in a closed economy is lower than the world price, and that economy opens itself to trade, the economy will tend to become a net exporter of that good or service.*

WINNERS AND LOSERS FROM TRADE

Why do politicians so often resist "free trade" and "globalization"? As noted in the introduction to this section, one reason could be that the assumptions underlying our comparative advantage model of trade may not hold in specific real-world situations. For example, we have assumed that a country's comparative advantage in any industry is based upon the country's given endowments of resources used in producing the output of that industry. Taking endowments as given is a natural assumption when the key resource for an industry is, huge expanses of arable land, but the assumption is more debatable when the key resource is something like computer programmers, the numbers of whom can be increased by changes in educational policy.[6]

Another reason may be that what is being called free trade is not primarily about the trade of goods and services. In recent times, as we will see later in this chapter, free trade agreements have sometimes been significantly about such issues as the rights of multinational corporations and the protection of intellectual property rights. These issues are quite distinct from the trade in goods and services that has been the focus of our analysis of the comparative advantage model. It is possible to oppose the strengthening of corporate rights and intellectual property rights without being opposed to free trade in goods and services.

But even if free trade is just about trade in goods and services, and even if it offers potential benefits for the economy as a whole, specific groups may not benefit. And politicians may respond to their concerns.

---

[6]To take a specific real-world example, the endowments relevant to comparative advantage in the production of regional jets are not clearly given in the same way that huge expanses of arable land are, and countries like Canada and Brazil have had difficulty reaching agreement on which country has comparative advantage in the production of regional jets. On the trade dispute between Canada and Brazil over regional jets, see, for example, Kathryn Leger, "Canada, Brazil Both Claim Win in Subsidy War," *National Post*, 27 July 2001.

The supply and demand analyses shown in Figures 15.6 and 15.7 are useful for understanding who gains and who loses when an economy opens up to trade. Look first at Figure 15.6, which shows the market for wine in Beaverland. When Beaverland opens its wine market to international competition, Beaverland purchasers enjoy a larger quantity of wine at a lower price. Clearly, Beaverland wine buyers benefit from the free trade in wine. In general, *domestic consumers of imported goods benefit from trade.* However, Beaverland wine producers will not be so happy about opening their market to international competition. The fall in wine prices to the international level implies that less-efficient domestic producers will go out of business and that those who remain will earn lower profits. Unemployment in the wine industry will rise and may persist over time, particularly if displaced wine workers cannot easily move to a new industry.[7] We see that, in general, *domestic producers of imported goods are hurt by free trade* (although in this example they can console themselves with cheap wine).

Consumers are helped, and producers hurt, when imports increase. The opposite conclusions apply for an increase in exports (see Figure 15.7). In the example of Beaverland, an opening of the lumber market raises the domestic price of lumber to the world price and creates the opportunity for Beaverland to export lumber. Domestic producers of lumber benefit from the increased market (they can now sell lumber abroad as well as at home) and from the higher price of their product. In short, *domestic producers of exported goods benefit from free trade.* Beaverland lumber purchasers will be less enthusiastic, however, since they must now pay the higher world price of lumber and can therefore purchase less. Thus *domestic consumers of exported goods are hurt by free trade.*

TABLE 15.1
Trade Winners and Losers

Winners

- Consumers of imported goods
- Producers of exported goods

Losers

- Consumers of exported goods
- Producers of imported goods

TARIFFS AND QUOTAS

So far we have used our supply and demand model of international trade to examine the consequences, for both consumers and producers, of moving from a closed to an open economy. Next we will use the supply and demand model to examine two measures that are legal barriers to imports and are commonly employed to protect domestic markets: *tariffs* and *import quotas*. A **tariff** is a tax imposed on an imported good, and an **import quota** is a legal limit placed on the quantity of a good that may be imported.

Before we begin our supply and demand analysis of tariffs and quotas, however, two points are worth mentioning. First, it is a mistake to view tariffs simply

tariff a tax imposed on an imported good

import quota a legal limit placed on the quantity of a good that may be imported

---

[7]The real wages paid to Beaverland wine industry workers will also tend to fall, reflecting the lower relative price of wine.

protective tariff a tax on imported goods; the intention is to shield domestic industry from import competition

revenue tariff a tax imposed on imported goods; for the purpose of collecting government revenue

as barriers to trade. The term **protective tariff** is used to describe a tariff that is intended to shield domestic industry from import competition. But there are also *revenue tariffs*. A **revenue tariff** is a tax imposed on imported goods for the purpose of collecting government revenue. For example, if a country such as Canada imposed a tariff on bananas it clearly would not be done to protect the domestic banana industry, because there is no such industry. Even protective tariffs generate revenue, provided that the tariff is not so high that it discourages imports altogether. As mentioned above in connection with Figure 15.5, countries such as Canada relied on tariffs as an important source of government revenue in their early stages of development.

A second point worth noting is that although we will focus on the impact of tariffs and quotas on international trade, it should be recognized that the protection provided to an industry by a tariff (which raises the relative price of the imported good) can also be provided to an industry through a subsidy (which lowers the relative price of the domestically produced good). We will see in the following section how trade agreements that aim to reduce tariffs also aim to control subsidies for this very reason.

Tariffs

The effects of tariffs and quotas can be explained using supply and demand diagrams. Suppose that Beaverland wine makers, dismayed by the penetration of their market by imported wine, persuade their government to impose a tariff— that is, a tax—on every bottle of wine imported into the country. Wine produced in Beaverland will be exempt from the tax. Figure 15.8 shows the likely effects of this tariff on the domestic Beaverland wine market (assuming it does not affect the foreign exchange rate). The lower of the two horizontal lines in the figure indicates the world price of wine, not including the tariff. The higher of the two lines indicates the price Beaverland consumers will actually pay for imported wine, including the tariff. We refer to the price of wine including the tariff as p_T.

FIGURE 15.8

The Market for Wine After the Imposition of an Import Tariff

The imposition of a tariff on imported wine raises the price of wine in Beaverland to the world price plus tariff, p_T, represented by the upper horizontal line. Domestic production of wine rises from q_S to q'_S, domestic purchases of wine fall from q_D to q'_D, and wine imports fall from $q_D - q_S$ to $q'_D - q'_S$. Beaverland consumers are worse off and Beaverland wine producers are better off. The Beaverland government collects revenue from the tariff equal to the area of the pale blue rectangle.

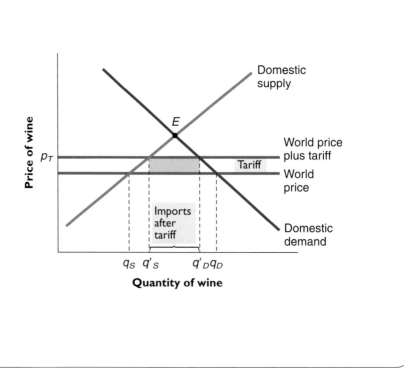

The vertical distance between the two lines equals the amount of the tariff that is imposed on each imported bottle of wine.

From the point of view of domestic Beaverland producers and consumers, the imposition of the tariff has the same effects as an equivalent increase in the world price of wine. Because the price (including the tariff) of imported wine has risen, Beaverland wine producers will be able to raise the price they charge for their wine to the world price plus tariff, p_T. Thus the price Beaverland consumers must pay—whether their wine is imported or not—equals p_T, represented by the upper horizontal line in Figure 15.8.

The rise in the price of wine created by the tariff affects the quantities of wine supplied and the quantities demanded by Beaverland residents. Domestic wine producers, facing a higher price for wine, increase their production from q_S to q'_S (see Figure 15.8). Beaverland consumers, also reacting to the higher price, reduce their wine purchases from q_D to q'_D. As a result, the quantity of imported wine—the difference between domestic purchases and domestic production—falls from $q_D - q_S$ to $q'_D - q'_S$.

Who are the winners and the losers from the tariff, then? The winners are the domestic wine producers, who sell more wine and receive a higher price for it. The clearest losers are Beaverland wine drinkers, who must now pay more for their wine. Another winner is the government, which collects revenue from the tariff. The pale blue area in Figure 15.8 shows the amount of revenue the government collects, equal to the quantity of wine imports after the imposition of the tariff, $q'_D - q'_S$, times the amount of the tariff.

A tariff on imported wine[8]	**EXAMPLE 15.1**

Suppose the demand for wine by Beaverland consumers is given by

$$\text{Demand} = 3000 - 0.5(\text{Price of wine}).$$

The supply of wine by Beaverland producers is

$$\text{Supply} = 1000 + 0.5(\text{Price of wine}).$$

a. Assuming that the Beaverland economy is closed to trade, find the equilibrium price and quantity in the Beaverland wine market.
b. Assume the economy opens to trade. If the world price of Beaverland wine is 1500, find Beaverland consumption, production, and imports of wine.
c. At the request of domestic producers, the Beaverland government imposes a tariff of 300 per imported bottle of wine. Find Beaverland consumption, production, and imports of wine after the imposition of the tariff. How much revenue does the tariff raise for the government?

To find the closed-economy price and quantity, we set supply equal to demand:

$$1000 + 0.5(\text{Price of wine}) = 3000 - 0.5(\text{Price of wine}).$$

Solving this equation for the price of a bottle of wine gives the equilibrium price, equal to 2000. Substituting the equilibrium price into either the supply equation or the demand equation, we find the equilibrium quantity of wine in the Beaverland market, equal to 2000. This equilibrium price and quantity correspond to a point like point E in Figure 15.8.

If the economy opens to trade, the domestic price of wine must equal the world price, which is 1500. At this price, domestic demand for wine is 3000 − 0.5(1500),

[8]If the price units in this example seem too high, think of the units as cents. If the quantities seem too low, think of them as quantities per hour.

or 2250; domestic supply is $1000 + 0.5(1500)$, or 1750. These quantities correspond to q_D and q_S, respectively, in Figure 15.8. Imports equal the difference between domestic quantities demanded and supplied, equal to $2250 - 1750$, or 500 bottles of wine.

The imposition of a tariff of 300 per bottle of wine raises the price from 1500 (the world price without the tariff) to 1800. To find Beaverland consumption and production at this price, we set the price equal to 1800 in the demand and supply equations. Thus the domestic demand for wine is $3000 - 0.5(1800)$, or 2100 bottles of wine, the domestic supply is $1000 + 0.5(1800)$, or 1900 bottles. Imports, the difference between the quantity demanded by Beaverland residents and the quantity supplied by domestic firms, equal $2100 - 1900$, or 200 bottles of wine, corresponding to $q'_D - q'_S$ in Figure 15.8. Thus the tariff has raised the price of wine by 300 and reduced imports by 300. The tariff revenue collected by the government equals 300 per imported bottle times 200 bottles or 60 000.

EXERCISE 15.1

Repeat parts (b) and (c) of Example 15.1 under the assumption that the world price of wine is 1200. What happens if the world price is 1800?

Quotas

An alternative to a tariff is a quota, or legal limit, on the number or value of foreign goods that can be imported. One means of enforcing a quota is to require importers to obtain a licence or permit for each good they bring into the country. The government then distributes exactly the number of permits as the number of goods that may be imported under the quota.

How does the imposition of a quota on wine affect the domestic market for wine? To see the effect of a quota on imported wine, see Figure 15.9, which is

FIGURE 15.9

The Market for Wine After the Imposition of an Import Quota

The figure shows the effects of the imposition of a quota that permits only $q'_D - q'_S$ bottles to be imported. The total supply of wine to the domestic economy equals the domestic supply curve shifted to the right by $q'_D - q'_S$ units (the fixed amount of imports). Market equilibrium occurs at point F. The effects of the quota on the domestic market are identical to those of the tariff analyzed in Figure 15.8. The price rises to p_T, domestic production of wine rises from q_S to q'_S, purchases fall from q_D to q'_D, and imports fall from $q_D - q_S$ to $q'_D - q'_S$.

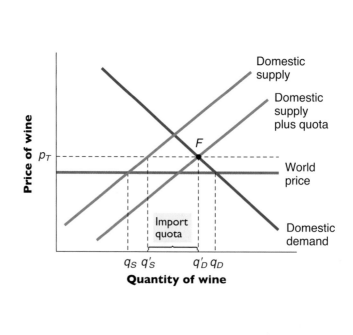

similar to Figure 15.8. As before, assume that at first there are no restrictions on trade. Consumers pay the world price for wine, and $q_D - q_S$ bottles are imported. Now suppose once more that domestic wine producers complain to the government about competition from foreign wine makers, and the government agrees to act. However, this time, instead of a tariff, the government imposes a quota on the amount of wine that can be imported. For comparability with the tariff analyzed in Figure 15.8, let's assume that the quota permits the same level of imports as entered the country under the tariff: specifically, $q'_D - q'_S$ bottles of wine. What effect does this ruling have on the domestic market for wine?

After the imposition of the quota, the supply of wine to the Beaverland market is the production of domestic firms plus the $q'_D - q'_S$ imported wine allowed under the quota. Figure 15.9 shows the supply of wine inclusive of the quota. The total supply curve, labelled "Domestic supply plus quota," is the same as the domestic supply curve except shifted $q'_D - q'_S$ units to the right. The domestic demand curve is the same as in Figure 15.8. Equilibrium in the domestic market for wine occurs at point F in Figure 15.9, at the intersection of the supply curve including the quota and the domestic demand curve. The figure shows that, relative to the initial situation with free trade, the quota (1) raises the domestic price of wine above the world price to the level marked p_T in Figure 15.9; (2) reduces domestic purchases of wine from q_D to q'_D; (3) increases domestic production of wine from q_S to q'_S; and (4) reduces imports to $q'_D - q'_S$, consistent with the quota. Like a tariff, the quota helps domestic producers by increasing their sales and the price they receive for their output, while hurting domestic consumers by forcing them to pay a higher price.

Interestingly, under our assumption that the quota is set so as to permit the same level of imports as the tariff, the effects on the domestic market of the tariff (Figure 15.8) and the quota (Figure 15.9) are not only similar, they are *equivalent*. Comparing Figures 15.8 and 15.9, you can see that the two policies have identical effects on the domestic price, domestic purchases, domestic production, and imports.

Although the market effects of a tariff and a quota are the same, there is one important difference between the two policies, which is that a tariff generates revenue for the government, while a quota does not.[9] With a quota, the revenue that would have gone to the government goes instead to those firms who hold the import licences. A holder of an import licence can purchase wine at the world price and resell it in the domestic market at price p_T, pocketing the difference. Thus, with a tariff the government collects the difference between the world price and the domestic market price of the good; with a quota, private firms or individuals collect that difference unless they are required to bid for import licences in competitive auctions.

Effects of an import quota

EXAMPLE 15.2

Suppose the supply of and demand for wine in Beaverland is as given in Example 15.1, and the government imposes an import quota of 200 bottles of wine. Find the equilibrium price in the domestic wine market, as well as the quantities produced by domestic firms and purchased by domestic consumers.

The supply of wine by domestic Beaverland producers was stated in Example 15.1 to be 1000 + 0.5(Price of wine). The quota allows 200 bottles of wine to be

---

[9]This is true unless the government sells rather than gives away import licences. If a perfectly competitive auction of import licenses can be organized, a tariff and a quota are also equivalent in terms of government revenue.

imported. Thus the total supply of wine, including both domestic production and imports, is 1000 + 0.5(Price of wine) + 200, or 1200 + 0.5(Price of wine). Setting the quantity supplied equal to the quantity demanded, we get

$$1200 + 0.5(\text{Price of wine}) = 3000 - 0.5(\text{Price of wine})$$

Solving for the unknown, we find that the price of wine in the domestic Beaverland market is 1800. Domestic production of wine is 1000 + 0.5(1800), or 1900 bottles of wine, while domestic demand is 3000 − 0.5(1800), or 2100 bottles of wine. The difference between demand and domestic production, 200 bottles of wine, is made up by imports.

Note that the domestic price, domestic production, and domestic demand are the same as in Example 15.1 on the effect of a tariff. Thus the tariff and the quota have the same effects on the domestic market for wine. The only difference between the two policies is that with a quota the government does not get the tariff revenue it got in Example 15.1. That revenue goes instead to the holders of import licences (assuming they get them for free rather than bidding for them) who can buy bottles of wine on the world market at 1500 and sell them in the domestic market at 1800.

> **RECAP**
>
> ## A SUPPLY AND DEMAND PERSPECTIVE ON TRADE
>
> - For a closed economy, the domestic supply of and demand for a good or service determine the equilibrium price and quantity of that good or service.
>
> - In an open economy, the price of a good or service traded on international markets equals the *world price*. If the domestic quantity supplied at the world price exceeds the domestic quantity demanded, the difference will be exported to the world market. If the domestic quantity demanded at the world price exceeds the domestic quantity supplied, the difference will be imported.
>
> - Generally, if the price of a good or service in a closed economy is lower than the world price, and the economy opens to trade, the country will become a net exporter of that good or service. If the closed-economy price is higher than the world price, and the economy opens to trade, the country will tend to become a net importer of the good or service.
>
> - Consumers of imported goods and producers of exported goods benefit from trade, while consumers of exported goods and producers of imported goods are hurt by trade.
>
> - The two most common types of trade barriers are *tariffs* and *import quotas*. A tariff raises the domestic price to the world price plus the tariff. The result is increased domestic production, reduced domestic consumption, and few imports. A quota has effects on the domestic market that are similar to a tariff. Although not analyzed here, subsidies can also duplicate the effects of tariffs.
>
> - *Revenue tariffs* are taxes on imported goods designed to raise government revenue rather than to protect domestic industry from imports.

15.3 TRADE INSTITUTIONS

To analyze real world-trade issues it is important to combine theoretical knowledge of trade with knowledge of trade institutions. In this section, we first examine two institutions with responsibility for Canada's international trade policy: the Department of Foreign Affairs and International Trade (DFAIT) and the Department of Finance. We then examine the evolution of international institutions affecting international trade.

DOMESTIC INSTITUTIONS: DFAIT AND THE DEPARTMENT OF FINANCE

We have seen that the Department of Finance (also known as Finance Canada) under the direction of the Minister of Finance is responsible for Canada's fiscal policy at the federal level and that the Bank of Canada under its governor is responsible for Canada's monetary policy. Canada's institutional arrangements for fiscal and monetary policy have close counterparts in most other countries, even if the terms used (for example, governor of the Bank of Canada as opposed to chairman of the Federal Reserve) are different. Institutional arrangements for international trade policy, however, vary considerably from one country to another.

In Canada, as of 2008, international trade policy is a responsibility of the **Department of Foreign Affairs and International Trade (DFAIT)**. DFAIT, however, is responsible not just for international trade policy, but for foreign policy in general and for services for Canadians travelling abroad as well. In the federal government cabinet, DFAIT is represented by the Minister of Foreign Affairs, the Minister of International Trade, and the Minister for International Cooperation who together represent the top level of the DFAIT organizational chart. The Minister of International Trade, as the title suggests, is responsible for international trade policy.

The international trade section of the DFAIT Web site is listed under the heading "Services for Canadian Business." It states that the department "helps Canadian companies succeed internationally, promotes investment and negotiates trade agreements."[10] The implication is that it is the job of the Minister of International Trade to develop opportunities for Canadian businesses and investors.

But trade policy is not solely the responsibility of the Minister of International Trade. The Department of Finance, among its other responsibilities, also plays a role in international trade policy. This department is the most powerful of the federal government departments, being involved in many areas. The Bank of Canada, which has a high degree of independence from the federal government, is one institution in which the Department of Finance plays a role; it is involved in the selection of the governor of the Bank of Canada and it represents the federal government in negotiating the inflation control agreement that binds the Bank of Canada. While the Department of Finance does not emphasize the role it plays in monetary policy, it does highlight the role it plays in international trade policy. For example, the department's Web site states that Finance Canada "plays an important role in negotiating our trade arrangements with other nations and monitoring how those arrangements serve Canada's interests."[11] It also declares, "One of the most important tools any government has for managing trade with other nations is the tariff. It's a kind of tax governments charge on imports of products and services. It's the job of Finance Canada to monitor our tariff policies and those of other nations, and to develop new policies that will best serve our economy."[12]

Department of Foreign Affairs and International Trade (DFAIT) a department of Canada's federal government led by multiple cabinet ministers; responsibility for international trade policy is shared between the Minister of International Trade and the Department of Finance

---

[10]See http://www.international.gc.ca/commerce/index.aspx (May 2008).
[11]See http://www.fin.gc.ca/access/int_iss_e.html (May 2008).
[12]See http://www.fin.gc.ca/access/taxe.html (May 2008).

Within the Department of Finance, international trade is of special concern to the International Trade and Finance Branch, and within that branch it is the focus of the International Trade Policy Division.

INTERNATIONAL INSTITUTIONS

In examining the international institutions that affect international trade, it is necessary to distinguish between the different levels of trade agreements: multilateral, regional, and those that are sector-specific.

Multilateral Agreements and the WTO

multilateral agreement
a document signed by representatives of many nations to express their acceptance of the principles set out in the document

A **multilateral agreement** typically refers to a document signed by representatives of many nations to express their acceptance of the principles set out in the document. Examples include the Kyoto Protocol, a multilateral environmental agreement regarding greenhouse gas emissions, and the Ottawa Convention, which bans anti-personnel landmines. International trade today is governed in part by a multilateral trade agreement that was first signed several decades ago.

More precisely, the major international institutions affecting finance and trade today date back to a July 1944 conference of 44 allied countries in the U.S. town of Bretton Woods, New Hampshire. With the end of World War II in sight, the conference delegates sought to develop institutions for international finance and trade in the postwar era. The International Monetary Fund (IMF) and the World Bank were established to deal with international finance issues: the IMF initially for exchange rate issues and the World Bank to provide financing and advice for economic development. To complement the IMF and the World Bank, the Bretton Woods conference proposed an International Trade Organization (ITO) that would establish rules and regulations for a more open international trading system.

General Agreement on Tariffs and Trade (GATT)
a multilateral agreement dating back to the late 1940s that, through numerous rounds of trade negotiations, led to reduced tariffs and quotas among many countries

As governments negotiated a charter for the ITO, parallel negotiations began under a *General Agreement on Tariffs and Trade* as a means of getting on with the job of reducing tariffs and opening markets. The **General Agreement on Tariffs and Trade (GATT)**, which came about in 1947–1948 among 23 countries including Canada, was a multilateral agreement with a preamble describing its purpose as being the "substantial reduction of tariffs and other barriers to trade and to the elimination of discriminatory treatment in international commerce."[13] Although a charter for the ITO itself was approved by the United Nations, approval was not obtained from the U.S. Congress and, hence, it never came into existence. But the GATT Treaty survived and evolved into an "unofficial, de facto international organization, also known informally as GATT."[14]

Three particularly noteworthy GATT principles that still apply are set out as Articles 1, 3, and 6, respectively, of the original GATT legal text of 1947.[15] The first of these is *most-favoured nation treatment*. Under **most-favoured nation (MFN) treatment**, a special arrangement such as a reduced tariff offered to one country (the most-favoured nation) in the interests of opening up a market must be offered to all other members of the agreement as well.

most-favoured nation (MFN) treatment an agreement that any special arrangement, such as a reduced tariff that is offered to one country (the most-favoured nation), in the interests of opening up a market must be offered to all other members

There are exceptions to MFN treatment. For example, GATT's Article 24 allows regional trading arrangements to be established if they promote trade among members without raising barriers to non-members. Also, since 1971 the GATT has made provision for a generalized system of preferences (GSP), allowing preference-giving countries to grant tariff rates below the MFN rates

---

[13]See http://www.wto.org/english/docs_e/legal_e/gatt47_01_e.htm (May 2008).
[14]See http://www.wto.org/English/thewto_e/whatis_e/tif_e/fact1_e.htm (May 2008).
[15]These and other principles are discussed at http://www.wto.org/english/thewto_e/whatis_e/tif_e/fact2_e.htm; the GATT legal text is available online at http://www.wto.org/english/docs_e/legal_e/gatt47_01_e.htm (May 2008).

(or even at zero rates) to the least developed countries so as to promote their export industries and accelerate their growth. In addition to the European Union countries, there are currently 12 preference-giving countries, of which Canada is one.

The second GATT principle worthy of mention is *national treatment*. In the context of international trade, **national treatment** means that once a good has entered a country it must be treated as equivalent to a domestically produced good of the same type, for purposes of taxation and regulation. The rationale for this principle is prevention of the undermining of tariff reductions by domestic policy measures that discriminate against foreign-produced goods. For example, if a country applies more stringent safety standards to foreign-produced automobiles than it does to domestically produced ones it is in violation of the principle of national treatment.

national treatment once a good has entered a country it must be treated as equivalent to a domestically produced good of the same type for purposes of taxation and regulation

The third noteworthy GATT principle is promotion of *fair competition*. Promoting **fair competition** means discouraging export subsidies and the dumping of products on foreign markets at below cost in order to gain market share. Under certain circumstances, the GATT permits its signatories to impose both *countervailing duties* on imports that have been subsidized and *antidumping duties* against imports that have been sold at a price below the one charged in the home market.

fair competition the practice of discouraging both export subsidies and the dumping of products on foreign markets at below cost in order to gain market share

Over the years, the GATT went through eight rounds of negotiations that responded both to unresolved issues from previous negotiations as well as to new issues, and involved an ever-expanding set of countries. The most famous rounds were the Kennedy Round of 1964–1967, involving 62 countries; the Tokyo Round of 1973–1979, involving 102 countries; and the Uruguay Round of 1986–1994, which was the eighth and final round and involved 123 countries.[16] The GATT, along with improvements in transportation and communication, among other factors, appears to have been an important contributor to ever rising trade-to-GDP ratios on a world level.[17]

Among other things, the Uruguay Round of the GATT produced an agreement to establish the *World Trade Organization*, which has headquarters in Geneva, Switzerland. The **World Trade Organization (WTO)** began operation in 1995 as an official international body governing world trade, and it superseded the role of the GATT as an unofficial, de facto trade organization. But the GATT, as an agreement, continues as the part of the WTO agreement dealing with trade in goods.

World Trade Organization (WTO) official international trade body headquartered in Geneva that began operation in 1995; superseded the GATT as an unofficial, de facto trade organization

In addition to the GATT, the WTO agreement incorporated a new General Agreement on Trade in Services (GATS) and an Agreement on Trade-Related Aspects of Intellectual Property Rights (TRIPS), and it provided for a dispute-settlement mechanism as well as for WTO reviews of governments' trade policies. Because of some of these measures, the WTO has been more controversial than the GATT ever was. The incorporation of GATS has raised concerns that domestic authority over services such as health, education, water, and electricity supply will be undermined. Likewise, critics see TRIPS as a tool by which certain rich countries will extract larger payments from other countries for patented and copyrighted material.

Under the auspices of the WTO, a ninth round of multilateral trade negotiations was to be launched in the U.S. city of Seattle in late 1999, but the meetings were disrupted by massive street protests and the round was launched instead in Doha, Qatar, in 2001. As of 2008, however, the Doha Round remains stalled, primarily because of differences between the interests of the advanced economies and those of the major developing ones.

---

[16]Details about the evolution of the GATT can be found at http://www.wto.org/English/thewto_e/whatis_e/tif_e/fact4_e.htm (May 2008).

[17]For a graph showing the growth of merchandise trade rel.ative to the growth of GDP at the world level, see http://www.wto.org/English/thewto_e/whatis_e/tif_e/fact3_e.htm (May 2008).

Regional Trade Agreements

The WTO has reported that, as of May 2008, all of its 152 members but one, Mongolia, were also members of *regional trade agreements*. A **regional trade agreement** aims to reduce restrictions on international trade between two or more countries, usually within a certain region. These trade agreements need not be limited to trade in goods and services; they may also deal with issues such as foreign investment and intellectual property protection.

regional trade agreement aims to reduce restrictions on international trade between two or more countries, usually within a certain region

Regional trade agreements have resulted in four major forms of regional trade arrangements, of which the least comprehensive is a *free trade area*. A **free trade area** involves two or more countries that agree to eliminate tariffs and other trade restrictions on most or all mutual trade of their own goods and services, but, at the same time, they may each have different tariffs on imports from outside countries. They must agree on *rules of origin* that prevent goods from outside countries from entering the member country with the lowest external tariff and from there being transported free of any additional tariff to the member with a higher tariff. Otherwise, if transport costs are negligible, the member with the higher tariff would collect no revenue from the evaded tariff and the volume of the good imported to this higher-tariff member would be the same as it would be if the tariff were reduced to the level of the member country with the lowest tariff.

free trade area involves two or more countries that agree to eliminate tariffs and other trade restrictions on most or all mutual trade of their own goods and services; they may each have different tariffs for imports from non-member countries

The Canada–U.S. Free Trade Agreement (CUSFTA) that came into effect in 1989 joined the United States and Canada into a free trade area. In 1994, the CUSFTA was replaced by the North American Free Trade Agreement (NAFTA) under which Canada, the United States, and Mexico formed the world's largest free trade area.

A *customs union* is characterized by a higher degree of trade integration than a free trade area. A **customs union** involves two or more countries that not only agree to eliminate tariffs and other trade restrictions on most or all mutual trade of their own goods and services, but also agree to a common set of trade barriers against imports from non-member countries. Members of a customs union have less freedom to set trade policy than members of a free trade area have. But because of their common set of trade barriers against non-member imports, they do not have to bother with rules of origin.

customs union two or more countries that not only agree to eliminate tariffs and other trade restrictions on most or all mutual trade but also agree to a common set of trade barriers to imports from non-member countries

The Mercosur agreement of 1991 involving Argentina, Brazil, Paraguay, and Uruguay was intended to lead to the formation of a customs union. The countries, however, have failed to implement their original intentions to such an extent that they are now more accurately described as forming a free trade area.

The third major type of regional trade arrangement, a *common market*, is characterized by an even higher degree of economic integration than a customs union imposes. A **common market** involves two or more countries that have agreed to eliminate trade restrictions on most or all mutual trade, to maintain a common set of trade barriers against imports from non-member countries, and to permit mobility of capital and labour among member countries.

common market two or more countries eliminating trade restrictions on most or all mutual trade, maintaining a common set of trade barriers against imports from non-member countries, and permitting mobility of capital and labour among member countries

Both the European Economic Community created in 1957 and the European Community into which it was subsumed in 1967 were often called "the Common Market." In economic terms, however, they were perhaps better characterized as being customs unions. With the establishment of the European Union under the Maastricht Treaty in 1993, however, it became appropriate to view the member countries as forming a common market.

A common market taken to the next level of economic integration, an *economic and monetary union*, is the fourth major type of regional trade arrangement. An **economic and monetary union** is a common market with a single currency. The process of economic integration among member countries is ongoing, but the European Union countries that have adopted the euro as their currency can be said to constitute an economic and monetary union.

economic and monetary union a common market with a single currency but made up of any number of member countries

Regardless of the type of regional trade arrangement that binds them, groups of countries that have joined together under a regional trade agreement are known as *trade blocs*. When a new trade bloc is formed, outsider countries often worry that they will suffer from *trade diversion*. **Trade diversion** occurs when a reduction of trade barriers among members of a trade bloc causes trade between them to take the place of trade with countries outside the bloc. The lowest-cost supplier for a particular product may exist outside of the trade bloc but be unable to compete with a higher-cost supplier within the bloc because of a tariff applying only to outside suppliers.

trade diversion a reduction of trade barriers among members of a trading bloc causes trade among them to take the place of trade with countries outside the bloc

Sector-Specific Trade Agreements

The trade agreements considered above, whether multilateral or regional, are broad ones covering wide ranges of goods and, in some cases, services. Some international trade agreements that have been important to Canada, however, were *sector-specific*. A **sector-specific trade agreement** deals with international trade in the products of a particular economic sector, such as the clothing and textile sector, the automotive industry, or the softwood lumber industry.

sector-specific trade agreement international trade agreement for the products of a particular economic sector, such as the softwood lumber industry

The Multifibre Arrangement (1974–1994) and its successor the WTO Agreement on Textiles and Clothing (1995–2004), for example, were multilateral agreements under which countries, mostly developed ones including Canada, whose markets were disrupted by imports of cheap textiles and clothing from another country, usually a developing one, were able to negotiate quota restrictions. In terms of our supply and demand analysis of winners and losers from trade measures, the main winners from the quotas were producers in countries such as Canada. The losers were producers in countries whose exports were restricted by the quotas and consumers in countries where imports were restricted.

The Canada–United States Automotive Products Trade Agreement (1965–2001), popularly known as the Auto Pact, is an example of a bilateral sector-specific trade agreement, and also an example of managed trade. Basically, it said that for every vehicle sold in Canada the auto companies had to assemble a vehicle in Canada. The Auto Pact resulted in larger, more efficient auto plants that exported freely to both countries, as opposed to smaller plants largely restricted by tariffs to producing for their domestic market only. Given our much smaller market, Canada's gains from the Auto Pact were particularly large. The losers were foreign auto producers such as the British who saw sharp reductions in their Canadian market share after the implementation of the Auto Pact. In 2001, the Auto Pact was abolished by the federal government in response to a WTO dispute panel ruling, following a complaint by Japan and the European Union, that the Auto Pact discriminated against vehicles produced outside North America.

A more recent example of a bilateral sector-specific trade agreement is the Canada–U.S. Softwood Lumber Agreement of 2006, the latest attempt to solve a trade dispute over softwood lumber exports from Canada to the United States that began back in the early 1980s. The dispute began with the U.S. lumber industry's argument that the Canadian system of forestry managment, under which forestry companies pay stumpage fees set by governments rather than by competitive auction as is typical in the United States, constituted a form of export subsidy that should be offset by countervailing duties. These countervailing duties mainly benefited the U.S. lumber industry. The Canadian lumber industry suffered, of course, but groups representing U.S. buyers such as the National Association of Home Builders and American Consumers for Affordable Homes have also seen themselves as losing through the restrictions on Canadian lumber exports.

RECAP ↑

TRADE INSTITUTIONS

Canada's international trade policy is the joint responsibility of the *Department of Foreign Affairs and International Trade* (DFAIT), particularly the Minister of International Trade, and of the Department of Finance.

The *General Agreement on Tariffs and Trade* (GATT) refers to a series of multilateral trade agreements but also to an unofficial, de facto international trade organization that was superseded by the *World Trade Organization* (WTO) in 1995. The GATT trade principles of *most-favoured nation* (MFN) treatment, *national treatment*, and *fair competition* continue to exist within the WTO. In addition to the GATT, the World Trade Organization (WTO) agreement incorporated a new General Agreement on Trade in Services (GATS) and a new Agreement on Trade-Related Aspects of Intellectual Property Rights (TRIPS), and it provided for a dispute-settlement mechanism.

Regional trade arrangements take four major forms: *free trade areas*, *customs unions*, *common markets*, and *economic and monetary unions*. Under the NAFTA, Canada forms a free trade area with the United States and Mexico.

The Auto Pact (1965–2001) and the Canada–U.S. Softwood Lumber Agreement of 2006 are examples of *sector-specific trade agreements*.

15.4 RELEVANT SHORT-RUN MACROECONOMIC THEORY

The comparative advantage theory of international trade presented in Chapter 2 and the supply and demand perspective on international trade presented in this chapter are both important for understanding real-world trade issues. But the short-run macroeconomic theory that we covered in Chapters 8 and 9 is also relevant to an understanding of international trade issues.

The Keynesian cross diagram of Chapter 8 is useful for analyzing an economy suffering from a recessionary gap. For example, Figure 8.5 showed how an increase in government purchases could be used to close a recessionary gap. Figure 15.10 is a similar diagram showing how an increase in net exports closes a recessionary gap.

In Figure 15.10, the expenditure line is given by *PAE* (planned aggregate expenditure) $= 950 + 0.8Y$, and it intersects the 45-degree line at E, equilibrium. The output associated with E is 4750 units. Potential output, Y^*, is 4800. Thus, there is a recessionary gap of 50 units. If net exports, *NX*, increase by 10, however, the expenditure line will shift upwards to $PAE = 960 + 0.8Y$ and the new equilibrium will be given by F. The increase in planned aggregate expenditure will eliminate the recessionary gap.

Figure 15.10 applies regardless of the reason that net exports increase. It could be, for example, that net exports increase because income in a trading partner goes up, causing that trading partner to increase its imports from the economy in question. But it could also be that the economy in question raises tariffs against the imports of its trading partners. All else being equal, the higher tariffs should cause its net exports to increase.

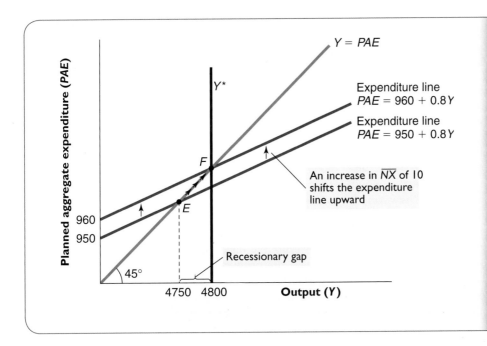

FIGURE 15.10

An Increase in Net Exports Eliminates a Recessionary Gap
The economy is initially at point *E*, with a recessionary gap of 50. A 10-unit increase in net exports raises autonomous expenditure by 10 units, shifting the expenditure line up and raising the equilibrium point from *E* to *F*. At point *F*, where output equals potential output ($Y = Y^* = 4800$), the output gap has been eliminated. (The figure is not drawn to scale.)

As these principles will also operate in reverse, they can be used to determine what monetary or fiscal measures need to be adopted in order to prevent a recessionary gap that otherwise might occur as the result of changes in trade policy. Suppose, for example, that an economy is initially in equilibrium with no recessionary gap and it drops tariffs against the imports of its trading partners. All else being equal, the lower tariffs should cause net exports to decline, planned aggregate expenditure to fall, and a recessionary gap to develop. Hence a policy of trade liberalization may require the simultaneous adoption of expansionary monetary and/or fiscal policy measures to ensure against a recessionary gap.[18] The Canada–U.S. Free Trade Agreement (FTA) of 1989, however, was introduced at the same time that the Bank of Canada was engaged in an extremely contractionary monetary policy to bring down the rate of inflation, and during the early stages of FTA implementation the federal government introduced the GST, widely seen as a contractionary fiscal policy measure.

We saw in Figure 15.5 that Canada's average tariff rate jumped during the Great Depression. Many countries raised their tariff rates during this period as they generally did not have a good grasp of how fiscal and monetary policy could be used to improve the economic situation. Many of them had the idea that if they could boost their net exports through trade protection they could stimulate their economies. Figure 15.10 suggests that this could work for one country. But if many countries try to boost net exports through trade protection they will fail: increased net exports for one country would mean reduced net exports for another. The belief that every country could increase net exports at once is an example of the *fallacy of composition*. This is one reason why economists generally oppose the use of trade protection as a means of increasing net exports and refer to it as a *beggar-thy-neighbour* policy.

We close this chapter with an Economic Naturalist that is an example of the use of short-run macroeconomic analysis in predicting the consequences of trade policy actions.

[18]This point has been emphasized many times by Joseph Stiglitz, a recipient of the Nobel Prize in Economics, in his role as a development economist.

ECONOMIC *Naturalist*   **15.1**   Correctly predicting Argentina's growth performance

Suppose a country that had been gradually moving towards freer trade suddenly reversed the process of trade liberalization. Would this increase in trade protection result in reduced economic growth?

The microeconomic reasoning about trade that we have studied with the production possibilities curve diagram suggests that an increase in trade protection would tend to reduce output. Another possibility, however, is suggested by the short-run macroeconomic reasoning we studied with the Keynesian cross diagram. If the economy is suffering from underutilization of resources, that is, if there is a recessionary gap, then it is possible to increase actual output to the level of potential output by increasing planned aggregate expenditure. One way to increase planned aggregate expenditure is to increase net exports. And an increase in trade protection that, say, reduces imports while not reducing exports will increase net exports. So macroeconomic reasoning suggests that

increased trade protection, though it may not be the best approach, could increase output.

During the 1990s, Argentina gradually moved towards freer trade. The country was sliding further and further into a deep recessionary gap when, in a *New York Times* column of January 1, 2002, economist Paul Krugman reasoned that Argentina would soon turn to greater trade protection. His comment was, "Turning your back on the world market is bad for long-run growth; Argentina's own history is the best proof."[19] With these words, he was recognizing the microeconomic reasoning we have studied with the production possibilities curve diagram, as in Figure 2.12.

Krugman predicted, however, that Argentina would impose "import quotas, turning its back on world markets", and he added that "...these retrograde policies will work, in the sense that they will produce a temporary improvement in the economic situation—just as similar

TABLE 15.2

Key Economic Indicators, Argentina, 1994–2006

1. Year	2. Trade Freedom Index	3. Trade balance as % of GDP	4. Growth of Real GDP Per Capita	5. U.S.$/peso Forex Rate	6. Real interest rate
1994	n.a.	−3.1	4.5	1.00	5.8
1995	58.4	−0.4	−4.0	1.00	14.6
1996	60.0	−0.7	4.3	1.00	10.8
1997	60.0	−2.2	6.9	1.00	8.5
1998	60.0	−2.5	2.7	1.00	10.1
1999	61.2	−1.7	−4.4	1.00	12.2
2000	62.0	−0.6	−1.8	1.00	11.9
2001	65.0	1.3	−5.4	1.00	29.1
2002	53.0	16.0	−11.7	0.35	26.1
2003	54.0	12.2	7.8	0.34	5.6
2004	61.6	7.9	8.0	0.34	2.6
2005	56.2	6.5	8.1	0.34	−3.6
2006	67.4	6.1	7.4	0.32	−1.9

SOURCES: Trade Freedom Index, http://www.heritage.org/research/features/index/downloads/2008PastScores.xls; U.S.$/peso foreign exchange rate, 1994–2006, adapted from monthly data, http://fx.sauder.ubc.ca/data.html; inflation, real GDP, and real GDP per capita, http://www.imf.org/external/pubs/ft/weo/2008/01/weodata/index.aspx; trade balance and nominal interest rate data, http://data.un.org

[19]Paul Krugman, "Crying with Argentina," *New York Times*, 1 January 2002, http://www.pkarchive.org/column/010102.html.

policies did back in the 1930s." These words, on the other hand, are a recognition of the short-run macroeconomic reasoning we studied with the Keynesian cross diagram. With them, Krugman was also suggesting that the macroeconomic reasoning was more relevant for predicting what would happen to Argentina's output in the short run than the microeconomic reasoning was.

In general terms, Krugman's prediction proved to be accurate. An index of Argentina's trade freedom (with 100 as a theoretical maximum) dropped from 65, before Krugman made his prediction and to 53 after it was made, as shown in column 2 of Table 15.2. Argentina's trade balance (net exports), which had averaged -1 percent of GDP from 1994–2001, averaged 14 percent of GDP in 2002–2003, as shown in column 3. In 2003, Argentina's real GDP per capita grew by 7.8 percent, and it continued to grow at over 7 percent per year from 2004 to 2006, as shown in column 4.

Factors other than increased trade protection also contributed to Argentina's strong economic recovery. The exchange rate, which had been pegged at U.S.$1/peso, was allowed to depreciate to about U.S.$0.34/peso, as shown in column 5. As we have seen in Chapter 12, exchange rate depreciation tends to boost net exports and, hence, planned aggregate expenditure and output also. Real interest rates, which averaged almost 30 percent in 2001, averaged less than 1 percent for the 2003–2006 period, as shown in column 6. We have seen in Chapters 9, 10, and 11 that lower real interest rates also boost planned aggregate expenditure (or aggregate demand) and, hence, output also.

Nevertheless, Krugman correctly predicted Argentina's economic recovery. He recognized the contribution that open trade can make to long-run growth. But at the same time he did not allow that recognition to cloud his short-run macroeconomic prediction about what a boost to net exports could do to eliminate a severe recessionary gap.

SUMMARY

15.1 Canada had a long-standing dependence on international trade, and today has the second highest ratio of trade to GDP among the G7 countries. Until the mid 1940s the United States and the United Kingdom were of roughly equal importance as trading partners of Canada, but since then, the U.S. role has grown to the point where the great bulk of Canadian trade is with the United States. Natural resource exports continue to be an important component of Canadian trade, but in recent years machinery and equipment has been Canada's largest export category. In the early stages of Canadian development tariffs were an important source of government revenue but today the value of tariff revenues is less than one percent of the value of imports.

15.2 The principle of comparative advantage has been used to argue that each country should specialize in the goods and services at which it is relatively most productive and then trade with other countries to obtain the goods and services its citizens desire.

15.2 In a closed economy, the relative price of a good or service is determined at the intersection of the supply curve of domestic producers and the demand curve of domestic consumers. In an open economy, the relative price of a good or service equals the world price—the price determined by supply and demand in the world economy. If the price of a good or service in a closed economy is greater than the world price, and the country opens its market to trade, it will become a net importer of that good or service. But if the closed-economy price is below the world price, and the country opens itself to trade, it will become a net exporter of that good or service.

15.2 Some groups are hurt by free trade. Groups that are hurt by trade may be able to induce the government to impose tariffs or quotas. A *tariff* is a tax on an imported good that has the effect of raising the domestic price of the good. A higher domestic price increases domestic supply, reduces domestic demand, and reduces imports of the good. A *quota*, which is a legal limit on the amount of a good that may be imported, has the same effects as a tariff, except that the government collects no tax revenue.

15.3 Canada's international trade policy is the joint responsibility of the Department of Foreign Affairs and International Trade (DFAIT), particularly the Minister of International Trade, and of the Department of Finance.

15.3 The General Agreement on Tariffs and Trade (GATT) refers to a series of multilateral trade agreements but also to an unofficial, de facto international trade organization that was superseded by the World Trade Organization in 1995.

15.3 The GATT continues to exist as an agreement featuring the principles of most-favoured nation (MFN) treatment, national treatment, and fair competition.

15.3 Regional trade arrangements take four major forms: free trade areas, customs unions, common markets, and economic and monetary unions. Under NAFTA, Canada forms a free trade area with the United States and Mexico.

15.3 The Auto Pact (1965–2001) and the Canada–U.S. Softwood Lumber Agreement of 2006 are examples of sector-specific trade agreements.

15.4 A policy of trade liberalization may require the simultaneous adoption of expansionary macroeconomic policy measures to ensure against a recessionary gap.

15.4 If many countries try to boost net exports through trade protection, they will encounter the problem that increased net exports for one country would mean reduced net exports for another.

KEY TERMS

closed economy (393)
common market (406)
customs union (406)
Department of Foreign Affairs and
    International Trade (DFAIT) (403)
economic and monetary union (406)
fair competition (405)
free trade area (406)

General Agreement on Tariffs and
    Trade (GATT) (404)
import quota (397)
most-favoured nation (MFN)
    treatment (404)
multilateral agreement (404)
national treatment (405)
open economy (393)

protective tariff (398)
regional trade agreement (406)
revenue tariff (398)
sector-specific trade agreement (407)
tariff (397)
trade diversion (407)
World Trade Organization (WTO) (405)
world price (395)

REVIEW QUESTIONS

1. Which two countries were Canada's leading trade partners during and prior to World War II and which four countries are Canada's major trade partners today?

2. True or false, and explain. If a country is more productive in every sector than a neighbouring country, then there is no benefit in trading with the neighbouring country.

3. Show graphically the effects of a tariff on imported automobiles on the domestic market for automobiles. Who is hurt by the tariff, and why? Who benefits, and why?

4. Show graphically the effects of a quota on imported automobiles on the domestic market for automobiles. Who does the quota hurt, and who benefits? Explain.

5. Explain why a free trade area requires rules of origin.

6. Discuss the winners and losers from the application of countervailing duties on Canadian lumber exports to the United States.

7. Use a Keynesian cross diagram to explain how a decrease in net exports would reduce an expansionary gap.

PROBLEMS

1. Suppose that a Canadian worker can produce 1000 pairs of shoes or 10 industrial robots per year. For simplicity, assume there are no costs other than labour costs and firms earn zero profits. Initially, the Canadian economy is closed. The domestic price of shoes is $30 per pair, so a Canadian worker can earn $30 000 annually by working in the shoe industry. The domestic price of a robot is $3000, so a Canadian worker can also earn $30 000 annually working in the robot industry.

   Now suppose that Canada opens trade with the rest of the world. Foreign workers can produce 500 pairs of shoes or one robot per year. The world price of shoes after Canada opens its markets is $10 per pair, and the world price of robots is $5000.

   a. What do foreign workers earn annually, in dollars?
   b. When it opens to trade, which good will Canada import and which will it export?
   c. Find the real income of Canadian workers after the opening to trade, measured in (1) the number of pairs of shoes annual worker income will buy and (2) the number of robots annual worker income will buy. Compare to the situation before the opening of trade. Does trading in goods produced by "cheap foreign labour" hurt Canadian workers?
   d. How might your conclusion in part (c) be modified if it is costly for workers to change industries?

2. The demand for automobiles in a certain country is given by

$$D = 12\,000 - 200P,$$

where P is the price of a car. Supply by domestic automobile producers is

$$S = 7000 + 50P.$$

a. Assuming that the economy is closed, find the equilibrium price and production of automobiles.
b. The economy opens to trade. The world price of automobiles is 18. Find the domestic quantities demanded and supplied, and the quantity of imports or exports. Who will favour the opening of the automobile market to trade, and who will oppose it?
c. The government imposes a tariff of 1 unit per car. Find the effects on domestic quantities demanded and supplied and on the quantity of imports or exports. Also find the revenue raised by the tariff. Who will favour the imposition of the tariff, and who will oppose it?
d. Can the government obtain the same results as you found in part (c) by imposing a quota on automobile imports? Explain.

3. Suppose the domestic demand and supply for automobiles is as given by Problem 2. The world price of automobiles is 16. Foreign car firms have a production cost of 15 per automobile, so they earn a profit of 1 per car.
a. How many cars will be imported, assuming this country trades freely?
b. Now suppose foreign car producers are asked "voluntarily" to limit their exports to the home country to half of free-trade levels. What will be the equilibrium price of cars in the domestic market if foreign producers comply? Find domestic quantities of cars supplied and demanded.
c. How will the voluntary export restriction affect the profits of foreign car producers?

ANSWER TO IN-CHAPTER EXERCISE

15.1 If the world price of wine is 1200, domestic demand for wine is $3000 - 0.5(1200)$, or 2400 bottles. Domestic supply is $1000 + 0.5(1200)$, or 1600 bottles. The difference between the quantity demanded and the quantity supplied, 800 bottles of wine, is imported.

  A tariff of 300 raises the domestic price of wine to 1500. Now domestic demand is $3000 - 0.5(1500)$, or 2250, and domestic supply is $1000 + 0.5(1500)$, or 1750. The difference, 500 bottles of wine, equals imports. Revenue for the government is 300 per bottle times 500 imported bottles, or 150 000.

  If the world price of wine is 1800 and there is no tariff, domestic demand is $3000 - 0.5(1800)$, or 2100; domestic supply is $1000 + 0.5(1800)$, or 1900; and imports are 200. A tariff of 300 raises the world price to 2100, which is greater than the domestic price when there is no trade (2000). No wine is imported in this case, and no tariff revenue is raised.

Chapter 16 Saving and Capital Formation

On your mother's or father's knee you probably heard the fable of the ant and the grasshopper. All summer the ant worked hard laying up food for the winter. The grasshopper mocked the ant's efforts and contented himself with basking in the sunshine, ignoring the ant's earnest warnings. When winter came the ant was well-fed, while the grasshopper starved. Moral: When times are good, the wise put aside something for the future.

Of course, there is also the modern ending to the fable, in which the grasshopper breaks his leg by tripping over the anthill, sues the ant for negligence, and ends up living comfortably on the ant's savings. (Nobody knows what happened to the ant.) Moral: Saving is risky; live for today.

The pitfalls of modern life notwithstanding, saving is important, both to individuals and to nations. People need to save to provide for their retirement and for other future needs, such as their children's education or a new home. Individual or a family savings can also provide a crucial buffer in the event of an economic emergency, such as the loss of a job. At the national level, the production of new capital goods—factories, equipment, and office buildings—is an important factor promoting economic growth and higher living standards. As we will see in this chapter, the resources necessary to produce new capital come primarily from a nation's collective saving.

Because saving is required for creating new capital goods, some people have expressed concern over the decline in Canada's personal saving rate since the early 1980s. Figure 16.1 shows Canada's personal saving rate (the percentage of personal disposable income saved) for the period from 1982, when the personal saving rate was at a peak of 20.1 percent, until 2007, when the personal saving rate had fallen to just 1.5 percent.

What was the significance of this precipitous decline? Alarmists saw the data as evidence of "grasshopperish" behaviour, and a threat to Canadians' future prosperity. The reality, as we will see, is more complex. Many Canadian families save very little and have accumulated little in the way of financial wealth. On the other hand, personal saving (more precisely, net saving by persons and unincorporated businesses) is only one domestic source of saving available to

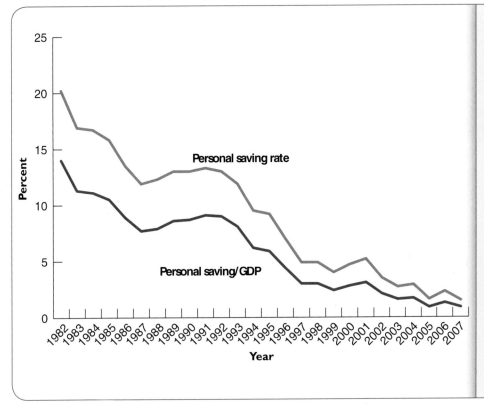

FIGURE 16.1

Personal Saving in Canada, 1982–2007
The personal saving rate, shown by the red line, is personal saving expressed as a percentage of personal disposable income. The decline in the personal saving rate from a peak of 20.1 percent in 1982 to a low of 1.5 percent in 2007 has raised concern in some circles. For some purposes it is convenient to consider the ratio of personal saving to GDP, as shown by the blue line.
SOURCE: Statistics Canada, CANSIM series V498187 (personal saving rate), V647354 (personal saving), and V498086 (GDP).

the Canadian economy. Corporations and governments also save, and they have saved considerably more than households in some years. Furthermore, the level of domestic saving in Canada does not set an upper limit to the level of investment in Canada; non-resident saving (essentially, net borrowing from abroad) can be used to finance investment in Canada, and it has been used to do so throughout much of Canadian history.

The evidence shows that the domestic saving of the Canadian economy, which economists call Canada's national saving, has climbed steadily since the 1990–1992 recession. In fact, since 2007 national saving has been sufficiently high to cover all investment in Canada and leave some over for lending to the rest of the world.

In this chapter we will look at saving and its links to investment. We begin by defining the concepts of saving and wealth and exploring the connection between them through simple examples about an individual. We will consider why people choose to save, rather than spend all their income. We then turn to national saving and gross saving. National saving is the collective saving of households and unincorporated businesses, corporations, and government. Gross saving is national saving plus non-resident saving. Because gross saving determines the capacity of an economy for gross investment, it is the most comprehensive measure of saving from a macroeconomic perspective. National saving and gross saving are linked to the concepts of national net worth and national wealth.

After examining national wealth, we discuss fixed capital formation. Most decisions to invest in fixed capital are made by firms. As we will see, a firm's decision to invest is in many respects analogous to its decision about whether to increase employment; firms will choose to expand their capital stocks when the benefits of doing so exceed the costs.

16.1   SAVING AND WEALTH

saving current income minus spending on current needs; a flow

saving rate saving divided by income

wealth the value of *assets* minus liabilities; also called net worth

assets anything of value that one *owns*

liabilities the debts one owes

In general, the **saving** of an economic unit—whether a household, a business, a university, or a nation—may be defined as its *current income* minus its *spending on current needs*. For example, if Kimberleigh earns $300 per week, spends $280 weekly on living expenses such as rent, food, clothes, and entertainment, and deposits the remaining $20 in the bank, her saving is $20 per week. The **saving rate** of any economic unit is its saving divided by its income. Since Kimberleigh saves $20 of her weekly income of $300, her saving rate is $20/$300, or 6.7 percent.

The saving of an economic unit measured over time contributes to its **wealth**, that is, the net value of all its assets minus all its liabilities, measured at a point in time. **Assets** are anything of value that one *owns*, either *financial* or *real*. Examples of financial assets that you or your family might own include cash, a chequing account, stocks, and bonds. Examples of real assets include a home or other real estate, jewellery, consumer durables like cars, and valuable collectibles. **Liabilities**, on the other hand, are the debts one *owes*. Examples of liabilities are credit card balances, student loans, and mortgages.

Accountants list the assets and liabilities of a family, a firm, a university, or any other economic unit on a *balance sheet*. Comparing the values of the assets and liabilities helps them to determine the economic unit's wealth, also called its *net worth*.

EXAMPLE 16.1   **Kimberleigh constructs her balance sheet**

To take stock of her financial position, Kimberleigh lists her assets and liabilities on a balance sheet. The result is shown in Table 16.1. What is Kimberleigh's wealth?

TABLE 16.1
Kimberleigh's Balance Sheet

Assets		Liabilities	
Cash	$ 80	Student loan	$3000
Chequing account	1200	Credit card balance	250
Shares of stock	1000		
Car (market value)	3500		
Furniture (market value)	500		
Total	**$6280**		**$3250**
		Net worth	**$3030**

Kimberleigh's financial assets are the cash in her wallet, the balance in her chequing account, and the current value of some shares of stock her parents gave her. Together her financial assets are worth $2280. She also lists $4000 in real assets, the sum of the market values of her car and her furniture. Kimberleigh's total assets, both financial and real, come to $6280. Her liabilities are the student loan she owes the bank and the balance due on her credit card, which total $3250. Kimberleigh's wealth, or net worth, then, is the value of her assets ($6280) minus the value of her liabilities ($3250), or $3030.

EXERCISE 16.1   **What would Kimberleigh's net worth be if her student loan were for $6500 rather than $3000? Construct a new balance sheet for her.**

Saving and wealth are related, because saving adds to wealth. To understand this relationship better, we must distinguish between *stocks* and *flows*.

STOCKS AND FLOWS

Saving is an example of a **flow**, a measure that is defined *per unit of time*. For example, Kimberleigh's saving is $20 *per week*. Wealth, in contrast, is a **stock**, a measure that is defined *at a point in time*. Kimberleigh's wealth of $3030, for example, is her wealth on a particular date—say, January 1, 2009.

To visualize the difference between stocks and flows, think of water running into a bathtub. The amount of water in the bathtub at any specific moment—for example, 40 litres at 7:15 P.M.—is a stock, because it is measured at a specific point in time. The rate at which the water flows into the tub—for example, 2 litres per minute—is a flow, because it is measured per unit of time. In many cases, a flow is the *rate of change* in a stock: if we know that there are 40 litres of water in the tub at 7:15 P.M., for example, and that water is flowing in at 2 litres per minute, we can easily determine that the stock of water will be changing at the rate of 2 litres per minute and will equal 42 litres at 7:16 P.M., 44 litres at 7:17 P.M., and so on, until the bathtub overflows.

The relationship between saving (a flow) and wealth (a stock) is similar to the relationship between the flow of water into a bathtub and the stock of water in the tub in that the *flow* of saving causes the *stock* of wealth to change at the same rate. Indeed, as Example 16.2 illustrates, every dollar that a person saves adds a dollar to his or her wealth.

flow a measure that is defined *per unit of time*

stock a measure that is defined *at a point in time*

The flow of saving increases the stock of wealth in the same way the flow of water through the faucet increases the amount of water in the tub.

The link between saving and wealth

EXAMPLE 16.2

Kimberleigh saves $20 per week. How does this saving affect her wealth? Does the change in her wealth depend on whether Kimberleigh uses her saving to accumulate assets or to pay down her liabilities?

Kimberleigh could use the $20 she saved this week to increase her assets—for example, by adding the $20 to her chequing account—or to reduce her liabilities—for example, by paying down her credit card balance. Suppose she adds the $20 to her chequing account, increasing her assets by $20. Since her liabilities are unchanged, her wealth also increases by $20, to $3050 (see Table 16.1).

If Kimberleigh decides to use the $20 she saved this week to pay down her credit card balance, she reduces it from $250 to $230. That action would reduce her liabilities by $20, leaving her assets unchanged. Since wealth equals assets minus liabilities, reducing her liabilities by $20 increases her wealth by $20, to $3050. Thus, saving $20 per week raises Kimberleigh's stock of wealth by $20 a week, regardless of whether she uses her saving to increase her assets or reduce her liabilities.

The link between saving and wealth (or net worth) for an individual has a counterpart at the national level. As we will see below, national saving is linked to national net worth.

CAPITAL GAINS AND LOSSES

Though saving increases wealth, it is not the only factor that determines wealth. Wealth can also change because of changes in the values of the real or financial assets one owns. Suppose Kimberleigh's shares of stock rise in value, from $1000 to $1500. This increase in the value of Kimberleigh's stock raises her total assets

TABLE 16.2
Kimberleigh's Balance Sheet After an Increase in the Value of Her Stocks

Assets		Liabilities	
Cash	$ 80	Student loan	$3000
Chequing account	1200	Credit card balance	250
Shares of stock	1500		
Car (market value)	3500		
Furniture (market value)	500		
Total	**$6780**		**$3250**
		Net worth	**$3530**

by $500 without affecting her liabilities. As a result, Kimberleigh's wealth rises by $500, from $3030 to $3530 (see Table 16.2).

capital gains increases in the value of existing assets

capital losses decreases in the value of existing assets

Changes in the value of existing assets are called **capital gains** when an asset's value increases and **capital losses** when an asset's value decreases.[1] Just as capital gains increase wealth, capital losses decrease wealth. Capital gains and losses are not counted as part of saving, however (which is in keeping with the fact that they are not counted as part of income in GDP accounting). Therefore, the total change in a person's wealth during any period equals the saving done during the period plus capital gains or minus capital losses during that period. In terms of an equation,

$$\text{Change in wealth} = \text{Saving} + \text{Capital gains} - \text{Capital losses}$$

EXERCISE 16.2

How would each of the following actions or events affect Kimberleigh's *saving* and her *wealth*?
a. **Kimberleigh deposits $20 in the bank at the end of the week as usual. She also charges $50 on her credit card, raising her credit card balance to $300.**
b. **Kimberleigh uses $300 from her chequing account to pay off her credit card bill.**
c. **Kimberleigh's old car is recognized as a classic. Its market value rises from $3500 to $4000.**
d. **Kimberleigh's furniture falls in value from $500 to $200.**

We have seen how saving is related to the accumulation of wealth. To understand why people save, however, we need to examine their motives for saving.

RECAP ↑

SAVING AND WEALTH

In general, *saving* is current income minus spending on current needs. *Wealth*, also called net worth, is the value of assets—anything of value that one owns—minus liabilities—the debts one owes. Saving is measured per unit of time (for example, dollars per week) and thus is a *flow*. Wealth is measured at a point in time and thus is a *stock*. In somewhat the same way the flow of water through the faucet increases the stock of water in a bathtub, the flow of saving increases the stock of wealth.

Wealth can also be increased by *capital gains* (increases in the value of existing assets) or reduced by *capital losses* (decreases in asset values).

[1]Capital gains and losses typically relate to changes in the value of financial assets or real estate. The normal decrease over time (related to quality deterioration or obsolescence) in the value of a real asset like a car is known as *depreciation*, which differs from a capital loss. To simplify matters, we ignore depreciation for now.

16.2 WHY DO PEOPLE SAVE?

As mentioned in the introduction, the total saving available to the Canadian economy comes from four different sectors or sources: persons (like Kimberleigh in our examples), corporations, governments, and non-residents. The savings of different sectors are generally determined by distinctive factors. The factors determining the saving of people (individuals or households) have been intensively studied by economists, and we will consider them first.

Economists have identified at least three broad reasons for saving. First, people save to meet certain long-term objectives, such as a more comfortable retirement. Some people save during their working years in the hope that in their retirement years they will be able to supplement their public pensions. Other long-term objectives might include college tuition for one's children and the purchase of a new home or car. Since many of these needs occur at fairly predictable stages in one's life, economists call this type of saving **life-cycle saving**.

A second reason to save is to protect oneself and family against unexpected setbacks—the loss of a job, for example. Personal financial advisors typically suggest that families maintain an emergency reserve (a "rainy-day fund") equal to three to six months' worth of income. Saving for protection against potential emergencies is called **precautionary saving**.

A third reason to save is to accumulate an estate to leave to one's heirs, usually one's children but possibly a favourite charity or other worthy cause. Saving for the purpose of leaving an inheritance, or bequest, is called **bequest saving**. Bequest saving is done primarily by people at the higher end of the income ladder. But because these people control a large share of the nation's wealth, bequest saving is an important part of overall saving.

To be sure, people usually do not mentally separate their saving into these three categories; rather, all three reasons for saving motivate most savers to varying degrees. The amount they choose to save, however, may depend on the economic environment. An economic variable of some relevance to saving decisions is the real interest rate.

life-cycle saving saving to meet long-term objectives, such as retirement, university attendance, or the purchase of a home

precautionary saving saving for protection against unexpected setbacks, such as the loss of a job

bequest saving saving done for the purpose of leaving an inheritance

SAVING AND THE REAL INTEREST RATE

Most people don't save by putting cash in a mattress. Instead, they make financial investments that they hope will provide a good return on their saving. For example, a savings account may pay interest on the account balance. More sophisticated financial investments, such as government bonds or shares of stock in a corporation (see Chapter 17), also pay returns in the form of interest payments, dividends, or capital gains. High returns are desirable, of course, because the higher the return, the faster one's savings will grow.

The rate of return that is most relevant to saving decisions is the *real interest rate,* denoted *r*. Recall from Chapter 6 that the real interest rate equals the market, or nominal, interest rate (*i*) minus the inflation rate (π).

The real interest rate is relevant to savers because it is the "reward" for saving. Suppose you are thinking of increasing your saving by $1000 this year, which you can do if you give up your habit of eating out once a week. If the real interest rate is 1 percent, then in a year your extra saving will give you extra purchasing power of $1010, measured in today's dollars. But if the real interest rate were 5 percent, your sacrifice of $1000 this year would be rewarded by $1050 in purchasing power next year. Obviously, all else being equal, you would be more willing to save today if you knew the reward next year would be greater. In either case the *cost* of the extra saving, giving up your weekly night out, is the same. But the *benefit* of the extra saving, in terms of increased purchasing power next year, is higher if the real interest rate is 5 percent rather than 1 percent.

COST–BENEFIT

While a higher real interest rate increases the reward for saving, which tends to strengthen people's willingness to save, another force counteracts that extra incentive. Recall that a major reason for saving is to attain specific goals: a comfortable retirement, a university or college education, or a first home. If the goal is a specific amount—say, $25 000 for a down payment on a home—then a higher rate of return means that households can save *less* and still reach their goal, because funds that are put aside will grow more quickly. For example, to accumulate $25 000 at the end of five years, at a 5 percent interest rate a person would have to save about $4309 per year. At a 10 percent interest rate, reaching the $25 000 goal would require saving only about $3723 per year. To the extent that people are *target savers* who save to reach a specific goal, higher interest rates actually decrease the amount they need to save.

In sum, a higher real interest rate has both positive and negative effects on saving—a positive effect because it increases the reward for saving and a negative effect because it reduces the amount people need to save each year to reach a given target. Empirical evidence suggests that, in practice, higher real interest rates lead to modest increases in saving.

"Someday, son, all this will be mine."

SAVING, SELF-CONTROL, AND DEMONSTRATION EFFECTS

The reasons for saving we just discussed are based on the notion that people are rational decision makers who choose their saving rates to maximize their welfare over the long run. Yet many psychologists, and some economists, have argued instead that people's saving behaviour is based as much on psychological as on economic factors. They stress that people sometimes lack the *self-control* to do what is in their own best interest. Many people have good intentions about saving, for example, but they lack the self-control to put aside as much as they ought to each month.

One way to strengthen self-control is to remove temptations from the immediate environment. A person who is not saving enough might arrange to use a payroll saving plan, through which a predetermined amount is deducted from each paycheque and set aside in a special account from which withdrawals are not permitted until retirement. Making saving automatic and withdrawals difficult reduces the temptation to spend all of current earnings or squander accumulated savings. In Canada, employer-sponsored pension plans (known as RPPs, for Registered Pension Plans) are an especially important way of making saving automatic.

One implication of the self-control hypothesis is that consumer credit arrangements that make borrowing and spending easier may reduce the amount that people save. For example, in recent years banks have encouraged people to borrow against the *equity* in their homes, that is, the value of the home less the value of the outstanding mortgage. Such financial innovations, by increasing the temptation to spend, may have reduced the personal saving rate. The increased availability of credit cards with high borrowing limits is another temptation.

Downward pressure on the saving rate may also occur when additional spending by some consumers stimulates additional spending by others. Such *demonstration effects* arise when people use the spending of others as a yardstick by which to measure the adequacy of their own living standards. When satisfaction depends in part on *relative* living standards, an upward spiral may result in which household spending is higher, and saving lower, than would be best for either the individual families involved or for the economy as a whole.

The idea that relative living standards or income levels affect personal saving rates was first developed into a formal theory by the Harvard economist James Duesenberry in the 1950s. He explained why aggregate personal saving rates do not increase with average disposable income, all else being equal, even though higher-income households have higher savings rates than do lower-income households.[2]

> **RECAP** ↰
>
> **WHY DO PEOPLE SAVE?**
>
> Motivations for personal saving include saving to meet long-term objectives such as retirement (*life-cycle saving*), saving for emergencies (*precautionary saving*), and saving to leave an inheritance or bequest (*bequest saving*). The amount that people save also depends on macroeconomic factors, such as the real interest rate. A higher real interest rate stimulates saving by increasing the reward for saving, but it can also depress saving by making it easier for savers to reach a specific savings target. On net, a higher real interest rate appears to lead to modest increases in saving.
>
> Psychological factors may also affect personal saving rates. If people have *self-control* problems, then financial arrangements (such as automatic payroll deductions) that make it more difficult to spend will increase their saving. People's saving decisions may also be influenced by *demonstration effects*, as when people feel compelled to spend at the same rate as their neighbours, even though they may not be able to afford to do so.

16.3 ECONOMY-WIDE SAVING AND WEALTH

Thus far we have been examining the concepts of saving and wealth from an individual's perspective. But macroeconomists are interested primarily in saving and wealth for the economy as a whole. In this section we will study the four major components of economy-wide saving published by Statistics Canada: personal, corporate, government, and non-resident saving.[3] We will also study Statistics Canada's economy-wide measures of wealth.

---

[2]Robert Frank, "The Mysterious Disappearance of James Duesenberry," *New York Times*, 9 June 2005.
[3]We focus on gross saving by these four sectors of the economy and, to keep things relatively simple, we ignore the concept of net lending by different sectors.

gross saving the sum of household, corporate, government, and non-resident saving

gross investment the sum of private-sector and government investment

The economy-wide measure of saving employed by Statistics Canada is **gross saving** and by definition it equals **gross investment**.[4] The concept of gross investment employed by Statistics Canada in connection with gross saving differs from the concept of private-sector investment that we encountered in Chapter 5 as a component of expenditure-based GDP, and for good reason.

Recall that GDP measurement came of age in the 1940s and was strongly influenced by Keynesian economics, which was focused on short-run macroeconomic issues. For examining short-run macroeconomic issues (see Part 3), it is important to distinguish between broad categories of expenditure like private-sector investment on the one hand and government purchases of goods and services (consisting of government current purchases and government investment) on the other. Private-sector investment is determined by factors such as profit expectations and interest rates, whereas government purchases of goods and services are controlled by the government. To analyze how fiscal and monetary policies may solve short-run macroeconomic problems, it makes sense to treat private-sector investment and government purchases of goods and services as two sharply distinct categories.

For examining long-run macroeconomic issues, however, it often makes sense to combine private-sector investment with government investment into one category of gross investment. As discussed in Chapter 14, both private-sector investment (particularly non-residential business fixed capital formation) and government investment contribute to the long-run growth of the economy. For example, if an airport is constructed by private-sector firms at the request of a government airport operator, the construction of the airport would count as government investment. If the same airport had been constructed by the same private-sector firms on behalf of a private airport operator, the airport would count as private-sector investment. But regardless of whether it is the government or the private sector that pays to have the airport built, the construction of the airport is infrastructure investment for the economy. Furthermore, both private-sector investment and government investment contribute to the stock of capital that is part of national wealth.

THE COMPONENTS OF GROSS SAVING

To understand all the sources of saving that are available to support gross investment in the Canadian economy, it is first necessary to distinguish gross saving from net saving.

How does net saving differ from gross saving? The personal saving rate shown in Figure 16.1, for example, is based upon the net saving of the persons and unincorporated businesses sector (or household sector). This net saving amounted to $13.4 billion in 2007, as shown in Table 16.3. It was actually smaller than another form of saving associated with the household sector—a capital consumption allowance of $45.1 billion. In general, a capital consumption allowance is an allowance for the using up of capital in the production of income—that is, for the depreciation of business and government fixed assets (and people's housing). Roughly speaking, it is the counterpart on the saving side to *replacement investment* on the investment side. For the household sector, major housing renovations are an important form of replacement investment. For the economy as a whole, net saving of the different sectors of the economy (including non-resident saving) plus their capital consumption allowances add up to gross saving, as Table 16.3 shows.

For many purposes it is useful to consider a large subset of gross saving known as gross domestic saving, or *national saving*. **National saving** is the sum of gross saving by the household sector, by the corporations and government business enterprises sector (also called the corporate sector), and by the government

national saving the sum of gross saving by the household sector, the corporate sector, and the government sector

---

[4]In practice, gross saving and gross investment are made equal by Statistics Canada using the same statistical discrepancy required to make the income-based measure of GDP equal to the expenditure-based measure.

TABLE 16.3
Gross Saving and Gross Investment, Canada, 2007

Components and Subcomponents	$ (billions)	Percent of gross saving or gross investment
I. GROSS SAVING (A+B+C+D)	**348.5**	**100.0**
A. Net domestic saving (1+2+3)	**165.1**	**47.3**
1. Persons and unincorporated business	13.4	3.9
2. Corporations and government business	118.0	33.8
3. Government	33.7	9.7
B. Capital consumption allowances (4+5+6)	**193.8**	**55.6**
4. Persons and unincorporated businesses	45.1	12.9
5. Corporations and government business enterprises	121.7	34.9
6. Government	27.0	7.8
C. Saving of non-residents	**−11.1**	**−3.2**
D. Statistical discrepancy	**0.7**	**0.2**
II. INVESTMENT IN FIXED CAPITAL AND INVENTORIES (E+F+G)	**348.5**	**100.0**
E. Persons and unincorporated businesses	**112.7**	**32.4**
F. Corporations and government business enterprises	**192.1**	**55.1**
G. Government	**43.7**	**12.6**

SOURCE: Adapted from the Statistics Canada publication *National Income and Expenditure Accounts,* Catalogue 13-001, Fourth Quarter 2007, Vol. 55, No. 4, March 2008, particularly Table 15.

sector. Note that the government sector includes not just the federal government, but also provincial and territorial governments, local governments, and public institutions like hospitals and universities.

Figure 16.2 shows trends in the three components of national saving (expressed as a percentage of GDP) for the period 1961–2007. Gross corporate saving is currently the most important component of national saving. In recent years, the rise in gross government saving has been offset by the decline in gross personal saving.

Sometimes economists divide national saving into two categories. *Private saving* is used to describe the sum of gross saving by the household and the corporate sectors. *Public saving* can then be used to mean gross government saving.

The difference between gross saving and national saving is known as *non-resident saving*. Positive non-resident saving refers to saving made available to the Canadian economy by transactors without residences or business locations in Canada. But non-resident saving can also be negative. In general, **non-resident saving** is the balance between saving provided to the Canadian economy by non-residents and saving provided to foreign economies by residents of Canada.

Non-resident saving relates to international flows of financial capital. Positive non-resident saving corresponds to an international capital inflow, whereas negative non-resident saving corresponds to an international capital outflow. In 2007, as shown in Table 16.3, saving by non-residents was negative, with Canada experiencing an international capital outflow of $11.1 billion. An international capital outflow happens when national saving exceeds gross investment in the economy.

As we explain in Chapter 17, an international capital outflow occurs when something called the *current account balance* (net exports as defined in Chapter 5 plus net international investment income and net international transfers) is positive, and an international capital inflow occurs when the current account balance is

non-resident saving the balance between saving provided to the Canadian economy by non-residents and saving provided to foreign economies by residents of Canada

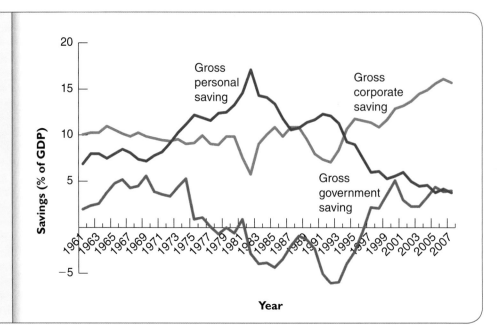

FIGURE 16.2

The Three Components of National Saving, 1961–2007

Of the three components of national saving, gross corporate saving is currently the most important. The rise in government saving since the mid-1990s has been offset by the decline in personal saving.
SOURCE: Adapted from CANSIM table 380-0032 and series v498086.

negative. So positive non-resident saving is a proxy for a current account deficit and negative non-resident saving is a proxy for a current account surplus.[5]

Figure 16.3 shows trends in gross saving, national saving, and non-resident saving for 1961–2007. All variables are expressed as percentages of GDP. As a percentage of Canadian GDP, gross saving (which equals gross investment, as we

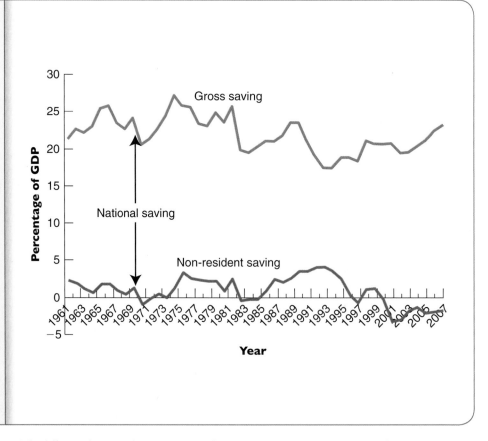

FIGURE 16.3

Gross Saving, National Saving, and Non-Resident Saving, 1961–2007

Gross saving (which equals gross investment) as a percentage of Canadian GDP has tended to drop during economic slowdowns but has not exhibited any pronounced long-term trend. Non-resident saving as a percentage of GDP has traditionally been positive, but since 1999 it has been negative. National saving is the difference between gross saving and non-resident saving.
SOURCE: Adapted from the Statistics Canada publication, *National Income and Gross Expenditure Accounts,* Catalogue 13-001, Fourth Quarter 2007, Vol. 55, No. 4, March 2008, Table 15.

[5]The difference between the two is an item known as net reinvested earnings on direct investment.

have mentioned) has tended to fluctuate within the 20–25 percent range. Non-resident saving has tended to fluctuate in the 0–4 percent range with no particular trend. Positive non-resident saving for most years means Canada typically experienced capital inflows for the 1961–1999 period. In other words, Canada was a capital importer because national saving was insufficient to develop our infrastructure and build our capital stock. In Figure 16.3, the gap between gross saving and non-resident saving in any given year gives national saving for the year.

To summarize saving terminology, suppose that we represent gross saving by S_{gross}, gross household saving by $S_{household}$, gross corporate saving by $S_{corporate}$, gross government or public saving by $S_{government}$, national saving by $S_{national}$, private saving by $S_{private}$, and non-resident saving by $S_{non\text{-}resident}$. Then we can decompose gross saving as follows:

$$S_{gross} = S_{household} + S_{corporate} + S_{government} + S_{non\text{-}resident} \qquad (16.1)$$

$$S_{gross} = S_{private} + S_{government} + S_{non\text{-}resident} \qquad (16.2)$$

$$S_{gross} = S_{national} + S_{non\text{-}resident} \qquad (16.3)$$

$$S_{gross} = S_{net} + \text{Capital consumption allowances} \qquad (16.4)$$

The determinants of personal saving were explained in some detail earlier in this chapter. We will deal with determinants of international capital flows in more detail in Chapter 17. Now we need to explain a few details about the other two components of gross saving—gross corporate and government saving.

MORE ABOUT CORPORATE AND GOVERNMENT SAVING

Most of us have no problem conceptualizing personal saving. Indeed, many of us learned about personal saving at a very young age, putting coins in a piggybank to save up for some special purchase. But the concepts of corporate and government saving seem a bit strange to people who think of saving as being conducted by individuals and investment being carried out by corporations. People find it surprising both that corporate saving could be the most important form of saving in the Canadian economy in 2007 (as shown in Figure 16.2) and that even government saving could exceed personal saving.

Corporate Saving

We have already mentioned one component of gross corporate saving—capital consumption allowances. The Statistics Canada estimates for capital consumption allowances are indirectly based upon business records employing the standard accounting practice that part of the revenue a firm receives cannot prudently be treated as profit because it represents reimbursement for the cost of capital goods that depreciate in value over time and will have to be replaced. The largest component of net corporate saving is undistributed profits (or unremitted profits, in the case of government business enterprises). Undistributed profits are typically, but not necessarily, plowed back into investment within the firm. If the corporate sector has a bad year—that is, if profits drop—then undistributed profits will drop, and with them net corporate savings.

Figure 16.4 shows gross corporate saving as a percentage of gross corporate investment for Canada during the period 1961–2007. When the percentage equals 100, gross corporate saving equals gross corporate investment. When the percentage exceeds 100, then gross corporate saving exceeds gross corporate investment.

In most years, the Canadian corporate sector has relied upon external funding to finance its gross investment, shown in Figure 16.4 by a percentage less than 100. But even during recession years, when gross corporate saving has plummeted, the Canadian corporate sector has always financed the bulk of its

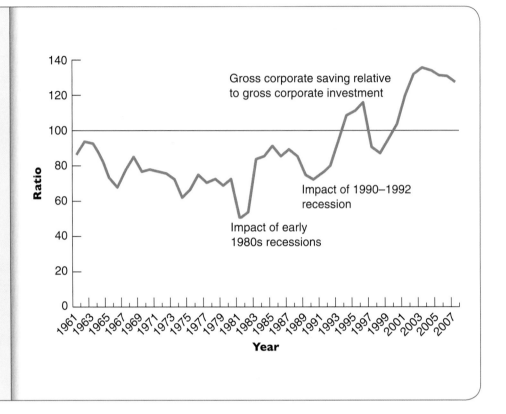

FIGURE 16.4

Ratio of Corporate Saving to Corporate Investment, 1961–2007
In most years, particularly during recessions, the Canadian corporate sector has relied upon external funding to finance its gross investment. But even during recession years, the Canadian corporate sector has always financed the bulk of its investment with internal corporate funding. Since the end of the 1990–1992 recession, gross corporate saving has tended to exceed gross corporate investment.
SOURCE: Adapted from CANSIM table 380-0032 and series v498086.

investment with internal funding. Since the end of the 1990–1992 recession, gross corporate saving has tended to exceed gross corporate investment, and by a large amount in some years.

Government Saving

Like gross corporate saving, gross government saving consists of a capital consumption allowance component and a net saving component shown in Table 16.4. The *net saving* component is closely related to the more widely known concept of the *government budget balance*.[6]

We first encountered the concept of the government budget balance in connection with Figure 4.7, which showed deficits when the federal government budget balance was zero and then surpluses more recently when the federal government budget balance has been positive. Roughly speaking, positive government saving corresponds to government surpluses and negative government saving corresponds to deficits.

Like corporate saving, government saving tends to decline during recessions. If personal incomes and corporate profits fall in a recession, then personal and corporate income taxes fall automatically, even without any change in income tax rates. Similarly, when unemployment rises in a recession, more people will end up drawing employment insurance benefits and social assistance, and government transfers will rise. So in a recession, government revenue tends to decline and government transfers tend to rise, a combination that spells a decline in government saving. Conversely, if incomes rise as the economy recovers, then income taxes

---

[6]The value of net government saving exceeds the value of the government budget surplus by the value of government investment. For example, if the government budget surplus is $25 billion, and government investment is $15 billion, then net government saving amounts to $40 billion. Net government saving, then, equals the amount of money the government makes available for investment, whether it is investment in other sectors of the economy (made possible by the budget surplus) or investment in the government sector.

TABLE 16.4

Government Revenue, Expenditure, and Savings, Canada, 2007

Components	$ (billions)	Percent of GDP
Revenue	**611.7**	**39.9**
Taxes on incomes	254.1	16.6
Contributions to social insurance plans	68.8	4.5
Taxes on production and imports	182.3	11.9
Other current transfers from persons	10.8	0.7
Investment income	49.4	3.2
Sales of goods and services	46.2	3.0
Expenditure	**577.8**	**37.7**
Gross current expenditure on goods and services	344.2	22.5
Current transfers	170.7	11.1
Interest on public debt	62.7	4.1
Net saving = Revenue − Expenditure	**33.7**	**2.2**
Capital consumption allowances	27.0	1.8
Gross saving = Net saving + CCA	**60.7**	**4.0**

SOURCE: Government Revenue, Expenditure and Savings, Canada, 2007. Adapted from the Statistics Canada publication *National Income and Expenditure Accounts*, Catalogue 13-001, Fourth Quarter 2007, Vol. 55 No. 4, March 2008, particularly Table 9.

automatically rise. Transfers will tend to fall as the economy recovers. As a consequence, net saving will tend to increase. (In Part 3, which dealt with short-run macroeconomics, we explained that budget items like income taxes and employment insurance are known as *automatic stabilizers*.)

Cyclical fluctuations in the economy are not the only economic influence on government saving. Another key influence is the level of interest rates. The government sector carries a substantial amount of debt (a stock) as a consequence of past deficits (flows). For the federal, provincial and territorial, and local governments of Canada, net debt amounted to $791 billion as the end of March 2005 (equivalent to 57.5 percent of GDP produced during 2005). When interest rates rise, any debt that has to be refinanced is subject to the higher rates, and so there is an increase in interest payments on the public debt, one of the three broad categories of government expenditures. All else being equal, a rise in interest rates will produce a decline in government saving.[7]

But a rise in the government debt-to-GDP ratio beyond some threshold level can also affect government saving. At the provincial level, especially high government debt-to-GDP ratios tend to result in higher borrowing costs to governments, as financial market participants demand an interest rate premium to cover the risk of default by the government. The higher borrowing costs provide governments with an incentive (or at least an excuse) to increase government saving.

Of course, levels of government saving do not just depend on economic factors. Politics also plays a role. For example, while strong economic growth from

---

[7]Recessions such as those in the early 1980s and during 1990–1992 were particularly hard on government saving because they were triggered by sharp rises in interest rates that continued well into the recessions.

1997 to 2000 helped produce a dramatic increase in federal government saving (specifically, a transformation from negative to positive saving), the expenditure cuts launched by then Finance Minister Paul Martin in his February 1995 federal budget also played an important role.

ECONOMY-WIDE WEALTH AND STOCK MEASURES

Recall that earlier in this chapter we examined the wealth of an imaginary individual named Kimberleigh. Using a balance sheet, we calculated her wealth or net worth by totalling the value of her financial assets (her cash, chequing account balance, and shares of stock) and the market value of her real assets (her car and furniture), and subtracting from the value of these assets the value of her liabilities (her student loan and credit card balance). We discussed how changes in her wealth from one time period to another would equal her saving during the time period plus any capital gains minus any capital losses.

For the economy as a whole, Statistics Canada calculates a national balance sheet. The non-financial (or "real") assets in the balance sheet are residential structures, non-residential structures, machinery and equipment, consumer durables, inventories, and land found in Canada.[8] The value of this stock of real assets is related to the value of past investment flows (or alternatively, the sum of past gross saving). Note, however, that while consumer durables count as real assets in the national balance sheet, their purchase does not count as investment in the national income and expenditure accounts. Also, land simply exists as a real asset and is not the product of investment. The value of these real assets is called the **national wealth** of Canada. As shown in Table 16.5, in 2006 Canada's national wealth totalled about $5.2 trillion.

national wealth the total value of the real assets in a country

> **TABLE 16.5**
> **National Balance Sheet, Canada, 2006**
>
> | Assets ($ Billions) | | Liabilities ($ Billions) | |
> |---|---|---|---|
> | **National wealth** (Non-financial or "real" assets) | 5157.5 | **Financial liabilities owed to Canadian residents** | **10 272.0** |
> | | | Financial liabilities owed to non-residents | 99.0 |
> | Financial assets | 10 074.0 | | |
> | Total | 15 231.5 | **Total** | **10 173.0** |
> | | | **Net worth =** Total assets − Liabilities | **5058.5** |
> | | | **Net foreign liabilities =** Net worth − National wealth | **−99.0** |
>
> SOURCE: Adapted from the Statistics Canada Web site, http://www.statcan.ca.

national net worth the total value of the real assets of a country adjusted for its net foreign liabilities

The **national net worth** of Canadians is calculated just as we calculated net worth for Kimberleigh—by adding up the value of real and financial assets and subtracting from the value of these assets the value of financial liabilities. Canada's national net worth in 2006 totalled about $5.1 trillion.

[8]Recall that in Chapter 5 we mentioned that economists sometimes use the term "real investment" to describe formation of new physical capital and inventories and to contrast it with financial investment. The "real assets" that make up national wealth are the stock counterparts to the flow of real investment.

If there were no financial transactions with the rest of the world, the financial assets and liabilities summed up over the whole economy would add to zero because the financial assets of some are always the financial liabilities of others. The national wealth of Canada and the national net worth of Canadians would be equal. But Canada has **net international liabilities** (also called net foreign debt). These are the value of financial claims of non-residents on Canadian wealth net of the value of financial claims of Canadian residents against foreign wealth. In 2006 Canada's net international liabilities amounted to about $99 billion (expressed in Table 16.5 as a negative number because it represents a claim against a portion of real wealth in Canada). Net foreign liabilities are subtracted from national wealth to get national net worth.

net international liabilities the value of financial claims of non-residents on Canadian wealth net of the value of financial claims of Canadian residents against foreign wealth

16.4 INVESTMENT AND CAPITAL FORMATION

FACTORS AFFECTING BUSINESS INVESTMENT IN FIXED CAPITAL

From the point of view of the economy as a whole, gross saving is important because it provides the funds needed for gross investment. Gross investment is important because it is associated with the accumulation of wealth, as mentioned above. It is also important because it is critical to increasing average labour productivity and improving standards of living.

But not all components of gross investment are equally critical to increasing average labour productivity. Inventory investment, for example, tends to account for a small share of gross investment (2.4 percent for Canada in 2007, and it turns negative when inventories decline), and is relatively unimportant for explaining differences in average labour productivity across countries and time periods.

Residential investment accounts for a significant share of gross investment (36.5 percent for Canada in 2007). But increases in residential investment are not closely associated with increases in average labour productivity. Spending on new housing is much like consumer spending on consumer durables like cars, household appliances, and furniture; increased spending is more a result of rising productivity than a cause of it.

As mentioned in Chapter 14, research has shown that government investment in fixed capital is important for increases in labour productivity. In a capitalist economy like Canada's, however, government fixed capital formation accounts for a relatively small share of gross investment (14.7 percent in 2007).

For Canada, business investment in non-residential structures (such as factory and office buildings, shopping malls, and warehouses) and machinery and equipment (such as assembly lines, mining and transportation equipment, computers, cash registers, and photocopiers) is much larger than government fixed capital formation as a share of gross investment (by a multiple of 4 in 2007). And, as with government fixed capital formation, research shows that it is clearly critical to increasing average labour productivity. We will therefore focus on determinants of non-residential business fixed capital formation—that is, on investment by firms in non-residential structures, machinery, and equipment.

What factors determine whether and how much firms choose to invest? Firms acquire new capital goods for the same reason they hire new workers: they expect that doing so will be profitable. According to the *cost–benefit principle*, the profitability of employing an extra worker depends primarily on two factors: the cost of employing the worker and the value of the worker's marginal product. In the same way, firms' willingness to acquire new factories and machines depends on the expected *cost* of using them and the expected *benefit,* equal to the value of the marginal product that they will provide.

COST–BENEFIT

| EXAMPLE 16.3 | **Does it pay Larry to buy a riding lawn mower?** |

Larry is thinking of going into the lawn care business. He can buy a $4000 riding mower by taking out a loan at 6 percent annual interest. With this mower and his own labour Larry can net $6000 per summer, after deducting costs such as gasoline and maintenance. Of the $6000 net revenues, 20 percent must be paid to the government in taxes. Assume that Larry could earn $4400 after taxes by working at another job. Assume also that the lawn mower can always be resold for its original purchase price of $4000. Does it pay Larry to buy the lawn mower?

To decide whether to invest in the capital good (the lawn mower), Larry would typically compare the financial benefits and costs. With the mower he can earn revenue of $6000, net of gasoline and maintenance costs. However, 20 percent of that, or $1200, must be paid in taxes, leaving Larry with $4800. Larry could earn $4400 after taxes by working at another job, so the financial benefit to Larry of buying the mower is the difference between $4800 and $4400, or $400; $400 is the value of the marginal product of the lawn mower.

Since we have assumed that the mower does not lose value over time and since gasoline and maintenance costs have already been deducted, the only remaining cost Larry should take into account is the interest on the loan for the mower. Larry must pay 6 percent interest on $4000, or $240 per year. Since this financial cost is less than the financial benefit of $400, the value of the mower's marginal product, Larry should buy the mower.

Larry's decision might change if the costs and benefits of his investment in the mower change, as Example 16.4 shows.

| EXAMPLE 16.4 | **Does it pay Larry to buy a riding lawn mower? (continued)** |

With all other assumptions the same as in Example 16.3, decide whether Larry should buy the mower:

    a. if the interest rate is 12 percent rather than 6 percent.
    b. if the purchase price of the mower is $7000 rather than $4000.
    c. if the tax rate on Larry's net revenues is 25 percent rather than 20 percent.

In each case, Larry must compare the financial costs and benefits of buying the mower.

    a. If the interest rate is 12 percent, then the interest cost will be 12 percent of $4000, or $480, which exceeds the value of the mower's marginal product ($400). Larry would not buy the mower.
    b. If the cost of the mower is $7000, then Larry must borrow $7000 instead of $4000. At 6 percent interest, his interest cost will be $420—too high to justify the purchase, since the value of the mower's marginal product is $400.
    c. If the tax rate on net revenues is 25 percent, then Larry must pay 25 percent of his $6000 net revenues, or $1500, in taxes. After taxes, his revenues from mowing will be $4500, which is only $100 more than he could make working at an alternative job. Furthermore, the $100 will not cover the $240 in interest that Larry would have to pay. So again, Larry would not buy the mower.

Repeat Example 16.3, but assume that, over the course of the year, wear and tear reduces the resale value of the lawn mower from $4000 to $3800. Does it pay Larry to buy the mower?

The examples involving Larry and the lawn mower illustrate most of the main factors firms must consider when deciding whether to invest in new capital goods. On the cost side, two important factors are the *price of capital goods* and the *real interest rate*. Clearly, the more expensive new capital goods are, the more reluctant firms will be to invest in them. Buying the mower was profitable for Larry when its price was $4000, but not when its price was $7000.

Why is the real interest rate a factor in investment decisions? The most straightforward case is when a firm has to borrow (as Larry did) to purchase its new capital. The real interest rate then determines the real cost to the firm of paying back its debt. Since financing costs are a major part of the total cost of owning and operating a piece of capital, much as mortgage payments are a major part of the cost of owning a home, increases in the real interest rate make the purchase of capital goods less attractive to firms, all else being equal.[9]

On the benefit side, the key factor in determining business investment is the *value of the marginal product* of the new capital, which should be calculated net of both operating and maintenance expenses and taxes paid on the revenues the capital generates. The value of the marginal product is affected by several factors. For example, a technological advance that allows a piece of capital to produce more goods and services would increase the value of its marginal product, as would lower taxes on the revenues produced by the new capital. An increase in the relative price of the good or service that the capital is used to produce will also increase the value of the marginal product and, hence, the desirability of the investment. For example, if the going price for lawn-mowing services were to rise, then, all else being equal, investing in the mower would become more profitable for Larry.

The examples of Larry and the lawn mower illustrate most of the main factors firms consider in making decisions about fixed capital formation. There are, however, other potentially important factors. For example, we have considered the impact of government taxation but not the impact of government expenditure. Yet provision of a subsidy to firms in the lawn care business (an increase in government expenditure falling under the category of transfers to business, sometimes called corporate welfare) could have the same impact on their investment as providing them with a tax cut. Increased government expenditure on roads could reduce the time Larry spends getting from one lawn care job to another, thereby enabling him to earn more revenue per year. Increased government expenditure on education could increase the pool of potential qualified employees Larry could draw upon to expand his business (putting the lawn mower to use in the evenings, say, after he has finished working for the day).

In general, the purpose of imposing taxes is to support government expenditures. It can be misleading to consider the impact of taxes without also considering the impact of the government expenditures that the taxes make possible. As the *scarcity problem* states, having more of one good thing (in this case, lower taxes) usually means having less of another (government expenditure).

---

[9]It should be recognized that statistical studies have generally found that business investment in plant and equipment is much less sensitive to changes in real interest rates than residential investment.

> **RECAP** ↑
>
> ### FACTORS THAT AFFECT INVESTMENT
>
> Any of the following factors will increase the willingness of firms to invest in new capital:
>
> 1. a decline in the price of new capital goods
> 2. a decline in the real interest rate
> 3. technological improvement that raises the marginal product of capital
> 4. lower taxes on the revenues generated by capital
> 5. a higher relative price for the firm's output
>
> This list of factors is not exhaustive, however. Increases in certain forms of government expenditure, for example, will also increase investment by firms in new capital.

ECONOMIC *Naturalist*   16.1

Did a decline in the gross saving rate in Canada produce a decline in corporate investment?

Gross saving in Canada fell from an average of 23 percent of GDP during 1961–1970 to an average of 19 percent of GDP during 1991–2000. In some circles this decline in the saving rate, attributed to substantial government deficits from around 1982 until the late 1990s, was alleged to have reduced private-sector investment (most importantly, corporate investment) and hence productivity growth in the Canadian economy. But are the allegations true?

The question has been examined by two Statistics Canada economists who make careful use of the saving and investment categories introduced in this chapter.[10] They point out that the level of gross saving for the whole Canadian economy has always been high relative to the level of gross investment by the Canadian corporate sector. To illustrate, in 2003 gross saving amounted to $245 billion. But investment in fixed capital by the corporate sector, at $132 billion, was only 54 percent of gross saving, and business investment in machinery and equipment, the category of investment most closely associated with productivity improvements (and the closest real-world counterpart to Larry's lawn mower), amounted to only $81 billion,

or 33 percent of gross saving. Obviously even a substantial decline in the gross saving rate could affect much else besides investment in fixed capital by the corporate sector or, more narrowly, business investment in machinery and equipment.

If gross saving has declined, so must some components of gross investment. Figure 16.5 shows that government fixed capital formation declined steadily over the 1961–2000 period, falling by about two percentage points as a share of GDP. Average business inventory investment was also lower in the 1990s than during 1960s by about one percentage point as a share of GDP. Business investment in machinery and equipment, the component of private-sector gross investment most clearly associated with average labour productivity growth, exhibited no downward trend as a percentage of GDP.

The Statistics Canada economists also pointed out that over this historical period the corporate sector generated enough funds internally to cover its gross fixed capital formation, and that gross corporate savings actually exceeded corporate gross fixed capital formation by a considerable margin during the 1990s.

---

[10]See John Baldwin and Tarek Harchaoui, "The Structure of Investment in Canada and Its Impact on Capital Accumulation," in John Baldwin et al., eds, *Productivity Growth in Canada*, (Ottawa: Statistics Canada, 2001) pp. 77–95.

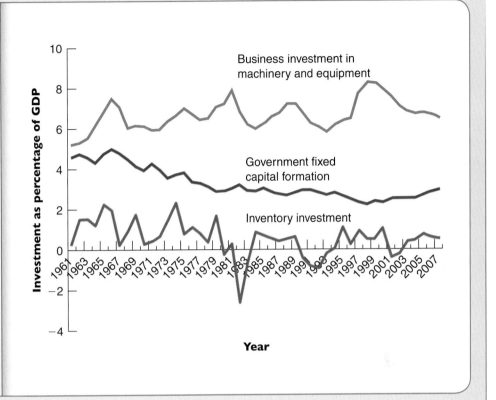

FIGURE 16.5

Long-Term Trends in Investment to GDP Ratios, 1961–2007

Gross investment in the Canadian economy dropped from 23 percent of GDP during 1961–1970 to 19 percent during 1991–2000. But not all components of gross investment declined. Business investment in machinery and equipment exhibited no downward trend. Government fixed capital formation as a share of GDP declined almost continuously from the 1960s to the 1990s.

SOURCE: Adapted from CANSIM series v498099, v498095, v498100, and v498086.

SUMMARY

16.1 In general, *saving* equals current income minus spending on current needs; the *saving rate* is the percentage of income that is saved. *Wealth*, or net worth, equals the market value of assets (real or financial items of value) minus liabilities (debts). Saving is a *flow*, being measured in dollars per unit of time, while wealth is a *stock*, measured in dollars at a point in time. As the amount of water in a bathtub changes according to the rate at which water flows in, the stock of wealth increases at the saving rate. Wealth also increases if the value of existing assets rises (*capital gains*) and decreases if the value of existing assets falls (*capital losses*).

16.2 Individuals and households save for a variety of reasons, including *life-cycle* objectives, such as saving for retirement or a new home; the need to be prepared for an emergency (*precautionary saving*); and the desire to leave an inheritance (*bequest saving*). The amount people save is also affected by the real interest rate, which is the "reward" for saving. Evidence suggests that higher real interest rates lead to modest increases in saving. Saving

can also be affected by psychological factors, such as the degree of self-control and the desire to consume at the level of one's neighbours (demonstration effects).

16.3 The *gross saving* of an economy is equal to its *gross investment*. Gross saving minus *national saving* equals non-resident saving, which can be positive or negative. Throughout most of the twentieth century, the non-resident sector was a net supplier of saving to the Canadian economy. But at the beginning of the 21st century, Canada's national saving exceeded its gross saving, meaning that Canada was a net supplier of saving to the rest of the world. The three components of national saving are personal (or household) saving, corporate saving, and government (or public) saving. Public saving refers to the saving of the government sector as a whole, not just saving associated with the federal government. The sum of household and corporate saving is called private saving. In recent years the level of household saving has been lower than the level of corporate saving, and the level of corporate saving has exceeded the level of real investment by the corporate sector. In the latter half of the 1990s, government saving turned positive, after about two decades of being negative.

16.3 The *national balance sheet* records assets and liabilities for Canada as a whole. Canada's *national wealth* corresponds to the value of real assets in Canada. Canada's *national net worth* is less than Canada's national wealth because Canada has *net international liabilities*.

16.4 Firms will invest in new capital goods if the benefits of doing so outweigh the costs. Two factors that determine the cost of investment are the price of new capital goods and the real interest rate. The higher the real interest rate, the more expensive it is to borrow, and the less likely firms are to invest. The benefit of investment is the value of the marginal product of new capital, which depends on factors such as the productivity of new capital goods and the relative price of the firm's output.

KEY TERMS

assets (416)
bequest saving (419)
capital gains (418)
capital losses (418)
flow (417)
gross investment (422)
gross saving (422)

liabilities (416)
life-cycle saving (419)
national net worth (428)
national saving (422)
national wealth (428)
net international liabilities (429)
non-resident saving (423)

precautionary saving (419)
saving (416)
saving rate (416)
stock (417)
wealth (416)

REVIEW QUESTIONS

1. Explain the relationship between an individual's saving and wealth, using the concepts of flows and stocks. Is saving the only means by which wealth can increase? Explain.

2. Give three basic motivations for saving. Illustrate each with an example. What other factors would psychologists cite as possibly being important for saving?

3. Define gross saving, national saving, and non-resident saving. How do these concepts relate to national wealth, national net worth, and net international liabilities?

4. Canadian household saving rates were low in the latter half of the 1990s. What implications would low saving rates have for individual households? What implications, if any, would they have for the Canadian economy as a whole?

5. What are the sources of gross corporate saving? What are some key economic factors influencing the level of government saving?

6. What are some key determinants of business investment? Could government spending on infrastructure influence the level of business investment?

PROBLEMS

1. a. Corey has a mountain bike worth $300, a credit card debt of $150, $200 in cash, a Wayne Gretzky hockey card worth $400, $1200 in a chequing account, and an electric bill due for $250. Construct Corey's balance sheet and calculate his net worth.
   For each remaining part, explain how the event affects Corey's assets, liabilities, and wealth.
   b. Corey goes to a hockey card convention and finds out that his hockey card is a worthless forgery.
   c. Corey uses $150 from his paycheque to pay off his credit card balance. The remainder of his earnings is spent.
   d. Corey writes a $150 cheque on his chequing account to pay off his credit card balance.
   Of the events in parts (b) to (d), which, if any, corresponds to saving on Corey's part?

2. State whether each of the following is a stock or a flow, and explain.
   a. the gross domestic product
   b. national saving
   c. the value of the Canadian housing stock on January 1, 2009
   d. the amount of Canadian currency in circulation as of this morning
   e. the government budget surplus or deficit
   f. the quantity of outstanding government debt on January 1, 2009

3. Ellie and Vince are a married couple, both with university degrees and jobs. How would you expect each of the following events to affect the amount they save each month? Explain your answers in terms of the basic motivations for saving.
   a. Ellie learns she is pregnant.
   b. Vince reads in the paper about possible layoffs in his industry.
   c. Vince had hoped that his parents would lend financial assistance toward the couple's planned purchase of a house, but he learns that they can't afford it.
   d. Ellie announces that she would like to go to law school in the next few years.
   e. A boom in the stock market greatly increases the value of the couple's retirement funds.
   f. Vince and Ellie agree that they would like to leave a substantial amount to local charities in their wills.

4. An individual who contributes money to a Registered Retirement Savings Plan, or RRSP, does not have to pay income taxes on a portion of the individual's personal income corresponding to the amount of the RRSP contribution, nor any current income taxes on the returns (interest, dividends, or capital gains) accruing to the funds in the RRSP. However, when the funds are withdrawn from the RRSP, the full amount withdrawn is treated as income in the withdrawal year and is taxed at the individual's current income tax rate. In contrast, an individual investing outside of an RRSP has to pay income taxes on the funds deposited and on returns earned by the funds in each year but does not have to pay taxes on withdrawals.
   a. Greg, who is five years from retirement, receives a $10 000 bonus at work. He is trying to decide whether to save this extra income in a savings account held as an RRSP or in a regular savings account. Both accounts earn 5 percent nominal interest, and Greg is in a 30 percent tax bracket in every year (including his retirement year). Compare the amounts that Greg will have in five years under each of the two saving strategies, net of all taxes. Is the RRSP a good deal for Greg? Assume that Greg's eligibility for public pension funds upon retirement is not affected by the size of the balance in his savings account (whether registered or not).

5. Use the economic data given to find national saving, private saving, public saving, and national saving as a percentage of GDP. Assume that saving amounts for all sectors represent gross rates, and assume that the government budget balance equals public saving. There is no government investment.
   Household saving = 200   Corporate saving = 400
   Government purchases of goods and services = 100
   Government transfers and interest payments = 100
   Tax collections = 150   GDP = 2200

6. Ellie and Vince are trying to decide whether to purchase a new home. The house they want is priced at $200 000. Annual expenses such as maintenance, taxes, and insurance equal 4 percent of the home's value. If properly maintained, the house's real value is not expected to change. The real interest rate in the economy is 6 percent, and Ellie and Vince can qualify to borrow the full amount of the purchase price (for simplicity, assume no down payment) at that rate.
   a. Ellie and Vince would be willing to pay $1500 monthly rent to live in a house of the same quality as the one they are thinking about purchasing. Should they buy the house?
   b. Does the answer to part (a) change if they were willing to pay $2000 monthly rent?
   c. Does the answer to part (a) change if the real interest rate is 4 percent instead of 6 percent?
   d. Does the answer to part (a) change if the developer offers to sell the house to Ellie and Vince for $150 000?
   e. Why do home-building companies dislike high interest rates?

7. The builder of a new movie theatre complex is trying to decide how many screens she wants. Below are her estimates of the number of patrons the complex will attract each year, depending on the number of screens available.

Number of screens	Total number of patrons
1	40 000
2	75 000
3	105 000
4	130 000
5	150 000

After paying the movie distributors and meeting all other non-interest expenses, the owner expects to net $2 per ticket sold. Construction costs are $1 000 000 per screen.

a. Make a table showing the value of marginal product for each screen from the first through the fifth. What property is illustrated by the behaviour of marginal product?
b. How many screens will be built if the real interest rate is 5.5 percent?
c. If the real interest rate is 7.5 percent?
d. If the real interest rate is 10 percent?
e. If the real interest rate is 5.5 percent, how far would construction costs have to fall before the builder would be willing to build a five-screen complex?

ANSWERS TO IN-CHAPTER EXERCISES

16.1 If Kimberleigh's student loan were for $6500 instead of $3000, her liabilities would be $6750 (the student loan plus the credit card balance) instead of $3250. The value of her assets, $6280, is unchanged. In this case Kimberleigh's wealth is negative, since assets of $6280 less liabilities of $6750 equals –$470. Negative wealth or net worth means one owes more than one owns.

16.2 a. Kimberleigh has set aside her usual $20, but she has also incurred a new liability of $50. So her net saving for the week is *minus* $30. Since her assets (her chequing account) have increased by $20 but her liabilities (her credit card balance) have increased by $50, her wealth has also declined by $30.

b. In paying off her credit card bill, Kimberleigh reduces her assets by $300 by drawing down her chequing account and reduces her liabilities by the same amount by reducing her credit card balance to zero. Thus there is no change in her wealth. There is also no change in her saving (note that Kimberleigh's income and spending on current needs have not changed).

c. The increase in the value of Kimberleigh's car raises her assets by $500. So her wealth also rises by $500. Changes in the value of existing assets are not treated as part of saving, however, so her saving is unchanged.

d. The decline in the value of Kimberleigh's furniture is a capital loss of $300. Her assets and wealth fall by $300. Her saving is unchanged.

16.3 The loss of value of $200 over the year is another financial cost of owning the mower, which Larry should take into account in making his decision. His total cost is now $240 in interest costs plus $200 in anticipated loss of value of the mower (known as depreciation), or $440. This exceeds the value of marginal product, $400, and so now Larry should not buy the mower.

Chapter 17 Financial Markets and International Capital Flows

A recent television ad for an online trading company showed an office worker, call him Ed, sitting in front of his computer. Instead of working, Ed is checking the prices of the stocks he bought over the Internet. Suddenly his eyes widen, as on the computer screen a graph shows the price of his stock shooting up like a rocket. With a whoop Ed heads down to his boss's office, delivers a few well-chosen insults, and quits his job. Unfortunately, when Ed returns to his desk to pack up his belongings, the computer screen shows that the price of his stock has fallen as quickly as it rose. The last we hear of Ed are his futile attempts to convince his boss that he was only kidding.

During periods such as that between January 1995 and August 2000, when the Toronto Stock Exchange 300 index rose from about 4000 to over 11 000, people often begin to think of the stock market as a place to gamble and, maybe, to strike it rich. Some people do get rich playing the market, and some people, like Ed, lose everything. But stock markets, as well as other financial markets, play a role in the economy that is not shared by the gambling establishments in Niagara Falls or Las Vegas. That role is to channel investment funds to potentially productive uses.

In Chapter 16, we discussed the importance of investment (or capital formation), which both economic logic and experience predict will tend to increase labour productivity and living standards. However, creating new capital does not guarantee a richer and more productive economy. History is full of examples of "white elephants," capital projects in which millions, and even billions, of dollars were invested with little economic benefit: nuclear power plants that were never opened, massive dams whose main effect was to divert water supplies and disrupt the local agriculture, dot-com companies that never amounted to anything.

A healthy economy channels investment funds in a productive way. In capitalist economies, like that of Canada, channeling investment funds into real capital investments is one role of the financial system: banks, stock markets, bond markets, and other financial markets and institutions. In the first part of this chapter, we discuss some major financial markets and institutions and their role in directing investment funds into real investments.

In today's world, saving often flows across national boundaries, as financial investors purchase financial assets in countries other than their own and borrowers look abroad for sources of financing. Flows of funds between lenders and borrowers located in different countries are referred to as *international capital flows*. We discuss the international dimension of saving and capital formation in the second and third sections of the chapter. As we will see, for many countries, including Canada until recently, foreign saving has provided an important supplement to domestic saving as a way to finance the formation of new capital.

This chapter should be viewed as an extension of Chapter 16 where we studied how saving is defined. In the first section of this chapter we analyze how that saving is channelled into investment. Non-resident saving was examined in Chapter 16, where we studied how it can allow an economy to achieve higher levels of investment than it otherwise would. In the second and third sections of this chapter we will again consider non-resident saving, that is, international capital flow, but in greater detail.

"White elephants," such as some nuclear power plants, are capital projects with large costs and small economic benefits

17.1 BANKS, BONDS, STOCKS, AND THE ALLOCATION OF FUNDS TO REAL INVESTMENT

We have emphasized the importance of a high rate of real (as opposed to financial) investment for economic growth and increased productivity.[1] A high rate of real investment (involving purchases of new factories and equipment and so on) is not sufficient, however. A successful economy not only invests vigorously but it applies its limited funds to investment projects that, on average, have a high rate of return.

In a capitalist economy like that of Canada, some investment funds are allocated by public sector decision makers to government fixed capital formation, as discussed in Chapters 5 and 16. But most investment funds are allocated either by private businesses reinvesting their profits or by the financial system. The Canadian financial system consists both of financial institutions, such as banks, and financial markets, such as bond markets and stock markets.

The financial system performs two major functions on behalf of financial investors (savers). First, it provides information to financial investors about which of the many possible uses of their funds are likely to prove most profitable, and hence pay the highest return. For example, financial intermediaries such as banks develop expertise in evaluating prospective borrowers, making it unnecessary for small financial investors to do that on their own. Similarly, stock and bond analysts evaluate the business prospects of a company issuing shares of stock or bonds, which affects the price the stock will sell for or the interest rate the company will have to offer on its bond.

Second, financial markets help financial investors share the risks of lending by permitting them to diversify their financial investments. When capital markets have not been developed, as in much of the less-developed world, the only way a person can save for the future is by acquiring real assets—as, for example, when a peasant farmer invests in a bigger barn or in more livestock. A central problem with such direct investments is that their risk is not diversified. When everything that a person owns is tied up in their farm, a single fire or other disaster would wipe them out financially. Where capital markets have been developed, such as in countries like Canada, they enable savers to buy a share in many different investments—thus, no single event can wipe out the entire value of their portfolio.

---

[1]Recall from Chapters 5 and 15 that economists sometimes use the term "real" in contrast to "financial" to distinguish investment in the national accounts sense (private and public investment in physical capital and inventories) from financial investment (purchases of stocks and bonds). This use of the term "real" means "inflation-adjusted."

Although it is important to recognize these two major functions that the financial system performs on behalf of financial investors, it is also important to recognize that even in well-regulated financial systems, financial investors may not always get particularly good advice, and may even be swindled from time to time. It is not easy to achieve a financial system that motivates its agents to provide quality service to investor customers but cuts off all opportunities for those agents to profit at the customer's expense. Furthermore, as the Enron and numerous other corporate scandals of recent years have demonstrated, the quality of advice provided by the financial system will be degraded if financial analysts are duped by corporations engaging in deceptive accounting practices.[2]

In this section, we briefly discuss three key components of the financial system: the banking system, the bond market, and the stock market. In doing so we elaborate on the role of the financial system as a whole in providing information about investment projects and in helping financial investors to share the risks of lending.

THE BANKING SYSTEM

Canada's banking system is based upon commercial banks (also known in Canada as chartered banks)—the 11 domestic banks and the more than 40 foreign bank subsidiaries operating in Canada. The six largest domestic banks, with their countrywide branch networks, are particularly important, as they account for about 90 percent of the assets of Canada's banking system.

"O.K., folks, let's move along. I'm sure you've all seen someone qualify for a loan before."

[2]For a fascinating analysis of the problems financial investors have in obtaining reliable information, see Robert Shiller, *Irrational Exuberance,* 2nd ed., (Princeton, N.J.: Princeton University Press, 2006). For a critical view of Canada's financial system, see Jim Stanford, *Paper Boom* (Ottawa: James Lorimer, 1999).

financial intermediaries
firms that extend credit to borrowers using funds raised from savers

COMPARATIVE
ADVANTAGE

Commercial banks are privately owned firms that accept deposits from individuals and businesses and use those deposits to make loans. Banks are the most important example of a class of institutions called **financial intermediaries**, firms that extend credit to borrowers using funds raised from savers. Other examples of financial intermediaries are trust companies, credit unions, and caisses populaires.

Why are financial intermediaries such as banks, which "stand between" financial investors and business borrowers, necessary? Why don't individual investors just lend directly to borrowers who want to invest in new capital projects? The main reason is that, through specialization, banks and other intermediaries develop a *comparative advantage* in evaluating the quality of borrowers—the information-gathering function that we referred to a moment ago. Most savers, particularly small investors, do not have the time or the knowledge to determine for themselves which borrowers are likely to most productively use the funds they receive.

Banks help financial investors by eliminating their need to gather information about potential borrowers and by directing their funds toward higher-return, more productive investments. Banks help borrowers as well by providing access to credit that might otherwise not be available.

BONDS AND STOCKS

Large and well-established corporations that wish to obtain funds for investment will sometimes go to banks. Unlike the typical small borrower, however, a larger firm usually has alternative ways of raising funds, notably through the corporate bond market and the stock market. We will therefore discuss some of the mechanics of bonds and stocks, then return to the role of bond and stock markets in allocating funds.

THE TIME VALUE OF MONEY REVISITED

In Chapter 1 we compared the value of a dollar today to the value of a dollar in the future. The *time value of money* implies that, if money can be invested in an interest-bearing account, a given dollar amount today is equivalent to a larger dollar amount in the future.

A dramatic example of the time value of money was provided by the case of an Ontario resident who made the news in the spring of 2004 when it was reported that he had decided to stash a winning $30 million lottery ticket in a safe-deposit box for almost a year before cashing it in. What was the opportunity cost of this decision? One financial reporter put it this way: "How about earnings of $675,000 in a one-year cashable guaranteed investment certificate with an annual interest rate of 2.25 per cent at the Royal Bank of Canada?"[3]

In general, what is the amount of money that would be required in the future to equal a given dollar amount today?

present value (PV), or *present discounted value,* is the value of a sum of money today—that is, the value in the current or initial period

future value (FV) is the value a sum of money grows to at some date in the future, when it compounds at a given interest rate

Suppose you have $100 and that you can get a 2 percent annual interest rate if you invest the $100 in an interest-bearing account. After one year the balance in the account will have a value of $102—the original sum of $100 plus the $2 of interest. If the interest rate remains at 2 percent, then the $102 to which the balance grew after one year will grow by 2 percent over the second year, to $104.04.

The logic of this example can be generalized. We can refer to *present discounted value* or, more succinctly, **present value (PV)**, as the value of a sum of money today. This can be contrasted with *future value*. **Future value (FV)** refers to how much a sum of money grows when it compounds at a given rate. If the interest rate is symbolized by i and the number of compounding periods by n,

[3]Rob Ferguson, "Long Wait Cost Lottery Winner Big Bucks," *Toronto Star*, 3 April 2004.

then the relationship between present value and future value can now be represented by Equation 17.1:

$$FV = PV \times (1 + i)^n \qquad (17.1)$$

Does Equation 17.1 fit with the example of $100 growing to $104.04 after two years when the interest rate is 2 percent? Let's check. The $100 corresponds to PV, the 2 percent (.02) corresponds to i, and the two years corresponds to n, the number of compounding periods. Substituting for PV, i, and n in Equation 17.1 indeed yields FV of $104.04—that is, $104.04 = $100 \times (1.02)^2$.

Another way to express the relationship between present value and future value is to divide both sides of Equation 17.1 by $(1 + i)^n$ to get:

$$FV = PV/(1 + i)^n \qquad (17.2)$$

To take a concrete example, what is the present value (PV) of $100 received three years from now when the interest rate is 2 percent? From Equation 17.2, we conclude that PV = $100/(1.02)^3 = $94.23.

When is a million dollars not worth a million dollars?

EXAMPLE 17.1

In the spring of 2004, the McDonald's fast food chain advertised that on one weekend it would give out 15 prizes of one million dollars each to lucky customers. The fine print of the advertising, however, revealed that each one million dollar prize would be paid out in instalments of $50 000 a year over a period of 20 years. What is the present value of such a prize?

To calculate the present value of the "one million dollar" prize you would add together the present values of each of the 20 instalments. If the relevant interest rate is 2.25 percent and if payments are made at the end of each year, then the value of the first instalment is $50 000/(1.0225), the value of the second instalment is $50 000/(1.0225)^2$, and so on, with the value of the final instalment being worth $50 000/(1.0225)^{20}$. It turns out that the present value of the "one million dollar" prize would be $798 186.

If you can grasp the time value of money, you should have no trouble understanding bond and stock price determination: both bond prices and stock prices involve present values of expected future payments.

Bonds

A **bond** is a legal promise to repay a debt, usually including both the **principal amount**, which is the amount originally lent, and regular interest payments. The promised interest rate when a bond is issued is called the **coupon rate**. The regular interest payments made to the bondholder are called coupon payments. The **coupon payment** of a bond that pays interest annually equals the coupon rate times the principal amount of the bond. For example, if the principal amount of a bond is $1 000 000 and its coupon rate is 5 percent, then the annual coupon payment made to the holder of the bond is (0.05)($1 000 000), or $50 000.

Corporations and governments frequently raise funds by issuing bonds and selling them to savers or financial investors. The coupon rate that a newly issued bond has to promise to be attractive to financial investors depends on a number of factors, including the bond's term and its credit risk. The *term* of a bond is the length of time before the debt it represents is fully repaid, a period that can range from 30 days to 30 years or more. Generally lenders will demand a higher interest rate to lend for a longer term. *Credit risk* is the risk that the borrower will go bankrupt and thus not repay the loan. A borrower viewed as risky will have to

bond a legal promise to repay a debt, usually including both the principal amount and regular interest payments

principal amount the amount originally lent

coupon rate the interest rate promised when a bond is issued

coupon payments regular interest payments made to the bondholder

pay a higher interest rate to compensate lenders for taking the chance of losing all or part of their financial investment. For example, so-called high-yield bonds, less formally known as "junk bonds," are bonds issued by firms judged to be risky by credit-rating agencies; these bonds pay higher interest rates than bonds issued by companies thought to be less risky.

Bondholders are not required to hold bonds until *maturity*, the time at which they are supposed to be repaid by the issuer, but are always free to sell their bonds in the *bond market*, an organized market run by professional bond traders.[4] The market value of a particular bond at any given point in time is called the *price* of the bond. As it turns out, there is a close relationship between the price of a bond at a given point of time and the interest rate prevailing in financial markets at that time, as illustrated by Example 17.2.

EXAMPLE 17.2	Bond prices and interest rates

On January 1, 2009, Tanya purchases a newly issued, 2-year government bond with a principal amount of $1000. The coupon rate on the bond is 5 percent, paid annually. Hence Tanya, or whoever owns the bond at the time, will receive a coupon payment of $50 (5 percent of $1000) on January 1, 2010, and $1050 (a $50 coupon payment plus repayment of the original $1000 lent) on January 1, 2011.

On January 1, 2010, after receiving her first year's coupon payment, Tanya decides to sell her bond to raise the funds to take a vacation. She offers her bond for sale in the bond market. How much can she expect to get for her "used" bond if the prevailing interest rate in the bond market is 6 percent? If the prevailing interest rate is 4 percent?

As we mentioned, the price of a "used" bond at any point in time depends on the prevailing interest rate. Suppose first that, on January 1, 2010, when Tanya takes her bond to the bond market, the prevailing interest rate on newly issued 1-year bonds is 6 percent. Would another financial investor be willing to pay Tanya the full $1000 principal amount of her bond? No, because the purchaser of Tanya's bond will receive $1050 in 1 year, when the bond matures; whereas if he uses his $1000 to buy a new 1-year bond paying 6 percent interest, he will receive $1060 ($1000 principal repayment plus $60 interest) in 1 year. So Tanya's bond is not worth $1000 to another financial investor.

How much would another investor be willing to pay for Tanya's bond? Since newly issued 1-year bonds pay a 6 percent return, he will buy Tanya's bond only at a price that allows him to earn at least that return. As the holder of Tanya's bond will receive $1050 ($1000 principal plus $50 interest) in 1 year, the price for her bond that allows the purchaser to earn a 6 percent return must satisfy the equation

$$\text{Bond price} \times 1.06 = \$1050.$$

Solving the equation for the bond price, we find that Tanya's bond will sell for $1050/1.06, or just under $991. To check this result, note that in 1 year the purchaser of the bond will receive $1050, or $59 more than he paid. His rate of return is $59/$991, or 6 percent, as expected.

What if the prevailing interest rate had been 4 percent rather than 6 percent? Then the price of Tanya's bond would satisfy the relationship (bond price × 1.04) = $1050, implying that the price of her bond would be $1050/1.04, or almost $1010.

What happens if the interest rate when Tanya wants to sell is 5 percent, the same as it was when she originally bought the bond? You should show that in this case the bond would sell at its face value of $1000.

---

[4]The analysis in the text does not apply to the special cases of Canada Savings Bonds and Canada Premium Bonds, two categories of federal government "bonds" that cannot be resold in markets but can only be redeemed at financial institutions for principal and accumulated interest. Neither of these are true "bonds" but are actually savings certificates.

This example illustrates a general principle: *bond prices and interest rates are inversely related.* When the interest rate being paid on newly issued bonds rises, the prices financial investors are willing to pay for existing bonds falls, and vice versa.

EXERCISE 17.1

Three-year government bonds are issued at a face value (principal amount) of $100 and a coupon rate of 7 percent, interest payable at the end of each year. One year prior to the maturation of these bonds, a newspaper head-line reads, "Bond Prices Plunge," and the story reveals that these 3-year bonds have fallen in price to $96. What has happened to interest rates? What is the 1-year interest rate at the time of the newspaper story?

Issuing bonds is one means by which a corporation or a government can obtain funds from financial investors. Another important way of raising funds, but one restricted to corporations, is by issuing stock to the public.

Stocks

A share of **stock** (or *equity*) is a claim to partial ownership of a firm. For example, if a corporation has 1 million shares of stock outstanding, ownership of one share is equivalent to ownership of one-millionth of the company. Stockholders receive returns on their financial investment in two forms. First, stockholders receive a regular payment called a **dividend** for each share of stock they own. Dividends are determined by the firm's management and usually depend on the firm's recent profits. Second, stockholders receive returns in the form of *capital gains* when the price of their stock increases (we discussed capital gains and losses in Chapter 16).

stock (or equity) a claim to partial ownership of a firm

dividend a regular payment received by stockholders for each share that they own

Prices of stocks are determined through trading on a stock exchange, such as the Toronto Stock Exchange. A stock's price rises and falls as the demand for the stock changes. Demand for stocks in turn depends on factors such as news about the prospects of the company. For example, the stock price of a pharmaceutical company that announces the discovery of an important new drug is likely to rise on the announcement, even if actual production and marketing of the drug is some time away, because financial investors expect the company to become more profitable in the future. Example 17.3 gives a numerical illustration of some key factors that affect stock prices.

How much should you pay for a share of FortuneCookie.com?   **EXAMPLE 17.3**

You have the opportunity to buy shares in a new company called FortuneCookie.com, which plans to sell gourmet fortune cookies over the Internet. Your stock-broker estimates that the company will pay $1 per share in dividends a year from now, and that in a year the market price of the company will be $80 per share. Assuming that you accept your broker's estimates as accurate, what is the most that you should be willing to pay today per share of FortuneCookie.com? How does your answer change if you expect a $5 dividend? If you expect a $1 dividend but an $84 stock price in one year?

Based on your broker's estimates, you conclude that in one year each share of FortuneCookie.com you own will be worth $81 in your pocket—the $1 dividend plus the $80 you could get by reselling the stock. Finding the maximum price you would pay for the stock today therefore boils down to asking how much you would invest today to have $81 a year from today. Answering this question in turn requires one more piece of information, which is the expected rate of return that you require in order to be willing to buy stock in this company.

How would you determine your required rate of return to hold stock in FortuneCookie.com? For the moment, let's imagine that you are not too worried about the potential riskiness of the stock, either because you think that it is a "sure thing" or because you are a devil-may-care type who is not bothered by risk. In that case, your required rate of return to hold FortuneCookie.com should be about the same as you can get on other financial investments, such as government bonds. The available return on other financial investments gives the *opportunity cost* of your funds. So, for example, if the interest rate currently being offered on government bonds is 6 percent, you should be willing to accept a 6 percent return to hold FortuneCookie.com as well. In that case, the maximum price you would pay today for a share of FortuneCookie.com satisfies the equation

$$\text{Stock price} \times 1.06 = \$81.$$

This equation defines the stock price you should be willing to pay if you are willing to accept a 6 percent return over the next year. Solving this equation yields stock price = $81/1.06 = $76.42. If you buy FortuneCookie.com for $76.42, then your return over the year will be ($81 − $76.42)/$76.42 = $4.58/$71.42 = 6 percent, which is the rate of return you required to buy the stock.

If, instead, the dividend is expected to be $5, then the total benefit of holding the stock in one year, equal to the expected dividend plus the expected price, is $5 + $80, or $85. Assuming again that you are willing to accept a 6 percent return to hold FortuneCookie.com, the price you are willing to pay for the stock today satisfies the relationship (stock price × 1.06) = $85. Solving this equation for the stock price yields stock price = $85/1.06 = $80.19. Comparing with the previous case, we see that a higher expected dividend in the future increases the value of the stock today. That's why good news about the future prospects of a company—such as the announcement by a pharmaceutical company that it has discovered a useful new drug—affects its stock price immediately.

If the expected future price of the stock is $84, with the dividend at $1, then the value of holding the stock in one year is once again $85, and the calculation is the same as the previous one. Again, the price you should be willing to pay for the stock is $80.19.

These examples show that an increase in the future dividend or in the future expected stock price raises the stock price today, whereas an increase in the return a financial investor requires to hold the stock lowers today's stock price. Since we expect required returns in the stock market to be closely tied to market interest rates, this last result implies that increases in interest rates tend to depress stock prices (as well as bond prices) and vice versa.

Our examples also took the future stock price as a given. But what determines the future stock price? Just as today's stock price depends on the dividend shareholders expect to receive this year and the stock price a year from now, the stock price a year from now depends on the dividend expected for next year and the stock price two years from now, and so on. Ultimately, then, today's stock price is affected not only by the dividend expected this year but future dividends as well. A company's ability to pay dividends depends on its earnings. Thus, as we noted in the example of the pharmaceutical company that announces the discovery of a new drug, news about future earnings—even earnings quite far in the future—is likely to affect a company's stock price immediately.

EXERCISE 17.2   **As in Example 17.3, you expect a share of FortuneCookie.com to be worth $80 per share in one year, and also to pay a dividend of $1 in one year. What should you be willing to pay for the stock today if the prevailing interest rate, equal to your required rate of return, is 4 percent? What if the interest**

rate is 8 percent? In general, how would you expect stock prices to react if economic news arrives that implies that interest rates will rise in the very near future?

In Example 17.3, we assumed that you were willing to accept a return of 6 percent to hold FortuneCookie.com, the same return that you could get on a government bond. However, financial investments in the stock market are quite risky in that returns to holding stocks can be quite variable and unpredictable. For example, although you expect a share of FortuneCookie.com to be worth $80 in one year, you also realize that there is a chance it might sell for as low as $50 or as high as $110 per share. Most financial investors dislike risk and unpredictability and thus have a higher required rate of return for holding risky assets like stocks than for holding relatively safe assets like government bonds. The difference between the required rate of return to hold risky assets and the rate of return on safe assets, like government bonds, is called the **risk premium**. Example 17.4 illustrates the effect of financial investors' dislike of risk on stock prices.

risk premium the rate of return that financial investors require to hold risky assets minus the rate of return on safe assets

Riskiness and stock prices

EXAMPLE 17.4

Continuing Example 17.3, suppose that FortuneCookie.com is expected to pay a $1 dividend and have a market price of $80 per share in one year. The interest rate on government bonds is 6 percent per year. However, to be willing to hold a risky asset like a share of FortuneCookie.com, you require an expected return four percentage points higher than the rate paid by safe assets like government bonds (a risk premium of 4 percent). Hence you require a 10 percent expected return to hold FortuneCookie.com. What is the most you would be willing to pay for the stock now? What do you conclude about the relationship between perceived riskiness and stock prices?

As a share of FortuneCookie.com is expected to pay $81 in one year and the required return is 10 percent, we have (stock price × 1.10) = $81. Solving for the stock price, we find the price to be $81/1.10 = $73.64, less than the price of $76.42 we found when there was no risk premium and the required rate of return was 6 percent (Example 17.3). We conclude that financial investors' dislike of risk, and the resulting risk premium, lowers the prices of risky assets like stocks.

To give a real-world example, in the spring of 2000, North American investors began to fear the risks associated with Internet-related (or "dot-com") companies, the real-world counterparts to our hypothetical FortuneCookie.com. Some observers have said that investors began to see through the hype that had been fed to them by dot-com entrepreneurs and by biased stock market analysts and brokers. In any case, the perceived riskiness of Internet-related shares rose, and this rise in perceived risk was one reason why share prices began to fall. The Forbes Internet index of 300 companies, for example, corresponded to a market value of over U.S.$1 trillion in early 2000, but by December 2000 its market value had dropped to under U.S.$400 billion, a fall of more than 60 percent. (Broad-based stock indices fell during the same period, but not by nearly as much as indices of Internet-related stocks.)

Having explained how bonds and stocks are priced, let us briefly consider the significance of bond and stock finance versus that of bank finance. Like banks, bond markets and stock markets provide a means of channelling funds from savers or financial investors to borrowers with investment opportunities.

In most developing economies, the financial systems depend heavily upon bank financing of real investment projects where financial markets, that is, bonds and stocks, have a minor role. Financial markets begin to play a greater role as the economies become more advanced. Some research indicates that "bank-led finance may be inevitable at certain stages of development, and that efforts to develop stock exchanges in some countries may have been premature...."[5]

Bank-led finance has also been more characteristic of some advanced economies, such as Japan's, than of others, such as that of the United States. When Japan was growing rapidly in the 1980s, the strengths of a bank-led financial system were widely noted. When Japan stagnated in the 1990s, however, the weaknesses of bank-led finance were highlighted, and in recent years the relative importance of bank finance in Japan has declined.

RECAP ↑

BONDS AND STOCKS

- Bond prices and interest rates are inversely related. That is, when the interest rate being paid on newly issued bonds rises, the price financial investors will pay for existing bonds falls, and vice versa.

- An increase in expected future dividends or in the expected future market price of a stock raises the current price of the stock.

- An increase in interest rates, implying an increase in the required rate of return to hold stocks, lowers the current price of stocks.

- An increase in perceived riskiness, as reflected in an increase in the risk premium, lowers the current price of stocks.

- Greater reliance on banks than on financial markets is characteristic of developing countries but some successful advanced economies have also been characterized by bank–led finance.

17.2 INTERNATIONAL CAPITAL FLOWS AND THE CURRENT ACCOUNT

Our discussion thus far has focused on financial markets operating within a given country, such as Canada. However, financial opportunities are not necessarily restricted by national boundaries. Only in a closed economy is there an absence of international trade and cross-border borrowing and lending. An open economy is characterized both by international trade and cross-border borrowing and lending. Over time, most economies have become more and more open and extensive financial markets have developed to facilitate cross-border borrowing and lending. Financial markets in which borrowers and lenders are residents of different countries are called *international* financial markets.

International financial markets differ from domestic financial markets in at least one important respect: unlike a domestic financial transaction, an international financial transaction is subject to the laws and regulations of at least two countries, the country that is home to the lender and the country that is home to the borrower. Thus the size of international financial markets depends on the degree of political and economic cooperation among countries. For example, during the relatively peaceful decades of the late nineteenth and early twentieth centuries, international financial markets were remarkably highly developed. Great

---

[5]Erik Berglof and Patrick Bolton, "The Great Divide and Beyond: Financial Architecture in Transition," http://www.worldbank.org/html/prddr/trans/octnovdec02/pgs8–12.htm (May 2008).

Britain, at the time the world's dominant economic power, was a major international lender, dispatching its savings for use around the globe, including Canada, which was a British colony. However, during the turbulent years 1914–1945, two world wars and the Great Depression substantially reduced both international finance and international trade in goods and services. It was only in the 1980s that international finance and trade returned to the levels achieved in the late nineteenth century.

In thinking about international financial markets, it is useful to understand that lending is economically equivalent to acquiring a real or financial asset, and borrowing is economically equivalent to selling a real or financial asset. For example, financial investors lend to companies by purchasing stocks or bonds, which are financial assets for the lender and financial liabilities for the borrowing firms. Similarly, lending to a government is accomplished in practice by acquiring a government bond—a financial asset for the lender, and a financial liability for the borrower, in this case the government. Lenders can also provide funds by acquiring real assets such as land; if I purchase a parcel of land from you, though I am not making a loan in the usual sense, I am providing you with funds that you can use for consuming or investing. In lieu of interest or dividends from a bond or a stock, I receive the rental value of the land that I purchased.

Purchases or sales of real and financial assets across international borders (economically equivalent to lending and borrowing across international borders) are known as **international capital flows.** From the perspective of a particular country, say Canada, purchases of domestic (Canadian) assets by foreigners are called **capital inflows;** purchases of foreign assets by domestic (Canadian) households and firms are called **capital outflows.** To remember these terms, it may help to keep in mind that capital inflows represent funds "flowing in" to the country (foreign savers buying domestic assets), while capital outflows are funds "flowing out" of the country (domestic savers buying foreign assets). The difference between the two flows is expressed as **net capital inflows**—capital inflows minus capital outflows—or **net capital outflows**—capital outflows minus capital inflows. Note that capital inflows and outflows are *not* counted as exports or imports, because they refer to the purchase of existing real and financial assets rather than currently produced goods and services.

From a macroeconomic perspective, international capital flows play two important roles. First, they allow countries whose real investment opportunities are greater than domestic saving to fill in the gap by borrowing from abroad. Second, they allow countries to run trade imbalances—situations in which the country's exports of goods and services do not equal its imports of goods and services—and, more generally, current account imbalances.

While international capital flows play these important roles, they also pose risks for both borrowing and lending countries, as we will discuss below.

TRADE BALANCE, CURRENT ACCOUNT, AND NET CAPITAL INFLOWS

In Chapter 5 we introduced the term *net exports* (NX), the value of a country's exports less the value of its imports. Another equivalent term for the value of a country's exports less the value of its imports is the **trade balance.** Because exports need not equal imports in each quarter or year, the trade balance (or net exports) need not always equal zero. If the trade balance is positive in a particular period, so that the value of exports exceeds the value of imports, a country is said to have a **trade surplus** for that period equal to the value of its exports minus the value of its imports. If the trade balance is negative, with imports greater than exports, the country is said to have a **trade deficit** equal to the value of its imports minus the value of its exports.

international capital flows purchases or sales of real and financial assets across international borders

capital inflows purchases of domestic assets by foreign households and firms

capital outflows purchases of foreign assets by domestic households and firms

net capital inflows capital inflows minus capital outflows

net capital outflows capital outflows minus capital inflows

trade balance (or net exports) the value of a country's exports less the value of its imports in a particular period (quarter or year)

trade surplus when exports exceed imports—the difference between the value of a country's exports and the value of its imports in a given period

trade deficit when imports exceed exports—the difference between the value of a country's imports and the value of its exports in a given period

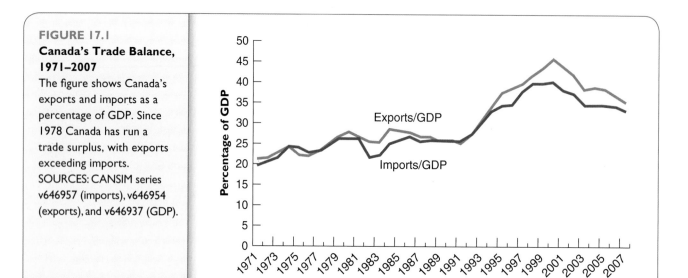

FIGURE 17.1

Canada's Trade Balance, 1971–2007

The figure shows Canada's exports and imports as a percentage of GDP. Since 1978 Canada has run a trade surplus, with exports exceeding imports.

SOURCES: CANSIM series v646957 (imports), v646954 (exports), and v646937 (GDP).

current account the record of payments and receipts arising from trade in goods and services, from international investment income, and from international transfers

Figure 17.1 shows the components of the Canadian trade balance since 1971 (see Figure 4.5 for data extending back to 1961). The red line represents Canada's exports as a percentage of GDP; the blue line, Canada's imports as a percentage of GDP. When exports exceed imports, the vertical distance between the two lines gives Canada's trade surplus as a percentage of GDP. When imports exceed exports, the vertical distance between the two lines represents Canada's trade deficit. Figure 17.1 shows that since 1978, exports have generally exceeded imports on an annual basis, indicating that Canada has typically had an annual trade surplus.

The trade balance is one component of a broader balance called the *current account*. In addition to the trade balance, the **current account** includes net international investment income and net international transfers. Table 17.1 shows Canada's balances on goods and services, investment income, and transfers for 2007. As can be seen, the current account balance was positive in 2007, reflecting a strongly positive trade balance (goods and services balance) more than offsetting the negative investment income balance. Figure 17.2 shows that Canada's current account balance has tended to be negative, even when its trade balance has been positive. Why would this be? We will address that question later in this section.

TABLE 17.1

Canada's Current Account Balance, 2007 ($ millions)

Goods and Services Balance	30 181
Investment Income Balance	−15 678
Transfers Balance	−320
Current Account Balance	14 183

SOURCE: CANSIM, Table 376-0001.

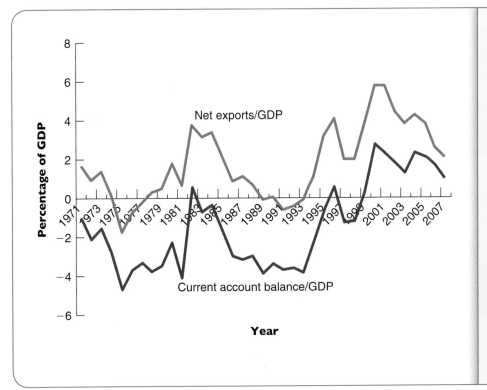

FIGURE 17.2

Canada's Net Exports and Current Account Balance as a Percentage of GDP, 1971–2007

In the past, Canada's current account balance has often been negative even while its net exports were positive due to negative investment income pulling down the current account balance. By the late 1990s, the strong performance of net exports was sufficient to make the current account balance positive.

SOURCES: Adapted from the CANSIM series v113713 (current account), v113714 (net exports), and v646937 (GDP).

Current Account and Net Capital Inflows

The first step to understanding international capital flows is recognizing the close link between them and the current account balance. There is a precise link between these two balances: in any given period, *the current account balance and net capital inflows sum to zero.* For future reference, let's write this relationship as an equation:

$$CA + KI = 0, \tag{17.3}$$

where CA is the current account balance and we use KI to stand for net capital inflows. The relationship given by Equation 17.3 is an identity, meaning that it is true by definition.

To see why Equation 17.3 holds, consider what happens when (for example) a Canadian resident purchases an imported good, say a Japanese automobile priced at $20 000. Suppose the Canadian buyer pays by cheque so that the Japanese car manufacturer now holds $20 000 in an account in a Canadian bank. What will the Japanese manufacturer do with this $20 000? There are two possibilities.

First, the Japanese company may use the $20 000 to buy Canadian-produced goods and services, such as Canadian-manufactured car parts or Whistler vacations for its executives. In this case, Canada has $20 000 in exports to balance the $20 000 automobile import. Because exports equal imports, Canada's current account is unaffected by these transactions (for these transactions, $CA = 0$). And because no assets are bought or sold, there are no capital inflows or outflows ($KI = 0$). So under this scenario, the condition that the current account balance plus net capital inflows equals zero, as stated in Equation 17.3, is satisfied.

Alternatively, the Japanese car producer might use the $20 000 to acquire Canadian assets, such as a Government of Canada bond or some land adjacent to its plant in Ontario. In this case, Canada compiles a current account deficit of $20 000, because the $20 000 car import is not offset by an export ($CA = -\$20\ 000$). But there is a corresponding capital inflow of $20 000, reflecting the purchase of a Canadian asset by the Japanese (KI = $20 000). So once again the current account balance and net capital inflows sum to zero, and Equation 17.3 is satisfied.[6]

There is also a third possibility, which is that the Japanese car company might trade its dollars to some other party outside Canada. For example, the company might trade its dollars to another Japanese firm or individual in exchange for Japanese yen. However, the acquirer of the dollars would then have the same two options as the car company—to buy Canadian goods and services or acquire Canadian assets—so that the equality of net capital inflows and the current account balance would continue to hold.

EXERCISE 17.3

A Canadian saver purchases a $20 000 Japanese government bond. Explain why Equation 17.3 is satisfied no matter what the Japanese government does with the $20 000 it receives for its bond.

With Equation 17.3, we have shown that net capital inflows are linked to the current account balance. Next we will show how net capital inflows combine with national saving to equal gross investment in an economy.

Recall from Chapter 16 that gross (or total) saving in the economy must equal gross (or total) investment, and that gross saving can be divided into national saving and non-resident saving. National saving is saving that originates within Canada from household, corporate, or government sources and can be denoted by $S_{national}$ or S, for simplicity. Non-resident saving originates outside Canada (on net). If non-resident saving is positive, then foreigners are bringing more funds into Canada than Canadians are taking out of the country; if non-resident saving is negative, then Canadians are taking more funds out of Canada than foreigners are bringing into the country. Non-resident saving is thus equal to net capital inflows. We can therefore denote non-resident saving by KI. If we denote gross investment by GI, then our statement that national saving plus non-resident saving equals gross investment can also be written as

$$S + KI = GI. \qquad (17.4)$$

Equation 17.4, a key result, states that in an open economy the pool of saving available for gross investment (GI) may include not only national saving (S) but funds from savers abroad as well (if KI is positive).

We now have the necessary background to answer an important question: what causes current account deficits?

Economists argue that *a low rate of national saving relative to investment* (or, equivalently, a high rate of investment relative to national saving) *is the primary cause of current account deficits*. To see the link between national saving, investment, and the current account deficit, recall the identity $CA + KI = 0$, from Equation 17.3, and $S + KI = GI$, from Equation 17.4. Together, these two equations imply that

$$S - GI = CA. \qquad (17.5)$$

According to Equation 17.5, if we hold gross investment (GI) constant, a high rate of national saving S implies a high level of the current account CA, while a low level of national saving implies a low level of the current account. Furthermore, if a country's national saving is less than its investment, or $S < GI$, then Equation 17.5 implies that the current account CA will be negative. That is, the country will have a current account deficit. The conclusion from Equation 17.5 is that, holding domestic investment constant, low national saving tends to be associated with a current account deficit ($CA < 0$), and high national saving is associated with a current account surplus ($CA > 0$).

A country with a current account deficit must also be receiving capital inflows, as we have seen. (Equation 17.3 tells us that if a current account deficit exists so

[6]If the Japanese company simply left the $20 000 in the Canadian bank it would still count as a capital inflow since the deposit would still be a Canadian asset acquired by foreigners.

that $CA < 0$, then it must be true that $KI > 0$—net capital inflows are positive.) Is a low national saving rate (relative to investment) consistent with the existence of net capital inflows? The answer is yes. A country with a low national saving rate will not have sufficient savings of its own to finance domestic investment. Thus there likely will be many good investment opportunities in the country available to foreign investors, leading to capital inflows. Equivalently, a shortage of domestic saving will tend to drive up the domestic real interest rate, which attracts capital flows from abroad.

RECAP

INTERNATIONAL CAPITAL FLOWS AND THE CURRENT ACCOUNT

Trade takes place in assets as well as in goods and services. Purchases of domestic assets (real or financial) by foreigners are called *capital inflows*, and purchases of foreign assets by residents are called *capital outflows*.

The *current account* is the balance of payments and receipts arising from trade in goods and services, from international investment income, and from international transfers. Because imports that are not financed by sales of exports must be financed by sales of assets, the current account balance and net capital inflows sum to zero. Canada has run trade surpluses consistently since 1978 but has only had consistent current account surpluses since 1999.

Economists generally argue that a low rate of national saving relative to investment (or, equivalently, a high rate of investment relative to national saving) is the primary cause of current account deficits.

ECONOMIC *Naturalist* 17.1 How could Canada have a current account deficit but a trade surplus?

As shown by Figure 17.2, over the last few decades, Canada's current account balance has tended to be negative even while its net exports have tended to be positive. How can this be?

Recall that the current account balance includes not only net exports, but also net investment income and net transfers. Net transfers represent foreign aid as well as private remittances across borders, and are a small part of the current account. The primary reason for the current account deficits must therefore lie in net investment income, which has been strongly negative for Canada's history, from −$208 million in 1926 to −$15.7 billion in 2007.

Investment income is composed of profits, interest, and dividends on *past* investments. If net investment income is negative, then more of these kinds of payments are leaving Canada than are entering. This would occur because of prior sales of Canadian assets to foreign residents. These sales entail the future repatriation of profits, interest, and dividends to the foreign owners of the Canadian assets.

If Canada's net exports are positive but relatively low, then negative net investment income will be sufficient to pull the current account into deficit. However, by the 1999–2007 period the sharp rise in Canada's net exports was adequate to bring the current account into surplus.

17.3 THE DETERMINANTS OF INTERNATIONAL CAPITAL FLOWS

We have seen how international capital flows are defined and how international capital inflows to a country are associated with its investment exceeding its national saving. Now let us examine the determinants of international capital flows further.

Recall that capital inflows are purchases of domestic assets by foreigners, while capital outflows are purchases of foreign assets by domestic residents. For example, capital inflows into Canada include foreign purchases of items such as the stocks and bonds of Canadian companies, Government of Canada bonds, and real assets such as land or buildings owned by Canadian residents. Why would foreigners want to acquire Canadian assets, and conversely, why would Canadians want to acquire assets abroad?

As we emphasized in connection with stock price determination, the basic factors that determine the attractiveness of an asset, either domestic or foreign, are *return* and *risk*. Financial investors seek high real returns; thus, with other factors (such as the degree of risk and the returns available abroad) held constant, a higher real interest rate in the home country promotes capital inflows by making domestic assets more attractive to foreigners. By the same token, a higher real interest rate in the home country reduces capital outflows by inducing domestic residents to invest their savings at home. Thus, all else being equal, a higher real interest rate at home leads to net capital inflows. Conversely, a low real interest rate at home tends to create net capital outflows, as financial investors look abroad for better opportunities. Figure 17.3 shows the relationship between a country's net capital inflows and the real rate of interest prevailing in that country. When the domestic real interest rate is high, net capital inflows are positive (foreign purchases of domestic assets exceed domestic purchases of foreign assets). But when the real interest rate is low, net capital inflows are negative (that is, the country experiences net capital outflows).[7]

The effect of risk on capital flows is the opposite of the effect of the real interest rate. For a given real interest rate, an increase in the riskiness of domestic assets reduces net capital inflows, as foreigners become less willing to buy the home country's assets, and domestic savers become more inclined to buy foreign assets. For example, political instability, which increases the risk of investing in

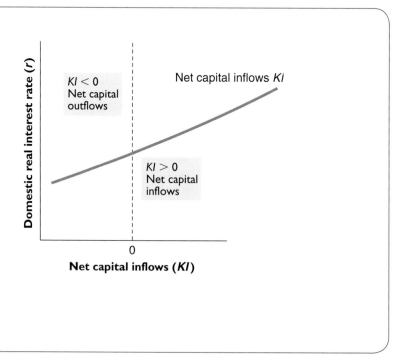

FIGURE 17.3

Net Capital Inflows and the Real Interest Rate
Holding constant the degree of risk and the real returns available abroad, a high real interest rate in the home country will induce foreigners to buy domestic assets, increasing capital inflows. A high real rate in the home country also reduces the incentive for domestic savers to buy foreign assets, reducing capital outflows. Thus, all else being equal, the higher the domestic real interest rate r, the higher will be net capital inflows KI.

[7]The KI curve for a small open economy like Canada's would be rather flat, given the units of measurement of the figure, indicating that a relatively small change in the real interest rate would induce a relatively large change in net capital inflows, and hence that Canadian real interest rates (at least long-term ones) cannot deviate greatly from "world" (or U.S.) real interest rates.

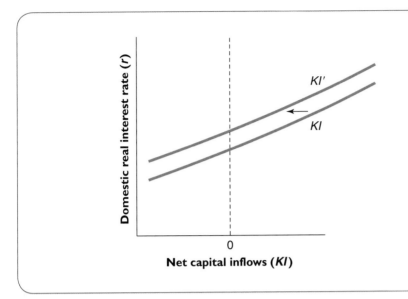

FIGURE 17.4

An Increase in Risk Reduces Net Capital Inflows

An increase in the riskiness of domestic assets arising, for example, from an increase in political instability reduces the willingness of foreign and domestic savers to hold domestic assets. The supply of capital inflows declines at each value of the domestic real interest rate, shifting the *KI* curve to the left.

a country, tends to reduce net capital inflows. Figure 17.4 shows the effect of an increase in risk on capital flows: At each value of the domestic real interest rate, an increase in risk reduces net capital inflows, shifting the capital inflows curve to the left.

EXERCISE 17.4

For given real interest rate and riskiness in the home country, how would you expect net capital inflows to be affected by an increase in real interest rates abroad? Show your answer graphically.

In Economic Naturalist 12.2 we examined the Asian currency crisis of 1997–1998 as an illustration of the risks associated with fixed or pegged exchange rates. Figure 17.4 could be used to illustrate the sharp reduction of net capital inflows that precipitated the crisis.

We now close this chapter, and this textbook, with an Economic Naturalist example that draws upon concepts and hypotheses from several chapters, but especially from this one and from Chapter 16.

ECONOMIC Naturalist 17.2   Why did the Argentine economy collapse in 2001–2002?

Argentina's economic growth following a deep recessionary gap in 2001–2002 was examined from an international trade perspective in Economic Naturalist 15.1. What was the recessionary gap like?

Table 15.1 showed that after posting three straight years of negative growth, the Argentine economy shrank again in 2002, with real GDP per capita dropping 11.7 percent. The unemployment rate exceeded 20 percent. There were riots in the streets of Buenos Aires, and the country went through five different presidents within the span of a few months. What led to this crisis?

Because Argentina is a developing economy with extensive human and natural resources, investment in new capital goods in Argentina could potentially be very profitable. However, Argentina's national saving rate was relatively low. To make up the difference between the demand for investment (new capital goods) and the domestic supply of saving, Argentina borrowed extensively from abroad; that is, capital inflows to Argentina were large. In other words, Argentina had strongly positive non-resident savings (to use the terminology of Chapter 16) or, in yet other words, it ran large current account deficits as is shown

TABLE 17.2

International Capital Flows and Real Interest Rates, Argentina, 1994–2006

1. Year	2. Current account balance/ GDP	3. Real interest rate
1994	−4.3	5.8
1995	−2.0	14.6
1996	−2.5	10.8
1997	−4.1	8.5
1998	−4.8	10.1
1999	−4.2	12.2
2000	−3.2	11.9
2001	−1.4	29.1
2002	8.9	26.1
2003	6.3	5.6
2004	2.1	2.6
2005	2.0	−3.6
2006	2.5	−1.9

SOURCES: Current account balance as a percentage of GDP and inflation rate from http://www.imf.org/external/pubs/ft/weo/2008/01/weodata/index.aspx; nominal interest rate data from http://data.un.org.

in column 2 of Table 17.2. These capital inflows helped Argentina to invest more and grow more rapidly than it otherwise might have. However, the rapid capital inflows also implied that, over time, Argentina was building up a large debt to foreigners (or, in the terminology of Table 16.5, large net foreign liabilities). Foreigners remained willing to lend to Argentina so long as they expected to earn good returns on their loans.

Unfortunately, in 1998 the situation in Argentina took a turn for the worse when the growth rate slowed considerably. Because of the fixed exchange rate (analyzed in Chapter 12) monetary policy could not be used to counter the slowdown. Partly as a result of the slowing economy, which automatically resulted in reduced tax receipts and raised transfer payments to individuals (as we saw in Chapter 16), the government budgetary situation worsened.

Decreased government saving resulted in a reduction of Argentina's national saving (composed of personal saving, corporate saving, and government saving, seen in connection with Figure 16.2), thereby increasing the need to borrow abroad. But at the same time, as a result of the Asian crisis of 1997–1998 (analyzed in Economic Naturalist 12.2) and subsequent crises involving Russia

and Brazil, foreign lenders had become more aware of the risks of lending to emerging market economies. They began to worry that Argentina—with its slowing economy, large current account deficit, and high foreign debt burden—was a riskier location for investment than they had thought.

Increased risk reduces the supply of capital inflows at any given real interest rate, as illustrated by Figure 17.4. Or, in other words, with increased risk higher real interest rates are required to maintain capital inflows. Real interest rates in Argentina reached 29 percent on an annual basis in 2001, as shown by column 3 of Table 17.2. But high real interest rates hamper investment and depress economic growth even further, as we learned in Chapters 9, 10, and 11. And beyond some point, higher real interest rates do not compensate the lender for the risk; it becomes apparent to the lender that the borrower is just not going to be able to repay the loan.

Eventually the Argentine economy collapsed and Argentina defaulted on its international debts. The Argentine example dramatically illustrates the opportunities and the risks that international capital flows represent both for borrower and for lender countries.

SUMMARY

17.1 Financial markets and institutions play the role of allocating funds to the most profitable-looking investment projects. The financial system performs two major functions on behalf of financial investors. First, it provides information to financial investors about which of the many possible uses of their funds are likely to prove most profitable, and thus pay the highest return. For example, financial intermediaries such as banks develop expertise in evaluating prospective borrowers, making it unnecessary for small financial investors to do that on their own. Similarly, stock and bond analysts evaluate the business prospects of a company issuing shares or bonds, and their evaluations affect the price the stock will sell for or the interest rate the company will have to offer on its bonds. Second, financial markets help financial investors share the risks of lending by permitting them to diversify their financial investments—they allow financial investors to avoid having all their "eggs in one basket."

17.1 Present value, or present discounted value, is the value of a sum of money today—that is, the value in the current or initial period. Future value is the value a sum of money grows to at some date in the future when it compounds at a given interest rate.

17.1 In addition to borrowing from banks, corporations can obtain financing by issuing bonds or stocks. A bond is a legal promise to replay a debt, including both the principal amount and regular interest payments. The prices of previously issued bonds decline when interest rates rise. A share of stock, is a claim to partial ownership of a firm. The price of a stock depends positively on the dividend the stock is expected to pay and on the expected future price of the stock, and negatively on the rate of return required by financial investors to hold the stock. The required rate of return is the sum of the return on safe assets and the additional return required to compensate financial investors for the riskiness of stocks, called the risk premium.

17.1 Some countries are characterized by bank–led finance; others rely more heavily upon financial markets (bonds and stocks) for channelling funds to investment.

17.2 The *trade balance,* or net exports, is the value of a country's exports less the value of its imports in a particular period. Exports need not equal imports in each period. If exports exceed imports, the difference is called a *trade surplus,* and if imports exceed exports the difference is called a *trade deficit.* The *current account* is the record of payments and receipts arising from trade in goods and services from international investment income and from international transfers. Trade takes place in assets as well as goods and services. Purchases of domestic assets (real or financial) by foreigners are called *capital inflows,* and purchases of foreign assets by domestic savers are called *capital outflows.* Because imports that are not financed by sales of exports must be financed by sales of assets, the current account balance and net capital inflows sum to zero.

17.2 A low rate of national saving relative to domestic investment (or a high rate of investment relative to national saving) is the primary cause of current account deficits. A country with low savings relative to investment opportunities will attract net capital inflows. Because the sum of the current account balance and capital inflows is zero, a high level of net capital inflows is consistent with a large current account deficit.

17.3 The higher the real interest rate in a country, and the lower the risk of investing there, the higher its net capital inflows. The availability of net capital inflows can expand a country's pool of savings, allowing for more domestic investment and increased growth.

17.3 Some emerging market economies have experienced severe economic crises as the result of sudden shifts in net capital inflows.

17.3 Lending countries have sometimes suffered substantial losses on international loans that have gone into default.

KEY TERMS

bond (441)
capital inflows (447)
capital outflows (447)
coupon payments (441)
coupon rate (441)
current account (448)
dividend (443)

financial intermediaries (440)
future value (FV) (440)
international capital flows (447)
net capital inflows (447)
net capital outflows (447)
present value (PV) (440)

principal amount (441)
risk premium (445)
stock (or equity) (443)
trade balance (or net exports) (447)
trade deficit (447)
trade surplus (447)

REVIEW QUESTIONS

1. Give two ways that the financial system can work on behalf of financial investors. Illustrate with examples.

2. Arjay plans to sell a bond that matures in one year and has a principal value of $1000. What factors determine the price he can expect to get for the bond?

3. Suppose that Amanda is less concerned about risk than the typical person. Are stocks a good financial investment for her? Why or why not?

4. Stock prices surge but the prices of government bonds remain stable. What can you infer from the behaviour of bond prices about the possible causes of the increase in stock values?

5. From the point of view of a given country, say, India, give an example of a capital inflow and a capital outflow.

6. Explain how a country could simultaneously run a trade surplus and a current account deficit.

7. How are capital inflows and outflows related to domestic investment in new capital goods?

8. Explain with examples why, in any period, a country's net capital inflows equal its current account deficit.

9. How would increased political instability in a country likely affect capital inflows, the domestic real interest rate, and investment in new capital goods? Show graphically.

PROBLEMS

1. Simon purchases a bond, newly issued by the Amalgamated Corporation, for $1000. The bond pays $60 to its holder at the end of the first and second years and pays $1060 upon its maturity at the end of the third year.
   a. What are the principal amount, the term, the coupon rate, and the coupon payment for Simon's bond?
   b. After receiving the second coupon payment (at the end of the second year), Simon decides to sell his bond in the bond market. What price can he expect for his bond if the one-year interest rate at that time is 3 percent? 8 percent? 10 percent?
   c. Can you think of a reason that the price of Simon's bond after two years might fall below $1000, even though the market interest rate equals the coupon rate?

2. Shares in Brothers Grimm, Inc., manufacturers of gingerbread houses, are expected to pay a dividend of $5 in one year and to sell for $100 per share at that time. How much should you be willing to pay today per share of Grimm:
   a. If the safe rate of interest is 5 percent and you believe that investing in Grimm carries no risk?
   b. If the safe rate of interest is 10 percent and you believe that investing in Grimm carries no risk?
   c. If the safe rate of interest is 5 percent but your risk premium is 3 percent?
   d. Repeat parts a to c, assuming that Grimm is not expected to pay a dividend but the expected price is unchanged.

3. Your financial investments consist of Canadian government bonds maturing in ten years and shares in a start-up company doing research in pharmaceuticals. How would you expect each of the following news items to affect the value of your assets? Explain.
   a. Interest rates on newly issued government bonds rise.
   b. Inflation is forecasted to be much lower than previously expected (*Hint:* Recall the Fisher effect from Chapter 6.) Assume for simplicity that this information does *not* affect your forecast of the dollar value of the pharmaceutical company's future dividends and stock price.
   In parts c to f, interest rates on newly issued government bonds are assumed to remain unchanged.
   c. Large swings in the stock market increase financial investors' concerns about market risk.
   d. The start-up company whose stock you own announces the development of a valuable new drug. However, the drug will not come to market for at least five years.
   e. The pharmaceutical company announces that it will not pay a dividend next year.
   f. The federal government announces a system of price controls on prescription drugs.

4. You have $1000 to invest and are considering buying some combination of the shares of two U.S. companies, DonkeyInc and ElephantInc. Shares of DonkeyInc will pay a 10 percent return if the Democrats are elected, an event you believe to have a 60 percent probability; otherwise the shares pay a zero return. Shares of ElephantInc will pay 8 percent if the Republicans are elected (a 40 percent probability), zero otherwise. Either the Democrats or the Republicans will be elected.
   a. If your only concern is maximizing your average expected return in U.S. dollars, with no regard for risk, how should you invest your $1000?
   b. What is your expected return if you invest $500 in each stock? (*Hint:* Consider what your return will be if the Democrats win and if the Republicans win, then weight each outcome by the probability that event occurs.)
   c. The strategy of investing $500 in each stock does *not* give the highest possible average expected return. Why might you choose it anyway?

d. Devise an investment strategy that guarantees at least a 4.4 percent return, no matter which party wins.

e. Devise an investment strategy that is riskless, that is, one in which the return on your $1000 does not depend at all on which party wins.

5. How do each of the following transactions affect (1) the current account surplus or deficit and (2) capital inflows or outflows for Canada? Show that in each case the identity that the current account balance plus net capital inflows equals zero applies.

a. A Canadian exporter sells software to Israel. She uses the Israeli shekels received to buy stock in an Israeli company.

b. A Mexican firm uses proceeds from its sale of oil to Canada to buy Canadian government debt.

c. A Mexican firm uses proceeds from its sale of oil to Canada to buy oil drilling equipment from a Canadian firm.

d. A Mexican firm receives Canadian dollars from selling oil to Canada. A French firm accepts the dollars as payment for drilling equipment. The French firm uses the dollars to buy Canadian government debt.

www.bombardier.com
Bombardier

e. A British financial investor writes a cheque on his bank account in Toronto to purchase shares of Bombardier stock (Bombardier is a Canadian company).

6. A country's domestic supply of saving, domestic demand for saving for purposes of capital formation, and supply of net capital inflows are given by the following equations:

$$S = 1500 + 2000r,$$
$$GI = 2000 - 4000r,$$
$$KI = -100 + 6000r.$$

a. Assuming that the market for saving and investment is in equilibrium, find national saving, net capital inflows, domestic investment, and the real interest rate.

b. Repeat part (a), assuming that desired national saving declines by 120 at each value of the real interest rate. What effect does a reduction in domestic saving have on capital inflows?

c. Concern about the economy's macroeconomic policies causes capital inflows to fall sharply so that now $KI = -700 + 6000r$. Repeat part (a). What does a reduction in capital inflows do to domestic investment and the real interest rate?

ANSWERS TO IN-CHAPTER EXERCISES

17.1 Since bond prices fell, interest rates must have risen. To find the interest rate, note that bond investors are willing to pay only $96 today for a bond that will pay back $107 (a coupon payment of $7 plus the principal amount of $100) in one year. To find the one-year return, divide $107 by $96 to get 1.115. Thus the interest rate must have risen to 11.5 percent.

17.2 The share of stock will be worth $81 in one year—the sum of its expected future price and the expected dividend. At an interest rate of 4 percent, its value today is $81/1.04 = $77.88. At an interest rate of 8 percent, the stock's current value is $81/1.08 = $75. Recall from Example 17.3 that when the interest rate is 6 percent, the value of a share of FortuneCookie.com is $76.42. Since higher interest rates imply lower stock values, news that interest rates are about to rise should cause the stock market to fall.

17.3 The purchase of the Japanese bond is a capital outflow for Canada, or $KI = -$20 000$. The Japanese government now holds $20 000. What will it do with these funds? There are basically three possibilities. First, it might use the funds to purchase Canadian goods and services (grain, for example). In that case the Canadian current account balance equals +$20 000, and the sum of the current account balance and capital inflows is zero. Second, the Japanese government might acquire Canadian assets, for example, deposits in Canadian banks. In that case a capital inflow to Canada of $20 000 offsets the original capital outflow. Both the current account balance and net capital outflows individually are zero, and so their sum is zero.

Finally, the Japanese government might use the $20 000 to purchase non-Canadian goods, services, or assets—oil from Saudi Arabia, for example. But then the non-Canadian recipient of the $20 000 is holding the funds, and it has the same options that the Japanese government did. Eventually, the funds will be used to purchase Canadian goods, services, or assets, satisfying Equation 17.3. Indeed, even if the recipient holds onto the funds (in cash, or as a Canadian bank deposit), they would still count as a capital inflow to Canada, as Canadian dollars or an account in a Canadian bank are Canadian assets acquired by foreigners.

17.4 An increase in the real interest rate abroad increases the relative attractiveness of foreign financial investments to both foreign and domestic savers. Net capital inflows to the home country will fall at each level of the domestic real interest rate. The supply curve of net capital inflows shifts left, as in Figure 17.4.

GLOSSARY

A

absolute advantage. one person has an absolute advantage over another if he or she takes fewer hours to perform a task than the other person does

accelerating inflation. when the inflation rate rises from one year to the next

adaptive expectations of inflation. a method of forming expectations about the inflation rate that involves looking to past experience, especially recent past experience

aggregate demand *(ADI)* **curve.** short for aggregate demand/inflation curve, shows the relationship between short-run equilibrium output Y and the rate of inflation π; the name of the curve reflects the fact that short-run equilibrium output is determined by, and equals, total planned spending in the economy; increases in inflation reduce planned spending and short-run equilibrium output, so the aggregate demand *(ADI)* curve is downward-sloping

aggregate demand curve. a relationship between overall spending in the economy and the aggregate price level

aggregate demand-aggregate supply model. a model of real output and overall price level determination

aggregate supply shock. either an inflation shock or a shock to potential output; adverse aggregate supply shocks of both types reduce output and increase inflation

aggregation. the adding up of individual economic variables to obtain economywide totals

anticipated inflation. when the rate of inflation turns out to be roughly what most people had expected

appreciation. an increase in the value of a currency relative to another currency

assets. anything of value that one *owns*

attainable point. any combination of goods that can be produced using currently available resources

automatic stabilizers. provisions in the law that imply automatic increases in government spending or decreases in taxes when real output declines

autonomous expenditure. the portion of planned aggregate expenditure that is independent of output

average benefit. total benefit of undertaking n units of an activity divided by n

average cost. total cost of undertaking n units of an activity divided by n

average labour productivity. output per employed worker

average propensity to consume *(APC)*. consumption divided by disposable income

B

balance-of-payments deficit. the net decline in a country's stock of international reserves over a year

balance-of-payments surplus. the net increase in a country's stock of international reserves over a year

Bank of Canada. Canada's central bank

bank rate. the interest rate that the Bank of Canada charges commercial banks for overnight loans, it corresponds to the upper limit of the Bank of Canada's operating band for the overnight rate; for decades, it was the Bank's official interest rate

bank reserves. cash or similar assets held by commercial banks for the purpose of meeting depositor withdrawals and payments

banking panic. a rush of withdrawals from the banking system made by depositors responding to news or rumours of impending bankruptcy of one or more banks

barter. the direct trade of goods or services for other goods or services

bequest saving. saving done for the purpose of leaving an inheritance

bond. a legal promise to repay a debt, usually including both the principal amount and regular interest payments

boom. a particularly strong and protracted phase of an expansion

C

capital consumption allowances. accounting allowances for the using up of fixed capital in the production process

capital gains. increases in the value of existing assets

capital good. a long-lived good, which is itself produced and used to produce other goods and services

capital inflows. purchases of domestic assets by foreign households and firms

capital losses. decreases in the values of existing assets

capital outflows. purchases of foreign assets by domestic households and firms

change in demand. a shift of the entire demand curve

change in supply. a shift of the entire supply curve

change in quantity demanded. a movement along the demand curve that occurs in response to a change in price

change in quantity supplied. a movement along the supply curve that occurs in response to a change in price

closed economy. an economy that does not trade with the rest of the world; also know as an autarky

commodity money. an asset with intrinsic value, such as a gold or silver coin, that is generally accepted as a means of payment for purchases and settling debts

common market. two or more countries eliminating trade restrictions on most or all mutual trade, maintaining a common set of trade barriers against imports from non-member countries, and permitting mobility of capital and labour among member countries

comparative advantage. one person has a comparative advantage over another if his or her opportunity cost of performing a task is lower than the other person's opportunity cost

complements. two goods are complements in consumption if an increase in the price of one causes a leftward shift in the demand curve for the other

compound interest. the payment of interest not only on the original deposit but on all previously accumulated interest

constant (or parameter). a quantity that is fixed in value

consumer price index (CPI). for any period, measures the cost in that period of a standard basket of goods and services relative to the cost of the same basket of goods and services in a fixed year, called the *base year*

consumption. spending by households on goods and services, such as food, clothing, and entertainment

consumption function. the relationship between consumption spending and its determinants, such as disposable (after-tax) income

contractionary policies. government policy actions designed to reduce planned spending and output

coupon payments. regular interest payments made to the bondholder

coupon rate. the interest rate promised when a bond is issued

current account. the record of payments and receipts arising from trade in goods and services, from international investment income, and from international transfers

customs union. two or more countries that not only agree to eliminate tariffs and other trade restrictions on most or all mutual trade but also agree to a common set of trade barriers to imports from non-member countries

cyclical unemployment. the extra unemployment brought about by periods of recession

D

deflating (a nominal quantity). the process of dividing a nominal quantity by a price index (such as the CPI) to express the quantity in real terms

deflation. a situation in which the prices of most goods and services are falling over time so that inflation is negative

demand curve. a curve or schedule showing the total quantity of a good of uniform quality that buyers want to buy at each price during a particular period of time provided that all other things are held constant

Department of Foreign Affairs and International Trade (DFAIT). a department of Canada's federal government led by multiple cabinet ministers; responsibility for international trade policy is shared between the Minister of International Trade and the Department of Finance

dependent variable. a variable in an equation whose value is *determined* by the value taken by another variable in the equation

depreciation. a decrease in the value of a currency relative to another currency

depression. a particularly severe or protracted recession

devaluation. a reduction in the official value of a currency (in a fixed-exchange-rate system)

diminishing returns to capital. if the amount of labour and other inputs employed is held constant, then the greater the amount of capital already in use, the less an additional unit of capital will tend to add to production

discouraged workers. people who say they would like to have a job but have not made an effort to find one in the past four weeks

discretionary fiscal policy. changes in government spending and taxation deliberately made to stabilize aggregate expenditure

disinflation. when the inflation rate falls from one year to the next

dividend. a regular payment received by stockholders for each share that they own

downward nominal wage rigidity hypothesis. the claim that low levels of inflation will reduce efficiency because real wage cuts will then typically require nominal wage cuts, which will be resisted

E

economic and monetary union. a common market with a single currency but made up of any number of member countries

economic efficiency. condition that occurs when all goods and services are produced and consumed at their respective socially optimal levels

economic surplus. the benefit of taking any action minus its cost

economics. the study of how people make choices under conditions of scarcity and of the results of those choices for society

economy-wide marginal tax rate. the amount by which taxes rise when income rises by $1

efficiency. obtaining the maximum possible output from a given amount of inputs

efficient point. any combination of goods for which currently available resources do not allow an increase in the production of one good without a reduction in the production of the other

efficient quantity. the quantity that results in the maximum possible economic surplus from producing and consuming the good

entrepreneurship. behaviour that results in new products, services, technological processes, or organizational innovations that are productivity-enhancing

equation. a mathematical expression that describes the relationship between two or more variables

equilibrium. a state that occurs when all of the forces that act on all the variables in a system are in balance, exactly offsetting each other so that none of the variables in the system has any tendency to change

equilibrium price and equilibrium quantity. the price and quantity of a good at the intersection of the supply and demand curves for the good

equity. a state of impartiality and fairness

European Central Bank (ECB). the central bank of the euro zone countries

excess demand, or shortage. the difference between the quantity supplied and the quantity demanded when the price of a good lies below the equilibrium price; buyers are dissatisfied when there is excess demand

excess supply, or surplus. the difference between the quantity supplied and the quantity demanded when the price of a good exceeds the equilibrium price; some sellers are dissatisfied when there is excess supply

expansion. a period in which the economy is growing at a rate significantly above normal

expansionary gap. a negative output gap, which occurs when actual output is higher than potential output

expansionary policies. government policy actions intended to increase planned spending and output

expectations-augmented Phillips curve model. distinguishes between a short-run Phillips curve and a long-run Phillips curve and argues that short-run Phillips curves shift when expectations about the inflation rate change

F

fallacy of composition. the argument that because something is true for a part, it also is true for the whole; the mistake of falsely assuming that what is true at the level of a particular individual, household, firm, or industry is necessarily true at a higher aggregate level

fair competition. the practice of discouraging both export subsidies and the dumping of products on foreign markets at below cost in order to gain market share

Federal Reserve System (the Fed). the central bank of the United States; also known as the Fed

fiat money. an asset with no intrinsic value, such as paper currency, that is generally accepted as a means of payment for purchases and the settling of debts

final goods or services. consumed by the ultimate user; because they are the end products of the production process, they are counted as part of GDP

financial intermediaries. firms that extend credit to borrowers using funds raised from savers

fiscal policy. decisions that determine the government's budget, including the amount and composition of government expenditures and government revenues

Fisher effect. the tendency for nominal interest rates to be high when inflation is high and low when inflation is low

fixed exchange rate. an exchange rate whose value is set by official government policy

flexible exchange rate. an exchange rate whose value is not officially fixed but varies according to the supply of and demand for the currency in the foreign exchange market

flow. a measure that is defined *per unit of time*

foreign exchange market. the market on which currencies of various nations are traded for one another

foreign trade effect. the hypothesis that net exports will be inversely related to the overall price level, and therefore that aggregate demand and the price level will be inversely related

fractional-reserve banking system. a banking system in which bank reserves are less than deposits so that the reserve-deposit ratio is less than 100 percent

free trade area. involves two or more countries that agree to eliminate tariffs and other trade restrictions on most or all mutual trade of their own goods and services; they may each have different tariffs for imports from non-member countries

frictional unemployment. the short-term unemployment associated with the process of matching workers with jobs

fundamental value of the exchange rate (or equilibrium exchange rate). the exchange rate that equates the quantities of the currency supplied and demanded in the foreign exchange market

future value *(FV)*. the value a sum of money grows at some date in the future, when it compounds at a given interest rate

G

GDP deflator. a measure of the price level of goods and services included in GDP

General Agreement on Tariffs and Trade (GATT). a multilateral agreement dating back to the late 1940s that, through numerous rounds of trade negotiations, led to reduced tariffs and quotas among many countries

government budget balance. the difference between government revenues and expenditures; it equals zero when revenues equal expenditure, is positive when revenues exceed expenditures, and is negative when revenues fall short of expenditures

government budget deficit. when government revenues fall short of expenditures; this is, the government budget balance is negative

government budget surplus. when government revenues exceed expenditures; that is, the government budget balance is positive

government deposit shifting. the transfer of government deposits by the central bank between the government's account at the central bank and the government's accounts at commercial banks

government purchases. purchases by federal, provincial, and municipal governments of final goods and services; government purchases do not include government transfer payments, nor do they include interest paid on the public debt

gross domestic product (GDP). the market value of the final goods and services produced in a country during a given period

gross investment. the sum of private-sector and government investment

gross national income (GNI). the market value of goods and services produced by factors of production owned by the residents of a country; formerly known as GNP

gross saving. the sum of household, corporate, government, and non-resident saving

H

high inflation. typically means inflation greater than 6 percent per year

hyperinflation. typically means inflation greater than 500 percent per year

I

import quota. a legal limit laced on the quantity of a good that may be imported

income-expenditure multiplier. the effect of a one-unit increase in autonomous aggregate demand on short-run equilibrium output

independent variable. a variable in an equation whose value *determines* the value taken by another variable in the equation

indexing. the practice of increasing a nominal quantity each period by an amount equal to the percentage increase in a specified price index; indexing prevents the purchasing power of the nominal quantity from being eroded by inflation

induced expenditure. the portion of planned aggregate expenditure that depends on output Y

inefficient point. any combination of goods for which currently available resources enable an increase in the production of one good without a reduction in the production of the other

inferior good. a good whose demand curve shifts leftward when the incomes of buyers increase

inflation adjustment (IA) line. a horizontal line showing the current rate of inflation, as determined by past expectations and pricing decisions

inflation shock. a sudden change in the normal behaviour of inflation, unrelated to the nation's output gap

inputs. goods or services used in the process of producing a different good or service

intermediate goods or services. used up in the production of final goods and services and therefore not counted as part of GDP

international capital flows. purchases or sales of real and financial assets across international borders

international reserves. foreign currency assets held by a government for the purpose of purchasing the domestic currency in the foreign exchange market

K

key policy rate. the interest rate employed by the central bank as its major policy tool; the key policy rate for the Bank

of Canada, which is also called its official interest rate, is the target for the overnight rate

L

labour force. the total number of employed and unemployed people in the economy

Large Value Transfer System (LVTS). an electronic wire system overseen by the Bank of Canada that allows major financial institutions operating in Canada to send large payments back and forth to each other

law of one price. if transportation costs are relatively small, the price of an internationally traded commodity will be the same in all locations

liabilities. the debts one *owes*

life-cycle saving. saving to meet long-term objectives, such as retirement, university attendance, or the purchase of a home

long-run aggregate supply (LRAS) curve. a relationship between potential output and the overall price level; the vertical *LRAS* curve indicates that potential output is independent of the overall price level

long-run aggregate supply (LRAS) line. a vertical line showing the economy's potential output Y*

long-run equilibrium. a situation in which actual output equals potential output and the inflation rate is stable; graphically, long-run equilibrium occurs when the *ADI* curve, the *IA* line, and the *LRAS* line all intersect at a single point

long-run Phillips curve. a relationship between the inflation rate and the unemployment rate in the long run; the vertical long-run Phillips curve is drawn at the natural rate of unemployment

low inflation. typically means inflation between 1 and 3 percent per year

M

M1. sum of currency outstanding and balances held in chequing accounts

M2. all the assets in M1 plus some additional assets that are usable in making payments but at greater cost or inconvenience than currency or chequing accounts

macroeconomic policies. government actions designed to affect the performance of the economy as a whole

macroeconomics. the study of the performance of national economies and the policies that governments use to try to improve that performance

marginal benefit. the increase in total benefit that results from carrying out one more unit of an activity

marginal cost. the increase in total cost that results from carrying out one additional unit of an activity

marginal propensity to consume (MPC). the amount by which consumption rises when disposable income rises by $1; we assume that $0 < MPC < 1$

marginal propensity to import. the amount by which imports rise when income rises by $1

market. the context in which potential buyers and sellers of a good or service can negotiate exchanges

market equilibrium. occurs when all buyers and sellers are satisfied with their respective quantities at the market price

medium of exchange. an asset used in purchasing goods and services

menu costs. the costs of changing prices

microeconomics. the study of individual choice under scarcity, and its implications for the behaviour of prices and quantities in individual markets

moderate inflation. typically means inflation between 3 and 6 percent per year

modern central banking theory. the view that the central bank changes its official interest rate directly and commercial banks respond by changing market interest rates

monetary policy. central bank management of interest rates to achieve macroeconomic objectives

money. any asset that can be used as a means of payment for purchases and to settle debts

most-favoured nation (MFN) treatment. an agreement that any special arrangement, such as a reduced tariff that is offered to one country (the most-favoured nation), in the interests of opening up a market must be offered to all other members

multilateral agreement. a document signed by representatives of many nations to express their acceptance of the principles set out in the document

N

national net worth. the total value of the real assets of a country adjusted for its net foreign liabilities

national saving. the sum of gross saving by the household sector, the corporate sector, and the government sector

national treatment. once a good has entered a country it must be treated as equivalent to a domestically produced good of the same type for purposes of taxation and regulation

national wealth. the total value of real assets in a country

natural rate of unemployment (or *u).** the part of the total unemployment rate that is attributable to frictional, structural, and seasonal unemployment; equivalently, the unemployment rate that prevails when cyclical unemployment is zero, so the economy has neither a recessionary nor an expansionary output gap

net capital inflows. capital inflows minus capital outflows

net capital outflows. capital outflows minus capital inflows

net exports. exports minus imports

net international liabilities. the value of financial claims of non-residents on Canadian wealth net of the value of financial claims of Canadian residents against foreign wealth

nominal exchange rate. the rate at which two currencies can be traded for each other

nominal GDP. a measure of GDP in which the quantities produced are valued at current-year prices; nominal GDP measures the *current dollar value* of production

nominal interest rate. the type of interest rate you usually encounter in everyday life—the price paid per dollar borrowed per year

nominal quantity. a quantity that is measured in terms of its current dollar value

non-resident saving. the balance between saving provided to the Canadian economy by non-residents and saving provided to foreign economies by residents of Canada

normal good. a good whose demand curve shifts rightward when the incomes of buyers increase

normative economics. economic statements that reflect subjective value judgments and that are based on ethical positions

O

Okun's law. states that each extra percentage point of cyclical unemployment is associated with about a 2-percentage-point increase in the output gap, measured in relation to potential output

100 percent reserve banking. a situation in which banks' reserves equal 100 percent of their deposits

open economy. an economy that trades with other countries

open-market operations. open-market purchases and open-market sales

open-market purchase. the purchase of government bonds from the public by the central bank for the purpose of increasing the supply of bank reserves

open-market sale. the sale by the central bank of government bonds for the purpose of reducing bank reserves

operating band. a term used by the Bank of Canada to describe the range of possible overnight interest rates: from 0.25 percentage points below the overnight rate target to 0.25 percentage points above the target

opportunity cost. the value of the next-best alternative that must be forgone in order to undertake the activity

output gap (or $Y^* - Y$). the difference between the economy's potential output and its actual output at a point in time

overnight rate. the market interest rate that financial institutions charge each other for overnight loans

overnight rate target. the interest rate that the Bank of Canada wants to prevail in the financial market where major Canadian institutions borrow and lend funds to settle daily transactions with one another

overvalued exchange rate. an exchange rate that has an officially fixed value greater than its fundamental value

P

participation rate. the labour force divided by the working-age population

parameter (or constant). a quantity that is fixed in value

peak. the beginning of a recession, the high point of economic activity prior to a downturn

Phillips curve. a term that typically refers to a statistical relationship between the inflation rate and the unemployment rate

planned aggregate expenditure *(PAE)*. total planned spending on final goods and services

policy reaction function. describes how the action a policy-maker takes depends on the state of the economy

positive economics. economic analysis that offers cause-and-effect explanations of economic relationships; the propositions, or hypotheses, that emerge from positive economics can, in principle, be confirmed or refuted by data; in principle, data can also be used to measure the magnitude of effects predicted by positive economics

***post hoc* fallacy.** the argument that because event A precedes event B, event A causes event B

potential output (or potential GDP or full-employment output or Y^*). the amount of output (real GDP) that an economy can produce when using its resources, such as capital and labour, at normal rates

power of compound growth. the fact that small differences in growth rates, maintained over long periods, will produce large differences in magnitude

precautionary saving. saving for protection against unexpected setbacks, such as the loss of a job

present value *(PV)*. or present discounted value, is the value of a sum of money today—that is, the value in the current or initial period

price index. a measure of the average price of a given class of goods or services relative to the price of the same goods and services in a base year

price level. the overall level of prices at a point in time as measured by a price index such as the CPI

price signal distortion hypothesis. the claim that any substantial amount of change in the price level will make it difficult for market participants to interpret the extent to which price changes involve relative price changes

principal amount. the amount originally lent

prime business rate. the interest rate that commerical banks charge to their least risky business borrowers; also called the prime rate

private-sector investment. spending by firms on final goods and services, primarily capital goods and housing

production possibilities curve. a graph that describes the maximum amount of one good that can be produced for every possible level of production of the other good

productivity. units of output per hour divided by units of input per hour

protective tariff. a tax on imported goods; the intention is to shield domestic industry from import competition

purchasing power parity (PPP). the theory that nominal exchange rates are determined as necessary for the law of one price to hold

Q

quantity demanded. the total amount of a good of uniform quality purchased at a single, specific price by all buyers during a particular period of time

quantity equation. an amount of money times its velocity equals nominal GDP; $M \times V = P \times Y$

quantity supplied. the total amount of a good of uniform quality that all sellers are willing to produce and sell at a single, specific price during a paricular period of time

R

rate of inflation. the annual percentage rate of change in the price level as measured, for example, by the CPI

rational person. someone with well-defined goals who tries to fulfill those goals as best as he or she can

real-balances effect. the hypothesis that overall wealth in the economy will be inversely related to the overall price level, and therefore that aggregate demand and the price level will be inversely related

real exchange rate. the price of the average domestic good or service *relative* to the price of the average foreign good or service, when prices are expressed in terms of a common currency

real GDP. a measure of GDP in which the quantities produced are valued at the prices in a base year rather than at current prices

real interest rate. the nominal interest rate minus the inflation rate

real quantity. a quantity that is measured in constant dollar terms

real wage. the wage paid to workers measured in terms of real purchasing power

recession (or contraction). a period in which the economy is growing at a rate significantly below normal

recessionary gap. a positive output gap, which occurs when potential output exceeds actual output

regional trade agreement. aims to reduce restrictions on international trade between two or more countries, usually within a certain region

relative price. the price of a specific good or service *in comparison* to the prices of other goods and services

reserve requirements. set by some central banks, the minimum values of the ratio of bank reserves to bank deposits that commercial banks are allowed to maintain; the Bank of Canada does not set reserve requirements

reserve-deposit ratio. bank reserves divided by deposits

revaluation. an increase in the official value of a currency (in a fixed-exchange-rate system)

revenue tariff. a tax imposed on imported goods; for the purpose of collecting government revenue

rise. vertical distance a straight line travels between any two points

risk premium. the rate of return that financial investors require to hold risky assets minus the rate of return on safe assets

rule of 72. a rule of thumb stating that to find the number of years it takes a magnitude to double when it is growing at a constant rate, divide 72 by the growth rate

run. horizontal distance a straight line travels between any two points

S

sale and repurchase agreement (SRA). a financial transaction, used to reinforce the overnight rate target, in which the bank of Canada sells Government of Canada bonds in the overnight market with an agreement to buy them back the next business day; SRAs are initiated by the Bank when overnight funds are trading below the target rate

saving. current income minus spending on current needs; a flow

saving rate. saving divided by income

sector-specific trade agreement. international trade agreement for the products of a particular economic sector, such as the softwood lumber industry

seasonal unemployment. unemployment associated with the seasons and/or weather

settlement balances. accounts held at the Bank of Canada by financial institutions for the purpose of settling their net payment obligations to one another

shortage. the difference between the quantity supplied and the quantity demanded when the price of a good lies below the equilibrium price; some buyers are dissatisfied when there is excess demand

short-run aggregate supply (SRAS) curve. a relationship between real output and the overall price level in the short run; the horizontal *SRAS* curve indicates that firms in the short run meet demand, on average, at existing prices

short-run equilibrium. a situation in which inflation equals the value determined by past expectations and pricing decisions, and output equals the level of short-run equilibrium output that is consistent with that inflation rate; graphically, short-run equilibrium occurs at the intersection of the *ADI* curve and the *IA* line

short-run equilibrium output. the level of output at which output *Y* equals planned aggregate expenditure; the level of output that prevails during the period in which prices are predetermined

short-run Phillips curve. a relationship between actual unemployment and the inflation rate for given inflationary expectations

slope. in a straight line, the ratio of the vertical distance the straight line travels between any two points (*rise*) to the corresponding horizontal distance (*run*)

speculative attack. a massive selling of domestic currency assets by financial investors

special purchase and resale agreement (SPRA). a financial transaction, used to reinforce the overnight rate target, in which the Bank of Canada buys Government of Canada bonds in the overnight market with an agreement to sell them back the next business day; SPRAs are initiated by the Bank when overnight funds are trading above the target rate

stabilization policies. government policies that are used to affect planned aggregate expenditure, with the objective of eliminating output gaps

stable inflation. when the inflation rate stays roughly constant from one year to the next

stagflation. the combination of a recessionary gap and a rising price level

stock. a measure that is defined *at a point in time*

stock (or equity). a claim to partial ownership of a firm

store of value. an asset that serves as a means of holding wealth

structural policy. government policies aimed at changing the underlying structure, or institutions, of the nation's economy

structural unemployment. unemployment that occurs when workers are unable to fill available jobs because they lack the skills, or do not live where jobs are available

substitutes. two goods are substitutes in consumption if an increase in the price of one causes a rightward shift in the demand curve for the other

sunk cost. a cost that is beyond recovery at the moment a decision must be made

supply curve. a curve or schedule showing the total quantity of a good of uniform quality that all sellers want to sell at each price during a particular period of time provided that all other things are held constant

T

tariff. a tax imposed on an imported good

technology. the stock of knowledge, useful in producing goods and services, that is available to a society

technological depletion hypothesis. the theory that the productivity slowdown after 1973 was due to the depletion of the backlog of technological advances made but not implemented during the 1930s and the Second World War

time value of money. the fact that a given dollar amount today is equivalent to a larger dollar amount in the future, because the money can be invested in an interest-bearing account in the meantime

trade balance (or net exports). the value of a country's exports less the value of its imports in a particular period (quarter or year)

trade deficit. when imports exceed exports—the difference between the value of a country's imports and the value of its exports in a given period

trade diversion. a reduction of trade barriers among members of a trading bloc causes trade among them to take the place of trade with countries outside the bloc

trade surplus. when exports exceed imports—the difference between the value of a country's exports and the value of its imports in a given period

trough. the end of a recession, the low point of economic activity prior to a recovery

U

unanticipated inflation. when the rate of inflation turns out to be substantially different from what most people had expected

unattainable point. any combination of goods that cannot be produced using currently available resources

undervalued exchange rate. an exchange rate that has an officially fixed value less than its fundamental value

unemployment rate. the number of unemployed people divided by the labour force

unit of account. a basic measure of economic value

V

value added. for any firm, the market value of its product or service minus the cost of inputs purchased from other firms

variable. a quantity that is free to take a range of different values

velocity of money. A measure of the speed at which money changes hands in transactions involving final goods and services; $V = (P \times Y)/M$

vertical intercept. in a straight line, the value taken by the dependent variable when the independent variable equals zero

W

wealth. the value of assets minus liabilities

wealth effect. the tendency of changes in asset prices to affect households' wealth and thus their spending on consumption goods and services

world price. the price at which a good or service is traded on international markets

World Trade Organization (WTO). official international trade body headquartered in Geneva that began operation in 1995; superseded the GATT as an unofficial, de facto trade organization

Z

zero bound on nominal interest rates hypothesis. the claim that because interest rates cannot go below zero, a central bank may be unable to stimulate the economy with rate cuts if the official interest rate is low to begin with

zero inflation. when the price level stays roughly constant from one year to the next

INDEX

CANADIAN MACROECONOMIC DATA TABLE, 1976–2007

What's happening to our standard of living? Are jobs readily available? Are we investing enough? Is our wealth increasing? Is the cost of living under control? These are examples of macroeconomic questions. From the millions of time series in Statistics Canada's CANSIM database, here are 28 of the most important ones for answering such questions.

		1976	1977	1978	1979	1980	1981	1982	1983	1984	1985	1986	1987	1988	1989
1	Consumption expenditure, $B	107.8	120.2	134.4	150.1	168.5	190.4	204.1	224.1	244.2	266.7	288.6	312.3	338.5	365.5
	(Share of GDP, %)	53.9	54.4	54.9	53.7	53.6	52.8	53.7	54.5	54.3	54.9	56.3	55.9	55.2	55.6
2	Private-sector investment, $B	42.4	45.0	48.2	60.5	63.0	78.7	61.1	69.4	79.2	86.9	93.5	108.2	123.6	134.6
	(Share of GDP, %)	21.2	20.3	19.7	21.6	20.0	21.8	16.1	16.9	17.6	17.9	18.2	19.4	20.2	20.5
3	Government purchases, $B	50.2	56.7	61.2	67.2	76.3	87.2	99.2	105.4	111.1	120.7	126.0	133.1	144.4	157.0
	(Share of GDP, %)	25.1	25.6	25.0	24.0	24.3	24.2	26.1	25.6	24.7	24.9	24.6	23.8	23.6	23.9
4	Net exports, $B	−1.4	−0.4	0.9	1.6	5.8	2.6	14.8	13.4	15.8	11.3	5.0	6.6	4.7	0.2
	(Share of GDP, %)	−0.7	−0.2	0.4	0.6	1.9	0.7	3.9	3.3	3.5	2.3	1.0	1.2	0.8	0.0
5	GDP at market prices, $B	200.0	221.0	244.9	279.6	314.4	360.5	379.9	411.4	449.6	485.7	512.5	558.9	613.1	657.7
6	GNP at market prices, $B	196.4	216.3	238.8	271.9	305.8	348.3	366.6	399.2	435.4	470.6	495.1	541.6	593.3	635.2
	(Percentage of GDP)	98.2	97.9	97.5	97.3	97.3	96.6	96.5	97.0	96.8	96.9	96.6	96.9	96.8	96.6
7	Personal disposable income, $B	127.8	141.7	160.1	180.7	205.6	238.6	263.5	275.5	299.2	323.0	340.4	362.2	395.2	432.8
	(Percentage of GDP)	63.9	64.1	65.4	64.6	65.4	66.2	69.4	67.0	66.5	66.5	66.4	64.8	64.5	65.8
8	Personal saving, $B	17.5	18.9	22.8	26.5	32.1	41.6	53.1	46.5	49.9	50.9	45.8	43.1	48.7	56.3
	(Share of gross saving, %)	35.6	36.1	40.7	38.6	44.4	46.5	72.5	57.2	54.2	50.1	42.3	34.9	34.7	36.7
9	Corporate saving, $B	8.0	6.7	6.9	10.0	10.2	2.9	−4.7	9.2	14.8	19.0	13.9	22.4	26.3	19.7
	(Share of gross saving, %)	16.3	12.9	12.4	14.5	14.1	3.2	−6.4	11.3	16.0	18.7	12.9	18.1	18.8	12.8
10	Government saving, $B	−2.1	−4.4	−6.8	−5.7	−8.5	−4.5	−19.0	−25.0	−26.6	−31.3	−28.2	−22.7	−17.9	−21.4
	(Share of gross saving, %)	−4.3	−8.4	−12.1	−8.3	−11.8	−5.0	−26.0	−30.8	−28.8	−30.8	−26.0	−18.4	−12.7	−14.0
11	Non-resident saving, $B	5.2	5.3	5.5	6.3	2.8	9.6	−1.4	−0.7	−0.8	4.7	12.9	11.9	16.1	23.5
	(Share of gross saving, %)	10.6	10.1	9.9	9.2	3.8	10.7	−1.9	−0.9	−0.9	4.7	11.9	9.6	11.5	15.3
12	Capital consumption, $B	22.5	24.9	27.8	32.1	37.2	43.0	46.7	49.6	53.3	58.4	62.6	66.3	70.5	75.9
	(Share of gross saving, %)	45.7	47.7	49.7	46.7	51.5	48.1	63.8	61.0	57.8	57.5	57.9	53.7	50.3	49.6
13	Gross investment, $B	49.2	52.3	55.9	68.6	72.3	89.4	73.3	81.3	92.2	101.6	108.1	123.5	140.1	153.1
	(Share of GDP, %)	24.6	23.6	22.8	24.5	23.0	24.8	19.3	19.8	20.5	20.9	21.1	22.1	22.9	23.3
14	National wealth, $B	738.4	822.4	924.5	1061.1	1210.5	1366.8	1453.1	1515.9	1598.7	1686.8	1815.2	1965.1	2140.1	2326.3
	(Percentage of GDP)	369.2	372.2	377.5	379.5	385.0	379.2	382.5	368.5	355.6	347.3	354.2	351.6	349.1	353.7
15	Current account balance, $B	−7.5	−7.4	−9.4	−9.8	−7.1	−15.0	2.3	−3.1	−1.7	−7.8	−15.5	−17.8	−18.3	−25.8
	(Percentage of GDP)	−3.8	−3.4	−3.8	−3.5	−2.3	−4.2	0.6	−0.8	−0.4	−1.6	−3.0	−3.2	−3.0	−3.9
16	Net int'l investment position, $B	−61.3	−68.7	−88.1	−103.2	−110.3	−135.7	−136.6	−144.3	−154.4	−177.8	−196.8	−212.6	−215.9	−232.1
	(Percentage of GDP)	−30.7	−31.1	−36.0	−36.9	−35.1	−37.7	−36.0	−35.1	−34.3	−36.6	−38.4	−38.0	−35.2	−35.3
17	National net worth, $B	677.1	753.8	836.4	957.9	1100.2	1231.0	1316.5	1371.6	1444.3	1509.0	1618.4	1752.5	1924.2	2094.2
	(Percentage of GDP)	338.6	341.1	341.6	342.6	350.0	341.5	346.6	333.4	321.2	310.7	315.8	313.5	313.8	318.4
18	Net federal debt-GDP ratio (%)	14.3	14.8	18.7	21.1	23.1	23.9	26.2	31.2	36.6	43.2	47.8	49.5	49.8	50.7
19	CPI inflation rate (%)	7.2	8.0	8.9	9.3	10.0	12.5	10.9	5.8	4.3	4.0	4.1	4.4	3.9	5.1
20	Short-term interest rate (%)	8.9	7.4	8.6	11.6	12.7	17.8	13.8	9.3	11.1	9.5	9.0	8.2	9.4	12.0
21	Exchange rate (U.S.$ per C$)	1.01	0.94	0.88	0.85	0.86	0.83	0.81	0.81	0.77	0.73	0.72	0.75	0.81	0.84
22	Population (millions)	23.4	23.7	24.0	24.2	24.5	24.8	25.1	25.4	25.6	25.8	26.1	26.4	26.8	27.3
23	Working-age population (millions)	17.1	17.4	17.8	18.1	18.5	18.8	19.1	19.4	19.6	19.8	20.1	20.3	20.6	20.9
24	Labour force (millions)	10.5	10.8	11.1	11.5	11.9	12.2	12.3	12.5	12.7	13.0	13.3	13.5	13.8	14.0
25	Employment (millions)	9.8	9.9	10.2	10.7	11.0	11.3	10.9	11.0	11.3	11.6	12.0	12.3	12.7	13.0
26	Labour productivity (2002$, 1000s)	56.3	57.2	57.7	57.4	56.9	57.3	57.5	58.6	60.5	61.6	61.2	62.0	63.2	63.4
27	Unemployment rate (%)	7.1	8.0	8.3	7.5	7.5	7.6	11.0	12.0	11.3	10.7	9.7	8.8	7.8	7.6
28	Growth of real GDP per capita (%)	3.8	2.3	2.9	2.8	0.9	2.2	−4.0	1.7	4.8	3.8	1.4	2.9	3.6	0.8
		1976	1977	1978	1979	1980	1981	1982	1983	1984	1985	1986	1987	1988	1989

Note: Series 1 to 17 are in billions of *current* (or *nominal*) dollars. For any given year, the data series numbered 1 through 4 sum to the series numbered 5 (except for a statistical discrepancy). They are also expressed as shares of GDP. Series 8 through 12 sum to series 13 (except for a statistical discrepancy). They are also expressed as shares of gross saving (which equals gross investment). Series 14, 16, and 17 measure *stocks* (at a point in time). They are also expressed as percentages of GDP. Series 18 compares a *stock* (debt) to a *flow* (GDP). Estimates listed below are as presented by Statistics Canada as of mid-August 2008; current estimates may differ. Further details are provided in the table of explanatory notes.

1990	1991	1992	1993	1994	1995	1996	1997	1998	1999	2000	2001	2002	2003	2004	2005	2006	2007	
385.4	398.3	411.2	428.2	445.9	460.9	480.4	510.7	531.2	560.9	596.0	620.6	655.7	686.6	719.9	759.2	803.3	852.8	1
56.7	*58.1*	*58.7*	*58.9*	*57.8*	*56.9*	*57.4*	*57.9*	*58.1*	*57.1*	*55.4*	*56.0*	*56.9*	*56.6*	*55.8*	*55.3*	*55.4*	*55.5*	
121.9	108.5	104.8	110.0	123.8	130.6	131.6	162.9	166.5	176.4	193.3	185.2	193.9	212.4	235.0	264.6	291.2	311.5	2
17.9	*15.8*	*15.0*	*15.1*	*16.1*	*16.1*	*15.7*	*18.5*	*18.2*	*18.0*	*18.0*	*16.7*	*16.8*	*17.5*	*18.2*	*19.3*	*20.1*	*20.3*	
171.7	182.5	188.7	191.0	193.2	193.9	191.7	191.9	199.3	209.1	224.6	239.0	253.0	268.5	279.9	297.2	319.8	342.2	3
25.3	*26.6*	*26.9*	*26.3*	*25.1*	*23.9*	*22.9*	*21.7*	*21.8*	*21.3*	*20.9*	*21.6*	*21.9*	*22.1*	*21.7*	*21.7*	*22.0*	*22.3*	
0.9	−3.9	−2.6	0.0	9.1	25.9	33.7	17.3	18.3	36.0	61.9	63.6	50.9	45.6	55.7	51.1	35.7	29.9	4
0.1	*−0.6*	*−0.4*	*0.0*	*1.2*	*3.2*	*4.0*	*2.0*	*2.0*	*3.7*	*5.8*	*5.7*	*4.4*	*3.8*	*4.3*	*3.7*	*2.5*	*1.9*	
679.9	685.4	700.5	727.2	770.9	810.4	836.9	882.7	915.0	982.4	1076.6	1108.2	1152.9	1213.2	1290.9	1372.6	1450.5	1535.6	5
655.5	662.5	675.1	702.0	742.9	781.9	808.5	855.0	884.6	949.2	1048.5	1076.7	1124.0	1184.6	1264.6	1348.1	1437.9	1514.5	6
96.4	*96.7*	*96.4*	*96.5*	*96.4*	*96.5*	*96.6*	*96.9*	*96.7*	*96.6*	*97.4*	*97.2*	*97.5*	*97.6*	*98.0*	*98.2*	*99.1*	*98.7*	
457.4	472.5	483.4	494.9	501.7	519.6	527.8	546.2	568.8	596.2	639.6	669.2	694.0	720.9	760.5	793.8	849.6	898.4	7
67.3	*68.9*	*69.0*	*68.1*	*65.1*	*64.1*	*63.1*	*61.9*	*62.2*	*60.7*	*59.4*	*60.4*	*60.2*	*59.4*	*58.9*	*57.8*	*58.6*	*58.1*	
59.3	62.7	62.9	58.7	47.4	47.9	37.0	26.6	27.6	23.9	29.9	34.5	24.0	19.1	24.1	16.1	26.2	23.8	8
41.7	*48.7*	*50.4*	*45.2*	*32.6*	*31.5*	*24.3*	*14.5*	*14.8*	*12.0*	*13.7*	*16.2*	*10.8*	*7.9*	*9.0*	*5.4*	*7.9*	*6.7*	
6.3	0.5	−3.2	5.2	23.0	32.9	29.8	28.7	23.9	34.1	52.2	51.6	59.1	72.3	83.5	100.3	107.7	104.1	9
4.4	*0.4*	*−2.6*	*4.0*	*15.8*	*21.6*	*19.6*	*15.7*	*12.8*	*17.1*	*24.0*	*24.3*	*26.6*	*29.8*	*31.2*	*33.3*	*32.4*	*29.1*	
−30.1	−48.4	−56.7	−58.0	−46.3	−38.2	−20.7	1.3	0.3	16.1	34.8	11.9	4.6	6.3	21.6	35.4	36.2	40.3	10
−21.1	*−37.6*	*−45.5*	*−44.7*	*−31.8*	*−25.2*	*−13.6*	*0.7*	*0.2*	*8.1*	*16.0*	*5.6*	*2.1*	*2.6*	*8.1*	*11.7*	*10.9*	*11.3*	
24.5	28.1	29.1	25.9	19.4	2.8	−6.0	9.7	11.3	−3.5	−35.0	−33.9	−22.0	−16.8	−28.7	−25.2	−22.0	−7.6	11
17.2	*21.8*	*23.4*	*20.0*	*13.3*	*1.9*	*−4.0*	*5.3*	*6.0*	*−1.8*	*−16.1*	*−15.9*	*−9.9*	*−6.9*	*−10.7*	*−8.3*	*−6.6*	*−2.1*	
82.2	85.9	89.6	94.0	99.6	105.0	110.8	116.6	122.7	129.0	137.4	147.5	155.6	161.8	167.8	176.0	185.2	195.2	12
57.8	*66.7*	*71.8*	*72.5*	*68.5*	*69.1*	*72.8*	*63.7*	*65.8*	*64.7*	*63.1*	*69.4*	*69.9*	*66.7*	*62.7*	*58.3*	*55.8*	*54.7*	
142.2	128.7	124.7	129.8	145.5	152.0	152.2	183.0	186.5	199.5	217.8	212.5	222.5	242.5	267.5	301.6	332.0	357.2	13
20.9	*18.8*	*17.8*	*17.8*	*18.9*	*18.8*	*18.2*	*20.7*	*20.4*	*20.3*	*20.2*	*19.2*	*19.3*	*20.0*	*20.7*	*22.0*	*22.9*	*23.3*	
2423.7	2489.8	2546.8	2654.6	2783.8	2852.9	2942.2	3077.4	3218.5	3382.3	3564.3	3737.3	3965.8	4167.5	4484.6	4814.1	5204.7	5632.3	14
356.5	*363.3*	*363.6*	*365.0*	*361.1*	*352.0*	*351.6*	*348.6*	*351.8*	*344.3*	*331.1*	*337.2*	*344.0*	*343.5*	*347.4*	*350.7*	*358.8*	*366.8*	
−23.1	−25.6	−25.4	−28.1	−17.7	−6.1	4.6	−11.4	−11.4	2.6	29.3	25.1	19.8	14.6	29.8	26.5	20.2	13.6	15
−3.4	*−3.7*	*−3.6*	*−3.9*	*−2.3*	*−0.8*	*0.5*	*−1.3*	*−1.2*	*0.3*	*2.7*	*2.3*	*1.7*	*1.2*	*2.3*	*1.9*	*1.4*	*0.9*	
−252.5	−267.4	−298.1	−323.7	−333.1	−324.2	−311.4	−290.2	−299.7	−243.7	−208.8	−203.4	−208.7	−216.7	−190.4	−159.5	−77.3	−125.0	16
−37.1	*−39.0*	*−42.6*	*−44.5*	*−43.2*	*−40.0*	*−37.2*	*−32.9*	*−32.8*	*−24.8*	*−19.4*	*−18.4*	*−18.1*	*−17.9*	*−14.8*	*−11.6*	*−5.3*	*−8.1*	
2172.5	2223.4	2251.1	2342.4	2466.6	2547.4	2662.3	2823.8	2962.1	3206.8	3461.7	3668.0	3906.1	4086.2	4252.5	4506.6	4878.8	5414.7	17
319.5	*324.4*	*321.4*	*322.1*	*320.0*	*314.3*	*318.1*	*319.9*	*323.7*	*326.4*	*321.5*	*331.0*	*338.8*	*336.8*	*329.4*	*328.3*	*336.4*	*352.6*	
53.4	57.6	61.2	64.8	66.6	68.0	69.2	66.7	63.6	58.5	52.2	49.2	46.4	43.4	40.6	38.1	35.4	33.1	18
4.8	5.6	1.4	1.9	0.1	2.2	1.5	1.7	1.0	1.8	2.7	2.5	2.2	2.8	1.8	2.2	2.0	2.2	19
12.8	8.8	6.5	4.9	5.4	7.0	4.3	3.2	4.7	4.7	5.5	3.9	2.5	2.9	2.2	2.7	4.0	4.2	20
0.86	0.87	0.83	0.78	0.73	0.73	0.73	0.72	0.67	0.67	0.67	0.65	0.64	0.71	0.77	0.83	0.88	0.93	21
27.7	28.0	28.4	28.7	29.0	29.3	29.6	29.9	30.2	30.4	30.7	31.0	31.4	31.6	32.0	32.3	32.6	33.0	22
21.2	21.5	21.9	22.2	22.4	22.7	23.0	23.4	23.7	24.0	24.3	24.6	24.9	25.3	25.4	25.8	26.2	26.6	23
14.2	14.3	14.4	14.5	14.6	14.8	14.9	15.2	15.4	15.7	16.0	16.2	16.7	17.0	17.2	17.3	17.6	17.9	24
13.1	12.9	12.8	12.9	13.1	13.4	13.5	13.8	14.1	14.5	14.9	15.1	15.4	15.7	15.9	16.2	16.5	16.9	25
63.1	62.8	64.0	65.2	66.9	67.6	68.1	69.5	70.6	72.6	74.5	74.9	75.3	74.9	76.0	77.1	77.9	78.2	26
8.1	10.3	11.2	11.4	10.4	9.4	9.7	9.1	8.3	7.6	6.8	7.2	7.7	7.6	7.2	6.8	6.3	6.0	27
−1.3	−3.3	−0.3	1.2	3.7	1.7	0.6	3.2	3.2	4.7	4.3	0.7	1.8	1.0	2.0	1.9	2.1	1.6	28
1990	1991	1992	1993	1994	1995	1996	1997	1998	1999	2000	2001	2002	2003	2004	2005	2006	2007	

CANADIAN MACROECONOMIC DATA: EXPLANATORY NOTES

Key variables from the Statistics Canada CANSIM Database	Meaning and Significance of the Key Variables
	These comments highlight the meaning and significance of the variables in the data table. Chapter listings below indicate the textbook chapters in which variables are introduced or most extensively discussed.
1. Consumption expenditure v498087	Largest of the four components of expenditure-based GDP. It consists of spending on durable goods, semi-durable goods, non-durable goods, and services. It depends on personal disposable income and the real interest rate, and is represented by the symbol **C**. Chapters 5 & 8
2. Private-sector investment v498097, v498096 and v498100	Consists of *non-residential business fixed capital formation*, *residential investment*, and *inventory investment*. Residential investment is especially sensitive to real interest rate changes. Private-sector investment involves "real" (i.e., non-financial) investment in factories, equipment, and the like, and does not refer to purchases of stocks and bonds. It is represented by the symbol **I**. Chapters 5 & 9
3. Government purchases v498092, v498093, and v498094	Can be divided into *government current purchases* and *government investment*. Government purchases differ from government budgetary expenditures, a broader category including both government purchases and two types of transfers (transfer payments and interest payments on the public debt). Government purchases are represented by the symbol **G**. Chapters 5 & 8
4. Net exports v498103 minus v498106	Canadian exports of goods and services to the rest of the world minus Canadian imports of goods and services from the rest of the world. Net exports for Canada have traditionally been positive. Both exports and imports have increased substantially as a percentage of GDP in recent decades. Net exports are represented by the symbol **NX**. Chapters 5, 8, 9, 11, 12 & 15
5. GDP at market prices v498086	Nominal *Gross Domestic Product* is a measure of the total output of the Canadian economy. It is the annual market value of all final goods and services produced in Canada. Expenditure-based GDP is theoretically the sum of **C + I + G + NX** (*Table 5.2*). GDP can also be calculated by the *income* (*Table 5.3*) and *value-added* approaches. The concept of production underlying GDP is the same as the concept of production underlying employment in the *Labour Force Survey*. GDP and its subcomponents are *flows*, not stocks. Chapter 5
6. GNP at market prices v499688	*Gross National Product* is the annual market value of all final goods and services produced by factors of production owned by the residents of Canada. *GNP − net international investment income = GDP*. For Canada, net international investment income is always negative; hence, for Canada GDP is always greater than GNP (subtracting a negative number from a magnitude adds to the magnitude). The new official term for the concept known as GNP is *gross national income* (GNI). Chapter 5
7. Personal disposable income v498186	A measure of income available to households for personal saving or for buying consumer goods and services. It does not include the value of public services received by households. Income taxes and social insurance contributions are deducted from personal income to get personal disposable income. Chapters 5 & 8
8. Personal saving v647354	Decisions about *net personal saving* have been explained by economists in terms of life-cycle, precautionary, and bequest motives. The term *personal saving rate* usually refers to personal saving expressed relative to personal disposable income, but personal saving is also expressed relative to GDP. Personal saving relative to GDP (and relative to personal disposable income) has declined in recent years. Chapter 16
9. Corporate saving v647355	The largest component of *net corporate saving* is undistributed profits (or *retained earnings*) that are typically, but not necessarily, invested back into the firm. If the corporate sector has a bad year—that is, if profits drop—then undistributed profits will tend to drop, and with them net corporate saving. Chapter 16
10. Government saving v647356	Because of *automatic stabilizers*, government revenue tends to decline in recessions and government transfers tend to rise. Hence, government saving tends to decline during recessions. Canada's *net government saving*, which is calculated for all levels of government, turned positive in 1997 after many years of being negative. Chapter 16
11. Non-resident saving v647357	Has traditionally added to the funds available for gross investment in Canada—that is, the Canadian economy has usually experienced *net capital inflows*. Net capital inflows add to Canada's net international liabilities. *Net capital outflows*, as Canada experienced during the 1999–2007 period, reduce the funds available for gross investment in Canada but act to reduce Canada's net international debt. Chapter 16
12. Capital consumption v647358	*Capital consumption allowances.* They are accounting allowances for depreciation—the using up of capital in the production of income. Gross measures (e.g., gross corporate saving) exceed their corresponding net measures (e.g., net corporate saving) by the amount of the relevant capital consumption allowances. (This usage of "net" differs from "net" used to describe the balance of positive and negative entries, as in net capital inflows or net international debt.) Chapters 5 & 16
13. Gross investment v647367	Total or economy-wide investment. It includes both private-sector and government "real" (or non-financial) investment. Except for a minor statistical discrepancy, it equals *gross saving*—personal, corporate, government, and non-resident saving, plus capital consumption allowances. Gross investment is a flow, not a stock. It is an extremely important category for the analysis of long-run economic growth. Chapters 5 & 16

Key variables from the Statistics Canada CANSIM Database	Meaning and Significance of the Key Variables
14. National wealth v34674	The value of the stock of non-financial (or "real") assets—factories, equipment, office buildings, shopping malls, warehouses, residential dwellings, inventories, land, and so on—located in Canada. It is stock that is largely the result of past flows of gross investment. Chapter 16
15. Current account balance v113713	The sum of net exports, net international investment income, and net transfers, as shown in *Table 17.1*. It is linked to non-resident saving. Canada's current account balance has tended to be negative while its net exports of goods and services have tended to be positive. During the 1999–2005 period, however, net exports were strongly positive and the current account balance turned positive. Chapters 16 & 17
16. Net international investment position v235422	A country's *net international investment position* represents the value of the financial claims of non-residents on domestic wealth, net of the value of financial claims of domestic residents against foreign wealth, and the position can be positive or negative. Canada's position has been persistently negative so it is common to refer to the position as Canada's *net international debt* or *net international liabilities*. When the current account balance (a flow) is positive, net international debt (a stock) tends to decline. Chapter 16
17. National net worth v34792	The value of the stock of non-financial (or "real") assets located in Canada minus the value of Canada's net international debt. Because Canada has net international debt, Canada's national net worth is less than Canada's national wealth. *Table 16.5* shows how the *national balance sheet* categories of national wealth, net international debt and national net worth are related. Chapter 16
18. Net federal debt-GDP ratio v151548 and v498086	Although *consolidated government debt* is a more comprehensive measure of government debt for Canada than *federal debt*, federal debt statistics become available more quickly. This ratio fell sharply during the 1997–2006 period due to federal surpluses and solid growth of nominal GDP. Reduction of the ratio does not require surpluses, but only that nominal GDP grow more rapidly than net federal debt. Usually it is the debt-to-GDP ratio that matters, not the absolute amount of the debt. Chapter 16
19. CPI inflation rate v41693271	Percentage change in the consumer price index (CPI). In Canada, inflation rates in the 1–3 percent range are typically called *low*, those from 3 to 6 percent are called *moderate*, and those 6 percent or higher are called *high*. When the inflation rate goes up and up, a country experiences *accelerating inflation*. *Disinflation* is the term for a declining rate of inflation. *Deflation*, or negative inflation, refers to a drop in the price level, the CPI. Canada's CPI has not dropped on an annual basis for decades. Chapters 6, 9, 11 & 12
20. Short-term interest rate v122484	The short-term interest rate is represented by the *nominal* interest rate on 3-month treasury bills (federal bonds). It changes, for example, when the Bank of Canada changes its overnight rate target. For a given inflation rate, changes in the nominal interest rate produce equal changes in the *real* (in the sense of "inflation-adjusted"; not in the sense of "non-financial") interest rate. Short-term interest rates vary more with the overnight rate target than do long-term rates. Chapters 6, 9, 10, 11 & 12
21. Exchange rate reciprocal of v37426	For Canada, the most important foreign exchange rate is that between the U.S. and Canadian dollars. Canada had a *fixed exchange rate* during the 1962–1970 period, but has had a *flexible exchange rate* since then. An increase in Canadian real interest rates relative to U.S. rates will tend to cause the Canadian dollar to appreciate (meaning it costs more U.S. cents to buy a loonie). Chapters 9, 11 & 12
22. Population v466668	Refers to the total population of Canada—33 million people in 2007. Population estimates provide the denominator for calculations like real GDP per capita. With positive population growth, growth of total output will exceed growth of output per capita. Population estimates from Statistics Canada exceed the Census counts (e.g., by 2.6% for 1996) due to under-enumeration in the Census. Chapters 4 & 14
23. Working-age population v2461077	The working-age population is that part of the Canadian population aged 15 and over. It divides into those in the *labour force* and those *not in the labour force*. Note that although Canadians aged 65 and over are typically retired, they are considered part of the working-age population. If they are retired, they are classified as *not in the labour force*. Chapter 5
24. Labour force v2461098	The labour force is the sum of the employed plus the unemployed, as shown in *Table 5.6*. The labour force divided by the working-age population gives the *labour force participation rate*, which is still somewhat higher for men than for women in Canada. Chapter 5
25. Employment v2461119	Total employment—that is, the total number of employed persons—exceeds the number of employees. In addition to employees, total employment includes employers and self-employed persons without paid help. For calculating the employment total, part-time workers are treated no differently than full-time workers. Employment divided by the working-age population gives the *employment-population ratio*, a measure of job creation. Chapter 5
26. Labour productivity v41707175 and v2461119	The level of average labour productivity is most simply measured by dividing real GDP by the level of employment. High-income countries have high average labour productivity levels. This series makes use of real GDP measured in constant 2002 dollars. Chapters 4 & 14
27. Unemployment rate v2461224	Calculated by dividing the unemployed by the labour force. Someone of working age is unemployed if he or she lacks a job but is looking for work. The unemployed and those not in the labour force are mutually exclusive categories. In recent years, less than half of Canada's unemployed have received employment insurance benefits. The unemployment rate rises during recessions. Chapter 5
28. Growth of real GDP per capita v41707175 and v466668	The most widely used indicator of the pace of improvement in living standards. Even small long-term differences between two countries in their growth rates of real GDP per capita will result in large differences between the living standards of the two countries. Chapter 14